Brief Contents

S0-AWF-827

Detailed Contents

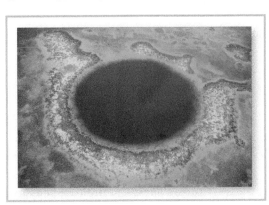

10 Tone and Purpose   421

PART

2

Additional Readings   621

Preface

Dear Colleagues:

One of my personal heroes is Oprah Winfrey. She embodies so much of what is wonderful about the human spirit—with her tenacity, generosity, awe-inspiring work ethic, and wisdom, she has influenced our world for the good in profound ways. She is one of our premier teachers. I shall always be grateful for her devotion to reading and for her active work to inspire others to love the printed word. Her devotion to literacy underscores two ideals in our profession: reading empowers an individual life, and our work as instructors is of great and urgent importance. Many of our students come to us needing to reinforce the basic skills that make master reading and clear thinking possible. Too often they struggle with text structure and feel uncertain about their comprehension. However, with solid instruction and guided practice, these students can discover the power and pleasure of reading. *The Master Reader*, Fourth Edition, has been designed to address these challenges.

New to This Edition

The following changes have been made to *The Master Reader*, Fourth Edition, to help students become master readers and critical thinkers.

- **Integration with—and enhanced feedback through—MyReadingLab.** A hallmark change in this edition is the book's integration with MyReadingLab. Students now have the option of taking both the Review and Mastery Tests that appear at the conclusion of each chapter in Part 1—as well as the Combined Skills Tests in Part 3—in MyReadingLab. By taking the Review Tests and Combined-Skills Tests in MyReadingLab, students will receive automatic feedback as to why certain answers are right and others wrong. The Mastery Tests do not include feedback online and therefore serve as a true test of students' mastery. This integration also offers the additional benefit of helping instructors more easily track and monitor their students' work through the tests and their mastery of the skills. In addition, there is also a fourth Mastery Test for each chapter located only in MyReadingLab.

- **Additional Opportunities for Practice and Instruction of *The Master Reader*, Fourth Edition, in MyReadingLab.** While the printed text contains five Combined Skills Tests in Part 3, an additional five Tests—with feedback—can also be found in MyReadingLab. In addition, the fourth Mastery Test for each Part 1 chapter can also be found on MyReadingLab.

- **New Information Literacy Applications.** Designed to help develop students' research capabilities—and focused by the skill being taught in that chapter—these new activities break information literacy down into manageable chunks. Located after the Practices and before the Review Tests, this feature helps students learn how to identify a need for new knowledge, how to locate and analyze new information, and how to apply that information to a specific situation.

- **New Summary Responses.** Appearing after Review Tests 3 and 4 in each chapter, the Summary Responses connect reading to writing, deepen students' comprehension, and lay the groundwork for responding to the "What Do You Think?" feature.

- **Chapter Review Cards.** These cards—which make studying more accessible and efficient by distilling chapter content down to the fundamentals—have now been integrated into each of the relevant chapters for greater ease of use.

- **New Passages and Readings Throughout.** As with every edition, we have replaced short passages as well as longer readings throughout the text to ensure that the reading is engaging to each new wave of students. The following are just some examples of the many new readings that now appear in the text:

  - "Prude or Prudent? The Debate Over Access to Plan B" by Kathleen Parker
  - "An Account of Alfred C. Cooley's Plight in the Face of Hurricane Katrina" by Sandra Offiah-Hawkins
  - "Night Diving" by Bucky McMahon
  - "Human Development" by Richard J. Gerrig with Philip G. Zimbardo
  - "The African Future: Health and Environment" by Craig, Graham, Kagan, Ozment, and Turner
  - "Finding Meaning" by Zimbardo, Johnson, and McCann
  - "Sociological Reasons for the High Divorce Rate" by John D. Carl
  - "The Politics of Immigrants: Power, Ethnicity, and Social Class" by James M. Henslin

- "Star Types" by Louis Giannetti
- "Do Lie Detectors Really Detect Lies?" by Zimbardo, Johnson, and McCann

Guiding Principles

The Master Reader, Fourth Edition, was written to develop in students the essential abilities that will enable them to become master readers and critical thinkers.

Practice and Feedback

Aristotle said, "What we have to learn to do, we learn by doing." We all know that the best way to learn is to do. Thus one of the primary aims of this text is to give students opportunity after opportunity to practice, practice, practice! Every concept introduced in the book is accompanied by an explanation of the concept, an example with an explanation of the example, and one or more practice exercises. Each chapter also contains brief skill applications, four review tests, three mastery tests, and a chapter review.

High-Interest Reading Selections

According to French poet, dramatist, and novelist, Victor Hugo, "To learn to read is to light a fire; every syllable that is spelled out is a spark." For developmental students we can fan the sparks by encouraging an enthusiasm for reading. For many, this enthusiasm can be stimulated by reading material that offers high-interest topics written in a fast-paced style. Every effort has been made to create reading passages in examples, reviews, and tests that students will find lively and engaging. Topics are taken from issues arising in popular culture and in current textbooks; some examples are gangs, movies, weight loss, sports figures, depression, interpersonal relationships, drug use, nutrition, inspirational and success stories, role models, stress management, and exercise—all written in active language using a variety of sentence patterns.

Integration of the Reading Process and Reading Skills

Master readers blend individual reading skills into a reading process such as SQ3R. Before reading, master readers skim for new or key vocabulary or main ideas. They create study questions and make connections to their prior knowledge. During reading, they check their comprehension. For example, they annotate the text. They notice thought patterns and the relationship between ideas. They read for the answers to the questions they created before reading. After reading, master readers use outlines, concept maps, and summaries to review what they have read and deepen their understanding. Students are taught to integrate each skill into a reading process in Part 1.

In Chapter 1, "A Reading System for Master Readers," students are introduced to SQ3R. In every other Part 1 chapter, students actively apply SQ3R reading strategies in "Before Reading About" and "After Reading About" activities. "Before Reading About" activities are prereading exercises that appear at the beginning of each chapter. These activities guide the student to review important concepts studied in earlier chapters, build on prior knowledge, and preview upcoming material. "After Reading About" activities are review activities that appear after the review tests in each chapter. These activities guide students to reflect on their achievements and assume responsibility for learning.

Comprehensive Approach

An ancient Chinese proverb states, "Skill comes from practice." *The Master Reader*, Fourth Edition, invites skill building by offering several levels of learning. First, students are given an abundance of practice. They are able to focus on individual reading skills through a chapter-by-chapter workbook approach. In each chapter of Part 1, Review Tests 3 and 4 offer a multiparagraph passage with items on all the skills taught up to that point. In addition, Chapter 1, "A Reading System for Master Readers," teaches students how to apply their reading skills to the reading process before, during, and after reading by using SQ3R. Students also learn to apply all the skills in combination in Part 2, "Additional Readings," and Part 3, "Combined-Skills Tests."

Chapter Features

Each chapter in Part 1 has several important features that help students become master readers.

> **Learning Outcomes.** Each chapter opens with learning outcomes to help students preview and assess their progress as they master chapter content.

"Before Reading About…". "Before Reading About…" activities appear at the beginning of Chapters 2–13 in Part 1. These activities are prereading exercises based on SQ3R: they review important concepts studied in earlier chapters, build on prior knowledge, and preview the chapter. The purpose of "Before Reading About…" is to actively teach students to develop a reading process that applies individual reading skills as they study.

"After Reading About…". "After Reading About…" activities appear after Review Test 4 in Chapters 2–13 of Part 1. Based on SQ3R, "After Reading About…" activities teach students to reflect on their achievements and assume responsibility for their own learning. These activities ask students reflective questions to check their comprehension of the skill taught in the chapter. Students learn to integrate individual reading skills into a reading process; they learn the value of reviewing material; and finally, students create a learning journal that enables them to see patterns in their behaviors and record their growth as readers.

Instruction, example, explanation, and practice. Each chapter skill is broken down into components, and each component is introduced and explained. Instruction is followed by an example, an explanation of the example, and a practice. Each section has its own instruction, example, explanation, and practice exercises.

Textbook
Skills

Textbook Skills. In the last section in each chapter, students are shown the ways in which the skills they are learning apply to reading textbooks. These activities, signaled by the icon to the left, present material from a textbook reading and direct students to apply the chapter's skill to the passage or visual. In a concerted effort to prepare students to be master readers in their content courses, activities that foster textbook skills across the curriculum are also carefully woven throughout the entire textbook. The Textbook Skills icon signals these activities.

Visual Vocabulary. The influence of technology and the media on reading is evident in the widespread use of graphics in newspapers, magazines, and textbooks. Throughout this textbook, visual vocabulary is presented as part of the reading process, and students interact with these visuals by completing captions or answering skill-based questions. The aim is to teach students to value photos, graphs, illustrations, and maps as important sources of information.

Review Tests. Each chapter has four Review Tests—which can also be found in MyReadingLab—where they are accompanied by feedback.

Review Tests 1 through 3 are designed to give ample opportunity for practice with the specific skill taught in the chapter; Review Test 4 offers a multiparagraph passage with combined-skills questions based on all the skills taught up to and including that particular chapter. Review Tests 3 and 4 also give "What Do You Think?" writing prompts so that teachers have the opportunity to guide students as they develop critical thinking skills.

Mastery Tests. Each chapter includes three Mastery Tests, which are also found in MyReadingLab. Most of the Mastery Tests are based on excerpts from science, history, psychology, social science, and literature textbooks. In addition, there is a fourth Mastery Test for each chapter that can be found only in MyReadingLab.

Chapter Review. A chapter review is included for each chapter, distilling the most important concepts down for students and helping them take responsibility for their own learning. In this edition, these chapter reviews appear with their relevant chapters.

The Pearson Teaching and Learning Package

The Master Reader, Fourth Edition, is supported by a series of innovative teaching and learning supplements. Ask your Pearson sales representative for a copy, or download the content for certain ancillaries at www.pearsonhighered.com/irc. Your sales representative will provide you with the username and password to access these materials.

MyReadingLab is an online, mastery-based system created specifically for students learning to become master readers. It not only offers students the opportunity to take the Review, Mastery, and Combined-Skills Tests from *The Master Reader* in an online setting (with feedback accompanying the Review and Combined-Skills Tests), it also offers a wealth of additional instruction (in different modalities), remediation, and practice. The site's flexible nature allows instructors to easily assign exercises and establish due dates according to their syllabus, or it can immerse students in a completely personalized, adaptive experience that targets the competencies on which they need to work to succeed. Regardless of the way MyReadingLab is integrated into the course, it offers instructors powerful and easy-to-use tracking and reporting features, facilitating the demonstration of improved and measurable learning outcomes among their students.

The Annotated Instructor's Edition (AIE) is a replica of the student text, with all answers included. ISBN 0-321-96560-4

The Instructor's Manual and Test Bank, prepared by Mary Dubbe and Loretta Rodgers, features teaching strategies for each textbook chapter, plus additional readings that engage students with a variety of learning styles and encourage active learning through class, group, and independent practices. Each chapter includes an introduction designed to hook the students, reproducible handouts, and study-strategy cards. Also included are a ten-item quiz for each chapter. A supplemental section provides a sample syllabus, readability calculations for each reading in *The Master Reader*, Fourth Edition, five book quizzes to encourage independent reading, and a scaffolded book review form. ISBN 0-321-96488-8

The PowerPoint Slides, developed by Mary Dubbe, offers a deck of book-specific slides to augment and complement an instructor's lecture, whether delivered live in classroom or online. ISBN 0-321-96493-4

The Lab Manual, prepared by Mary Dubbe, is designed as a student workbook and provides a collection of 65 activities that provide additional practice, enrichment, and assessment for the skills presented in *The Master Reader*, Fourth Edition. The activities for each chapter include practice exercises, one review test, and two mastery tests that mirror the design of *The Master Reader*, Fourth Edition, and emphasize the reading skills and applications students need in order to succeed in college. The lab activities give students realistic practice, encourage them to use the strategies they have learned, and offer an opportunity for students to continue to build a base of general, background knowledge. This lab manual can be used to strengthen students' reading skills, to allow them to assess their own progress, and to measure their success and readiness for college level reading. ISBN 0-321-98855-8

Alternative Formats

The Master Reader, Fourth Edition, is offered in several different formats to give instructors and students the flexibility of using the very same material in different settings and at different price points:

A la Carte. This unbound, binder-ready version of the text gives students the option of integrating their own notes with textbook material, and it enables them to only carry only the relevant chapter of the text to class.

It is available at two-thirds of the net price of the bound text. ISBN 0-321-96490-X

CourseSmart eText. Available through www.coursesmart.com, this on-line version of the text—which offers complete page fidelity with the print edition—is available at different, discounted price points depending on the duration of access. ISBN 0-321-96489-6

Acknowledgments

As I worked on the fourth edition of this reading series, I felt an overwhelming sense of gratitude and humility for the opportunity to serve the learning community as a textbook author. I would like to thank the entire Pearson team for their dedication to providing the best possible materials to foster literacy. To every person, from the editorial team to the representatives in the field, all demonstrate a passion for students, teachers, and learning. It is a joy to be part of such a team. Special thanks are due to the following: Eric Stano, Editor-in-Chief, Developmental Reading and Writing; Kathy Smith with Cenveo® Publisher Services for her tireless devotion to excellence; and Ellen MacElree and the entire production team for their work ethic and gracious attitudes. I would also like to thank Mary Dubbe and Loretta Rodgers for authoring the Lab Manual and the Instructor's Manual that supplement this reading series.

For nearly twenty-five years, I worked with the most amazing group of faculty from across the State of Florida as an item-writer, reviewer, or scorer of state-wide assessment exams for student learning and professional certification. The work that we accomplished together continues to inform me as a teacher, writer, and consultant. I owe a debt of gratitude to this group who sacrificed much for the good of our students.

Finally, I would like to gratefully recognize the invaluable insights provided by the following colleagues and reviewers. I deeply appreciate their investment of time and energy: Denise Clay, Fullerton College; Wayne Conrad, El Centro College; Tomekia Cooper, Albany Technical College; Jan Eveler, El Paso Community College; Annie Gonzalez, Laredo Community College; Charles Hill, McLennan Community College; Yolanda Nieves, Wilbur Wright College; Cindy A. Renfro, Houston Community College; Margarita Sanchez, McLennan Community College; Michael Vensel, Miami Dade College; and Shari Waldrop, Navarro College.

D. J. Henry
Daytona Beach, Florida

Becoming a Master Reader

A Reading System for Master Readers

CHAPTER 1

LO LEARNING OUTCOMES

After studying this chapter, you should be able to:

- **LO1** Define Prior Knowledge
- **LO2** Use the Three Phases of the Reading Process with SQ3R
- **LO3** Survey and Question Before Reading
- **LO4** Read and Annotate During Reading
- **LO5** Recite and Review After Reading
- **LO6** Develop Textbook Skills: Use SQ3R to Master Textbook Reading
- **LO7** Apply Information Literacy Skills: Academic, Personal, and Career Applications of the Reading Process

Many people think that reading involves simply passing our eyes over the words in the order they appear on the page. However, reading is an active process during which you draw information from the text to create meaning. When you understand what you've read, you've achieved **comprehension** of the material.

Comprehension is an understanding of what has been read.

Once we understand the **reading process**, we can follow specific steps and apply strategies that will make us master readers. The most important aspect of being a master reader is being an *active reader*.

Active reading means that you ask questions, find answers, and react to the author's ideas. For example, an active reader often marks, or annotates, key ideas by underlining the text or writing notes in the margin. (For more information about annotating a text, see pages 622–623.) In addition, an active reader often checks comprehension by summarizing, or briefly restating the author's major points. (For more information about summarizing, see pages 623–625.) The activities in this chapter are designed to give you the skills you need to become an active reader.

Define Prior Knowledge

We all have learned a large body of information throughout a lifetime of experience. This body of information is called **prior knowledge**.

Knowledge is gained from experience and stored in memory. For example, a small child hears her father repeat the word *no* frequently as he takes away dangerous objects, removes her from unsafe situations, or wants her to stop certain behaviors. The child quickly learns and will remember the meaning of *no*.

> **Prior knowledge** is the large body of information that is learned throughout a lifetime of experience.

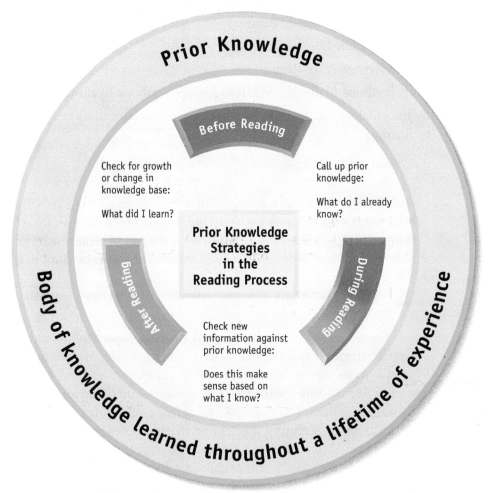

EXAMPLE Read the following passage taken from a college science textbook. In the space provided, list any topics from the passage about which you already have prior knowledge.

Textbook Skills

The Lunar Surface

[1]When Galileo first pointed his telescope toward the Moon, he saw two different types of terrains—dark lowlands and brighter, highly cratered highlands. [2]Because the dark regions resembled seas on Earth, they were called maria (*mar* = sea, singular, mare). [3]Today, we know that the maria are not oceans but, instead, are flat plains that resulted from immense outpourings of fluid basaltic lavas. [4]By contrast, the light-colored areas resemble Earth's continents, so the first observers dubbed them terrae (Latin for "land"). [5]These areas are now generally referred to as lunar highlands, because they are elevated several kilometers above the maria. [6]Together, the arrangement of terrae and maria result in the well-known "face of the moon."

—Lutgens, Frederick K., Tarbuck, Edward J., and Tasa, Dennis, *Foundations of Earth Science*, 5th ed., p. 409.

_____

_____

_____

EXPLANATION If you know something about the terrain of the moon, basaltic lava, or the actual length of a kilometer, then this passage makes more sense to you than it does to someone who does not possess such prior knowledge. However, even if you do not know much about those topics, you may have helpful prior knowledge about some of the other ideas in the passage. For example, most of us have seen and perhaps wondered about the "face of the moon." Our prior knowledge that comes from observing the moon with our own eyes connects with new information in the passage.

The more prior knowledge we have about a topic, the more likely we are to understand that topic. This is why master readers build their knowledge base by reading often! ◄

Practice 1

Read the passage from a college health textbook. Then answer the questions that follow it.

Textbook Skills

From Everyday Problems to Emotionally Crippling Behavior

[1]Neuroses are the most common type of mental problem. [2]Although neuroses can cause emotional suffering, neurotic individuals usually can carry out day-to-day activities. [3]Anxiety and phobia are examples of

neuroses; they are generally viewed as cognitive distortions or unsatisfactory ways of reacting to life situations.

[4]Anxiety is often brought on by an imagined fear of impending danger. [5]Americans experience anxiety more than any other mental health problem. [6]Most anxiety is normal and may play an important role in anticipating situations. [7]For example, the fear of being attacked on a deserted street at night may cause a person to take appropriate actions to avoid such a possibility. [8]You have probably experienced anxiety before taking a final exam. [9]Some of the symptoms you may have had are sweating, dry mouth, heavy breathing, and insomnia. [10]This type of anxiety is in response to a realistic situation.

[11]However, some people suffer anxiety over a long period of time and without any apparent cause. [12]A person who has a phobia, for example, has an unreasonable fear of some object or situation. [13]Simple phobias include fear of heights or fear of bees and usually do not interfere with daily activities. [14]Some phobias, however, are more severe and can cause people to lead constricted lives. [15]Because of their irrational fears, some people do not leave the house. [16]Anxiety becomes a serious mental health problem when individuals suffering from it are so emotionally crippled that they cannot continue at school, hold a job, or otherwise lead a satisfying and productive life.

—Pruitt, B. E. and Stein, Jane J., *Healthstyles: Decisions for Living Well*, 2nd ed., pp. 58–59.

1. What did you already know about neuroses such as anxiety and phobias? That is, what was your prior knowledge? Phobia can have you fearing learning your house

2. When you think of anxiety and phobias, what do you think of? Describe ideas and experiences that come to mind. Panic Attacks

3. Was this an easy passage to understand? How does your prior knowledge affect your understanding of this passage? yes

4. List any parts of the passage you had no prior knowledge of: Anxiety so serious you cannot continue school or work

LO2 ## Use the Three Phases of the Reading Process with SQ3R

Triggering prior knowledge is a reading skill that you as an active reader can turn into a reading strategy by using it in your reading process. In each of the remaining chapters in Part One, you will be encouraged to begin thinking about how you can connect the reading skills that you are learning to the reading process. Master readers use reading skills as comprehension strategies throughout the reading process.

Master readers break reading into a three-step process. Each step uses its own thinking activities.

1. Before reading, look over, or *preview,* the material. (Previewing brings up prior knowledge.) Ask questions about the material you are about to read.

2. During reading, *test* your understanding of the material.

3. After reading, *review and react* to what you have learned.

One well-known way to apply this reading process is called SQ3R.

SQ3R stands for Survey, Question, Read, Recite, and Review.

SQ3R activates prior knowledge and offers strategies for each phase of the reading process. The graphic illustrates the phases of the reading process through SQ3R. Master readers repeat or move among phases as needed to repair comprehension.

Survey and Question Before Reading

Survey

Quickly look over, or **skim**, the reading passage for clues about how it is organized and what it is going to present or teach you.

To skim effectively, look at *italic* and **bold** type and take note of titles, the introduction, and headings. Also look at pictures and graphs. Finally, read the first paragraph, summaries, and questions. Each of these clues provides important information.

Question

To aid in comprehension, ask questions before you read. The list of prereading questions that follows can be used in most reading situations.

- What is the topic or subject of the passage? (See Chapter 3.)
- How is the material organized? (See Chapters 6 and 7.)
- What do I already know about this idea? (What is my prior knowledge?)
- What is my purpose for reading?
- What is my reading plan? Do I need to read everything, or can I just skim for the information I need?
- What are the most important parts to remember?

▶ **EXAMPLE** The excerpted passage below is from a college business textbook. Before you read it word for word, skim the passage and fill in the following information:

1. What is the topic of this passage? _____

2. What do I already know about this topic? _____

3. What is my purpose for reading? That is, why am I reading this? What do I need to remember? _____

_____

4. What ideas in the passage are in *italic* and/or **bold** type? _____

_____

_____

What Is the Accounting Process?

[1]When people think of accounting, most think of the systematic recording of a company's every financial transaction. [2]This precise process is a small but important part of accounting called **bookkeeping.** [3]The process of bookkeeping centers on the fundamental concept that what a company owns (*assets*) must equal what it owes to its creditors (*liabilities*) plus what it owes to its owners (*owners' equity*). [4]This balance is illustrated in the **fundamental accounting equation:** assets = liabilities + owners' equity.

[5]To maintain the balance of assets and liabilities plus owners' equity, accountants use a recording system called double entry bookkeeping. [6]**Double entry bookkeeping** recognizes that for every transaction that affects an asset, an equal transaction must also affect either a liability or owners' equity.

—Adapted from Solomon, Michael, Poatsy, Mary Anne, and Martin, Kendall. *Better Business*, 2nd ed., p. 494.

EXPLANATION

1. The title of the passage, "What Is the Accounting Process?," gives a clue to the topic of the passage. By also quickly looking at the terms in italic and bold type, you can see that this passage is about a company's accounting process.

2. Prior knowledge varies from person to person. Some readers may draw up their own budgets at home and thus already may have some experience and understanding about accounting principles. Others will have minimal experience and therefore have little prior knowledge about the topic.

3. Wording of one's purpose for reading will vary from person to person. A sample answer: I need to remember what important concepts make up the accounting process.

4. The words in *italic* or **bold** type are *bookkeeping, assets, liabilities, owners' equity, fundamental accounting equation,* and *double entry bookkeeping.*

Read and Annotate During Reading

After you have surveyed and asked questions about the text, it's time to read the entire passage. Use the following helpful practices while reading.

Read

As you read, think about the importance of the information by continuing to ask questions. For example:

- Does this new information agree with what I already knew?
- Do I need to change my mind about what I thought I knew?
- What is the significance of this information? Do I need to remember this?

In addition to asking questions while you read, acknowledge and resolve any confusion as it occurs.

- Create questions based on the headings, subheadings, and words in *italics* and **bold** type.
- Reread the parts you don't understand.
- Reread whenever your mind drifts during reading.
- Read ahead to see if an idea becomes clearer.
- Determine the meaning of words from their context.
- Look up new or difficult words.
- Think about ideas even when they differ from your own.

Annotate

Make the material your own. Make sure you understand it by repeating the information.

- Create a picture in your mind or on paper.
- Restate the ideas in your own words.
- Mark your text by underlining, circling, or highlighting topics, key terms, and main ideas. (See pages 622–625 for more about how to annotate.)
- Write out answers to the questions you created based on the headings, sub-headings, and highlighted words.
- Write a summary of the passage or section.

> **EXAMPLE**

A. Before you read the following excerpt from a college science textbook, survey the passage and answer the following questions.

1. What is the topic of the passage? _____

2. What do I already know about the topic of this passage? What is my prior knowledge? _____

3. What is important about this passage? What do I need to remember?

_____

_____

Textbook Skills

4. What are the words in **bold** type (which will help me remember what I need to know)? _____

B. Once you have surveyed the information, read the passage. During reading, check your understanding by writing answers to the questions based on the ideas in **bold** type.

5. What new or difficult words do I need to look up?

_____

_____

6. What are circadian rhythms?

_____

_____

7. What is an example of circadian rhythms?

_____

_____

Biological Rhythms

[1]Many different types of animals show **circadian rhythms**—patterns of activity that approximate the length of a day. [2]For example, fruit flies (*Dacus tryoni*) always mate at about the same time in the evening; they continue to show this cyclical pattern of mating even when external cues indicating the time of day are not available. [3]This pattern enables the flies to mate under cover of darkness, when the danger of predation is reduced.

[4]Another common cycle in the animal world is a **circannual rhythm**, a cycle lasting approximately one year. [5]A circannual pattern makes it possible for an animal to engage in a behavior during the appropriate season. [6]For example, the golden-mantled ground squirrel (*Citellus lateralis*) enters into hibernation approximately the same time every year, during the late fall. [7]Like the fruit flies, the ground squirrel

maintains its rhythm when kept in a laboratory, isolated from external factors that could indicate the season. [8]For example, ground squirrels kept in rooms with constant temperature and unchanging light-dark cycles showed a consistent hibernation schedule over a 4-year period.

—Maier, Richard A., *Comparative Animal Behavior*, p. 431.

8. What is a circannual rhythm?

_____

_____

9. What is an example of a circannual rhythm?

_____

10. What do you need to reread to understand?

_____

_____

EXPLANATIONS Compare your answers to the ones below. Keep in mind that your wording and examples may be different.

A. Before Reading: Survey and Question

1. The topic of the passage is biological rhythms.
2. Answers to this question will vary.
3. Answers to this question will vary. A possible answer is: I need to know the two types of biological rhythms and examples of each type.
4. The terms in **bold** type are: biological rhythms, circadian rhythms, and circannual rhythm.

B. During Reading: Read and Annotate

5. Answers to this question will vary.
6. Circadian rhythms are patterns of activity that approximate the length of a day.
7. Fruit flies (*Dacus tryoni*) always mate about the same time in the evening.
8. A circannual rhythm is a cycle of behavior lasting approximately one year that allows an animal to engage in a behavior during the appropriate season.

9. The golden-mantled ground squirrel hibernates every year in the late fall.

10. Answers to this question will vary. ◀

LO5 Recite and Review After Reading

Recite

As part of your review, take time to think and write about what you have read.

- Connect new information to your prior knowledge about the topic.
- Form opinions about the material and the author.
- Notice changes in your opinions based on the new information.
- Write about what you have read.

Review

Once you have read the entire selection, go back over the material to review it.

- Summarize the most important parts (for more information about how to summarize, see pages 623–625).
- Return to and answer the questions raised by headings and subheadings.
- Review new words and their meanings based on the way they were used in the passage.

Practice 2

Now that you have learned about each of the three phases of the reading process, practice putting all three together. Think before, during, and after reading. Apply SQ3R to the following passage. Remember the steps:

- **Survey:** Look over the whole passage.
- **Question:** Ask questions about the content. Predict how the new information fits together with or differs from what you already know about the topic.
- **Read:** Continue to question, look up new words, reread, and create pictures in your mind.
- **Recite:** Take notes; write out questions and answers, definitions of words, and new information.

- **Review:** Think about what you have read and written. Use journals to capture your opinions and feelings about what you have read.

A. **Before Reading: Survey and Question.** Skim the passage taken from a college law textbook, and then answer the following questions.

1. What is the topic of this passage? _The First Amendment and Freedom of Religion_

2. What do I already know about this topic? _you lack freedom of religion_

3. What do I need to remember? _the gov't cant do nothing about 1st Amendment law_

4. What ideas in the passage are in *italic* and/or **bold** type? _Establishment clause, exercise clause_

5-6. *Before you go on:* Use the terms you listed in item 4 to create questions. Write the questions in the blank boxes labeled 5 and 6. Write your answers to these questions in the boxes during reading.

B. **During Reading: Read and Recite.** As you read, answer the questions you created from the words in **bold** type.

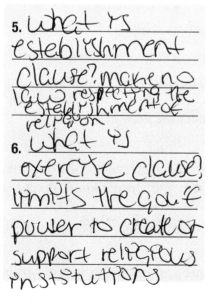

5. _what is establishment clause? make no law respecting the establishment of religion_

6. _what is exercise clause? limits the gov't power to create or support religious institutions_

The First Amendment and Freedom of Religion

[1]The First Amendment contains two provisions relating to religious freedom. [2]The government can make no law respecting the establishment of a religion (the **Establishment Clause**), nor can it make any law prohibiting the free exercise of religion (**Free Exercise Clause**). [3]The Establishment Clause limits the government's power to create or support religious institutions and led to the philosophy of separation of church and state. [4]The Free Exercise Clause limits the right of government to interfere in a person's practice of his or her religion.

[5]As with many freedoms, situations occur where governmental interests and freedom of religion clash. [6]Recently, for example, a parent challenged

Textbook
Skills

the recitation of the Pledge of Allegiance in public schools because the pledge contains the words "under God." [7]Lower courts held that this violates the First Amendment. [8]Although the Supreme Court agreed to hear the case, it eventually decided that the petitioner, who did not have legal custody of his daughter, did not have the right (referred to as standing) to bring the lawsuit. [9]The Court did not rule on the First Amendment issue. [10]The case is *Elk Grove Unified Sch. Dist. v. Newdow,* 124 S. Ct. 2301 (2004).

[11]A leading case in the area of religious freedom is *Lemon v. Kurtzman,* 403 U.S. 602 (1971). [12]This case involved a state law allowing financial support to religious schools, although it limited the use of the money to teachers and supplies for nonreligious courses. [13]The Court held the law unconstitutional because of the entanglement of church and state.

—Hames, Joanne B. and Ekern, Yvonne,
Introduction to Law, 4th ed., p. 109.

C. After Reading: Review

7. Why is the Establishment Clause important? *Because the government cant make no laws respecting establishment of religion or make any law prohibiting free exercise of religion*

8. Identify a time when the Free Exercise Clause becomes an issue. *In court*

Textbook
Skills

LO6 Develop Textbook Skills: Use SQ3R to Master Textbook Reading

You can use the SQ3R reading system to increase your comprehension and retention of information from all types of reading materials, from newspapers to novels. As a college student, you will find SQ3R to be a particularly helpful study method when trying to master information in your textbooks. Most textbooks are designed with special features to help readers understand and learn the vast amount of information within them. Master readers actively use these features as they preview, read, and review textbook material. The following chart lists and explains several features common to most textbooks.

Textbook Features

BOOK FEATURES

Table of Contents	The table of contents, located in the front of the book, is a list of the chapters in the order in which they appear, along with their corresponding page numbers.
Index	The index, located in the back of the book, is an alphabetical list of all the specific topics discussed in the textbook, along with the precise page numbers that deal with each topic.
Glossary	A glossary is an alphabetical list of specialized words and their meanings. Glossaries can be located in a number of places in a textbook, including at the back of the book, in the chapter's preview material, in the margins of the pages where the words are first used, or at the end of the chapter as review material.
Preface	The preface is a type of introduction that discusses the textbook's overall purpose, format, and special features.
Appendices	Appendices are sections of additional material designed to supplement or support your learning; they appear at the back of many textbooks.

CHAPTER FEATURES

Introductions and Previews	Each chapter usually begins with a brief overview of the chapter's contents. Sometimes, this section also includes key questions or objectives to keep in mind as you read.
Headings and Subheadings	Textbook authors divide complex information into smaller sections to organize the ideas. Each section is labeled with a heading. Some sections are divided into subgroups and are given subheadings.
Information Boxes	Information boxes are used to highlight important information; they frequently contain key concepts, definitions, activities, real-life connections, or summaries.
Summaries	A summary is a brief section at the end of a chapter that restates the chapter's main idea and major supporting details.
Review Questions	At the end of a section, the author may supply a set of questions designed to test your comprehension.
Typographical Features	Authors frequently use **bold** and *italic* type to draw attention to important ideas and terms.
Graphics	Graphs, tables, diagrams, maps, photographs, and other graphic aids support the information explained in the paragraphs. Graphics make the information more visually interesting and accessible to visual learners.

Master readers actively use textbook features throughout the process of reading an assignment. For example, a master reader sets up a reading session or a series of sessions to complete a reading assignment. Each reading session is broken into the three reading phases. The time spent in each phase of the process varies based on the reading assignment.

Before Reading: A master reader may begin a reading session with five to ten minutes of before-reading activities such as skimming, noting new or special terms, creating questions, and setting a purpose for the reading session.

During Reading: Then, the master reader reads for a set amount of time, such as thirty minutes. The duration of a reading session depends on many factors such as length or difficulty of the material, time-management issues, and reader interest. For example, the difficulty of the text may require several shorter sessions of reading smaller chunks of the assignment. Master readers avoid marathon sessions that lead to fatigue and loss of concentration. During reading, the master reader stays focused by highlighting the text, taking notes, and repairing any confusion when it occurs.

After Reading: The master reader spends five to fifteen minutes completing notes or writing a summary with information that fulfills the purpose for reading (which was established before reading).

> **EXAMPLE** The following study plan outlines how one student plans to apply SQ3R to the process of reading textbooks. Test your understanding of the steps you can take to use SQ3R to understand textbook material. Fill in the blanks with information that best completes each idea. Answer the question that follows the chart.

Before Reading [5–10 minutes]—**(1)** _____ and **(2)** _____

- ▪ Preview textbook: Skim preface and table of contents, and locate index.

- ▪ Preview a chapter: Read chapter **(3)** _____. Preview material, including information boxes, graphics, and end-of-chapter questions.

- ▪ Turn chapter **(4)** _____, **(5)** _____, and terms in **bold** or *italic* type into questions.

- ▪ Preview **(6)** _____ questions.

During Reading [around 30 minutes]—**(7)** _____

- ▪ Annotate to understand; underline **(8)** _____.
- ▪ Note definitions/examples of terms in **(9)** _____ or **(10)** _____ type.

- Repair **(11)** __________; check glossaries and indexes for more information.
- Reread or read ahead for clarification. Study graphics to understand key concepts.

After Reading [5–15 minutes]—(12) __________ **and (13)** __________

- Use notes to test recall. Use two-column notes. Consider the following headings: Topics and Details, Terms and Definitions, or Questions and Answers. Create flashcards for important terms.
- Answer **(14)** ______________ at the end of the chapter.
- Write a **(15)** __________ that paraphrases the chapter.

  How can SQ3R help me read a textbook? ______________________________

  ____

  ____

EXPLANATIONS Compare your answers to the ones given here.

Before Reading (1) *Survey* and **(2)** *Question.* Several ways to preview the textbook include the following: read the chapter **(3)** *introduction,* turn chapter **(4)** *headings* and **(5)** *subheadings* into questions, and preview **(6)** *end-of-chapter review* questions.

During Reading (7) *Read;* underline **(8)** *key ideas* and note the definitions and examples of terms in **(9)** *bold* or **(10)** *italic* type. Also repair **(11)** *confusion.*

After Reading (12) *Review* and **(13)** *Recite.* Answer **(14)** *review questions* and write a **(15)** *summary* using your own words.

How can SQ3R help me read a textbook? Although answers will vary, in general, SQ3R breaks the reading assignment into three phases of previewing, reading, and reviewing information. By asking questions, recording ideas, and reciting information, I am more likely to understand and remember information.

Practice 3

The following selection is a section of a chapter from a geography textbook. Use SQ3R to comprehend the passage. Skim the passage and answer the Before Reading questions. During reading, underline key concepts and definitions. After reading, complete the three-column notes with information from the passage.

Survey and Question Before Reading

1. What do I need to know? _Types of Rocks_

    _____

    _____

2. What is my purpose for reading? _Learn about the difference of each rock_

Textbook
Skills

Rock Formation

[1]Although by human standards Earth's surface moves very slowly—by at most a few centimeters per year—this movement produces Earth's great diversity of rocks. [2]As Earth's crust moves, its materials are eroded and deposited, heated and cooled, buried and exposed.

Types of Rocks

[3]Rocks can be grouped into three basic categories that reflect how they form:

[4]**Igneous rocks** are formed when molten crustal material cools and solidifies. [5]The name derives from the Greek word for fire, which is the same root as for the English word ignite. [6]Examples of igneous rocks are basalt, which is common in volcanic areas, including much of the ocean floor, and granite, which is common in continental areas.

[7]**Sedimentary rocks** result when rocks eroded from higher elevations (mountains, hills, plains) accumulate at lower elevations (like swamps and ocean bottoms). [8]When subjected to high pressure and the presence of cementing materials to bind their grains together, rocks like sandstone, shale, conglomerate, and limestone are formed.

[9]**Metamorphic rocks** are created when rocks are exposed to great pressure and heat, altering them into more compact, crystalline rocks. [10]In Greek the name means "to change form." [11]Examples include marble (which metamorphosed from limestone) and slate (which metamorphosed from shale).

Minerals

[12]Minerals are natural substances that comprise rocks. [13]Each type of mineral has specific chemical and crystalline properties. [14]Earth's rocks are diverse in part because the crust contains thousands of minerals. [15]The

density of rocks depends on the kinds of materials they contain. [16]Denser rocks are dominated by compounds of silicon, magnesium, and iron minerals; they are called **sima** (for *silicon-magnesium*). [17]Less dense rocks are dominated by compounds of silicon and aluminum minerals; they are called **sial** (for *silicon-aluminum*).

[18]Denser sima rocks make up much of the oceanic crust. [19]Less dense sial rocks make up much of the continental crust. [20]The lower density and greater thickness of sial rocks cause the continents to have higher surface elevations than the oceanic crust, just as a less dense dry log will float higher in water than a denser wet one.

[21]The formation and distribution of many minerals is caused by the movements of Earth's crust. [22]Vast areas of the continental crust, known as **shields**, have not been significantly eroded or changed for millions of years.

[23]Shield areas often contain rich concentrations of minerals, such as metal ores and fossil fuels. [24]Shields are located in the core of large continents such as Africa, Asia, and North America. [25]Many of the world's mining districts exist where these continental shields are exposed at the surface.

—Bergman, Edward and Renwick, William, *Introduction to Geography: People, Places, and Environment*, 4th ed., pp. 101–103.

Review and Recite After Reading

Complete the following notes with information from the passage. Then answer the summary question.

Chapter 3   Rock Formations   **Textbook Notes pages 102–103**

Term	Definition	Examples
3. _Igneous_	are formed when molten crustal material cools and solidifies	basalt, granite
4. _Sedimentary_	5. _results when rocks eroded from_ higher elevations and collect at lower elevations	sandstone, shale conglomerate, limestone
6. _Metamorphic_	are formed when rocks are exposed to great pressure and heat, altering them into more compact, crystalline rocks	7. _Marble Slate_

Minerals	are natural elements that comprise rocks	silicon, magnesium, aluminum, metal ores, fossil fuels
Sima	8. are denser rocks dominated by compounds of _silicon_ _magnesium_, and iron minerals	make up much of oceanic crust
9. _sial_	are less dense rocks dominated by compounds of silicon and aluminum minerals	make up much of continental crust
Shields	are vast areas of continental crust that contain rich concentrations of minerals	core of large continents such as Africa, Asia, North America

Summary: What role do minerals play in rock formation and what are the three types of rocks?

10. The role minerals play in rock formation is as earth crust moves the materials are eroded & deposited, heated and cooled, buried and exposed. Three types rocks are Igneous, sedimentary, Metamorphic

Granite, _____ rock, has become a popular building material for kitchen countertops.

a. an igneous
b. a sedimentary
c. a metamorphic

Apply Information Literacy Skills

 Academic, Personal, and Career Applications of the Reading Process

Information literacy is the set of skills needed to find, retrieve, analyze, and use information. Masterful use of the reading process is an information literacy skill that can be applied to academic, personal, and career issues or situations.

Academic Application

Assume you are taking a college communications course. Your professor has assigned your class to become familiar with the nonverbal indicators of low stakes deception. Read the following table and complete the reading activities.

- **Before Reading**: Skim the table, "Nonverbal Indicators of Deception: Low Stakes," and create two pre-reading questions.
- **During Reading**: Highlight or annotate the details that you think will answer your pre-reading questions.
- **After Reading**: In the space following the passage, summarize the most important idea from the passage.

What do I already know? _____

What do I need to know? _____

_____

Table 1.1   Nonverbal Indicators of Deception: Low Stakes

	Deceivers Exhibit	
	More	*Less*
Vocal Cues		
	Pausing	Lengthy answers
	Pauses	
	Time before pausing	
	Lengthy pauses	
	Hesitations	

Nonfluencies
    Sentence changes
    Word repetitions
    Intruding sounds

Rapid speaking rate

Overall vocal nervousness
    Voice sounds tense or stressed

Gestures	Self-adaptors (touching face and body, hand shrugs)	Head movement
	Object-adaptors (touching or playing with objects in room)	Head nodding
		Foot movements
	Overall bodily nervousness	Illustrators
		Leg movements
Eye Behaviors	Time spent looking away	Eye contact
	Averted gazes	duration
	Pupil dilation	
	Blinking	
Smiling	Masked smiles	Felt happy smiles

—Leathers, Dale and Eaves, Michael H., *Successful
Nonverbal Communication: Principles
and Applications,* 4th ed., p. 242.

VISUAL *VOCABULARY*

Eye contact is a _____ that indicates honesty.

   a. gesture
   b. behavior

Summary: _____

_____

_____

_____

Personal Application

Assume you are a parent of a toddler, and you are introducing your child to TV. As a loving and concerned parent, you want to make sure you are selecting age appropriate and educational programs for your child to watch. You do an Internet search using the phrase "best educational TV shows for toddlers," which generates the following results.

■ **Before Reading**: Skim the screenshot and record a question you have as a consumer.

■ **During Reading**: Highlight the details that answer your pre-reading question.

■ **After Reading**: In the space below, record what sources you think will provide reliable information and why.

Pre-Reading Questions: _____

_____

—Google and the Google logo are registered trademarks of Google, Inc., used with permission.

Reliable sources and why: _____

_____

_____

_____

Career Application

Assume you are a marketing assistant for a nationwide overstock company. The head of your department has issued a memo that addresses a new direction in advertisement that the company would like to pursue. Read the email and respond to the following prompts:

- **Before Reading**: Skim the memo and write a pre-reading question.
- **During Reading**: Highlight the details that answer your pre-reading question.
- **After Reading**: In the space following the passage, reply to the memo by summarizing how you will work to expand your company's advertising.

Pre-Reading Question: _____

_____

_____

To: James Anderson, Marketing Assistant
From: Joana Patterson, Director of Market Research
Date: September 27, 2013
Subject: Expanding Company Advertising in Media

Market research and analysis indicate the necessity for advertising through the growing range of media. In order for our company to stay competitive and relevant in today's market, we need to make our presence known on the Internet. Focus groups and surveys have shown that the majority of our target market uses the Internet as their primary means for comparison shopping. Also, it is important to use the Internet as a tool to reach new customers.

The company needs to focus advertising on our target market's most frequently visited sites. Based on the focus groups and surveys, the following list ranks sites by popularity:

Google

Bing

Facebook

Reply: _____

_____

_____

_____

_____

_____

_____

_____

_____

_____

REVIEW TEST 1

Score (number correct) _____ x 20 = _____ %

Visit MyReadingLab to take this test online and receive feedback and guidance on your answers.

Before, During, and After Reading

A. Before you read, survey the following passage from a college health textbook, and then answer the questions listed here.

1. What is the topic of this passage? *Eating Disorders*

_____

2. What are the ideas in **bold** type? _____

_____

3. What do I already know about this idea? _____

_____

Textbook
Skills

4. What do I need to remember? *eating disorders are not healthy*

B.   Read the passage. As you read, answer the questions in the box.

Eating Disorders

[1]On occasion, over one-third of all Americans fit the description of obesity and diet obsessiveness. [2]For an increasing number of people, particularly young women, this obsessive relationship with food develops into an eating disorder.

[3]**Anorexia nervosa** is a persistent, chronic eating disorder characterized by deliberate food restriction and severe, life-threatening weight loss. [4]Anorexia involves self-starvation motivated by an intense fear of gaining weight along with an extremely distorted body image. [5]Usually people with anorexia achieve their weight loss through initial reduction in total food intake, particularly of high-calorie foods. [6]What they do eat, they often purge through vomiting or using laxatives.

[7]**Bulimia nervosa** often involves binging and purging. [8]People with bulimia binge and then take inappropriate measures, such as secret vomiting, to lose the calories they have just acquired. [9]People with bulimia are obsessed with their bodies, weight gain, and how they appear to others. [10]Unlike those with anorexia, people with bulimia are often "hidden" from the public eye because their weight may vary only slightly or fall within normal range.

[11]**Binge eating disorder** (BED) also involves frequent bouts of binge eating. [12]People who suffer with BED binge like their bulimic counterparts, but they do not take excessive measures to lose the weight that they gain. [13]Often they are clinically obese, and they tend to binge much more often than the typically obese person who may consume too many calories but spaces his or her eating over a more normal daily eating pattern.

—Adapted from Donatelle, Rebecca J.
and Davis, Lorraine G., *Health:*
The Basics, 7th ed., pp. 299–301.

5. What does **obsessiveness** mean?

_____

_____

_____

6. What are the traits of anorexia nervosa?

life threatening weight loss, fear of gaining weight

_____

7. What are the traits of bulimia nervosa?

Secret vomiting obsessed with weight gain

_____

_____

8. What are the traits of binge eating disorder?

Clinically obese, eating more than typically obese person

_____

_____

After Reading

9. What are the differences among the three types of eating disorders?

Anorexia is when forcing yourself lose weight. Bulimia is when you care how your body looks offer & secret vomiting.

10. What is the main cause of eating disorders? care what other people think about

---

REVIEW TEST 2

Score (number correct) _____ x 20 = _____ %

Visit MyReadingLab to take this test online and receive feedback and guidance on your answers.

Textbook
Skills

Read the following two passages from a chapter in a college criminal justice textbook. The first passage is the list of learning objectives on the first page of the chapter; the second passage is the summary at the end of the chapter. Use the appropriate steps in SQ3R to read the material and complete the activities.

Survey and Question Before Reading

1. What is the topic of this passage? Policing · Legal Aspects

2. How many subtopics are in the chapter? 2

Chapter 5 Policing: Legal Aspects

Learning Objectives

[1]After reading this chapter, you should be able to:

- [2]Identify legal restraints on police action, and list instances of the abuse of police power.
- [3]Explain how the Bill of Rights and democratically inspired legal restraints help protect personal freedoms in our society.

- [4]Describe the circumstances under which police officers may properly conduct searches or seize property.
- [5]Define arrest, and describe how popular depictions of the arrest process may not be consistent with legal understandings of the term.
- [6]Describe the intelligence function, including police interrogations, and explain the role of Miranda warnings.

Summary: Policing: Legal Aspects

- [7]Legal restraints on police action stem primarily from the U.S. Constitution's Bill of Rights, especially the Fourth, Fifth, and Sixth Amendments, which (along with the Fourteenth Amendment) require due process of law. [8]Most due process requirements of relevance to police work concern three major areas: (1) evidence and investigation (often called search and seizure), (2) arrest, and (3) interrogation. [9]Each of these areas has been addressed by a number of important U.S. Supreme Court decisions, and this chapter discusses those decisions and their significance for police work.

- [10]The Bill of Rights was designed to protect citizens against abuses of police power. [11]It does so by guaranteeing due process of law for everyone suspected of having committed a crime and by ensuring the availability of constitutional rights to all citizens, regardless of state or local law or procedure. [12]Within the context of criminal case processing, due process requirements mandate that all justice system officials, not only the police, respect the rights of accused individuals throughout the criminal justice process.

- [13]The Fourth Amendment to the Constitution declares that people must be secure in their homes and in their persons against unreasonable searches and seizures. [14]Consequently, law enforcement officers are generally required to demonstrate probable cause in order to obtain a search warrant if they are to conduct searches and seize the property of criminal suspects legally. [15]The Supreme Court has established that police officers, in order to protect themselves from attack, have the right to search a person being arrested and to search the area under the arrestee's immediate control.

- [16]An arrest takes place whenever a law enforcement officer restricts a person's freedom to leave. [17]Arrests may occur when an officer comes upon a crime in progress, but most jurisdictions also allow warrantless arrests for felonies when a crime is not in progress, as long as probable cause can later be demonstrated.

- [18]Information that is useful for law enforcement purposes is called *intelligence,* and as this chapter has shown, intelligence gathering is vital to police work. [19]The need for useful information often leads police investigators to question suspects, informants, and potentially knowledgeable citizens. [20]When suspects who are in custody become subject to interrogation, they must be advised of their Miranda rights before questioning begins. [21]The Miranda warnings, which were mandated by the Supreme Court in the 1966 case of *Miranda v. Arizona,* are listed in this chapter. [22]They ensure that suspects know their rights—including the right to remain silent—in the face of police interrogation.

—Schmalleger, Frank J., *Criminal Justice,*
9th ed., p. 114 (Learning Objectives)
and 153 (Summary).

After Reading

Complete the following SQ3R Study Guide with information from the passage.

SQ3R Study Guide: Policing: Legal Aspects

3. Primary source of legal restraints on police action: _Stem primarily from U.S constitution Bills of Rights._

4. _Bill of Rights_ : guarantees due process of law and ensures constitutional rights to all citizens

5. Due process requirements: _evidence, investigation ~~xxxxxxxxxxxxxxxx~~ Arrest, interrogation_

6. Fourth Amendment: _declare that people must be secure in their homes in their persons against unreasonable search + seizing_

7. Requirement for conducting search and seizing property: _Search warrant_

8. Arrest: _Takes place whenever a law enforcement officer restricts A person's freedom to leave_

9. Intelligence: *information that useful for law enforcement*
10. Miranda warning: *were mandated by the supreme court in the 1966 case Miranda v. Arizona*

VISUAL *VOCABULARY*

The police are _____ to give the Miranda Warning upon arrest.

   a. inclined
   b. obliged

REVIEW TEST 3

Score (number correct) _____ x 25 = _____ %

Visit MyReadingLab to take this test online and receive feedback and guidance on your answers.

Reading Textbook Selections

Textbook Skills

Before Reading: Survey the following passage from a college education textbook. Study the words in the Vocabulary Preview; then skim the passage, noting terms in **bold** or *italic* type. Answer the Before Reading questions that follow the passage. Then read the passage and answer the After Reading questions that follow.

Vocabulary Preview

preferences (sentence 9): favored choices
solitary (sentence 11): private, alone, independent

distinction (sentence 19): difference, trait
dimension (sentence chart): aspect, feature, trait
facets (sentence 21): aspect, feature, trait
cognitive (sentence 21): mental
spatial (sentence 21): physical space

Learning Preferences

[1]Since the late 1970s, a great deal has been written about differences in students' learning preferences. [2]Learning preferences are often called *learning styles* in these writings, but I believe preferences is a more accurate label because the "styles" are determined by your preferences for particular learning environments—for example, where, when, with whom, or with what lighting, food, or music you like to study. [3]I like to study and write during large blocks of time—all day, if I don't have classes. [4]I usually make some kind of commitment or deadline every week so that I have to work in long stretches to finish the work before that deadline. [5]Then I take a day off. [6]When I plan or think, I have to see my thinking in writing. [7]I have a colleague who draws diagrams of relationships when she listens to a speaker or plans a paper. [8]You may be similar or very different, but we all may work effectively. [9]But are these **preferences** important for learning?

[10]Some proponents of learning styles believe that students learn more when they study in their preferred setting and manner. [11]And there is evidence that very bright students need less structure and prefer quiet, **solitary** learning. [12]But most educational psychologists are skeptical about the value of learning preferences. [13]"The reason researchers roll their eyes at learning styles research is the utter failure to find that assessing children's learning styles and matching to instructional methods has any effect on their learning" (Stahl, 2002, p. 99).

[14]Students, especially younger ones, may not be the best judges of how they should learn. [15]Sometimes, students, particularly those who have difficulty, prefer what is easy and comfortable; real learning can be hard and uncomfortable. [16]Sometimes, students prefer to learn in a certain way because they have no alternatives; it is the only way they know how to approach the task. [17]These students may benefit from developing new—and perhaps more effective—ways to learn. [18]One final consideration: Many of the learning styles advocates imply that the differences in the learner are what matter.

Visual/Verbal Distinctions

[19]There is one learning styles **distinction** that has research support. [20]Richard Mayer has been studying the distinction between visual and verbal learners, with a focus on learning from computer-based multimedia. [21]He is finding that there is a visualizer-verbalizer dimension and that it has three **facets:** *cognitive spatial* ability (low or high), *cognitive style* (visualizer vs. verbalizer), and *learning preference* (verbal learner vs. visual learner), as shown in the following table.

Three Facets of the Visualizer-Verbalizer Dimension

There are three **dimensions** to visual versus verbal learning: ability, style, and preference. Individuals can be high or low on any or all of these dimensions.

Facet	Types of Learners	Definition
Cognitive Ability	High spatial ability	Good abilities to create, remember, and manipulate images and spatial information
	Low spatial ability	Poor abilities to create, remember, and manipulate images and spatial information
Cognitive Style	Visualizer	Thinks using images and visual information
	Verbalizer	Thinks using words and verbal information
Learning Preference	Visual learner	Prefers instruction using pictures
	Verbal learner	Prefers instruction using words

—Mayer, Richard E., *Journal of Educational Psychology*, American Psychological Association, © 2003. Reproduced with the permission of American Psychological Association.

[22]The picture is more complex than simply categorizing a student as either a visual or a verbal learner. [23]Students might have preferences for learning with pictures, but their low spatial ability could make using pictures to learn less effective. [24]These differences can be reliably measured, but research has not identified the effects of teaching to these styles.

—Woolfolk, Anita E., *Educational Psychology*, 10th ed., pp. 124–127.

Before Reading

1. What do I already know about learning styles? _____

_____

_____

_____

2. What do I need to learn? _____

_____

After Reading

3. According to the chart, the three dimensions to visual versus verbal learning

   are _____, _____, and _____.

4. Which of the terms—verbalizer or visualizer—describes you as a learner?

   Explain why. _____

   _____

SUMMARY RESPONSE

Respond to the passage by answering the following question: What is the author's most important idea? Restate the author's ideas in your own words. Begin your summary response with the following: *The most important idea of "Learning Preferences" by Woolfolk is . . .*

WHAT DO YOU THINK?

Assume you have been asked to become a peer counselor in the learning center of your college or university. You have been asked to prepare a report about your learning preferences. Refer to the chart in the passage, and consider the following:

- Identify and describe the ways in which you or someone you know is a visualizer-verbalizer.
- Give examples based on experiences and observations.

REVIEW TEST 4

Score (number correct) _____ x 10 = _____ %

Visit MyReadingLab to take this test online and receive feedback and guidance on your answers.

Textbook Skills

Before Reading: Survey the following passage from the college textbook *Criminal Justice Today*. Study the words in the Vocabulary Preview. Then skim the passage and answer the Before Reading questions that follow the passage. Next, read the passage and answer the After Reading questions that follow.

Vocabulary Preview

ingestible (sentence 2): able to be absorbed into the body
social convention (sentence 6): rule, principle, standard, custom
inherent (sentence 6): basic, natural, inbuilt
legitimate (sentence 25): legal, lawful
psychoactive (sentence 29): drugs or medications having a significant effect on mood or behavior
anesthetic (sentence 31): substance that dulls pain
advocated (sentence 33): supported, promoted
strictures (sentence 35): limits, restrictions, severe criticism

What Is a Drug?

¹Before we begin any comprehensive discussion of drugs, we must first grapple with the concept of what a drug is. ²In common usage, a *drug* may be any **ingestible** substance that has a noticeable effect on the mind or body. ³Drugs may enter the body via injection, inhalation, swallowing, or even direct absorption through the skin or mucous membranes. ⁴Some drugs, like penicillin and tranquilizers, are useful in medical treatment, while others, like heroin and cocaine, are attractive only to *recreational drug* users or to those who are addicted to them.

⁵In determining which substances should be called "drugs," it is important to recognize the role that social definitions of any phenomenon play in our understanding of it. ⁶Hence, what Americans today consider to be a drug depends more on **social convention** or agreed-on definitions than it does on any **inherent** property of the substance itself. ⁷The history of marijuana provides a case in point. ⁸Before the early twentieth century, marijuana was freely available in the United States. ⁹Although alcohol was the recreational drug of choice at the time, marijuana found a following among some artists and musicians. ¹⁰Marijuana was also occasionally used

for medical purposes to "calm the nerves" and to treat hysteria. [11]Howard Becker, in his classic study of the early Federal Bureau of Narcotics (forerunner of the Drug Enforcement Administration, or DEA), demonstrates how federal agencies worked to outlaw marijuana in order to increase their power. [12]Federally funded publications voiced calls for laws against the substance. [13]And movies like *Reefer Madness* led the drive toward classifying marijuana as a dangerous drug. [14]The 1939 Marijuana Tax Act was the result, and marijuana has been thought of as a drug worthy of federal and local enforcement efforts ever since.

[15]Both the law and social convention make strong distinctions between drugs that are socially acceptable and those that are not. [16]Some substances with profound effects on the mind and body are not even thought of as drugs. [17]Gasoline fumes, chemical vapors of many kinds, perfumes, certain vitamins, sugar-rich foods, and toxic chemicals may all have profound effects. [18]Even so, most people do not think of these substances as drugs. [19]And they are rarely regulated by the criminal law.

[20]Recent social awareness has reclassified alcohol, caffeine, and nicotine as "drugs." [21]However, before the 1960s it is doubtful that most Americans would have applied that word to these three substances. [22]Even today, alcohol, caffeine, and nicotine are readily available throughout the country, with only minimal controls on their manufacture and distribution. [23]As a result, these three drugs continue to enjoy favored status in both our law and culture. [24]Nonetheless, alcohol abuse and addiction are commonplace in American society, and anyone who has tried to quit smoking knows the power that nicotine can wield.

[25]Occupying a middle ground on the continuum between acceptability and illegality are substances that have a **legitimate** medical use and are usually available only with a prescription. [26]Antibiotics, diet pills, and, in particular, tranquilizers, stimulants, and mood-altering chemicals (like the popular drug Prozac) are culturally acceptable but typically can be attained legally only with a physician's prescription. [27]The majority of Americans clearly recognize these substances as drugs, albeit useful ones.

[28]Powerful drugs, those with the ability to produce substantially altered states of consciousness and with a high potential for addiction, occupy the forefront in social and legal condemnation. [29]Among them are *psychoactive substances* like heroin, peyote, mescaline, LSD, and cocaine. [30]Even here, however, legitimate uses for such drugs may exist. [31]Cocaine is used in the treatment of certain medical conditions and can be applied

as a topical **anesthetic** during medical interventions. [32]LSD has been employed experimentally to investigate the nature of human consciousness, and peyote and mescaline may be used legally by members of the Native American Church in religious services. [33]Even heroin has been **advocated** as beneficial in relieving the suffering associated with some forms of terminal illness. [34]Hence, answers to the question of "What is a drug?" depend to a large extent on the social definitions and conventions operating at a given time and in a given place. [35]Some of the clearest definitional statements relating to controlled substances can be found in the law, although informal **strictures** and definitions guide much of everyday drug use.

—Schmalleger, Frank J., *Criminal Justice Today: An Introductory Text for the 21st Century*, 10th ed., p. 578.

Before Reading

1. What is the topic of this passage? _____

2. What is my purpose for reading? _____

_____

After Reading

Complete the following chart with information from the passage.

The Continuum of Acceptability and Illegality of Drugs

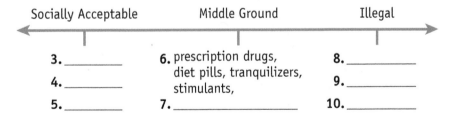

Socially Acceptable	Middle Ground	Illegal
3._____	6. prescription drugs, diet pills, tranquilizers, stimulants,	8._____
4._____		9._____
5._____	7._____	10._____

SUMMARY RESPONSE

Respond to the passage by answering the following question: What is the author's most important idea? Restate the author's ideas in your own words. Begin your summary response with the following: *The most important idea of "What Is a Drug?" by Schmalleger is . . .*

WHAT DO YOU THINK?

Would you be in favor of "reclassifying" any drugs that are currently considered illegal? Would you be in favor of reclassifying any drugs that are currently considered legal? Which ones and why? Assume you are a volunteer with your local police department, and one of your duties is to help educate the public about important local issues. You are to speak at a middle school about drugs. Refer to the passage, and consider the following:

- Identify what drugs are, along with their uses and risks.
- Distinguish between drugs that are legally and socially acceptable, and those that are not.
- Give examples of how knowledge can reclassify what is considered a drug.

After Reading About a System for Master Readers

Before you move on to the Mastery Tests on a reading system for master readers, take time to reflect on your learning and performance by answering the following questions. Write your answers in your notebook.

- How has my knowledge base or prior knowledge changed about a reading system such as SQ3R?
- Based on my studies, how do I think I will perform on the Mastery Test(s)? Why do I think my scores will be above average, average, or below average? (Note: An additional fourth Mastery Test may be found in MyReadingLab.)
- Would I recommend this chapter to other students who want to learn more about a reading system such as SQ3R. Why or why not?

Test your understanding of what you have learned about a reading system for master readers by completing the Chapter 1 Review.

Name _____ Section _____

Date _____ **Score** (number correct) _____ x 20 = _____ %

Visit MyReadingLab to take this test online and receive feedback and guidance on your answers.

Textbook Skills

Using SQ3R, read the following passage from a college environmental science textbook.

Outdoor Air Pollution

[1]When we think of outdoor air pollution, we tend to envision smokestacks belching smoke from industrial plants. [2]However, natural processes produce a great deal of air pollution.

[3]Fires from burning vegetation generate soot and gases, and over 60 million ha (150 million acres) of forest and grassland burn in a typical year. [4]Volcanic eruptions release large quantities of particulate matter and sulfur dioxide into the troposphere, and major eruptions may blow matter into the stratosphere. [5]Winds sweeping over arid terrain can send huge amounts of dust aloft—sometimes even from one continent to another. [6]In July 2009, the bustling city of Tehran came to a standstill when windstorms blew sand and dust from drought-stricken Iraq into Iran, enveloping half of the country. [7]Businesses, schools, and government offices were closed for several days, airplane flights were cancelled, and people were warned to stay indoors to safeguard their health.

[8]Some natural impacts are made worse by human activity and land use policies. [9]Farming and grazing practices that strip vegetation from the soil promote wind erosion and dust storms. [10]Suppression of fire allows fuel to build up and eventually leads to more-destructive fires. [11]And in the tropics, many farmers set fires to clear forest for agriculture.

[12]Human activity introduces many sources of air pollution. [13]Air pollution can emanate from *point sources* or *nonpoint sources*. [14]A point source describes a specific location from which large quantities of pollutants are discharged, such as a coal-fired power plant. [15]Nonpoint sources are more diffuse, consisting of many small, widely spread sources (such as thousands of automobiles).

—Withgott, Jay H. and Brennan, Scott R.,
Essential Environment, 2nd ed., pp. 282–283.

1. What is the topic of this passage? _____

2–5. Complete the concept map that follows with information from the passage.

Outdoor Air Pollution

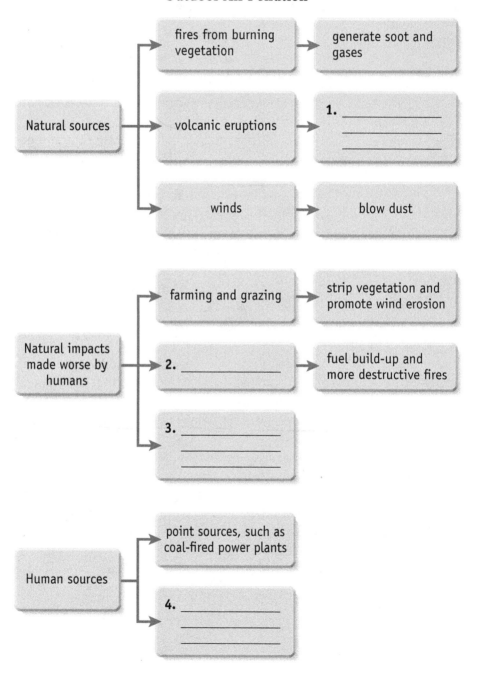

Natural sources
→ fires from burning vegetation → generate soot and gases
→ volcanic eruptions → 1. _____
→ winds → blow dust

Natural impacts made worse by humans
→ farming and grazing → strip vegetation and promote wind erosion
→ 2. _____ → fuel build-up and more destructive fires
→ 3. _____

Human sources
→ point sources, such as coal-fired power plants
→ 4. _____

Name _____ Section _____

Date _____ **Score** (number correct) _____ x 20 = _____ %

Visit MyReadingLab to take this test online and receive feedback and guidance on your answers.

Textbook Skills

Using SQ3R, read the following passage from a college sociology textbook.

Groups Within Society

[1]How important has your family been to you?

[2]Your first group, the family, has given you your basic orientations to life. [3]Later, among friends, you have found more intimacy and an expanded sense of belonging. [4]These groups are what sociologist Charles Cooley called **primary groups**. [5]By providing intimate, face-to-face interaction, they give us an identity, a feeling of who we are. [6]As Cooley (1909) put it,

[7]By primary groups I mean those characterized by intimate face-to-face association and cooperation. [8]They are primary in several senses, but chiefly in that they are fundamental in forming the social nature and ideals of the individual.

[9]Cooley, who developed the concept *looking glass self,* called primary groups the "springs of life." [10]By this, he meant that primary groups, such as family and friends, are essential to our emotional well-being. [11]As humans, we have an intense need for face-to-face interaction that generates feelings of self-esteem. [12]By offering a sense of belonging and a feeling of being appreciated—and sometimes even loved—primary groups are uniquely equipped to meet this basic need. [13]From our opening vignette, you can see that gangs are also primary groups.

[14]Primary groups are also significant because their values and attitudes become fused into our identity. [15]We internalize their views, which then become the lenses through which we view life. [16]Even when we are adults—no matter how far we move away from our childhood roots—early primary groups remain "inside" us. [17]There, they continue to form part of the perspective from which we look out onto the world. [18]Ultimately, then, it is difficult, if not impossible, for us to separate the self from our primary groups, for inside us the self and these groups merge into a "we."

[19]Compared with primary groups, **secondary groups** are larger, more anonymous, and more formal and impersonal. [20]These groups are based on shared interests or activities, and their members are likely to interact on the basis of specific statuses, such as president, manager, worker,

or student. [21]Examples include college classes, the American Sociological Association, and the Democratic Party. [22]Contemporary society could not function without secondary groups. [23]They are part of the way we get our education, make our living, spend our money, and use our leisure time.

[24]As necessary as secondary groups are for contemporary life, they often fail to satisfy our deep needs for intimate association. [25]Consequently, secondary groups tend to break down into primary groups. [26]At school and work, we form friendships. [27]Our interaction with our friends is so important that we sometimes feel that if it weren't for them, school or work "would drive us crazy." [28]The primary groups that we form within secondary groups, then, serve as a buffer between ourselves and the demands that secondary groups place on us.

—Henslin, James M., *Sociology: A Down-to-Earth Approach*, 11th ed., p. 151.

1. What is the topic of this passage? _____

_____

2–5. Complete the following chart with information from the passage.

Term	Definition	Examples
2. _____	**3.** _____	family and friends
	_____	
	_____	
	_____	
Secondary groups	**4.** _____	**5.** _____
	_____	_____
	_____	_____
	_____	

Name _____ Section _____

Date _____ **Score** (number correct) _____ x 25 = _____ %

Visit MyReadingLab to take this test online and receive feedback and guidance on your answers.

Using SQ3R, read the following passage from a college psychology textbook.

Textbook Skills

Nonassertiveness, Aggressiveness, and Assertiveness

[1]The nature of assertive communication can be better understood by distinguishing it from nonassertiveness and aggressiveness.

[2]**Nonassertiveness** refers to a lack of assertiveness in certain types of or in all communication situations. [3]People who are nonassertive fail to assert their rights. [4]In many instances, these people do what others tell them to do—parents, employers, and the like—without questioning and without concern for what is best for them. [5]They operate with a "You win, I lose" philosophy. [6]Nonassertive people often ask permission from others to do what is their perfect right. [7]Social situations create anxiety for these individuals, and their self-esteem is generally low.

[8]**Aggressiveness** is the other extreme. [9]Aggressive people operate with an "I win, you lose" philosophy; they care little for what the other person wants and focus only on their own needs. [10]Some people communicate aggressively only under certain conditions or in certain situations (for example, after being taken advantage of over a long period of time) while others communicate aggressively in all or at least most situations. [11]Aggressive communicators think little of the opinions, values, or beliefs of others and yet are extremely sensitive to others' criticism of their own behaviors. [12]Consequently, they frequently get into arguments with others.

[13]**Assertive behavior**—behavior that enables you to act in your own best interests without denying or infringing upon the rights of others—is the generally desired alternative to nonassertiveness or aggressiveness. [14]Assertive people operate with an "I win, you win" philosophy; they assume that both people can gain something from an interpersonal interaction.

1. What are the traits of nonassertive behavior?

_____

_____

_____

_____

_____

2. What are the traits of aggressive behavior?

_____

_____

_____

_____

3. What are the traits of assertive behavior?

_____

_____

_____

43

4. What is the purpose of this passage?

_____

_____

_____

_____

_____

_____

[15]Assertive people are willing to assert their own rights. [16]Unlike their aggressive counterparts, however, they don't hurt others in the process. [17]Assertive people speak their minds and welcome others' doing likewise.

—DeVito, Joseph A., *The Interpersonal Communication Book*, 10th ed., p. 149.

VISUAL *VOCABULARY*

Road rage is an example of which type of behavior?

_____

a. assertive
b. nonassertive
c. aggressive

1 Summary of Key Concepts of a Reading System for Master Readers

 Assess your comprehension of prior knowledge and the reading process.

- Comprehension is _____.

- Prior knowledge is _____

  _____.

- Use prior knowledge to _____.

  - Activate _____ by asking _____

    _____

  - Check _____ against prior knowledge by asking, _____

    _____

  - Check for _____ by asking,

    _____

- The reading process has three phases: _____

  _____

- SQ3R, an acronym for a reading process, stands for _____

  _____. SQ3R activates prior knowledge and

  offers strategies for each phase of the reading process:

  - **Before Reading,** _____: Skim _____

    _____. _____: Ask _____

    _____

  - **During Reading:** _____. _____ key words

    and ideas. Repair confusion. Reread.

- **After Reading:** ——————: Answer questions such as ——————

  ————————————————————————————————

  ——————————: Recall ——————————————. Summarize.

- Textbook features help readers understand and learn the vast amount of information in a textbook. A few examples are as follows:

  - Table of Contents: ——————————————————————

  - Index: ——————————————————————————————

  - Glossary: ——————————————————————————————

  - Preface: ——————————————————————————————

    ————————————————————————————————

  - Appendices: ——————————————————————————

  - Typographical features: ——————————————————————

    ————————————————————————————————

  - Graphics: ——————————————————————————————

    ————————————————————————————————

Test Your Comprehension of A Reading System for Master Readers

Respond to the following prompt and questions.

LO1 LO2
LO3 LO4
LO5 LO6
LO7

Describe your reading process. How did you read before you studied this chapter? Will you change your reading process? If so, how? If not, why not?

————————————————————————————————

————————————————————————————————

————————————————————————————————

————————————————————————————————

Vocabulary Skills

Copyright © 2015 Pearson Education, Inc.

(LO) LEARNING OUTCOMES

After studying this chapter, you should be able to:

LO1 Define Vocabulary

LO2 Analyze Context Clues Using SAGE: Synonyms, Antonyms, General Sense of the Passage, and Examples

LO3 Develop Textbook Skills: Using a Glossary

LO4 Analyze Word Parts: Roots, Prefixes, Suffixes

LO5 Develop Textbooks Skills: Discipline-Specific Vocabulary

LO6 Develop Textbooks Skills: Visual Vocabulary

LO7 Apply Information Literacy Skills: Academic, Personal, and Career Applications of Vocabulary

Before Reading About Vocabulary Skills

Chapter 1 taught you the importance of surveying material before you begin reading by skimming the information for **bold** or *italic* type. Throughout this textbook, key ideas are emphasized in bold or italic print where they appear in the passage; often they are also set apart visually in a box that gives the definition or examples of the term. Skim the chapter for key ideas in boxes that will help you understand vocabulary skills. Refer to these boxes and create at least six questions that you can answer as you read the chapter. Write your questions in the following spaces (record the page number for the key term in each question):

_____? (page _____)

_____? (page _____)

_____? (page _____)

_____? (page _____)

_____? (page _____)

_____? (page _____)

Compare the questions you created with the following questions. Then, write the ones that seem most helpful in your notebook, leaving enough space after each question to record the answers as you read and study the chapter.

What is vocabulary? (page 48) What is a context clue? (page 49) What are the signal words for synonyms? (page 49) What are the signal words for antonyms? (page 51) What are the signal words for examples? (page 54) What is a glossary? (page 55) What are roots, prefixes, and suffixes? (page 59) How will knowing about these vocabulary skills help me develop my vocabulary? (pages 48 and 59)

Define Vocabulary

Words are the building blocks of meaning. Have you ever watched a child with a set of building blocks such as Legos? Hundreds of separate pieces can be joined together to create buildings, planes, cars, or even spaceships. Words are like that, too. A word is the smallest unit of thought. Words properly joined create meaning.

Vocabulary is all the words used or understood by a person.

How many words do you have in your **vocabulary**? If you are like most people, by the time you are 18 years old, you know about 60,000 words. During your college studies, you will most likely learn an additional 20,000 words. Each subject you study will have its own set of words. There are several ways to study vocabulary.

Analyze Context Clues Using SAGE: Synonyms, Antonyms, General Sense of the Passage, and Examples

Master readers interact with new words in a number of ways. One way is to use **context clues**. The meaning of a word is shaped by its context. The word *context* means "surroundings." Master readers use context clues to learn new words.

> A **context clue** is the information that surrounds a new word, used to understand its meaning.

There are four types of context clues:

- Synonyms
- Antonyms
- General context
- Examples

Notice that when the first letters of each context clue are put together, they spell the word **SAGE**. The word *sage* means "wise." Using context clues is a wise—a SAGE—reading strategy.

Synonyms

A **synonym** is a word that has the same or nearly the same meaning as another word. Many times, an author will place a synonym near a new or difficult word as a context clue to the word's meaning. Usually, a synonym is set off with a pair of commas, a pair of dashes, or a pair of parentheses before and after it.

Synonym Signal Words

or   that is

> **EXAMPLES** Each of the following sentences has a key word in **bold** type. In each sentence, underline the signal words and then circle the synonym for the word in **bold**.

1. To ensure personal safety, be **cognizant**, or aware, of your surroundings.

2. Many crimes are committed against women who are **oblivious**, that is, uninformed and ignorant, about how to protect themselves.

Self-defense training makes women _____ of tactics they can use to ensure their safety.

   a. fearful
   b. cognizant
   c. skilled

EXPLANATIONS

1. The signal word *or* clues the reader that the synonym for *cognizant* is *aware*.

2. The signal words *that is* clue the reader that the synonyms for *oblivious* are *uninformed* and *ignorant*. ◀

Practice 1

Each of the following sentences contains a word that is a synonym for the word in **bold** type. Underline the signal words and circle the synonym in each sentence.

1. Idris is known for his **discreet**, or tactful, manner of handling personnel issues.

2. **Indigent**, that is, poverty-stricken, people do not have access to health care.

3. Rocky's poetry has a **lyrical**, or musical, quality.

Antonyms

An **antonym** is a word that has the opposite meaning of another word. Antonyms help you see the shade of a word's meaning by showing you what the original word is *not*. The following contrast words often act as signals that an antonym is being used.

Antonym Signal Words

but	not	unlike
however	on the other hand	yet
in contrast		

Sometimes antonyms can be found next to the new word. In those cases, commas, dashes, or parentheses set them off. At other times, antonyms are placed in other parts of the sentence to emphasize the contrast between the ideas.

> **EXAMPLES** In each sentence, underline the signal words and circle the antonym for the word in **bold** type. In the blank, write the letter of the word that best defines the word in **bold**.

_____ **1.** Marcel **facilitated** the study group's progress with his thoughtful questions; in contrast, Randy hindered their ability to concentrate with his inappropriate jokes.
a. assisted   c. deepened
b. impeded   d. recorded

_____ **2.** After purchasing a painting by the famous artist Monet, Charlene discovered the piece was a **facsimile**, not an original.
a. innovation   c. rarity
b. copy   d. spare

EXPLANATIONS

1. The signal words *in contrast* clue the reader to the antonym *hindered*. The best definition of the word *facilitated* is (a) "assisted."

2. The signal word *not* clues the reader to the antonym *original*. The best definition of the word *facsimile* is (b) "copy." <

Practice 2

In each sentence, underline the signal words and circle the antonym for the word in **bold** type. In the blank, write the letter of the word that best defines the word in **bold**.

_____ **1.** The explanation the defense offered for the crime seems **credible**. It is not at all far-fetched, as the prosecution accuses.
a. mature   c. trustworthy
b. absurd   d. crazy

_____ **2.** The candidate gave a long, **discursive** speech when instead she should have made the speech short and direct.

    a. entertaining   c. important
    b. boring   d. rambling

_____ **3.** Before cosmetic surgery, Rory's face was **craggy** with age lines, but now after surgery, his complexion is smooth again.

    a. sagging   c. rough
    b. damaging   d. ugly

General Context

Often you will find that the author has not provided a synonym clue or an antonym clue. In that case, you will have to rely on the general context of the passage to figure out the meaning of the unfamiliar word. This requires you to read the entire sentence, or to read ahead for a few sentences, for information that will help you understand the new word.

Information about the word can be included in the passage in several ways. Sometimes a definition of the word may be provided. Vivid word pictures or descriptions of a situation can provide a sense of the word's meaning. Sometimes you may need to figure out the meaning of an unknown word by using logic and reasoning skills.

◇ EXAMPLES In the blank, write the letter of the word that best defines the word in **bold** type.

**Textbook
Skills**

_____ **1. Chronically** ill people may never regain the full level of health they experienced before the onset of their illnesses, and they may face a continuing loss of function and the constant threat of ever more serious medical problems as their illness progresses.

—Pruitt, B. E. and Stein, Jane J., *HealthStyles:
Decisions for Living Well,* 2nd ed., p. 344.

    a. slightly   c. briefly
    b. permanently   d. effectively

_____ **2.** Nitrogen is one of the most **essential** nutrients for life, and it increases the fertility of soil and water.

—Smith, Thomas and Smith, Robert Leo,
Elements of Ecology, 4th ed., p. 349.

    a. minor   c. necessary
    b. optional   d. possible

1. The best meaning of the word *chronically* is (b) "permanently." Clues from the sentence are the words and phrases *never regain*, *continuing loss*, *constant*, *ever more serious*, and *progresses*.

2. The best meaning of the word *essential* is (c) "necessary." A clue word is *most*, which describes the word *essential*. The way the word *essential* is used in the sentence also provides a clue, for it describes *nutrients*. Even if the meaning of *nutrients* is not clear, the reader knows from the rest of the sentence that nutrients improve soil and water (by increasing their fertility). Thus the reader can conclude that the *most essential nutrients* are necessary.

Practice 3

Each of the following sentences has a word in **bold** type. In the blank, write the letter of the word that best defines the word in **bold**.

Textbook Skills

_____ 1. Parental restrictiveness and harsh criticism are also associated with a greater likelihood of a teenager smoking. **Conversely**, affection, emotional support, and participation in meaningful conversations at home more often result in the teenager not smoking.

—Pruitt, B. E. and Stein, Jane J., *HealthStyles: Decisions for Living Well*, 2nd ed., p. 181.

   a. additionally   c. surprisingly
   b. in contrast   d. as a result

_____ 2. Fear **galvanized** my entire body, and I ran faster than I have ever run before, my heart thumping wildly.
   a. froze   c. stimulated
   b. broke   d. strained

_____ 3. The statement "Bill is **at least** 21 years old" can also be expressed or translated into the following mathematical language: $b \geq 21$.
   a. less than or equal to   c. less than
   b. greater than or equal to   d. equal to

Examples

Many times an author will show the meaning of a new or difficult word by providing an example. Signal words indicate that an example is coming.

> **Example Signal Words**
>
> consists of   for example   for instance   including   such as

Colons and dashes can also indicate examples.

> **⊘ EXAMPLE** Using example clues, choose the correct meaning of the words in **bold** type.

_____ **1.** Some people believe that the pesticides used on foods cause serious physical **impairments** such as weakened kidneys and a more fragile immune system.
a. improvements   c. injuries
b. laws   d. pairings

_____ **2.** Some students find **collaborative** learning helps them understand and retain information; for example, Nicole, Vejay, and Chad meet every Tuesday and Thursday in the library to compare notes and help each other prepare for tests.
a. additional   c. independent
b. intense   d. shared

EXPLANATIONS

1. The examples "weakened kidneys and a more fragile immune system" are clearly physical conditions that threaten people's health. Thus, the best meaning of the word *impairments* is (c) "injuries."

2. The example illustrates behaviors such as "compare notes" and "help each other prepare" that indicate sharing. Thus, the best meaning of the word *collaborative* is (d) "shared." ⊘

Practice 4

Using example clues, choose the correct meaning of the word in **bold** type.

Textbook
Skills

_____ **1.** Enslaved people were considered the plantation owner's **chattel**, just as wagons, farm animals, furniture, and household goods were.
a. help   c. property
b. rewards   d. payment

Textbook Skills

_____ **2.** Aquifers are composed of water-permeable **sediments** such as silt, sand, or gravel, which are saturated with water.

—Audesirk, Gerald, Audesirk, Teresa, and Byers, Bruce E., *Biology: Life on Earth,* 9th ed., p. 541.

a. particles   c. containers
b. drops   d. liquids

LO3 Develop Textbook Skills: Using a Glossary

Textbook Skills

Each subject or content area, such as science, mathematics, or English, has its own specialized vocabulary. As you learned in Chapter 1 (p. 16), some text-books provide an extra section in the back of the book called a *glossary* that alphabetically lists all the specialized terms with their definitions as they were used throughout the textbook. Other textbooks may provide short glossaries within each chapter; in these cases, the glossaries may appear in the margins or in highlighted boxes, listing the words in the order that they appear on the page. The meanings given in a glossary are limited to the way in which the word or term is used in that content area.

> A **glossary** is a list of selected terms with their definitions as used in a specific area of study.

Glossaries provide excellent opportunities to use strategies before and after reading. Before reading, skim the section for specialized terms (usually these words are in **bold** or *italic* print). Checking the words and their meanings triggers prior knowledge or establishes meaning that will deepen your comprehension. In addition, you can create vocabulary review lists using glossary terms by paraphrasing or restating the definition in your own words. These vocabulary lists can be used after reading to review and test your recall of the material.

> **EXAMPLE** The following selection is from a college psychology textbook. Before reading, use the glossary to complete your vocabulary review list. Then read the passage. After reading, answer the questions.

Physiological Stress Reactions

[1]How would you respond if you arrived at a class and discovered that you were about to have a pop quiz? [2]You would probably agree that

GLOSSARY

Acute stress A transient state of arousal with typically clear onset and offset patterns.

Chronic stress A continuous state of arousal in which an individual perceives demands as greater than the inner and outer resources available for dealing with them.

Fight-or-flight response A sequence of internal activities triggered when an organism is faced with a threat; prepares the body for combat and struggle or for running away to safety; recent evidence suggests that the response is characteristic only of males.

this would cause you some stress, but what does that mean for your body's reactions? [3]Many of the physiological responses we described for emotional situations are also relevant to day-to-day instances of stress. [4]Such transient states of arousal, with typically clear onset and offset patterns, are examples of **acute stress.** [5]**Chronic stress,** on the other hand, is a state of enduring arousal, continuing over time, in which demands are perceived as greater than the inner and outer resources available for dealing with them. [6]An example of chronic stress might be a continuous frustration with your inability to find time to do all the things you want to do.

Emergency Reactions to Acute Threats

[7]In the 1920s, Walter Cannon outlined the first scientific description of the way animals and humans respond to danger. [8]He found that a sequence of activity is triggered in the nerves and glands to prepare the body either to defend itself and struggle or to run away to safety. [9]Cannon called this dual stress response the **fight-or-flight response.** [10]At the center of this stress response is the *hypothalamus,* which is involved in a variety of emotional responses. [11]The hypothalamus has sometimes been referred to as the *stress center* because of its twin functions in emergencies: (1) it controls the autonomic nervous system (ANS) and (2) it activates the pituitary gland.

—Gerrig, Richard J. and Zimbardo, Philip G.,
Psychology and Life, 16th ed., p. 6.

Before Reading

1. The process that readies the body to deal with danger and conflict is known as _____.

2. _____ is a temporary state that arises from day-to-day instances of stress.

3. Ongoing stress that challenges available resources is known as _____.

After Reading

_____ **4.** The hypothalamus is also known as the
   a. stress center.
   b. autonomic nervous system.
   c. the pituitary gland.

_____ **5.** Physiological stress reactions primarily involve
   a. the mind.
   b. the body.
   c. the emotions.

EXPLANATION

1. The process that readies the body to deal with danger and conflict is known as *fight-or-flight*. Note that the paraphrase (restatement) of the definition for fight-or-flight draws on information given in the glossary.

2. *Acute stress* is a temporary state that arises from day-to-day instances of stress.

3. Ongoing stress that challenges available resources is known as *chronic stress*.

4. The hypothalamus is also known as the (a) "stress center."

5. Physiological stress reactions primarily involve (b) "the body." ◀

Practice 5

Textbook Skills

The following selection is from a college psychology textbook. Before reading, use the glossary to complete your vocabulary review list. Then read the passage. After reading, answer the questions.

Dependence and Addiction

[1]**Psychoactive drugs** are chemicals that affect mental processes and behavior by temporarily changing conscious awareness. [2]Once in the brain, they attach themselves to synaptic receptors, blocking or stimulating certain reactions. [3]By doing so, they profoundly alter the brain's communication system, affecting perception, memory, mood, and behavior. [4]However, continued use of a given drug creates **tolerance**—greater dosages are required to achieve the same effect. . . . [5]Hand in hand with tolerance is **physiological dependence**, a process in which the body becomes adjusted to and dependent on the substance, in part because

GLOSSARY

Psychoactive drugs
Chemicals that affect mental processes and behavior by temporarily changing conscious awareness of reality.

Tolerance A situation that occurs with continued use of a drug in which an individual requires greater dosages to achieve the same effect.

Physiological dependence The process by which the body becomes adjusted to and dependent on a drug.

Addiction A condition in which the body requires a drug in order to function without physical and psychological reactions to its absence; often the outcome of tolerance and dependence.

Psychological dependence The psychological need or craving for a drug.

neurotransmitters are depleted by the frequent presence of the drug. [6]The tragic outcome of tolerance and dependence is **addiction**. [7]A person who is addicted requires the drug in his or her body and suffers painful withdrawal symptoms (shakes, sweats, nausea, and, in the case of alcohol withdrawal, even death) if the drug is not present.

[8]When an individual finds the use of a drug so desirable or pleasurable that a *craving* develops, with or without addiction, the condition is known as **psychological dependence**. [9]Psychological dependence can occur with any drug. [10]The result of drug dependence is that a person's lifestyle comes to revolve around drug use so wholly that his or her capacity to function is limited or impaired. [11]In addition, the expense involved in maintaining a drug habit of daily—and increasing—amounts often drives an addict to robbery, assault, prostitution, or drug peddling. [12]One of the gravest dangers currently facing addicts is the threat of getting AIDS by sharing hypodermic needles—intravenous drug users can unknowingly share bodily fluids with those who have this deadly immune deficiency disease.

[13]Teenagers who use illicit drugs to relieve emotional distress and to cope with daily stressors suffer long-term negative consequences.

—Gerrig, Richard J. and Zimbardo, Philip G., *Psychology and Life*, 16th ed., p. 174.

Before Reading

1. _____ The body requires a drug and suffers painful withdrawal symptoms if the drug is not present.

2. _____ Chemicals that affect an individual's thought processes and actions by temporarily altering the person's awareness of reality.

3. _____ The mental and emotional need or craving for a drug.

4. _____ The body's need for a drug.

5. _____ Greater amounts of the drug are needed for the same effect.

After Reading

Complete the following summary. Fill in the blanks with the appropriate word from the glossary.

Continued use of **(6)** _____ leads to several serious outcomes. First, psychoactive drugs alter a person's sense of reality, "affecting perception, memory, mood, and behavior." Ongoing use of the drug causes **(7)** _____, a state in which the body needs more of the drug to produce the same effect. As the body develops tolerance, the body also develops **(8)** _____ upon the drug. Tragically, the result of tolerance and dependence is **(9)** _____. In addition, a person can suffer from **(10)** _____, when a "craving" for a drug "develops with or without addiction."

LO4
Analyze Word Parts: Roots, Prefixes, Suffixes

Just as ideas are made up of words, words also are made up of smaller parts. *Word parts* can help you learn vocabulary more easily and quickly. In addition, knowing the meaning of the parts of words helps you understand a new word when you see it in context.

Many words are divided into the following three parts: *roots, prefixes*, and *suffixes*.

Root	The basic or main part of a word. Prefixes and suffixes are added to roots to make a new word. Example: *derm* means "skin."
Prefix	A group of letters with a specific meaning added to the beginning of a word (root) to make a new word. Example: the **hypo** in **hypo**dermic means "under."
Suffix	A group of letters with a specific meaning added to the end of a word (root) to make a new word. Example: the **ic** in hypoderm**ic** means "of, like, related to, being."

Master readers understand how the three word parts join together to make additional words.

Roots

The **root** is the basic or main part of a word. Many times a root combined with other word parts will create a whole family of closely related words. Even when the root word is joined with other word parts to form new words, the meaning of the root does not change. Knowing the commonly used roots will help you master many new and difficult words. A list of common roots is available on MyReadingLab.

⊙ **EXAMPLES** Study the following word parts. Using the meaning of the root *clamere* and the context of each sentence, put each word into the sentence that best fits its meaning. Use each word once.

Prefix:	*re-*	(again, back)
Root:	*clamere, claim, clam*	(call out, shout)
Suffix:	*-ant*	(one who does)

> claimant   reclaim

1. The city may ask to _____ the land it had leased to the shoe factory.

2. A _____ is a person who files a loss with an insurance company.

EXPLANATIONS Both words contain the root *clamere* ("call out," "shout"), and each word uses the meaning differently. The additional word parts—the prefix and the suffix—created the different meanings.

1. The word *reclaim* combines the prefix *re-*, which means "again" or "back," with the root *claim*, which means "call out." *Reclaim* means "call back." The city may want to reclaim or call back control of the land it had leased.

2. The word *claimant* combines the root *claim*, which means "call out," with the suffix *-ant*, which means "one who does." A claimant is "one who calls out" for the insurance company to pay for the loss. ⊙

Practice 6

Study the following word parts. Using the meaning of the root *dexter* and context clues, put each word into the sentence that best fits its meaning. Use each word once.

Prefix: *ambi-* (both)
Root: *dexter* (on the right, skillful)
Suffix: *-ous* (of, like, related to, being)
     -ity (a quality)

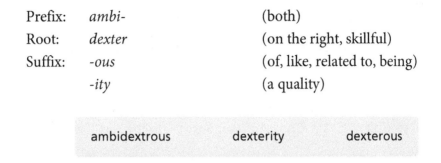

| ambidextrous | dexterity | dexterous |

1. Jolene is _____; she can write and pitch a ball with either her right or her left hand.

2. Miguel, a _____ mechanic, can rapidly rebuild an engine.

3. An Olympic gymnast must possess extraordinary _____.

Prefixes

A **prefix** is a group of letters with a specific meaning added to the beginning of a word or root to make a new word. Although the basic meaning of a root is not changed, a prefix changes the meaning of the word as a whole.

The importance of prefixes can be seen in the family of words that comes from the root *struct*, which means "build." Look over the following examples of prefixes and their meanings. Note the change in the meaning of the whole word based on the meaning of the prefix.

Prefix	Meaning	Root	Meaning	Example
con-	with, together	*struct*	build	*construct* (to build)
de-	down away, reverse			*destruct* (to destroy)
in-	in, into			*instruct* (to teach)

> **EXAMPLES** Using the meanings of the prefixes, root, and context clues, put each word into the sentence that best fits its meaning. Use each word once.

Prefix	Meaning	Root	Meaning
dis-	apart, in different directions	*sect*	cut
inter-	among, between, in the midst		

| dissect | intersect |

1. Some ethicists believe that biology students should learn to _____ using a computer program instead of real animals, such as frogs or cats.

2. My house sits on the corner where the roads New Trail and Rio Pinar _____.

EXPLANATIONS Compare your answers to the explanations below.

1. Some ethicists believe that biology students should learn how to cut apart, *dissect,* animals such as frogs and cats by using a computer program.

2. My house sits on the corner of two roads, New Trail and Rio Pinar, where they *intersect,* cross one another. ◀

Practice 7

Study the meaning of each of the following prefixes and roots.

Prefix	Meaning	Root	Meaning
circum-	around	*spect*	to look
intro-	inside, to the inside	*stance*	stand, position
retro-	backward		

Create at least three words by joining these prefixes and roots.

1. _____

2. _____

3. _____

Suffixes

A **suffix** is a group of letters with a specific meaning added to the end of a word or root to make a new word. Although the basic meaning of a root does not change, a suffix can change the type of word and the way a word is used. (A list of common suffixes is available on MyReadingLab.) Look at the following set of examples.

Root	Meaning	Suffix	Meaning	Word
psych	mind	*-ical*	quality	*psychological*
		-ist	person	*psychologist*
		-ology	study of	*psychology*

Note that sometimes a word will use more than one suffix. For example, the word *psychologist* combines the root *psych* ("mind") with two suffixes: *-ology* ("study of") and *-ist* ("person"). Thus *psychologist* means "a person who studies the mind." The word *psychological* combines the root *psych* ("mind") with two suffixes: *-ology* ("study of") and *-ical* ("quality"). Thus the word *psychological* means "the study of the qualities of the mind." Note also that the *y* in the suffix *-ology* is dropped because the additional suffixes begin with an *i*, which takes the place of the *y*.

▷ EXAMPLES Using the meanings of the root and the suffixes, and the context clues, put each of the words in the box below into the sentence that best fits its meaning. Use each word once.

Root	Meaning	Suffix	Meaning
err	wander, stray, deviate	*-ancy*	quality or state of
		-ant	one who, that which
		-or	a condition

errant   errors

1. News reporters are expected to avoid _____ in their reports.

2. Acting the part of the _____ son, Nathan often rebelled against his parents' wishes.

EXPLANATIONS

1. News reporters are expected to avoid *errors*, that is, wandering or deviating from the facts that serve as a basis for the report.

2. Acting the part of the *errant* son, Nathan often strayed or deviated from his parents' wishes. ◁

Practice 8

Using the meanings of the roots and the suffixes, and the context clues, put each word in the box into the sentence that best fits its meaning. Use each word once. Slight changes in spelling may be necessary.

Root	Meaning	Suffix	Meaning
icon	image, symbol	*-graph*	writing
		-ic	of, like, related to, being
		-ology	study of, science

iconic	iconography	iconology

1. Ted's interest in _____ has taken him to Egypt to visit the pyramids.

2. Lady Gaga's musical abilities and controversial behaviors have turned her into an _____ pop figure.

3. Ancient Egyptians practiced _____ by creating a writing system using pictures for concepts instead of letters for sounds; their writing system is known as hieroglyphics.

LO5 Develop Textbook Skills: Discipline-Specific Vocabulary

Textbook Skills

During your college career, you will take classes in a variety of different course areas, or disciplines. Each discipline has special words that it uses to describe the concepts of its area of study. In other words, each discipline has its own vocabulary. This is part of the reason why reading a biology textbook may seem like a very different experience than reading an economics textbook. Courses in different disciplines may use the same words, but the words sometimes take on new or different meanings within the context of each course area. For example, when a biology textbook talks about a "consumer," it is referring to any organism that eats either plants or animals for food; but when an economics textbook talks about a "consumer," it is referring to any individual who uses a product or service. Although the word is used similarly, the different definitions are a result of their discipline-specific applications.

To help you incorporate these new words into your vocabulary, textbooks usually provide context clues. Word parts can also be an essential tool for deciphering discipline-specific vocabulary. Many academic disciplines, especially in the sciences, use a language that relies heavily on Latin roots, suffixes, and prefixes.

> **EXAMPLE** Read the following text from the college textbook *Biology: Life on Earth.* Then answer the questions, using context clues and the information about word parts as needed.

Energy Enters Community Through Photosynthesis

[1]During photosynthesis, pigments such as chlorophyll absorb specific wavelengths of sunlight. [2]This solar energy is then used in reactions that store energy in chemical bonds, producing sugar and other high-energy molecules. [3]Photosynthetic organisms, from mighty oak trees to single-celled diatoms in the ocean, are called autotrophs or producers, because they produce food for themselves using nonliving nutrients and sunlight. [4]In doing so, they directly or indirectly produce food for nearly all other forms of life as well. [5]Organisms that cannot photosynthesize, called heterotrophs or consumers, must acquire energy and many of their nutrients prepackaged in the molecules that comprise the bodies of other organisms.

—Audesirk, Gerald, Audesirk, Teresa,
and Byers, Bruce E., *Biology: Life
on Earth,* 8th ed., p. 561.

Prefix	Meaning	Root	Meaning	Suffix	Meaning
auto-	self	*tithenai*	to do		
dia-	two	*tome*	segment	*-s*	more than one
eco-	habitat, environment	*troph*	to nourish	*-sis*	action, production
hetere-	other, different			*-ic*	pertaining to
photo-	light				
syn-	together				

_____ 1. What is the best meaning of the word **photosynthesis**?
   a. high-energy molecules   c. solar energy
   b. organisms that use light   d. the action of using light
      to produce food   to produce food

_____ 2. What is the best meaning of **diatoms**?
   a. multi-cell organisms   c. sea creatures
   b. single-cell organisms with   d. mineral deposits
      two-sided cell walls

_____ 3. What is the best meaning of **ecosystem**?
   a. environment   c. nutritional
   b. security   d. plants

_____ 4. What is the best meaning of **trophic**?
   a. environment   c. feeding level
   b. light levels   d. energy supply

5. How would you define **autotrophs** and **heterotrophs**? Explain how you created your definitions. _____

_____

_____

_____

EXPLANATION

1. Word parts and the general sense of the passage reveal the meaning of *photosynthesis*. The prefix *photo* means light; the prefix *syn* means "together"; the root *tithenai* means "to do," and the suffix *sis* indicates that the action of producing something is occurring. In addition, the author offers a defining phrase "use solar energy to make food." When combined, these word parts mean (d) "the action of using light to produce food."

2. Word parts and the general sense of the passage reveal the meaning of *diatoms*: the prefix *dia* means "two"; the root *tome* means "segment," and the suffix *s* indicates "more than one." The author states that diatoms are single-celled organisms, so the word parts indicate that the single cell must have two parts. Thus, the best meaning of *diatoms* is (b) "single-cell organisms with two-sided cell walls."

3. Word parts reveal the meaning of *ecosystem*. The prefix *eco* means "habitat or environment." Thus (a) "environment" is the correct answer.

4. Word parts reveal the meaning of *trophic*. The root *troph* means "to nourish," and the suffix *ic* means "pertaining to." Thus (c) "feeding level" is the correct answer.

5. Although the wording of your answers may vary, you should have come to the following conclusion: "Autotrophs are organisms that can produce their own food." The suffix *auto* means "self," and the root *troph* means "to nourish." "Heterotrophs are organisms that are fed by others." The prefix *hetere* means "other," and the root *troph* means "to nourish." ◀

Practice 9

Study the following passage from a college environmental science textbook. Then complete the activity "Key Term Review," using context clues and the information given about word parts, as needed.

Temperature and the Movement of Air

[1]Every breath we take reaffirms our connection to the **atmosphere,** the layer of gases that surrounds Earth. [2]The atmosphere that seems to stretch so high above us is actually just 1/100th of Earth's diameter, like the fuzzy skin of a peach. [3]It consists of four layers that differ in temperature, density, and composition. Movement of air within the bottommost layer, the **troposphere,** is largely responsible for the planet's weather.

[4]Land and surface water absorb solar energy and then radiate heat, causing some water to evaporate. [5]Air near Earth's surface therefore tends to be warmer and moister than air at higher altitudes. [6]These differences set into motion a process of **convective circulation.** [7]Warm air, being less dense, rises and creates vertical currents. [8]As air rises into regions of lesser atmospheric pressure, it expands and cools. [9]Once the air cools, it becomes denser and descends, replacing warm air that is rising. [10]The descending air picks up heat and moisture near ground level and prepares to rise again, continuing the process. [11]Convective circulation influences both weather and climate.

[12]Under most conditions, air in the troposphere decreases in temperature as altitude increases. [13]Because warm air rises, vertical mixing results. [14]Occasionally, however, a layer of cool air may form beneath a layer of warmer air. [15]This departure from the normal temperature profile is known as a **temperature inversion,** or **thermal inversion.** [16]The band of air in which temperature rises with altitude is called an **inversion layer** (because the normal direction of temperature change is inverted). [17]Thermal inversions can occur in different ways, sometimes involving cool air at ground level and sometimes producing an inversion layer higher above the ground. [18]One common type of inversion occurs in mountain valleys where slopes block morning sunlight, keeping ground-level air within the valley shaded and cool.

[19]Because the cooler air at the bottom of an inversion layer is denser than the warmer air above it, it resists vertical mixing and remains stable. [20]Vertical mixing allows air pollution to be carried upward and diluted, but thermal inversions trap pollutants near the ground. [21]An inversion persisting for several days sparked a "killer smog" crisis in London, England, in 1952. [22]The inversion trapped pollutants from factories and coal-burning stoves, creating foul conditions that killed 4,000 people—and by some estimates up to 12,000.

—Adapted from Withgott, Jay H. and Laposata, Matthew,
Essential Environment: The Science Behind the Stories, pp. 279, 280–281.

Prefix	Meaning	Root	Meaning	Suffix	Meaning
atmos-	vapor, gas	sphere	round figure	-al	of; having
con-	together	therm	heat	-ic	having to do with
in-	back in toward	vectio	carried	-ion	act or process of
tropos-	a turning	vertere	to turn	-ive	relating to

Key Term Review

Match the following terms to their definitions.

_____ **1.** atmospheric

_____ **2.** convective

_____ **3.** inversion

_____ **4.** thermal

_____ **5.** troposphere

a. carrying together; mixing
b. having heat
c. bottom layer of air that surrounds the earth
d. having to do with the gases that surround the earth
e. the process of turning back in; reversing

Complete the Summary

Fill in the blanks with terms from the Key Term Review.

Under normal **(6)** _____ conditions, air in the **(7)** _____, the bottom layer of the atmosphere, is warmer near Earth's surface than at higher altitudes. The warmer air tends to rise, cool, sink back down, warm, and then rise again. This mixing of air is called **(8)** _____ circulation. However, sometimes a layer of cooler air forms at the surface beneath warm air. This reversal of normal warm-cold air temperatures, called a **(9)** _____ **(10)** _____, can trap pollutants near the ground.

LO6 Develop Textbook Skills: Visual Vocabulary

Textbook Skills

Textbooks often make information clearer by giving a visual image such as a graph, chart, or photograph. Take time to study the visual images and captions in this section to figure out how each one ties in to the information given in words.

▶ **EXAMPLE** Study the following image and its caption. Then answer the questions that follow. If necessary, review the passage "Temperature and the Movement of Air" (page 71).

(a) Normal conditions

(b) Thermal inversion

— Withgott, Jay H. and Laposata, Matthew, *Essential Environment: The Science Behind the Stories*, p. 280.

During a _____ inversion, dense cool air remains near the ground, and air warms with altitude within the inversion layer. Little mixing occurs, and pollutants are trapped near the surface.

_____ **1.** Which term best completes the caption?

    a. convective   c. thermal

    b. troposphere   d. atmospheric

2. How does this image add to your understanding of the passage?

_____

_____

1. *Thermal* correctly completes the caption.

2. The image illustrates how cool polluted air can be trapped near the ground under warmer air. ◀

Practice 10

Study the following image and its caption. Then read the passage and answer the questions that follow.

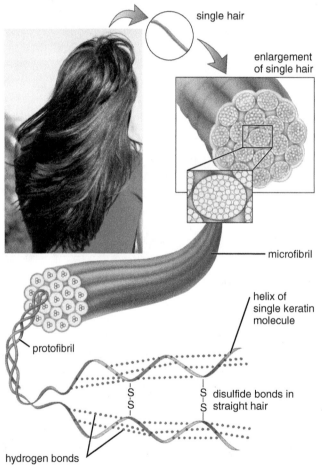

single hair

enlargement
of single hair

microfibril

helix of
single keratin
molecule

protofibril

S–S
S–S

S
S disulfide bonds in
straight hair

hydrogen bonds

▲ FIGURE E3-3 **The structure of hair** At the microscopic level, a single hair is organized into bundles of protofibrils within larger bundles called microfibrils. Each protofibril consists of keratin molecules held in a helical shape by hydrogen bonds, with different keratin strands cross–linked by disulfide bonds. These bonds give hair both elasticity and strength. Straight hair is depicted here.

Proteins and Hair Texture

[1]Pull out a strand of hair, and notice the root or follicle that was embedded in the scalp. [2]Hair is composed mostly of a helical protein called keratin. [3]Living cells in the hair follicle produce new keratin at the rate of 10 turns of the protein helix every second.

—Figure and text from Audesirk, Gerald, Audesirk, Teresa, and Byers, Bruce E., *Biology: Life on Earth,* 9th ed., p. 501.

_____ 1. The best definition of **helical** in this context is
   a. spiral.
   b. circular.
   c. triangular.
   d. square.

2. How does the graphic add to your understanding of the passage?

_____

_____

Apply Information Literacy Skills

 # Academic, Personal, and Career Applications of Vocabulary

Masterful use of vocabulary skills is a key element of information literacy. Information literacy is the ability to recognize a need for new information, such as new vocabulary. You need to be able to identify new words or terms, locate and evaluate their definitions, and usefully apply that information to your situation. For example, in your academic, personal, and career lives, you will come across many unfamiliar words. Thus, you can use the skills you have learned in this chapter in several ways:

- Recognize your own need to know a word or term.
- Discover how to find the meanings of new words or terms.
- Apply the new word or term to the specific situation.

Academic Application

Assume you are taking a college biology course. Your textbook provides three vocabulary resources. (1) Key terms are highlighted in bold print and defined in the text. (2) Each chapter summary lists key vocabulary and identifies the page number where the term appears in the text. (3) The last section of the textbook is a glossary of all the key terms highlighted in bold in the text.

- **Before Reading**: (1) Skim the passage. Note the terms in **bold** and *italics*. (2) Identify three key terms to learn. (3) Create a vocabulary learning plan and word chart to use before, during, and after reading. Consider use of context clues (SAGE), word parts, an online dictionary, and/or textbook resources.

- **During Reading**: Highlight the definitions of the key terms identified before reading.

- **After Reading**: In the space following the passage, complete the word chart with details from the passage.

Key Terms: _____

_____

Vocabulary Learning Plan: _____

_____

_____

_____

If I Can't See Things Far Away, Am I Nearsighted or Farsighted?

[1]It seems that whenever people who wear glasses or contact lenses get together and discuss their vision, one of them says something like, "Nearby objects appear blurry to me, but I can't remember if that means I'm nearsighted or farsighted." [2]Or, someone else may say, "My glasses allow me to see faraway away objects more clearly, so does that mean I am farsighted?" [3]Here we will explain the meaning of nearsightedness and farsightedness as we explore the basis of eye-focusing disorders.

[4]The eye that focuses images correctly on the retina is said to have **emmetropia** (em"e-tro'pe-ah), literally, "harmonious vision." [5]Such an eye is shown in part (a) of the figure.

[6]Nearsightedness is formally called **myopia** (mi"o'pe-ah; "short vision"). [7]It occurs when the parallel *light* rays from distant objects fail to reach the retina and instead are focused in front of it; see part (b) in the figure. [8]Therefore, *distant* objects appear blurry to myopic people. [9]Nearby objects

are in focus, however, because the lens "accommodates" (bulges) to focus the image properly on the retina. [10]Myopia results from an eyeball that is too long, a lens that is too strong, or a cornea that is too curved. [11]Correction requires *concave* corrective lenses that diverge the light rays before they enter the eye, so that they converge farther back. [12]To answer the first question posed above, *near*sighted people see *near* objects clearly and need corrective lenses to focus distant objects.

[13]Farsightedness is formally called **hyperopia** (hi" per-o 'pe-ah; "far vision"). [14]It occurs when the parallel light rays from distant objects are focused *behind* the retina—at least in the resting eye in which the lens is flat and the ciliary muscle is relaxed; see part (c) in the figure. [15]Hyperopia usually results from an eyeball that is too short or a "lazy" lens. [16]People with hyperopia can see distant objects clearly because their ciliary muscles contract continuously to increase the light-bending power of the lens, which moves the focal point forward onto the retina. [17]However, the diverging rays from *nearby* objects are focused so far behind

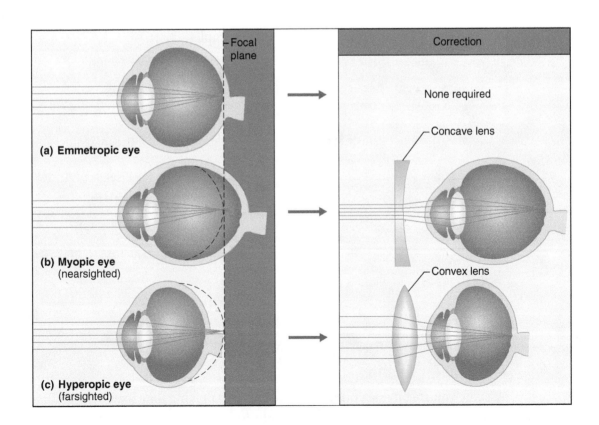

the retina that even at full "bulge," the lens cannot focus the image on the retina. [18]Therefore, nearby objects appear blurry. [19]Furthermore, hyperopic individuals are subject to eyestrain as their endlessly contracting ciliary muscles tire from overwork. [20]Correction to hyperopia requires *convex* corrective lenses that converge the light rays before they enter the eye. [21]To answer the second question posed at the beginning of this essay, *farsighted* people can see *faraway* objects clearly and require corrective lenses to focus on nearby objects.

[22]Unequal curvatures in different parts of the cornea or lens cause **astigmatism** (ah-stig'mah-tizm). [23]In this condition, blurry images occur because points of light are focused not as points on the retina but as lines (*astigma* = not a point). [24]Special cylindrically ground lenses or contacts are used to correct this problem. [25]Eyes that are myopic or hyperopic and astigmatic require a more complex correction.

—Marieb, Elaine N., *Essentials of Human Anatomy and Physiology,* 10th ed., pp. 290.

After Reading: Complete the following chart with three key terms identified before reading. List the resources you used to complete chart.

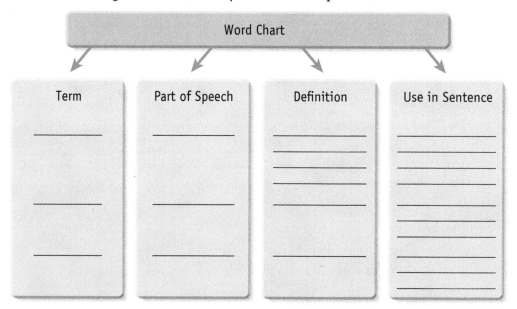

Term	Part of Speech	Definition	Use in Sentence

Personal Application

Assume you are buying your first home and are applying for a loan with a mortgage company. Before you buy, you want to learn more about mortgages and what you can expect. You have found information on a government website.

- **Before Reading**: Skim the terms and circle at least two words about which you want to learn more.
- **During Reading**: Underline the definitions for each term you circled before reading.
- **After Reading**: Use your own words to state the meaning of the words you annotated before and during reading. If needed, go to http://www .merriam-webster.com for more information about the words you identified.

Understanding Your Mortgage

Mortgage statements come in many different forms. However, most contain similar terms and information. Here are some commonly used terms and their definitions that may help you better understand your mortgage statement.

Understanding Your Mortgage Statement

1 **Mortgage Company Contact Information** – name, address, and phone number of the mortgage company. Some statements will also identify the loan officer that originated the loan along with their contact information.

2 **Loan Number** – shows the account number for your loan.

3 **Interest Rate** – the amount charged for the use of borrowing money for your mortgage, expressed as a percentage of the principal.

4 **Taxes Paid/ Escrow Balance** – shows how much property tax has been paid by the lender for the year and how much money is remaining in the escrow account. An escrow account provides the lender with the funds – included in each monthly payment – needed for such expenses as property taxes, homeowners insurance, mortgage insurance, etc.

5 **Total Monthly Payment** – displays total amount due for each specific line item. The total monthly payment generally includes payments for: principal, interest, taxes, and insurance. In some cases, the borrower may decide not to escrow the taxes and insurance and pay them separately from the mortgage payment.

6 **Principal Payment** – displays dollar amount of principal included in the monthly payment. Principal is the amount of money owed on the loan, not including interest.

7 **Interest Payment** – displays dollar amount of interest included in the monthly payment. Interest is a fee charged for the use of borrowing money for the mortgage.

8 **Escrow** – displays dollar amount sent to escrow account in the monthly payment, if the borrower decides to have the mortgage company set aside an escrow.

Source: "Understanding Your Mortgage Statement." 19 March 2011. <http://www.makinghomeaffordable .gov/learning-center/key-concepts/mortgage-statement/Documents/example_mortgage_statement.pdf>

After Reading: Definition of Key Terms

1. _____

   _____

2. _____

   _____

Career Application

Assume you have just been hired as a full-time employee who receives health care benefits. The HR department of your company has sent you the following memo about how to file a health insurance claim.

- **Before Reading**: Skim the text and underline the key terms you need to know. Use an online dictionary to look up the meanings of these words.
- **During Reading**: Highlight details related to the key terms you identified before reading.
- **After Reading**: In the space following the passage, use your own words to state the meaning of the key words you identified before reading.

Filing a Health Insurance Claim

When do you need to file a medical claim?

[1]Participating providers have agreed to file your claims for you. [2]When you receive care from a non-participating provider, you will need to file your claim yourself. [3]Before you can file a claim, you need to receive an itemized bill from your health care provider.

How do you file a medical claim?

[4]First, you must receive the proper itemized bill from your health care provider before you can file a claim. [5]Then, you must complete the Blue Cross & Blue Shield Medical Claim Form. [6]Be sure to read the instructions on the claim form carefully and complete the entire form to avoid delays in processing.

With whom do you file a medical claim?

[7]You should send your completed medical claim forms to: Blue Cross & Blue Shield of Mississippi P.O. Box 12345 Jackson, MS 39123 or fax claims to 601-664-5342.

*How do you file a claim when the Plan is not
your primary source of medical coverage?*

[8]First, file a claim with your "primary" plan and request an Explanation of Benefits (EOB) from that plan. [9]Your second step is to file the claim with your "secondary" plan, which in this case is the State and School Employees' Health Plan. [10]When you file with the Plan, please be sure to include a copy of your primary plan's EOB with your paperwork.

[11]If Medicare is your primary coverage, you would use this same claims filing process when filing for secondary coverage under the Plan.

*I would like to have a claim reviewed.
How do I begin the appeals process?*

[12]You have 180 days to submit a written request for a review after receiving notice of denial from Blue Cross & Blue Shield of Mississippi. [13]If you do not request a review within this timeframe, you will lose your right to review.

*Here Are Some Tips to Help You File
Your Next Claim . . . .*

- [14]Keep all receipts from non-participating pharmacies and physicians.
- [15]File your claim promptly.
- [16]Use the correct form. [17](Remember, there are separate claim forms for medical and prescription drug benefits.)
- [18]Complete the entire form.
- [19]Make a copy of your completed form to keep for your own records.
- [20]Mail the claim form to the correct address or fax claims to 601-646-1234.

—Adapted from Mississippi Department of
Transportation, Filing a Health Insurance Claim.

Key Terms and Definitions: _____

_____

_____

_____

_____

REVIEW TEST 1

Score (number correct) _____ x 10 = _____ %

Visit MyReadingLab to take this test online and receive feedback and guidance on your answers.

Context Clues

Read the following passage from the college textbook *Foundations of Earth Science*. Answer the questions that follow.

Textbook
Skills

Earth's Internal Structure

[1]Earth's interior has three basic divisions—the iron rich **core**; the thin primitive crust; and Earth's largest layer, called the **mantle**, which is located between the core and the crust.

Earth's Crust [2]The crust, Earth's relatively thin, rocky outer skin, is of two types—**continental** crust and oceanic crust. [3]Both share the word crust, but the similarity ends there. [4]The oceanic crust is roughly 7 kilometers (4 miles) thick and composed of the dark igneous rock basalt. [5]By contrast, the continental crust averages 35 to 40 kilometers (22 to 25 miles) thick but may exceed 70 kilometers (40 miles) in some mountainous regions such as the Rockies and Himalayas. [6]Unlike the oceanic crust, which has a relatively **homogeneous** chemical composition, the continental crust consists of many rock types. [7]Although the upper crust has an average composition of a granitic rock called **granodiorite**, it varies considerably from place to place.

[8]Continental rocks have an average density of about 2.7 grams per cubic centimeter, and some are 4 billion years old. [9]The rocks of the oceanic crust are younger (180 million years or less) and denser (about 3.0 grams per cubic centimeter) than continental rocks.

Earth's Mantle [10]More than 82 percent of Earth's volume is contained in the mantle, a solid, rocky shell that extends to a depth of about 2900 kilometers (1800 miles). [11]The boundary between the crust and mantle represents a marked change in chemical composition. [12]The dominant rock type in the uppermost mantle is **peridotite**, which is richer in the metals magnesium and iron than the minerals found in either the continental or oceanic crust.

[13]The upper mantle extends from the crust-mantle boundary down to a depth of about 660 kilometers (410 miles). [14]The upper mantle can be

divided into three different parts. [15]The top portion of the upper mantle is part of the stiff **lithosphere**, and beneath that is the weaker asthenosphere. [16]The bottom part of the upper mantle is called the transition zone.

[17]The lithosphere (sphere of rock) consists of the entire crust and uppermost mantle and forms Earth's relatively cool, rigid outer shell. [18]Averaging about 100 kilometers (62 miles) in thickness, the lithosphere is more than 250 kilometers (155 miles) thick below the oldest portions of the continents. [19]Beneath this stiff layer to a depth of about 350 kilometers (217 miles) lies a soft, comparatively weak layer known as the **asthenosphere** ("weak sphere"). [20]The top portion of the asthenosphere has a temperature/pressure regime that results in a small amount of melting. [21]Within this very weak zone, the lithosphere is mechanically detached from the layer below. [22]The result is that the lithosphere is able to move independently of the asthenosphere, a fact we will consider in the next chapter.

[23]It is important to emphasize that the strength of various Earth materials is a function of both their composition and the temperature and pressure of their environment. [24]The entire lithosphere does not behave like a brittle solid similar to rocks found on the surface. [25]Rather, the rocks of the lithosphere get progressively hotter and weaker (more easily deformed) with increasing depth. [26]At the depth of the uppermost asthenosphere, the rocks are close enough to their melting temperature that they are very easily deformed, and some melting may actually occur. [27]Thus, the upper most asthenosphere is weak because it is near its melting point, just as hot wax is weaker than cold wax.

[28]From 660 kilometers (410 miles) deep to the top of the core, at a depth of 2900 kilometers (1800 miles), is the lower mantle. [29]Because of an increase in pressure (caused by the weight of the rock above), the mantle gradually strengthens with depth. [30]Despite their strength however, the rocks within the lower mantle are very hot and capable of very gradual flow.

Earth's Core [31]The composition of the core is thought to be an iron-nickel alloy with minor amounts of oxygen, silicon, and sulfur-elements that readily form compounds with iron. [32]At the extreme pressure found in the core, this iron-rich material has an average density of nearly 11 grams per cubic centimeter and approaches 14 times the density of water at Earth's center.

[33]The core is divided into two regions that exhibit very different mechanical strengths. [34]The outer core is a liquid layer 2270 kilometers (1410 miles) thick. [35]It is the movement of metallic iron within this zone that generates Earth's magnetic field. [36]The inner core is a sphere with a radius of 1216 kilometers (754 miles). [37]Despite its higher temperature, the iron in the inner core is solid due to the immense pressures that exist in the center of the planet.

—Lutgens, Frederick K., Tarbuck, Edward J., and Tasa, Dennis, *Foundations of Earth Science,* 5th ed., pp. 176–177.

_____ 1. What is the best meaning of the word **continental** in sentence 2?
   a. of or related to land   c. of or related to oceans
   b. of or related to colonies   d. of or related to Europe

_____ 2. Identify the context clue used for **continental** in sentence 2.
   a. synonym   c. general sense of the passage
   b. antonym   d. example

_____ 3. What is the best meaning of **homogeneous** in sentence 6?
   a. different than   c. of the same kind
   b. liquid   d. solid

_____ 4. Identify the context clue used for **homogeneous** in sentence 6.
   a. synonym   c. general sense of the passage
   b. antonym   d. example

Match the following glossary words to their definitions

_____ 5. asthenosphere

_____ 6. core

_____ 7. granodiorite

_____ 8. mantle

_____ 9. lithosphere

_____ 10. peridotite

a. a solid rocky shell, extends about 1800 miles below crust

b. dominant rock in uppermost mantle; made of magnesium and iron

c. innermost layer of Earth; mostly of iron-nickel alloy

d. middle, weaker layer of the upper mantle

e. a granitic rock that composes the upper crust

f. rigid outer layer of Earth; includes the crust and upper mantle

REVIEW TEST 2

Score (number correct) _____ x 10 = _____ %

Visit MyReadingLab to take this test online and receive feedback and guidance on your answers.

Context Clues

Choose the best definition for each word in **bold** type. Then, identify the context clue used in each passage. A clue may be used more than once.

Context Clues

> Synonym
> Antonym
> General context
> Example

_____ **1.** Jerry and Marie were **incredulous** when they heard that they had purchased the sole winning lottery ticket; they were skeptical that they could have won the entire $34 million jackpot.
    a. excited   c. disbelieving
    b. secretive   d. hysterical

2. Context clue: _____

_____ **3.** The Underground Railroad was a route made up of a series of **clandestine** safe houses for African Americans fleeing the injustice of slavery in the South.
    a. exposed   c. dangerous
    b. secret   d. poor

4. Context clue: _____

_____ **5.** Some people who are infected with West Nile virus develop mild flulike symptoms that disappear within a few days. However, in rare cases, West Nile virus leads to more **virulent** infections that could cause long-term disability or even death.
    a. weak   c. contagious
    b. hidden   d. dangerous

6. Context clue: _____

_____ **7.** The play *The Taming of the Shrew* by William Shakespeare is known for its **trenchant**, or biting, wit about the battle of the sexes.
  a. subtle   c. bland
  b. cutting   d. rude

8. Context clue: _____

_____ **9.** Often, humans are driven by their **temporal** needs for safety, food, housing, and other possessions and measure their success by how well these needs are met.
  a. long-term   c. spiritual
  b. sordid   d. worldly

10. Context clue: _____

REVIEW TEST 3

Score (number correct) _____ x 10 = _____ %

Visit MyReadingLab to take this test online and receive feedback and guidance on your answers.

Vocabulary Skills

Textbook
Skills

Before Reading: Study the glossary and survey the passage from a college sociology textbook. Locate the terms from the glossary in the passage; circle the terms and underline the definitions as they are worded in context. Then read the passage and respond to the After Reading questions and activities.

Glossary

megacity: a city of 10 million or more residents

megalopolis: an urban area consisting of at least two metropolises and their many suburbs

metropolis: a central city surrounded by smaller cities and their suburbs

metropolitan statistical area: a central city and the urbanized counties adjacent to it

urbanization: the process by which an increasing proportion of the population live in cities and have growing influence on the culture

The Process of Urbanization

[1]Although cities are not new to the world scene, urbanization is. [2]**Urbanization** refers to masses of people moving to cities, and these cities

having a growing influence on society. [3]Urbanization is taking place all over the world. [4]In 1800, only 3 percent of the world's population lived in cities (Hauser and Schnore 1965). [5]Then in 2007, for the first time in history, more people lived in cities than in rural areas. [6]Urbanization is uneven across the globe. [7]For the industrialized world, it is 77 percent, and for the Least Industrialized Nations, it is 41 percent (Haub 2006; Robb 2007). [8]Without the Industrial Revolution, this remarkable growth could not have taken place, for an extensive infrastructure is needed to support hundreds of thousands and even millions of people in a relatively small area.

[9]To understand the city's attraction, we need to consider the "pulls" of urban life. [10]Because of its exquisite division of labor, the city offers incredible variety—music ranging from rap and salsa to country and classical, shops that feature imported delicacies from around the world and those that sell special foods for vegetarians and diabetics. [11]Cities also offer anonymity, which so many find refreshing in light of the tighter controls of village and small-town life. [12]And, of course, the city offers work.

[13]Some cities have grown so large and have so much influence over a region that the term city is no longer adequate to describe them. [14]The term **metropolis** is used instead. [15]This term refers to a central city surrounded by smaller cities and their suburbs. [16]They are linked by transportation and communication and connected economically, and sometimes politically, through county boards and regional governing bodies. [17]St. Louis is an example.

[18]Although this name, St. Louis, properly refers to a city of 340,000 people in Missouri, it also refers to another 2 million people who live in more than a hundred separate towns in both Missouri and Illinois. [19]Altogether, the region is known as the "St. Louis or Bi-State Area." [20]Although these towns are independent politically, they form an economic unit. [21]They are linked by work (many people in the smaller towns work in St. Louis or are served by industries from St. Louis), by communications (they share the same area newspaper and radio and television stations), and by transportation (they use the same interstate highways, the Bi-State Bus system, and international airport). [22]As symbolic interactionists would note, shared symbols (the Arch, the Mississippi River, Busch Brewery, the Cardinals, the Rams, the Blues—both the hockey team and the music) provide the residents a common identity.

[23]Most of the towns run into one another, and if you were to drive through this metropolis, you would not know that you were leaving one

town and entering another—unless you had lived there for some time and were aware of the fierce small town identifications and rivalries that coexist within this overarching identity.

[24]Some metropolises have grown so large and influential that the term **megalopolis** is used to describe them. [25]This term refers to an overlapping area consisting of at least two metropolises and their many suburbs. [26]Of the twenty or so megalopolises in the United States, the three largest are the Eastern seaboard running from Maine to Virginia, the area in Florida between Miami, Orlando, and Tampa, and California's coastal area between San Francisco and San Diego. [27]The California megalopolis extends into Mexico and includes Tijuana and its suburbs.

[28]This process of urban areas turning into a metropolis, and a metropolis developing into a megalopolis, occurs worldwide. [29]When a city's population hits 10 million, it is called a **megacity.** [30]In 1950, New York City was the only megacity in the world. [31]Today there are 19. [32]The figure entitled "How Many Millions of People Live in the World's Largest Megacities?" shows the world's 10 largest megacities. [33]Note that most megacities are located in the Least Industrialized Nations.

—Henslin, James M., *Sociology: A Down-to-Earth Approach*, 9th ed., p. 606.

After Reading

Use the word parts and terms in the word bank to complete the word web based on information from the glossary and the passage.

city	mega-	megalopolis	metropolis	-polis-
large	megacity	metro-	mother	urbanization

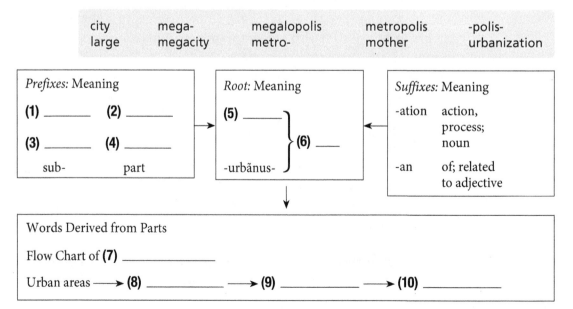

Prefixes: Meaning

(1) _____   (2) _____

(3) _____   (4) _____

sub-   part

Root: Meaning

(5) _____

(6) _____

-urbānus-

Suffixes: Meaning

-ation   action, process; noun

-an   of; related to adjective

Words Derived from Parts

Flow Chart of **(7)** _____

Urban areas ⟶ **(8)** _____ ⟶ **(9)** _____ ⟶ **(10)** _____

VISUAL *VOCABULARY*

Fill in the blank with a word from the glossary that completes the caption.

The U.S. Census Bureau divides the country into 274 _____

_____ (MSAs). Each MSA consists of a central city of at least

50,000 people and the urbanized areas linked to it. About three of five

Americans live in just fifty or so MSAs.

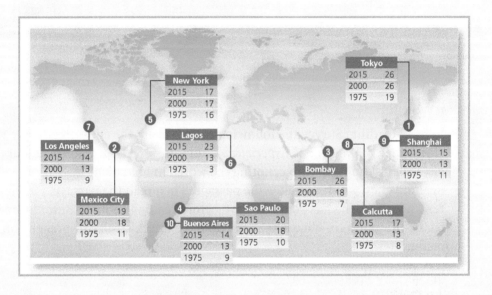

—Henslin, James M., *Sociology: A Down-to-Earth
Approach,* 9th ed., Figure 20.10.

SUMMARY RESPONSE

Restate the author's most important idea in your own words using some of the
words in bold print. Begin your summary response with the following: *The
most important idea of "The Process of Urbanization" by Henslin is . . .*

WHAT DO YOU THINK?

What type of community do you live in? How has urbanization affected your
area? Write an article for local publication that describes your vision for how

the city should grow or control growth. Consider the following:

- Describe your community.
- Identify strengths in your community.
- Identify problems in your community.

REVIEW TEST 4

Score (number correct) _____ x 10 = _____ %

Visit MyReadingLab to take this test online and receive feedback and guidance on your answers.

Vocabulary Skills

Before Reading: Survey the following passage from the college textbook *World Civilizations: The Global Experience.* Study the words in the Vocabulary Preview; then skim the passage, noting the words in bold print. Answer the Before Reading questions that follow the passage. Then read the passage. Finally, after reading, check the answers you gave before reading to make sure they are accurate. Respond to What Do You Think? to check your comprehension after reading.

Vocabulary Preview

Republic (sentence 2): State
Muslim (sentence 3): a believer of Islam
hold (sentence 21): the interior of a ship below deck; the cargo deck of a ship
singular (sentence 22): individual

Textbook
Skills

Africa and the Africans in the Age of the Atlantic Slave Trade

¹Sometimes a single, extraordinary life can represent the forces and patterns of a whole historical era. ²Born in the early 19th century, Mahommah Gardo Baquaqua was a young man from the trading town of Djougou in what is now the Benin **Republic** in west Africa. ³A **Muslim**, he could speak Arabic, Hausa, and a number of other languages, as was common among the trading peoples from which he came. ⁴At a young age, Baquaqua was captured and **enslaved** during a war with a neighboring African state; after gaining his freedom, he

was enslaved again, and around 1845 he was sold into the Atlantic slave trade.

[5]Baquaqua was taken first to northeastern Brazil and from there was purchased by a ship captain from Rio de Janeiro. [6]After a number of voyages along the Brazilian coast, his ship eventually sailed for New York. [7]After a failed attempt to use the American courts to gain his freedom (a strategy that many slaves attempted), Baquaqua fled to Boston with the help of local **abolitionists.** [8]In that city he was **befriended** by anti-slavery Baptist missionaries. [9]With them, he sailed for Haiti. [10]Eventually he learned French and English and studied at a college in upstate New York in order to prepare for missionary work in his native Africa. [11]His life was not easy. [12]Eventually, because of racial incidents, he moved to Canada.

[13]Although Baquaqua had left the Baptist college, he did not abandon his desire to return to Africa, and he continued to seek ways to make that voyage. [14]In 1854, in an attempt to get the money he needed to realize his dream, he published his **autobiography,** [15]*An Interesting Narrative: Biography of Mahommah G. Baquaqua.* [16]In it he was able to provide his personal observations on his experiences. [17]On the slave ship, he reported:

> [18]O the loathsomeness and filth of that horrible place will never be **effaced** from my memory; nay as long as my memory holds her seat in this **distracted** brain, will I remember that. [19]My heart, even at this day, sickens at the thought of it. [20]Let those humane individuals, who are in favor of slavery, only allow themselves to take the slave's position in the noisome hold of a slave ship, just for one trip from Africa to America, and without going into the horrors of slavery further than this, if they do not come out thorough-going abolitionists, then I have no more to say in favor of abolition.

[21]The only place worse than the **hold** of a slave ship, said Baquaqua, was the place to which slave owners would be condemned in the next life. [22]We do not know whether Baquaqua finally returned to the land of his birth, but the life of this African, while **singular** in many aspects, represents the stories of millions of Africans in the age of the slave trade, and these make up an important part of world history.

—Stearns, Peter N., Adas, Michael B., Schwartz, Stuart B., and Gilbert, Marc Jason, *World Civilizations: The Global Experience, Combined Volume, Atlas Edition,* 5th ed., pp. 542–543.

Before Reading

A. Use context clues to state in your own words the definition of the following terms. Indicate the context clue you used.

1. In sentence 4, what does the word **enslaved** mean? _____

2. Identify the context clue used for the word **enslaved** in sentence 4.

    _____

3. In sentence 7, what does the word **abolitionists** mean? _____

    _____

4. Identify the context clue used for the word **abolitionists** in sentences 7 and 20.

    _____

5. In sentence 8, what does the word **befriended** mean? _____

    _____

6. Identify the context clue used for the word **befriended** in sentence 8. ____

    _____

7. In sentence 18, what does the word **distracted** mean? _____

    _____

8. Identify the context clue used for the word **distracted** in sentence 18. ____

    _____

B. Study the following chart of word parts. Use context clues and the word parts to answer the questions that follow.

Prefix	Meaning	Root	Meaning	Suffix	Meaning
auto-	self	*bio*	life	*-ed*	completed action
ef-	out	*fac*	face	*-y*	quality, state
		graph	write		

_____ **9.** What does the word **effaced** in sentence 18 mean?
   a. carved   c. seen
   b. wiped out   d. endured

10. What does the word **autobiography** in sentence 14 mean? _____

_____

SUMMARY RESPONSE

Restate the author's most important idea in your own words using some of the words in bold print. Begin your summary response with the following: *The most important idea of "Africa and the Africans in the Age of the Atlantic Slave Trade" by Sterns, Adas, Schwartz, and Gilbert is . . .*

WHAT DO YOU THINK?

Write an autobiographical or biographical essay. Consider the following:

- Describe the ways your life or someone you know represents an important aspect of our era.
- Use vocabulary specific to our time.
- Identify universal issues that impact you personally.

After Reading About Vocabulary Skills

Before you move on to the Mastery Tests on vocabulary skills for master readers, take time to reflect on your learning and performance by answering the following questions. Write your answers in your notebook.

- How has my knowledge base or prior knowledge about vocabulary and glossary skills changed?
- Based on my studies, how do I think I will perform on the Mastery Test(s)? Why do I think my scores will be above average, average, or below average? (Note: An additional fourth Mastery Test may be found in MyReadingLab.)

■ Would I recommend this chapter to other students who want to learn more about vocabulary skills? Why or why not?

Test your understanding of what you have learned about Vocabulary and Dictionary Skills for Master Readers by completing the Chapter 2 Review.

Name _____ Section _____

Date _____ **Score** (number correct) _____ x 10 = _____ %

Visit MyReadingLab to take this test online and receive feedback and guidance on your answers.

Read the following passage from the college textbook *Psychology and Life.* Answer the questions that follow.

Sleep Apnea

Textbook Skills

[1]Sleep apnea is a sleep disorder that causes the person to stop breathing while asleep. [2]When this happens, the blood's oxygen level drops and emergency hormones are **secreted**, which then causes the sleeper to awaken and begin breathing again. [3]Most people have a few apnea **episodes** a night. [4]However, someone with sleep apnea disorder can have hundreds of such cycles every night. [5]Sometimes apnea episodes frighten the sleeper. [6]But often they are so brief that the sleeper fails to credit **accumulating** or mounting sleepiness to them.

[7]Consider, for example, the case of a famous psychologist who, because of undetected sleep apnea, could not stay awake during research meetings and lectures. [8]When his wife made him aware of his disturbing nighttime behavior, he went to a sleep disorder clinic. [9]The treatment he received **reinvigorated** or revived his career (Zimbardo, personal communication, 1991). [10]In other cases, people have lost their jobs, friends, and even spouses.

[11]Sleep apnea is also frequent in premature infants. [12]These babies sometimes need physical **stimulation** to start breathing again. [13]Because of their immature respiratory system, these infants must remain attached to monitors in intensive care nurseries as long as the problem continues.

—Gerrig, Richard J. and Zimbardo, Philip G.,
Psychology and Life, 16th ed., p. 165.

_____ **1.** What is the best meaning of the word **secreted** in sentence 2?
   a. hidden   c. suppressed
   b. produced   d. disturbed

_____ **2.** Identify the context clue used for **secreted** in sentence 2.
   a. synonym   c. general context
   b. antonym   d. example

_____ **3.** What is the best meaning of the word **episodes** in sentence 3?
   a. scares   c. reasons
   b. events   d. treatments

_____ **4.** Identify the context clue used for **episodes** in sentence 3.
   a. synonym
   c. general context
   b. antonym
   d. example

_____ **5.** What is the best meaning of the word **accumulating** in sentence 6?
   a. lessening
   c. increasing
   b. embarrassing
   d. confusing

_____ **6.** Identify the context clue used for **accumulating** in sentence 6.
   a. synonym
   c. general context
   b. antonym
   d. example

_____ **7.** What is the best meaning of the word **reinvigorated** in sentence 9?
   a. repressed
   c. cured
   b. ruined again
   d. strengthened again

_____ **8.** Identify the context clue used for **reinvigorated** in sentence 9.
   a. synonym
   c. general context
   b. antonym
   d. example

_____ **9.** What is the best meaning of the word **stimulation** in sentence 12?
   a. encouragement
   c. pain
   b. hindrance
   d. relief

_____ **10.** Identify the context clue used for **stimulation** in sentence 12.
   a. synonym
   c. general context
   b. antonym
   d. example

Name _____ Section _____

Date _____ **Score** (number correct) _____ x 10 = _____ %

Visit MyReadingLab to take this test online and receive feedback and guidance on your answers.

Read the following passage adapted from the college humanities textbook *The Creative Impulse: An Introduction to the Arts*. Using context clues, write the definition for each word in **bold** type. Choose definitions from the box. You will not use all the definitions. Then identify the context clue you used to determine the meaning of each word.

Cave Painting

Textbook
Skills

[1]The Cave of Lascaux (lahs-KOH) in France lies slightly over a mile from the little town of Montignac, in the valley of the Vézère (vay-Zair) River. [2]The cave itself was discovered in 1940 by a group of children who, while investigating a tree uprooted by a storm, scrambled down a **fissure** (crevice) into a world undisturbed for thousands of years. [3]The cave was sealed in 1963 to protect it from **atmospheric** damage, and visitors now see Lascaux II, an exact replica, which is sited in a quarry 600 feet away.

[4]Perhaps a **sanctuary** for the performance of sacred rites and ceremonies, the Main Hall, or Hall of the Bulls, elicits a sense of power and grandeur. [5]The thundering herd moves below a sky formed by the rolling contours of the stone ceiling of the cave, sweeping our eyes forward as we travel into the cave itself. [6]At the entrance of the main hall, the 8-foot "unicorn" begins a larger-than-lifesize **montage** of bulls, horses, and deer, which are up to 12 feet tall. [7]Their shapes intermingle with one another, and their colors radiate warmth and power. [8]These magnificent creatures remind us that their creators were capable technicians, who, with artistic skills at least equal to our own, were able to capture the essence, that is heart, beneath the visible surface of their world. [9]The paintings in the Main Hall were created over a long period of time and by a succession of artists. [10]Yet their **cumulative** or combined effect in this 30- by 100-foot domed gallery is that of a single work, carefully composed for maximum dramatic and communicative impact.

—Sporre, Dennis J., *The Creative Impulse:
An Introduction to the Arts*, 8th ed., pp. 38–39.

ancient	composite	environmental	spirit
collective	crack	shelter	sweeping

Context Clues

Synonym
Antonym
General context
Example

1. In sentence 2, **fissure** means _____.

2. Context clue used for **fissure**: _____

3. In sentence 3, **atmospheric** means _____.

4. Context clue used for **atmospheric**: _____

5. In sentence 4, **sanctuary** means _____.

6. Context clue used for **sanctuary**: _____

7. In sentence 6, **montage** means _____.

8. Context clue used for **montage**: _____

9. In sentence 10, **cumulative** means _____.

10. Context clue used for **cumulative**: _____

This painting in the Cave
of Lascaux, France, is a

_____ of larger-
than-lifesize animals.

Name _____ Section _____

Date _____ **Score** (number correct) _____ x 20 = _____ %

Visit MyReadingLab to take this test online and receive feedback and guidance on your answers.

Read the following passage from the college textbook *Economics*. Answer the questions that follow the passage.

Oligopoly

[1]An **oligopoly** is an industry dominated by a few large firms. [2]They are not like small competitive firms, but they are also not **monopolists**. [3]There is great variety in oligopolistic industries, so economists have developed a number of different models of oligopoly to describe their behavior and results. [4]Oligopoly has the following major characteristics:

- [5]A few firms produce most of the output in an industry. [6]These firms are thus usually large with respect to the market, and dominate its activities. [7]Examples include automobiles, computers, steel, aluminum, cigarettes, and chewing gum. [8]In some cases, there may be fewer than ten firms in the entire industry. [9]In others, there may be hundreds of companies, but four or five firms dominate.

- [10]The product of an oligopoly may be **homogeneous** or differentiated. [11]If it is a consumer good, it is usually differentiated to gain consumers' attention and loyalty (e.g., automobiles). [12]And, if it is a raw material sold to other firms, it is usually homogeneous (e.g., steel, copper, or aluminum).

- [13]There may be technological reasons for domination of an industry by a few firms. [14]Large-scale operations may enjoy lower costs. [15]Economies of scale may allow only a few firms to constitute the entire industry, given the size of the market. [16]Firms may also have grown large due to mergers. [17]As a result, entry into such markets is difficult. [18]Because of the substantial initial investment, a firm must be large to enter.

- [19]The firms in an oligopolistic industry are **interdependent**; their pricing and output decisions affect the other firms in the industry. [20]Each firm must pay close attention to the actions of its rivals. [21]This creates a constant possibility for price wars (aggressive price cutting to increase sales) among oligopolists or **collusion** to avoid those price wars. [22]It can also lead to price leadership or a reluctance to alter price. [23]Despite this interdependence, oligopoly firms do have some control over their prices.

- [24]Oligopolies usually have a significant amount of nonprice competition, such as product differentiation and advertising.

> —Riddell, Tom, Shackelford, Jean A., Stamos, Stephen C., and Schneider, Geoffrey, *Economics: A Tool for Critically Understanding Society*, 9th ed., p. 181.

Use context clues and the word parts in the chart below to state in your own words the definitions of the following words from the passage.

Prefix	Meaning	Root	Meaning	Suffix	Meaning
col-	with	*genus*	kind	-ent	in a condition that
homo-	same	*lūdere*	to play	-ion	the act of
inter-	between, among	*pendere*	to hang on	-ist	one that
mono-	single	*pōlein*	to sell	-ous	of; characterized by
oligo-	few				

1. In sentence 1, what does the word **oligopoly** mean? _____

   _____

2. In sentence 2, what does the word **monopolists** mean? _____

   _____

3. In sentence 10, what does the word **homogeneous** mean? _____

   _____

4. In sentence 19, what does the word **interdependent** mean? _____

   _____

5. In sentence 21, what does the word **collusion** mean? _____

   _____

2 Summary of Key Concepts of Vocabulary Skills

LO1 LO2
LO3 LO4

Assess your comprehension of vocabulary skills.

- **Vocabulary** is _____.

- The acronym SAGE identifies four of the most common types of context clues: The four context clues and their definitions are as follows:

Context Clue	Definition
■ _____	_____
	_____
■ _____	_____
	_____
	_____
■ _____	_____
	_____
	_____
	_____
■ _____	_____
	_____
	_____

- The three basic word parts and their definitions are as follows:

Word Part	Definition
■ _____	_____
■ _____	_____
	_____
	_____
	_____
■ _____	_____
	_____
	_____
	_____

- Each subject matter has its own _____.

- A glossary is _____

  _____, often provided as an extra section in

  _____.

Test Your Comprehension of Vocabulary Skills

Respond to the following prompts.

LO2 LO3 LO4 LO5 Demonstrate your use of context clues. Use the headings below and create a chart based on the four types of context clues. Then complete the chart with new words you have come across recently.

Type of Clue	New Word	Meaning of Word	Source Sentence of Word

LO4 Demonstrate your ability to decode the meaning of words using word parts. Use the blank word web below to create your own web of words linked by word parts. Use a family of words you have come across recently.

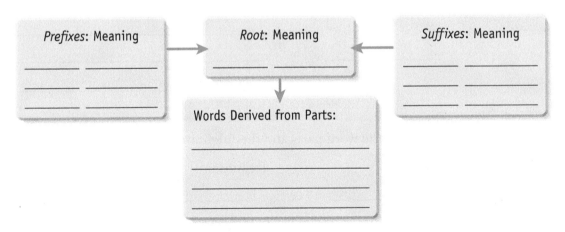

LO5 Create a glossary of terms for a subject you are currently studying; use the headings below to create your glossary. Then complete the chart with new words you have come across recently.

Word	Definition	Source Sentence of Word

Stated Main Ideas

(LO) LEARNING OUTCOMES

After studying this chapter, you should be able to:

- (LO1) Identify the Traits of a Main Idea
- (LO2) Identify the Topic of a Paragraph
- (LO3) Identify a Topic Sentence
- (LO4) Analyze the Flow of Ideas and Identify Placement of Topic Sentences
- (LO5) Recognize the Central Idea and Thesis Statement
- (LO6) Develop Textbook Skills: Identify Topics, Main Ideas, and Central Ideas in Textbook Passages
- (LO7) Apply Information Literacy Skills: Academic, Personal, and Career Applications of Stated Main Ideas

Before Reading About Stated Main Ideas

Effective use of the reading process relies on developing questions about the material that will guide you as you read. Using the chapter learning outcomes above, create at least five questions that you can answer as you study the chapter. Write your questions in the following spaces:

_____? (page _____)

_____? (page _____)

_____? (page _____)

_____? (page _____)

_____? (page _____)

Compare the questions you created based on the chapter learning outcomes with the following questions. Then write the ones that seem the most helpful in your notebook, leaving enough space after each question to record the answers as you read and study the chapter.

What are the traits of a main idea? (p. 100) What is the difference between a topic and a topic sentence? (p. 105) How is the flow of ideas related to the placement of topic sentences? (p. 109) What is the central idea? (p. 118) What is the difference between the central idea and thesis statement? (p. 119)

Identify the Traits of a Main Idea

> A **main idea** is the author's controlling point about the topic. It usually includes the topic and the author's attitude or opinion about the topic, or the author's approach to the topic.

To identify the main idea, ask yourself two questions:

- Who or what is the paragraph about? The answer is the *topic*. The topic can be stated in just a few words.
- What is the author's controlling point about the topic? The answer is the *main idea*. The main idea is stated in one sentence.

Consider these questions as you read the following paragraph from the college textbook *Essentials of Human Communication.*

Textbook
Skills

Communication Context

[1]The context of communication influences what you say and how you say it. [2]You communicate differently depending on the context you're in. [3]The communication context consists of at least four aspects. [4]The *physical context* refers to the tangible environment, the room, park, or auditorium; you don't talk the same way at a noisy football game as you do at a quiet funeral. [5]The *cultural context* refers to lifestyles, beliefs, values, behavior, and communication of a group; it is the rules of a group of people for considering something is right or wrong. [6]The *social-psychological context* refers to the status relationships among speakers, the formality of the situation; you don't talk the same way in the cafeteria as you would at a formal dinner at your boss's house. [7]The *temporal context* refers to the position in which a message fits into a sequence of events; you don't talk the same way after someone tells of the death of a close relative as you do after someone tells of winning the lottery.

—DeVito, Joseph A., *Essentials of Human Communication,* 4th ed., p. 7.

- *Who or what is the paragraph about*? The topic of the paragraph is "the communication context."

- *What is the author's controlling point about the topic*? The controlling point is that it "consists of at least four aspects." Putting topic and controlling point together, the main idea is "The communication context consists of at least four parts."

To better understand the traits of a main idea, compare a passage to a well-planned house of ideas. The *topic* or general subject matter is the roof. The roof covers all the rooms of the house. The *main idea* is the frame of the house, and the supporting details are the different rooms. The following diagram shows the relationship of the ideas:

Topic: the communication context

Main Idea (stated in a topic sentence):

The communication context consists of at least four aspects.

Supporting Details:

| The physical context | The cultural context | The social-psychological context | The temporal context |

Each of the supporting details explains one aspect of the communication process.

LO2 Identify the Topic of a Paragraph

When you ask the question "Who or what is the paragraph about?" you must be sure that your answer is neither too general nor too specific. A general subject needs specific ideas to support or explain it. However, no single paragraph can discuss all the specific ideas linked to a general idea. So an author narrows the general subject to a topic that needs a specific set of ideas to support it. For example, the very general subject "humor" can be narrowed to "stand-up comics." And the specific details related to stand-up comics might include different comics, ranging from Chris Rock to Aziz Ansari to Louis C. K. However, a piece of writing dealing with the general topic "humor" will include a very different set of specific ideas than the narrower topic of "stand-up comics." The more general category of humor might include jokes and television sitcoms, for example.

Often an author shows the relationship between the topic and the specific details by repeating the topic throughout the paragraph as new pieces of information are introduced. To identify the topic, a master reader often skims the material for this recurring idea. Skimming for the topic allows you to grasp the relationship among a general subject, the topic, and specific details.

> **EXAMPLE** Skim the following paragraph. Circle the topic as it recurs throughout the paragraph. Answer the question that follows.

A Question of Manners

[1]Bad manners seem to dominate today's culture. [2]In fact, bad manners have become so common in everyday life that even pop psychologist Dr. Phil devoted an entire segment of his television show to confronting people about their inconsiderate behaviors. [3]Some people are rude enough to loudly conduct cell phone conversations about private matters in public places such as restaurants, stores, and theatres. [4]Some customers feel no shame in speaking rudely, even abusively, to sales clerks and food servers. [5]Frequently, automobile drivers change lanes or turn without signaling, ride too near to the bumpers of other cars, and make rude hand gestures as they pass.

_____ Which of the following best states the topic?
   a. manners
   b. bad manners
   c. confronting people about their inconsiderate behaviors

EXPLANATION "Manners" is too general, for it could cover good manners, business manners, or eating manners. "Confronting people about their inconsiderate behaviors" is too specific. This idea is a supporting detail, just one piece of evidence for the claim that bad manners dominate today's culture.

The topic of this paragraph is (b) "bad manners." You should have circled the following phrases: "Bad manners" (sentences 1 and 2), "inconsiderate behaviors" (sentence 2), "rudely" (sentence 4), and "rude" (sentences 3 and 5). Notice how the author uses the synonyms "rude" and "rudely" to restate the topic "bad manners." <

Practice 1

Skim each of the following paragraphs and circle the topic as it recurs throughout the paragraph. Then identify the idea that correctly states the topic. (*Hint:* one idea is too general to be the topic; another idea is too specific.)

_____ **1.** [1]Reflexology is a form of natural healing based on the belief that reflexes in the hands, feet, and ears correspond to specific parts, glands, and organs of the body. [2]By applying pressure on these reflexes, reflexology aids the natural function of the related body areas by relieving tension and improving circulation. [3]Ancient humans stimulated reflexes naturally by working and building with their hands and walking barefoot over rough ground. [4]Modern humans have lost much of nature's way of maintaining a balanced and healthy equilibrium. [5]Reflexology aids natural health and vitality in several ways.

    a. glands and organs
    b. natural forms of healing
    c. reflexology

VISUAL *VOCABULARY*

A _____ uses a method of massage that eases tension through the use of finger pressure, especially to the feet.

    a. reflex
    b. reflexologist
    c. reflexology

Textbook Skills

_____ **2.** [1]Just as we must critically evaluate information we read, we must also use critical thinking skills as we view images. [2]Every day we are bombarded with images—pictures on billboards, commercials on television, graphs and charts in newspapers and textbooks, to name just a few examples. [3]Most images slide by without our noticing them, or so we think. [4]But images, sometimes even more than text, can influence us. [5]Their creators have purposes, some worthy, some not. [6]And understanding those purposes requires that we think critically. [7]The methods of viewing images critically are the same as those we use for reading text critically. [8]For example, we preview, analyze, interpret, and (often) evaluate images.

—Aaron, Jane E., *The Little, Brown Compact Handbook*, 4th ed., p. 64.

a. viewing images critically
b. graphs and charts
c. images

 ## Identify a Topic Sentence

Most paragraphs have three parts:

- A topic (the general idea or subject)
- A main idea (the controlling point the author is making about the topic, often stated in a topic sentence)
- Supporting details (the specific ideas to support the main idea)

Think again of the house of ideas that a writer builds. Remember, the main idea *frames* the specific ideas. Think of all the different rooms in a house: the kitchen, bedroom, bathroom, living room. Each room is a different part of the house. The frame determines the space for each room and the flow of traffic between rooms. Similarly, the main idea determines how much detail is given and how each detail flows into the next. The main idea of a paragraph is usually stated in a single sentence called the **topic sentence**. The topic sentence—the stated main idea—is unique in two ways.

First, the topic sentence contains two types of information: the topic and the author's controlling point, which restricts or qualifies the topic. At times, the controlling point may be expressed as the author's opinion using biased words. (For more information on biased words see Chapter 9, "Fact and Opinion.") For example, in the topic sentence "Bad manners seem to dominate today's culture," the biased words "bad," "seem," and "dominate" limit and control the general topic "manners."

Other times, the controlling point may express the author's thought pattern, the way in which the thoughts are going to be organized. (For more information on words that indicate thought patterns, see Chapters 7 and 8.) For example, the topic sentence "Just as we must critically evaluate information we read, we must also use critical thinking skills as we view images" uses the phrase "just as" to reveal that the author will control the topic by comparing our responses to text and images.

Often, an author will use both biased words and a thought pattern to qualify or limit the topic. For example, the topic sentence "Reflexology aids natural health and vitality in several ways" combines the biased word "aids" and the phrase "several ways" to indicate a list of positive examples and explanations has been provided.

These qualifiers—words that convey the author's bias or thought pattern—helped you correctly identify the topic in the previous section. An important difference between the topic and the topic sentence is that the topic sentence states the author's main idea in a complete sentence.

A **topic sentence** is a single sentence that states the topic and words that qualify the topic by revealing the author's opinion or approach to the topic.

The second unique trait of the topic sentence is its scope: the topic sentence is a general statement that all the other sentences in the paragraph explain or support. A topic sentence states an author's opinion or thought process, which must be explained further with specific supporting details. For example, in the paragraph about the communication context, the topic and the author's controlling point about the topic are stated in the first sentence. Each of the other sentences in the paragraph states and describes the four aspects of communication context:

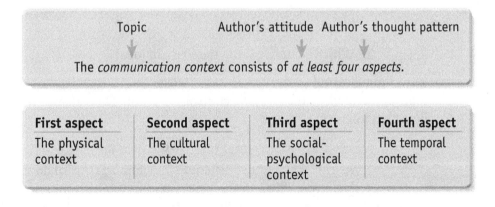

First aspect	Second aspect	Third aspect	Fourth aspect
The physical context	The cultural context	The social-psychological context	The temporal context

Supporting details are specific ideas that *develop, explain,* or *support* the main idea.

The supporting details of a paragraph are framed by the main idea, and all work together to explain or support the author's view of the topic. As a master reader, you will see that every paragraph has a topic, a main idea, and supporting details. It is much easier to tell the difference between these three parts of a passage once you understand how each part works. A topic, as the general subject of the paragraph, can be expressed in a word or phrase. The main idea contains both the topic and the author's controlling point about the topic and can be stated in one sentence called the topic sentence. The supporting details are all the sentences that state reasons and explanations for the main idea. To locate the topic sentence of a paragraph, ask yourself two questions:

- Which sentence contains qualifiers that reveal the author's controlling point— that is, the author's attitude about the topic or approach to the topic?

- Do all the specific details in the passage support this statement?

> **EXAMPLES**

A. The following group of ideas contains a topic, a main idea, and two supporting details. Circle the topic and underline the author's controlling point. Then answer the questions.

   a. A tsunami (tsoo-nah-me) can be the most disastrous of all ocean waves.
   b. Tsunamis are powerful sea waves caused by seismic activity such as volcano eruptions, landslides, or earthquakes on the sea floor.
   c. These waves, reaching heights over 100 feet and traveling as rapidly as 500 miles per hour, killed tens of thousands of people in the past century.

   _____ **1.** Which of the following best states the topic?
            a. a tsunami   c. an ocean wave
            b. seismic activity

   _____ **2.** Which sentence is the stated main idea?

B. Read the following paragraph from a college humanities textbook. Circle the topic and underline the author's controlling point. Then answer the two questions that follow it.

Love

[1]We can scarcely overestimate the importance of love, yesterday and today, in our lives, in the world, and in the humanities. [2]One of the world's most beautiful buildings, the glorious Taj Mahal mausoleum in Agra, India, is evidence of the love of one man, Shah Mumtaz, for

his favorite wife. ³Without the theme of love, all of the arts would be diminished. ⁴Even the successive marriages of the frequently divorced give evidence that people believe so strongly in love they keep looking for it and that, no matter what their other achievements, they probably believe they have wasted their lives if they cannot say they have loved and been loved at some point. ⁵In countless poems, novels, operas, films, and plays, love is shown as the source of both pleasure and pain, often at the same time.

—Janaro, Richard P., *The Art of Being Human*, 10th ed., p. 409.

1. What is the topic? _____

2. Which sentence states the author's main idea? _____

EXPLANATIONS

A. The topic is (a) "a tsunami." The first item (a) is the main idea. Note that the main idea is stated as a topic sentence and contains both the topic, "tsunami," and the author's controlling point about the topic, "most disastrous of all ocean waves." The second and third items give two details that support the main idea, by describing the disastrous traits of a tsunami.

B. Every idea in the paragraph has to do with love. Sentence 1 states the main idea as a topic sentence: "We can scarcely overestimate the importance of love, yesterday and today, in our lives, in the world, and in the humanities." Notice that the topic sentence states the topic, and it states the author's controlling point about the topic. All the other sentences give reasons or evidence that love is important. ◀

Practice 2

Textbook Skills

The following groups of ideas come from the college textbook *Biology: Life on Earth*. Each group contains a main idea and two supporting details. In each group, first identify the topic; then identify the stated main idea. (*Hint:* circle the topic and underline the author's controlling point in each group.)

Group 1

a. Living things are defined by distinct characteristics.
b. Living things are composed of cells that have a complex organized structure.

c. Living things acquire and use materials and energy from their environment and convert them into different forms.

—Audesirk, Gerald, Audesirk, Teresa, and Byers, Bruce E.,
Biology: Life on Earth, 8th ed., p. 11.

_____ **1.** Which of the following best states the topic?

    a. cells   c. materials and energy

    b. traits of living things   d. living things

_____ **2.** Which sentence is the stated main idea?

Group 2

a. All cells contain genes, units of heredity that provide the information needed to control the life of the cell and the small structures called organelles that are specialized to carry out specific functions such as moving the cell, obtaining energy, or synthesizing large molecules.

b. Even a single cell has an elaborate internal structure.

c. Cells are always surrounded by a thin plasma membrane that encloses the cytoplasm (organelles and the fluid surrounding them) and separates the cell from the outside world.

—Audesirk, Gerald, Audesirk, Teresa, and Byers, Bruce E.,
Biology: Life on Earth, 8th ed., p. 11.

_____ **3.** Which of the following best states the topic?

    a. cells   c. hereditary information

    b. organelles   d. the internal structure of cells

_____ **4.** Which sentence is the stated main idea?

Read the following paragraph from the college textbook *Biology: Life on Earth*. Circle the topic and underline the author's controlling point. Then answer the questions that follow.

How Do Scientists Categorize the Diversity of Life?

[1]Although all living things share the general characteristics discussed earlier, evolution has produced an amazing variety of life-forms. [2]Organisms can be grouped into three major categories, called domains: Bacteria, Archaea, and Eukarya. [3]This classification reflects fundamental differences among the cell types that compose these organisms. [4]Members of both the Bacteria and the Archaea usually consist of single, simple cells. [5]Members of the Eukarya have bodies composed of one or more highly complex cells. [6]This domain includes three major subdivisions or

kingdoms: the Fungi, Plantae, and Animalia, as well as a diverse collection of mostly single-celled organisms collectively known as "protists." [7]There are exceptions to any simple set of criteria used to characterize the domains and kingdoms, but three characteristics are particularly useful: cell type, the number of cells in each organism, and how it acquires energy.

—Audesirk, Gerald, Audesirk, Teresa, and Byers, Bruce E.,
Biology: Life on Earth, 8th ed., pp. 14–15.

5. What is the topic of the paragraph? _____

6. Which sentence is the topic sentence that states the main idea? _____

VISUAL *VOCABULARY*

Trichophyton rubrum fungus
This fungus infects tissues such as skin, nails, and hair in humans and other animals. This organism is classified as part of the _____ domain.

   a. Bacteria
   b. Archaea
   c. Eukarya

Analyze the Flow of Ideas and Identify Placement of Topic Sentences

So far, many of the paragraphs you have worked on in this textbook have placed the topic sentence/main idea as the first sentence in the paragraph. However, not all paragraphs put the main idea first. In fact, a topic sentence can be placed at the *beginning* of a paragraph, *within* a paragraph, at the *end* of a paragraph, or at both the beginning and the end of a paragraph. The placement of the topic sentence controls the flow of ideas. In a sense, when a writer builds a house of ideas, the floor plan—the flow of ideas—changes based on where in the paragraph the topic sentence is located. One of the first things a master reader looks for is the location of the topic sentence.

Topic Sentence at the Beginning of a Paragraph

A topic sentence that begins a paragraph signals a move from general ideas to specific ideas. This flow from general to specific, in which an author begins with a general statement and moves to specific reasons and supports, is also known as deductive reasoning. Articles and news stories in magazines and newspapers typically use the deductive flow of ideas. The following chart shows this flow from general to specific ideas.

Main idea: Topic sentence
Supporting detail
Supporting detail
Supporting detail
Supporting detail

> **EXAMPLE** Read the paragraph and identify its topic sentence. Remember to ask, "Does this sentence cover all the ideas in the passage?"

Textbook
Skills

Cancer

[1]Cancer is a far-reaching malady. [2]Statistics tell us that it affects three of four families. [3]About a third of all Americans living today will contract cancer in their lifetime. [4]And cancer kills more children between ages three and fourteen years than any other disease. [5]Someone dies from cancer in the United States approximately every minute.

—Adapted from Karren, Keith J., *Mind/Body Health: The Effects of Attitudes, Emotions, and Relationships*, 2nd ed., p. 13.

Topic sentence: _____

EXPLANATION The topic sentence of this paragraph is sentence 1: "Cancer is a far-reaching malady." All the other sentences explain the extent of cancer's effects.

Topic Sentence Within a Paragraph

Topic sentences within a paragraph can be near the beginning or in the middle of the paragraph.

Near the Beginning

A paragraph does not always start with the topic sentence. Instead, it may begin with a general overview of the topic. These introductory sentences are used to get the reader interested in the topic. They also lead the reader to the topic sentence. Sometimes introductory sentences tell how the ideas in one paragraph tie in to the ideas of earlier paragraphs. At other times, the introductory sentences give background information about the topic.

The flow of ideas remains deductive as it moves from general ideas (the introduction) and main idea (topic sentence) to specific ideas (supporting details). Human interest stories and editorials in magazines and newspapers, as well as academic papers, often rely on this flow of ideas. The following diagram shows this flow from general to specific ideas:

> Introductory sentence(s)
> Main idea: Topic sentence
> Supporting detail
> Supporting detail
> Supporting detail

> **EXAMPLE** Read the following paragraph and identify its topic sentence. Remember to ask, "Does this sentence cover all the ideas in the passage?"

Textbook
Skills

Understanding and Meeting Guest Needs

[1]The first step in delivering high-quality service is to learn and fully understand what customers want in a particular tourism service. [2]Tourism managers can uncover specific needs and expectations of customers in a number of ways. [3]First, marketing research can be used to gather information from potential and existing customers. [4]Many companies regularly survey members of their target market to better understand the changing needs and desires of segments they hope to serve. [5]For example, when PepsiCo acquired Taco Bell, management conducted a study of fast-food customers (any fast-food customer, not simply customers who liked Mexican food). [6]From this survey, PepsiCo concluded that fast-food customers had expectations about four things, which can be remembered by the acronym FACT. [7]Customers wanted their fast food really *Fast;* they expected their orders to be *Accurately* delivered; they wanted the premises to be

Clean; and they expected foods and beverages to be served at appropriate *Temperatures.* [8]With this knowledge, top management redesigned the entire Taco Bell system to better deliver these expected qualities.

> —Cook, Roy A., Yale, Laura J., and Marqua, Joseph J.,
> *Tourism: The Business of Travel,* 4th ed., pp. 69–70.

Topic sentence: _____

EXPLANATION Sentence 2 is the topic sentence of this paragraph. Sentence 1 offers background information about the general topic "meeting guest needs." The purpose of sentence 1 is to get the reader's attention and tie the upcoming ideas with previously discussed ideas. Sentences 3 through 8 offer supporting details that explain and illustrate how a company can "meet guest needs." ◁

In the Middle

At times, an author begins a paragraph with a few attention-grabbing details. These details are placed first to stir the reader's interest in the topic. The flow of ideas no longer follows the deductive pattern of thinking because the material now moves from specific ideas (supporting details) to a general idea (the topic sentence) to specific ideas (additional supporting details). Creative essays and special interest stories that strive to excite reader interest often employ this approach. Often television news stories begin with shocking details to hook the viewer and prevent channel surfing. The following diagram shows this flow of ideas:

> Supporting detail
> Supporting detail
> Main idea: Topic sentence
> Supporting detail
> Supporting detail

▷ **EXAMPLE** Read the following paragraph and identify its topic sentence. Remember to ask, "Does this sentence cover all the ideas in the passage?"

Textbook
Skills

Unwanted Guests

[1]In the late 1600s, Dutch microscopist Anton van Leeuwenhoek scraped white matter from between his teeth and viewed it through a microscope

that he had constructed himself. [2]To his consternation, he saw millions of cells that he called "animalcules," single-celled organisms that we now recognize as bacteria. [3]Annoyed at the presence of these life-forms in his mouth, he attempted to kill them with vinegar and hot coffee—with little success. [4]The warm, moist environment of the human mouth, particularly the crevices of the teeth and gums, is an ideal habitat for a variety of bacteria. [5]Some produce slime layers that help them and others adhere to the tooth. [6]Each divides repeatedly to form a colony of offspring. [7]Thick layers of bacteria, slime, and glycoproteins from saliva make up the white substance, called plaque, that Leeuwenhoek scraped from his teeth. [8]Sugar in foods and beverages nourishes the bacteria, which break down the sugar into lactic acid. [9]The acid eats away at the tooth enamel, producing tiny crevices in which the bacteria multiply further, eventually producing a cavity. [10]So, although he didn't know why, Leeuwenhoek was right to be concerned about the "animalcules" in his mouth!

—Audesirk, Gerald, Audesirk, Teresa, and Byers, Bruce E.,
Biology: Life on Earth, 9th ed., p. 74.

Topic sentence: _____

EXPLANATION Sentences 1 through 3 offer an attention-grabbing story that captures the reader's interest while setting up the topic. Sentence 4 is the topic sentence. Sentences 5 through 10 give details about the bacteria that live in the mouth. ◀

Topic Sentence at the End of a Paragraph

Sometimes an author waits until the end of the paragraph to state the topic sentence and main idea. This approach can be very effective, for it allows the details to build up to the main idea. The pattern is sometimes called climactic order.

The flow of ideas is known as inductive as the author's thoughts move from specific (supporting details) to general (the topic sentence). Inductive reasoning is often used in math and science to generate hypotheses and theories, and to discover relationships between details. In addition, inductive reasoning is often used in argument (for more about argument, see Chapters 12 and 13). Politicians and advertisers use this approach to convince people to agree with their ideas or to buy their products. If a politician begins with a general statement such as "Taxes must be raised," the audience members may strongly disagree. If, however, the politician begins with the details and leads up to the main idea, people are more likely to agree. For example, people are more likely to agree that roads need to be repaired, even if it means raising taxes. Inductive reasoning is the process of arriving at a general understanding based on specific details. The following diagram shows the ideas moving from specific to general.

Supporting detail
Supporting detail
Supporting detail
Supporting detail
Main idea: Topic sentence

EXAMPLE Read the following paragraph and identify its topic sentence. Remember to ask, "Does this sentence cover all the ideas in the passage?"

Roofies and Rape

¹Charlene sat perched on a bar stool as she sipped her drink and chatted flirtatiously with the cute stranger who had introduced himself as Roger. ²After a few minutes of conversation, she excused herself for a quick trip to the restroom. ³While she was gone, Roger dropped a little white pill into her glass and stirred until it dissolved. ⁴When she returned, she finished her drink. ⁵About ten minutes later, Charlene began to feel dizzy, disoriented, and nauseated; she felt simultaneously too hot and too cold. ⁶Roger asked her if she felt all right and offered to drive her home. ⁷Because she had difficulty speaking and moving, Roger easily guided her out of the bar and into his car. ⁸Shortly thereafter, she passed out. ⁹Roger took her to a remote wooded area, raped her, and left her there. ¹⁰The next morning, she had no memory of what had happened. ¹¹Charlene became one of the thousands of victims of Rohypnol, also known as "roofies." ¹²Rohypnol is used as a "date rape" drug, which causes a victim to pass out so she cannot resist or recall what happened to her.

Topic sentence: _____

EXPLANATION Sentences 1 through 11 tell the story of one woman's experience with Rohypnol. Sentence 12 states the main idea. Starting the passage with the details of the incident draws readers into the situation and heightens their interest. Ending the passage with the main idea is very powerful.

Topic Sentence at the Beginning and the End of a Paragraph

A paragraph may start and end by stating one main idea in two different sentences. Even though these two sentences state the same idea, they usually word the idea in different ways. A topic sentence presents the main idea at the beginning of the paragraph. Then, at the end of the paragraph, the main idea is stated again, this time using different words. This flow of ideas is based on the age-old advice given to writers to "tell the reader what you are going to say; say it; then tell the reader what you said." Many essays written by college students rely on this presentation of ideas. The following diagram shows this flow of ideas:

Main idea: Topic sentence
Supporting detail
Supporting detail
Supporting detail
Supporting detail
Supporting detail
Supporting detail
Main idea: Topic sentence

> **EXAMPLE** Read the following paragraph and identify its topic sentences. Remember to ask, "Do these sentences cover all the ideas in the passage?"

Recreational Therapy

[1]Recreational therapy benefits the physical and mental health of many patients. [2]Recreational therapy includes music, art, drama, and dance. [3]Patients who benefit from recreational therapy include those who suffer from substance abuse, eating disorders, violent abuse, homelessness, autism, and complications due to aging. [4]This type of therapy improves a person's physical, mental, social, and emotional abilities. [5]Recreational therapy promotes good health and well-being, which leads to a higher quality of life. [6]This therapy also reduces the need for extended healthcare services by nurturing independent living skills. [7]Recreational therapy is an excellent method to improve or maintain physical and mental health.

Topic sentences: _____

EXPLANATION Sentences 1 and 7 both state the main idea of the passage: Recreational therapy benefits patients. Notice how the wording changes at the end of the passage. Repeating the main idea makes the point much stronger and more likely to be remembered. ◄

Practice 3

Textbook
Skills

Read the following series of paragraphs taken from the same section of the college textbook *Business*. Identify the topic sentence of each paragraph. Remember to ask, "Which sentence covers all the details in each paragraph?"

The Business Environment

1No doubt business today is faster paced, more complex, and more demanding than ever before. **2**In less than a decade, the hunt for new goods and services has been accelerated by product life cycles measured in weeks or months rather than years. **3**Individual consumers and business customers want high-quality goods and services—often customized and with lower prices and immediate delivery. **4**Sales offices, service providers, and production facilities are shifting geographically as new markets and resources emerge in other countries. **5**Employees want flexible working hours and opportunities to work at home. **6**Stockholder expectations also add pressure for productivity increases, growth in market share, and larger profits. **7**At the same time, however, a more vocal public demands greater honesty, fair competition, and respect for the environment.

—Griffin, Ricky W. and Ebert, Ronald J., *Business*, 8th ed., p. 44.

Topic sentence(s): _____

Redrawing Corporate Boundaries

1Successful companies are responding to these challenges in new, often unprecedented ways. **2**To stay competitive, they are redrawing traditional organizational boundaries. **3**Today, firms join together with other companies, even with competitors, to develop new goods and services. **4**Some of these relationships are permanent. **5**But others are temporary alliances formed on short notice so that, working together, partners can produce and deliver products with shorter lead times than either firm could manage alone. **6**Increasingly, the most successful firms are getting leaner by focusing on their core competencies. **7**Core competencies are the skills and resources with which they compete best and create the most value for owners. [8]They *outsource* noncore business processes. [9]They pay suppliers and distributors to perform these secondary processes and thereby increase their reliance on suppliers. [10]These new business models call for unprecedented coordination—not only among internal activities, but also among customers, suppliers, and strategic partners.

—Griffin, Ricky W. and Ebert, Ronald J.,
Business, 8th ed., pp. 44–45.

Topic sentence(s): _____

Outsourcing

[1]Outsourcing is the strategy of paying suppliers and distributors to perform certain business processes or to provide needed materials or services. [2]For example, the cafeteria at a large bank may be important to employees and some customers. [3]But running it is not the bank's main line of business and expertise. [4]Bankers need to focus on money management and financial services, not foodservice operations. [5]That's why most banks outsource cafeteria operations to foodservice management companies whose main line of business includes cafeterias. [6]The result, ideally, is more attention to banking by bankers, better food service for cafeteria customers, and formation of a new supplier-client relationship (foodservice company/bank). [7]Firms today outsource numerous activities. [8]These include payroll, employee training, and research and development. [9]Outsourcing is an increasingly popular strategy because it helps firms focus on their core activities and avoid getting sidetracked onto secondary activities.

—Griffin, Ricky W. and Ebert, Ronald J.,
Business, 8th ed., pp. 45–46.

Topic sentence(s): _____

LO5 Recognize the Central Idea and the Thesis Statement

Just as a single paragraph has a main idea, longer passages made up of two or more paragraphs also have a main idea. You encounter these longer passages in articles, essays, and textbooks. In longer passages, the main idea is called the **central idea**. Often the author will state the central idea in a single sentence called the **thesis statement**.

> The **central idea** is the main idea of a passage made up of two
>   or more paragraphs.
> The **thesis statement** is a sentence that states the topic and
>   the author's controlling point about the topic for a passage
>   of two or more paragraphs.

You find the central idea of longer passages the same way you locate the main idea or topic sentence of a paragraph. The thesis statement is the one sentence that is general enough to include all the ideas in the passage.

> **EXAMPLE**   Read the following passage from a college criminal justice textbook and identify the thesis statement, which states the central idea.

Textbook
Skills

Arrest

[1]Officers seize not only property but people as well, a process referred to as *arrest*. [2]Most people think of arrest in terms of what they see on popular TV crime shows: The suspect is chased, subdued, and "cuffed" after committing some loathsome act in view of the camera. [3]Some arrests do occur that way. [4]In reality, however, most arrests are far more mundane.

[5]In technical terms, an arrest occurs whenever a law enforcement officer restricts a person's freedom to leave. [6]The officer may not yell, "You're under arrest!" [7]No Miranda warnings may be offered, and in fact, the suspect may not even consider himself or herself to be in custody. [8]Arrests, and the decisions to enforce them, evolve as the situations between officers and suspects develop. [9]A situation usually begins with polite conversation and a request by the officer for information. [10]Only when the suspect tries to leave and tests the limits of the police response may the suspect discover that he or she is really in custody.

[11]In the 1980 case of *U.S. v. Mendenhall*, Justice Potter Stewart set forth the "free to leave" test for determining whether a person has been arrested. [12]Stewart wrote, "A person has been 'seized' within the meaning of the Fourth Amendment only if in view of all the circumstances surrounding the incident, a reasonable person would have believed that he was not free to leave." [13]The "free to leave" test has been repeatedly adopted by the Court as the test for a seizure. [14]In 1994, in the case of *Stansbury v. California*, the Court once again used such a test in determining the point at which an arrest had been made. [15]In *Stansbury*, where the focus was on the interrogation of a suspected child molester and murderer,

the Court ruled, "In determining whether an individual was in custody, a court must examine all of the circumstances surrounding the interrogation, but the ultimate inquiry is simply whether there [was] a formal arrest or restraint on freedom of movement of the degree associated with a formal arrest."

—Adapted from Schmalleger, Frank J., *Criminal Justice*, 9th ed., pp. 128–129.

Thesis statement: _____

EXPLANATION The first paragraph hooks the reader's interest in the topic of an arrest. Sentence 5, the first sentence of the second paragraph, is the central idea of the passage. Note that sentence 5 includes the topic "arrest" and the author's controlling point about the topic: "An arrest occurs whenever a law enforcement officer restricts a person's freedom to leave." The rest of the passage includes supporting details that explain this definition and cite legal examples. ◀

Practice 4

Read the following passage from a college history textbook. Identify the thesis statement, which states the central idea.

Textbook Skills

God Kings

¹Divine kingship was the cornerstone of Egyptian life. ²Initially, the king was the incarnation of Horus, a sky and falcon god; later, the king was identified with the sun god Ra, as well as with Osiris, the god of the dead. ³As divine incarnation, the king was obliged above all to care for his people. ⁴It was he who ensured the annual flooding of the Nile, which brought water to the parched land. ⁵His commands preserved *maat*, the ideal state of the universe and society, a condition of harmony and justice. ⁶In the poetry of the Old Kingdom, the king was the divine herdsman, while the people were the cattle of god:

⁷Well tended are men, the cattle of god.
⁸He made heaven and earth according to their desire and repelled the demon of the waters . . .
⁹He made for the rulers (even) in the egg, a supporter to support the back of the disabled.

¹⁰Unlike the rulers in Mesopotamia, the kings of the Old Kingdom were not warriors but divine administrators. ¹¹Protected by the Sahara, Egypt had few external enemies and no standing army. ¹²A vast bureaucracy of literate court officials and provincial administrators

assisted the god-king. ¹³They wielded wide authority as religious leaders, judicial officers, and when necessary, military leaders. ¹⁴A host of subordinate overseers, scribes, metalworkers, stonemasons, artisans, and tax collectors rounded out the royal administration. ¹⁵At the local level, governors administered provinces called *nomes*, the basic unit of Egyptian local government.

—Adapted from Kishlansky, Mark, Geary, Patrick, and O'Brien, Patricia, *Civilization in the West,* 4th ed., pp. 18–19.

Central idea: _____

LO6 Develop Textbook Skills: Identify Topics, Main Ideas, and Central Ideas in Textbook Passages

Textbook Skills

Textbooks identify topics in the title of each chapter. An excellent study strategy is to read a textbook's table of contents, including all of the chapters' titles, which list the general topics covered in the textbook. In addition to providing topics in chapter titles, textbooks also identify topics within each chapter. Other publications, such as newspapers and magazines, also use titles and headings to point out topics.

Textbook authors often state the topic of a passage or paragraph in a heading. For example, titles of graphs often help readers identify the main idea of the graph by stating the topic. Identifying the topic in a heading makes it easier to identify the central idea and supporting details.

⊳ **EXAMPLE** Read the following passage from a sociology textbook. Then answer the questions that follow it.

Textbook Skills

Glimpsing the Future: The Shifting U.S. Racial–Ethnic Mix

¹During the next twenty-five years, the population of the United States is expected to grow by about 22 percent. ²To see what the U.S. population will look like at that time, can we simply add 22 percent to our current racial–ethnic mix? ³The answer is a resounding no. ⁴Some groups will grow much more than others, giving us a different-looking United States.

⁵Some of the changes in the U.S. racial–ethnic mix will be dramatic. ⁶In twenty-five years, one of every nineteen Americans is expected to have an Asian background, and in the most dramatic change, almost

one of four is expected to be of Latino ancestry. [7]The basic causes of this fundamental shift are the racial–ethnic groups' different rates of immigration and birth. [8]Both will change the groups' proportions of the U.S. population, but immigration is by far the more important. [9]The proportion of non-Hispanic whites is expected to shrink, that of Native Americans to remain the same, that of African Americans to increase slightly, and that of Latinos to increase sharply.

—Adapted excerpt and graphs from Henslin, James M., *Sociology: A Down-to-Earth Approach,* 11th ed., p. 345.

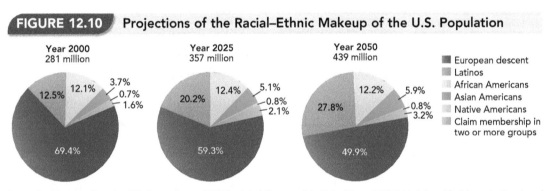

FIGURE 12.10   **Projections of the Racial–Ethnic Makeup of the U.S. Population**

Source: By the author. Based on U.S. Census Bureau 2009; *Statistical Abstract of the United States* 2011:Table 3. I modified the projections based on the new census category of membership in two or more groups and trends in interethnic marriage.

1. The topic of the passage is _____.

2. Sentence 1 is _____
   a. the central idea.
   b. a supporting detail.

3. Sentence 4 is _____
   a. the central idea.
   b. a supporting detail.

4. The topic of the graphs is _____

   _____.

5. According to the graphs, the percentage of which group will increase the most by 2050? _____
   a. Individuals of European descent
   b. Latinos
   c. African Americans
   d. Asian Americans

EXPLANATION

1. The topic is the shifting racial–ethnic mix in the United States. The topic is stated in the title.

2. Sentence 1 is a supporting detail. It helps lead up to the central idea by introducing the topic.

3. Sentence 4 is the central idea; it states the topic and the author's primary point about the topic: some racial–ethnic groups will grow more than others, giving us a different-looking United States. Notice that this passage states the central idea in the middle. The reader can use the heading, which identifies the topic, to help locate the central idea.

4. The topic of the graphs is the projected racial–ethnic makeup of the U.S. population. The topic is stated in the title of the graphs.

5. According to the graphs, the population of Latinos will increase by 15.3 percent by 2050, far more than any other group. ◀

Practice 5

Read the following passage from a college biology textbook. Then answer the questions that follow it.

Textbook
Skills

The Scientific Method Is the Basis of Scientific Inquiry

¹A biologist's job is to answer questions about life. ²What causes cancer? ³Why are frog populations shrinking worldwide? ⁴What happens when a sperm and egg meet? ⁵How does HIV cause AIDS? ⁶When did the earliest mammals appear? ⁷How do bees fly? ⁸The list of questions is both endless and endlessly fascinating.

⁹Anyone can ask an interesting question about life. ¹⁰A biologist, however, is distinguished by the manner in which he or she goes about finding answers. ¹¹A biologist is a scientist and accepts only answers that are supported by evidence, and then only by a certain kind of evidence. ¹²Scientific evidence consists of observations or measurements that are easily shared with others and that can be repeated by anyone who has the appropriate tools. ¹³The process by which this kind of evidence is gathered is known as the **scientific method.**

¹⁴The scientific method proceeds step-by-step. ¹⁵It begins when someone makes an **observation** of an interesting pattern or phenomenon.

[16]The observation, in turn, stimulates the observer to ask a **question** about what was observed. [17]Then, after a period of contemplation (that perhaps also includes reflecting on the scientific work of others who have considered related questions), the person proposes an answer to the question, an explanation for the observation. [18]This proposed explanation is a **hypothesis.** [19]A good hypothesis leads to a **prediction,** typically expressed in "if . . . then" language. [20]The prediction is tested with further observations or with experiments. [21]These experiments produce results that either support or refute the hypothesis, and a **conclusion** is drawn about it. [22]A single experiment is never an adequate basis for a conclusion; the experiment must be repeated not only by the original experimenter but also by others.

[23]You may find it easier to visualize the steps of the scientific method through an example from everyday life. [24]Imagine this scenario: Late to an appointment, you rush to your car and make the *observation* that it won't start. [25]This observation leads directly to a *question:* Why won't the car start? [26]You quickly form a *hypothesis:* The battery is dead. [27]Your hypothesis leads in turn to an if-then *prediction:* If the battery is dead, then a new battery will cause the car to start. [28]Next, you design an *experiment* to test your prediction: You replace your battery with the battery from your roommate's new car and try to start your car again. [29]Your car starts immediately, and you reach the *conclusion* that your dead battery hypothesis is correct.

—Audesirk, Teresa, Audesirk, Gerald, and
Byers, Bruce E., *Life on Earth,* 5th ed.,
Figure 1–3 (p. 363) and pp. 3–4.

1. The topic of the passage is _____

_____.

_____   **2.** Sentence 1 is
    a. the central idea.   b. a supporting detail.

_____   **3.** Sentence 8 is
    a. the central idea.   b. a supporting detail.

_____   **4.** Sentence 11 is
    a. the central idea.   b. a supporting detail.

_____   **5.** Sentence 12 is
    a. the central idea.   b. a supporting detail.

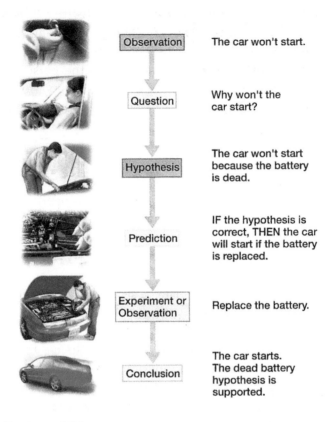

	Observation	The car won't start.
	Question	Why won't the car start?
	Hypothesis	The car won't start because the battery is dead.
	Prediction	IF the hypothesis is correct, THEN the car will start if the battery is replaced.
	Experiment or Observation	Replace the battery.
	Conclusion	The car starts. The dead battery hypothesis is supported.

_____ **6.** Sentence 13 is

      a. the central idea.   b. a supporting detail.

7. Based on the information in the passage, state the main idea of the figure by completing the following caption for the figure: The scientific method in

_____.

Apply Information Literacy Skills

 ## Academic, Personal, and Career Applications of Stated Main Ideas

The ability to identify a stated main idea is another component of information literacy. Along with having strong vocabulary skills, being able to locate and evaluate a stated main idea is a vital part of accessing information. Information

literacy is the ability to recognize the need to know the main idea, and then to locate, evaluate, and effectively apply that information to your situation. In your academic, personal, and career lives, you will come across various forms of documents such as essays, articles, reports, memos, or e-mails. You will be expected to understand and respond to the stated main idea of these documents. Thus, you will use the skills that you have learned in this chapter in several ways:

- Recognize your own need to know a stated main idea.
- Locate a stated main idea.
- Restate the author's stated main idea in your own words.
- Apply the stated main idea to your specific situation.

Academic Application

Assume you are taking a college American Government course. Your class is studying how political opinions are formed. You have been assigned to read the following textbook passage. Part of your study plan is to record the main idea of the passage.

- **Before Reading:** Skim the passage. Circle the topic as it recurs. Create a question based on the topic. Keep in mind that the topic may recur with the use of synonyms.
- **During Reading:** Underline the topic sentence and details that answer the pre-reading question.
- **After Reading:** In the space following the passage, restate the author's main idea by answering your pre-reading question with information from the passage.

Pre-Reading Question: _____

_____

The Mass Media

¹Over the years, more and more Americans have turned away from traditional news sources, such as nightly news broadcasts on the major networks and daily newspapers, in favor of different outlets. ²TV talk shows, talk radio, online magazines, and blogs are important sources of political news for many people. ³Cable news, the Internet, and social media are almost omnipresent in the lives of modern Americans. ⁴American teenagers, for example, consume almost eleven hours of media content each day.

[5]Cable and Internet news sources are often skewed. [6]Consuming slanted views may affect the way citizens process political information, form opinions on public policy, obtain political knowledge, and receive new ideas. [7]One recent study, for example, revealed that Americans who get most of their news from cable news outlets such as Fox News and MSNBC are even less knowledgeable about political issues than citizens who consume no political news. [8]Individuals who rely on alternative sources such as *The Daily Show* and *The Colbert Report,* as well as Sunday morning talk shows and National Public Radio, are generally more knowledgeable.

—O'Connor, Karen, *American Government: Roots and Reform* 2012 Election Edition, pp. 319–320.

Author's Main Idea: _____

_____

_____

Personal Application

Assume you are the parent of a teenage daughter, and you have just read the following article. As a concerned parent, you use this opportunity to talk with your daughter about peer pressure and body image issues. You want to understand how your daughter sees herself, and how she deals with group mentality.

- **Before Reading:** Skim the passage. Then rate this article from 1 to 5, with 5 being most helpful and 1 being least helpful. Evaluate the source.
- **During Reading:** Underline the topic sentence and the most important details of support.
- **After Reading:** In the space following the passage, in your own words, state the main idea and key points you would like to discuss with your daughter.

'Thigh Gap': New Teen Body Obsession?

[1]A new body trend is apparently becoming an obsession among teenage girls.

[2]It's the thigh gap—a clear space, or gap, that can be seen between the thighs when a girl is standing with her knees together. [3]Some runway models have it, and teen girls want it.

[4]"Good Morning America" sat down with four high school juniors from a New Jersey Chapter of Students Against Destructive Decisions to discuss this latest trend.

[5]The four girls told ABC News' Juju Chang that they all had friends that were intent on achieving the thigh gap.

[6]Emily Rozansky told Chang that, for many teens, the thigh gap symbolized "the ideal body shape."

[7]Social media sites such as Tumblr, Facebook and Twitter have devotees who flood the zone with images of thigh gaps, bony collarbones and confidence-crushing messages disguised as "inspiration" for staying thin.

[8]Some of the most popular pictures showcase very thin girls with protruding hip bones and a thigh gap.

[9]The teens told Chang that the sites make them feel they have to conform.

[10]Angela DePalma, 16, said: "I see those pictures on Tumblr and stuff and I think that wow, like, they look so good. [11]And then I realize how unhealthy that is."

[12]Tumblr says it discourages blogs that actively promote or glorify self-harm.

[13]According to teen psychologist Barbara Greenberg, statistics show that 80 percent of girls dislike their bodies by the time they are 17 years old. [14]That, combined with a tendency to overshare, makes teen girls vulnerable to even the most subtle messages.

[15]A quick online search brings up page after page of thigh gap inspiration photos and supporters. [16]Experts say the images alone can lead to self-destructive behavior, especially since the thigh gap is, for most girls, an unrealistic standard of beauty.

[17]Greenberg said teens who were pursuing a thigh gap were "setting themselves up for not only an unattainable goal but for an unsustainable goal.

[18]"Even if they reach it, it's going to be very hard for them to maintain it," she said.

[19]Surprisingly, some girls' motivation to have a thigh gap isn't to make themselves more desirable to boys. [20]The New Jersey students told Chang that some boys don't even notice it.

[21]It's strictly a girl thing, affecting popularity and status, they said.

—"Thigh Gap: New Teen Body Obsession?" from Health, Medical Unit. Copyright © March 25, 2013. Reproduced by the permission of ABC NEWS.

Main Idea and Key Points: _____

_____

_____

_____

Career Application

Assume you are a manager of a local surf store that sells California lifestyle apparel. As store manager, it is your duty to read all store e-mails, manage all operational tasks, and keep your team focused.

- **Before Reading:** Skim the e-mail. In the space provided, predict the primary store goal for this week of work.
- **During Reading:** Underline the stated main ideas. (*Hint:* the subject box usually states the topic.)
- **After Reading:** In the space following the passage, reply to your district manager's e-mail, to let him/her know you understand how to manage the workload of the week.

Pre-Reading Prediction: _____

_____

From: ssjones.district.manager89@sunstyle.net

To: mdavis.storemanager23@sunstyle.net

Subject: Weekly Agenda/Store Goals

Hi Malcolm,

Please review the workload calendar for this week. As you see, Friday marks a new store set that will showcase a few of the many new fall fashions that are arriving in our stores for back to school shopping! You will receive the visual updates for the new store set in Thursday's mail pack. All operational tasks are to be executed by the close of Thursday. Keep in mind there are many shipments coming to your store this week, and we don't want to overfill the racks, making it impossible for the customers to shop. I also want to give you notice that I will be visiting all stores in our district next week to review quarterly sales reports. Please contact me if you have any further questions.

Monday	Markdowns: Swimsuits, sandals, board shorts, and tank tops
Tuesday	Receive and stock new merchandise
Wednesday	Receive and stock new merchandise
Thursday	• Receive and stock new merchandise
	• Remove all signage
	• Review mail pack

Friday	New store set
Saturday	Make sure all sales assistants are promoting the new arrivals!
Sunday	Prepare end of week sales report

Reply: _____

_____

_____

_____

_____

REVIEW TEST 1

Score (number correct) _____ x 20 = _____ %

Visit MyReadingLab to take this test online and receive feedback and guidance on your answers.

Topics, Main Ideas, and Supporting Details

A. Each of the following groups of ideas includes one topic, one main idea, and two supporting details. In each group, first identify the topic. Then identify the stated main idea. (*Hint:* circle the topic and underline the author's controlling point in each group.)

Textbook Skills

Group 1

A. People use several methods to avoid conflict.

B. In addition, quick acceptance of a suggested solution avoids conflict.

C. For example, some stop themselves from raising controversial aspects of an issue.

> —Adapted from Folger, Joseph P., Poole, Marshall Scott, and Stutman, Randall K., *Working Through Conflict*, 4th ed., p. 24.

_____ **1.** Which of the following best states the topic?
   a. avoiding controversial issues   c. avoiding conflict
   b. quick acceptance of a solution

_____ **2.** Which sentence best states the main idea?

Group 2

A. The difference between sun and shade plants has practical importance.

B. Look in a nursery catalog and you will find plants keyed by symbols to indicate their adaptation to full sun, partial shade, and full shade.

C. Foresters and landscape designers base a part of their management plans on the shade tolerance or intolerance of plants.

—Adapted from Smith, Thomas and Smith, Robert Leo,
Elements of Ecology, 4th ed., p. 48.

_____ 3. Which of the following best states the topic?
   a. plants   c. landscape designers
   b. sun and shade plants

_____ 4. Which sentence best states the main idea?

B. Read the paragraph from a college education textbook. Then, answer the questions that follow it.

Classroom Tests

[1]Teacher-made tests are a traditional and indispensable part of evaluation. [2]They serve several functions, including, of course, measuring achievement. [3]The items on a test provide the teacher with the opportunity to select for the student those aspects of the unit of study that are most important and thus reinforce learning of the material one last time during the study of the unit. [4]Furthermore, students' attention is entirely devoted to the test for the duration of the time, resulting in some of the most intense learning that occurs in a classroom. [5]This is a strong rationale for writing powerful tests.

—Wilen, William, Ishler, Margaret, Hutchinson, Janice, and Kindsvatter, Richard, *Dynamics of Effective Teaching*, 4th ed., p. 354.

_____ 5. Which sentence states the main idea of the paragraph?
   a. sentence 1   c. sentence 3
   b. sentence 2   d. sentence 5

REVIEW TEST 2

Score (number correct) _____ x 10 = _____ %

Visit MyReadingLab to take this test online and receive feedback and guidance on your answers.

The following passage is the summary of a chapter in a college criminal justice textbook. Read the passage. Then answer the questions that follow.

Textbook
Skills

Summary

[1]Laws are rules of conduct, usually found enacted in the form of statutes, that regulate relationships between people and also between parties. [2]One of the primary functions of the law is to maintain public order. [3]Laws also serve to regulate human interaction, enforce moral beliefs, define the economic environment of a society, enhance predictability, promote orderly social change, sustain individual rights, identify wrongdoers and redress wrongs, and mandate punishment and retribution. [4]Because laws are made by those in power and are influenced by those with access to power brokers, they tend to reflect and support the interests of society's most powerful members.

[5]The rule of law, which is sometimes referred to as the supremacy of law, encompasses the principle that an orderly society must be governed by established principles and known codes that are applied uniformly and fairly to all of its members. [6]It means that no one is above the law, and it mandates that even those who make or enforce the law must also abide by it. [7]The rule of law is regarded as a vital underpinning in Western democracies, for without it disorder and chaos might prevail.

[8]There are various types of law, including criminal law, civil law, administrative law, case law, and procedural law. [9]Criminal law is that form of the law that defines and specifies punishments for offenses of a public nature or for wrongs committed against the state or against society. [10]Violations of the criminal law can be of many different types and can vary in severity. [11]Five categories of violations are: (1) felonies, (2) misdemeanors, (3) offenses, (4) treason and espionage, and (5) inchoate offenses.

[12]From the perspective of Western jurisprudence, all crimes can be said to share certain features. [13]Taken together, these features make up the legal essence of the concept of crime. [14]The essence of crime consists of three conjoined elements. [15]These elements are: (1) the criminal act, which in legal parlance is termed the *actus reus*; (2) a culpable mental state, or *mens rea*; and (3) a concurrence of the two. [16]Hence the essence of criminal conduct consists of a concurrence of a criminal act with a culpable mental state. [17]Five additional principles, added to these three, allow us to fully appreciate contemporary understandings of crime: (1) causation, (2) resulting harm, (3) legality, (4) punishment, and (5) necessary attendant circumstances.

[18]Our legal system recognizes four broad categories of defenses to a criminal charge. [19]An alibi, if shown to be valid, means that the defendant could not have committed the crime in question because he or she was not present at the time of the crime. [20]When a defendant offers a justification

as a defense, he or she admits committing the act in question but claims that it was necessary to avoid some greater evil. [21]A defendant who offers an excuse as a defense claims that some personal condition or circumstance at the time of the act was such that he or she should not be held accountable under the criminal law. [22]Procedural defenses make the claim that the defendant was in some significant way discriminated against in the justice process or that some important aspect of official procedure was not properly followed in the investigation or prosecution of the crime charged.

—Adapted from Schmalleger, Frank J., *Criminal Justice*, 9th ed., pp. 85–86.

_____ **1.** Which of the following best states the topic of the first paragraph (sentences 1–4)?

a. laws   c. relationships
b. conduct   d. public order

2. The topic sentence of the first paragraph (sentences 1–4) is _____.

_____ **3.** Which of the following best states the topic of the second paragraph (sentences 5–7)?

a. principles   c. orderly societies
b. rule of law   d. Western democracies

4. The topic sentence of the second paragraph (sentences 5–7) is _____.

_____ **5.** Which of the following best states the topic of the third paragraph (sentences 8–11)?

a. types of law   c. felonies
b. misdemeanors   d. criminal law

6. The topic sentence of the third paragraph (sentences 8–11) is _____.

_____ **7.** Which of the following best states the topic of the fourth paragraph (sentences 12–17)?

a. Western jurisprudence   c. essence of crime
b. criminal acts   d. additional principles

8. The topic sentence of the fourth paragraph (sentences 12–17) is _____.

_____ **9.** Which of the following best states the topic of the fifth paragraph (sentences 18–22)?

a. alibis   c. criminal defenses
b. excuses   d. justifications

10. The topic sentence of the fifth paragraph (sentences 18–22) is _____.

REVIEW TEST 3

Score (number correct) _____ x 10 = _____ %

Visit MyReadingLab to take this test online and receive feedback and guidance on your answers.

Topics and Main Ideas

Before Reading: Survey the following passage adapted from the college textbook *Psychology and Life*. Skim the passage, noting the words in bold print. Answer the Before Reading questions that follow the passage. Then read the passage. Next answer the After Reading questions. Use the discussion and writing topics as activities to do after reading.

Vocabulary Preview

incredibly (1): extremely
mania (3): craze, obsession
psychopathy (6): mental disorder
clinical (11): medically shown or proven by medical testing

Depression: A Mood Disorder

Textbook
Skills

¹There have almost certainly been times in your life when you would have described yourself as terribly depressed or **incredibly** happy. ²For some people, however, extremes in mood disrupt normal life experiences. ³A mood disorder is an emotional disturbance, such as a severe depression or depression **alternating** with **mania.** ⁴Researchers estimate that about 19 percent of adults have suffered from mood disorders. ⁵One common type of mood disorder is the major depressive disorder.

⁶Depression has been characterized as the "common cold of **psychopathy**" for two reasons. ⁷First, it occurs frequently, and, second, almost everyone has experienced elements of the full-scale disorder at some time in their life. ⁸Everyone has, at one time or another, experienced grief after the loss of a loved one or felt sad or upset when failing to achieve a desired goal. ⁹These sad feelings are only one symptom experienced by people suffering from a major depressive disorder.

¹⁰People suffering with depression differ in terms of the **severity** and duration of their symptoms. ¹¹Many people struggle with **clinical** depression for only several weeks at one point in their lives. ¹²Others suffer depression **episodically** or chronically for many years. ¹³Estimates of the prevalence of mood disorders reveal that about 21 percent of females and 13 percent of males suffer a major depression at some time in their lives.

¹⁴Depression takes an enormous toll on those who suffer, their families, and society. ¹⁵One European study found that people with **chronic**

depression spend a fifth of their entire adult lives in the hospital. [16]Twenty percent of sufferers are totally disabled by their symptoms and do not ever work again. [17]In the United States, depression accounts for the majority of all mental hospital admissions. [18]Still, many experts believe that the disorder is under-diagnosed and under-treated. [19]Fewer than half of those who struggle with major depressive disorder receive any professional help.

—Gerrig, Richard J. and Zimbardo, Philip G., *Psychology and Life*, 16th ed., pp. 482–484.

Before Reading

Vocabulary in Context

_____ 1. The word **alternating** in sentence 3 means
   a. remaining.   c. shutting out.
   b. taking turns.   d. encouraging.

_____ 2. The word **severity** in sentence 10 means
   a. gentleness.   c. visibility.
   b. length.   d. harshness.

_____ 3. The word **episodically** in sentence 12 means
   a. continually.   c. regularly.
   b. deeply.   d. rarely.

_____ 4. The word **chronic** in sentence 15 means
   a. constant.   c. treatable.
   b. mild.   d. occasional.

Topics and Main Ideas

_____ 5. What is the topic of the passage?
   a. grief   c. normal life
   b. major depressive disorder   d. mental hospital admissions

After Reading

Main Ideas and Supporting Details

_____ 6. Which sentence states the central idea of the passage?
   a. sentence 1   c. sentence 10
   b. sentence 5   d. sentence 14

_____ 7. What is the topic of the third paragraph (sentences 10–13)?
   a. people suffering from depression
   b. differences in the severity and duration of the symptoms of depression
   c. the number of males and females suffering from depression

_____ **8.** Which sentence states the main idea of the third paragraph?

    a. sentence 10   c. sentence 12

    b. sentence 11   d. sentence 13

9–10. Label each of the following two sentences from the fourth paragraph (sentences 14–19). Write **A** if it states the main idea or **B** if it supplies a supporting detail.

_____ **9.** Depression takes an enormous toll on those who suffer, their families, and society.

_____ **10.** Fewer than half of those who struggle with major depressive disorder receive any professional help.

SUMMARY RESPONSE

Respond to the passage by restating the topic sentence in your own words. Be sure to identify the topic and the author's attitude about the topic. Begin your summary response with the following: *The most important idea of "Depression: A Mood Disorder" by Gerrig and Zimbardo is . . .*

WHAT DO YOU THINK?

Assume you are taking a college psychology course and your professor has assigned a short essay with the following prompt: "Predict or guess the difference between the terms *episodic depression* and *chronic depression*." Consider the following:

- Use the details from the passage and from a dictionary to define each term.
- Illustrate the differences using examples.
- Identify the major causes of depression.

REVIEW TEST 4

Score (number correct) _____ x 10 = _____ %

Visit MyReadingLab to take this test online and receive feedback and guidance on your answers.

Topics and Main Ideas

Before Reading: Survey the following passage adapted from the college textbook *Cross-Cultural Psychology*. Skim the passage, noting the words in bold print. Answer the Before Reading questions that follow the passage. Then read the passage. Next answer the After Reading questions. Use the discussion and writing topics as activities to do after reading.

Vocabulary Preview

psychological (1): mental, emotional
formulated (2): made, created
assumptions (3): beliefs, ideas
phenomenon (3): event, occurrence

Textbook
Skills

Cross-Cultural Sensitivity

[1]One type of **psychological** knowledge represents a collection of *popular beliefs,* often called **folk theories.** [2]This knowledge is a type of "everyday **psychology**" that is **formulated** by the people and for the people. [3]These popular beliefs are shared **assumptions** about certain aspects of human psychological **phenomena.** [4]These assumptions vary from being general, such as the belief in the ability of dreams to predict the future, to quite specific, that a particular item of clothing will bring good luck. [5]We can increase our cross-cultural sensitivity by understanding the psychological power of popular beliefs.

[6]When Jeff, an exchange student from Oregon, was invited to a birthday party, he was thrilled. [7]This was the first party he would attend in Russia, and he knew how well Russians mastered the art of celebration. [8]The day of the birthday, he dug out a nice souvenir from his suitcase, then caught a taxicab and decided to stop by a flower market to buy a nice bouquet—he was invited by a female student and he thought flowers would be a nice addition to the souvenir he brought from Portland. [9]He could not anticipate that the flowers would cause so much anxiety and frustration an hour later. [10]He bought a dozen roses—a nice gesture according to U.S. standards. [11]But when he presented flowers to the host, he noticed how visibly upset she became when she put the flowers into a vase. [12]He even saw her crying in the kitchen. [13]A couple of friends were trying to comfort her. [14]Jeff began to wonder if his behavior had been the cause of the young woman's crying. [15]What he learned, as he later said, was one of the strangest experiences in his life. [16]He said that the young woman was extremely upset because he brought an even number of flowers. [17]**Coincidentally,** she had recently survived a deadly illness and was extremely sensitive to the issue of death and dying. [18]Apparently, Russians bring an even number of flowers to funerals, memorial services in church, and cemeteries. [19]An odd number of flowers is designed for dates, weddings, and other happy celebrations. [20]Apparently the

flowers—the number of them, in fact—that Jeff brought to the party became a disturbing signal that brought the woman's traumatic experience back to her memory.

[21]In general, Russians will not react in the same dramatic way if you bring an even number of flowers to their celebrations. [22]However, you will notice that one flower—out of the dozen or half-a-dozen you bring—disappears from the vase. [23]Fears, phobias, and superstitions are at times rooted in folk customs and practices.

—Adapted from Shiraev, Eric B. and Levy, David A. *Cross-Cultural Psychology: Critical Thinking and Contemporary Applications*, 3rd ed., pp. 11, 264.

Before Reading

Vocabulary in Context

Use your own words to define each of the following terms. Identify the context clue you used to make meaning of the word.

1. The word **theories** in sentence 1 means _____.

2. Context clue used for **theories**: _____

3. The word **coincidentally** in sentence 17 means _____.

4. Context clue used for **coincidentally**: _____

Topics and Main Ideas

5. What is the topic of the passage? _____

After Reading

Main Ideas and Supporting Details

6. Which sentence states the central idea of the passage? _____

_____ **7.** What is the topic of the second paragraph (sentences 6–20)?
   a. the young woman's near death experience
   b. Jeff's strange experience
   c. a birthday party

8–10. Label each of the following sentences from the third paragraph (sentences 21–23). Write **A** if it states the main idea or **B** if it supplies a supporting detail.

_____ **8.** In general, Russians will not react in the same dramatic way if you bring an even number of flowers to their celebrations.

_____ **9.** However, you will notice that one flower—out of the dozen or half-a-dozen you bring—disappears from the vase.

_____ **10.** Fears, phobias, and superstitions are at times rooted in folk customs and practices.

SUMMARY RESPONSE

Respond to the passage by restating the topic sentence in your own words. Be sure to identify the topic and the author's attitude about the topic. Begin your summary response with the following: _The most important idea of "Cross-Cultural Sensitivity" by Shiraev and Levy is . . ._

WHAT DO YOU THINK?

Assume you are a friend to the young woman who became upset with Jeff's gesture of giving a dozen roses. Write an e-mail to her in which you give her advice and comfort. Consider discussing the following ideas in your e-mail:

- Determine if Jeff was wrong to bring the flowers to the birthday party.
- Explain why or why not.
- Explain "cross-cultural sensitivity."

After Reading About Stated Main Ideas

Before you move on to the Mastery Tests on stated main ideas, take time to reflect on your learning and performance by answering the following questions. Write your answers in your notebook.

- How has my knowledge base or prior knowledge about stated main ideas changed?
- Based on my studies, how do I think I will perform on the Mastery Test(s)? Why do I think my scores will be above average, average, or below average? (Note: An additional fourth Mastery Test may be found in MyReadingLab.)
- Would I recommend this chapter to other students who want to learn more about stated main ideas? Why or why not?

Test your understanding of what you have learned about stated main ideas by completing the Chapter 3 Review.

Name _____ Section _____

Date _____ **Score** (number correct) _____ x 25 = _____ %

Visit MyReadingLab to take this test online and receive feedback and guidance on your answers.

A. Skim each of the following paragraphs and circle the topic as it recurs through-out the paragraph. Then identify the idea that correctly states the topic. (*Hint:* one idea is too general to be the topic; another idea is too specific.)

Textbook
Skills

Animals

[1]It is difficult to devise a concise definition of the term "animal." [2]No single feature fully characterizes animals, so the group is defined by a list of characteristics. [3]None of these characteristics is unique to animals, but together they distinguish animals from members of other kingdoms:

- [4]Animals are multicellular.
- [5]Animals obtain their energy by consuming the bodies of other organisms.
- [6]Animals typically reproduce sexually. [7]Although animal species exhibit a tremendous diversity of reproductive styles, most are capable of sexual reproduction.
- [8]Animal cells lack a cell wall.
- [9]Animals are motile (able to move about) during some stage of their lives. [10]Even the relatively stationary sponges have a free-swimming larval stage (a juvenile form).
- [11]Most animals are able to respond rapidly to external stimuli as a result of the activity of nerve cells, muscle tissue, or both.

—Audesirk, Gerald, Audesirk, Teresa, and Byers, Bruce E.,
Biology: Life on Earth, 8th ed., p. 301.

_____ **1.** Which idea correctly states the topic?
  a. animals   c. characteristics of animals
  b. animal kingdoms

VISUAL *VOCABULARY*

Sponges, such as the Erect Rope sponge and the Encrusting sponge, are often described as the most primitive of _____.

   a. life forms
   b. creatures
   c. animals

B. The following group of ideas is from a college psychology textbook. Read the ideas, and answer the questions that follow.

Textbook Skills

A. Implicit memories are of three major types.

B. An implicit memory is a memory that cannot be voluntarily called to mind but still influences behavior or thinking in certain ways.

C. One type of implicit memory is habits, which are well-learned responses that are carried out without conscious thought.

—Kosslyn, Stephen M. and Rosenberg, Robin S., *Fundamentals of Psychology: The Brain, The Person, The World*, p. 206.

_____ **2.** Statement A is
   a. the main idea.   b. a supporting detail.

_____ **3.** Statement B is
   a. the main idea.   b. a supporting detail.

_____ **4.** Statement C is
   a. the main idea.   b. a supporting detail.

Name _____ Section _____

Date _____ **Score** (number correct) _____ x 33.3 = _____ %

Visit MyReadingLab to take this test online and receive feedback and guidance on your answers.

Identify the topic sentence in each of the following paragraphs.

A. Paragraph from a college accounting textbook

Textbook
Skills

Estate Planning: Living Wills and Power of Attorney

¹A living will is a simple legal document in which individuals state their preferences if they become mentally or physically disabled. ²For example, many individuals have a living will that expresses their desire not to be placed on life support if they become terminally ill. ³In this case, a living will also has financial implications because an estate could be charged with large medical bills resulting from life support. ⁴In this way, those who do not want to be kept alive by life support can ensure that their estate is used in the way that they prefer. ⁵A power of attorney is a legal document granting a person the power to make decisions for you in the event that you are incapacitated. ⁶For example, you may name a family member or a close friend to make your investment and housing decisions if you become ill. ⁷A durable power of attorney for health care is a legal document granting a person the power to make specific health care decisions for you. ⁸While a living will states many of your preferences, a situation may arise that is not covered by your living will. ⁹A durable power of attorney for health care means that the necessary decisions will be made by someone who knows your preferences, rather than by a health care facility. ¹⁰Estate planning involves these decisions about a living will and power of attorney.

—Adapted from Madura, Jeff. *Personal Finance*, 3rd ed., p. 543.

Topic sentence(s): _____

B. Paragraph from a college health textbook

Caffeine Addiction

Textbook
Skills

¹As the effects of caffeine wear off, users may feel let down. ²They may feel mentally or physically depressed, exhausted, and weak. ³To offset this, people commonly choose to drink another cup of coffee. ⁴Habitual use leads to tolerance and psychological dependence. ⁵Until the mid-1970s,

caffeine was not medically recognized as addictive. [6]Chronic caffeine use and the behaviors linked to it was called "coffee nerves." [7]This syndrome is now recognized as caffeine intoxication, or **caffeinism**. [8]Symptoms of caffeinism include chronic insomnia, jitters, irritability, nervousness, anxiety, and involuntary muscle twitches. [9]Withdrawing the caffeine may make the effects worse and lead to severe headaches. [10](Some physicians ask their patients to take a simple test for caffeine addiction: don't consume anything containing caffeine, and if you get a severe headache within four hours, you are addicted.) [11]Caffeine meets the requirements for addiction, which are tolerance, psychological dependence, and withdrawal symptoms; thus, it can be classified as addictive.

—Adapted from Donatelle, Rebecca J.,
Health: The Basics, 5th ed., p. 215.

Topic sentence(s): _____

C. Paragraph from a college psychology textbook

Touch and Skin Senses

**Textbook
Skills**

[1]The skin is a remarkably versatile organ. [2]In addition to protecting you against surface injury, holding in body fluids, and helping control body temperature, it contains nerve endings that produce sensations of pressure, warmth, and cold. [3]These sensations are called cutaneous senses (skin senses). [4]Because you receive so much sensory information through your skin, many different types of receptor cells operate close to the surface of the body. [5]Two examples are the *Meissner corpuscles* and *Merkel disks*. [6]The Meissner corpuscles respond best when something rubs against the skin, and the Merkel disks are most active when a small object exerts steady pressure against the skin.

—Gerrig, Richard J. and Zimbardo, Philip G.,
Psychology and Life, 16th ed., pp. 108–109.

Topic sentence(s): _____

Name _____ Section _____

Date _____ **Score** (number correct) _____ x 25 = _____ %

Visit MyReadingLab to take this test online and receive feedback and guidance on your answers.

Read the passage below. Then answer the questions that follow it.

The Theater of Sophocles

Textbook
Skills

¹For the citizens of Athens, Greece, in the fifth century B.C., theater was both a religious and a civic occasion. ²Seated in the open air in a hillside amphitheater, as many as 17,000 spectators could watch a performance that must have somewhat resembled an opera or musical. ³Plays were presented only twice a year on religious festivals. ⁴These festivals were related to Dionysius, the god of wine and crops; in January there was the Lenaea, the festival of the winepress, when plays, especially comedies, were performed. ⁵But the major theatrical event of the year came in March at the Great Dionysia. ⁶This was a citywide celebration that included sacrifices, prize ceremonies, and spectacular processions as well as three days of drama.

⁷Each day at dawn a different author presented a trilogy of tragic plays. ⁸A trilogy was made up of three related dramas that depicted an important mythic or legendary event. ⁹Each intense tragic trilogy was followed by a satyr play, an obscene parody of a mythic story. ¹⁰In a satyr play the chorus dressed as satyrs, unruly followers of Dionysius who were half goat or horse and half human.

¹¹The Greeks loved competition and believed it fostered excellence; even theater was a competitive event—not unlike the Olympic games. ¹²A panel of five judges voted each year at the Great Dionysia for the best dramatic presentation, and a substantial cash prize was given to the winning poet-playwright (all plays were written in verse). ¹³Any aspiring writer who has ever lost a literary contest may be comforted to know that Sophocles, who triumphed in the competition twenty-four times, seems not to have won the annual prize for *Oedipus the King*. ¹⁴Although this play ultimately proved to be the most celebrated Greek tragedy ever written, it lost the award to a revival of Aeschylus, a playwright who had recently died.

—Adapted from Kennedy, X. J. and Gioia, Dana, *Literature: An Introduction to Fiction, Poetry, and Drama*, 8th ed., p. 1375.

1. What is the topic of the passage? _____

_____ **2.** Which sentence (or sentences) state(s) the central idea of the passage?

a. sentence 1

c. sentence 10

b. sentence 3

d. sentences 1 and 14

_____ **3.** Which sentence (or sentences) state(s) the main idea of the second paragraph?

a. sentence 7

c. sentence 9

b. sentence 8

d. sentence 10

_____ **4.** Which sentence (or sentences) state(s) the main idea of the third paragraph?

a. sentences 11 and 14

c. sentence 12

b. sentence 11

d. sentence 14

VISUAL *VOCABULARY*

This ancient _____ is the Theatre of Dionysus, built between 342–326 B.C., in Athens, Greece.

a. competition

b. amphitheater

c. region

3 Summary of Key Concepts of Stated Main Ideas

 Assess your comprehension of stated main ideas. Complete the following two-column notes with information from the chapter.

- What are the traits of a main idea? _____

  _____

- How does a reader identify a topic of a passage? _____

  _____

  _____

Reading Concept	Definition
Topic Sentence	_____ _____
Central Idea	_____ _____
Thesis Statement	_____ _____
Various Locations of the Stated Main Idea	_____ _____
Deductive Thinking	_____ _____
Inductive Thinking	_____ _____

Test Your Comprehension of Stated Main Ideas

Respond to the following questions and prompts.

(LO4) In your own words, what is the difference between deductive and inductive thinking? _____

_____

_____

(LO3) (LO5) In your own words, what is the difference between a topic sentence and a thesis statement? _____

_____

(LO4) Draw and label four graphs that show the possible locations of stated main ideas.

(LO1) (LO2) Identify and discuss the two most important ideas in this chapter that will
(LO3) (LO4)
(LO5) (LO6) help you improve your reading comprehension. _____
(LO7)

_____

_____

Implied Main Ideas and Implied Central Ideas

4 CHAPTER

LO LEARNING OUTCOMES

After studying this chapter, you should be able to:

- **LO1** Define the Term *Implied Main Idea*
- **LO2** Analyze Supporting Details and Thought Patterns to Determine Implied Main Ideas
- **LO3** Determine the Implied Main Ideas of Paragraphs
- **LO4** Create a Summary from the Supporting Details
- **LO5** Determine and State the Implied Central Idea
- **LO6** Develop Textbook Skills: How to Read a Map
- **LO7** Recognize Experience and Perspective
- **LO8** Apply Information Literacy Skills: Academic, Personal, and Career Applications of Implied Main Ideas

Before Reading About Implied Main Ideas and Implied Central Ideas

Take a moment to study the chapter learning outcomes. Underline key words that refer to ideas you have already studied in previous chapters. Each of these key words represents a great deal of knowledge upon which you will build as you learn about implied main ideas and implied central ideas. These key terms have been listed below. In the given spaces, write what you already know about each one.

- Main ideas: _____

  _____

- Supporting details: _____

  _____

  _____

  _____

- A summary: _____

- Central ideas: _____

_____

Compare what you wrote to the following paragraph, which summarizes this vital prior knowledge:

> Main ideas are stated in a topic sentence. A topic sentence includes a topic and the author's controlling point. Supporting details explain the main idea. There are two types of supporting details. Major supporting details directly explain the topic sentence (or thesis statement), and minor supporting details explain the major supporting details. A summary condenses a paragraph or passage to its main idea. Central ideas are the main ideas of longer passages. Stated central ideas are called *thesis statements*.

Recopy the list of key words in your notebook; leave several blank lines between each idea. As you work through this chapter, record how you apply each idea in the list to the new information you learn about implied main ideas and implied central ideas.

LO1   Define the Term *Implied Main Idea*

As you learned in Chapter 3, sometimes authors state the main idea of a paragraph in a topic sentence. However, other paragraphs do not include a stated main idea. Even though the main idea is not stated in a single sentence, the paragraph still has a main idea. In these cases, the details clearly suggest or imply the author's main idea.

> An **implied main idea** is a main idea that is not stated directly but is strongly suggested by the supporting details in the passage.

When the main idea is not stated, you must figure out the author's controlling point about a topic. One approach is to study the facts, examples, descriptions, and explanations given—the supporting details. Another approach is to identify the author's thought pattern, a logical flow of ideas between sentences. A master reader often uses both approaches. Learning how to develop a main idea based on the supporting details and thought patterns will help you develop several skills. You will learn how to study information, value the meaning of supporting details, recognize the relationships among ideas, and use your own words to express an implied main idea.

Many different types of nonfiction reading material use implied main ideas. For example, you will often need to formulate the implied main idea of essays, articles, and textbook paragraphs and sections. The following passage is taken from a college marketing textbook. Read the passage, asking yourself, "What is the main idea?"

Positioning

[1]The Apple iPod, with over 200 million units sold, controls the leading position in the global digital music player industry. [2]Launched by Apple Computers in 2001, the iPod has enjoyed success from building on the Apple brand and using the Apple computer as a digital hub for consumers. [3]The idea of a digital hub is that consumers will purchase additional Apple products to connect to their Apple computer. [4]Beyond iPod, iTunes, iPhone, and iPad, there is iLife, iWork, iWeb, and iPhoto, not to mention Apple TV (renamed from iTV). [5]While the iPod basically performs the same functions as the many different brands of MP3 players, it separates itself from other brands by being used by many different influential celebrities, from presidents to rock stars, and by generally being considered "cool." [6]Being positioned as cool and being associated with celebrities have made the product iconic in countries across the world. [7]Just as being popular has helped the iPod increase sales, it is that ubiquity that could, potentially, cause at least some of its consumers to look for less common brands of MP3s to express their individuality. [8]That is where the digital hub strategy is designed to keep adding new and relevant products to the overall Apple offering.

—Levens, Michael R., *Marketing: Defined, Explained, Applied*, 2nd ed., p. 139.

Did you notice that every sentence in this paragraph is a supporting detail? No single sentence covers all the other ideas. To figure out the implied main idea, ask the following questions:

Questions for Finding the Implied Main Idea

- What is the topic, or subject, of the paragraph?
- What are the major supporting details?
- Based on the details about the topic, what point or main idea is the author trying to get across?

Apply these three questions to the passage "Positioning" by writing your responses to each question in the following blanks.

1. What is the topic of the paragraph? _____

2. What are the major supporting details?

   _____

   _____

   _____

   _____

   _____

   _____

   _____

   _____

3. What is the main idea the author is trying to get across?

   _____

   _____

   _____

In order to formulate a main idea statement for this passage, you had to consider each of the details within it. First, the author discusses how popular the iPod is. Next, he explains that part of the popularity is due to the digital hub strategy, which connects the Apple computer (the "hub") to the iPod and other Apple products. Third, the iPod also sells well by separating itself from other brands because it is considered "cool," yet, interestingly, the author maintains that this very "coolness" may lead consumers away from the iPod. In the end, though, Apple will continue to sell products because its digital hub strategy will add new products to the hub.

Asking and answering these questions allows you to think about the impact of each detail and how the details fit together to create the author's most important point. Searching for an implied main idea is like a treasure hunt. You must carefully read the clues provided by the author. The following examples and practices are designed to strengthen this important skill.

Analyze Supporting Details and Thought Patterns to Determine Implied Main Ideas

Remember that the main idea of a paragraph is like a frame of a house. Just as a frame includes all the rooms, a main idea must cover all the details in a paragraph. Therefore, the implied main idea will be general enough to cover all the details, but it will not be so broad that it becomes an overgeneralization or a sweeping statement that suggests details not given; nor can it be so narrow that some of the given details are not covered. Instead, the implied main idea must cover *all* the details given.

Having the skill of identifying a stated main idea will also help you grasp the implied main idea. You learned in Chapter 3 that the stated main idea (the topic sentence) has two parts. A main idea is made up of the topic and the author's controlling point about the topic. One trait of the controlling point is the author's opinion or bias. A second trait is the author's thought pattern. Consider, for example, the topic sentence "Older people benefit from volunteer work for several reasons." "Older people" and "volunteer work" make up the topic. "Benefit" states the opinion, and "several reasons" states the thought pattern. When you read material that implies the main idea, you should mentally create a topic sentence based on the details in the material.

Textbook
Skills

⊙ EXAMPLE Read the following list of supporting details from a criminal justice textbook. Circle the topic as it recurs throughout the list of details. Underline transition words which join ideas within a sentence and between sentences. Double underline the biased (opinion) words. Then choose the statement that best expresses the author's controlling point about the topic.

- Lay witnesses are non-expert witnesses who may be called to testify in court for either the prosecution or the defense.

- Lay witnesses may be eyewitnesses who saw the crime being committed or who came upon the crime scene shortly after the crime had occurred.

- Another type of lay witness is the character witness.

- A character witness frequently provides information about the personality, family life, business acumen, and so on of the defendant.

- Of course the victim may also be a lay witness, providing detailed and sometimes lengthy testimony about the defendant and the crime.

—Schmalleger, Frank J., *Criminal Justice Today: An Introductory*
Text for the 21st Century, 10th ed., p. 338.

_____   Which statement best expresses the implied main idea?

    a. Character witnesses offer important information on behalf of the defendant.

    b. Witnesses are important to both the prosecution and the defense.

    c. Several types of lay witnesses, or non-expert witnesses, may be called to testify for the prosecution or the defense.

    d. Eyewitnesses and victims frequently provide details about the defendant and the crime.

EXPLANATION The best statement of the implied main idea is (c), "Several types of lay witnesses, or non-expert witnesses, may be called to testify for the prosecution or the defense." Option (a) is too general, and options (b) and (d) state specific details. The terms _lay witness, witness, eyewitness, character witness,_ and _victim_ state the various forms of the topic and should have been circled. The words _another type, frequently, also,_ and _sometimes_ are transition words that should have been underlined. These transition words reveal the author has organized ideas by classification or types. The phrase _another type_ suggests that this list of details describes types of lay witnesses. The word _may_ is a biased word that suggests a possibility rather than a factual event and, therefore, should be double underlined. ◀

Practice 1

Read the following groups of supporting details. Circle the topic as it recurs throughout the list of details. Underline transition words to help you locate the major details. Also, double underline the biased words to determine the author's opinion. Then select the sentence that best expresses the implied main idea.

Group 1

- Many people volunteer within their communities because they want to make a difference.
- Others volunteer so that they can develop new skills.
- One reason some volunteer is to explore career paths.
- In addition, volunteering is a good way for young people to have fun working with friends.
- Finally, volunteers feel good about themselves.

_____ **1.** Which statement best expresses the implied main idea?
   a. Volunteer work is a good way to build a résumé.
   b. Volunteering provides an excellent opportunity to meet new people.
   c. People engage in volunteer work for several reasons.
   d. Volunteer work is very rewarding.

Textbook Skills

Group 2

- Ancient Roman entertainment included public fights between gladiators.
- Many gladiators were volunteers who willingly gave up their rights and property and pledged not only to suffer intensely but to die fighting.
- Romans valued a concept called *virtus* (honor above life).
- *Virtus* was a specifically male trait and was most often applied to a gladiator who had fought well or continued to struggle even after defeat.
- If a gladiator displayed *virtus* but was clearly losing, he could raise one finger in a plea for mercy.
- Usually, Romans granted *missio* or mercy for gladiators who displayed *virtus* so that they could live to fight another day.

—Adapted from Sporre, Dennis J., *The Creative Impulse:
An Introduction to the Arts,* 8th ed., p. 133.

_____ **2.** Which statement best expresses the implied main idea?
   a. Ancient Romans enjoyed violent entertainment.
   b. Ancient Romans valued honor above life.
   c. Ancient Romans were often merciful.
   d. Ancient Romans were virtuous.

Textbook Skills

Group 3

- A person who is supporting a family will normally incur more expenses than a single person without dependents.
- As people get older, they tend to spend more money on expensive houses, cars, and vacations.
- In addition, people's consumption behavior varies greatly.
- For example, at one extreme are people who spend their entire paycheck within a few days of receiving it; at the other extreme are "big savers" who reduce their spending and focus on saving for the future.

—Adapted from Madura, Jeff. *Personal Finance,*
2nd ed., p. 32.

_____ **3.** Which statement best expresses the implied main idea?
  a. Some people are better at managing their money than others.
  b. The size of one's family affects cash outflows.
  c. Several factors affect cash outflows.
  d. People spend more money as they age.

Group 4

- Nomadic Native American tribes followed migratory prey and the seasonal changes of plant life.
- Nomadic Native American tribes needed housing structures that were easily erected and dismantled.
- For example, tipis were easily erected and dismantled.
- Agricultural Native American tribes, on the other hand, could enjoy more permanent dwellings, like pueblos.

_____ **4.** Which statement best expresses the implied main idea?
  a. Native American tribes were constantly on the move.
  b. The lifestyle of a Native American tribe influenced the types of dwellings they inhabited.
  c. Native American tribes were excellent architects.
  d. Native American tribes lived in substandard housing.

LO3 Determine the Implied Main Ideas of Paragraphs

So far, you have learned to recognize the implied main idea by studying the specific details in a group of sentences. In this next step, the sentences will form a paragraph, but the skill of recognizing the implied main idea is exactly the same. The implied main idea of paragraphs must not be too broad or too narrow, so study the supporting details and look for thought patterns and opinions that suggest the main idea.

> **EXAMPLE** Read the following paragraph. Circle the topic as it recurs throughout the paragraph. Underline transition words to help you locate the major details. Also, double underline biased words to determine the author's opinion. Then select the sentence that best expresses the implied main idea.

Textbook
Skills

The Faces of Fetal Alcohol Syndrome

[1]"The guilt is tremendous . . . I did it again and again . . . I don't know how to tell them. [2]It was something I could have prevented." [3]Debbie has

had seven children. [4]One of her older daughters, Corey, has been diagnosed with fetal alcohol syndrome (FAS), the most serious type of alcohol damage. [5]At age three she was hyperactive and talked like a one-year-old. [6]Doctors believe that Debbie's youngest child Sabrina is almost certainly a victim as well. [7]Her face bears the characteristic features of FAS, including small eyes, a short nose, and a small head. [8]At 7 months, she was weak, began having seizures, and could not eat solid food because she was unable to close her mouth around the spoon. [9]As this pregnant mother repeatedly got drunk, so did her developing children.

—Audesirk, Teresa, Audesirk, Gerald, and Byers, Bruce E.,
Life on Earth, 5th ed., p. 486.

_____ Which sentence best states the implied main idea?
  a. The effects of Fetal Alcohol Syndrome can be avoided.
  b. Pregnant women can consume alcohol in moderate amounts.
  c. Pregnant mothers who frequently consume alcohol cause preventable physical and mental damage to their developing children.

EXPLANATION Implied main ideas require that the reader be actively involved in the meaning-making process. The author states the damage caused to developing children by their mothers' prenatal consumption of alcohol in the following expression: "most serious type of alcohol damage." The author reinforces the point by describing the physical and mental traits of FAS in sentences 5 and 7. Item (c) is the best statement of the implied main idea of this paragraph. Item (a) is too narrow, and item (b) jumps to the wrong conclusion based on the evidence in the paragraph. Nowhere in the paragraph does the author imply that occasional or moderate consumption of alcohol is safe or leads to FAS. ◁

Practice 2

Read the following paragraphs. In each paragraph, circle the topic as it recurs throughout the paragraph. Underline transition words to help you locate the major details. Also, double underline the biased words to determine the author's opinion. Then select the sentence that best expresses the implied main idea.

Opposition to Capital Punishment

Textbook
Skills

[1]The first recorded effort to eliminate the death penalty occurred at the home of Benjamin Franklin in 1787. [2]At a meeting there on March 9 of that year, Dr. Benjamin Rush, a signer of the Declaration of Independence

and a leading medical pioneer, read a paper against capital punishment to a small but influential audience. [3]Although his immediate efforts came to nothing, his arguments laid the groundwork for many debates that followed. [4]Michigan, widely regarded as the first abolitionist state, joined the Union in 1837 without a death penalty. [5]A number of other states, including Alaska, Hawaii, Massachusetts, Minnesota, West Virginia, and Wisconsin, have since spurned death as a possible sanction for criminal acts. [6]However, the death penalty remains a sentencing option in 38 of the states and in all federal jurisdictions.

—Adapted from Schmalleger, Frank J., *Criminal Justice Today: An Introductory Text for the 21st Century*, 10th ed., p. 409.

_____ 1. Which sentence best states the implied main idea?
   a. Many oppose capital punishment.
   b. Capital punishment should not be a viable sanction for criminal acts.
   c. Dr. Benjamin Rush was the first to publicly oppose capital punishment.
   d. Attempts have been made to abolish capital punishment since the founding of the United States.

[1]The *personal* aspects of emotional intelligence are a set of components that include awareness and management of our own emotions. [2]People who are able to monitor their feelings as they arise are less likely to be ruled by them. [3]However, managing emotions does not mean suppressing them; nor does it mean giving free rein to every feeling. [4]Instead, effective management of emotions involves expressing them appropriately. [5]Emotion management also involves engaging in activities that cheer us up, soothe our hurts, or reassure us when we feel anxious. [6]The *interpersonal* aspects of emotional intelligence make up the second set of components. [7]Empathy, or sensitivity to others' feelings, is one such component. [8]One key indicator of empathy is the ability to read others' nonverbal behavior— the gestures, vocal inflections, tones of voice, and facial expressions of others. [9]Another of the interpersonal components is the capacity to manage relationships. [10]However, it is related to both the personal aspects of emotional intelligence and to empathy. [11]In other words, to effectively manage the emotional give-and-take involved in social relationships, we have to be able to manage our own feelings and be sensitive to those of others.

—Adapted from Wood, Samuel E., Wood, Ellen Green, and Boyd, Denise, *Mastering the World of Psychology*, 3rd ed., p. 237.

_____ **2.** Which sentence best states the implied main idea?
 a. Emotional intelligence includes two sets of components.
 b. Emotional intelligence is made up of personal aspects.
 c. Emotional intelligence is made up of interpersonal aspects.
 d. Emotional intelligence is the ability to manage emotions effectively.

 ## Create a Summary from the Supporting Details

You have developed the skill of figuring out implied main ideas, which will serve you well throughout college. The next step is to state the implied main idea in your own words. When you are reading and studying, you must be able to summarize the most important details in a one-sentence statement; in other words, you must create a topic sentence.

To formulate this one-sentence summary, find the topic, determine the author's opinion by examining the biased words, and use the thought pattern to locate the major details. Then combine these ideas in a single sentence. The summary sentence includes the topic and the author's controlling point, just like a topic sentence. The statement you come up with must not be too narrow, for it must cover all the details given. On the other hand, it must not be too broad or go beyond the supporting details.

Remember that a main idea is always written as a complete sentence.

▷ **EXAMPLE** Read the following paragraph. Circle the topic as it recurs throughout the paragraph. Underline words that reveal thought patterns and bias to discover the controlling point. Then write a sentence that best states the implied main idea. Remember: not too narrow, not too broad—find that perfect fit!

The Cost of Owning a Horse

¹People invest in horses for a variety of reasons, including riding for pleasure or therapy, competing in shows, farming, breeding, and racing. ²The first cost incurred is, of course, the purchase of the horse. ³Depending on the pedigree, health, and prior training of the horse, prices vary from a few hundred to several thousand dollars. ⁴The ongoing cost of boarding the horse must be considered as well. ⁵Boarding costs vary based on location and the type of services. ⁶For example, some facilities offer just a pasture while others offer full-service stall boarding and daily exercise. ⁷A third major expense involved in owning a horse is feed. ⁸Horses are usually fed a grain mix, grass hay, and salt and minerals. ⁹Next, health care costs include dewormings four times a year and a variety of vaccinations. ¹⁰In addition, medical attention associated with breeding and emergencies

can cause sizeable increases in expenses. [11]Farrier costs must also be considered; this expense includes at a minimum trimming the hooves every couple of months, but may require, depending on the type of activity and the owner's taste, shoeing the horse or resetting the horse's shoes. [12]Another cost that must be taken into account is the cost of stall bedding. [13]The dollar amount varies based on different bedding sources and quantity used. [14]Finally, the costs for equipment most often include items needed for grooming, feeding, and cleaning such as brushes, buckets, shovels, and forks; in addition, tack must be bought and kept in good repair.

Implied main idea: _____

_____

A synonym for **farrier** is _____.

   a. veterinarian

   b. groomer

   c. blacksmith

▶ A **farrier** making a horse shoe.

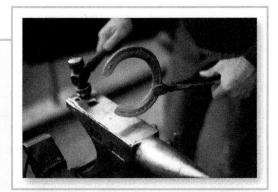

EXPLANATION   The following sentence is one way to state the main idea of the paragraph: "Many expenses are involved in owning a horse." Keep in mind that using your own words to formulate an implied main idea means that the wording of answers will vary. ◀

Practice 3

Read the following paragraphs. Annotate the text. Then write a sentence that states the implied main idea.

From *Narrative of the Life of Frederick Douglass, an American Slave. Written by Himself*

[1]I was born in Tuckahoe, near Hillsborough, and about twelve miles from Easton, in Talbot county, Maryland. [2]I have no accurate knowledge

of my age, never having seen any authentic record containing it. [3]By far the larger part of the slaves know as little of their ages as horses know of theirs, and it is the wish of most masters within my knowledge to keep their slaves thus ignorant. [4]I do not remember to have ever met a slave who could tell of his birthday. [5]They seldom come nearer to it than planting-time, harvest-time, cherry-time, spring-time, or fall-time. [6]A want of information concerning my own was a source of unhappiness to me even during childhood. [7]The white children could tell their ages. [8]I could not tell why I ought to be deprived of the same privilege. [9]I was not allowed to make any inquiries of my master concerning it. [10]He deemed all such inquiries on the part of a slave improper and impertinent, and evidence of a restless spirit. [11]The nearest estimate I can give makes me now between twenty-seven and twenty-eight years of age. [12]I come to this, from hearing my master say, some time during 1835, I was about seventeen years old.

—From Douglass, Frederick, *Narrative of the Life of Frederick Douglass, an American Slave. Written by Himself,* 1845. pp. 1–2.

1. Implied main idea: _____

_____

The Mayan World

[1]The Classic Maya developed a sophisticated mathematics and were among the first peoples in the world to invent the concept of zero. [2]In addition to the 52-year calendar they shared with other Mesoamerican societies, the Maya developed an absolute calendar, known as the Long Count. [3]The Long Count calendar—like the Jewish, Christian, or Muslim calendars—was anchored to a fixed starting point in the past. [4]The calendar had great religious as well as practical significance for the Maya. [5]They viewed the movements of the celestial bodies to which the calendar was tied—including the sun, moon, and Venus—as deities. [6]The complexity and accuracy of their calendar reflect Maya skills in astronomical observation. [7]They adjusted their lunar calendar for the actual length of the lunar cycle (29.53 days) and may have had provisions like our leap years for the actual length of the solar year. [8]The calendar's association with divine forces and the esoteric knowledge required to master it must have been important sources of prestige and power for its elite guardians.

—Craig, Albert M., Graham, William A., Kagan, Donald, Ozment, Steven, and Turner, Frank M., *The Heritage of World Civilizations, Brief,* 5th ed., p. 320.

2. Implied main idea: _____

_____

_____

LO5 ## Determine and State the Implied Central Idea

Just as a single paragraph can have an implied main idea, longer passages made up of two or more paragraphs can also have an implied main idea. As you learned in Chapter 3, the stated main idea or central idea of these longer passages is called the *thesis statement*. When the main idea of several paragraphs is implied, it is called the **implied central idea**. You use the same skills to formulate the implied central idea of a longer passage that you use to formulate the implied main idea of a paragraph.

> **The implied central idea** is the main idea suggested by the details of a passage made up of two or more paragraphs.

Annotating the text is a helpful tool in determining the implied central idea. Just as you did to grasp the implied main idea for paragraphs, circle the topic. Underline the signal words for thought patterns. Remember, transition words introduce supporting details. An author often pairs a transition word with a major supporting detail. Consider the following examples: *the first reason, a second cause, the final effect, another similarity, an additional difference,* and so on. When you see phrases such as these, your one-sentence summary may include the following kinds of phrases: *several effects, a few differences,* and so on.

A longer passage often contains paragraphs with stated main ideas. The stated main idea of a paragraph is a one-sentence summary of that paragraph and can be used as part of your summary of the implied central idea.

> **EXAMPLE** Read the following passage from a college criminal justice textbook. Annotate the text. Then write a sentence that states the implied central idea of the entire passage.

Types of Terrorism

[1]It is important to distinguish between two major forms of terrorism: domestic and international. [2]Such distinctions are generally made in terms of the origin, base of operations, and objectives of a terrorist organization.

[3]**Domestic terrorism** refers to the unlawful use of force or violence by a group or an individual who is based and operates entirely within the United States and its territories without foreign direction and whose acts are directed against elements of the U.S. government or population. [4]**International terrorism**, in contrast, is the unlawful use of force or violence by a group or an individual who has some connection to a foreign power or whose activities transcend national boundaries against people or property to intimidate or coerce a government, the civilian population, or any segment thereof in furtherance of political or social objectives. [5]International terrorism is sometimes mistakenly called foreign terrorism, a term that, strictly speaking, refers only to acts of terrorism that occur outside the United States.

[6]Another new kind of terrorism, called **cyberterrorism**, is lurking on the horizon. [7]Cyberterrorism makes use of high technology, especially computers and the Internet, in the planning and carrying out of terrorist attacks. [8]The term was coined in the 1980s by Barry Collin, a senior research fellow at the Institute for Security and Intelligence in California, who used it to refer to the convergence of cyberspace and terrorism. [9]It was later popularized by a 1996 RAND report that warned of an emerging "new terrorism" distinguished by how terrorist groups organize and by how they use technology. [10]The report warned of a coming "netwar" or "infowar" consisting of coordinated cyberattacks on our nation's economic, business, and military infrastructure. [11]A year later, FBI Agent Mark M. Pollitt offered a working definition of *cyberterrorism*, saying that it is "the premeditated, politically motivated attack against information, computer systems, computer programs, and data which results in violence against noncombatant targets by subnational groups or clandestine agents."

—Schmalleger, Frank J., *Criminal Justice: A Brief Introduction*, 9th ed., p. 55.

Implied central idea: _____

_____

_____

EXPLANATION Terrorism is the topic of this passage. The topic sentences of both paragraphs tell the reader the two major points the author is using to limit the topic. In the first paragraph, sentence 1 is the topic sentence, and it focuses on the fact that there are two major forms of terrorism: domestic and international. The additional details in that paragraph define the two forms and make distinctions between them. In the second paragraph, sentence 6 is the topic sentence, and it focuses on "another new kind of terrorism, called *cyberterrorism* . . . lurking on the horizon." By combining these two main ideas, a master reader creates a one-sentence summary of the passage.

Although answers will vary, one possible answer is "Domestic and international terrorism are two major forms of terrorism, but a new kind—cyberterrorism—is likely in the future." This sentence covers the major supporting details, but does not go beyond the information given in the passage. ◀

Practice 4

Textbook
Skills

Read the following passage from a college sociology textbook. Write a sentence that states the implied central idea.

¹Prostitution is illegal because it is a social problem that has a corrosive effect on society—it has widespread implications that go beyond prostitutes and their customers. ²Prostitution keeps pimps and madams (who are constantly on the lookout for new employees) in business and can corrupt police officers who are bribed to look the other way. ³Most importantly, it can feed into larger, more harmful organized crimes, such as the drug trade.

⁴Any neighborhood with the presence of prostitution will be hurt. ⁵Property values will decrease substantially. ⁶Not only will the prostitution activity be unwanted, but it will also attract undesirable people to the neighborhood. ⁷Residents who have children will relocate, and prospective home buyers will look elsewhere.

⁸Prostitution can rapidly spread disease and is an enormous health risk. ⁹Because of the many sexual partners that a prostitute encounters on a regular basis, one prostitute who carries an STD could infect dozens of people. ¹⁰If the disease goes undetected and those clients have other sexual partners, more could be infected as well.

¹¹Prostitution is immoral and undermines an accepted sense of decency. ¹²The selling of sex and the sex acts that are performed by prostitutes violate long-held beliefs about intimacy and sexuality. ¹³Prostitution ruins marriages, tears families apart, and leads to corruption in the home and community.

¹⁴Women are often treated in a manner in which they are objectified, and prostitution only serves to continue—and even enhance this mind-set. ¹⁵The profession itself is degrading to women, and because of the stigma attached to prostitution, women are often seen and treated as second class citizens.

—Carl, John D., *Think Social Problems.*

Implied central idea: _____

_____

LO6 Develop Textbook Skills: How to Read a Map

Textbook Skills

Many academic courses, particularly in the social sciences, rely on maps to communicate important geographical, political, social, and economic information. Maps provide information about what occurs in time and space. Not only do maps show the exact locations of particular places, but they also document the movements of civilizations, people, ideas, and trade. To analyze a map, follow these basic steps:

- **Read the title and caption to identify the main topic of the map.** Is the map illustrating a political idea, physical features, or a particular theme? Read the title and caption before you study the map to focus your attention on the cartographer's purpose for the map.

- **Activate your prior knowledge.** What do you already know about the topic, the region, and the time period? How does this map fit in with what you already know? What do you need to know to understand the map?

- **Discern the orientation of the map.** The orientation, the direction in which the map is pointed, is usually shown by a compass. Most current maps place north at the top of the map.

- **Identify the date of the map.** Because our world (and our understanding of our world) is ever-changing politically and socially, older maps may not be relevant. In addition, a map may be illustrating a historical perspective.

- **Understand and apply the legend.** The legend, or key, which shows the meaning of the colors, symbols, and other markings on the map, is crucial to understanding what the map represents.

- **Understand and apply the scale.** The scale tells you the relationship between the distance on the map and the corresponding distance on the ground. For example, one inch may represent 100 miles. Understanding the scale enables the reader to visualize the size of and distance between places.

> **EXAMPLE** The following map is from the textbook *World Civilizations: The Global Experience*. Read the map and answer the questions. Then state the implied main idea of the map in one sentence.

European Population Density, c. 1600

—Stearns, Peter N., Adas, Michael B., Schwartz, Stuart B., and Gilbert, Marc Jason, *World Civilizations: The Global Experience, Combined Volume, Atlas Edition*, 5th ed., Map 22.2 (p. 490).

1. What is the title and date of the map? _____

   _____

2. According to the legend, what do the colors represent? _____

   _____

3. Name three densely populated regions of Europe. _____

   _____

4. Why might most of the most heavily populated areas be located alongside rivers, oceans, or seas? _____

_____

Implied main idea of the map: _____

_____

EXPLANATION Compare your answers to the following.

(1) The date of the map is included in its title "European Population Density, c. 1600." Based on the date, the reader understands that this map offers a historical view of the region. (2) The legend indicates four levels of "people per square mile." (3) The map indicates more than three regions that are densely populated, so answers may vary, but should include three of the following: Ireland, England, France, United Netherlands, Holy Roman Empire, and Papal States. (4) Answers may vary, but prior knowledge supports the idea that during this time water provided the major means of transportation of people and trade, so the following statement is an appropriate answer: "Waterways make trade easier, and people settle along trade routes." Although your interpretation of the main idea of the map may vary, based on the title, the legend, and the answers to the preceding questions, the implied main idea of the map is as follows: "In 1600, European population density was greater alongside rivers, oceans, and seas." Quite often, to properly analyze a map, a master reader uses prior knowledge (see page 4 in this textbook for more information about this term). ◄

Practice 5

Study the map from the textbook *Introduction to Geography: People, Places, and Environment.* Answer the questions, and write a sentence that states the implied main idea of the map.

1. What prior knowledge is needed to understand the implied main idea of the map? _____

2. According to the caption, what is the topic of the map? _____

_____

3. According to the legend, what is the unit of measurement? _____

_____

4. What is the implied main idea of the map? _____

_____

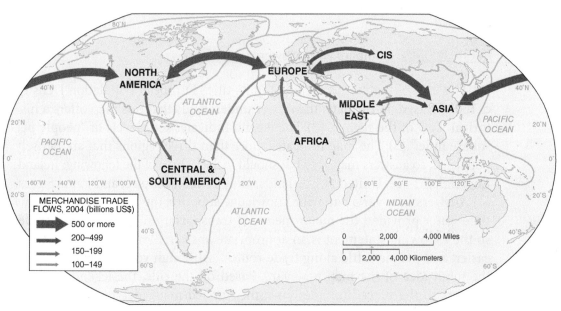

"Figure 12.32 World Merchandise Trade by Region"

—Bergman, Edward and Renwick, William, *Introduction to Geography: People, Places, and Environment,* 4th ed., Figure 12.32.

LO7   Recognize Experience and Perspective

As you have worked through this chapter, hopefully you have had some lively discussions about the possible answers for activities that asked you to state implied main ideas. Often a set of details will suggest many things to many people. Determining main ideas requires that the reader bring personal understandings and experience to the task. Thus people with different perspectives may disagree about what the details suggest. Another complex aspect of determining main ideas is that authors may choose to give a collection of details because the idea suggested is difficult to sum up in one sentence. The author intends several meanings to coexist. The important point to remember is that the main idea you formulate should be strongly supported by the details in the paragraph or longer passage.

Apply Information Literacy Skills

LO8 Academic, Personal, and Career Applications of Implied Main Ideas

The ability to identify an implied main idea is another information literacy skill. In addition to locating the stated main idea, being able to determine the implied main idea is an important problem-solving tool that will help you comprehend information. In your academic, personal, and career lives, you will come across many forms of reading material with implied main ideas. Some examples are fiction, poetry, songs, instructions, manuals, non-fiction books, reports, memos, letters, or articles. You will be expected to or will want to understand and respond to the implied main idea of these materials. Thus, you will use the skills that you have learned in this chapter in several ways to:

- Recognize your own need to know an implied main idea.
- State an implied main idea.
- Apply the implied main idea to your specific situation.

Academic Application

Assume you are taking a college environmental science course. You have been assigned the following chapter. Preview the list of learning objectives and complete the activities that follow.

- **Before Reading:** Recall what you already know about climate change. Write a sentence that states the implied main idea of the picture.
- **During Reading:** Underline key terms that indicate the implied central idea of the chapter.
- **After Reading:** In the space following the chapter opener image write one sentence that states the central idea of the chapter implied by the learning objectives.

Implied main idea of the photograph: _____

_____

_____

—Withgott, Jay H. and Laposata, Matthew, *Essential Environment: The Science Behind the Stories,* 4th ed.

Topic sentence stating implied central idea of the chapter: _____

_____

_____

Personal Application

Assume you write a blog about health issues, and you want to educate your readers about the cold and the flu. During your research about this topic, you found the following information. Read the article and complete the activities that follow:

- ▪ **Before Reading:** Skim the information.
- ▪ **During Reading:** Highlight the key points that are relevant to your search.

■ **After Reading:** Write a sentence that states the implied main idea of your research.

Cold Versus Flu

What is the difference between a cold and the flu?

The flu and the common cold are both respiratory illnesses, but they are caused by different viruses. In general, the flu is worse than the common cold, and symptoms are more common and intense. Colds are usually milder than the flu. People with colds are more likely to have a runny or stuffy nose.

How can you tell the difference between a cold and the flu?

Because colds and flu share many symptoms, special tests that usually must be done within the first few days of illness can be carried out, when needed to tell if a person has the flu.

What are the symptoms of the flu versus the symptoms of a cold?

In general, the flu is worse than the common cold, and symptoms such as fever, body aches, extreme tiredness, and dry cough are more common and intense. Colds are usually milder than the flu. People with colds are more likely to have a runny or stuffy nose. Colds generally do not result in serious health problems, such as pneumonia, bacterial infections, or hospitalizations.

—"Seasonal Influenza." Centers for Disease Control and Prevention.

Symptoms	Cold Lasts up to 2 weeks	Flu Lasts a few days to less than 2 weeks
Fever or feeling feverish/chills	Mild	High/severe
Cough	Mild	Intense dry cough
Runny or stuffy nose	Early sign	Yes
Sneezing	Yes	Yes
Sore throat	Early sign	Yes
Muscle or body aches	Mild	Intense
Headaches	Mild	Severe
Fatigue	Mild	Very tired
Vomiting and diarrhea	No	Possible

—"Seasonal Influenza (Flu)"; "Common Cold and Runny Nose."
CDC. Table by D. J. Henry.

Implied main idea: _____

_____

_____

Career Application

Assume you are the principal of a middle school in Alabama. You have found the following information regarding a government energy program that would pay for a renewable energy system for your school. This sounds like a great opportunity for your school to apply for.

- ▪ **Before Reading:** Skim the passage. Predict the benefit of switching to renewable energy.
- ▪ **During Reading:** Underline key words that imply the main idea.
- ▪ **After Reading:** In the space at the end of the passage, write a sentence that states the implied main idea of this loan program.

Program Information

Funding Source Alabama	State Revolving Loan Fund
Program Type	State Loan Program

Through a public-private partnership with PowerSouth, Alabama's Local Government Energy Loan Program offers zero-interest loans to local governments, K-12 schools, and public colleges and universities for renewable energy systems and energy efficiency improvements that will eventually have a payback through utility savings. Under the program, municipal and county governments, and colleges and universities may borrow up to $350,000 for eligible projects, and K-12 schools may receive up to $350,000 per campus or $500,000 per school system for eligible projects. Eligible renewable energy resources generally include biomass, hydropower, geothermal energy, wind energy, and solar energy.

The application is available on the program web site. An energy audit must be completed to identify necessary improvements. Following installation, the loan recipient must be benchmarked using the Energy Star Portfolio Manager program.

—U.S. Department of Energy.

Implied main idea: _____

_____

REVIEW TEST 1

Score (number correct) _____ x 25 = _____ %

Visit MyReadingLab to take this test online and receive feedback and guidance on your answers.

Implied Main Ideas

A. Read each group of supporting details. Annotate the text. Then choose the sentence that best expresses the implied main idea for each group.

1. Supporting details:

   - **Education**. About 1 in 4 adults with an advanced degree engage in a high level of overall physical activity, compared with 1 in 7 of those with less than a high school diploma.

   - **Income**. Adults with incomes below the poverty level are three times as likely to be physically inactive as adults in the highest income group.

   - **Marital Status**. Married women are more likely than never-married women to engage in a high level of overall physical activity.

   - **Geography**. Adults in the South are more likely to be physically inactive than adults in any other region.

   - This information is based on approximately 32,000 interviews with adults ages 18 and over, regardless of employment status, from the National Health Interview Survey, conducted by CDC's National Center for Health Statistics (NCHS).

      —"HHS Issues New Report on Americans' Overall Physical Activity Levels,"
      National Center for Health Statistics, Centers for Disease Control.

   _____ Which statement best expresses the implied main idea?

   a. According to the National Center for Health Statistics, several factors affect the levels of physical activity of Americans.

   b. People who live in the South are lazier than those who live in any other region.

   c. Married women are in better physical condition than single women.

   d. Exercise is an important aspect of a healthy lifestyle.

2. Supporting details:

- Graffiti consists of inscriptions, slogans and drawings scratched, scribbled or painted on a wall or other public or private surface.
- Graffiti is most often thought of as an eyesore.
- Graffiti generates fear of neighborhood crime and instability.
- It is costly, destructive, and lowers property values.
- Graffiti sends a message that people of the community are not concerned about the appearance of their neighborhoods.
- It is also against the law!

—Adapted from "What Is Graffiti?" Graffiti Control Program,
The City of San Diego.

_____ Which sentence best states the implied main idea?
a. Graffiti should be considered as a right to free speech.
b. Graffiti is not art; it is vandalism.
c. Graffiti lowers the value of property.
d. Graffiti is illegal.

B. Read the following paragraph. Annotate the text. In the space provided, write the letter of the best statement of the implied main idea.

Building Healthy Bones

[1]The main mineral in bones is calcium, one of whose functions is to add strength and stiffness to bones, which they need to support the body. [2]To lengthen long bones during growth, the body builds a scaffold of protein and fills this scaffold in with calcium-rich mineral. [3]From the ages of 11 through 24, an individual needs about 1,200 milligrams (mg) of calcium each day. [4]Bone also needs vitamin D, to move calcium from the intestine to the bloodstream and into bone. [5]Vitamin D can be obtained from short, normal day-to-day exposure of arms and legs to sun and from foods fortified with the vitamin. [6]Also needed are vitamin A, vitamin C, magnesium and zinc, as well as protein for the growing bone scaffold. [7]Many foods provide these nutrients. [8]Growing bone is especially sensitive to the impact of weight and pull of muscle during exercise, and responds by building stronger, denser bones. [9]That's why it's especially important to be physically active on a regular basis. [10]Bone building activities include sports and exercise such as football, basketball, baseball, jogging, dancing,

jumping rope, inline skating, skateboarding, bicycling, ballet, hiking, skiing, karate, swimming, rowing a canoe, bowling, and weight-training.

—Adapted from Farely, Dixie. "Bone Builders: Support Your Bones with Healthy Habits." *FDA Consumer Magazine.* U.S. Food and Drug Administration.

_____ **3.** The best statement of the implied main idea is
   a. Healthy diet leads to healthy bones.
   b. Calcium is necessary to building healthy bones.
   c. One must eat a well-balanced diet and exercise regularly to build healthy bones.
   d. Many people develop weak bones due to poor diet and lack of exercise.

C. Study the following map from the textbook *Cultural Anthropology*. Write a sentence that states the implied main idea of the map.

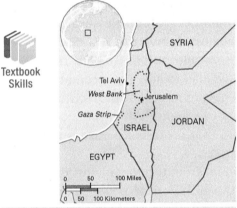

Textbook Skills

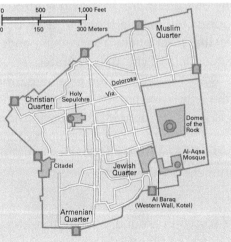

4. Implied main idea: _____

_____

_____

_____

◄ Sacred Sites in the Old City of Jerusalem, Israel. Jerusalem is the holiest city of Judaism, the third holiest city of Islam, and holy to some Christian denominations. The section called the Old City is surrounded by walls that have been built, razed, relocated, and rebuilt over several hundred years. The Old City contains four quarters: Armenian, Christian, Jewish, and Muslim, and many sacred sites such as the Kotel and the Via Dolorosa.

—Miller, Barbara, *Cultural Anthropology*, 4th ed., Map 13.5 (p. 356).

REVIEW TEST 2

Score (number correct) _____ x 25 = _____ %

Visit MyReadingLab to take this test online and receive feedback and guidance on your answers.

Read the following passage from a college sociology textbook. Answer the questions that follow the passage.

Textbook
Skills

Who Rules the United States?

[1]With lobbyists and PACs wielding such influence, just whom do U.S. senators and representatives really represent? [2]This question has led to a lively debate among sociologists.

The Functionalist Perspective: Pluralism

[3]Functionalists view the state as having arisen out of the basic needs of the social group. [4]To protect themselves from oppressors, people formed a government and gave it the monopoly on violence. [5]The risk is that the state can turn that force against its own citizens. [6]States have a tendency to become muggers. [7]Thus, people must find a balance between having no government—which would lead to anarchy, a condition of disorder and violence—and having a government that protects them from violence, but that also may turn against them. [8]When functioning well, then, the state is a balanced system that protects its citizens both from one another and from government.

[9]What keeps the U.S. government from turning against its citizens? [10]Functionalists say that pluralism, a diffusion of power among many special-interest groups, prevents any one group from gaining control of the government and using it to oppress the people (Bentley 1908; Dahl 1961, 1982; Lemann 2008). [11]To keep the government from coming under the control of any one group, the founders of the United States set up three branches of government: the executive branch (the president), the judiciary branch (the courts), and the legislative branch (the Senate and House of Representatives). [12]Each is sworn to uphold the Constitution, which guarantees rights to citizens, and each can nullify the actions of the other two. [13]This system, known as checks and balances, was designed to ensure that no one branch of government dominates the others.

The Conflict Perspective: The Power Elite

[14]If you focus on the lobbyists scurrying around Washington, stress conflict theorists, you get a blurred image of superficial activities. [15]What

really counts is the big picture, not its fragments. [16]The important question is, Who holds the power that determines the country's overarching policies? [17]For example, who determines interest rates—and their impact on the price of our homes? [18]Who sets policies that encourage the transfer of jobs from the United States to countries where labor costs less? [19]And the ultimate question of power: Who is behind the decision to go to war?

[20]Sociologist C. Wright Mills (1956) took the position that the country's most important matters are not decided by lobbyists or even by Congress. [21]Rather, the decisions that have the greatest impact on the lives of Americans—and people across the globe—are made by a power elite. [22]The power elite consists of the top leaders of the largest corporations, the most powerful generals and admirals of the armed forces, and certain elite politicians—the president, the president's cabinet, and senior members of Congress who chair the major committees. [23]It is they who wield power, who make the decisions that direct the country and shake the world.

[24]Are the three groups that make up the power elite—the top business, political, and military leaders—equal in power? [25]Mills said that they were not, but he didn't point to the president and his staff or even to the generals and admirals as the most powerful. [26]Instead, he said that the corporate leaders are the most dominant. [27]Because all three segments of the power elite view capitalism as essential to the welfare of the country, Mills said that business interests take center stage in setting national policy.

[28]Sociologist William Domhoff (1990, 2006) uses the term ruling class to refer to the power elite. [29]He focuses on the 1 percent of Americans who belong to the super-rich, the powerful capitalist class. [30]Members of this class control our top corporations and foundations, even the boards that oversee our major universities. [31]It is no accident, says Domhoff, that from this group come most members of the president's cabinet and the ambassadors to the most powerful countries of the world.

Which View Is Right?

[32]The functionalist and conflict views of power in U.S. society cannot be reconciled. [33]Either competing interests block any single group from being dominant, as functionalists assert, or a power elite oversees the major decisions of the United States, as conflict theorists maintain. [34]The answer may have to do with the level you look at. [35]Perhaps at the middle level of power—which consists of Congress, other legislators, interest-group leaders, and local opinion leaders—the competing groups do keep each other at bay, and none can dominate. [36]If so, the functionalist view would apply to this level. [37]But which level holds the key to U.S. power?

[38]Perhaps the functionalists have not looked high enough, and activities at the peak remain invisible to them. [39]On that level, does an elite dominate? [40]To protect its mutual interests, does a small group make the major decisions of the United States?

[41]Sociologists passionately argue this issue, but with mixed data, we don't yet know the answer. [42]We await further research.

—Henslin, James M., *Sociology: A Down-to-Earth Approach,* 11th ed., pp. 426–427.

_____   **1.** Which sentence best states the implied central idea of paragraphs 2 through 3 (sentences 3–13)?

a. Functionalists view the state as having arisen out of the basic needs of the social group.

b. Functionalists think that groups must work to keep the U.S. government from turning against its people.

c. Functionalists believe that as different groups in society pursue their interests, power is balanced, and no one group can take over the government.

d. Functionalists believe that the U.S. Constitution set up three branches of government and a system of checks and balances.

_____   **2.** Which sentence best states the implied central idea of paragraphs 4 through 7 (sentences 14–31)?

a. Conflict theorists believe that the country's most important matters are decided by members of Congress and the people who lobby them.

b. Conflict theorists view conflict as an important element in distributing power in our society.

c. Conflict theorists think that power should be concentrated in an elite because they are best suited to run the country.

d. Conflict theorists say that a power elite with similar backgrounds direct the country, but it is dominated by corporate leaders.

_____   **3.** Which sentence best states the implied main idea of paragraph 8 (sentences 32–40)?

a. The functionalist and conflict views of power in U.S. society can never be reconciled.

b. The functionalist and conflict perspectives are opposing views, but the functionalists may not have considered the group at the highest level of power.

c. The conflict theorist perspective of power in U.S. society seems to take into account all levels of society.

d. The functionalists and the conflict theorists seem to disagree over who holds the most power in U.S. society.

_____ **4.** Which sentence best states the implied central idea of the entire passage?

    a. The functionalist view of power is Constitution-based, but the conflict view of power is not.

    b. The conflict view of power seems more accurate than the functionalist view of power.

    c. The functionalist and conflict perspectives are two opposing views of power that need more study.

    d. The functionalist and conflict perspectives of power are debated by sociologists, with neither side winning.

REVIEW TEST 3

Score (number correct) _____ x 10 = _____ %

Visit MyReadingLab to take this test online and receive feedback and guidance on your answers.

Implied Main Ideas

Before you read, skim the following passage. Answer the Before Reading questions. Read the passage and annotate the text. Then answer the After Reading questions.

Vocabulary Preview

ornamental (5): decorative, attractive
pigments (10): colors
spectrum (12): range
synthesize (17): manufacture
foliage (35): plant life

The Awe in Autumn: Why Leaves Change Their Color

[1]Did you know that the state of Maine is the most heavily forested state in the union? [2]It's true. [3]Over 90 percent of the state's land mass is devoted to growing trees. [4]That's 17 million acres! [5]In addition, we have a wide variety of trees, with over 50 native species, and many more **ornamental** trees in various neighborhoods. [6]With such an abundance of trees, it is no wonder that we have such a breathtaking season.

[7]Every autumn, magic **transformations** begin as trees begin to prepare for winter. [8]In certain regions, such as our own, the shedding of

leaves is preceded by a spectacular color show. [9]Formerly green leaves turn to brilliant shades of yellow, orange, and red. [10]These color changes are the result of transformations in leaf **pigments**.

[11]All during the spring and summer, leaves serve as factories where most of the foods necessary for the trees' growth are manufactured. [12]This food-making process takes place inside the leaf in numerous cells that contain the pigment chlorophyll, which actually masks the true color of the leaf by absorbing all other light colors and reflecting only the green light **spectrum**—thus the leaves appear to our eyes as green.

[13]The energy of the light absorbed by chlorophyll is converted into chemical energy stored in carbohydrates (sugars and starches). [14]By the plant absorbing water and nutrients through its roots, and absorbing carbon dioxide from the air, the chemical process of photosynthesis takes place. [15]This chemical change drives the biochemical reactions that cause plants to grow, flower, and produce seed. [16]Chlorophyll is not a very stable compound; bright sunlight causes it to **decompose**. [17]To maintain the amount of chlorophyll in their leaves, plants continuously **synthesize** it. [18]The synthesis of chlorophyll in plants requires sunlight and warm temperatures. [19]During the summer months, chlorophyll is continuously broken down and regenerated in the leaves of the trees.

[20]The shortening of the days and the cooler temperatures at night trigger several changes within the tree. [21]One of these changes is the growth of a corky membrane between the branch and the leaf stem. [22]This membrane interferes with the flow of nutrients into the leaf. [23]As this nutrient flow is interrupted, the production of chlorophyll in the leaf declines, and the green color begins to fade.

[24]The different chemical components that are always present inside the structure of the individual leaf will determine its fleeting brilliant color in the fall. [25]But weather also plays a factor in determining color. [26]The degree of color may vary from tree to tree. [27]For example, leaves directly exposed to the sun may turn red, while those on the shady side of the same tree may appear yellow or orange. [28]Also, the colors on the same tree may vary from year to year, depending upon the combination of weather conditions.

[29]According to the tree experts at several universities, including North Carolina State, the U.S. Department of Agriculture, and the U.S. Forestry Service, the most vivid colors appear after a warm, dry summer and early autumn rains, which will help prevent early leaf fall. [30]Long periods of wet weather in late fall will produce a rather drab coloration. [31]Droughts favor the chemical formation of anthocyanin, which is the chemical that is

most responsible for the brilliant reds and purples. [32]Drought conditions, especially in late summer, also favor red pigment formation due to the reduction of nitrate absorption through the tree's roots.

[33]The best colors seem to be displayed when relatively warm and sunny days are followed by cold nights through early October. [34]Light frost will enhance the colors, but a hard, killing frost will hasten the actual fall of the leaves from the trees. [35]The right combination of temperature, rainfall, and sunshine can prolong the autumn **foliage** brilliance by as much as two weeks.

—"The Awe in Autumn: Why Leaves Change Their Color," *Maine-ly Weather*, Fall/Winter 2002–2003, National Weather Service, NOAA.

Before Reading

Vocabulary in Context

_____ **1.** The best definition of the word **transformations** in sentence 7 is
    a. mysteries.   c. shows.
    b. changes.   d. seasons.

_____ **2.** The best meaning of the word **decompose** in sentence 16 is
    a. stabilize.   c. decay.
    b. grow.   d. stink.

Thought Patterns

_____ **3.** What is the thought pattern suggested by the title of the passage?
    a. cause and effect   c. spatial order
    b. classification   d. comparison

Stated Main Ideas

_____ **4.** Which sentence is the topic sentence in the fifth paragraph (sentences 20–23)?
    a. sentence 20   c. sentence 22
    b. sentence 21   d. sentence 23

After Reading

Supporting Details

_____ **5.** According to tree experts from universities and government agencies,
    a. autumn is a breathtaking season.
    b. trees go through magic transformations.

c. the most vivid colors appear after a warm, dry summer.

d. carbohydrates are sugars and starches.

_____ **6.** Based on the passage, chlorophyll

a. causes the color of the leaves to turn brilliant colors.

b. is a stable compound.

c. is a pigment which masks the true color of the leaf.

d. is a corky membrane between the branch and the leaf stem.

Concept Maps and Charts

7. Complete the concept map with information from the passage.

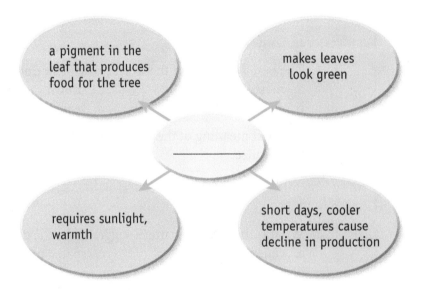

a pigment in the leaf that produces food for the tree

makes leaves look green

_____

requires sunlight, warmth

short days, cooler temperatures cause decline in production

Implied Main Ideas and Implied Central Idea

_____ **8.** Which sentence best states the implied central idea of the third, fourth, and fifth paragraphs (sentences 11–23)?

a. The production of chlorophyll affects the color of the leaves on a tree.

b. Chlorophyll produces food for the tree.

c. When chlorophyll production declines, leaves lose their green color.

d. Cooler weather slows down the production of chlorophyll.

_____   **9.** Which sentence best states the implied main idea of the eighth paragraph (sentences 33–35)?

      a. A hard frost will cause autumn leaves to fall from trees early in the season.

      b. Warm and sunny days produce brilliant colors.

      c. Climate plays a significant role in the brilliance of the autumn colors.

      d. Many factors affect the brilliance of the autumn colors.

_____   **10.** Which sentence best states the implied central idea of the reading passage?

      a. Autumn is a beautiful season.

      b. Chlorophyll is a major component in the process of leaves turning colors.

      c. Several factors work together to produce the awe-inspiring colors of fall.

      d. Weather is a major factor that affects the quality of the color of autumn leaves.

SUMMARY RESPONSE

Respond to the passage by stating the implied main idea in a thesis sentence. Be sure to identify the topic and the author's attitude about the topic. Begin your summary response with the following: *The most important idea of "The Awe in Autumn: Why Leaves Change Their Color" by the National Weather Service is . . .*

WHAT DO YOU THINK?

Assume you are a real estate salesperson, and your firm is launching a national ad campaign to persuade people to move to your region and buy a home or commercial property. Write a couple of paragraphs that describe the appealing aspects of the seasons in your area. Consider the following:

- Describe outdoor activities available for the changing seasons.
- Describe the different community events that occur as seasons change.
- Summarize the various scenic trails or state parks new residents may enjoy.

REVIEW TEST 4

Score (number correct) _____ x 10 = _____ %

Visit MyReadingLab to take this test online and receive feedback and guidance on your answers.

Implied Main Ideas

Before you read, skim the following passage. Answer the Before Reading questions. Read the passage and annotate the text. Then answer the After Reading questions.

Vocabulary Preview

scavenged (5): hunted, searched
migrating (6): traveling, moving
manipulate (15): use, operate
mechanisms (22): means, methods
hierarchies (23): levels of power or importance

Textbook
Skills

The Food-Producing Revolution

[1]For the first thousands of millennia of their existence, modern humans, known as *Homo sapiens sapiens* ("most intelligent people"), did not produce food. [2]Between 200,000 and 100,000 years ago, *Homo sapiens sapiens* first appeared in Africa and began to spread to other continents. [3]Scientists refer to this stage of human history as the Paleolithic Age, or Old Stone Age, because people made tools by cracking rocks and using their sharp edges to cut and chop. [4]*Homo sapiens sapiens'* use of tools demonstrated adaptation to new environments and practical needs. [5]They **scavenged** for wild food and became shrewd observers of the natural environment. [6]They followed **migrating** herds of animals, hunting with increasing efficiency as their weapons improved. [7]They also created beautiful works of art by carving bone and painting on cave walls. [8]By 45,000 years ago, these humans had reached most of Earth's **habitable** regions, except for Australia, the islands of the South Pacific, and North and South America.

[9]The end of the last Ice Age about 15,000 years ago ushered in an era of momentous change: the food-producing revolution. [10]As the Earth's climate became warmer, causing changes in vegetation, humans began to interact with the natural environment in new ways. [11]The warmer climate allowed cereal grasses to spread quickly over large areas; hunter-gatherers learned to collect these wild grains and grind them up for food. [12]Some groups of hunter-gatherers settled in semi-permanent camps near rivers and wetlands, where wild grains grew. [13]When people learned that

the seeds of wild grasses could be transplanted and grown in new areas, the domestication of plants was under way (see Map).

[14]At the same time that people discovered the benefits of planting seeds, they also began domesticating pigs, sheep, goats, and cattle, which eventually replaced wild game as the main source of meat. [15]**Domestication** occurs when humans **manipulate** the breeding of animals in order to serve their own purposes—for example, making wool (lacking on wild sheep), laying extra eggs (not done by undomesticated chickens), and producing extra milk (wild cows produce only enough milk for their offspring). [16]The first signs of goat domestication occurred about 8900 B.C.E. in the Zagros Mountains in Southwest Asia. Pigs, which adapt very well to human settlements because they eat garbage, were first domesticated around 7000 B.C.E. [17]By around 6500 B.C.E. domesticated cattle, goats, and sheep had become widespread.

[18]Farming and herding required hard work. [19]Even simple agricultural methods could produce about fifty times more food than hunting and gathering. [20]Thanks to the increased food supply, more newborns survived past infancy. [21]Populations expanded, and so did human settlements. [22]With the mastery of food production, human societies developed the **mechanisms** not only to feed themselves, but also to produce a surplus, which could then be traded for other resources. [23]Such economic activity allowed for economic specialization and fostered the growth of social, political, and religious **hierarchies**.

—Adapted from Levack, Brian, Muir, Edward, Veldman, Meredith, and Maas, Michael, *The West: Encounters & Transformation,* Atlas Edition, Combined Edition, 2nd ed., Map 1.1, pp. 13–14, 27.

Before Reading

Vocabulary in Context

1–2. Study the following chart of word parts and the context in which the words are used. Then use your own words to define the terms.

Root	Meaning	Suffix	Meaning
habitare	possess	*-able*	quality, degree
domus	house	*-ation*	action, process

1. In sentence 8, **habitable** means _____

2. In sentence 15, **domestication** means _____

_____

The Beginnings of Food Production

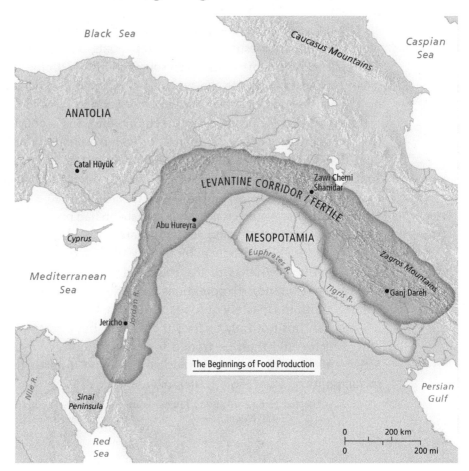

The Beginnings of Food Production

After Reading

Thought Patterns

_____ **3.** The overall thought pattern used in this passage is
   a. time order.   c. definition and example.
   b. comparison and contrast.   d. space order.

Stated Main Ideas

_____ **4.** The sentence that states the main idea of the second paragraph
   (sentences 9–13) is
   a. sentence 9.   c. sentence 11.
   b. sentence 10.   d. sentence 12.

Supporting Details and Concept Maps

5–7. Complete the following concept map with details from the passage and the map.

Chronology: Beginnings of Civilization

200,000 to 100,000 years ago   Modern humans first appear in Africa.

45,000 years ago   **5.** _____

_____

15,000 years ago   Ice Age ends.

6. _____

8900 B.C.E.   First signs of goat domestication occurred.

7000 B.C.E.   Pigs were domesticated.

6500 B.C.E.   **7.** _____

_____

Implied Main Ideas and Implied Central Ideas

_____   **8.** Which sentence best states the implied main idea of the fourth paragraph (sentences 18–23)?
   a. Domesticating plants and animals was a difficult process.
   b. The benefits of farming and herding were worth the effort.
   c. Farming and herding increased trade.
   d. Farming and herding lengthened the life expectancy of infants.

_____   **9.** Which sentence best states the implied central idea of the passage?
   a. Food production requires great effort.
   b. Domestication of plants and animals occurred about 15,000 years ago.
   c. Increased food supplies lengthened the life of humans.
   d. Food production made civilization possible.

Reading a Map

10. Study the map. State in one sentence the implied main idea of the map.

_____

_____

SUMMARY RESPONSE

Respond to the passage by stating the implied main idea in a thesis sentence. Be sure to identify the topic and the author's attitude about the topic. Begin your summary response with the following: *The most important idea of "The Food-Producing Revolution" by Levack, Muir, Veldman and Maas is . . .*

WHAT DO YOU THINK?

Assume you are a concerned citizen who wants to help a particular group of people who are suffering from hunger. Write a letter to the editor of your local newspaper that calls on the public to help this group of people. Explain the problem and ask for action. Consider the following:

- Explain the problem and ask for action.
- Explain why you think famine and hunger are still a global problem.
- Describe what steps we can take to unite as a country or as individuals to offer relief.

After Reading About Implied Main Ideas and Implied Central Ideas

Before you move on to the Mastery Tests on implied main ideas and implied central ideas, take time to reflect on your learning and performance by answering the following questions. Write your answers in your notebook.

- How has my knowledge base or prior knowledge about implied main ideas changed?
- Based on my studies, how do I think I will perform on the Mastery Test(s)? Why do I think my scores will be above average, average, or below average? (Note: An additional fourth Mastery Test may be found in MyReadingLab.)
- Would I recommend this chapter to other students who want to learn more about implied main ideas? Why or why not?

Test your understanding of what you have learned about implied main ideas for master readers by completing the Chapter 4 Review.

Name _____ Section _____

Date _____ **Score** (number correct) _____ x 50 = _____ %

Visit MyReadingLab to take this test online and receive feedback and guidance on your answers.

A. Study the map and its caption from a college history textbook. Then write a sentence that states the implied main idea of the map.

Textbook Skills

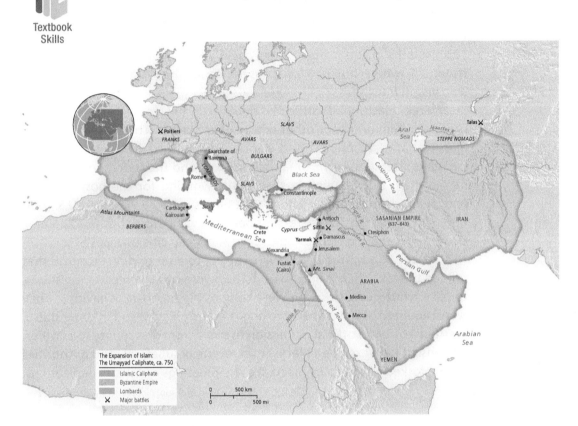

The Expansion of Islam:
The Umayyad Caliphate, ca. 750

- Islamic Caliphate
- Byzantine Empire
- Lombards
- X Major battles

▲ Islam originated in the early seventh century among the inhabitants of the Arabian peninsula. Through conquest and expansion, Muslims created a single Islamic Empire stretching from Spain to central Asia by 750.

—Adapted from Levack, Brian, Muir, Edward, Veldman, Meredith, and Maas, Michael, *The West: Encounters & Transformations*, Atlas Edition, Combined Edition, 2nd ed., Map 7.3, pp. 219, 221.

1. Implied main idea of map: _____

_____

_____

B. Determine the central idea stated in a thesis sentence for the following passage from a college history textbook. Annotate the text. Using your own words, write the central idea in the space provided.

Textbook
Skills

The Struggles of Free Blacks

[1]In addition to the 4 million blacks in bondage, there were approximately 500,000 free African Americans in 1860, about half of them living in slave states. [2]Public facilities were strictly segregated, and after the 1830s, blacks in the United States could vote only in four New England states. [3]Nowhere but in Massachusetts could they testify in court cases involving whites.

[4]Free blacks had difficulty finding decent jobs; most employers preferred immigrants or other whites over blacks. [5]The blacks were usually relegated to menial and poorly paid occupations. [6]Many states excluded blacks entirely from public schools, and the federal government barred them from serving in the militia, working for the postal service, and laying claim to public lands. [7]Free blacks were even denied U.S. passports. [8]In effect, they were stateless persons even before the 1857 Supreme Court ruling that no Negro could claim American citizenship.

[9]In the South, free blacks were subject to a set of direct controls that tended to make them semi-slaves. [10]They were often forced to register or to have white guardians who were responsible for their behavior. [11]They were required to carry papers proving their free status, and in some states, they had to obtain official permission to move from one county to another. [12]Licensing laws excluded blacks from several occupations, and authorities often blocked attempts by blacks to hold meetings or form organizations.

—Adapted from Divine, Robert A., Frederickson, George M., Williams, R. Hal, and Breen, T. H., *The American Story,* 1st ed., pp. 427–428.

2. Central idea stated in a thesis sentence: _____

_____

_____

Name _____ Section _____

Date _____ **Score** (number correct) _____ x 25 = _____ %

Visit MyReadingLab to take this test online and receive feedback and guidance on your answers.

Read the following textbook passages. Annotate the texts. Then either write the letter of the best statement of the implied main idea or use your own words to state the implied central idea.

Sound Effects

Textbook
Skills

[1]Although the function of sound effects is primarily atmospheric, they can also be precise sources of meaning in film. [2]Cinematic sound is a constructed experience: multiple layers of sound are synthesized (mixed) in a studio rather than recorded in reality, for most film sounds are not even present during the actual shooting. [3]Often these sounds are completely unlike their on-screen counterparts. [4]For example, the crunch of a blade penetrating a security officer's skull in *Terminator 2: Judgment Day* is actually a recording of a dog biting into a dog biscuit.

[5]A sound editor gathers all the different sounds necessary for a movie. [6]Many of these are prerecorded and stored in sound libraries—sounds like thunderstorms, a squeaky door, the wind howling, and so on. [7]A popular theory of sound design in Hollywood is known colloquially as "see a dog, hear a dog." [8]That is, if a dog appears on screen, the audience hears traditional dog sounds, such as the clink-clank of his leash or barking. [9]Then the sound mixer decides on the relative loudness of each piece of sound. [10]The mixer also decides what sounds go into what separate channels of a stereophonic sound system. [11]Most movie theaters have five separate speakers: center, left-front, right-front, left-back, and right-back. [12]Dolby sound systems, perfected in the 1990s, have as many as six or seven separate speakers.

—Giannetti, Louis, *Understanding Movies*, 12th ed., pp. 207–208.

_____ 1. Which sentence best states the implied central idea?
   a. Sound effects are constructed in a studio by a sound editor, who gathers sounds, and a sound mixer, who synthesizes them.
   b. Sound effects are primarily atmospheric, but they can also provide meaning in a film.
   c. Sound effects are not recorded during the actual shooting, and different sounds are used.
   d. Sound editors and sound mixers are two different jobs associated with sound effects.

Textbook
Skills

Writing and Speaking

[1]Writing and speechmaking have much in common: both require careful thought about your subject, purpose, and audience. [2]Thus the mental and physical activities that go into the writing process can also help you prepare and deliver a successful speech.

[3]Despite many similarities, however, writing for readers is not the same as speaking to listeners. [4]Whereas a reader can go back and reread a written message, a listener cannot stop a speech to rehear a section. [5]Several studies have reported that immediately after hearing a short talk, most listeners cannot recall half of what was said.

[6]Effective speakers adapt to their audience's listening ability by restating and repeating their ideas. [7]They use simple words, short sentences, personal pronouns, and informal language. [8]In formal writing, these strategies might seem out of place and too informal. [9]But in speaking, they improve listeners' comprehension.

—Adapted from Fowler, H. Ramsey and Aaron, Jane E., *The Little, Brown Handbook*, 9th ed., p. 905.

2. Implied central idea of paragraphs 1 and 2: _____

_____

_____

3. Implied main idea of paragraph 3: _____

_____

Textbook
Skills

Advertisements' Purpose

[1]*Business ads* try to influence people's attitudes and behaviors toward the product and services a business sells. [2]Most of these ads try to persuade consumers to buy something. [3]But sometimes a business tries to improve its image through advertising.

[4]*Public service ads* promote behaviors and attitudes that are beneficial to society and its members. [5]These ads may be either national or local and usually are the product of donated labor and media time or space.

[6]*Political ads* aim to persuade voters to elect a candidate to political office or to influence the public on legislative matters. [7]These advertisements are run at the local, state, and national levels.

—Adapted from Folkerts, Jean and Lacy, Stephen, *The Media in Your Life: An Introduction to Mass Communication*, 2nd ed., p. 428.

4. Implied central idea: _____

_____

_____

Name _____ Section_____

Date _____ **Score** (number correct) _____ x 25 = _____ %

Visit MyReadingLab to take this test online and receive feedback and guidance on your answers.

Read the following selections. Annotate the texts. In the spaces provided, use your own words to state the implied main idea of each one.

A poem

Dark house, by which once more I stand (1850)
by Alfred Lord Tennyson

Dark house, by which once more I stand
    Here in the long unlovely street,
    Doors, where my heart was used to beat
So quickly, waiting for a hand,

A hand that can be clasped no more—
    Behold me, for I cannot sleep,
    And like a guilty thing I creep
At earliest morning to the door.

He is not here; but far away
    The noise of life begins again,
    And ghastly through the drizzling rain
On the bald street breaks the blank day.

—Tennyson, Alfred Lord. *In Memoriam* (London: E Moxon, 1850).

1. Implied main idea: _____

_____

Textbook
Skills

Paragraph from a college science textbook

Lives Up in Smoke

[1]Mark Twain once said "Quitting smoking is easy, I've done it a thousand times." [2]Researchers have found that, like cocaine and heroin, nicotine activates the brain's reward center. [3]The brain adjusts by becoming less sensitive, requiring larger quantities of nicotine to experience the same rewarding effect, and causing the reward center to feel understimulated when nicotine is withdrawn. [4]Withdrawal symptoms include nicotine craving, depression, anxiety, irritability, difficulty concentrating, headaches, and disturbed sleep. [5]Although at least 70% of smokers would like to quit, only about 2.5% of smokers are successful each year.

—Audesirk, Teresa, Audesirk, Gerald, and Byers, Bruce E.,
Life on Earth, 5th ed., p. 390.

2. Implied main idea: _____

_____

Paragraph from a college history textbook

[1]The NIRA and other New Deal legislation, such as the Wagner Act of 1935, which established the National Labor Relations Board and the Fair Labor Standards Act of 1938, provided a larger role in the American economy for organized labor. [2]It became easier for unions to organize. [3]Union membership grew steadily, and American unionism took on a new character. [4]Previously, most unions had organized by craft and had been affiliated with the American Federation of Labor (AFL). [5]In the 1930s, however, whole industries composed of workers in various crafts were organized in a single union. [6]The most important of these organizations were the United Mine Workers and United Automobile Workers. [7]These new unions organized themselves into the Congress of Industrial Organizations (CIO). [8]The CIO and the AFL were rivals until they merged in the 1950s. [9]These organizations introduced a powerful new force into the American economic scene.

—Craig, Albert M., Graham, William A., Kagan, Donald, Ozment, Steven, and Turner, Frank M., *The Heritage of World Civilizations, Brief,* 5th ed., p. 774.

3. Implied main idea: _____

_____

_____

Visual graphic or concept map from a college health textbook

Personality Types		
Type A Impatient, Competitive, Aggressive, Highly Motivated, and Sometimes Hostile	**Type B** Patient, Nonaggressive, and Easygoing	**Type C** Competitive, Highly Motivated, High Level of Confidence, and Maintains a Constant Level of Emotional Control
High Risk for Heart Disease	Low Risk for Heart Disease	Low Risk for Heart Disease

4. Implied main idea: _____

_____

4 Summary of Key Concepts of Implied Main Ideas and Implied Central Ideas

LO3 LO5

- To state an implied main idea of a paragraph, create a _____, a one-sentence summary of the details.

- To state an implied central idea of a longer passage, create a _____, a one-sentence summary of several paragraphs.

LO1 LO2 LO3 LO5

Assess your comprehension of implied main ideas and implied central ideas. Complete the following two-column notes, set up as question-answers, with information from the chapter.

Implied Main Ideas	
What is an implied main idea?	_____ _____ _____ _____
What three questions can help determine an implied main idea?	_____ _____ _____ _____
What should be annotated in a passage to help determine a main idea?	_____ _____ _____ _____
What is an implied central idea?	_____ _____ _____ _____

Test Your Comprehension of Implied Main Ideas and Implied Central Ideas

LO1 LO2 LO3 Respond to the following questions and prompts.

How can the skills you use to identify the stated main idea help you determine the implied main idea or implied central idea? _____

_____

_____

_____

LO6 Describe how you will use what you have learned about implied main ideas and implied central ideas in your reading process to comprehend textbook material.

_____

_____

_____

LO1 LO2 LO3 LO4 Study the following concept map. Then write the implied main idea suggested by the details in the map.

```
                    ┌──────────────┐
                    │  Gardening   │
                    └──────────────┘
          ↙               ↓                ↘
┌──────────────┐  ┌──────────────┐  ┌──────────────┐
│  Increases   │  │   Relieves   │  │Provides Useful│
│Property Value│  │    Stress    │  │   Exercise   │
└──────────────┘  └──────────────┘  └──────────────┘
```

Implied main idea: _____

_____

LO1 LO2 LO3 LO4 LO5 LO6 LO7 Identify and discuss the two most important ideas in this chapter that will help you improve your reading comprehension. _____

_____

_____

Supporting Details

LO LEARNING OUTCOMES

After studying this chapter, you should be able to:

- **LO1** Create Questions to Locate Supporting Details
- **LO2** Distinguish Between Major and Minor Details
- **LO3** Create a Summary from Annotations
- **LO4** Develop Textbook Skills: Chapter-End Questions in a Textbook
- **LO5** Apply Information Literacy Skills: Academic, Personal, and Career Applications of Supporting Details

Before Reading About Supporting Details

In Chapter 3, you learned several important ideas that will help you as you work through this chapter. Use the following questions to call up your prior knowledge about supporting details.

What is a main idea? (page 100) _____

_____

_____

What are the three parts of most paragraphs? (page 104) _____,

_____, and _____.

Define supporting details. (page 105) _____

_____

What are the different possible locations of topic sentences? (pages 110–117)

_____

_____

What is a central idea? (page 118) _____

_____

 ## Create Questions to Locate Supporting Details

To locate supporting details, a master reader turns the main idea into a question by asking one of the following reporter's questions: *who, what, when, where, why,* or *how.* The answer to this question will yield a specific set of supporting details. For example, the question *why* is often answered by listing and explaining reasons or causes. The question *how* is answered by explaining a process. The answer to the question *when* is based on time order. A master writer strives to answer some or all of these questions with the details in the paragraph. You may want to try out several of the reporter's questions as you turn the main idea into a question. Experiment to discover which question is best answered by the details.

> **Supporting details** explain, develop, and illustrate the main idea.

Take, for example, the subject "youth joining gangs." For this topic an author might choose to write about ways parents can prevent their child from becoming involved in gangs. The main idea of such a paragraph may read as follows:

Main idea: To prevent their children from joining gangs, parents must take the following two steps.

Using the word *how* turns the main idea into this question: "How can parents prevent their children from joining gangs?" Read the following paragraph for the answers to this question.

Parental Love:
The First Line of Defense in the War Against Gangs

¹To prevent their children from joining gangs, parents must take the following two steps. ²First, and most important, parents should spend time with their children. ³One-on-one time with a parent who is giving undivided attention builds trust, establishes communication, and fosters self-esteem. ⁴Likewise, family trips to parks, libraries, museums,

or the beach create a sense of belonging so that children are not tempted to seek acceptance elsewhere. ⁵Second, parents should set and abide by reasonable rules. ⁶Establishing boundaries that ensure safety and teach respect for authority is an expression of love. ⁷Parents who expect children to value an education, abide by a curfew, and choose friends wisely are thwarting the chances that their children will join a gang.

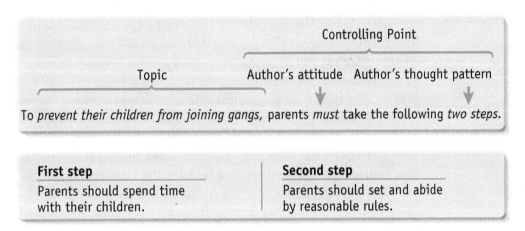

Controlling Point

Topic   Author's attitude   Author's thought pattern

To *prevent their children from joining gangs,* parents *must* take the following *two steps.*

First step	**Second step**
Parents should spend time with their children.	Parents should set and abide by reasonable rules.

The supporting details for this main idea answer the question "how?" by listing the two steps that are likely to prevent a child from joining a gang. Then the paragraph discusses why these steps may help.

Note the relationship between the author's controlling point and the supporting details. Notice that the details about situations directly explain the main idea. However, additional supporting details were given in the paragraph that are not listed. Each of the main supporting details needed further explanation. This paragraph shows us that there are two kinds of supporting details: details that explain the main idea and details that explain other details.

> **EXAMPLE** Read the paragraph. Turn the topic sentence into a question using one of the reporter's questions (Who? What? When? Where? Why? How?). Write the question in the space. Fill in the chart with the answers to the questions you have created.

The Traits of Attention Deficit Hyperactivity Disorder

¹Attention Deficit Hyperactivity Disorder (ADHD) has three basic traits. ²One trait of ADHD children is **inattention.** ³They have a hard time keeping their minds on any one thing and may get bored with a task

after only a few minutes. [4]If they are doing something they really enjoy, they have no trouble paying attention. [5]But focusing deliberate, conscious attention to organizing and completing a task or learning something new is difficult. [6]Homework is particularly hard for these children. [7]They will forget to write down an assignment, or leave it at school. [8]They will forget to bring a book home, or bring the wrong one. [9]The homework, if finally finished, is full of errors and erasures. [10]Homework is often accompanied by frustration for both parent and child. [11]Another trait of ADHD children is **hyperactivity**. [12]These children seem to be constantly in motion. [13]They dash around touching or playing with whatever is in sight, or talk incessantly. [14]Sitting still at dinner or during a school lesson or story can be a difficult task. [15]They squirm and fidget in their seats or roam around the room. [16]Or they may wiggle their feet, touch everything, or noisily tap their pencil. [17]The third trait of ADHD children is **impulsivity**. [18]They seem unable to curb their immediate reactions or think before they act. [19]They will often blurt out inappropriate comments, display their emotions without restraint, and act without regard for the later consequences of their conduct. [20]Their impulsivity may make it hard for them to wait for things they want or to take their turn in games. [21]They may grab a toy from another child or hit when they're upset. [22]Even as teenagers or adults, they may impulsively choose to do things that have an immediate but small payoff rather than engage in activities that may take more effort yet provide much greater but delayed rewards.

—Adapted from "Attention Deficit Hyperactivity Disorder."
National Institute of Mental Health.

Question based on topic sentence: _____

Topic sentence: _____

First trait	**Second trait**	**Third trait**
(1) _____	(2) _____	(3) _____

EXPLANATION Using the reporter's question *What?*, you should have turned the topic sentence into the following question: *What are the three basic traits of ADHD?* The answer to this question yields the supporting details. Compare your answers to the following: (1) Inattention, (2) Hyperactivity, and (3) Impulsivity.

Practice 1

Read the paragraph. Turn the topic sentence into a question using one of the reporter's questions (Who? What? When? Where? Why? How?). Write the question in the space. Fill in the chart with the answers to the question you have created.

Ozone and Your Health

[1]Ozone is a gas that occurs both in the Earth's upper atmosphere and at ground level. [2]Ozone can be helpful or harmful, depending on where it is found. [3]The helpful ozone occurs naturally in the Earth's upper atmosphere—10 to 30 miles above the Earth's surface. [4]At this level, it shields us from the sun's harmful ultraviolet rays. [5]The harmful ozone is found in the Earth's lower atmosphere, near ground level. [6]Harmful ozone is formed when pollutants emitted by cars, power plants, industrial boilers, refineries, chemical plants, and other sources react chemically in the presence of sunlight. [7]Ozone at the ground level can harm your health. [8]First, ozone can irritate your respiratory system, causing you to start coughing, feel an irritation in your throat or experience an uncomfortable sensation in your chest. [9]Second, ozone can reduce lung function and make it more difficult for you to breathe as deeply and vigorously as you normally would. [10]When this happens, you may notice that breathing starts to feel uncomfortable. [11]If you are exercising or working outdoors, you may notice that you are taking more rapid and shallow breaths than normal. [12]Third, ozone can aggravate asthma. [13]When ozone levels are high, more people with asthma have attacks that require a doctor's attention or the use of additional medication. [14]One reason this happens is that ozone makes people more sensitive to allergens, which are the most common triggers for asthma attacks. [15]Also, asthmatics are more severely affected by the reduced lung function and irritation that ozone causes in the respiratory system. [16]Fourth, ozone can inflame and damage cells that line your lungs. [17]Within a few days, the damaged cells are replaced and the old cells are shed—much in the way your skin peels after a sunburn. [18]Fifth, ozone may aggravate chronic lung diseases such as emphysema and bronchitis and reduce the immune system's ability to fight off bacterial infections in the respiratory system. [19]Sixth, ozone may cause permanent lung damage. [20]Repeated short-term ozone damage to children's developing lungs may lead to reduced lung function in adulthood. [21]In adults, ozone exposure may

accelerate the natural decline in lung function that occurs as part of the
normal aging process.

—Adapted from "Ozone and Your Health." *AIRNow*.
Environmental Protection Agency.

Question based on topic sentence: _____

_____

Topic sentence: _____

Harmful Effects:

(1) _____ **(2)** _____ **(3)** _____ **(4)** _____ **(5)** _____ **(6)** _____

_____ _____ _____ _____ _____ _____

_____ _____ _____ _____ _____ _____

_____ _____ _____ _____ _____ _____

LO2 Distinguish Between Major and Minor Details

A supporting detail will always be one of two types:

> A **major detail** directly explains, develops, or illustrates the *main idea*.
> A **minor detail** explains, develops, or illustrates a *major detail*.

A **major detail** is directly tied to the main idea. Without the major details,
the author's main idea would not be clear because the major details are the
principal points the author is making about the topic.

In contrast, a **minor detail** explains a major detail. The minor details
could be left out, and the main idea would still be clear. Thus minor details are
not as important as major details. Minor details are used to add interest and to
give further descriptions, examples, testimonies, analysis, illustrations, and reasons for the major details. To better understand the flow of ideas, study the
following diagram:

Topic: General subject

Main idea:
- Is often stated as a topic sentence
- Explains the author's point about the general subject
- Is a more general statement than any of the supporting details

general

Major detail:
- Explains or sets forth the main idea
- Provides primary support to the main idea
- Is more general than a minor detail

Minor detail:
- Explains a major detail
- Provides secondary support to the main idea
- Is the most specific idea in the passage

specific

As ideas move from general to specific details, the author often uses signal words to introduce a new detail. These signal words—such as *first, second, next, in addition,* or *finally*—can help you identify major and minor details.

> **EXAMPLE** See if you can tell the difference between major and minor details. Read the following paragraph. Then complete the exercise that follows.

Terrestrial and Jovian Planets

¹Planets fall quite nicely into two groups: the terrestrial (Earthlike) planets (Mercury, Venus, Earth, and Mars), and the Jovian (Jupiter-like) planets (Jupiter, Saturn, Uranus, and Neptune). ²Pluto was recently demoted to a dwarf planet—a new class of solar system objects that have an orbit around the Sun but share their space with other celestial bodies. ³The most obvious difference between the terrestrial and the Jovian planets is their size. ⁴The largest terrestrial planets (Earth and Venus) have diameters only one quarter as great as the diameter of the smallest Jovian planet (Neptune). ⁵Also, their masses are only 1/17 as great as Neptune's. ⁶Hence, the Jovian planets are often called giants. ⁷In addition to their size, planets are distinguished based on their location. ⁸Because of their relative locations, the four Jovian planets are also referred to as the **outer planets**.

[9]In contrast, the terrestrial planets are called the **inner planets**. [10]As we will see, there appears to be a correlation between the location of these planets within the solar system and their sizes.

—Lutgens, Frederick K., Tarbuck, Edward J., and Tasa, Dennis, *Foundations of Earth Science*, 5th ed., p. 407.

VISUAL *VOCABULARY*

Saturn, known for its rings of debris and ice, is classified as a

_____ planet and also referred

to as an _____ planet.

   a. Terrestrial
   b. Jovian
   c. inner
   d. outer

Complete the following outline of the paragraph by supplying the appropriate major and minor details.

Stated main idea: Planets fall quite nicely into two groups: the terrestrial (Earthlike) planets (Mercury, Venus, Earth, and Mars), and the Jovian (Jupiter-like) planets (Jupiter, Saturn, Uranus, and Neptune).

A.   _____

      _____

   1. The largest terrestrial planets (Earth and Venus) have diameters only one quarter as great as the diameter of the smallest Jovian planet (Neptune).
   2. Also, their masses are only 1/17 as great as Neptune's.
   3. Hence, the Jovian planets are often called giants.

B.   _____

   1. _____

      _____

2. In contrast, the terrestrial planets are called the inner planets.

3. As we will see, there appears to be a correlation between the location of these planets within the solar system and their sizes.

EXPLANATION This paragraph provides two major supporting details that help explain the main idea: sentences 3 and 7 state these two major supporting details that describe the classification of planets based on size and location. Sentences 4, 5, and 6 are minor details that explain the differences between the two types of planets based on size. Sentences 8 and 9 are minor details; they explain the differences between the types of planets based on location. Sentence 10 is a minor detail; it suggests a relationship between the size and location of a planet. Interestingly, sentence 2 is a detail that does not directly relate to the two types of planets discussed in the paragraph. The author may have felt this detail was necessary, however, since Pluto, long thought of as a planet, has just recently been reclassified and is no longer considered a planet at all. Thus, sentence 2 acknowledges that some readers have prior knowledge about Pluto's former status as a planet. Sentence 2 preempts reader confusion and readjusts prior knowledge to current scientific standards.

Practice 2

Read the following paragraph. Then identify the major and minor details by completing the outline that follows it.

Weight Loss in Our Pets

[1]Weight management is an important aspect of ensuring a long, healthy, and happy life for our pets. [2]As a caring pet owner, you need to be aware of the various reasons pets lose weight and when weight loss signals trouble. [3]Of course, at times, some weight loss is expected. [4]For example, dropping a pound or so may be perfectly normal, particularly if your pet has put on a few extra pounds over the years. [5]In addition, some pets lose weight during those hot summer months when soaring temperatures can curb an appetite. [6]Likewise, some pets lose weight during the frigid winter months as they burn more calories to keep warm. [7]And female pets who are nursing mothers may lose weight as they burn calories to produce milk. [8]Another major cause of weight loss is the environment. [9]Even healthy pets that are boarded may lose weight because of the stress of a different environment. [10]What you feed your pet is a key aspect of the animal's environment; diet plays a vital role in weight

management because poor quality, spoiled, or inedible food can result in undernourishment and weight loss. [11]Finally, many underlying medical conditions are often signaled by sudden or dramatic weight loss. [12]A few examples of conditions to be on guard against are dental disease, gastro-intestinal disorders (which may include parasites), diabetes, liver or kidney disease, heart disease, and cancer. [13]Any one of these conditions can inter-fere with eating and the absorption of nutrients.

Stated main idea: As a caring pet owner, you need to be aware of the vari-ous reasons pets lose weight and when weight loss signals trouble.

A. _____

1. For example, dropping a pound or so may be perfectly normal, particularly if your pet has put on a few extra pounds over the years.

2. In addition, some pets lose weight during those hot summer months when soaring temperatures can curb an appetite.

3. Likewise, some pets lose weight during the frigid winter months as they burn more calories to keep warm.

4. _____

_____

B. _____

1. _____

_____

2. What you feed your pet is a key aspect of the animal's environment; diet plays a vital role in weight management because poor quality, spoiled, or inedible food can result in undernourishment and weight loss.

C. _____

_____

1. A few examples of conditions to be on guard against are dental disease, gastrointestinal disorders (which may include parasites), diabetes, liver or kidney disease, heart disease, and cancer.

2. Any one of these conditions can interfere with eating and the absorption of nutrients.

LO3   Create a Summary from Annotations

Reading for main ideas and major supporting details is an excellent study technique. Writing down main ideas and major supporting details in a summary after you read is an effective strategy that will deepen your understanding and provide you with study notes for review and reflection. (Chapter 1 presented a number of reading strategies.) A **summary** condenses a paragraph or passage down to only its primary points by restating the main idea, major supporting details, and important examples. Often, you will want to paraphrase or restate the ideas in your own words; other times, you may need to use the exact language of the text to ensure accuracy. For example, scientific or medical terms have precise meanings that must be memorized; thus your summaries of these types of ideas would include the original language of the text.

> A **summary** is a brief, clear restatement of the most important points of a paragraph or passage.

Different lengths of text require different lengths of summaries. For example, a paragraph can be summarized in one sentence or a few sentences. A passage of several paragraphs can be reduced to one paragraph, and a much longer selection such as a chapter in a textbook may require a summary of a page or two in length.

To help create a summary after reading, you can **annotate**, or mark, your text *during reading*. For example, as you read, circle the main idea and underline the major supporting details and important examples. To learn more about annotating a text see pages 622–623 in Part 2.

> **EXAMPLE**   Read the following paragraph from a college textbook on education. Annotate the text by circling the main idea and underlining the major supporting details and the important examples. Then complete the summary by filling in the blanks with information from the passage.

State Standards-Based Tests

[1]Test results in some states are not reported in ways that are useful to teachers as they make instructional decisions. [2]Many state tests simply place students in one of four categories—below basic, basic, proficient, and advanced. [3]These types of results do not provide information about performance within a particular subject area. [4]In science, for example, the tests do not reveal whether students lack understanding in earth science,

biological science, or both. [5]In other words, the results are evaluative and summative, not educative. [6]"Educative feedback is immediate, relevant, and useful, and it promotes student learning" (Reeves, 2004, p. 9). [7]Teachers and other educators have expressed disappointment that many state standards-based tests do not provide educative feedback.

—Adapted from Powell, Sara Davis, *Your Introduction to Education,* 2nd ed., p. 137.

Summary

Test results in some states _____

_____

_____

_____

For example, _____

_____

EXPLANATION The main idea of the paragraph is "Test results in some states are not reported in ways that are useful to teachers as they make instructional decisions." Including important details in your summary clarifies why test result reports are not useful. The comments on educative feedback are minor details that you do not need to include.

Compare your summary to the following: Test results in some states are not reported in ways that are useful to teachers. They simply place students in one of four categories—below basic, basic, proficient, and advanced—and do not provide information about performance within a particular subject area. For example, in science, the tests do not reveal whether students lack understanding in earth science, biological science, or both. ◀

Practice 3

Read the following passage from a college textbook about tourism. Annotate the text by circling the central idea and underlining the major supporting details and important examples. Then compose a summary of the passage.

Textbook
Skills

[1]For decades, tourism researchers have grouped tourist motivations as push or pull factors. [2]The notion is that travelers are both "pushed" to travel by personality traits or individual needs and wants, and "pulled" to

travel by appealing attributes of travel destinations. [3]Traditionally, the push motivations have been thought useful for explaining the desire for travel while the pull motivations have been thought useful for explaining the actual destination choice.

[4]This "theory" of travel motivation highlights the fact that tourists are pushed (motivated) to travel by many factors simultaneously, and destinations pull (attract) visitors with a combination of resources. [5]For instance, a tourist generates the desire to escape from his mundane day-to-day routine and seeks a destination that seems to offer the "ticket" to that escape. [6]Research has shown that push and pull factors are matched by travelers. [7]For example, studies have found a large percentage of travelers are motivated to travel by a desire to be pampered, comfortable, and entertained. [8]Destinations that generate the most "pull" for this group of travelers are cities and beach resorts.

[9]Several "push" factors have been identified and researched as personality traits (such as novelty seeking). [10]An additional and particularly appropriate personality trait theory that relates to tourism is optimal arousal theory. [11]Briefly, the core of this theory is that each of us has some optimal level of arousal at which we feel most comfortable. [12]For some, that level is quite low, leading to a relaxed, slower-paced lifestyle, whereas for many, the optimal arousal level is very high, driving individuals constantly to seek new and challenging activities. [13]A person who is stressed out by work may desire to reduce arousal by seeking a quiet seaside resort to spend some quiet time with a loved one. [14]Another who is bored by the routine of his job and life may instead decide to travel to Europe and test his mettle on the ski slopes of the Alps.

—Cook, Roy A., Yale, Laura J., and Marqua, Joseph J.,
Tourism: The Business of Travel,
4th ed, pp. 34–35.

_____

_____

_____

_____

_____

Drafting a Summary: Implied Main Ideas

At times, an author may choose to imply a main idea instead of directly stating it. As you learned in Chapter 4, you can use supporting details to create a topic sentence or thesis statement when the main idea or central point is implied. Annotating your text will also help you create a summary for passages with an implied main idea.

First, identify the topic of the passage. Underline recurring words or phrases. Locate each heading or major supporting detail in the passage. (Remember, minor details explain or support major details. Thus, when creating a summary, you can ignore these minor details.) Assign a number or letter to each of the headings or major details you identified. Next, for each piece of information you have marked, ask the question "What controlling point or opinion about the topic does this detail reveal?" Often, a main heading can be turned into a question that will help you determine the implied main idea. Then, write a brief answer to each question in the margin next to the detail you marked. Next, after you finish reading, create a topic sentence or thesis statement for the passage. Finally, use only a few brief sentences to create the entire summary.

⊘ EXAMPLE Read the following passage taken from a college psychology text-book. As you read, complete the following steps. Then create a summary of the passage in the space provided after the passage.

Step 1.   Annotate the text: Underline the recurring key terms or phrases and label the major supporting details with a number or letter.

Step 2.   Turn the main heading into a question to determine the implied main idea. If needed, turn major details into questions that reveal the author's controlling point.

Step 3.   Answer each question in your own words.

Step 4.   Create a thesis statement based on the main heading and/or supporting details.

Step 5.   Write a summary that combines the thesis statement and the major supporting details into one sentence or a few brief sentences.

Three Ways to Measure Memory

Textbook
Skills

[1]We have all had the embarrassing experience of being unable to recall the name of a person whom we are sure that we have already met. [2]This happens to everyone because recognition is an easier memory task than recall. [3]In **recall**, a person must produce required information

simply by searching memory. [4]Trying to remember someone's name, the items on a shopping list, or the words of a speech or a poem is a recall task. [5]A recall task may be made a little easier if cues are provided to jog memory. [6]A **retrieval cue** is any stimulus or bit of information that aids in retrieving a particular memory. [7]Think about how you might respond to these two test questions:

[8]What are the four basic memory processes?

[9]The four processes involved in memory are e____, s____, c____, and r____.

[10]Both questions require you to recall information. [11]However, most students would find the second question easier to answer because it includes four retrieval cues.

[12]**Recognition** is exactly what the name implies. [13]A person simply recognizes something as familiar—a face, a name, a taste, a melody. [14]Multiple-choice, matching, and true false questions are examples of test items based on recognition. [15]The main difference between recall and recognition is that a recognition task does not require you to supply the information but only to recognize it when you see it. [16]The correct answer is included along with other items in a recognition question.

[17]There is another, more sensitive way to measure memory. [18]With the **relearning method**, retention is expressed as the percentage of time saved when material is relearned relative to the time required to learn the material originally. [19]Suppose it took you 40 minutes to memorize a list of words, and one month later you were tested on those words, using recall or recognition. [20]If you could not recall or recognize a single word, would this mean that you had absolutely no memory of anything on the list? [21]Or could it mean that the recall and recognition tasks were not sensitive enough to measure what little information you may have stored? [22]How could a researcher measure such a remnant of former learning? [23]Using the relearning method, a researcher could time how long it would take you to relearn the list of words. [24]If it took 20 minutes to relearn the list, this would represent a 50% savings over the original learning time of 40 minutes. [25]The percentage of time saved—the savings score—reflects how much material remains in long-term memory.

[26]College students demonstrate the relearning method each semester when they study for comprehensive final exams. [27]Relearning material for a final exam takes less time than it took to learn the material originally.

—Adapted from Wood, Samuel E., Wood, Ellen Green, and Boyd, Denise, *Mastering the World of Psychology*, 3rd ed., pp. 184–185.

Summary: _____

_____

_____

_____

_____

_____

EXPLANATION Think about the following question based on the title of the passage: "What are the three ways to measure memory?" To answer this question, you should have located and numbered the major supporting details, which also state the central idea of the passage. The author used bold print to highlight the three major details that answer the question. By using your own words to combine the thesis statement and the major supporting details, you create your summary. Compare your summary to the following: The three ways to measure memory include recall, recognition, and the relearning method. Recall is the task of producing information by searching memory. Often a retrieval cue, a bit of information or stimulus, aids in the recall of information from long-term memory. Recognition is the task of identifying material as familiar. Finally, the relearning method measures the percentage of time saved when material is relearned compared to the time needed to learn the material originally. ◀

Practice 4

Read the following passage from a college textbook about human anatomy. Then create a summary of the passage in the space provided after the passage.

Textbook
Skills

Muscle Tissue

[1]Muscle tissues are highly specialized to contract, or shorten, to produce movement.

[2]**Skeletal muscle** tissue is packaged by connective tissue sheets into organs called skeletal muscles, which are attached to the skeleton. [3]These muscles, which can be controlled voluntarily (or consciously), form the flesh of the body, the so-called muscular system. [4]When the skeletal muscles contract, they pull on bones or skin. [5]The result of their action is gross body movements—or changes in our facial expressions. [6]The cells of skeletal muscle are long, cylindrical, multinucleate, and they have obvious striations (stripes). [7]Because skeletal muscle cells are elongated to provide a long axis for contraction, they are often called muscle fibers.

[8]**Cardiac muscle** is found only in the heart. [9]As it contracts, the heart acts as a pump and propels blood through the blood vessels. [10]Like skeletal muscle, cardiac muscle has striations, but cardiac cells are uni-nucleate, relatively short, branching cells that fit tightly together (like clasped fingers) at junctions called intercalated disks. [11]These intercalated disks contain gap junctions that allow ions to pass freely from cell to cell, resulting in rapid conduction of the exciting electrical impulse across the heart. [12]Cardiac muscle is under involuntary control, which means that we cannot consciously control the activity of the heart. [13](There are, however, rare individuals who claim they have such an ability.)

[14]**Smooth muscle**, or visceral muscle, is so called because no striations are visible. [15]The individual cells have a single nucleus and are spindle-shaped (pointed at each end). [16]Smooth muscle is found in the walls of hollow organs such as the stomach, uterus, and blood vessels. [17]As smooth muscle in its walls contracts, the cavity of an organ alternately becomes smaller (constricts on smooth muscle contraction) or enlarges (dilates on smooth muscle relaxation) so that substances are propelled through the organ along a specific pathway. [18]Smooth muscle contracts much more slowly than the other two muscle types. [19]Peristalsis (per"ĭstal'sis), a wave-like motion that keeps food moving through the small intestine, is typical of its activity.

—Marieb, Elaine N., *Essentials of Human Anatomy and Physiology*, 9th ed., pp. 66, 98.

Summary: _____

_____

_____

_____

_____

LO4 Develop Textbook Skills: Chapter-End Questions in a Textbook

Textbooks often provide questions at the end of a chapter or section to help you identify and remember the most important points. These questions typically ask you to summarize the main idea and major supporting details. The chapter-end questions may also ask you to note one or two minor supporting details as examples. Annotating your text by circling the main idea and underlining major supporting details and examples as you read will help you answer chapter-end questions and summarize what you are learning.

⊘ **EXAMPLE** Read the following paragraph and chapter-end question about the paragraph from a college communications textbook. Circle the topic sentence and underline the major supporting details and the important examples. Then answer the question.

Textbook
Skills

Types of Media

¹The mass media fall broadly into two categories or groups. ²These two groups have certain elements in common, yet they possess different physical traits. ³The first group, **print**, includes newspapers, magazines, newsletters, and books. ⁴Their words create images in the mind as well as convey information. ⁵The second group is **electronics and film**. ⁶This group includes radio, recordings, television, still and motion pictures, and video. ⁷These media send their messages through visual and audio impact on the senses, sometimes with great emotional power.

Chapter-End Question: What are the two basic categories of media? Name at least two media in each category.

—Adapted from Agee, Warren K., Ault, Philip H., and Emery, Edwin, *Introduction to Mass Communication,* 12th ed., pp. 6, 20.

Answer:

_____

_____

EXPLANATION By answering this question, you are restating the main idea and the major supporting details. In the second part of the question, the textbook author asks you to name two examples. All of this information can be stated in one sentence: "The two basic categories of media are (1) print, which includes magazines and books, and (2) electronics and film, which includes radio and television." ⊙

Practice 5

Read the following paragraph and chapter-end question about the paragraph from a college communications textbook. Circle the topic sentence and underline the major supporting details. Then answer the question.

Textbook
Skills

Friendship

[1]Friendship is an interpersonal relationship between two persons that is mutually productive and is characterized by mutual positive regard. [2]Several types of friendships exist. [3]One type of friendship is known as reciprocity, characterized by loyalty, self-sacrifice, mutual affection, and generosity. [4]A second type is based on receptivity, characterized by a comfortable and positive imbalance in the giving and receiving of rewards; each person's needs are satisfied by the exchange. [5]Another type of friendship identified as association is a transitory relationship, more like a friendly relationship than a true friendship. [6]Friendships meet our needs and give us a variety of values, among which are the values of utility, affirmation, ego support, stimulation, and security. [7]Interestingly, women share more and are more intimate with same-sex friends than are men. [8]Men's friendships are often built around shared activities rather than shared intimacies. [9]By understanding the nature and function of friendship, the types of friendships, and the ways in which friendships differ between men and women, we can improve the effectiveness of our interpersonal communication with our friends.

Chapter-End Question: What is friendship, its types and purposes, and the ways it differs between men and women?

—DeVito, Joseph A., *The Interpersonal Communication Book*, 11th ed., pp. 282–283.

Answer:

_____

_____

_____

_____

Apply Information Literacy Skills

 ## Academic, Personal, and Career Applications of Supporting Details

The ability to identify supporting details is a part of information literacy. Now that you have mastered the ability to locate and determine the stated and implied main idea, you can also use supporting details to access and connect information. Understanding how to locate and evaluate supporting details will help in your academic, personal, and career lives. You will come across a wide range of documents such as essays, articles, reports, memos, or emails. You will be expected to pay attention to the supporting details in these documents. Thus, you will use the skills that you have learned in this chapter in several ways:

- Identify your own need to know the supporting details.
- Locate key supporting details.
- Summarize the main idea and supporting details.

Academic Application

Assume you are taking a college social psychology course. You are working with several classmates on a group presentation to be given in class. Your group chose to present on the process of breaking up. You begin your research with information from your textbook.

- **Before Reading:** In the table of contents, highlight the title of the section that relates to your topic. Then skim the passage from that section. Create a pre-reading question to guide your reading.
- **During Reading:** Annotate the text: Underline the topic sentence and major supporting details that answer the pre-reading question.
- **After Reading:** In the notecard following the passage, write a summary of the main idea and major supporting details.

Pre-Reading Question: _____

Ending a romantic relationship is one of life's more painful experiences. Researchers continue to examine what makes people end a relationship and the disengagement strategies they use to do so. For example, Steve Duck (1982) reminds us that relationship dissolution is not a single event but a process with many steps. Duck theorizes that four stages of dissolution exist, ranging from the intrapersonal (the individual thinks a lot about his or her dissatisfaction with the relationship) to the dyadic (the individual discusses the breakup with the partner) to the social (the breakup is announced to other people) and back to the intrapersonal (the individual recovers from the breakup and forms an internal account of how and why it happened). In terms of the last stage in the process, John Harvey and his colleagues have found that the honest version of "why the relationship ended" that we present to close friends can be very different from the official version that we present to coworkers or neighbors.

—Adapted from Aronson, Elliot, Wilson, Timothy D., and Akert, Robin M., *Social Psychology,* 8th ed., pp. xiv–xv, 292.

Summary Notecard: _____

_____

_____

Personal Application

Assume you are a single parent of a minor child, and you need to provide health insurance for your family. You are researching the types of health care coverage for which you may be eligible, and have found the following information about Medicaid.

- **Before Reading:** Skim the description for any key words that indicate what this program covers and who is eligible.
- **During Reading:** Underline the major details in the article that explain the eligibility for the program and how to receive its benefits.
- **After Reading:** In the space following the passage, restate the major details. Then create two questions to ask to learn additional specific details about Medicaid.

Medicaid Program Description

The Medicaid Program is a Federally funded program, which provides health coverage to U.S. residents, within certain groups, based on income and resource limits set by Congress. Medicaid provides a complete package of medical coverage for those who qualify. Generally, eligible recipients of benefits include low-income families with children, low-income elderly, and persons with disabilities. Persons who are entitled to Medicare Part A and/or Part B are also eligible. Mandatory medical services included under Medicaid are: inpatient and outpatient hospital services; physician services; laboratory and x-ray services; long-term care facilities (nursing homes); family planning; services for early periodic screening, diagnosis and treatment (EPSDT) of those under age 21. To receive benefits, you must complete an application. We will make a decision and you will be notified within 45 days (with some exceptions) after you apply. If your application is based on disability, it may take up to 90 days. Coverage can start as early as 3 months before the month you apply. This is why you should get this form to us as soon as you can.

—<Benefits.gov>

Major Details: _____

_____

_____

Career Application

Assume you are interested in becoming a personal trainer. To help you make your decision, you have found the following information on a government website.

- **Before Reading:** Skim the information. Create two pre-reading questions to guide your hunt for relevant information.
- **During Reading:** Underline the details that answer your pre-reading questions.
- **After Reading:** In the space following the passage, record the details that answer your pre-reading questions.

Pre-Reading Questions: _____

_____

_____

How to Become a Fitness Trainer or Instructor

The education and training required for fitness trainers and instructors vary by type of specialty, and employers often hire those with certification. Personal fitness trainers, group fitness instructors, and specialized fitness instructors each need different preparation. Requirements vary by facility. Personal fitness trainers often start out by taking classes to become certified. Then they work alongside an experienced trainer before training clients alone. Many group fitness instructors often take training and become certified. Then, they must audition for instructor positions before they begin teaching classes. Training for specialized fitness instructors can vary greatly. For example, the duration of programs for yoga instructors can range from a few days to more than 2 years. The Yoga Alliance has training standards requiring at least 200 hours with a specified number of hours in techniques, teaching methods, anatomy, physiology, philosophy, and other areas.

Certification: Employers prefer to hire certified fitness trainers and instructors. Personal trainers are often required to be certified to begin working with clients or with members of a gym or other type of health club. Group fitness instructors may be allowed to begin without certification, but employers often encourage or require them to become certified. Most trainers or instructors need certification in cardiopulmonary resuscitation (CPR) before applying for certification in physical fitness. Many organizations offer certification. The National Commission for Certifying Agencies (NCCA) lists certifying organizations that are accredited.

All certification exams have a written part. Some also have a practical part. The exams measure the candidate's knowledge of human physiology, understanding of proper exercise techniques, assessment of clients' fitness levels, and development of appropriate exercise programs.

No specific education or training is required for certification. Many certifying organizations offer study materials, including books, CDs, other audio and visual materials, and exam preparation workshops and seminars.

Advanced certification requires an associate's or bachelor's degree in an exercise-related subject that presents more specialized instruction, such as training athletes, working with people who are injured or ill, or advising clients on general health.

Education: Almost all trainers and instructors have at least a high school diploma before entering the occupation. An increasing number of employers require fitness workers to have an associate's or bachelor's degree related to a health or fitness field, such as exercise science, kinesiology, or physical education. Programs often include courses in nutrition, exercise techniques, and group fitness.

Important Qualities: Fitness trainers and instructors must have customer-service skills, listening skills, motivational skills, problem solving skills, speaking skills, physical fitness.

—Bureau of Labor Statistics, U.S. Department of Labor, *Occupational Outlook Handbook, 2012–13 Edition*, Fitness Trainers and Instructors.

Details answering pre-reading questions: _____

_____

_____

_____

_____

_____

REVIEW TEST 1

Score (number correct) _____ x 20 = _____ %

Visit MyReadingLab to take this test online and receive feedback and guidance on your answers.

Main Idea and Supporting Details

Read the paragraph and then answer the questions.

Textbook
Skills

Nutrient Density

[1]You should choose mostly nutrient-dense foods from each food group. [2]Nutrient density refers to the amount of nutrients a food contains

in relationship to the number of calories it contains. **3**More nutrient-dense foods provide more nutrients per calorie (and in each bite) than less nutrient-dense foods, and so are better choices for meeting your DRIs (Dietary Reference Intakes) without exceeding your daily calorie needs. **4**The foundation of your diet should be nutrient-dense foods with little solid fats and added sugars. **5**Solid fats are solid at room temperature and contain a high percentage of heart-unhealthy saturated and/or trans fatty acids. **6**Solid fats include butter, beef fat, chicken fat, pork fat (lard), stick margarine, and shortening. **7**The fat in milk is also considered a solid fat, as it is solid at room temperature. **8**Because of the homogenization process involved in processing milk, the solid fat is evenly dispersed and suspended in fluid milk, which masks its solid density. **9**Saturated fat–laden coconut, palm, and palm kernel oils, as well as partially hydrogenated oils, which contain trans fatty acids, are also considered solid fats. **10**Added sugars include sources such as brown sugar, corn syrup, molasses, and table sugar. **11**Foods within each food group that contain solid fats and added sugars should be eaten in moderation because they add calories that are less nutrient dense to your diet.

—Adapted from Blake, Joan Salge, *Nutrition and You,* 2nd ed., p. 40.

_____ **1.** Sentence 1 is
   a. a main idea.
   b. a major supporting detail.
   c. a minor supporting detail.

_____ **2.** Sentence 2 is
   a. a main idea.
   b. a major supporting detail.
   c. a minor supporting detail.

_____ **3.** Sentence 4 is
   a. a main idea.
   b. a major supporting detail.
   c. a minor supporting detail.

_____ **4.** Sentence 5 is
   a. a main idea.
   b. a major supporting detail.
   c. a minor supporting detail.

_____ **5.** Sentence 10 is
   a. a main idea.
   b. a major supporting detail.
   c. a minor supporting detail.

VISUAL *VOCABULARY*

Homogenized milk is ———— milk.

   a. natural
   b. processed
   c. fat free

REVIEW TEST 2

Score (number correct) ———— x 10 = ———— %

Visit MyReadingLab to take this test online and receive feedback and guidance on your answers.

Main Ideas, Supporting Details, and Summarizing

Read the following passage from a college geography textbook. Answer the questions that follow.

Textbook
Skills

The Differences Between Folk Culture and Popular Culture

[1]The term **folk culture** refers to a culture that preserves traditions. [2]Folk groups are often bound by a distinctive religion, national background, or language, and are conservative and resistant to change. [3]Most folk-culture groups are rural, and relative isolation helps these groups maintain their integrity. [4]Folk-culture groups, however, also include urban neighborhoods of immigrants struggling to preserve their native cultures in their new homes. [5]Folk culture suggests that any culture identified by the term is a lingering remnant of something that is embattled by the tide of modern change.

[6]Folk geographic studies in the United States range from studies of folk songs, folk foods, folk medicine, and folklore to objects of folk material as diverse as locally produced pottery, clothing, tombstones, farm fencing, and even knives and guns. [7]In North America, the Amish provide an example of a folk culture. [8]The Amish are notable because they wear plain clothing and shun modern education and technology.

⁹**Popular culture**, by contrast, is the culture of people who embrace innovation and conform to changing norms. ¹⁰Popular culture may originate anywhere. ¹¹And it tends to diffuse rapidly, especially wherever people have time, money, and inclination to indulge in it.

¹²Popular material culture usually means mass culture. ¹³For example, items such as clothing, processed food, CDs, and household goods are mass produced for mass distribution. ¹⁴Whereas folk culture is often produced or done by people at-large (folk singing and dancing, cooking, costumes, woodcarving, etc.), popular culture, by contrast, is usually produced by corporations and purchased.

—Adapted from Bergman, Edward and Renwick, William, *Introduction to Geography: People, Places, and Environment,* 4th ed., pp. 221–223.

_____ **1.** Sentence 1 states _____ of the first paragraph (sentences 1–5).
   a. the main idea   c. a minor supporting detail
   b. a major supporting detail

_____ **2.** Sentence 2 states _____ of the first paragraph (sentences 1–5).
   a. the main idea   c. a minor supporting detail
   b. a major supporting detail

_____ **3.** Sentence 7 states _____ of the second paragraph (sentences 6–8).
   a. the main idea   c. a minor supporting detail
   b. a major supporting detail

_____ **4.** Sentence 9 states _____ of the third paragraph (sentences 9–11).
   a. the main idea   c. a minor supporting detail
   b. a major supporting detail

_____ **5.** Sentence 13 states _____ of the fourth paragraph (sentences 12–14).
   a. the main idea   c. a minor supporting detail
   b. a major supporting detail

Complete the following summary with information from the passage.

(**6**) _____ differs from (**7**) _____. On the one hand, folk culture refers to a culture that (**8**) _____.

On the other hand, popular culture refers to the culture that (**9**) _____

_____. Folk culture is produced by local people in rural regions, while popular culture is mass produced, mass distributed, and sold to the masses by (**10**) _____.

REVIEW TEST 3

Score (number correct) _____ x 10 = _____ %

Visit MyReadingLab to take this test online and receive feedback and guidance on your answers.

Main Ideas, Supporting Details, and Summarizing

Textbook Skills

Before you read the following passage from a college sociology textbook, skim the material and answer the Before Reading questions. Read the passage. Then answer the After Reading questions.

Vocabulary Preview

incompatible (1): mismatched, opposed
fragile (10): weak, unstable, breakable
perceptions (16): views, insights, understandings
interpersonal (19): between people
relative (20): in relation to

Conflict Defined

[1]Conflict is the interaction of interdependent people who perceive **incompatible** goals and interference from each other in achieving those goals. [2]This definition has the advantage of providing a much clearer focus than definitions that view conflict simply as disagreement, as competition, or as the presence of opposing interests.

[3]The most important feature of conflict is that it is based in interaction. [4]Conflicts are formed and sustained by the behaviors of the parties involved and their verbal and nonverbal reactions to one another. [5]Conflict interaction takes many forms, and each form presents special problems and requires special handling. [6]The most familiar type of conflict interaction is marked by shouting matches or open competition in which each party tries to defeat the other. [7]But conflicts may also be more subtle. [8]People may react to conflict by suppressing it. [9]A husband and wife may communicate in ways that allow them to avoid confrontation. [10]Either they are afraid the conflict may damage a **fragile** relationship, or they convince themselves that the issue "isn't worth fighting over." [11]This response is as much a part of the conflict process as fights and shouting matches.

[12]People in conflict perceive that they have incompatible goals or interests; they also believe that others are a barrier to achieving their goals. [13]The key word here is *perceive*. [14]Regardless of whether goals are actually incompatible, if the parties believe them to be incompatible, then conditions are ripe for conflict. [15]Regardless of whether one employee really stands in the way of a co-worker's promotion, if the co-worker

interprets the employee's behavior as interfering with his promotion, then a conflict is likely to occur. [16]Communication is important; it is the key to shaping and maintaining the **perceptions** that guide conflict behavior.

[17]Communication problems can be an important cause of conflict. [18]Conflict may result from misunderstandings that occur when people have different communication styles. [19]For example, Tannen argues that men and women have different approaches to **interpersonal** communication. [20]Men are mostly task-oriented; they are concerned with establishing their position **relative** to others in conversations. [21]In contrast, women use conversations to build relationships and establish connections with others. [22]As a result, men and women may interpret the same act in very different ways. [23]When a man makes a demand during a conflict, he might mean to signal that he is strong and has a definite position. [24]A woman hearing this demand is likely to focus more on its **implications** for their relationship. [25]Thus she may interpret it as a signal that it will be very difficult to deal with this man. [26]As a result, the woman may become more competitive toward her male partner than she would have had she seen his demand in the man's terms. [27]According to Tannen, stylistic differences of this sort create communication barriers that make misunderstanding—and the conflict that results from it—**inevitable** in male-female relationships. [28]Similar communication problems can occur across almost any social divide, such as those between people of different cultures, ages, educational backgrounds, and socioeconomic classes.

—Adapted from Folger, Joseph P., Poole, Marshall Scott, and Stutman, Randall K., *Working Through Conflict*, 4th ed., pp. 5–6.

Before Reading

Vocabulary in Context

_____ **1.** In sentence 24 of the passage, the word **implications** means
   a. conflicts.
   b. meanings.
   c. accusations.
   d. levels.

_____ **2.** In sentence 27 of the passage, the word **inevitable** means
   a. delayed.
   b. long term.
   c. hidden.
   d. unavoidable.

After Reading

Main Ideas

_____ **3.** Which sentence states the central idea of the passage?
   a. sentence 1
   b. sentence 2
   c. sentence 3
   d. sentence 4

_____ **4.** Which sentence is the topic sentence of the fourth paragraph (sentences 17–28)?

     a. sentence 17   c. sentence 20

     b. sentence 18   d. sentence 27

Supporting Details

_____ **5.** Sentence 7 is

     a. a major supporting detail.   b. a minor supporting detail.

_____ **6.** Sentence 9 is

     a. a major supporting detail.   b. a minor supporting detail.

_____ **7.** Sentence 15 is

     a. a major supporting detail.   b. a minor supporting detail.

8–10. Complete the summary with information from the passage.

Conflict is the _____ of interdependent people who perceive incompatible goals and interference from each other in achieving those goals. Perceptions based on _____ reactions, nonverbal reactions, and differing interpersonal _____ styles are key sources of conflict.

SUMMARY RESPONSE

Restate the author's central idea in your own words. Include key major details in your summary. Begin your summary response with the following: *The central idea of "Conflict Defined" by Folger, Poole, & Stutman is . . .*

WHAT DO YOU THINK?

Assume you are a supervisor of a sales staff at a local retail store, and two employees under your supervision are in conflict with each other. Assume you have met with them both privately and individually to understand and resolve the conflict. Write a memo to be sent to both employees and placed in their personnel files. Consider the following:

- Describe the conflict.
- Suggest steps that you expect both people to take to resolve the issue.

REVIEW TEST 4

Score (number correct) _____ x 10 = _____ %

Visit MyReadingLab to take this test online and receive feedback and guidance on your answers.

Main Ideas and Supporting Details

Before Reading: Survey the following passage from the college textbook, *The Heritage of World Civilization*. Skim the passage, noting the words in bold print. Answer the Before Reading questions that follow the passage. Then read the passage. Next, answer the After Reading questions. Use the discussion and writing topics as activities to do after reading.

Vocabulary Preview

HIV/AIDS (1): Collection of symptoms and infections resulting from the specific damage to the immune system caused by the human immunodeficiency virus (HIV)

variations (3): differences

embarked (5): set out; began

prevalence (8): wide existence; common occurrence

absenteeism (9): continual failure to appear

gamut (11): range

grass-roots (12): done by people at the local level

The African Future: Health and Environment

[1]A variety of health and environmental challenges face Africa, the most **notorious** of which is **HIV/AIDS**. [2]In late 2008, an estimated 22.4 million people in sub-Saharan Africa were living with HIV. [3]There are significant regional **variations** in HIV infection rates: In general, rates are highest in southern Africa and lowest in West Africa. [4]Governments have varied tremendously in their responses to HIV/AIDS. [5]Uganda, for example, **embarked** on an aggressive public education campaign in the 1990s, which seems to have helped reduce infection rates there. [6]In contrast, in early 2000, South African President Mbeki publicly questioned whether HIV causes AIDS and made statements that contributed to an atmosphere of denial and shame surrounding HIV/AIDS in South Africa.

[7]Other diseases, while less likely to capture headlines in the West, sicken or kill millions of Africans every year. [8]The World Health Organization declared the prevalence of tuberculosis an emergency in Africa

in 2005. [9]Malaria and other tropical diseases reduce life expectancy, increase school and job **absenteeism,** and reduce economic productivity almost everywhere in Africa. [10]Only very recently have significant global health **initiatives,** such as the Global Network for Neglected Tropical Diseases (established in 2006), begun to target Africa's interrelated health challenges.

[11]African environmental challenges run the **gamut** from wildlife poaching to soil erosion to improper disposal of hazardous waste. [12]Africans have been in the forefront of the environmental justice movement, with activists including Ken Saro-Wiwa and Nobel laureate Wangari Maathai, leader of Kenya's Green Belt Movement, building **grass-roots** environmental campaigns.

—Craig, Albert M., Graham, William A., Kagan, Donald, Ozment, Steven, and Turner, Frank M.,
The Heritage of World Civilizations, Brief, 5th ed., pp. 881–882.

Before Reading

Vocabulary in Context

1–2. Use your own words to define the following term. Identify the context clue you used to make meaning of the word.

The word **initiatives** in sentence 10 means _____

Context clue used: _____

3. Study the following chart of word parts.

Root	Meaning	Suffix	Meaning
notoria	news	*-ous*	characterized by

Use context clues and the word parts to state the definition of the word **notorious**

in sentence 1: _____

Topic

4. What is the topic of the passage? _____

After Reading

Main Ideas and Supporting Details

Complete the following study notes with information from the passage.

Thesis Statement: A variety of health and environmental challenges face Africa.

Major Supports	Minor Supports
Most notorious health challenge: (5) _____	Significant regional variations, with highest rates in south and lowest in west (6) _____ _____
Challenges from (7) _____	Tuberculosis declared an emergency (8) _____ _____ _____
	Recent global initiatives have begun to target health challenges.
(9) _____	(10) _____ _____
	Africans in forefront of environmental justice movement, building grass-roots campaigns

SUMMARY RESPONSE

Restate the author's main idea in your own words. Include key major details in your summary. Begin your summary response with the following: *The main idea of "The African Future: Health and Environment" by Craig, Graham, Kagan, Ozment, and Turner is . . .*

WHAT DO YOU THINK?

Africa has a past characterized by colonialism and a present marked by problems, including war and poverty. Assume your school is holding an Africa Awareness day. You have been asked to prepare a brief presentation on one challenge facing people in African countries today. Choose one African country to research and write about. Consider the following:

- Identify the biggest challenge that your selected country faces presently.

- Describe how the country's government is responding, or not responding, to the problem that you have identified.
- Describe any initiatives that may be in place or proposed by outside organizations.

After Reading About Supporting Details

Before you move on to the Mastery Tests on supporting details, take time to reflect on your learning and performance by answering the following questions. Write your answers in your notebook.

- How has my knowledge base or prior knowledge about supporting details changed?
- Based on my studies, how do I think I will perform on the Mastery Test(s)? Why do I think my scores will be above average, average, or below average? (Note: An additional Mastery Test may be found in MyReadingLab.)
- Would I recommend this chapter to other students who want to learn more about supporting details? Why or why not?

Test your understanding of what you have learned about supporting details for Master Readers by completing the Chapter 5 Review.

Name _____ Section_____

Date _____ **Score** (number correct) _____ x 10 = _____ %

Visit MyReadingLab to take this test online and receive feedback and guidance on your answers.

Textbook Skills

Read this passage from a college marketing textbook. Then complete the summary that follows it.

Media Types

[1]With so many types of media from which to choose, how do marketers decide which ones to use?

[2]Four factors enter into the media decision. [3]**Media efficiency** measures how effective a media vehicle is at reaching a particular customer segment, compared to the cost. [4]Because media budgets are not infinite, marketers weigh efficiency carefully. [5]More efficient forms of media are less expensive, but less able to finely target niche demographics or behavioral segments. [6]**Media impact** is a qualitative assessment of the value of a message exposed in a particular medium. [7]For example, consumers might view an ad in the *New York Times* as having more credibility than if it appeared in the *National Enquirer*. [8]Marketing research companies collect measures of **media engagement**, which evaluates how attentively audiences read, watch, or listen to media. [9]Two television shows might deliver audiences of equal size, but viewers of one show might be significantly more engaged and involved in their experience than viewers of another show. [10]For example, viewers of drama shows, such as *NCIS* or *Grey's Anatomy*, are more actively involved in the show from week to week than are viewers of other genres such as news or comedy. [11]**Product or service characteristics** are also taken into account. [12]Does the product need to be demonstrated for consumers to understand what it does? [13]If so, visual media such as television or online advertising are required. [14]Are customers located in a fairly tight geographic area? [15]If so, local newspapers or local radio would be a great solution. [16]Each type of medium has relative advantages and disadvantages that are weighed when developing a media mix.

—Adapted from Levens, Michael R., *Marketing: Defined, Explained, Applied,* 2nd ed., p. 258.

_____ **1.** Sentence 1 is
   a. a main idea.
   b. a major supporting detail.
   c. a minor supporting detail.

_____ **2.** Sentence 2 is
   a. a main idea.
   b. a major supporting detail.
   c. a minor supporting detail.

_____ **3.** Sentence 3 is
   a. a main idea.
   b. a major supporting detail.
   c. a minor supporting detail.

_____ **4.** Sentence 7 is
   a. a main idea.
   b. a major supporting detail.
   c. a minor supporting detail.

_____ **5.** Sentence 11 is
   a. a main idea.
   b. a major supporting detail.
   c. a minor supporting detail.

6–10. Complete the summary with information from the paragraph.

(6) _____ factors enter into the marketers' decision on which media to use. **(7)** _____ measures how effective a media vehicle is at reaching a particular customer compared to the cost. Media impact assesses the **(8)** _____ of a message exposed in a particular medium. Measures of **(9)** _____ evaluate how attentively audiences read, watch, or listen to media. Product or **(10)** _____ characteristics, such as whether the product needs to be demonstrated or whether customers are in a tight geographic area, are also taken into account.

Name _____ Section_____

Date _____ **Score** (number correct) _____ x 20 = _____ %

Visit MyReadingLab to take this test online and receive feedback and guidance on your answers.

Read this passage from a college psychology textbook. Then answer the questions that follow it.

Textbook Skills

Finding Meaning

[1]Viktor Frankl was a well-respected neurologist in Austria when Nazi forces deported him and his family to a concentration camp. [2]They, along with thousands of other Jews, were subjected to various forms of deprivation, torture, and unspeakable atrocities, and many—including Frankl's wife and parents—died in the camps. [3]Frankl, however, survived, and after the war ended, he made a significant contribution to the field of psychology with his work on the importance of finding meaning in seemingly inexplicable events such as what he had experienced in the camps. [4]In his seminal work, *Man's Search for Meaning* (Frankl, 1959), he says, "When we are no longer able to change a situation—just think of an incurable disease such as inoperable cancer—we are challenged to change ourselves."

[5]Frankl's hypothesis spawned research investigating the benefit of finding meaning in loss, which has identified two specific types of meaning, **sense making** and **benefit finding**. [6]Following a significant negative life event, people try to make sense of the event in some way so it fits our perception of the world as predictable, controllable, and nonrandom (Tait & Silver, 1989; Tedeschi & Calhoun, 1996). [7]For example, a death might be explained as inevitable if the person had been battling a long illness or if he or she had a history of heavy smoking. [8]In the wake of Hurricane Katrina, discussions of long-standing problems with New Orleans' levees reflected a similar attempt for sense making. [9]Individuals with strong religious beliefs may make sense of loss by attributing it to God's will. [10]A second path to finding meaning lies in recognizing some benefit that ultimately came from the loss, such as a renewed sense of appreciation for life or other loved ones, or discovery of a new path in life.

[11]Successful coping appears to involve both sense making and benefit finding, although at different times. [12]Sense making is the first task people struggle with, but ultimately working through the loss and regaining momentum in life seems to hinge on resolving this first question and moving on to the second (Janoff-Bulman & Frantz, 1997). [13]This may explain why people who have lost a child, individuals coping with an

accidental or violent death of a loved one, and others dealing with a loss that defies our perception of the natural order of life often have a harder time recovering from the loss (Davis et al., 1998).

—Zimbardo, Philip G., Johnson, Robert L., and Hamilton, Vivian McCann, *Psychology: Core Concepts,* 7th ed., pp. 632–633.

_____ **1.** Sentence 3 is
  a. a main idea.
  b. a major supporting detail.
  c. a minor supporting detail.

_____ **2.** Sentence 5 is
  a. a main idea.
  b. a major supporting detail.
  c. a minor supporting detail.

_____ **3.** Sentence 7 is
  a. a main idea.
  b. a major supporting detail.
  c. a minor supporting detail.

_____ **4.** Sentence 10 is
  a. a main idea.
  b. a major supporting detail.
  c. a minor supporting detail.

_____ **5.** Sentence 11 is
  a. a main idea.
  b. a major supporting detail.
  c. a minor supporting detail.

Name _____ Section_____

Date _____ **Score** (number correct) _____ x 20 = _____ %

Visit MyReadingLab to take this test online and receive feedback and guidance on your answers.

Read this passage from a college history textbook. Then answer the questions that follow it.

Textbook Skills

The Jazz Age

[1]"The music from the trumpet at the Negro's lips is honey mixed with liquid fire." [2]With these words, Langston Hughes described the new music called jazz. [3]But among black intellectuals, Hughes's opinion was in the minority. [4]Many black Americans distanced themselves from the sensuous music that brought white attention to black culture. [5]Jazz music's improvisational style, they argued, only reinforced the stereotype that black people were impetuous and lacked intellectual discipline. [6]Other black people criticized this "folk art" because it was born in brothels and performed in speakeasies—illegal bars that opened during the decade of Prohibition, when the government outlawed alcohol. [7]But jazz was not just a musical innovation. [8]At a time when all other social institutions in the United States were segregated, a few jazz clubs brought together music lovers of all races.

[9]Some historians consider jazz the only truly American art form. [10]Rather than deriving from another culture, it was born in the United States from a blend of European and African percussion, horn, and piano melodies. [11]Many jazz artists were trained in the disciplined formality of classical piano. [12]Most jazz was feel-good music, embracing a bewildering array of forms—from spirituals and the mournful tones of the blues to the aggressive percussion of marching band rhythms, from the asymmetry of ragtime to the staid patterns of European tradition. [13]Jazz offered deep, throaty voices, and provocative brass, woodwind, and percussion sounds. [14]Building on written scores, band members improvised during performances. [15]Thus jazz was always in motion, always transforming something familiar into something new. [16]Hughes felt that jazz embodied a cultural richness that opened new doors for black Americans. [17]Through jazz, Hughes commented, "Josephine Baker goes to Paris, Robeson to London, Jean Toomer to a Quaker Meeting House, Garvey to Atlanta Federal Penitentiary . . . and Duke Ellington to fame and fortune."

—Carson, Clayborne, Lapsansky-Werner, Emma J., and Nash, Gary B., *The Struggle for Freedom: A History of African Americans, Volume II*, p. 363.

_____ **1.** Sentence 1 is

    a. a main idea.   c. a minor supporting detail.

    b. a major supporting detail.

_____ **2** Sentence 3 is

    a. a main idea.   c. a minor supporting detail.

    b. a major supporting detail.

_____ **3.** Sentence 10 is

    a. a main idea.   c. a minor supporting detail.

    b. a major supporting detail.

_____ **4.** Sentence 13 is

    a. a main idea.   c. a minor supporting detail.

    b. a major supporting detail.

_____ **5.** Sentence 16 is

    a. a main idea.   c. a minor supporting detail.

    b. a major supporting detail.

VISUAL *VOCABULARY*

Jazz **percussionist** Hamid Drake performs at the 2008 New Orleans Jazz and Heritage Festival.

A **percussionist** _____.

    a. plays the drums

    b. makes music by striking instruments

    c. is a set of drums

5 Summary of Key Concepts of Supporting Details

 Assess your comprehension of supporting details. Fill in the blanks with information from the chapter.

- To locate supporting details in a passage, a master reader turns the _____ into a _____.

- A major supporting detail _____

  _____.

- A minor supporting detail _____

  _____.

- A _____ is a _____

  _____.

- Often you will want to _____, or restate, ideas in your own words.

- _____ or marking your text _____ reading

  will help you create a _____ after you read.

- To create a summary for a passage with a stated main idea, _____

  _____.

- To create a summary for a passage with an implied main idea, _____

  _____.

Test Your Comprehension of Supporting Details

Respond to the following questions and prompts.

 In your own words, how do major and minor supporting details differ?

_____

_____

_____

_____

LO2 LO3 In the space below, outline the steps for creating a summary for stated and implied main ideas. See pages 205–211.

_____

_____

_____

_____

_____

_____

_____

_____

_____

_____

_____

_____

_____

_____

_____

_____

LO1 LO2 Summarize the two most important ideas in this chapter that will help you
LO3 LO4 improve your reading comprehension. _____
LO5

_____

_____

Outlines and Concept Maps

6

LO LEARNING OUTCOMES

After studying this chapter, you should be able to:

- **LO1** Create Outlines
- **LO2** Create Concept Maps
- **LO3** Develop Textbook Skills: The Table of Contents in a Textbook
- **LO4** Apply Information Literacy Skills: Academic, Personal, and Career Applications of Outlines and Concept Maps

Before Reading About Outlines and Concept Maps

In Chapter 5, you learned several important ideas that will help you use outlines and concept maps effectively. To review, reread the diagram about the flow of ideas on page 201 in Chapter 5. Next, skim this chapter for key ideas in boxes about outlines, concept maps, and the table of contents in a textbook. Refer to the diagrams and boxes and create at least three questions that you can answer as you read the chapter. Write your questions in the following spaces (record the page number for the key term in each question):

_____

_____? (page _____)

_____

_____? (page _____)

_____? (page _____)

Compare the questions you created with those that follow. Then write the ones that seem most helpful in your notebook, leaving enough space after each question to record the answers as you read and study the chapter.

How does an outline show the relationships among the main idea, major supporting details, and minor supporting details? Where are main ideas used in an outline, concept map, and table of contents? Where are major supporting

237

details used in an outline, concept map, and table of contents? Where are minor supporting details used in an outline, concept map, and table of contents? What is the difference between a formal outline and an informal outline?

LO1   Create Outlines

An outline shows how information in a paragraph or passage moves from a general idea to specific supporting details; thus it helps you make sense of the ways ideas relate to one another. A master reader uses an outline to see the main idea, major supporting details, and minor supporting details.

> An **outline** shows the relationships among the main idea, major supporting details, and minor supporting details.

Outlines can be formal or informal. A **formal** or **traditional outline** uses Roman numerals to indicate the main idea, capital letters to indicate the major details, and Arabic numbers to indicate minor details. It can be composed of full sentences or of topics or sentence parts that begin with a capital letter. A formal outline is particularly useful for studying complex reading material. Sometimes, you may choose to use an **informal outline** and record only the main ideas and the major supporting details. Because these outlines are informal, they may vary according to each student's notetaking style. Elements may or may not be capitalized. Also, one person might label the main idea with the number *1* and the major supporting details with letters *a, b, c, d,* and so on. Another person might not label the main idea at all and might label each major supporting detail with either letters or numbers.

▶ **EXAMPLE** Read the following paragraph from a college finance textbook. Fill in the details to complete the outline. Then answer the questions that follow it.

Textbook
Skills

Income and Types of Jobs

[1]Income varies by job type. [2]Jobs that require specialized skills tend to pay much higher salaries than those that require skills that can be obtained very quickly and easily. [3]The income level associated with specific skills is also affected by the demand for those skills. [4]For example, the demand for people with a nursing license has been very high in recent years, so hospitals have been forced to pay high salaries to outbid other

hospitals for nurses. [5]Conversely, the demand for people with a history or English literature degree is low because more students major in these areas than there are jobs.

—Madura, Jeff. *Personal Finance*, 3rd ed., p. 27.

Outline

I. (**Main idea**) _____

   A. Jobs that require specialized skills tend to pay much higher salaries than those that require skills that can be obtained very quickly and easily.

   B. _____

      _____

     1. _____

      _____

      _____

      _____

     2. Conversely, the demand for people with a history or English literature degree is low because more students major in these areas than there are jobs.

Questions

_____ **1.** Sentences 4 and 5 are
    a. major supporting details.
    b. minor supporting details.

_____ **2.** The outline used in this activity is an example of
    a. an informal outline.
    b. a formal outline.

EXPLANATION The main idea of this paragraph is stated in sentence 1: "Income varies by job type." The author suggests that a list of supporting details will be presented and explained with the phrase "varies by job type." The second major detail, stated in sentence 3, is signaled with the word *also*. Sentences 4 and 5 are minor supporting details, introduced with the words *for example* and *conversely*. This outline is an example of a formal outline that includes the main idea, the major supporting details, and the minor supporting details of one paragraph.

An informal outline of the information looks like the following:

Stated main idea: Income varies by job type.

1. Jobs that require specialized skills tend to pay much higher salaries than those that require skills that can be obtained very quickly and easily.

2. The income level associated with specific skills is also affected by the demand for those skills.

Notice how this informal outline of the main idea and the major supporting details—without the minor supporting details—condenses the material into a summary of the author's primary points. ⓦ

Practice 1

Read the following paragraph from a college textbook on education. Then answer the questions that follow it.

Torts

Textbook
Skills

[1]A tort is a civil wrong not arising out of a contract. [2]Tort law forms the basis of an important area of legal practice, commonly known as personal injury practice. [3]Parties who are injured because of a tort committed by another are usually entitled to recover damages for their injuries. [4]The three major categories of torts are: intentional torts, negligence, and strict liability. [5]Intentional torts require that an individual intentionally do an act knowing that it will cause harm or act with reckless disregard for the act's consequences. [6]Intentional torts include assault, battery, false imprisonment, false arrest, defamation, invasion of privacy, intentional infliction of emotional distress, malicious prosecution, abuse of process, trespass, conversion, and fraud. [7]In addition, a series of business torts and actions based on civil rights violations also exist. [8]The second general category of torts is negligence. [9]Negligence is a tort resulting from damages caused by one who fails to act as a reasonably prudent person would act under the same or similar circumstances. [10]This is the most common tort that gives rise to lawsuits; it stems from many different factual situations, including automobile accidents, medical and other professional malpractice, accidents occurring on premises, and defective products. [11]The third category of torts is strict liability. [12]Strict liability imposes liability on parties even though they did nothing wrong. [13]It applies to injuries resulting from keeping dangerous animals, engaging in abnormally dangerous activities, and manufacturing or distributing defective products.

—Hames, Joanne B. and Ekern, Yvonne, *Introduction to Law*,
4th ed., pp. 165–166.

1–5. Complete the following outline.

I. (Stated main idea) _____

_____

A. Intentional torts

    1. Require that an individual intentionally do an act knowing that it will cause harm or act with reckless disregard for the act's consequences

    2. _____

_____

_____

    3. Business torts and actions based on civil rights violations exist

B. Negligence

    1. Results from damages caused by one who fails to act as a reasonably prudent person would under the same or similar circumstances

    2. Most common tort that gives rise to lawsuits

    3. _____

_____

C. _____

    1. _____

    2. Applies to injuries resulting from keeping dangerous animals, engaging in abnormally dangerous activities, and manufacturing or distributing defective products

VISUAL *VOCABULARY*

Reading someone's text messages without their approval is an example of _____.

    a. intentional tort
    b. negligence
    c. strict liability

Create Concept Maps

An outline is one way to see the details that support a main idea. Another way to see details is through the use of a concept map. A **concept map** is a diagram that shows the flow of ideas from the main idea to the supporting details. Think of what you already know about a map. Someone can tell you how to get somewhere, but it is much easier to understand the directions if you can see how each road connects to the others by studying a map. Likewise, a concept map shows how ideas connect to one another.

> A **concept map** is a diagram that shows the flow of ideas from the main idea to the supporting details.

To make a concept map, a master reader places the main idea in a box or circle as a heading and then places the major supporting details in boxes or circles beneath the main idea. Often arrows or lines are used to show the flow of ideas.

> **EXAMPLE**   Read the following passage. Then complete the concept map by filling in the major and minor supporting details from the paragraph.

The Dangers of Texting While Driving

[1]Putting the brakes on the distracted driving epidemic will require both dedication and creative thinking, and the FCC is committed to doing its part to address this growing crisis.

Distracted Driving Is Dangerous

[2]The popularity of mobile devices has had some unintended and even dangerous consequences. [3]We now know that mobile communications is linked to a significant increase in distracted driving, resulting in injury and loss of life. [4]The National Highway Traffic Safety Administration reported in 2010 that driver distraction was the cause of 18 percent of all fatal crashes—3,092 people killed and 18 percent of crashes resulting in an injury—416,000 people wounded. [5]According to AAA, nearly 50 percent of teens admit to texting while driving. [6]Distracted driving endangers life and property and the current levels of injury and loss are unacceptable.

What You Can Do

[7]*Give Clear Instructions* [8]Give teen drivers simple, clear instructions not to use their wireless devices while driving. [9]According to CTIA, the easiest way to say it is: "On the road, off the phone." [10]Before new drivers

get their licenses, discuss the fact that taking their eyes off the road—even for a few seconds—could cost someone injury or even death.

[11]*Lead by Example* [12]Children learn from their parents' behavior. No one should text and drive. [13]Be an example for your children and if you need to text or talk on the phone, pull over to a safe place.

[14]*Become Informed and Be Active* [15]Review the information in our Clearinghouse and the literature on the web sites mentioned above. [16]Set rules for yourself and your household regarding distracted driving. [17]Tell family, friends and organizations to which you belong about the importance of driving without distractions. [18]Take information to your children's schools and ask that it be shared with students and parents.

—Federal Communications Commission. "FCC Consumer Advisory: The Dangers of Texting while Driving." Consumer & Government Affairs Bureau.

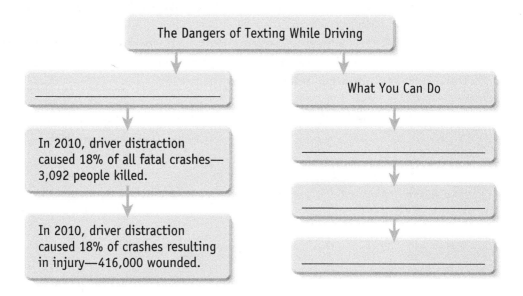

EXPLANATION The author of this passage used bold and italic print to emphasize the important ideas in the passage. The title of the passage states the topic and the author's controlling point. The two subheadings in bold print state the two major supporting details. The details in italic print highlight important minor details—action steps citizens can take in response to the dangers of texting while driving.

Practice 2

Read the following passage from a college English handbook. Then fill in the concept map with the central idea and major supporting details from the reading.

Using Online Chat

[1]You may be familiar with chat conversations from using instant messaging with friends and family. [2]In academic settings, chat will likely occur with coursework such as *WebCT* or *Blackboard*. [3]Collaborating via chat discussions will be more productive if you follow these tips:

- [4]*Use the chat space for brainstorming topics and exchanging impressions.* [5]The pace of online chat rarely allows lengthy consideration and articulation of messages.

- [6]*Focus on a thread or common topic.* [7]Online chat can be the electronic equivalent of a busy hallway outside a classroom, with different conversations occurring in the same space. [8]If you have trouble keeping up with all the messages, concentrate on the ones that relate to your interest.

- [9]*Write as quickly and fluidly as possible.* [10]Don't worry about producing perfect prose.

- [11]*Observe the standard of conduct expected in your group.* [12]If someone upsets or irritates you, remember that the person is, like you, an individual deserving of respect.

- [13]*Save transcripts of online chats.* [14]Then you'll be able to refer to them later. [15](If you are unsure how to save transcripts, ask your instructor.)

—Fowler, H. Ramsey and Aaron, Jane E., *The Little, Brown Handbook,* 9th ed., p. 233.

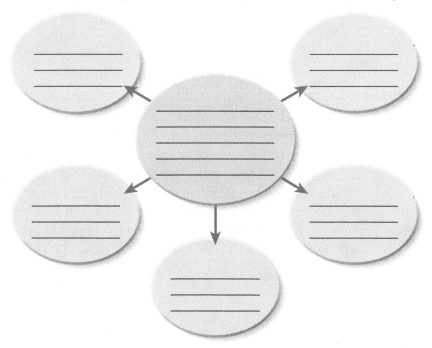

Develop Textbook Skills: The Table of Contents in a Textbook

LO3

Textbook
Skills

The table of contents is a special kind of outline that is based on topics and sub-topics. A **topic** is the *general subject,* so a **subtopic** is a *smaller part* of the topic. The general subject of the textbook is stated in the textbook's title. For example, the title *Health in America: A Multicultural Perspective* tells us that the book is about health concerns from the view of different cultures. Textbooks divide the general subject into smaller sections or subtopics. These subtopics form the chapters of the textbook. Because a large amount of information is found in each chapter, chapters are further divided into smaller parts or subtopics, and each subtopic is labeled with a heading. The table of contents lists the general subjects and subtopics of each chapter. Many textbooks provide a brief table of contents that divides the textbook into sections and lists the chapter titles for each section. There also may be a separate detailed table of contents that lists the subtopics for each chapter. A master reader examines the table of contents of a textbook to understand how the author has organized the information and to determine where specific information can be found.

> **EXAMPLE** Survey, or look over, the following brief table of contents. Then answer the questions.

1. What is the general topic of this textbook? _____

_____

2. How many parts did the author use to divide the general topic? _____

3. How many chapters are in each part? _____ What is the approximate

length of each chapter? _____ pages.

4. Write a one-sentence summary using the topic and subtopics for Part Two.

_____

_____

EXPLANATIONS The general topic of this textbook is stated in its title: *Messages: Building Interpersonal Communication Skills.* The author divides the general topic into three parts: "Messages about the Self and Others," "Messages: Spoken and Unspoken," and "Messages in Context." Each part is divided into four chapters. Knowing the length of each chapter helps you set aside the proper amount of

Messages: Building Interpersonal Communication Skills, 6th ed.

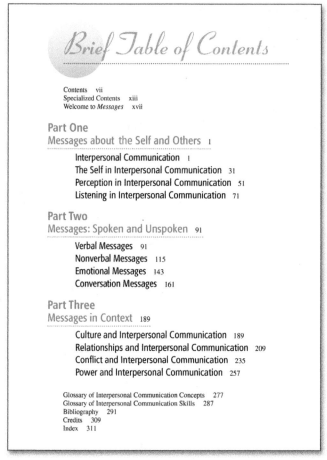

—DeVito, Joseph A., *Messages: Building Interpersonal Communication Skills*, 6th ed., pp. v–vi.

time needed to read and study. In this textbook, each chapter is about twenty to thirty pages in length. One way to get a general sense of the ideas in a chapter or part is by writing a summary. Compare your summary to the following: Spoken and unspoken messages include verbal messages, nonverbal messages, emotional messages, and conversation messages. ◀

Practice 3

Study the following detailed table of contents for Chapter 1 of *Messages: Building Interpersonal Communication Skills*, 6th ed.

1. What is the topic of the chapter? _____

2. How many subtopics are listed for the section "Principles of Interpersonal Communication"? _____

3. On what page does the discussion about competence in interpersonal communication begin? _____

4. What are the major supporting details of this chapter? _____

_____

_____

_____

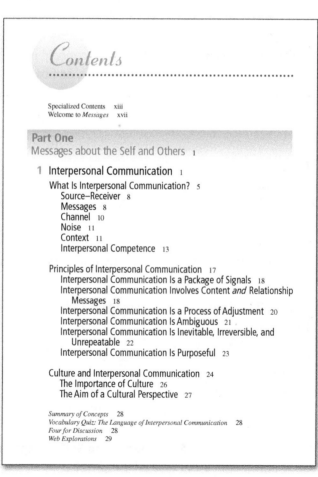

—DeVito, Joseph A., *Messages: Building Interpersonal Communication Skills*, 6th ed., p. vii.

Apply Information Literacy Skills

 ## Academic, Personal, and Career Applications of Outlines and Concept Maps

The ability to use outlines and concept maps is an information literacy skill that you can apply to your academic, personal, and career lives. Now that you have learned how to locate and identify supporting details, you can apply that skill to help you create outlines and concept maps. Outlines and concept maps enable you to organize and visualize information. For example, in your academic life, outlines and concept maps are useful study and writing tools. In your personal life, the ability to outline or make a concept map will help you in many aspects, such as weighing the pros and cons of an important decision, even down to small events like making a grocery list. In your career life, outlines and concept maps become tools to sum up or illustrate business plans, project timelines, or flow of resources. Thus, you will use the skills that you have learned in this chapter in several ways:

- Recognize your own need to use outlines and concept maps.
- Evaluate information to determine main ideas and key supports.
- Illustrate the flow of information from main ideas to supporting details for a specific purpose.

Academic Application

Assume you are taking a college health course. You are studying for a unit exam on self-esteem and self-acceptance. The follow paragraph is a chapter summary from the unit in your textbook.

- **Before Reading:** Skim the passage. Circle key terms you need to know for the exam.
- **During Reading:** Underline key details related to each key term you need to know.
- **After Reading:** In the space following the passage, create an outline or concept map with the key terms and details that you need to know.

Self-Esteem and Self-Acceptance

Important factors that affect your ability to nurture yourself and maintain healthy relationships with others include the way you define yourself *(self-concept)* and the way you evaluate yourself *(self-esteem)*.

Your self-concept is like a mental mirror that reflects how you view your physical features, emotional states, talents, likes and dislikes, values, and roles. A person might define herself as an activist, mother, honor student, athlete, or musician. How you feel about yourself or evaluate yourself constitutes your self-esteem. You might consider yourself an excellent student, a horrible singer, a great lover, or a "10" in terms of appearance. Taken together, such judgments indicate your level of self-esteem or self-evaluation.

Your perception and acceptance of yourself influences your relationship choices. If you feel unattractive, insecure, or inferior to others, you may choose not to interact with other people or to avoid social events. Or you may unconsciously seek out individuals who confirm your negative view of yourself by treating you poorly. Conversely, if you are secure about your unique characteristics and talents, that positive self-concept will make it easier to form relationships with people who support and nurture you and to interact with a variety of people in a healthy, balanced way.

—Donatelle, Rebecca, J., *Access to Health*,
13th ed., p. 114.

Outline or Concept Map:

I. _____

    A. _____

    B. _____

    C. constitutes your self-esteem

II. Self-esteem

    A. _____

    B. _____

III. Perception and acceptance of yourself influences your relationship choices

    A. _____

        _____

    B. _____

        _____

Personal Application

Assume you have decided to begin exercising and eating healthier meals. Your personal trainer, Chrissy Wallis Henry, posted the following information to help you and other clients with your plans for a healthier lifestyle in her fitness blog.

- **Before Reading:** Skim the posting. Record two examples of your current unhealthy lifestyle.
- **During Reading:** Underline details to include in your plan for a healthier lifestyle.
- **After Reading:** Complete the concept map with three steps in your plan.

My current unhealthy lifestyle: _____

_____

Eat Your Way to Higher Performance, a Better Physique, and a Healthier Mind & Body

My best advice is create a plan (or have one created for you), based on your training, sleeping and goals. Then stick to it. Without question. Remember, this is YOUR GOAL. Set one that is measurable and achievable.

1. Eat more protein. You need protein such as eggs, pork loin, chicken, and salmon. Ideally, protein will be free range, organic, and grass-fed or line caught.
2. Eat more veggies. For nutrient density (think nutrients per calorie), you simply can't beat green veggies. Have a salad at every meal. Put veggies on it that you like. Ranch is not a veggie.
3. Eat less fruit. Fruit is nature's candy; treat it as such. Look for fruits low on the glycemic index scale and glycemic load, such as berries.
4. Eat fats. Animal fats, fats from fruit oils (coconut, avocado, olive oils), some nuts and seeds. Fats are super easy to overdo.
5. Just like fruits, they are tasty. Only cook in fats when necessary. Grill or bake meats. Eat salads raw or with very little balsamic vinegar.
6. Sleep. Yup. I know this isn't "nutrition," but since we're talking performance and health, sleep is critical—8 hours.
7. No sugar. No sweetener. No fake sugars.
8. No alcohol. Please don't go on a bender and ask me why you feel like crap.
9. No soy. There are so many reasons why soy is not ideal; here are my top two: a) It's near impossible to find non-GMO soy. I'd rather not eat genetically mutated foods, but if you STILL insist— b) Soy raises

your estrogen. Let's be honest, ladies—do we NEED any MORE estrogen? And men—Manboobs.

10. Take fish oil. Fish oil is a great anti-inflammation supplement linked to heart health, brain heath, and a laundry list of other benefits.

11. Grains. O, Grains. A LOT of people have already said this better than me, so I'm going to suggest a few easy reads; if you ignore EVERY-THING else, please just eliminate grains and gluten.

- *Wheatbelly*, the website of cardiologist Dr. William Davis.
- "The Grain Manifesto" from the website *Whole9*.
- "Meats Not Grains—To Live Sustainably" on fitness author Robb Wolfe's website.
- "Why Grains Are Unhealthy" by fitness expert Mark Sessions on his website *Mark's Daily Apple*.

—Adapted from Henry, Chrissy Wallis. "Eat Your Way to Higher Performance, a Better Physique, and a Healthier Mind & Body."CWH Fitness. 9. May 2012. cwhfitness.com.

After Reading

Complete the concept map to plan for a healthier lifestyle.

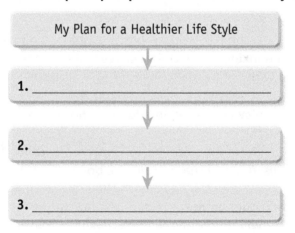

My Plan for a Healthier Life Style

1. _____

2. _____

3. _____

Career Application

Assume you are the youth program coordinator for your church or temple. You have been given the assignment to organize the pre-kindergarten program. The following memo addresses the tasks that you will accomplish.

- **Before Reading:** Skim the memo. Circle the key objectives of the memo.
- **During Reading:** Underline key details that describe how to implement the objectives.

- **After Reading:** In the space at the end of the passage, create an outline or concept map to help organize the objectives and plan how to execute them.

Dear Youth Program Coordinator,

I hope this finds you well. As you have observed, our youth program has many new members that are Pre-K children. You have suggested that our youth program could use some fine-tuning in order to best serve these children. As you will see below, I have outlined three changes to our program: 1) adding more low-level shelving stocked with 2) activities geared toward the children's skill level that are linked to a piece of scripture, and 3) offering healthier snack options.

First, we will build low-level shelving that is stocked with activities and projects appropriate for the children's age. As you know, kids this age really love to be independent and helpers. The objective is for the children to apply those skills to their spiritual education. By stocking materials on their level, they will do more for themselves, such as gather and put away materials. Each child has a different way that he/she will want to participate in the group. Therefore, the children will learn that they are each a unique and an important member of their group who has something valuable to contribute.

Second, by tying projects to spiritual content, we will promote critical thinking in the children. We will label the shelves where the activities go with their corresponding spiritual content. By doing this they will not only get to practice reading, but they will also be applying the lesson as they play and work. In addition, they are learning the practical skill that everything has a place and a purpose.

Third, I would like to provide our children with healthy snack options. An ideal snack offers the body a source of protein, a healthy carbohydrate, or a fat. Let's teach the kids that our bodies are important, and we should be mindful about what we put into them. Healthier choices now will, hopefully, lead to healthier choices later. Overall, what I am hopeful to instill in our children is the ability to think critically about their lives and education.

Thank you in advance,

Joe Martinez

Youth Program Director

Outline or Concept Map

I. Objective to promote spiritual critical thinking.

A. _____

   1. _____

   2. Children learn to help the group.

      a. _____

      b. _____

B. Apply spiritual content to projects and activities.

   1. _____

   2. _____

   3. _____

C. _____

   1. _____

   2. _____

   3. Identify and apply healthy eating habits.

REVIEW TEST 1

Score (number correct) _____ x 10 = _____ %

Visit MyReadingLab to take this test online and receive feedback and guidance on your answers.

Main Ideas, Major and Minor Supporting Details, and Outlines

Read the following passage from a college business textbook. Then complete the outline with the major and minor details from the passage.

Textbook
Skills

Consumer Rights

[1]Much of the current interest in business responsibility toward customers can be traced to the rise of consumerism–social activism dedicated to protecting the rights of consumers in their dealings with businesses. [2]The first formal declaration of consumer rights protection came in the early 1960s when President John F. Kennedy identified four basic consumer

rights. [3]Since that time, general agreement on two additional rights has also emerged; these rights are also backed by numerous federal and state laws. Legally, consumers have six basic rights:

- [4]*Consumers have a right to safe products.* [5]Businesses can't knowingly sell products that they suspect of being defective. [6]For example, a central legal argument in the recent problems involving Firestone tires was whether or not company officials knew in advance that the firm was selling defective tires.
- [7]*Consumers have a right to be informed about all relevant aspects of a product.* [8]For example, apparel manufacturers are now required to provide full disclosure on all fabrics used (cotton, silk, polyester, and so forth) and instructions for care (dry-clean, machine wash, hand wash).
- [9]*Consumers have a right to be heard.* [10]Labels on most products sold today have either a telephone number or address through which customers can file complaints or make inquiries.
- [11]*Consumers have a right to choose what they buy.* [12]Customers getting auto-repair service are allowed to know and make choices about pricing and warranties on new versus used parts. [13]Similarly, with the consent of their doctors, people have the right to choose between name-brand medications versus generic products that might be cheaper.
- [14]*Consumers have a right to be educated about purchases.* [15]All prescription drugs now come with detailed information regarding dosage, possible side effects, and potential interactions with other medications.
- [16]*Consumers have a right to courteous service.* [17]This right, of course, is hard to legislate. [18]But as consumers become increasingly knowledgeable, they're more willing to complain about bad service. [19]Consumer hotlines can also be used to voice service-related issues.

[20]American Home Products provides an instructive example of what can happen to a firm that violates one or more of these consumer rights. [21]For several years the firm aggressively marketed the drug Pondimin, a diet pill containing fenfluramine. [22]During its heyday, doctors were writing 18 million prescriptions a year for Pondimin and other medications containing fenfluramine. [23]The FDA subsequently discovered a link between the pills and heart-valve disease. [24]A class action lawsuit against the firm charged that the drug was unsafe and that users had not been provided with complete information about possible side effects. [25]American Home

Products eventually agreed to pay $3.75 billion to individuals who had used the drug.

—Griffin, Ricky W. and Ebert, Ronald J.,
Business, 8th ed., p. 75.

Stated central idea: (1) _____

   A. (2) _____

      1. (3) _____

      _____

      2. For example, a central legal argument in the recent problems involving Firestone tires was whether or not company officials knew in advance that the firm was selling defective tires.

   B. (4) _____

      1. For example, apparel manufacturers are now required to provide full disclosure on all fabrics used (cotton, silk, polyester, and so forth).

      2. Also required are instructions for care (dry-clean, machine wash, hand wash).

   C. (5) _____

      1. Labels on most products sold today have either a telephone number or address.

      2. Thus, customers can file complaints or make inquiries.

   D. (6) _____

      1. Customers getting auto-repair service are allowed to know and make choices about pricing and warranties on new versus used parts.

      2. (7) _____

      _____

      _____

   E. (8) _____

      1. All prescription drugs now come with detailed information.

      2. Information may include dosage, possible side effects, and potential interactions with other medications.

F. **(9)** _____

    1. **(10)** _____

    2. But as consumers become increasingly knowledgeable, they're more willing to complain about bad service.

    3. Consumer hotlines can also be used to voice service-related issues.

REVIEW TEST 2

Score (number correct) _____ x 25 = _____ %

Visit MyReadingLab to take this test online and receive feedback and guidance on your answers.

Supporting Details, Outlines, and Concept Maps

Read the following paragraph from a college ecology textbook. Complete the concept map with the main idea and the major supporting details from the paragraph.

Textbook
Skills

Coral Reefs

[1]Lying in the warm, shallow waters about tropical islands and continental land masses are colorful rich oases, the coral reefs. [2]They are a unique buildup of dead skeletal material from a variety of organisms, including coral, certain types of algae, and mollusks. [3]Built only underwater at shallow depths, coral reefs need a stable foundation upon which to grow. [4]Such foundations are provided by shallow continental shelves and submerged volcanoes. [5]Coral reefs are of three types. [6](1) *Fringing reefs* grow seaward from the rocky shores of islands and continents. [7](2) *Barrier reefs* parallel shorelines of continents and islands and are separated from land by shallow lagoons. [8](3) *Atolls* are horseshoe-shaped rings of coral reefs and islands surrounding a lagoon, formed when a volcanic mountain subsided. [9]Such lagoons are about 40m deep, usually connect to the open sea by breaks in the reef, and may hold small islands of patch reefs. [10]Reefs build up to sea level.

—Adapted from Smith, Thomas and Smith, Robert Leo,
Elements of Ecology, 4th ed., p. 504.

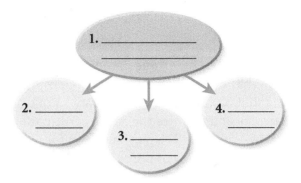

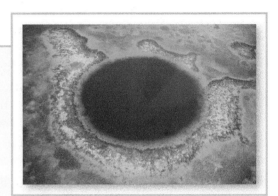

VISUAL *VOCABULARY*

Belize's Lighthouse Reef is _____ that
surrounds the Blue Hole, a sunken cave
system that is a haven for marine life
and scuba divers.

   a. a fringe

   b. a barrier

   c. an atoll

REVIEW TEST 3

Score (number correct) _____ x 10 = _____ %

Visit MyReadingLab to take this test online and receive feedback and guidance on your answers.

Supporting Details and Outlines

Before you read the following passage from a college textbook about tourism,
skim the material and answer the Before Reading questions. Read the passage.
Then answer the After Reading questions and activities.

Vocabulary Preview

reportorial (1): having the traits of reporting news or facts
vanguard (3): the leading position in a movement, field, or trend
platoons (3): bodies of people with a common purpose or goal
atmospherics (9): the mood, tone, environment, climate
raucous (14): loud, noisy

The Art of Travel Writing

by William R. Gray

[1]Over the past three decades or so, travel writing—like other nonfiction—has undergone a transformation from a more **reportorial** style to one that is propelled by the literary voice of the author. [2]This approach is personal and features the active participation of the writer in the subject matter—and thus is highly involving for readers, who feel they are being taken on a journey of discovery.

[3]Writers such as Edward Abbey, John McPhee, William Least Heat-Moon (particularly in *Blue Highways*), and Paul Theroux were in the **vanguard** of this approach to nonfiction writing, and today there are literally **platoons** of excellent writers following their lead. [4]And the great travel magazines overflow each issue with generally superb writing.

[5]In teaching my writing courses—including travel writing—and speaking at conferences, I try to instill the key elements that contribute to quality nonfiction writing, and all of these apply most emphatically to travel. [6]Focusing on these attributes helps elevate the quality of the writing, the personal involvement of the author, and draws readers in—and as writers we always need to keep our readers in the forefront of our minds.

- [7]Keen Observer: always seek the descriptive element, the penetrating detail that truly brings your subject to life and illuminates its uniqueness. [8]When interviewing someone, avoid the obvious descriptors such as color of hair and eyes; instead focus on timbre of voice, tilt of head, the gesture or mannerism that reveals character, the way light and shadow play across the face. [9]Likewise with place, use imagery—to evoke essential qualities; **atmospherics** and color are integral—the play of clouds, the tone of wind; use color dramatically—a cobalt sky; a sunset the color of apricots.

- [10]Active Participant: be both dynamically and intimately involved with your subject; follow every lead and participate in every activity appropriate to the place you are writing about. [11]Get up early, stay up late, and experience new things all day long.

- [12]Depth of Feeling: develop empathy for your subject; seek to experience it emotionally and do not hesitate to reveal something of yourself—how events and people affect you.

- [13]Openness to Experience: seek the **harrowing**, the exhilarating, the unusual. [14]Canoe through the crocodile-infested waters; climb the treacherous cliff; stay up all night with the **raucous** carnival celebrants. [15]In other words, be open to doing everything that might contribute to your understanding of the place you are writing about. [16]Be spontaneous—one of these activities may form the basis of the lead to your story.

- [17]Desire to Seek Knowledge and Understanding: strive to know your subject deeply; it's the way it is today because of the **confluence** of history, geology, exploration, warfare, cultural traditions, racial configuration, tourism, and a dozen other factors. [18]Understanding these elements will give perspective to your writing and help make it insightful and profound.

- [19]Desire to Seek a High Level in the Craft of Writing: use a strong first person point of view and a clear literary style to elevate and distinguish your writing. [20]Begin with an effective, original lead and end meaningfully. [21]Always be aware of **diction**, sentence variety, and quality of transitions. [22]Write so creatively and imaginatively that you leave your readers impatiently waiting to devour your next piece of writing.

—Cook, Roy A., Yale, Laura J., and Marqua, Joseph J.,
Tourism: The Business of Travel, 4th ed., pp. 121–122.

Before Reading

Vocabulary in Context

_____   **1.** In sentence 13 of the passage, the word **harrowing** means
       a. fun.   c. frightening.
       b. pleasant.   d. fulfilling.

_____   **2.** In sentence 17 of the passage, the word **confluence** means
       a. meeting.   c. departure.
       b. multitude.   d. being.

_____   **3.** In sentence 21 of the passage, the word **diction** means
       a. speech.   c. accent.
       b. wording.   d. organization.

After Reading

Main Ideas and Supporting Details

4–10. Complete the following outline with the central idea and major supporting details of the passage.

Stated central idea: (4) _____

_____

_____

- **(5)** _____

- **(6)** _____

- **(7)** _____

- **(8)** _____

- **(9)** Desire to Seek Knowledge and Understanding

- **(10)** Desire to Seek a High Level in the Craft of Writing

SUMMARY RESPONSE

Restate the author's central idea in your own words. Include key major details in your summary. Begin your summary response with the following: *The central idea of "The Art of Travel Writing" by William Gray is . . .*

WHAT DO YOU THINK?

Assume you are a travel writer and an online travel blog has asked you to write an article about a place of your choosing. As you write and revise, use the elements of effective travel writing suggested by William R. Gray. Consider the following approaches to your writing:

- Avoid obvious descriptors.
- Use imagery.
- Use an active voice.

REVIEW TEST 4

Score (number correct) _____ x 10 = _____ %

Visit MyReadingLab to take this test online and receive feedback and guidance on your answers.

Supporting Details and Concept Maps

Before Reading: Survey the following passage adapted from the college textbook *The Interpersonal Communication Book*. Skim the passage, noting the words in bold print. Answer the Before Reading questions that follow the passage. Then read the passage. Next answer the After Reading questions. Use the discussion and writing topics as activities to do after reading.

Vocabulary Preview

implications (4): meanings
subsequent (8): following, later
alibi (16): explanation, excuse
assurance (17): promise, guarantee

Textbook
Skills

Repairing Conversational Problems: The Excuse

[1]At times you may say the wrong thing; then, because you can't erase the message (communication really is irreversible), you may try to account for it. [2]Perhaps the most common method for doing so is the excuse. [3]You learn early in life that when you do something that others will view negatively, an excuse is in order to justify your performance. [4]*Excuses*, central to all forms of communication and interaction, are "explanations or actions that lessen the negative **implications** of an actor's performance, thereby maintaining a positive image for oneself and others" (Snyder, 1984; Snyder, Higgins, & Stucky, 1983).

[5]Excuses seem especially in order when you say or are accused of saying something that runs **counter** to what is expected, sanctioned, or considered "right" by the people with whom you're talking. [6]Ideally, the excuse lessens the negative impact of the message.

Some Motives for Excuse Making

[7]The major motive for excuse making seems to be to maintain your self-esteem, to project a positive image to yourself and to others. [8]Excuses also represent an effort to reduce stress: You may feel that if you can offer an excuse—especially a good one that is accepted by those around you—it will reduce the negative reaction and the **subsequent** stress that accompanies a poor performance.

[9]Excuses also may enable you to maintain effective interpersonal relationships even after some negative behavior. [10]For example, after criticizing a friend's behavior and observing the negative reaction to your criticism, you might offer an excuse such as, "Please forgive me; I'm really exhausted. [11]I'm just not thinking straight." [12]Excuses enable you to place your messages—even your possible failures—in a more favorable light.

Types of Excuses

[13]Think of the recent excuses you have used or heard. [14]Did they fall into any of these three classes (Snyder, 1984)?

- [15]*I didn't do it:* Here you deny that you have done what you're being accused of. [16]You may then bring up an **alibi** to prove you couldn't have done it, or perhaps you may accuse another person of doing what you're being blamed for ("I never said that" or "I wasn't even near the place when it happened"). [17]These "I didn't do it" types are the worst excuses, because they fail to acknowledge responsibility and offer no **assurance** that this failure will not happen again.
- [18]*It wasn't so bad:* Here you admit to doing it but claim the offense was not really so bad or perhaps that there was justification for the behavior ("I only padded the expense account, and even then only modestly" or "Sure, I hit him, but he was asking for it").
- [19]*Yes, but:* Here you claim that **extenuating circumstances** accounted for the behavior; for example, that you weren't in control of yourself at the time or that you didn't intend to do what you did ("It was the liquor talking" or "I never intended to hurt him; I was actually trying to help").

—Adapted from DeVito, Joseph A., *The Interpersonal Communication Book*, 11th ed., pp. 210–211.

Before Reading

Vocabulary in Context

Use your own words to define the following terms. Identify the context clue you used to make meaning of the word.

1. The word **counter** in sentence 5 means _____

2. Context clue used for **counter** _____

_____

3. The phrase **extenuating circumstances** in sentence 19 means _____

_____

4. Context clue used for **extenuating circumstances** _____

_____

After Reading

Main Ideas and Supporting Details

Complete the following graphic organizer with information from the passage.

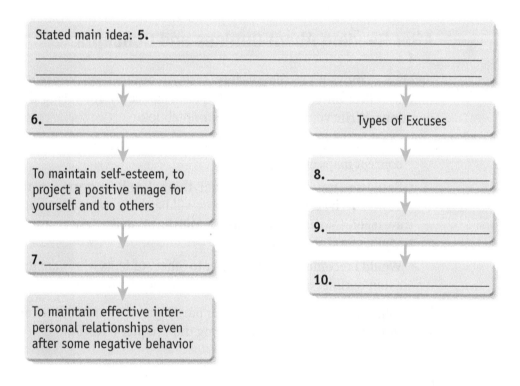

Stated main idea: **5.** _____

_____

_____

6. _____

To maintain self-esteem, to project a positive image for yourself and to others

7. _____

To maintain effective inter-personal relationships even after some negative behavior

Types of Excuses

8. _____

9. _____

10. _____

SUMMARY RESPONSE

Restate the author's central idea in your own words. Include key major details in your summary. Begin your summary response with the following: *The central idea of "Repairing Conversation Problems: The Excuse" by Joseph A. DeVito is . . .*

WHAT DO YOU THINK?

Assume you are a manager of a local retail store. Write an article for your company's newsletter to educate workers about excuse making. Consider the following approaches to your newsletter:

- Explain possible motives.
- Describe types of excuses.
- Explain the impact that excuse making will have on chances for promotion.
- Suggest a solution to avoid the need for excuses.

After Reading About Outlines and Concepts

Before you move on to the Mastery Tests on outlines and concept maps, take time to reflect on your learning and performance by answering the following questions. Write your answers in your notebook.

- How has my knowledge base or prior knowledge about outlines and concept maps changed?
- Based on my studies, how do I think I will perform on the Mastery Test(s)? Why do I think my scores will be above average, average, or below average? (Note: An additional fourth Mastery Test may be found in MyReadingLab.)
- Would I recommend this chapter to other students who want to learn more about outlines and concept maps? Why or why not?

Test your understanding of what you have learned about outlines and concept maps for master readers by completing the Chapter 6 Review.

Name _____ Section_____

Date _____ **Score** (number correct) _____ x 10 = _____ %

Visit MyReadingLab to take this test online and receive feedback and guidance on your answers.

A. Read the following passage from a college business textbook.

Textbook
Skills

Cookies in Online Business

[1]Some companies use **cookies**, small text files written to a user's hard disk that track customer preferences and Web clicks or store previous responses to online forms. [2]This allows a company to customize its Web storefront for each customer. [3]For example, by using cookies, Yahoo! collects a significant amount of data about its users—almost 12 terabytes of data a day. [4]When processing these data, sophisticated analysis programs try to predict consumer behavior. [5]Then this valuable information can be sold to marketing firms or used to justify high prices for Yahoo! ad space. [6]Some people feel this practice compromises their security. [7]Just that perception, whether it is truthful or not, can cost a company business. [8]So, should a company use cookies or not? [9]Some companies, such as Yahoo!, say yes. Others, such as Google, refuse to collect such information about their users.

—Adapted from Solomon, Michael, Poatsy, Mary Anne, and Martin, Kendall. *Better Business*, 2nd ed., p. 311.

1–5. Complete the summary with information from the paragraph.

Cookies are **(1)** _____

_____

allowing a company to customize its Web storefront for each customer—for example, **(2)** _____

_____ **3.** Sentence 1 is
    a. a main idea.
    b. a major supporting detail.
    c. a minor supporting detail.

_____ **4.** Sentence 6 is
    a. a main idea.
    b. a major supporting detail.
    c. a minor supporting detail.

5. What words signaling time order introduce the two major supporting details that explain the purpose of collecting data with cookies? _____

B. Read the following paragraph from a college environmental science textbook.

Toxic Substances Can Threaten Ecosystem Services

[1]Toxicants can alter the biological composition of ecosystems and the manner in which organisms interact with one another and their environment. [2]In so doing, harmful compounds can threaten the ecosystem services provided by nature. [3]For example, pesticide exposure has been implicated as a factor in the recent declines in honeybee populations. [4]Honeybees pollinate over 100 economically important crops. [5]Therefore, reduced pollination by wild bees has increased costs for farmers by forcing them to hire professional beekeepers to pollinate their crops.

—Adapted from Withgott, Jay H. and Laposata, Matthew, *Essential Environment: The Science Behind the Stories*, p. 217.

6–10. Complete the summary with information from the paragraph.

Toxicants **(6)** _____

_____

thereby threatening the ecosystem services provided by nature—for example,

(7) _____

_____

_____ **8.** Sentence 3 is
    a. a main idea.
    b. a major supporting detail.
    c. a minor supporting detail.

_____ **9.** Sentence 4 is
    a. a main idea.
    b. a major supporting detail.
    c. a minor supporting detail.

10. What time signal word introduces the final minor supporting detail?

_____

Name _____ Section_____

Date _____ **Score** (number correct) _____ x 10 = _____ %

Visit MyReadingLab to take this test online and receive feedback and guidance on your answers.

Textbook
Skills

Read the following paragraph from a college psychology textbook. Then answer the questions that follow it.

What Is Substance Abuse?

[1]What is the difference between drug use and substance abuse? [2]The impact on people's lives is one way to gauge use versus abuse. [3]People who experience negative effects as a result of their drug use cross the line into substance abuse. [4]A **substance abuser** is a person who overuses and relies on drugs to deal with everyday life. [5]Most substance abusers use alcohol or tobacco, but the whole range of psychoactive drugs and combinations of these drugs presents possibilities for substance abuse. [6]A person is a substance abuser if all three of the following statements apply:

- [7]The person has used the substance for at least a month.
- [8]The use has caused legal, personal, social, or vocational problems.
- [9]The person repeatedly uses the substance even in situations when doing so is hazardous, such as when driving a car.

[10]Missing work or school, spending too much money on drugs, damaging personal relationships, and getting into legal trouble are all signs of substance abuse. [11]When substance abusers try to decrease or quit their drug use, they may experience withdrawal symptoms. [12]**Withdrawal symptoms** are the reactions experienced when a substance abuser stops using a drug with dependence properties. [13]For example, an alcoholic may experience the "shakes" as he or she attempts to quit drinking alcohol.

—Adapted from Lefton, Lester A. and Brannon, Linda, *Psychology*, 8th ed., pp. 215–216.

_____ **1.** Which sentence states the main idea of the passage?
- a. sentence 1
- b. sentence 2
- c. sentence 3
- d. sentence 8

_____ **2.** In general, the major details of this passage are
- a. facts that show the number of people who are substance abusers.
- b. ways to avoid substance abuse.
- c. reasons for substance abuse.
- d. definitions of substance abuse, substance abuser, and withdrawal symptoms.

_____ **3.** In the passage, sentence 4 is
- a. a main idea.
- b. a major supporting detail.
- c. a minor supporting detail.

_____ **4.** In the passage, sentence 7 is

a. a main idea.   c. a minor supporting detail.

b. a major supporting detail.

5–10. Complete the informal outline with the key terms, definitions, and examples from the paragraph.

Main idea: Drug abuse can be measured by the impact on the lives of users.

A. _____: Negative effects as a result of drug use

Example: Missing work or school, spending too much money on drugs, damaging personal relationships, and getting into legal trouble are all signs of substance abuse.

B. Substance abuser: _____

_____

Example: _____

_____

_____

C. _____: _____

_____

Example: _____

_____

Which word or phrase best states the meaning of **psychoactive**?

_____

a. mind-altering

b. satisfying

c. addictive

▶ Caffeine is one example of a commonly used **psychoactive** drug.

Name _____ Section_____

Date _____ **Score** (number correct) _____ x 10 = _____ %

Visit MyReadingLab to take this test online and receive feedback and guidance on your answers.

Read the following passage from a college humanities textbook.

Textbook Skills

The Difference Between Problems and Issues

[1]To be able to think clearly and effectively, you must be able to understand and recognize problems and issues. [2]Problems and issues differ in some respects. [3]A problem is a situation that we regard as unacceptable. [4]In contrast, an issue is a matter about which intelligent, informed people disagree to some extent. [5]Solving problems, therefore, means deciding what action will change the situation for the best. [6]On the other hand, resolving issues means deciding what belief or viewpoint is the most reasonable.

[7]Whenever you are uncertain whether to treat a particular challenge as a problem or an issue, apply this test: Ask whether the matter involved tends to arouse partisan feelings and to divide informed, intelligent people. [8]If it does not, treat it as a problem. [9]If it does, treat it as an issue. [10]Here are some sample problems: a student trying to study in a noisy dormitory, a child frightened by the prospect of going to the hospital, a businesswoman dealing with sexual harassment. [11]Here are some sample issues: a public school teacher leading students in prayer in a public school classroom, a member of Congress proposing a cut in Social Security benefits for the elderly, an anthropologist stating that human beings are violent by nature.

—Adapted from Ruggerio, Vincent Ryan, *The Art of Thinking: A Guide to Critical and Creative Thought,* 7th ed., p. 109.

_____ **1.** Sentence 2 is a
    a. main idea.
    b. major supporting detail.
    c. minor supporting detail.

_____ **2.** Sentence 3 is a
    a. main idea.
    b. major supporting detail.
    c. minor supporting detail.

_____ **3.** Sentence 4 is a
    a. main idea.
    b. major supporting detail.
    c. minor supporting detail.

_____ **4.** Sentence 8 is a
    a. main idea.
    b. major supporting detail.
    c. minor supporting detail.

_____ **5.** Sentence 11 is a
  a. main idea.
  b. major supporting detail.
  c. minor supporting detail.

6–10. Complete the concept map (a contrast chart) with information from the passage.

Differences between:	6. _____	Issues
Definitions	an unacceptable situation	7. _____ _____ _____ _____
Goals	positive actions	8. _____
Traits	9. _____ _____ _____	arouse feelings and divide people
Examples	10. _____ _____ _____ _____ _____ _____ _____ _____	a public school teacher leading students in prayer in a public classroom, a member of Congress proposing a cut in Social Security benefits for the elderly, an anthropologist stating that human beings are violent by nature

VISUAL _VOCABULARY_

This photograph entitled "Pro-Life Demonstrators Face Pro-Choice Demonstrators" illustrates a significant _____ in the United States.

  a. problem
  b. issue

6 Summary of Key Concepts of Outlines and Concept Maps

LO1 LO2 Assess your comprehension of outlines and concept maps. Complete the chart with information from the chapter.

Outlines and Concept Maps: Question-Answer Two-Column Notes	
What is the purpose of an outline?	_____ _____ _____
Which signal words may an author use to introduce a main idea?	_____ _____ _____ _____
Which signal words may an author use to introduce a supporting detail?	_____ _____ _____ _____
How does a formal outline use Roman numerals and numbers?	A formal outline uses _____ to indicate the _____, _____ to indicate the _____, and _____ _____ to indicate the _____ _____.
What is a concept map?	A concept map is a _____ _____ _____

Test Your Comprehension of Outlines and Concept Maps

Respond to the following questions and prompts.

LO1 LO2 LO3 In the space below, create an outline and a concept map for the following terms from a college anatomy and physiology textbook.

Skeletal Muscle; Smooth Muscle; Muscle Types; Cardiac Muscle; Producing Movement; Maintaining Posture; Muscle Functions; Stabilizing Joints

_____   _____

                      _____

                      _____

                      _____

                      _____

                      _____

                      _____

                      _____

                      _____

_____

LO1 LO2 LO3 LO4 Summarize the two most important ideas in this chapter that will help you improve your reading comprehension. _____

_____

_____

Transitions and Thought Patterns

🔵 LEARNING OUTCOMES

After studying this chapter you should be able to:

LO1 Recognize Transition Words to Determine Relationships Within a Sentence

LO2 Recognize Thought Patterns to Determine Relationships Between Sentences

LO3 Develop Textbook Skills: Thought Patterns in Textbooks

LO4 Apply Information Literacy Skills: Academic, Personal, and Career Applications of Transitions and Thought Patterns

Before Reading About Transitions and Thought Patterns

Using the reporter's questions (Who? What? When? Where? Why? How?), refer to the chapter learning outcomes and create at least three questions that you can answer as you study the chapter. Write your questions in the following spaces:

_____

_____

_____

Now take a few minutes to skim the chapter for ideas and terms that you have studied in previous chapters. List those ideas in the following spaces:

_____

_____

Compare the questions you created based on the chapter learning outcomes with the following questions. Then write the ones that seem the most helpful in your notebook, leaving enough space after each question to record the answers as you read and study the chapter.

What are transitions? What are thought patterns? What is the relationship between transitions and thought patterns? How do thought patterns use transition words?

On page 278, the terms *main idea* and *supporting details* are discussed in relationship to transitions and thought patterns. Consider the following study questions based on these ideas: How can transitions help me understand the author's main idea? How can transitions help me create an outline?

 ## Recognize Transition Words to Determine Relationships Within a Sentence

Read the following set of ideas. Which word makes the relationship between the ideas clear?

Marcus was asked to leave the movie _____ he was talking loudly.

   a. however   b. because   c. finally

The word that makes the relationship between ideas within the sentence clear is (b) *because.* The first part of the sentence states what happened to Marcus. The second part of the sentence explains why he was asked to leave the theatre. The word *because* best signals the cause and effect relationship between Marcus's behavior and the result of his behavior.

Transitions are key words and phrases that signal the logical relationships among ideas both within a sentence and between sentences. **Transitions** help you make sense of an author's idea in two basic ways. First, transitions join ideas within a sentence. Second, transitions establish **thought patterns** so readers can understand the logical flow of ideas between sentences.

> **Transitions** are words and phrases that signal thought patterns by showing the logical relationships among ideas both within a sentence and between sentences.
> A **thought pattern** is established by using transitions to show the logical relationship between ideas in a paragraph or passage.

Some transition words have similar meanings. *For example, also, too,* and *furthermore* all signal the relationship of addition or listing. Sometimes a single word can serve as two different types of transitions, depending on how it is used. For example, the word *since* can reveal time order, or it can signal a cause. Notice the difference in the following two sentences.

Since I began studying every day, my understanding and my grades have improved dramatically.

Since you have the flu, please stay home from work to avoid spreading the disease.

> **EXAMPLE** Complete the following ideas with a transition that shows the relationship among ideas within each sentence. Fill in each blank with a word from the box. Use each word once.

adjacent	another	during	one type

1. In the ancient Aztec culture, priests offered cacao seeds and chocolate drinks to their gods _____ sacred ceremonies.

2. One way to shop for a vehicle is to visit local dealerships; _____ way is to use online resources such as AutoTrader.com.

3. Fear of failure is _____ of attitude that drives academic cheating.

4. The registrar's office is _____ to the financial aid office.

EXPLANATION

1. The word *during* indicates *when* the Aztec priests offered the cacao seeds and chocolate drinks to their gods.

2. *Another* signals the *addition* of the second idea in this sentence.

3. The phrase *one type* suggests that other types of thinking also motivate academic cheating.

4. The word *adjacent* signals that the registrar's office is located *next to* the financial aid office.

Practice 1

Complete the following ideas with a transition that shows the relationship among ideas within each sentence. Fill in each blank with a word from the box. Use each word once.

| furthermore | in the foreground | one category | subsequently |

1. An American citizen is entitled to a fair and speedy trial whether _____ found guilty or innocent.

2. Walking—a safe, efficient, and popular method of attaining and maintaining physical fitness—strengthens the heart and lungs; _____, it builds bones and tones muscles.

3. In Monet's 1877 painting *Arrival of a Train*, the smoke of the trains _____ of the painting blurs the cathedral, which is barely visible past the smoke.

4. The white lie is only _____ of the myriad types of lies that do much harm.

Master readers look for transition words, study their meaning in context, and use them as keys to unlock the author's thought pattern.

LO2 Recognize Thought Patterns to Determine Relationships Between Sentences

Not only do transitions reveal the relationships among ideas within a sentence, they also show the relationship of ideas between sentences.

Walking strengthens the heart and lungs. It *also* builds and tones muscles.

▷ **EXAMPLE** Complete each of the following ideas with a transition that makes the relationship between the sentences clear. Fill in each blank with a word from the box. Use each word or phrase once.

| as a result | finally | for example | next |

1. According to the National Weather Service, frostbite is the damage caused to body tissue due to freezing. _____, frostbite causes a loss of feeling and white or pale coloring of the affected areas.

2. Your family should have an emergency or disaster kit on hand. _____, you should have water, non-perishable food, and first aid supplies.

3. Four test-taking tips may prove helpful if you experience test anxiety. First, keep a positive attitude. _____, to gain confidence and build up points, answer the easy questions before you answer tougher ones.

4. Third, don't let the hard questions stump you; circle them, move on, and come back to them later if you can. _____, take time to proof-read for careless errors.

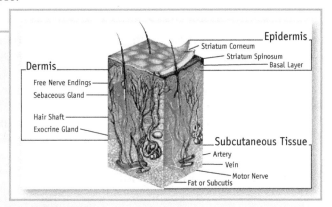

VISUAL VOCABULARY

The root **dermis** means

_____.

a. degree
b. skin
c. layer of skin or tissue

▶ **Cross-Section of the Three Layers of Human Skin**

First-degree frostbite injuries involve the epidermis, and fourth-degree injuries involve the epidermis, dermis, and subcutaneous tissue.

—Adapted from *Occupational Dermatoses*, Page 3, Slide 14, 21 Apr. 2001; National Institute for Occupational Safety and Health Photolibrary, CDC.

EXPLANATION

1. The transition *as a result* indicates that the second sentence offers specific symptoms of frostbite.

2. The transition phrase *for example* logically introduces example items to include in a family disaster kit.

3–4. Items 3 and 4 list four test-taking tips. In item 3, the transition *next* logically introduces the second tip, and in item 4, the transition *finally* introduces the last of the four test-taking tips. ◀

Practice 2

Complete the following ideas with transitions. Fill in each blank with a word from the box. Use each word once.

immediately	meanwhile	next	on	out

Andre began choking. **(1)** _____ Daine wrapped his arms around Andre's waist. **(2)** _____, Daine made a fist with his right hand. He then placed the thumb side of his fist **(3)** _____ the middle of Andre's abdomen just above his navel and well below the lower tip of his breastbone. **(4)** _____, he grasped the fist with the other hand. He pressed his fist into Andre's abdomen with a quick upward thrust. After several quick, hard thrusts, the piece of food that had been blocking Andre's airway flew **(5)** _____ of his mouth.

You will recall that a paragraph is made up of a group of ideas. Major details support the main idea, and minor details support the major details. Transitions make the relationship between these three levels of ideas clear, smooth, and easy to follow.

Before beginning to write, an author must ask, "What thought pattern best expresses these ideas?" or "How should these ideas be organized so that the reader can follow and understand my point?" A **thought pattern** (also called a **pattern of organization**) allows the author to arrange the supporting details in a clear and smooth flow by using transition words.

> **Thought patterns** (or **patterns of organization**) are signaled by using transitions to show the logical relationship among ideas in a paragraph, passage, or textbook chapter.

As you learned in Chapter 3, a main idea is made up of a topic and the author's controlling point about the topic. One way an author controls the topic is by using a specific thought pattern. Read the following paragraph. Identify the topic sentence by circling the topic and underlining the controlling point.

Textbook
Skills

Smokers and the Risk of Cancer

[1]If you are a smoker, your risk of developing lung cancer depends on several factors. [2]First, the amount you smoke per day is important. [3]Someone who smokes two packs a day is 15 to 25 times more likely to

develop lung cancer than a nonsmoker. [4]Smoking as little as one cigar per day can double the risk of several cancers, including that of the oral cavity (lip, tongue, mouth, and throat), esophagus, larynx, and lungs. [5]The risks increase with the number of cigars smoked per day. [6]A second factor is when you started smoking; if you started in your teens, you have a greater chance of developing lung cancer than people who start later. [7]And a third risk factor is whether you inhale deeply when you smoke. [8]Smokers are also more susceptible to the cancer-causing effects of exposure to other irritants, such as asbestos and radon, than are nonsmokers.

—Adapted from Donatelle, Rebecca, J., *Access to Health*, 12th ed., p. 389.

The topic is smokers' risk of developing lung cancer, and the controlling point is the phrase "depends on several factors." The phrase "depends on" states the author's opinion. The words "several factors" state the author's thought pattern. The author's controlling point limits the supporting details to listing and describing the three factors affecting the risk of cancer. The transition words *First, second,* and *third* signal each of the supporting details. Authors often introduce supporting details with transition words based on the controlling point. Creating an outline using transition words is an excellent way to grasp an author's thought pattern.

> **EXAMPLE** Read the following paragraph. Complete the informal outline, then answer the question.

Textbook
Skills

Types of Coping Styles

[1]Each of us can learn to control stress by adopting coping strategies that are consistent with our lifestyles. [2]According to Lazarus and Folkman (1984; Folkman and Lazarus, 1991), there are two types of coping responses. [3]The first type of coping style, **problem-focused coping,** is directed toward the source of the stress. [4]For example, if the stress is job-related, a person might try to change conditions at the job site or take courses to acquire skills that would enable him or her to obtain a different job. [5]The second type of coping style, **emotion-focused coping,** is directed toward a person's own personal reaction to a stressor. [6]For example, a person might try to relax and forget about the problem or find solace in the company of friends.

—Adapted from Carlson, Neil R. and Buskist, William, *Psychology: The Science of Behavior*, 5th ed., p. 552.

Topic sentence: _____

    A. _____

For example, if the stress is job-related, a person might try to change conditions at the job site or take courses to acquire skills that would enable him or her to obtain a different job.

B. _____

_____

For example, a person might try to relax and forget about the problem or find solace in the company of friends.

_____ What is the author's thought pattern?
    a. time order   b. classification

EXPLANATION Compare your outline to the following:

Topic sentence: There are two types of coping responses.

A. Problem-focused coping is directed toward the source of the stress.

For example, if the stress is job-related, a person might try to change conditions at the job site or take courses to acquire skills that would enable him or her to obtain a different job.

B. Emotion-focused coping is directed toward a person's own personal reaction to a stressor.

For example, a person might try to relax and forget about the problem or find solace in the company of friends.

The topic is "coping responses." The thought pattern is signaled by the phrase "two types." The transitions clearly carry out the thought pattern by introducing the major supporting details (the two types of coping responses) with the phrases "first type" and "second type." In addition, the author provides minor details in the form of examples, and each example is introduced with the phrase "for example." In this paragraph, these transitions establish the (b) classification thought pattern, which is discussed later in the chapter. ◉

Practice 3

Read the following paragraph. Then complete the informal outline.

Textbook
Skills

Biodiversity Loss and Species Extinction

[1]Biodiversity at all levels is being lost to human impact, most irretrievably in the extinction of species. [2]Once vanished, a species can never

return. [3]**Extinction** occurs when the last member of a species dies and the species ceases to exist, as apparently was the case with Monteverde's golden toad. [4]The disappearance of a particular population from a given area, but not the entire species globally, is referred to as **extirpation**. [5]For example, the tiger has been extirpated from most of its historic range, but it is not yet extinct. [6]However, extirpation is an erosive process that can, over time, lead to extinction.

—Withgott, Jay H. and Brennan, Scott R., *Essential Environment: The Science Behind the Stories*, 3rd ed., p. 165.

Topic sentence: _____

_____

a. _____

_____

b. _____

_____

1. _____

_____

2. _____

_____

In this chapter, we discuss four common thought patterns and the transition words and phrases used to signal each:

- The time order pattern
- The space order pattern
- The listing pattern
- The classification pattern

Some additional common thought patterns are covered in Chapter 8.

The Time Order Pattern

The **time order** thought pattern generally shows a chain of events. The actions or events are listed in the order in which they occur. This is called *chronological* *order.* Two types of chronological order are narration and process. An author uses narration to describe a chain of points such as a significant event in history or a story. The second type of chronological order is process. Process is used to give directions to a task in order, like in steps, stages, or directions.

Narration: A Chain of Events

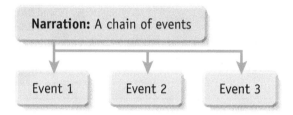

Transitions of **time** signal that the writer is describing when things occurred and in what order. The writer presents an event and then shows when each of the additional details or events flowed from the first event. Thus the details follow a logical order based on time.

Stretching your muscles *before* they are warmed up may cause injury.

Notice that this sentence warns about the relationship between stretching muscles, warming up muscles, and possible injury to muscles. The transition word tells us the order in which certain actions should occur and why. Muscles should be warmed up *before* they are stretched to avoid injury.

Transitions Used in the Time Order Pattern for Events or Stages

after	during	last	often	then
afterward	eventually	later	previously	ultimately
as	finally	meanwhile	second	until
before	first	next	since	when
currently	immediately	now	soon	while

▶ **EXAMPLE** Determine the logical order of the following seven sentences from a college history textbook. Write **1** in front of the sentence that should come first, **2** by the sentence that should come second, **3** by the sentence that should come third, and so on. (**Hint:** Circle the time transition words.)

The Beringia Land Bridge

_____ Eventually, this process dramatically lowered ocean levels.

_____ Ultimately, a land bridge emerged in the area of the Bering Strait.

_____ Today, 56 miles of ocean separate Siberia from Alaska.

_____ At times this land bridge between Asia and America, *Beringia*, may have been 1,000 miles wide.

_____ In turn, these ice caps spread over vast reaches of land.

_____ Year after year water being drawn from the oceans formed into mighty ice caps.

_____ The world was a much colder place 75,000 years ago; a great ice age, known as the Wisconsin glaciation, had begun.

—Adapted from Martin et al., *America and Its People*, 3rd ed., p. 5.

EXPLANATION Compare your answers to the sentences arranged in the order used by the author of a college history textbook. The transitions are in **bold** type. ◄

Textbook
Skills

The Beringia Land Bridge

[1]The world was a much colder place 75,000 years ago; a great ice age, known as the Wisconsin glaciation, had begun. [2]**Year after year** water being drawn from the oceans formed into mighty ice caps. [3]**In turn**, these ice caps spread over vast reaches of land. [4]**Eventually**, this process dramatically lowered ocean levels. [5]**Ultimately**, a land bridge emerged in the area of the Bering Strait. [6]**At times** this land bridge between Asia and America, *Beringia*, may have been 1,000 miles wide. [7]**Today**, 56 miles of ocean separate Siberia from Alaska.

—Adapted from Martin, James Kirby, Roberts, Randy J., Mintz, Steven, McMurry, Linda O., and Jones, James H., *America and Its Peoples, Volume 1: A Mosaic in the Making*, 3rd ed., p. 5.

Practice 4

Determine the logical order for the following six sentences. Write **1** by the sentence that should come first, **2** by the sentence that should come second, **3** by the sentence that should come third, and so on. (**Hint:** Circle the time transition words.)

Textbook
Skills

Initiating

_____ During the first stage of a relationship, we make conscious and unconscious judgments about others.

_____2_____ Although we are cautious at this stage, we have usually sized up the other person within 15 seconds.

_____4_____ Immediately, he stereotyped and classified available women according to his own personal preferences.

_____ Finally, he began a conversation by asking, "Would you like a drink?" "Are you waiting for someone?" "You look like you need company," or "It was nice of you to save me this seat."

_____3_____ For example, David entered a singles' bar and scanned the room for prospective dancing partners.

_____ After narrowing the field to two women, David planned his approach.

—Adapted from Barker, Larry Lee and Gaut, Deborah A., *Communication*, 8th ed., p. 131.

Process: Steps, Stages, or Directions

The process thought pattern for steps, stages, or directions shows actions that can be repeated at any time with similar results. This pattern is used to provide steps or give directions for completing a task.

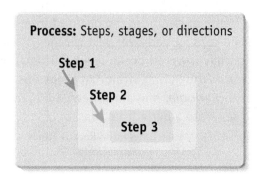

Read the following topic sentences. Circle the words that signal process time order.

1. Follow six simple steps to lose weight.

2. Photosynthesis is the process by which plants harness light energy from the sun.

3. Effective communication occurs through the cycle of sending and receiving messages.

Sentence 1 uses the word *steps* to introduce directions for the reader to follow. Sentence 2 uses the word *process* to indicate that these are stages plants undergo in photosynthesis. Sentence 3 signals a pattern of giving and receiving messages in communication using the word *cycle*. In paragraphs that developed these topic sentences, transitions of time order would likely signal the supporting details.

Transitions Used in the Time Order Pattern for Process

after	during	later	previously	ultimately
afterward	eventually	meanwhile	second	until
as	finally	next	since	when
before	first	now	soon	while
currently	last	often	then	

> **EXAMPLE** The following passage from the government website Small Business Administration uses the time order process to offer advice to people who are starting up their own small businesses. Read the passage and list the major steps to time management for small business owners. (**Hint:** Circle the time order transition words.)

Making Time

¹The first step in learning how to manage your time is to develop a general work schedule. ²Your work schedule should include time for yourself as well as time for the maintenance of your business.

³After you've defined the major elements of your workload, the next step is to prioritize them by identifying critical deadlines, routine maintenance items, and fun/relaxation time. ⁴Answering questions like "How much time do I have to make this decision, finish this task, or contact this person?" will help you to start identifying what needs to be done immediately versus what can wait. ⁵Setting priorities depends on deadlines, how many people you must call to get the information you need, and whether you can delegate or get assistance from others. ⁶If you are involved in group projects, reserve additional time for communication and problem-solving.

⁷Once you have identified your priorities, look at all of your options for achieving them. ⁸Evaluate and move forward with the ones you feel are the most useful for you. ⁹The only time to consider changing approaches mid-task is when you know the change will save time. ¹⁰If you are in doubt, it is usually best to consider staying in the direction you started.

[11]By setting up your work schedule and identifying your priorities, you have already started down the road to more effective time management.

—U.S. Small Business Association. "Manage Your Business." 18 March 2010.

VISUAL *VOCABULARY*

A successful business person must **prioritize** goals. The best synonym for **prioritize**

is _____.

a. complete
b. rank
c. identify

I. _____

_____

II. _____

_____

_____

III. _____

_____

EXPLANATION Compare your answers to the following:

I. The first step in learning how to manage your time is to develop a general work schedule.

II. After you've defined the major elements of your workload, the next step is to prioritize them by identifying critical deadlines, routine maintenance items, and fun/relaxation time.

III. Once you have identified your priorities, look at all of your options for achieving them. ◀

Practice 5

The following passage uses the time order pattern for steps or directions to organize its ideas. Complete the list of steps that follows it by giving the missing details in their proper order. (**Hint:** Circle the time order transition words.)

Textbook
Skills

Creating a Budget

[1]The best way to manage your money and still be able to buy some of the extras you want is to create a budget. [2]A budget is a detailed financial plan used to allocate money for a specific time period. [3]A budget reflects your goals and specifies where your money goes in order to reach these goals. [4]Control and prioritize your spending to match these goals. [5]Be as precise and honest as you can when you are creating and working with a budget.

[6]The first step in creating a budget is to identify goals. [7]Remember, effective goals must be in writing and should provide direction for creating your budget. [8]Next attach financial goals to these personal goals.

[9]The next step in creating a budget is to determine your income by including all money that you receive on an annual (yearly) basis. [10]Then divide by 12 to determine your monthly income. [11]To make it easier to set up the budget, you only need to know your net income. [12]The net income from your paycheck is the amount you have after your employer takes out all taxes and deductions.

[13]After you have identified your monthly income, it is time to determine your expenses. [14]Estimate how much you spend every month in categories such as housing, food, and transportation. [15]The idea is to track exactly where your money is being spent. [16]Ideally, you need to track all of your expenses over the next few months.

[17]First budgets are not perfect. [18]Adjust your personal budget monthly as you identify specific income and expenses.

—Adapted from Anderson, Lydia E. and Bolt, Sandra B., *Professionalism: Skills for Workplace Success*, 2nd ed., pp. 26–27, 29.

Step 1: Identify goals.

Step 2: _____

Step 3: _____

_____

Step 4: _____

Step 5: _____

_____

Estimate how much you spend every month in categories such as housing, food, and transportation.

Step 6: _____

Step 7: Adjust your personal budget monthly as you identify specific income and expenses.

The Space Order Pattern

The **space order pattern** allows authors to describe a person, place, or thing based on its location or the way it is arranged in space. In the space order pattern, also known as spatial order, the writer often uses descriptive details to help readers create vivid mental pictures of the subject being described. An author may choose to describe an object from top to bottom, from bottom to top, from right to left, from left to right, from near to far, from far to near, from inside to outside, or from outside to inside.

Space Order: Descriptive Details

Descriptive detail 1 → Descriptive detail 2 → Descriptive detail 3

Transition words of **space order** signal that the details follow a logical order based on two elements: (1) how the object, place, or person is arranged in space, and (2) the starting point from which the author chooses to begin the description.

Transition Words Used in the Space Order Pattern

above	at the side	below	center	front	middle	there
across	at the top	beneath	close to	here	nearby	under
adjacent	back	beside	down	in	next to	underneath
around	backup	beyond	far away	inside	outside	within
at the bottom	behind	by	farther	left	right	

> **EXAMPLE** Determine a logical order for the following six sentences. Write **1** by the sentence that should come first, **2** in front of the sentence that should come second, **3** in front of the sentence that should come third, **4** in front of the sentence that should come fourth, **5** in front of the sentence that should come fifth, and **6** in front of the sentence that should come last. (**Hint:** Circle the space order transition words.)

_____ In a tropical rain forest, vertical stratification, or layering, provides several discernible strata or layers of plant growth.

_____ At the upper canopy level, the treetops range from 100 to 160 feet, out of which emergents may soar to 200 feet.

_____ The middle layer contains another level of treetops that are covered with vines and air plants.

_____ The lowest and the thinnest layer is the forest floor of seedlings, shoots, and herbaceous plants.

_____ Between the middle layer and the forest floor is the shrub understory; thus very little light passes through the dense middle layer to the forest floor.

_____ This upper canopy is uneven, allowing sunlight to filter through treetops to the middle layer.

EXPLANATION Compare your answers to the sentences arranged in the proper order in the paragraph below. The transition words are in **bold** print.

> [1]**In** a tropical rain forest, vertical stratification, or layering, provides several discernible strata or layers of plant growth. [2]**At the upper** canopy level, the treetops range from 100 to 160 feet, **out of** which emergents may soar to 200 feet. [3]This **upper** canopy is uneven, allowing sunlight to filter through treetops to the middle layer. [4]The **middle** layer contains another level of treetops that are covered with vines and air plants. [5]**Between the middle layer and the forest floor** is the shrub **understory**; thus very little light passes through the dense **middle** layer to the forest **floor**. [6]The **lowest** and the thinnest layer is the forest **floor** of seedlings, shoots, and herbaceous plants. ◀

Practice 6

Textbook Skills

Determine a logical order for the following five sentences. Write **1** in front of the sentence that should come first, **2** in front of the sentence that should come second, **3** in front of the sentence that should come third, **4** in front of the sentence that should come fourth, and **5** in front of the sentence that should come last. (**Hint:** Circle the space order transition words.)

The Anatomy of a Generalized Cell

_____ In turn, the cytoplasm is enclosed by the plasma membrane.

_____ The plasma membrane forms the outer cell boundary.

_____ The nucleus is surrounded by the semifluid cytoplasm.

_____ The nucleus is usually located near the center of the cell.

_____ In general, all cells have three main regions; the nucleus (nu´kle-us), _cytoplasm_ (si´to-plazm´´), and a plasma membrane.

—Marieb, Elaine N., _Essentials of Human Anatomy and Physiology_, 9th ed., p. 66 and figure.

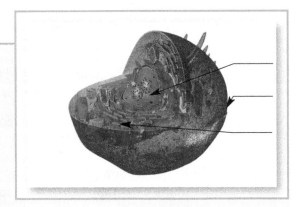

VISUAL _VOCABULARY_

Label the three regions of a generalized cell.

a. cytoplasm
b. nucleus
c. plasma membrane

The Listing Pattern

Often authors want to present an orderly series or set of reasons, details, or points. These details are listed in an order that the author has chosen. Changing the order of the details does not change their meaning. Transitions of addition, such as _and, also,_ and _furthermore,_ are generally used to indicate a **listing pattern**.

Listing Pattern

Idea 1
Idea 2
Idea 3

Transitions of **addition** signal that the writer is adding to an earlier thought. The writer presents an idea and then _adds_ other ideas to deepen or clarify the first idea. Thus, transitions of addition are used to establish the listing pattern.

Addition Transitions Used in the Listing Pattern

also	final	for one thing	last of all	second
and	finally	furthermore	moreover	third
another	first	in addition	next	
besides	first of all	last	one	

> **EXAMPLE** Refer to the box of addition transitions used in the listing pattern. Complete the following paragraph with transitions that show the appropriate relationship between sentences.

Benefits of Weightlifting

Weightlifting is an exercise that offers many benefits. **(1)** _____, increased muscle mass causes the body to burn fat, and lowered body fat reduces several health risks. **(2)** _____, weightlifting builds bone density and thus reduces the risk of osteoporosis (brittle bones). **(3)** _____, weightlifting increases strength, independence, and self-confidence.

EXPLANATION Compare your answers to the following:

Benefits of Weightlifting

[1]Weightlifting is an exercise that offers many benefits. [2]**First,** increased muscle mass causes the body to burn fat, and lowered body fat reduces several health risks. [3]**In addition,** weightlifting builds bone density and thus reduces the risk of osteoporosis (brittle bones). [4]**Finally,** weightlifting increases strength, independence, and self-confidence.

The paragraph on the benefits of weightlifting begins with a general idea that is then followed by three major supporting details. Each detail requires a transition to show addition. ◁

Practice 7

The following paragraph adapted from a college health textbook uses the listing thought pattern. Finish the outline that follows it by listing the major supporting details in their proper order. (**Hint:** Circle the addition transition words.)

Against the Development of GM Foods

Textbook
Skills

[1]Many researchers and health advocates are opposed to the further development and widespread use of genetically modified foods, which they feel carry health risks and could have a negative impact on the ecosystem. [2]For one thing, there haven't been enough independent studies of GM products to confirm that they are safe for consumption. [3]Also, there are potential health risks if GM products approved for animal feed or other uses are mistakenly or inadvertently used in the production of food for human consumption. [4]In addition, the use of GM crops cannot be completely controlled, so they have the potential to damage the environment. [5]For example, inadvertent cross-pollination could lead to the creation of "super weeds"; insect-resistant crops could harm insect species that are not pests; and insect- and disease-resistant crops could prompt the evolution of even more virulent species, which would then require more aggressive control measures, such as the increased use of chemical sprays. [6]Furthermore, because corporations create and patent GM seeds, they will control the market, meaning that poor farmers in the developing world would become reliant on these corporations. [7]This circumstance would be more likely to increase world hunger than to alleviate it. [8]Finally, creating and patenting new life forms is unethical. The introduction of foreign genes into a plant—particularly genes taken from an animal—is offensive to many religious and cultural groups and upsets the balance of nature.

—Adapted from Donatelle, Rebecca, J.,
Access to Health, 12th ed., p. 243.

Against the Development of GM Foods

Many researchers and health advocates are opposed to the further development and widespread use of genetically modified foods, which they feel carry health risks and could have a negative impact on the ecosystem.

A. _____

_____

B. _____

_____

_____

C. _____

_____

D. _____

_____

_____

E. _____

_____

The Classification Pattern

Authors use the **classification pattern** to sort ideas into smaller groups and describe the traits of each group. Each smaller group, called a *subgroup*, is based on shared traits or characteristics. The author lists each subgroup and describes its traits.

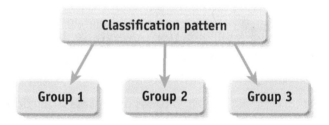

Because groups and subgroups are listed, transitions of addition are also used in this thought pattern. These transitions are coupled with words that indicate classes or groups. Examples of classification signal words are *first type, second kind, another group, order,* and *traits.*

Transitions Used in the Classification Pattern	
another (group, kind, type)	first (group, category, kind, type)
characteristics	second (group, class, kind, type)

> **EXAMPLE** Determine a logical order for the following sentences. Write **1** in front of the sentence that should come first, **2** in front of the sentence that should come second, **3** in front of the sentence that should come third, and **4** in front of the sentence that should come last. (**Hint:** Circle the classification signal words.)

Textbook
Skills

Types of Process Addictions

_____ Another type of process addiction is money addiction, which includes gambling, spending, and borrowing; money addicts develop tolerance and also experience withdrawal symptoms such as depression, anxiety, and anger.

_____ One type of process addiction is work addiction, marked by the compulsive use of work and the work persona to fulfill needs of intimacy, power, and success.

_____ A third type of this kind of addiction is exercise addiction; addictive exercisers abuse exercise the same way that alcoholics abuse alcohol and face effects similar to those found in other addictions: alienation of family and friends, injuries from overdoing it, and a craving for more.

_____ Process addictions are behaviors known to be addictive because they are mood-altering.

—Adapted from Donatelle, Rebecca, J., *Access to Health*,
7th ed., pp. 317–320.

EXPLANATION Compare your answers to the sentences arranged in their proper order in the paragraph below. The transition words are in **bold** type.

Types of Process Addictions

[1]Process addictions are behaviors known to be addictive because they are mood-altering. [2]**One type** of process addiction is work addiction, marked by the compulsive use of work and the work persona to fulfill needs of intimacy, power, and success. [3]**Another type** of process addiction is money addiction, which includes gambling, spending, and borrowing; money addicts develop tolerance and also experience withdrawal symptoms such as depression, anxiety, and anger. [4]A **third type** of this kind of addiction is exercise addiction; addictive exercisers abuse exercise the same way that alcoholics abuse alcohol and face effects similar to those found in other addictions: alienation of family and friends, injuries from overdoing it, and a craving for more.

In this paragraph, transitions of addition work with the classification signal words. In this case, *one*, *another*, and *third* convey the order of the types listed.

Practice 8

The following passage uses the classification pattern of organization. Fill in the outline that follows by giving the missing major details in their proper order. (**Hint:** Circle the classification transition words.)

Types of Volcanoes

1Geologists generally group volcanoes into four main kinds— cinder cones, composite volcanoes, shield volcanoes, and lava domes. **2**The first type, the cinder cone volcanoes, are the simplest type of volcano. **3**They are built from particles and blobs of congealed lava ejected from a single vent. **4**As the gas-charged lava is blown violently into the air, it breaks into small fragments that solidify and fall as *cinders* around the vent to form a circular or oval cone. **5**Most cinder cones have a bowl-shaped *crater* at the summit and rarely rise more than a thousand feet or so above their surroundings.

6The second type of volcano is the *composite* volcano. **7**The essential feature of a composite volcano is a conduit system through which magma from a reservoir deep in the Earth's crust rises to the surface. **8**The volcano is built up by the accumulation of material erupted through the conduit and increases in size as lava, cinders, ash, and so on, are added to its slopes. **9**Most composite volcanoes have a crater at the summit which contains a central vent or a clustered group of vents. **10**Lavas either flow through breaks in the crater wall or issue from fissures on the flanks of the cone. **11**Lava, solidified within the fissures, forms dikes that act as ribs, which greatly strengthen the cone.

12Shield volcanoes, the third type of volcano, are built almost entirely of fluid lava flows. **13**Flow after flow pours out in all directions from a central summit vent, or group of vents, building a broad, gently sloping cone of flat, domical shape, with a profile much like that of a warrior's shield. **14**They are built up slowly by the accretion of thousands of highly fluid lava flows called basalt lava that spread widely over great distances, and then cool as thin, gently dipping sheets. **15**Lavas also commonly erupt from vents along fractures (rift zones) that develop on the flanks of the cone.

16The fourth type, volcanic or lava domes, are formed by relatively small, bulbous masses of lava too viscous to flow any great distance; consequently, on extrusion, the lava piles over and around its vent. **17**A dome grows largely by expansion from within. **18**As it grows, its outer surface cools and hardens, then shatters, spilling loose fragments down its sides.

[19]Some domes form craggy knobs or spines over the volcanic vent, whereas others form short, steep-sided lava flows known as "coulees." [20]Volcanic domes commonly occur within the craters or on the flanks of large composite volcanoes.

—Adapted from Tilling, "Volcanoes," U.S. Geological Survey.

Types of Volcanoes

I. _____

II. _____

III. _____

IV. _____

VISUAL *VOCABULARY*

Which type of volcano is this Hawaiian volcano?

_____

a. cinder cone
b. shield
c. composite
d. lava dome

Textbook Skills

LO3 Develop Textbook Skills: Thought Patterns in Textbooks

Textbook authors often use transitions to make relationships between ideas clear and easy to understand. However, often an author will use more than one type of transition. For example, classification combines words that indicate addition and types. Sometimes addition and time words are used in the same paragraph or passage for a specific purpose. Furthermore, authors may mix thought patterns in the same paragraph or passage. Finally, be aware that relationships between ideas still exist even when transition words are not explicitly stated. The master reader looks for the author's primary thought pattern.

> **EXAMPLE** Read the following paragraphs from college textbooks. Circle the transitions or signal words used in each paragraph. Then identify the primary thought pattern used in the paragraph.

A.   **Reinforcement**

[1]A positive reinforcement is a reward that is given to increase the likelihood that a behavior change will occur. [2]Most positive reinforcers can be classified under five headings. [3]The first type is consumable reinforcers, which are delicious edibles, such as candy, cookies, or gourmet meals. [4]Second, activity reinforcers are opportunities to do something enjoyable, such as to watch TV, go on a vacation, or go swimming. [5]Third, manipulative reinforcers are incentives, such as getting a lower rent in exchange for mowing the lawn or the promise of a better grade for doing an extra-credit project. [6]A fourth type of positive reinforcer is the possessional reinforcers, which are tangible rewards, such as a new TV or a sports car. [7]The final type consists of social reinforcers that express signs of appreciation, approval, or love, such as loving looks, affectionate hugs, and praise.

—Adapted from Donatelle, Rebecca J., *Health: The Basics*, 5th ed., p. 21.

_____ The primary thought pattern of the paragraph is
      a. time order.   b. classification.

B.   **Interpersonal Perception**

[1]Interpersonal perception is a continuous series of processes that blend into one another. [2]For convenience of discussion we can separate them into five stages. [3]During the first stage, you sense, you pick up some kind of stimulation. [4]Next, you organize the stimuli in some way. [5]Third, you interpret and evaluate what you perceive. [6]Then, you store it in memory, and finally, in stage five, you retrieve it when needed.

—Adapted from DeVito, Joseph A., *The Interpersonal Communication Book*, 10th ed., p. 91.

_____ The primary thought pattern of the paragraph is
      a. time order.   b. listing.

EXPLANATION Compare your answers to the following answers.

Passage A, "Reinforcement," is organized by (b) classification.

Passage B, "Interpersonal Perception," is organized by (a) time order. ◀

Practice 9

Read the following paragraph taken from a college anthropology textbook. Circle the transitions or signal words used in the passage. Then identify the primary thought pattern.

Nonhuman Communication

[1]Systems of communication are not unique to human beings, nor is communication by sound. [2]Other animal species communicate in a variety of ways. [3]One way is by sound. [4]A bird may communicate by a call that "this is my territory"; a squirrel may utter a cry that leads other squirrels to flee from danger. [5]Another means of animal communication is odor. [6]An ant releases a chemical when it dies, and its fellows then carry it away to the compost heap. [7]Apparently the communication is highly effective; a healthy ant painted with the death chemical will be dragged to the funeral heap again and again. [8]Bees use another means of communication, body movement, to convey the location of food sources. [9]Karl von Frisch discovered that the black Austrian honeybee—by choosing a round dance, a wagging dance, or a short, straight run—can communicate not only the precise direction of the source of food but also its distance from the hive.

—Ember, Carol R., Ember, Melvin R., and Peregrine, Peter, *Human Evolution and Culture: Highlights of Anthropology*, 7th ed., p. 224.

_____ The primary thought pattern used in the paragraph is
   a. time order.   b. listing.

Apply Information Literacy Skills

LO4 # Academic, Personal, and Career Applications of Transitions and Thought Patterns

As you learned in Chapter 6, understanding how knowledge is organized is a basic information literacy skill. Transitions and thought patterns also help organize information and ideas by focusing attention on key concepts and relationships. Transitions and thought patterns connect specific details to logically support a main idea. The transitions, or signal words, of a thought pattern help you predict what is to come. When you understand an idea's structure, you can monitor your comprehension as you read. Transitions and thought patterns show how ideas are connected. In academic, personal, and career situations you will use the skills that you have learned in this chapter in several ways:

- Recognize your own need to identify transitions and thought patterns.
- Analyze information to see the relationships among ideas.
- Determine the author's use of a thought pattern to develop a main idea.

Academic Application

Assume you are taking a college course in sociology. You are required to give an in-class speech about a topic of your choice. You have chosen to speak about culture.

- **Before Reading:** Skim the table of contents and identify the page numbers of the sections you need to read to define culture. Use the topic and thought pattern to create a pre-reading question to guide your reading.
- **During Reading:** Annotate the details in the passage that answer your pre-reading question.
- **After Reading:** In the space following the passage, fill in the concept map with details you will use in your speech.

Before Reading: Page numbers of relevant information: _____

Pre-Reading Question: _____

—Henslin, James M., *Sociology: A Down-to-Earth Approach,* 11th ed.

What Is Culture?

[1]What is culture? [2]The concept is sometimes easier to grasp by description than by definition. [3]For example, suppose you meet a young woman from India who has just arrived in the United States. [4]That her culture is different from yours is immediately evident. [5]You first see it in her clothing, jewelry, makeup, and hairstyle. [6]Next you hear it in her speech. [7]It then becomes apparent by her gestures. [8]Later, you might hear her express unfamiliar beliefs about relationships or what is valuable in life. [9]All of these characteristics are indicative of culture—the language, beliefs, values, norms, behaviors, and even material objects that are passed from one generation to the next.

[10]In northern Africa, I was surrounded by a culture quite different from mine. [11]It was evident in everything I saw and heard. [12]The **material culture**—such things as jewelry, art, buildings, weapons, machines, and even eating utensils, hairstyles, and clothing provided a sharp contrast to what I was used to seeing. [13]There is nothing inherently "natural" about material culture. [14]That is, it is no more natural (or unnatural) to wear gowns on the street than it is to wear jeans.

[15]I also found myself immersed in an unfamiliar **nonmaterial culture,** that is, a group's ways of thinking (its beliefs, values, and other assumptions about the world) and doing (its **common patterns of behavior,** including language, gestures, and other forms of interaction). [16]North African assumptions that it is acceptable to stare at others in public and to push people aside to buy tickets are examples of nonmaterial culture. [17]So are U.S. assumptions that it is wrong to do either of these things. [18]Like material culture, neither custom is "right." [19]People simply become comfortable with the customs they learn during childhood, and—as when I visited northern Africa—uncomfortable when their basic assumptions about life are challenged.

—Henslin, James M., *Sociology: A Down-to-Earth Approach*, 11th ed., p. 36.

After Reading Concept Map of Key Ideas

Terms	Definitions	Examples
Culture	_____	_____
	_____	_____
	_____	_____
_____	_____	jewelry, art, buildings, weapons, machines, and even eating utensils, hairstyles, and clothing
	_____	
_____	a group's ways of thinking and doing	_____
_____		_____

Personal Application

Assume you are planning your family vacation to Florida, and your children want to visit a theme park, but your husband wants to stay on the water. You want to plan a trip that explores all your family's interests. You begin your vacation destination research by comparing theme parks on the Internet. Predict the search term used that produced the following results in the screen shot below. Then complete the reading activities.

Key search term: _____

_____

- **Before Reading:** List the activities you want to experience at a theme park.
- **During Reading:** Annotate the information to highlight details that will help you decide which theme park to visit.
- **After Reading:** In the space following the passage, choose the right theme park for your family. State your reasons.

Features I want in a theme park: _____

_____

_____

Decision: _____

_____

_____

_____

Compare Florida Amusement Parks

Sort By Number of Roller Co... ▼ High to Low

Busch Gardens Tampa Bay

4.3 ☆☆☆☆☆ 6 ratings

| Number of Roller Coasters | 8 | Adult Admission Price | $85 |
| Location | | Tampa, Florida | |

PARK TICKETS

☐ COMPARE   SEE DETAILS ›

Universal's Islands of Adventure

3.1 ☆☆☆☆☆ 7 ratings

| Number of Roller Coasters | 5 | Adult Admission Price | $88 |
| Location | | Orlando, Florida | |

PARK TICKETS

☐ COMPARE   SEE DETAILS ›

SeaWorld Orlando

3.7 ☆☆☆☆☆ 6 ratings

| Number of Roller Coasters | 4 | Adult Admission Price | $89 |
| Location | | Orlando, Florida | |

BUY NOW

☐ COMPARE   SEE DETAILS ›

Legoland Florida

3.8 ☆☆☆☆☆ 4 ratings

| Number of Roller Coasters | 4 | Adult Admission Price | $79 |
| Location | | Winter Haven, Florida | |

PARK TICKETS

☐ COMPARE   SEE DETAILS ›

Disney's Magic Kingdom

3.5 ☆☆☆☆☆ 2 ratings

| Number of Roller Coasters | 3 | Adult Admission Price | $89 |
| Location | | Lake Buena Vista, Florida | |

PARK TICKETS

☐ COMPARE   SEE DETAILS ›

Santa's Enchanted Forest

☆☆☆☆☆

| Number of Roller Coasters | 3 | Adult Admission Price | $27 |
| Location | | Miami, Florida | |

PARK TICKETS

☐ COMPARE   SEE DETAILS ›

—<http://amusement-parks.findthebest.com/d/a/Florida>

Career Application

Assume you are the manager of a corporate media and appliance store. You would like to help your staff meet their sales goals, so that your team will be awarded their quarterly bonus. You have made copies of the following article for your staff to read when they begin their next shifts.

- **Before Reading:** Skim the memo. Write a pre-reading question to guide your thinking.
- **During Reading:** Annotate the key details.
- **After Reading:** In the space following the passage fill in the concept map with key details to review with your employees when they begin their next shift.

Pre-Reading Question: _____

_____

_____

To: Assistant Managers and Full-time Sales Staff

From: Monica Brown, Store Manager

RE: Appliance Sales Tips article; please read before your next shift.

Appliance Sales Techniques

By Marilyn Lindblad, Demand Media

Home appliances are big-ticket items that last a long time—a gas range can last 15 years, and a refrigerator has a life expectancy of 13 years. Many homeowners replace an appliance before it reaches the end of its useful life because they don't like the way the old appliances look, and they realize that new appliances are more efficient and innovative. Several sales techniques help appliance sales businesses persuade customers to replace their appliances with new models.

Bundling

Bundling appliances means that the more appliances a customer buys, the more money she saves. Stores offer savings when a customer purchases a "bundle"—two or more appliances—at once. A customer could get a volume discount of 5 percent for two appliances, 10 percent for three or 15 percent for four. The store moves its inventory and makes a profit, and the customer gets a good deal.

Demonstrations

Another way to attract customers to the store and create demand for new appliances is to feature cooking demonstrations at the store. A local celebrity chef or a gregarious employee who can cook entertains shoppers while creating a meal that highlights the features and benefits of new cook-tops, stoves, convection ovens and microwave ovens. On a smaller scale, store staff uses a featured oven to bake cookies or serve ice cream and beverages from a featured refrigerator-freezer.

Extras

Adding extra value is another effective sales technique. Extended service warranties give customers peace of mind that, once they buy an appliance, they won't have to pay for unexpected repairs. Offering financing that gives customers up to 90 days to pay for the merchandise without incurring finance charges is another enhancement that helps sales staff close the deal. Offering free delivery and set-up of the customer's new appliances and free removal of the old ones makes buying new appliances even easier.

Online Marketing

An appliance dealer should maintain an online presence that includes social networking and e-commerce. Social networking sites enable dealers to connect with their customers and promote new products and special sales. An e-commerce site captures sales from customers who prefer to shop online. It also provides information for customers who like to research appliances before they buy.

—Reproduced with permission from Demand Media.

Bundling	
Demonstrations	
Extras	
Online Marketing	

REVIEW TEST 1

Score (number correct) _____ x 10 = _____ %

Visit MyReadingLab to take this test online and receive feedback and guidance on your answers.

Transitions and Thought Patterns

Fill in each blank with a transition from the box. Use each transition once. Then answer the questions that follow the paragraph.

already	and	in addition	when
also	another	one	

Barriers to Memory

It is likely that you will remember things that support your position **(1)** _____ forget or distort information that contradicts your current beliefs. **(2)** _____ reason, of course, may be selective attention; you focus on things you want to hear or things you expect to hear. Distortion can **(3)** _____ be explained, in part, through schema theory. Ideas that fit into your existing framework are stored more readily than bits of information that don't make sense in light of what you **(4)** _____ know. **(5)** _____, threatening or unpleasant experiences are often blocked, or repressed, while positive images remain vivid. **(6)** _____ reason why you forget is that the information you are trying to store in long-term memory becomes mixed with information already in your memory system. **(7)** _____ these two information sets become confused, there is a "backward" impact of new learning on the material stored earlier.

—Adapted from Brownell, Judi, *Listening: Attitudes,
Principles, and Skills,* 2nd ed., pp. 155–156.

_____ **8.** The relationship signaled by the word **already** is
  a. time order.   b. classification.

_____ **9.** The relationship signaled by the transition word **one** is
  a. addition.   b. space order.

_____ **10.** The overall thought pattern of the paragraph is
  a. listing.   b. time order.

REVIEW TEST 2

Score (number correct) _____ x 10 = _____ %

Visit MyReadingLab to take this test online and receive feedback and guidance on your answers.

Transitions

Select a transition word for each of the blanks. Then identify the type of transition you chose.

A. The thief had bought thousands of dollars worth of goods with Aimee's credit

card _____ she even knew it was missing.

_____ **1.** The best transition word for sentence A is
   a. meanwhile.   c. before.
   b. after.

_____ **2.** The relationship between the ideas in sentence A is one of
   a. classification.   b. time order.

B. Every cell has a plasma membrane which forms its _____ border
   and sets the cell off from its fluid environment.

_____ **3.** The best transition word for the sentence above is
   a. another.   c. one.
   b. outside.

_____ **4.** The relationship between the ideas above is one of
   a. space order.   b. addition.

C. Everything inside a cell _____ the plasma membrane and the
   nucleus is called the cytoplasm.

_____ **5.** The best transition word for the sentence above is
   a. between.   c. since.
   b. before.

_____ **6.** The relationship between the ideas above is one of
   a. listing.   b. space order.

D. Poetry can be broken into two very broad groups. The first type, dramatic poetry,

   tells a story using characters, setting, and conflict. The _____, lyric
   poetry, directly expresses the emotions of the poet.

_____ **7.** The best transition word or phrase for the sentences in section D is
    a. additional part.   c. later time.
    b. second type.

_____ **8.** The relationship between the ideas in the sentences in section D is one of
    a. classification.   b. time order.

E.   [1]For producing electricity, hydropower has two clear advantages over fossil fuels. [2]First, it is renewable; as long as precipitation falls from the sky and fills rivers and reservoirs, we can use water to turn turbines. [3]The _____ advantage of hydropower over fossil fuels is its cleanliness. [4]No carbon compounds are burned in the production of hydropower, so no carbon dioxide or other pollutants are emitted into the atmosphere. [5]Of course, fossil fuels are used in constructing and maintaining dams. [6]More-over, recent evidence indicates that reservoirs release the greenhouse gas methane as a result of anaerobic decay in deep water. [7]Overall, hydro-power accounts for only a fraction of the greenhouse gas emissions typical of fossil fuel combustion.

—Withgott, Jay H. and Brennan, Scott R., *Essential Environment: The Science Behind the Stories*, 3rd ed., p. 363.

_____ **9.** The best transition word for the blank in sentence 3 is
    a. later.   c. second.
    b. addition.

_____ **10.** The main thought pattern of the paragraph is
    a. time order.   b. listing.

VISUAL *VOCABULARY*

The Grand Coulee Dam in Washington State, the largest electric power-producing facility in the United States, is an example of hydropower. The best meaning of **hydro** is

_____.

  a. electric   c. wind
  b. pressure   d. water

REVIEW TEST 3

Score (number correct) _____ x 5 = _____ %

Visit MyReadingLab to take this test online and receive feedback and guidance on your answers.

Transitions and Thought Patterns

Textbook Skills

The following passage appears in a college psychology textbook. Before you read, skim the passage and answer the Before Reading questions. Read the passage. Then answer the After Reading questions.

Categorizing Personality by Types

[1]We are always categorizing people according to distinguishing features. [2]These include college class, academic major, sex, and race. [3]Some personality theorists also group people into distinct, nonoverlapping categories that are called personality **types**. [4]Personality types are all-or-none **phenomena**, not matters of degree: If a person is assigned to one type, he or she could not belong to any other type within that system. [5]Many people like to use personality types in everyday life because they help simplify the complex process of understanding other people.

[6]One of the earliest type theories was originated in the 5th century B.C. by Hippocrates, the Greek physician who gave medicine the Hippocratic Oath. [7]He theorized that the body contained four basic fluids, or **humors**, each associated with a particular temperament, a pattern of emotions and behaviors. [8]In the 2nd century A.D., a later Greek physician, Galen, suggested that an individual's personality depended on which humor was predominant in his or her body. [9]Galen paired Hippocrates's body humors with personality temperaments according to the following scheme:

- [10]**Blood**. Sanguine temperament: cheerful and active
- [11]**Phlegm**. **Phlegmatic** temperament: apathetic and sluggish
- [12]**Black bile**. Melancholy temperament: sad and brooding
- [13]**Yellow bile**. Choleric temperament: irritable and excitable

[14]The theory proposed by Galen was believed for centuries, up through the Middle Ages, although it has not held up to modern scrutiny.

[15]In modern times, William Sheldon (1898–1977) originated a type theory that related physique to temperament. [16]Sheldon (1942) assigned people to three categories based on their body builds: *endomorphic* (fat, soft, round), *mesomorphic* (muscular, rectangular, strong), or *ectomorphic*

(thin, long, fragile). [17]Sheldon believed that endomorphs are relaxed, fond of eating, and sociable. [18]Mesomorphs are physical people, filled with energy, courage, and assertive tendencies. [19]Ectomorphs are brainy, artistic, and introverted; they would think about life, rather than consuming it or acting on it. [20]For a period of time, Sheldon's theory was sufficiently influential that nude "posture" photographs were taken of thousands of students at U.S. colleges like Yale and Wellesley to allow researchers to study the relationships between body type and life factors. [21]However, like Hippocrates's much earlier theory, Sheldon's notion of body types has proven to be of very little value in predicting an individual's behavior (Tyler, 1965).

[22]More recently, Frank Sulloway (1996) has proposed a contemporary type theory based on birth order. [23]Are you the firstborn child (or only child) in your family, or are you a laterborn child? [24]Because you can take on only one of these birth positions, Sulloway's theory fits the criteria for being a type theory. [25](For people with unusual family constellations—for example, a very large age gap between two children—Sulloway still provides ways of categorizing individuals.) [26]Sulloway makes birth-order predictions based on Darwin's idea that organisms diversify to find niches in which they will survive. [27]According to Sulloway, firstborns have a ready-made niche: They immediately command their parents' love and attention; they seek to maintain that initial attachment by identifying and complying with their parents. [28]By contrast, laterborn children need to find a different niche—one in which they don't so clearly follow their parents' example. [29]As a consequence, Sulloway characterizes laterborns as "born to rebel": "they seek to excel in those domains where older siblings have not already established superiority. [30]Laterborns typically cultivate openness to experience—a useful strategy for anyone who wishes to find a novel and successful niche in life" (Sulloway, 1996, p. 353).

—Gerrig, Richard J. and Zimbardo, Philip G.,
Psychology and Life, 19th ed., p. 407.

Before Reading

Vocabulary in Context

_____ **1.** The word **phenomena** in sentence 4 means

    a. spectacles.   c. facts.

    b. experiences.   d. features.

_____ **2.** The best meaning of the word **humors** in sentence 7 is
   a. funny qualities.   c. effects of body fluids.
   b. emotions.   d. behaviors.

_____ **3.** The best synonym for the word **phlegmatic** in sentence 10 is
   a. unmotivated.   c. calm.
   b. sickly.   d. determined.

After Reading

Concept Maps and Graphic Organizers

4–15. Complete the following two-column notes with information from the passage.

Categorizing Personality by Types	
Theorist	**Theories of Personality Type**
4. _____	**5.** _____ cheerful and active
	6. Phlegm. Phlegmatic temperament: _____
	Black bile. Melancholy temperament: sad and brooding
	7. _____ _____
8. _____	**9.** _____ (fat, soft, round)
	10. Mesomorphic _____ _____
	11. _____
12. _____	**13.** _____ command parents' love and attention; identify and comply with parents
	14. _____ are born to rebel; they seek to excel in those domains where older siblings have not already established superiority

Central Ideas

_____ **15.** Which sentence states the central idea of the essay?

a. sentence 1   c. sentence 3

b. sentence 2   d. sentence 5

Supporting Details

_____ **16.** Sentence 20 states a

a. a main idea.   c. minor supporting detail.

b. major supporting detail.

Transitions and Thought Patterns

_____ **17.** What thought pattern does the word **types** in sentence 3 signal?

a time order   c. space order

b. classification

_____ **18.** What is the relationship of ideas within sentence 16?

a. listing   c. space order

b. time order

_____ **19.** What is the relationship of ideas between sentence 7 and sentence 8?

a. time order   c. listing

b. classification

_____ **20.** Based on the title, the main thought pattern of the passage is

a. time order.   c. classification.

b. space order.

SUMMARY RESPONSE

Restate the author's central idea in your own words. Include the two major thought patterns used by the authors in your summary. Begin your summary response with the following: _The central idea of "Categorizing Personality Types" by Gerrig and Zimbardo is . . ._

WHAT DO YOU THINK?

Assume you are taking a college psychology class, and your teacher has given you the following assignment: Choose a fictional character from a television show, movie, book, graphic novel, etc., and categorize his or her personality type. Consider the following prompts to help your writing process:

- Analyze the character using each of the personality types described in the passage.
- Describe the moods and behaviors of the character to support your use of each label.

REVIEW TEST 4

Score (number correct) _____ x 10 = _____ %

Visit MyReadingLab to take this test online and receive feedback and guidance on your answers.

Transitions and Thought Patterns

Before Reading: Survey the following passage from the college textbook *Life on Earth*. Skim the passage, noting the words in **bold** print. Answer the Before Reading questions that follow the passage. Then read the passage. Next, answer the After Reading questions. Use the discussion and writing topics as after reading activities.

Vocabulary Preview

mammalian (3): related to mammals, animals that have a spine and milk glands

mechanoreceptor (3): a nerve ending that responds to a mechanical stimulus (as in a change of pressure)

auditory (12): hearing

cerebellum (12): located at the back of the brain, the control center for muscle tone, balance, and coordination of movement

pharynx (14): a hollow tube that begins behind the nose and ends at the top of the windpipe

membrane (17): a thin barrier that surrounds a cell or parts of a cell

receptors (20): receivers

basilar (21): located at the base of a structure

cilia (22): short, hairlike projections from the surface of certain cells. The movement of cilia aids the movement of cells and fluids

embedded (23): fixed in, set in

gelatinous (23): a jelly-like texture, quality, or consistency

potentials (25): stored energies

axons (26): large extensions of nerve cells, reaching from the cell body to the ends of other nerve cells or muscles

Textbook
Skills

The Perception of Sound Is a Specialized Type of Mechanoreception

[1]Sound is produced by any vibrating object—a drum, vocal cords, or the speaker of your CD player. [2]These vibrations, or sound waves, are transmitted through the air and intercepted by our ears, which convert them to signals that our brains interpret as the direction, pitch, and loudness of sound. [3]The **mammalian** ear consists of a variety of structures (for example, the outer ear and eardrum) that transmit vibrations to specialized **mechanoreceptor** cells deep in the inner ear.

The Ear Converts Sound Waves into Electrical Signals

[4]The ear of humans and most other vertebrates consists of three parts: the outer, middle, and inner ear. [5]The *outer ear* consists of the *pinna* and *auditory canal*. [6]The pinna is the flap of skin-covered cartilage attached to the surface of the head. [7]The pinna collects sound waves and modifies them in various ways. [8]Humans and other fairly large animals determine sound direction by differences in *when* sound arrives at the two ears and in *how loud* it is in each ear. [9]The shape and mobility of the pinna further contribute to sound localization. [10]Bats have probably the most precise sound localization in the animal kingdom. [11]Insect-eating bats emit extremely high-pitched shrieks that reflect off moths and other insect prey. [12]Large ears, a highly developed **auditory** cortex, and an enormous **cerebellum** (for precise control of flying) combine to allow the bats to intercept their flying prey in pitch darkness.

[13]The air-filled auditory canal conducts the sound waves to the *middle ear*, consisting of the *tympanic membrane,* or *eardrum;* three tiny bones called the *hammer, anvil,* and *stirrup;* and the auditory tube (also called the *Eustachian tube*). [14]The auditory tube connects the middle ear to the **pharynx** and equalizes the air pressure between the middle ear and the atmosphere.

[15]Sound waves traveling down the auditory canal vibrate the tympanic membrane, which in turn vibrates the hammer, the anvil, and the stirrup. [16]These bones transmit vibrations to the *inner ear,* which contains the spiral-shaped *cochlea.* [17]The stirrup bone transmits vibrations to the fluid within the cochlea by vibrating a **membrane** on the cochlea called the *oval window.* [18]The *round window* is a second membrane that allows fluid within the cochlea to shift back and forth as the stirrup bone vibrates the oval window.

Sound Is Converted into Electrical Signals in the Cochlea

[19]The cochlea, in cross section, consists of three fluid-filled canals. [20]The central canal houses the **receptors** and the supporting structures

that activate them in response to sound vibrations. [21]The floor of this central canal is the *basilar membrane*, on top of which sit mechanoreceptors called *hair cells*. [22]Hair cells have small cell bodies topped by hairlike projections that resemble stiff **cilia**. [23]Some of these hairs are **embedded** in a **gelatinous** structure called the *tectorial membrane*.

[24]The oval window passes vibrations from the bones of the middle ear to the fluid in the cochlea, which in turn vibrates the basilar membrane relative to the tectorial membrane. [25]This movement bends the hairs of the hair cells, producing receptor **potentials**. [26]The hair cells _____ release **neurotransmitters** onto neurons whose **axons** form the auditory nerve. [27]Action potentials triggered in these axons travel to auditory processing centers within the brain.

[28]The structures of the inner ear allow us to perceive *loudness* (the magnitude of sound vibrations) and *pitch* (the frequency of sound vibrations). [29]Soft sounds cause small vibrations, which bend the hairs only slightly and result in a small receptor potential and a low rate of action potentials in axons of the auditory nerve. [30]Loud sounds cause large vibrations, which cause greater bending of the hairs, a larger receptor potential, and a high rate of action potentials in the axons of the auditory nerve. [31]Loud sounds sustained for a long time can damage the hair cells, resulting in hearing loss, a fate suffered by many rock musicians and their fans. [32]In fact, many sounds in our everyday environment have the potential to damage hearing, especially if exposure to them is prolonged.

[33]The perception of pitch is a little more complex. [34]The basilar membrane resembles a harp in shape and stiffness: narrow and stiff at the end near the oval window but wider and more flexible near the tip of the cochlea. [35]In a harp, the short, tight strings produce high notes and the long, looser strings produce low notes. [36]In the basilar membrane, the **progressive** change in shape and stiffness causes each portion to vibrate most strongly to a particular frequency of sound: high notes near the oval window and low notes near the tip of the cochlea. [37]The brain interprets signals from hair cells near the oval window as high-pitched sound, whereas signals from hair cells located progressively closer to the tip of the cochlea are interpreted as increasingly lower in pitch. [38]Young people with undamaged cochleas can detect sounds from about 30 vibrations per second (very low pitched) to about 20,000 vibrations per second (very high pitched).

—Audesirk, Teresa, Audesirk, Gerald, and Byers, Bruce E.,
Life on Earth, 5th ed., pp. 476–477.

Before Reading

Vocabulary

1–2. Study the following chart of word parts. Read the sentences in which the words appear for context clues. Then use your own words to define the terms.

Prefix	Meaning	Root	Meaning	Suffix	Meaning
pro-	before	*gress*	to step	*-er*	doer
trans-	across	*mitt*	to send	*-ive*	of, relating to, the quality or nature of
		neuron	nerve cell		

1. In sentence 26, **neurotransmitters** are _____

_____ .

2. In sentence 36, **progressive** means _____

_____ .

After Reading

3–5. Central Idea and Supporting Details

Complete the following study notes with information from the passage and the illustration of the ear in the Visual Vocabulary activity.

Thesis Statement: (3) _____

_____ .

Questions Based on Major Supporting Details	Answers Based on Minor Supporting Details
What does the outer ear consist of?	the flap-like pinna and the auditory canal
What does the middle ear consist of?	the tympanic membrane (eardrum); three bones called the hammer, **(4)** _____, and stirrup; and the auditory tube (Eustachian tube)
What does the inner ear consist of?	the **(5)** _____ (three fluid-filled chambers); the basilar membrane; hair cells, and the auditory nerve

VISUAL *VOCABULARY*

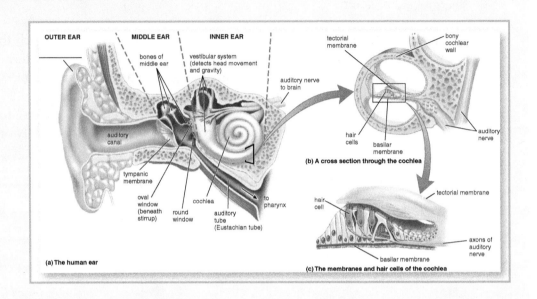

▲ **The Human Ear**

—Audesirk, Teresa, Audesirk, Gerald, and Byers, Bruce E.,
Life on Earth, 5th ed., Figure 24-16a (p. 476).

Transitions and Thought Patterns

_____ **6.** The main thought pattern for the fifth paragraph (sentences 19–23) is
    a. time order.   c. listing.
    b. space order.

_____ **7.** What is the relationship of ideas within sentence 4?
    a. time order   c. classification
    b. space order

_____ **8.** What is the main relationship of ideas between sentences 13 and 14?
    a. space order   c. listing
    b. time order

_____ **9.** Which is the best transition word(s) for the blank in sentence 26?
   a. then   c. in addition
   b. after

_____ **10.** What is the relationship of ideas in sentence 34?
   a. time order   c. classification
   b. space order

SUMMARY RESPONSE

Restate the author's central idea in your own words. Include the two major thought patterns used by the authors in your summary. Begin your summary response with the following: *The central idea of "The Perception of Sound Is a Specialized Type of Mechanoreception" by Audesirk, Audesirk, and Byers is . . .*

WHAT DO YOU THINK?

Assume you are writing a series of articles for your college newspaper about the relationship between classroom learning and real life. This week, you are writing about biology's relevance to the real world. Write about particular lifestyle choices that may damage human hearing. Consider the following prompts to help your writing process:

- Use details from the passage to explain the lifestyle dangers that damage hearing.
- List several actions your readers should take to protect their hearing.

After Reading About Transitions and Thought Patterns

Before you move on to the Mastery Tests on transitions and thought patterns, take time to reflect on your learning and performance by answering the following questions. Write your answers in your notebook.

- How has my knowledge base or prior knowledge about transitions and thought patterns changed?
- Based on my studies, how do I think I will perform on the Mastery Test(s)? Why do I think my scores will be above average, average, or below average? (Note: An additional fourth Mastery Test may be found in MyReadingLab.)

■ Would I recommend this chapter to other students who want to learn more about transitions and thought patterns? Why or why not?

Test your understanding of what you have learned about transitions and thought patterns for master readers by completing the Chapter 7 Review.

Name _____ Section_____

Date _____ **Score** (number correct) _____ x 10 = _____ %

Visit MyReadingLab to take this test online and receive feedback and guidance on your answers.

A. The following information is from a college science textbook. Determine a logical order for the ideas to create a paragraph that makes sense. Indicate the proper order of ideas by writing **1, 2, 3, 4,** and **5** in the spaces provided.

Textbook
Skills

_____ Prey have evolved a number of defense mechanisms.

_____ A fourth and more subtle defense is the timing of reproduction so that most of the offspring are produced in a short period of time.

_____ One defense mechanism is cryptic coloration, which includes colors, patterns, shapes, and postures that allow prey to blend into the background.

_____ A third defense mechanism employs physical means; for example, clams, armadillos, turtles, and numerous beetles all withdraw into their armor coat or shell when danger approaches.

_____ Another defense is behavioral, such as alarm calls and distraction displays.

—Adapted from Smith, Thomas and Smith, Robert Leo,
Elements of Ecology, 4th ed., pp. 198–199.

_____ **6.** What overall thought pattern is shown in the paragraph?
   a. time order
   b. listing

VISUAL *VOCABULARY*

The best synonym for the phrase **cryptic coloration** is

_____ .

   a. camouflage
   b. hidden
   c. colorful

▶ An excellent example of **cryptic coloration** is the Peppered Moth.

B. Read the following paragraph from a college communications textbook. Fill in each blank (**7–9**) with the correct transition from the box. Use each transition once.

also	in addition	last

Persuasive Proof

Textbook
Skills

In a persuasive speech, your support is proof, and your proof is material that offers evidence, argument, and motivational appeal. **(7)** _____, your support establishes your credibility and reputation. You can persuade your audience with several types of support. First, logical support is built on specific examples and general concepts. Logical supports **(8)** _____ come from comparisons and contrasts, from causes and effects, and from signs. Second, motivational support appeals to the emotions of your audience. These supports appeal to their desire for status, financial gain, or increased self-esteem. The **(9)** _____ type, credibility appeals, are built on your own personal reputation or trustworthiness. This type of appeal rests on your skill, high moral character, and personal charm.

—Adapted from DeVito, Joseph A., *Essentials of Human Communication*, 4th ed., p. 308.

_____ **10.** What thought pattern is used in the paragraph?
  a. classification
  b. time order

Name _____ Section_____

Date _____ **Score** (number correct) _____ x 10 = _____ %

Visit MyReadingLab to take this test online and receive feedback and guidance on your answers.

A. Read the following paragraph from a college biology textbook.

How Do Biologists Study Life?

Textbook Skills

[1]Biology is the science of life. [2]Knowledge in biology is acquired through the scientific method. [3]First, an observation is made, which leads to a question. [4]Then a hypothesis is formulated that suggests a possible answer to the question. [5]The hypothesis is used to predict the outcome of further observations or experiments. [6]A conclusion is then drawn about the hypothesis. [7]Conclusions are based only on results that can be shared, verified, and repeated. [8]A scientific theory is a general explanation of natural phenomena, developed through extensive and reproducible experiments and observations.

—Audesirk, Teresa, Audesirk, Gerald, and Byers,
Bruce E., *Life on Earth,* 5th ed., p. 13.

_____ **1.** The relationship between sentence 3 and sentence 4 is based on
  a. time.   b. addition.

_____ **2.** The overall thought pattern that organizes the paragraph is
  a. classification.   b. time order.

B. Read the following information from a college mathematics textbook.

Types of Real Numbers

Textbook Skills

[1]The set of real numbers is the set of all numbers corresponding to points on the number line. [2]In addition, real numbers consist of several levels of relationships among various kinds of numbers. [3]First, real numbers are divided into two subsets: rational numbers and irrational numbers. [4]Rational numbers are next classified either as rational numbers that are not integers (such as 2/3, –4/5, and 8.2) or as integers. [5]Three types of integers exist: positive integers (1, 2, 3 . . .), zero (0), and negative integers (–1, –2, –3 . . .). [6]Every rational number has a point on the number line. [7]However, there are points on the line for which there are no rational numbers. [8]These points correspond to the second subset of real numbers—irrational numbers. [9]One example is the number π, which is

used to find the area and the circumference of a circle. [10]_____ example of an irrational number is the square root of 2, named $\sqrt{2}$.

—Adapted from Bittinger, Marvin L. and Beecher, Judith A., *Introductory and Intermediate Algebra: A Combined Approach*, 2nd ed., pp. 14–17.

_____ **3.** Which transition word best fits the blank in sentence 10?
  a. First   c. Another
  b. Third

_____ **4.** What is the thought pattern used in the paragraph?
  a. classification
  b. time order

Complete the concept map with the information from the passage.

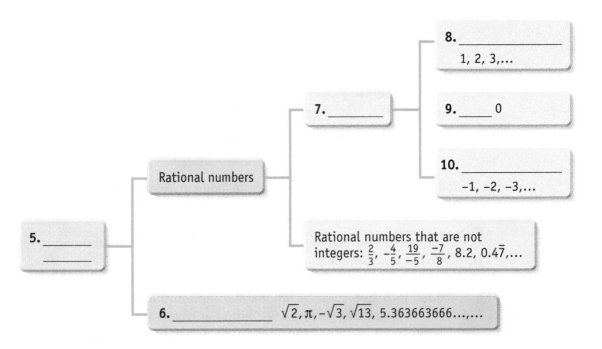

8. _____
1, 2, 3,...

7. _____

9. _____ 0

10. _____
–1, –2, –3,...

Rational numbers

Rational numbers that are not integers: $\frac{2}{3}$, $-\frac{4}{5}$, $\frac{19}{-5}$, $\frac{-7}{8}$, 8.2, 0.4$\overline{7}$,...

5. _____

6. _____ $\sqrt{2}, \pi, -\sqrt{3}, \sqrt{13}$, 5.363663666...,...

—Adapted from Bittinger, Marvin L. and Beecher, Judith A., *Introductory and Intermediate Algebra: A Combined Approach*, 2nd ed., p. 17.

Name _____ Section_____

Date _____ **Score** (number correct) _____ x 10 = _____ %

Visit MyReadingLab to take this test online and receive feedback and guidance on your answers

A. Read the following passage from a college health textbook.

Choosing a Romantic Partner

¹The choice of a relationship partner is influenced by more than just the chemical and psychological processes described in researchers' theories of love. ²One important factor is proximity, or being in the same place at the same time. ³The more often that you see a person in your hometown, at social gatherings, or at work, the more likely that interaction will occur. ⁴Thus, if you live in New York, you'll probably end up with another New Yorker. ⁵(With the advent of the Internet, however, geographic proximity has become less important.)

⁶You _____ choose a partner based on similarities (in attitudes, values, intellect, interests, education, and socioeconomic status); the old adage that "opposites attract" usually isn't true. ⁷If your potential partner expresses interest or liking, you may react with mutual regard known as reciprocity. ⁸The more you express interest, the safer it is for someone else to return the regard, and the cycle spirals onward.

⁹A final factor that plays a significant role in selecting a partner is physical attraction. ¹⁰Whether such attraction is caused by a chemical reaction or a socially learned behavior, men and women appear to have different attraction criteria. ¹¹This attraction is complex and influenced by social, biological, and cultural factors.

—Donatelle, Rebecca, J., *Access to Health*, 12th ed., pp. 122–123.

_____ **1.** What is the relationship between the ideas in sentence 3?
   a. listing order   b. time order

_____ **2.** Which transition word best fits the blank in line 6?
   a. also   c. then
   b. next

_____ **3.** In this passage, the author
   a. explains step by step how to choose a partner.
   b. lists factors that influence the choice of a partner.

B. Read the following passage from a college government textbook.

Interest Groups

¹Interest groups are everywhere in the American political system. ²Political scientists loosely categorize interest groups into clusters. ³An examination of the four distinct types of interest groups gives a good picture of much of the American interest group system.

[4]One type of group focuses on economic interests. [5]All economic interests are ultimately concerned with wages, prices, and profits. [6]In the American economy, the government does not determine these directly. [7]More commonly the government affects economic interests through regulations and taxes, among other things. [8]Business executives, factory workers, and farmers seek to affect government's impact on their livelihoods.

[9]Another type of interest group is made up of the environmentalists. [10]Environmental groups have promoted pollution-control policies, wilderness protection, and population control. [11]They have fought against strip mining, supersonic aircraft, the Alaskan oil pipeline, offshore oil drilling, and nuclear power plants.

[12]The next kind of interest group fights for equality interests. [13]The Fourteenth Amendment assures equal protection under the law. [14]American history, though, shows that this is easier said than done. [15]Interest groups representing minorities and women have made equal rights their main policy goal.

[16]The fourth type of interest group deals with consumers and public interests. [17]Today, over 2,000 organized groups are championing various causes or ideas in the public interest. [18]If products are made safer by the lobbying of consumer protection groups, it is not the members of such groups alone that benefit; everyone should be better off. [19]In addition to consumer groups, other groups speaking for those who cannot speak for themselves seek to protect children, animals, and the mentally ill.

—Adapted from Edwards, George C. III, Wattenberg, Martin P., and Lineberry, Robert L., *Government in America: People, Politics, and Policy*, 5th ed., Brief Version, pp. 253–258.

_____ 4. The overall thought pattern for the passage is
      a. time order.   b. classification.

5. The second major supporting detail is signaled by the transition word(s)

_____ .

6–10. Complete the outline with information from the paragraph.

Main idea stated in a topic sentence: _____

_____

_____

Major supporting details:

a. _____

b. _____

c. _____

d. _____

7 Summary of Key Concepts of Transitions and Thought Patterns

LO1 LO2 Assess your comprehension of transitions and thought patterns. Complete the following two-column notes of terms and definitions with information from the chapter.

Term	Definition/Examples
Transitions	
Thought pattern	
Time order: Narration Time order: Process	
Listing pattern	
Examples of signal words for listing	
Classification pattern	
Examples of classification signal words	
Space order pattern	
Examples of words used to establish space order pattern	

Test Your Comprehension of Transitions and Thought Patterns

Respond to the following questions and prompts.

(LO1) In your own words, what is a transition? _____

_____

_____

(LO2) In your own words, what is a thought pattern? _____

_____

(LO3) In the space below, illustrate the thought pattern of the following ideas from a college human anatomy textbook by creating an outline or concept map.

[1]Burns are classified according to their severity (depth) as first-, second-, or third-degree burns. [2]In first-degree burns, only the epidermis is damaged. [3]The area becomes red and swollen. [4]First-degree burns are not usually serious and generally heal in two to three days without any special attention. [5]Sunburn is usually a first-degree burn. [6]Second-degree burns involve injury to the epidermis and the upper region of the dermis. [7]The skin is red and painful, and *blisters* appear. [8]Because sufficient numbers of epithelial cells are still present, regrowth can occur. [9]First- and second-degree burns are referred to as partial-thickness burns. [10]Third-degree burns destroy the entire thickness of the skin, so these burns are also called full-thickness burns. [11]In third-degree burns, regeneration is not possible, and skin grafting must be done to cover the underlying exposed tissues.

—Adapted from Lutgens, Frederick K., Tarbuck, Edward J., and Tasa, Dennis, *Foundations of Earth Science*, 5th ed., pp. 4–6.

(LO1) (LO2) (LO3) (LO4) Summarize the two most important ideas in this chapter that will help you improve your reading comprehension. _____

_____

_____

More Thought Patterns

LO LEARNING OUTCOMES

After studying this chapter, you should be able to:

LO1 Recognize the Comparison-and-Contrast Pattern and Signal Words

LO2 Recognize the Cause-and-Effect Pattern and Signal Words

LO3 Recognize the Generalization-and-Example Pattern and Signal Words

LO4 Recognize the Definition-and-Example Pattern and Signal Words

LO5 Develop Textbook Skills: Thought Patterns in Textbooks

LO6 Apply Information Literacy Skills: Academic, Personal, and Career Applications of More Thought Patterns

Before Reading About More Thought Patterns

In Chapter 7, you learned several important ideas that will help you as you work through this chapter. Use the following questions to call up your prior knowledge about transitions and thought patterns.

What are transitions? (Refer to page 274.) _____

_____

_____

What are thought patterns? (Refer to page 274.) _____

_____

_____

What is important to know about mixed thought patterns? Give an example from Chapter 7. (Refer to page 296.) _____

327

You have learned that transitions and thought patterns show the relationships of ideas within sentences as well as between sentences and paragraphs, and you studied four common types: time order, space order, listing, and classification. In this chapter, we will explore some other common thought patterns:

- The comparison-and-contrast patterns
- The cause-and-effect pattern
- The generalization-and-example pattern
- The definition-and-example pattern

 ## Recognize the Comparison-and-Contrast Pattern and Signal Words

Many ideas become clearer when they are thought of in relation to one another. For example, comparing the prices of different phone plans makes us smarter shoppers. Likewise, noting the difference between mature and immature behavior helps us grow. The comparison-and-contrast patterns enable us to see these relationships. This section discusses both comparison and contrast, starting with comparison. The discussion then turns to the important and effective comparison-and-contrast pattern, in which these two basic ways of organizing ideas are combined when writing an explanation, a description, or an analysis.

Comparison

Comparison points out the ways in which two or more ideas are alike. Sample signal words are listed in the box.

Words and Phrases of Comparison

a kind of	comparable	in like manner	likewise	same
alike	equally	in the same way	matching	similar
as	in a similar fashion	just as	near to	similarity
as well as	in character with	like	resemble	similarly

When comparison is used to organize an entire paragraph, the pattern looks like this.

Comparison Pattern

Idea 1		Idea 2
Idea 1	*like*	Idea 2
Idea 1	*like*	Idea 2
Idea 1	*like*	Idea 2

Words and phrases of comparison state the relationship of ideas within and between sentences.

> **EXAMPLE** Fill in each blank with a signal word or phrase that shows comparison.

1. Earning a promotion is _____ running a marathon.

2. An aspiring employee must work to achieve _____ a competitive athlete trains to win.

3. A raise in rank and salary is _____ trophy.

EXPLANATION Each of the example sentences compares two topics to make a point: *earning a promotion* and *running a marathon*. Note that the relationship within each sentence helps to establish a comparison pattern for a three-sentence paragraph as illustrated in the following chart. Compare your choice of words of comparison with the ones given in the chart. ◄

Comparison Pattern: Promotion and Marathon

Idea 1		Idea 2
earning a promotion	(1) *like*	running a marathon
aspiring employee works	(2) *in the same way*	competitive athlete trains
raise	(3) *a kind of*	trophy

Practice 1

Determine the logical order for the following four sentences. Write **1** by the sentence that should come first, **2** by the sentence that should come second, **3** by the sentence that should come third, and **4** by the sentence that should come last. Then use the information to fill in the chart.

_____ The careers of Jennifer Lopez and Beyoncé Knowles are similar in several respects.

_____ An overall similarity between these two mega-stars is their financial success; both are extraordinarily rich, with growing incomes.

_____ Both women also enjoy success as singers, record producers, actors, and fashion icons.

_____ Both Lopez and Knowles are known world-wide by their single names: J-Lo and Beyoncé.

Similarities between Jennifer Lopez and Beyoncé Knowles	
Jennifer Lopez	**Beyoncé Knowles**
5. _____	6. _____
_____	_____
7. _____	8. _____
_____	_____
9. _____	10. _____

Contrast

Contrast points out the ways in which two or more ideas are different. Sample signal words are listed in the box below.

Words and Phrases of Contrast				
all	counter to	differently	instead	than
although	despite	even though	nevertheless	to the contrary
as opposed to	differ	however	on the contrary	unlike
at the same time	difference	in contrast	on the one hand	while
but	different	in spite of	on the other hand	yet
conversely	different from	incompatible with	still	

When contrast is used to organize an entire paragraph, the pattern looks like this.

Contrast Pattern		
Idea 1		**Idea 2**
Idea 1	_differs from_	Idea 2
Idea 1	_differs from_	Idea 2
Idea 1	_differs from_	Idea 2

Words and phrases of contrast state the relationship of ideas within and between sentences.

> EXAMPLE Fill in each blank with a word or phrase that shows contrast.

Optimists and pessimists **(1)** _____ in their outlooks on life. Optimists tend to look for positive outcomes, **(2)** _____ pessimists almost always expect the worst. But outlook is not the only way in which the two **(3)** _____. Research has shown that optimists tend to live longer **(4)** _____ pessimists. Pessimists experience more health issues, more pain, and less energy **(5)** _____ optimists. One possible explanation is that optimists and pessimists have **(6)** _____ levels of T cells, which increase the functioning of the body's immune system. Another possible reason is that, **(7)** _____ pessimists, optimists tend to take preventive health measures. Optimists and pessimists also **(8)**_____ in their social lives. **(9)** _____, optimists tend to take part in social activities and succeed in their endeavors. **(10)** _____, pessimists do not.

—Based on Ciccarelli, Saundra K. and White, Noland J.,
Psychology: An Exploration, pp. 321–322.

Contrast Pattern: Difference Between Optimists and Pessimists

Idea 1 Optimists		Idea 2 Pessimists
look for positive outcomes	(1) *differ*	almost always expect the
outlook	(2) *while*	worst outlook
live longer	(3) *differ*	more health issues, pain, less
	(4) *than*	energy
	(5) *than*	
level of T cells	(6) *different*	level of T cells
preventive health measures	(7) *unlike*	preventive health measure
social lives	(8) *differ*	social lives
take part in social activities	(9) *on the one hand*	do not
and succeed	(10) *on the other hand*	

EXPLANATION Every sentence in the paragraph contrasts two topics to make a point. Note that the relationships within and between sentences establish a contrast pattern for the paragraph as illustrated in the following chart. Compare your choice of words of contrast with the ones given in the chart. ◀

Practice 2

Determine a logical order for the following five sentences. Write **1** by the sentence that should come first, **2** in front of the sentence that should come second, **3** by the sentence that should come third, and so on. Then use the information to fill in the chart.

Cultural Differences and Touch

Textbook Skills

_____ Thus, on the one hand, southern Europeans may view the Japanese as cold, distant, and uninvolved.

_____ On the other hand, the Japanese may view the southern Europeans as pushy, aggressive, and too intimate.

_____ Members of a contact culture, such as southern Europeans, maintain close distances and touch each other in conversation, face each other directly, and maintain eye contact.

_____ In contrast, members of a noncontact culture, such as the Japanese, maintain greater distances in their interactions, rarely touch each other, avoid facing each other, and have much less direct eye contact.

Cultural Differences and Touch

Contact Cultures	Noncontact Cultures
1. Southern European	1. _____
2. maintain close distances and touch each other in conversation, face each other directly, and maintain eye contact	2. _____ _____ _____
3. _____ _____ _____	3. The Japanese may view the southern Europeans as pushy, aggressive, and too intimate.

_____ Some cultures are contact cultures, as opposed to others that are non-contact cultures.

—DeVito, Joseph A., *The Interpersonal Communication Book*, 10th ed., p. 193.

Comparison and Contrast

The **comparison-and-contrast pattern** shows how two things are similar and how they are different.

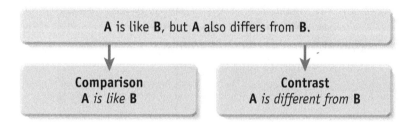

The following short paragraph offers an example of a comparison and contrast between two types of weight training. Read the paragraph and circle the comparison and contrast words and phrases.

> [1]Although exercising with free weights is similar to exercising with machine weights, important differences exist between the two methods. [2]Both methods offer resistance training, and both improve posture, build bones and muscles, and improve one's overall well-being. [3]However, free weights and machine weights differ in cost and convenience. [4]On the one hand, free weights are inexpensive and portable. [5]On the other hand, machines, such as Bowflex and Nautilus, costs hundreds of dollars and require a fixed location.

Did you circle the following nine signal words and phrases: *although, similar, differences, both, both, however, differ, on the one hand,* and *on the other hand*? These signal words and phrases state the relationship within and between sentences and establish the paragraph's thought pattern.

⊘ **EXAMPLE** Read the following paragraph from a college sociology textbook. Circle the comparison-and-contrast words; then answer the questions that follow the paragraph.

Textbook
Skills

Men and Women and Hormones

[1]Scientists don't know why women and men differ but believe that hormones provide part of the explanation. [2]All males and females share three sex hormones. [3]Estrogen is dominant in females and is produced by the ovaries. [4]Progesterone is present in high levels during pregnancy and is also secreted by the ovaries. [5]Testosterone is dominant in males, where it is produced by the testes. [6]All of these hormones are produced in very small quantities in both sexes before puberty.

[7]After puberty, different levels of these hormones in females and males produce different changes in bodily processes. [8]For example, testosterone, the main male sex hormone, strengthens muscles but threatens the heart. [9]Thus males are at twice the risk of heart disease as are females. [10]The main female sex hormones, especially estrogen, make blood vessels more elastic and strengthen the immune system. [11]Thus females are more resistant to infection.

—Adapted from Benokraitis, Nijole V., *Marriages and Families: Changes, Choices, and Constraints*, 4th ed., p. 75.

1. What two ideas are being compared and contrasted? _____

   _____

2. List four different comparison-and-contrast words or phrases in the

   paragraph. _____

   _____

EXPLANATION (1) The paragraph compares and contrasts men's hormones and women's hormones. (2) You were correct to choose any four of these comparison-and-contrast words: *differ, but, share, both, all, different, as, more.*

Practice 3

This paragraph from a college sociology textbook uses comparison and contrast. Read the paragraph and then answer the questions that follow.

Textbook
Skills

[1]The *authoritative* parent and the *authoritarian* parent may seem similar in purpose but differ in style. [2]The similar spelling of the terms *authoritative* and *authoritarian* requires that you read these terms carefully. [3]The first part of both words, which comes from the word *authority,*

suggests that these parents are willing to "take charge" of their children. [4]However, they take charge in quite different ways. [5]On the one hand, authoritative parents are warm (accepting) and firm (controlling). [6]They use reason to gain compliance. [7]They explain rules and encourage verbal give-and-take with their children. [8]They are flexible in setting limits and are responsive to their children's needs. [9]They encourage independent thinking and are accepting of opposing points of view. [10]During a conflict, an authoritative parent might ask a child, "What do you think we should do?" [11]In contrast, authoritarian parents value obedience above all. [12]They limit their child's freedom by imposing many rules, which they strictly enforce. [13]They favor punishment and forceful measures and mainly use power to gain compliance. [14]They value order and tradition and do not compromise. [15]They do not encourage verbal give-and-take with their children. [16]During a conflict, this parent is likely to assert power with statements such as "Because I said so."

—Adapted from Jaffee, Michael L., *Understanding Parenting*, 2nd ed., pp. 158, 160.

1. What two ideas are being discussed? _____

   and _____

2. How are authoritative and authoritarian parents similar? _____

   _____

3. Complete the following chart with information from the passage:

The *authoritative* parent and the *authoritarian* parent may seem similar in purpose but differ in style.

Both **authoritative** and **authoritarian** parents "take charge" of a child.

Contrast	
Authoritative Parents	**Authoritarian Parents**
encourage independent thinking	value obedience above all
use reason to gain compliance	_____
are flexible	_____
	are inflexible
_____	say, "Because I said so."
_____	

Recognize the Cause-and-Effect Pattern and Signal Words

Sometimes an author talks about *why* something happened or *what* results came from an event. A **cause** states why something happens; an **effect** states a result or outcome. Sample signal words are listed in the box.

Cause-and-Effect Words			
accordingly	by reason	leads to	so
as a result	consequently	on account of	thereby
because	due to	results in	therefore
because of	if . . . then	since	thus

Here are some examples:

> **Because** Zahira is the oldest of eight siblings, she has developed many leadership skills.

> **Due to** a collision involving 34 vehicles, all lanes of Interstate 4 have been shut down for hours.

Each of the example sentences has two topics: one topic causes or has an effect on the second topic. The cause or effect is the author's main point. For example, the two topics in the first sentence are Zahira's birth order and her leadership skills. The stated main idea is that being the oldest of eight siblings is the cause of her leadership skills. The cause is introduced by the word *because*. In the second sentence the two topics are the collision of 34 vehicles and the closing of Interstate 4; the author focuses on the cause by using the signal phrase *due to*.

Note that cause and effect has a strong connection to time, and many of the transitions for this pattern have a time element. Although many cause-and-effect transition words have similar meanings and may be interchangeable, authors carefully choose the transition that best fits the context.

> **EXAMPLE** Read the following paragraph. Fill in each blank (1–5) with a cause-and-effect word or phrase from the box. Each is used only once.

| because | due to | leads to | result | therefore |

The State of Knowledge about Climate Science

Scientists know with virtual certainty several causes and effects of climate change. The composition of Earth's atmosphere is changing **(1)** _____ of human activities. Increasing levels of greenhouse gases like carbon dioxide (CO_2) in the atmosphere since pre-industrial times are well-documented and understood. The atmospheric buildup of CO_2 and other greenhouse gases is largely the **(2)** _____ of human activities such as the burning of fossil fuels. An "unequivocal" warming trend of about 1.0 to 1.7°F occurred from 1906–2005. Warming occurred in both the Northern and Southern Hemispheres, and over the oceans. The major greenhouse gases emitted **(3)** _____ human activities remain in the atmosphere for periods ranging from decades to centuries. It is **(4)** _____ virtually certain that atmospheric concentrations of greenhouse gases will continue to rise over the next few decades. Increasing greenhouse gas concentrations **(5)** _____ the warming of the planet.

—U.S. Environmental Protection Agency. "Climate Change: State of Knowledge." 28 Sept. 2009.

VISUAL *VOCABULARY*

The best meaning of **radiation** is _____.

a. gases
b. atmosphere
c. heat

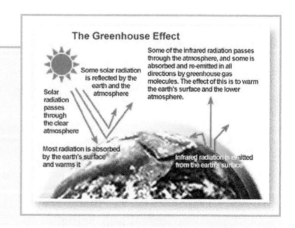

The Greenhouse Effect

EXPLANATION   Compare your answers to the following: (1) because, (2) result, (3) due to, (4) therefore, (5) leads to. ◀

Common Cause-and-Effect Patterns

The writer using cause and effect introduces an idea or event, and then provides supporting details to show how that idea *results in* or *leads to* another idea. Many times, the second idea comes about because of the first idea. Thus the first idea is the cause and the following ideas are the effects.

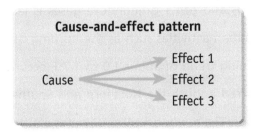

For example, read the following topic sentence:

Music therapy leads to the improvement of a person's physical and psychological well-being.

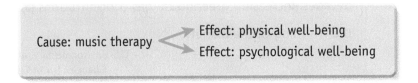

Often an author will begin with an effect and then give the causes.

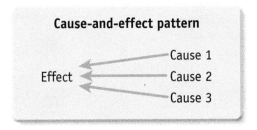

For example, read the following topic sentence.

Some people turn to music therapy due to a loss of physical or psychological well-being.

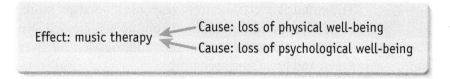

Effect: music therapy ← Cause: loss of physical well-being
← Cause: loss of psychological well-being

Sometimes the author may wish to emphasize a chain reaction.

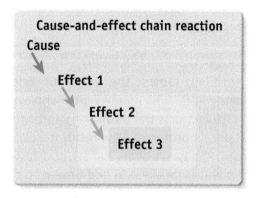

Cause-and-effect chain reaction
Cause
↓
Effect 1
↓
Effect 2
↓
Effect 3

For example, read the following topic sentence.

Music therapy reduces stress and anxiety, which leads to positive emotional states and can ultimately result in feelings of control and empowerment.

Cause-and-effect chain reaction
Cause: music therapy → Effect: reduces stress and anxiety →
Effect: positive emotional states → Effect: feelings of control and empowerment

⊙ EXAMPLE Determine a logical order for the following three sentences from a college health textbook. Write **1** by the sentence that should come first, **2** in front of the sentence that should come second, and **3** by the sentence that should come last.

Textbook
Skills

_____ First, CRH instructs the pituitary gland and the adrenal glands to secrete special stress hormones.

_____ Hostility causes the body to release corticotrophin-releasing-hormone (CRH), which starts the whole sequence of stress hormones.

_____ The result is a classic stress response: blood pressure rises, the heart beats harder and faster, blood volume is increased, blood moves from the skin and organs to the brain and muscles, the liver releases stored sugar, and breathing speeds up.

> —Karren, Keith J., Hafen, Brent Q., Smith, Lee, and Frandsen, Kathryn, *Mind/Body Health: The Effects of Attitudes, Emotions, and Relationships,* 2nd ed., p. 218.

EXPLANATION Here are the sentences arranged in their proper order. The transition and signal words are in bold type.

The Bodily Effects of Hostility

[1]Hostility **causes** the body to release corticotrophin-releasing-hormone (CRH), which starts the whole sequence of stress hormones. [2]**First**, CRH instructs the pituitary gland and the adrenal glands to secrete special stress hormones. [3]The **result** is a classic stress response: blood pressure rises, the heart beats harder and faster, blood volume is increased, blood moves from the skin and organs to the brain and muscles, the liver releases stored sugar, and breathing speeds up.

> —Karren, Keith J., Hafen, Brent Q., Smith, Lee, and Frandsen, Kathryn, *Mind/Body Health: The Effects of Attitudes, Emotions, and Relationships,* 2nd ed., p. 218.

In this paragraph, the cause-and-effect signal words are *causes* and *result*. The listing word *first* indicates the order of the cause-and-effect discussion. The addition word *and* is used to list the bodily effects of hostility. This paragraph actually uses two thought patterns to make the point—listing, as well as cause and effect. Even though two patterns are used, the cause-and-effect pattern is the primary organizing pattern. ◀

Practice 4

This excerpt from a college history textbook uses the cause-and-effect thought pattern to organize information. Read the paragraph, circle the cause-and-effect signal words in it, and complete the concept map that follows.

Textbook
Skills

The Great Depression

[1]The financial collapse of 1929 triggered the Great Depression in America, although there were other underlying domestic causes. [2]One reason

was that manufacturing firms had not made sufficient capital investment. [3]Another cause was the disproportionate amount of profits going to about 5 percent of the U.S. population, thus undermining the purchasing power of other consumers. [4]Agriculture was a fourth cause; it had been in trouble for years. [5]Finally, the economic difficulties in Europe and Latin America, which predated those in the United States, meant foreigners were less able to purchase U.S.-made products.

—Adapted from Craig, Albert M., Graham, William A., Kagan, Donald, Ozment, Steven, and Turner, Frank M., *The Heritage of World Civilizations, Brief,* 5th ed., p. 773.

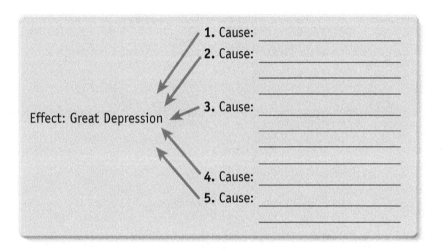

L03 ## Recognize the Generalization-and-Example Pattern and Signal Words

Curiosity can quickly lead to danger: Rayanne, a curious five-year-old, found a hairpin on the floor and stuck it in an electrical outlet to see what would happen.

Some people may read this sentence and think that the author's focus is on Rayanne. However, the author's general point is about curiosity, not Rayanne. In the first part of the sentence the author has made a generalization: "Curiosity can quickly lead to danger." Adding an **example word** or phrase makes it clear that the author is using Rayanne as only one example of the general dangers of curiosity.

Read the sentence about Rayanne again. Note how the use of the signal word makes the relationship between ideas clear.

Curiosity can quickly lead to danger; *for instance,* Rayanne, a curious five-year-old, found a hairpin on the floor and stuck it in an electrical outlet to see what would happen.

In the generalization-and-example thought pattern, the author makes a general statement and then offers an example or a series of examples to clarify the generalization.

The Generalization-and-Example Pattern

Statement of a general idea
   Example
   Example

Example words signal that a writer is giving an instance of a general idea.

Words and Phrases That Introduce Examples

an illustration	for instance	once	to illustrate
for example	including	such as	typically

> EXAMPLE Read each of the following items and fill in the blanks with an appropriate example word or phrase.

1. History is full of people who overcame significant challenges and went on to achieve success; _____, Abraham Lincoln lost at least six major elections for various political offices before becoming the sixteenth president of the United States.

2. Women can now earn some of the highest salaries. _____, in 2012, *Forbes* reported that Oprah Winfrey earned $165 million.

3. Television programs _____ *Sesame Street* and *Blue's Clues* have helped educate millions of children.

EXPLANATION Many words and phrases that introduce examples are easily interchanged. Compare your choices with the following: (1) *for example,* (2) *For instance*, and (3) *such as*. Notice that in the first two of these three examples, the phrases *for example* and *for instance* are similar in meaning, signaling that at least one example will be offered. The use of the transition phrase *such as* in the third example, however, tends to signal a list. Even though transition words or phrases have similar meanings, authors carefully choose transitions based on style and meaning. ◄

Practice 5

Determine a logical order for the following three sentences. Write a **1** by the sentence that should come first, a **2** in front of the sentence that should come second, and **3** by the sentence that should come last.

_____ The $250,000–$450,000 million loss in crops that occurred in 2010 further exemplifies the damage of such a Florida freeze.

_____ Sunny, warm Florida can experience crop-damaging cold spells.

_____ In one instance, the temperature in agricultural areas during January 2010 dipped as low as 17 degrees.

L04 Recognize the Definition-and-Example Pattern and Signal Words

Textbooks are full of new words and special terms. Even if the word is common, it can take on a special meaning in a specific course. To help students understand the ideas, authors often include a definition of the new or special term. Then to make sure the meaning of the word or concept is clear, the author will also give examples.

Textbook Skills

> **Euphemisms** are rephrasings of harsh terms; they attempt to avoid offending or to skirt an unpleasant issue. For instance, the Federal Reserve Board is fond of calling a bad market "a market imbalance." A bereaved person might rather hear, "I was sorry to hear of your grandmother's passing" than "I was sorry to hear your grandmother died."
>
> —Faigley, Lester, *The Penguin Handbook*, p. 506.

In the paragraph above, the term *euphemisms* is defined first. Then the author gives two examples to make the term clear to the reader.

■ The **definition** explains the meaning of new, difficult, or special terms. Definitions include words like *is, are,* and *means*: "Euphemisms *are*

> **The Definition Pattern**
>
> Term and definition
>   Example
>   Example

rephrasings of harsh terms; they attempt to avoid offending or to skirt an unpleasant issue."

- The **examples** follow a definition to show how the word is used or applied in the content course. Examples are signaled by words like *for instance* and *such as:* "For instance, the Federal Reserve Board is fond of calling a bad market 'a market imbalance.'"

Textbook Skills

> EXAMPLE Determine a logical order for the following three sentences. Write a **1** by the sentence that should come first, a **2** in front of the sentence that should come second, and a **3** by the sentence that should come last. Then read the explanation.

_____ They also help clarify and intensify your verbal messages.

_____ *Illustrators* are physical gestures that go along with and literally illustrate the verbal message; they make your communications more vivid and help to maintain your listener's attention.

_____ In saying, "Let's go up," for example, you probably move your head and perhaps your finger in an upward direction.

—DeVito, Joseph A., *The Interpersonal Communication Book*, 10th ed., p. 182.

EXPLANATION The sentences have been arranged in the proper order in the paragraph below. The definition, example, and transition words are in **bold** type.

Illustrators, One Type of Body Gesture

Illustrators **are** physical gestures that go along with and literally illustrate the verbal message; they make your communications more vivid and help to maintain your listener's attention. They **also** help clarify and intensify your verbal messages. In saying, "Let's go up," **for example,** you probably move your head and perhaps your finger in an upward direction.

This sequence of ideas begins by introducing the term *illustrators*. The term is linked to its definition with the verb *are*. The author signals two additional traits of illustrators with the addition word *also*. The sentence that contains *for example* logically follows the definition and additional traits of the term *illustrators*. ◖

Practice 6

Read the paragraph. Finish the definition concept table that follows it by adding the missing details in the proper order.

Affect Displays, A Type of Gesture

Textbook Skills

[1]Affect displays are the movements of the face that convey emotional meaning—the expressions that show anger and fear, happiness and surprise, eagerness and fatigue. [2]They're the facial muscles that give you away when you try to present a false image and that lead people to say "You look angry. [3]What's wrong?" [4]We can, however, consciously control affect displays, as actors do when they play a role. [5]Affect displays may be unintentional (as when they give you away) or intentional (as when you want to show anger, love, or surprise).

—DeVito, Joseph A., *The Interpersonal Communication Book*, 10th ed., p. 182.

Term: _____

↓

Definition: _____

↓

Example: _____
_____

↓

Example: _____

↓

Example: _____

VISUAL *VOCABULARY*

Provide captions for the two photographs that correctly label the types of gestures represented by each of the images.

_____   _____

LO5 # Develop Textbook Skills: Thought Patterns in Textbooks

Textbook Skills

Textbook authors rely heavily on the use of transitions and thought patterns to make information clear and easier to understand.

> **EXAMPLE** The following topic sentences have been taken from college textbooks. Identify the *primary* thought pattern that each sentence suggests.

_____ **1.** After 1660, the Virginia economy steadily declined for several reasons.
   a. cause and effect   c. definition and example
   b. comparison and contrast

_____ **2.** Domain-specific knowledge is knowledge that pertains to a particular task or subject; for example, knowing that the shortstop plays between second and third base is specific to the domain of baseball.

a. cause and effect   c. definition and example

b. comparison and contrast

EXPLANATION Topic sentence 1, taken from a history textbook, uses (a) cause and effect, signaled by the phrase *for several reasons*. Topic sentence 2, from an education textbook, is organized according to (c) definition and example, using the verb *is* in the definition and the phrase *for example* to introduce the example. ◀

Practice 7

The following topic sentences have been taken from college textbooks (in social science, mathematics, health, and literature). Identify the primary thought pattern that each sentence suggests.

_____ **1.** A stereotype, a fixed impression about a group, may influence your views of individual group members because you may see individuals only as members of a group rather than as unique individuals.

a. cause and effect   c. definition and example

b. comparison and contrast

_____ **2.** Note that the expressions $x + y$ and $y + x$ have the same values no matter what the variables stand for; they are equivalent.

a. cause and effect   c. generalization and example

b. comparison

_____ **3.** Excessive time pressure, excessive responsibility, lack of support, or excessive expectations of yourself and those around you may result in overload.

a. cause and effect   c. definition and example

b. comparison and contrast

_____ **4.** Poets have long been fond of retelling myths, narrowly defined as traditional stories about the deeds of immortal beings; myths tell us stories of gods or heroes—their battles, their lives, their loves, and often their suffering—all on a scale of magnificence larger than our life.

a. cause and effect   c. definition and example

b. comparison and contrast

Apply Information Literacy Skills

 ## Academic, Personal, and Career Applications of More Thought Patterns

As you learned in Chapter 7, transitions and thought patterns organize information by directing your attention to key concepts and the relationships among ideas. Transitions and thought patterns connect specific details to logically support a main idea. The signal words of a thought pattern help you predict what is to come. When you understand the structure of an idea, you can monitor your comprehension as you read. Transitions and thought patterns show how ideas are connected. In academic, personal, and career situations, you will use the skills that you have learned in this chapter in several ways:

- Recognize your own need to identify transitions and thought patterns.
- Analyze information to see the relationships among ideas.
- Determine the author's use of a thought pattern to develop a main idea.

Academic Application

Assume you are taking a college geography course, and your class is studying natural Earth cycles and the effects humans have on these cycles.

- **Before Reading:** Skim the passage. Determine the thought pattern used to organize the information in the passage. *(Hint: note the transition words that signal the thought pattern.)*
- **During Reading:** Underline the central idea and double underline the key details that support the central idea of the passage.
- **After Reading:** In the space following the passage, create an outline or concept map that reflects the thought pattern of the passage. Organize the key details that support the central idea.

Thought Pattern: _____.

Pre-Reading Question: _____

_____

Fire and Forest Management in the
Western United States

In the chaparral woodlands of California and many other forest ecosystems of the western United States fire is an important natural part of ecosystems. Unfortunately, people have built homes and businesses in forested areas. Conflagrations like the 2006 fires near Sedona, Arizona, destroy entire communities, cause vast property damage, and occasionally take lives. Fire has also been an increasing problem in western Canada recently, and one major fire that started in the United States burned across the border into British Columbia. When a fire starts near a populated area, the natural reaction is to extinguish it at once. Paradoxically, this action to halt fire actually makes fire-prone conditions worse. In the chaparral, plant growth produces flammable biomass that does not decay as rapidly as it is produced, so it accumulates over time. The longer it accumulates, the more fuel is available for severe fires. If a fire starts in a recently burned area, little fuel is available, the fire burns slowly at cooler temperatures, and it does not spread widely. But if a fire starts where one has not burned for a long time, a hot, dangerous fire is likely.

Consequently, many areas that routinely would burn naturally have not burned, and fuel accumulations—dry leaves and dead wood—are unusually large. When a fire starts during dry, windy conditions, it becomes very dangerous and uncontrollable. Its high temperatures make it much more destructive than fires during moist conditions.

Decades of firefighting in the western United States have not eliminated fires; they have only allowed fuel to accumulate. Normal, "natural" fires, low temperature and slow burning, have been eliminated and replaced by infrequent but catastrophic conflagrations. Fire managers now use controlled burns in some areas to reduce fuel accumulations.

—Bergman, Edward and Renwick, William, *Introduction to Geography: People, Places & Environment*, p. 150.

After Reading Outline or Concept Map of Key Ideas:

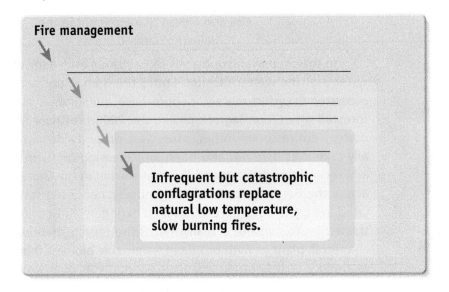

Fire management

Infrequent but catastrophic conflagrations replace natural low temperature, slow burning fires.

Personal Application

Assume you want to buy a tablet for your personal use. You want to choose the best tablet for your lifestyle and budget. You have found the following information on the Internet using the search phrase, "compare tablets by price."

- **Before Reading:** List the features you want in a tablet.
- **During Reading:** Annotate the information to highlight details that will help you decide which tablet to buy.
- **After Reading:** In the space following the passage, choose the tablet you would like to buy. State your reasons.

Features I want in a tablet: _____

_____

Decision: _____

_____

_____

Product name	Google Nexus 7 (16GB)	Amazon Kindle Fire HD 8.9	Apple iPad Mini	Samsung Galaxy Tab 2 7.0 (8GB)	Microsoft Surface RT
	PLAY CNET VIDEO	PLAY CNET VIDEO	PLAY CNET VIDEO	PLAY CNET VIDEO	PLAY CNET VIDEO
Price	$199 to $229 at 3 stores	$269 at 1 store	$329 to $337 at 4 stores	$149 to $235 at 11 stores	$304 to $399 at 4 stores
RAM installed size	1 GB	Info unavailable	Info unavailable	1 GB	2 GB
OS provided	Android 4.1 Jelly Bean	Info unavailable	Apple iOS	Android 4.0	Microsoft Windows RT
Clock speed	1300 MHz	1.5 GHz	Info unavailable	1 GHz	Info unavailable
Weight	12 oz	20 oz	0.68 lbs	12.1 oz	676 g
Height	4.7 in	9.4 in	7.87 in	7.6 in	6.8 in
Input device type	Camera Touch-screen	Info unavailable	Info unavailable	Touch-screen	Detachable keyboard
Wireless connectivity	Bluetooth NFC Wi-Fi		Bluetooth 4.0	Bluetooth 3.0	
Built-in devices	Display Speakerphone Touchscreen Digital camera	Info unavailable	Info unavailable	Display Touchscreen Digital camera Digital player	keyboard Display

—Comparing Tablets from CNET Networks. Reproduced with the permission of The YGS group.

Career Application

Assume you are looking for employment and a career counselor shared the following information with you.

- **Before Reading:** Skim the information. Then write two pre-reading questions to guide your thinking.

- **During Reading:** Annotate the details that answer your pre-reading questions.

- **After Reading:** Record your answers to your pre-reading questions.

Pre-Reading Questions: _____

_____

_____

Your Online Image May Hurt Your Employment Opportunities

Employers often research job applicants by surfing the Internet and social networks, such as Facebook, before interviewing or hiring an applicant. Often, what employers learn makes them question your suitability as a possible employee. Types of questionable online content include the following:

- Discussing or boasting about alcohol or drug use.
- Gossiping about or harshly criticizing past, current, or prospective employers or coworkers.
- Sharing inappropriate or offensive images, including photos of you and friends drinking, wearing inappropriate clothing, or engaging in sexually suggestive acts.
- Using offensive language (you or friends):
  - Using discriminatory comments such as derogatory terms based on gender, sexual orientation, race or ethnicity.
  - Using profanity or sexually suggestive language.

Three simple steps can improve your online image:

1. **Create a positive online identity of yourself.** Don't post anything you wouldn't want an employer to see. Everything online is public information. Delete past postings of yours or your friends with inappropriate content. Advise friends against making inappropriate postings on your site.
2. **Create a professional online identity.** Join online professional groups, such as LinkedIn, related to your career. Ask people to "recommend" you on these sites.
3. **Proofread your postings.** Most people on social networks often ignore the standard rules of English. However, employers frequently reject job applicants due to poor communication skills.

After Reading Response: _____

_____

_____

REVIEW TEST 1

Score (number correct)) _____ x 10 = _____ %

Visit MyReadingLab to take this test online and receive feedback and guidance on your answers.

Transition Words and Thought Patterns

A. Circle the signal words used in these sentences from a college psychology text. Then identify the organizational pattern in each, as follows:

Textbook Skills

a. cause and effect   c. definition and example

b. comparison or contrast or both

_____ **1.** Social negotiation is an aspect of the learning process that relies on collaboration with others and respect for different points of view. For example, during class discussions, while students talk and listen to each other, they learn to establish and defend their own positions and respect the opinions of others.

—Adapted from Woolfolk, Anita E., *Educational Psychology*, 8th ed., pp. 335, 369, 370.

_____ **2.** Higher mental processes develop through social negotiation and interaction, so collaboration in learning is valued.

—Adapted from Woolfolk, p. 335.

_____ **3.** A reward is an attractive object or event supplied as a result of a particular behavior. In contrast, an incentive is an object or event that encourages or discourages the behavior. The promise of an A may be an incentive for a student to work hard at studying, while actually receiving the A is her reward.

—Adapted from Woolfolk, pp. 369–370.

_____ **4.** If we are consistently reinforced for certain behaviors, then we may develop habits or tendencies to act in certain ways.

—Adapted from Woolfolk, p. 370.

B. Read the following passage from a college health textbook. Then answer the questions that follow.

Beliefs and Attitudes

¹Even if you know why you should change a specific behavior, your beliefs and attitudes about the value of your actions will significantly affect what you do. ²We often assume that _____ rational people realize there is a risk in what they are doing, then they will act to reduce that risk. ³But this is not necessarily true. ⁴Consider, for example, the number of physicians and other health professionals who smoke, fail to manage stress, consume high-fat diets, and act in other unhealthy ways. ⁵They surely know better, but their "knowing" is disconnected from their "doing." ⁶Why is this so? ⁷Two strong influences on behaviors are beliefs and attitudes.

⁸A **belief** is an appraisal of the relationship between some object, action, or idea and some attribute of that object, action, or idea (_____, smoking is expensive, dirty, causes cancer—or it is relaxing). ⁹Beliefs may develop from direct experience (such as whether you have trouble breathing after smoking for several years). ¹⁰Or they may develop from second-hand experience or knowledge conveyed by other people (for example, if you see your grandfather die of lung cancer after he smoked for years). ¹¹Although most of us have a general idea about what makes up a belief, we may be a bit unsure about what makes up an attitude. ¹²We often hear or say comments such as "He's got a rotten attitude" or "She needs an attitude adjustment." ¹³However, we may still be unable to define attitude. ¹⁴**Attitude** is a relatively stable set of beliefs, feelings, and behaviors in relation to something or someone.

—Adapted from Donatelle, Rebecca, J. and Davis, Lorraine G., *Access to Health*, 7th ed., pp. 19–20.

5. Fill in the blank in sentence 2 with a transition word or phrase that makes sense.

_____ 6. The relationship of ideas within sentence 2 is one of
   a. generalization and example.   c. cause and effect.
   b. comparison and contrast.

_____ **7.** The primary thought pattern of organization for the first paragraph is

    a. generalization and example.   c. cause and effect.

    b. comparison and contrast.

8. Fill in the blank in sentence 8 with a transition word or phrase that makes sense.

_____ **9.** The relationship of ideas between sentence 12 and sentence 13 is one of

    a. definition and example.   c. cause and effect.

    b. comparison and contrast.

_____ **10.** The primary thought pattern for the second paragraph is

    a. definition and example.   c. cause and effect.

    b. comparison or contrast or both.

REVIEW TEST 2

Score (number correct) _____ x 20 = _____ %

Visit MyReadingLab to take this test online and receive feedback and guidance on your answers.

Read the passage and complete the concept map with information from the passage.

Tension-Type Headaches

Textbook
Skills

[1]Tension-type headaches are typically due to chemical and neuronal imbalances in the brain and/or muscular tension in the back of the neck or scalp that results in pain in the forehead, temples, or back of the head or neck. [2]There is a wide range in the frequency and severity of symptoms, with occurrences categorized as episodic (occurring less than once a month and triggered by stress, anxiety, fatigue, or anger), frequent (occurring 1 to 15 days per month along with migraines), and chronic (occurring more than 15 days per month, with varying pain, and often associated with depression or other emotional problems). [3]Possible triggers also include red wine, lack of sleep, fasting, menstruation, or certain food additives or preservatives.

—Adapted from Donatelle, Rebecca J. and Davis, Lorraine G., *Health: The Basics*, 7th ed., p. 562.

1–5. Complete the following cause-and-effect concept map with information from the passage.

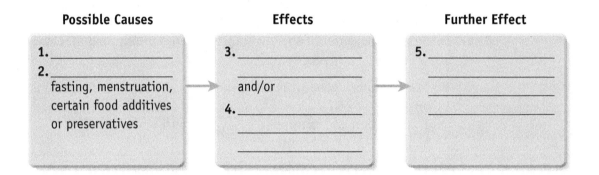

Possible Causes	Effects	Further Effect
1. _____ 2. _____ fasting, menstruation, certain food additives or preservatives	3. _____ and/or 4. _____	5. _____

REVIEW TEST 3

Score (number correct) _____ x 10 = _____ %

Visit MyReadingLab to take this test online and receive feedback and guidance on your answers.

Transitions and Thought Patterns

Textbook Skills

Before you read the following essay from the college textbook *Psychology and Life*, skim the passage and answer the Before Reading questions. Read the essay. Then answer the After Reading questions.

Vocabulary Preview

affiliate (7): associate, connect with
aesthetic (12): artistic
hierarchy (1, 13): ladder, series of levels
actualization (14): realization, fulfillment
transcendence (16): the state of going beyond usual limits

A Hierarchy of Needs

[1]Humanist psychologist Abraham Maslow (1970) formulated the theory that basic motives form a **hierarchy** of needs. [2]In Maslow's view, the needs are arranged in a sequence from primitive to advanced, and

the needs at each level must be satisfied before the next level can be reached. [3]At the bottom (primitive level) of this hierarchy are the basic biological needs, such as hunger and thirst. [4]They must be met before any other needs can begin to operate. [5]When *biological needs* are pressing, other needs are put on hold and are unlikely to influence your actions. [6]When they are reasonably well satisfied, the needs at the next level—*safety needs*—motivate you. [7]When you are no longer concerned about danger, you become motivated by *attachment needs*—needs to belong, to **affiliate** with others, to love, and to be loved. [8]If you are well fed and safe and if you feel a sense of belonging, you move up to *esteem needs*—to like oneself, to see oneself as **competent** and effective, and to do what is necessary to earn the esteem of others.

[9]Humans are thinking beings, with complex brains that demand the stimulation of thought. [10]You are motivated by strong ***cognitive*** needs to know your past, to comprehend the puzzles of current existence, and to predict the future. [11]It is the force of these needs that enables scientists to spend their lives discovering new knowledge. [12]At the next level of Maslow's hierarchy comes the human desire for beauty and order, in the form of **aesthetic** needs that give rise to the creative side of humanity.

[13]At the top of the **hierarchy** are people who are nourished, safe, loved and loving, secure, thinking, and creating. [14]These people have moved beyond basic human needs in the quest for the fullest development of their abilities, or *self-**actualization***. [15]A self-actualizing person has many positive traits such as being self-aware, self-accepting, socially responsive, creative, and open to change. [16] *Needs for **transcendence*** may lead to higher states of awareness and a cosmic vision of one's part in the universe. [17]Very few people move beyond the self to achieve union with spiritual forces.

[18]Maslow's theory is a particularly upbeat view of human motivation. [19]At the core of the theory is the need for each individual to grow and actualize his or her highest potential. [20]Can we maintain such an unfailingly positive view? [21]The data suggests that we cannot. [22]Alongside the needs Maslow recognized, we find that people express power, dominance, and aggression. [23]You also know from your own experience that Maslow's strict hierarchy breaks down. [24]You're likely, for example, to have ignored hunger on occasion to follow higher-level needs. [25]Even with these limitations, however, Maslow's scheme may enable you to bring some order to different aspects of your motivational experiences.

—Gerrig, Richard J. and Zimbardo, Philip G., *Psychology and Life*,
16th ed., pp. 388–389.

VISUAL *VOCABULARY*

VISUAL *VOCABULARY*

Which level of Maslow's
hierarchy of needs is
represented by the picture?

_____

Before Reading

Vocabulary in Context

_____   **1.** The word **competent** in sentence 8 means
      a. prideful.   c. capable.
      b. happy.   d. clear.

_____   **2.** The best synonym for **cognitive** in sentence 10 is
      a. emotional.   c. demanding.
      b. thinking.   d. planning.

After Reading

Concept Maps

3–4. Finish the concept map on the next page with information from the passage.

Central Idea and Main Idea

_____   **5.** Which sentence states the central idea of the passage?
      a. sentence 1   c. sentence 17
      b. sentence 2   d. sentence 24

Supporting Details

_____   **6.** Sentence 7 is
      a. a major supporting detail.
      b. a minor supporting detail.

Transcendence
Spiritual needs for
cosmic identification

Self-Actualization
Needs to fulfill potential,
have meaningful goals

Aesthetic

4. _____

  _____

Cognitive
Needs for knowledge,
understanding, novelty

Esteem
Needs for confidence, sense
of worth and competence, self-
esteem and respect of others

Attachment
Needs to belong, to affiliate,
to love and be loved

Safety
Needs for security, comfort,
tranquility, freedom from fear

3. _____

Needs for food, water, oxygen, rest,
sexual expression, release from tension

▲ **Maslow's Hierarchy of Needs**

According to Maslow, needs at the lower level of the hierarchy dominate an
individual's motivation as long as they are unsatisfied. Once these needs are
adequately met, the higher needs occupy the individual's attention.

—Gerrig, Richard J. and Zimbardo, Philip G., *Psychology and Life*,
16th ed., Figure 12.7 (p. 390).

Transitions

_____ **7.** The word *if* in sentence 8 is a signal word that shows
- a. comparison.
- b. cause and effect.
- c. time order.

_____ **8.** The word *however* in sentence 25 signals
- a. cause and effect.
- b. contrast.
- c. addition.

Thought Patterns

_____ **9.** The primary thought pattern for the entire passage is
- a. classification.
- b. cause and effect.
- c. comparison and contrast.

_____ **10.** The thought pattern for the second paragraph (sentences 9–12) is
- a. cause and effect.
- b. definition and example.
- c. listing.

SUMMARY RESPONSE

Restate the author's central idea in your own words. In your summary, follow the thought pattern used by the author. Begin your summary response with the following: *The central idea of "A Hierarchy of Needs" by Gerrig and Zimbardo is . . .*

WHAT DO YOU THINK?

Assume you are taking a college course in psychology, and your professor has assigned a weekly essay response to your textbook reading. Choose one of the following topics and write a few paragraphs in response to Maslow's hierarchy:

- Describe your motivations or the motivations of someone you know based on Maslow's hierarchy of needs.
- Use generalizations, definitions, and examples in your response.

REVIEW TEST 4

Score (number correct) _____ x 10 = _____ %

Visit MyReadingLab to take this test online and receive feedback and guidance on your answers.

Transitions and Thought Patterns

Before Reading: Survey the following passage adapted from the college textbook *The Interpersonal Communication Book*. Skim the passage, noting the words in bold print. Answer the Before Reading questions that follow the passage. Then read the passage. Next, answer the After Reading questions. Use the discussion and writing topics as activities to do after reading.

Vocabulary Preview

solidifies (6): strengthens
camaraderie (6): friendship
exhortation (11): urging, advice, warning
ethical (17): moral, principled, right

Textbook
Skills

Gossip

[1] Gossip is social talk that involves making evaluations about persons who are not present during the conversation; it generally occurs when two people talk about a third party (Eder & Enke, 1991). [2] As you obviously know, a large part of your conversation at work and in social situations is spent gossiping (Lachnit, 2001; Waddington, 2004; Carey, 2005). [3] In fact, one study estimates that approximately two-thirds of people's conversation time is devoted to social topics, and that most of these topics can be considered gossip (Dunbar, 2004). [4] Gossiping seems universal among all cultures (Laing, 1993), and among some it's a commonly accepted ritual (Hall, 1993).

[5] Lots of reasons have been suggested for the popularity and persistence of gossip. [6] One reason often given is that gossip bonds people together and **solidifies** their relationship; it creates a sense of **camaraderie** (Greengard, 2001; Hafen, 2004). [7] At the same time, of course, it helps to create an in-group (those doing the gossiping) and an out-group (those being gossiped about). [8] Gossip also serves a persuasive function in teaching people the cultural rules of their society. [9] That is, when you gossip about the wrong things that so-and-so did, you're in effect identifying the rules that should be followed and perhaps even the consequences that follow when the rules are broken. [10] Gossip enables you to learn what is

and what is not acceptable behavior (Baumeister, Zhang, & Vohs, 2004). [11]Within an organization, gossip helps to regulate organization behavior: Gossip enables workers to learn who the organizational heroes are, what they did, and how they were rewarded—and carries an implicit **exhortation** to do likewise. [12]And, of course, negative gossip enables workers to learn who broke the rules and what punishments resulted from such rule-breaking—again, with an accompanying implicit **admonition** to avoid such behaviors (Hafen, 2004).

[13]People often engage in gossip for some kind of reward; for example, to hear more gossip, gain social status or control, have fun, cement social bonds, or make social comparisons (Rosnow, 1977; Miller & Wilcox, 1986; Leaper & Holliday, 1995; Wert & Salovey, 2004). [14]Research is not consistent on the consequences of gossip for the person gossiping. [15]One research study argues that gossiping leads others to see you more negatively, regardless of whether your gossip is positive or negative and whether you're sharing this gossip with strangers or friends (Turner, Mazur, Wendel, & Winslow, 2003). [16]Another study finds that positive gossip leads to acceptance by your peers and greater friendship intimacy (Cristina, 2001).

[17]As you might expect, gossiping often has **ethical** implications, and in many instances gossip would be considered unethical. [18]Some such instances: when gossip is used to unfairly hurt another person, when you know it's not true, when no one has the right to such personal information, or when you've promised secrecy (Bok, 1983).

—DeVito, Joseph A., *The Interpersonal Communication
Book*, 11th ed., pp. 212–213.

Before Reading

Vocabulary in Context

1. In sentence 12, **admonition** means _____.

2. Context clue used for **admonition** _____

_____

After Reading

3–6 Central Idea, Supporting Details, and Outlines

Complete the following outline with information from the passage.

Thesis Statement: (3) _____

_____

_____

I. Gossip

    A. Definition: **(4)** _____

       _____

      1. Two-thirds of conversation time is considered gossip.

      2. Gossip is a universal ritual among all cultures.

    B. Reasons for gossip

      1. Gossip bonds people and solidifies relationships.

      2. Gossip creates an in-group and an out-group.

      3. **(5)** _____

    C. **(6)** _____

      1. Gossiping may lead others to see you negatively.

      2. Gossiping may lead to acceptance and intimacy.

Transitions and Thought Patterns

_____   **7.** The main thought pattern for the first paragraph (sentences 1–4) is
      a. comparison.   c. definition and example.
      b. cause and effect.

_____   **8.** The main thought pattern for the second paragraph (sentences 5–12) is
      a. comparison.   c. definition and example.
      b. cause and effect.

_____   **9.** What is the relationship of ideas between sentences 8 and 9?
      a. cause and effect   c. generalization and example
      b. contrast

_____   **10.** What is the relationship of ideas within sentence 13?
      a. definition and example   c. contrast
      b. generalization and example

Restate the author's central idea in your own words. In your summary, follow the thought pattern used by the author. Begin your summary response with the following: *The central idea of "Gossip" from* The Interpersonal Communication Book *by DeVito is . . .*

Assume you have taken the role of a mentor to a younger person through your public service work with a youth organization such as the Boys Club, the Girls Club, Boys Scouts, Girl Scouts, or the YMCA. Write an article to post on the organization's local Web page about the causes and effects of gossip—particularly in the context of online social networks. Consider the following ideas from the passage to guide your writing:

- Define the term *gossip.*
- List reasons why gossip occurs.
- Summarize the effects of gossip.

After Reading About More Thought Patterns

Before you move on to the Mastery Tests on thought patterns, take time to reflect on your learning and performance by answering the following questions. Write your answers in your notebook.

- How has my knowledge base or prior knowledge about more thought patterns changed?
- Based on my studies, how do I think I will perform on the Mastery Test(s)? Why do I think my scores will be above average, average, or below average? (Note: An additional fourth Mastery Test may be found in MyReadingLab.)
- Would I recommend this chapter to other students who want to learn about thought patterns? Why or why not?

Test your understanding of what you have learned about thought patterns for master readers by completing the Chapter 8 Review.

Name _____ Section_____

Date _____ **Score** (number correct) _____ x 10 = _____ %

Visit MyReadingLab to take this test online and receive feedback and guidance on your answers.

Read the following paragraph from a college social science textbook. Fill in the blanks (**1–5**) with transition words from the box. Then, answer the questions following the paragraph.

differences	effect	more	same	than

Differences in the Effects of Drugs

Textbook Skills

Some differences in drug effects may be related to an interaction between the drug itself and the specific traits of the person taking the drug. One characteristic is a person's weight. In general, a heavier person will require a greater amount of a drug **(1)** _____ a lighter person to receive the same drug **(2)** _____. It is for this reason that drug dosages are expressed as a ratio of drug amount to weight. Another characteristic is gender. Even if a man and a woman are exactly the **(3)** _____ weight, differences in drug effects can still result on the basis of gender **(4)** _____ in body composition and sex hormones. Women have, on average, a higher proportion of fat, due to a greater fat-to-muscle ratio, and a lower proportion of water than men. When we look at the effects of alcohol consumption in terms of gender, we find that the lower water content in women makes them feel **(5)** _____ intoxicated than men, even if the same amount of alcohol is consumed.

—Adapted from Levinthal, Charles F., *Drugs, Behaviors, and Modern Society*, 3rd ed., pp. 58–59.

_____ **6.** The transition used to fill blank (1) signals
  a. cause and effect.
  b. generalization and example.
  c. comparison and contrast.

_____ **7.** The transition used to fill blank (2) signals
   a. cause and effect.
   b. generalization and example.
   c. comparison and contrast.

_____ **8.** The transition used to fill blank (3) signals
   a. cause and effect.
   b. definition and example.
   c. comparison and contrast.

_____ **9.** The transition used to fill blank (4) signals
   a. cause and effect.
   b. generalization and example.
   c. comparison and contrast.

_____ **10.** The transition used to fill blank (5) signals
   a. cause and effect.
   b. definition.
   c. comparison and contrast.

Name _____ Section_____

Date _____ **Score** (number correct) _____ x 10 = _____ %

Visit MyReadingLab to take this test online and receive feedback and guidance on your answers.

A. Write the appropriate numbers in the spaces provided to complete the correct order of the ideas. Then answer the question that follows the list.

Physical Effects of Modern Life

_____ One of the most pervasive problems is shortened muscles, tendons, and ligaments.

___5___ For example, continual sitting at work and leisure results in shortened muscles, tendons, and ligaments and eventually results in restricted movements.

_____ However, our daily activities have changed drastically.

_____ Our modern living patterns are directly responsible for a host of health problems.

___3___ First, our basic body structure and function have not changed since the days of prehistoric humans.

_____ It is not unusual for adults in their mid-twenties to be so restricted that touching their toes while keeping the knees straight is impossible or painful.

___7___ In addition to restricted movement, chronic sitting affects the spine.

_____ The result will be a sitting-type posture when one is standing or walking; this posture produces pain and tension because body parts are not positioned naturally.

___8___ The spine will condition itself to the demand of chronic sitting and lose its ability to remain erect.

—Adapted from Girdano, Daniel A., Dusek, Dorothy E., and Everly, Jr., George S., *Controlling Stress and Tension*, 6th ed., p. 248.

_____ **6.** The primary thought pattern is
  a. generalization and example.
  b. comparison and contrast.
  c. cause and effect.

B. Read the following paragraph from a college textbook on tourism. Then complete the concept map.

The Development of Cancun

[1]In the early 1970s, several remote areas of the world saw that tourism could be profitable; however, they did not want to destroy the exotic environment that surrounded them. [2]One such place was Cancun, Mexico. [3]Cancun was a prime beach location, but the number of tourists was quite low. [4]Developers recognized Cancun's potential and drew up a master plan that placed priority on environmental protection. [5]Unfortunately, Mexico began to experience political and economical instability. [6]The recession caused the government and business leaders to scramble, trying to find a way to bring money into the economy—specifically, U.S. dollars. [7]Tourism in Mexico was one of the few industries that showed signs of growth. [8]However, in an effort to make a quick profit, Cancun's environmentally friendly attractions were sacrificed to make room for large-scale development. [9]As a result, the few natives that were living in the assigned resort area were relocated to the mountains where they live in cardboard shacks without plumbing. [10]The beaches surrounding Cancun are becoming cluttered with garbage, and the reef off of the coastline is damaged by ships coming into the wharf. [11]Water treatment is insufficient and it is practically impossible to meet the growing capacity requirement of the tourists.

—Walker, John R. and Walker, Josielyn T., *Tourism: Concepts and Practices*, pp. 381–382.

Causes		Effects
7. _____ _____ _____	Cancun's large-scale, rapid development →	natives were relocated 9. _____ _____ reef is damaged by ships
8. _____ _____ _____ _____		10. _____ _____

Read the following passages from college textbooks. Then answer the questior
and complete the outline and the concept table.

**Textbook
Skills**

Quakes, Aftershocks, and Foreshocks

[1]Earthquakes are produced by the rapid release of elastic energy stored in rock that has been deformed by differential stresses. [2]Once the strength of the rock is exceeded, it suddenly ruptures, causing the vibrations of an earthquake.

[3]Strong earthquakes are followed by numerous smaller tremors, called aftershocks, that gradually diminish in frequency and intensity over a period of several months. [4]Within 24 hours of the massive 1964 Alaskan earthquake, 28 aftershocks were recorded, 10 of which had magnitudes that exceeded 6. [5]More than 10,000 aftershocks with magnitudes of 3.5 or above occurred in the following 69 days and thousands of minor tremors were recorded over a span of 18 months. [6]Because aftershocks happen mainly on the section of the fault that has slipped, they provide geologists with data that is useful in establishing the dimensions of the rupture surface.

[7]Although aftershocks are weaker than the main earthquake, they can trigger the destruction of already weakened structures. [8]This occurred in northwestern Armenia (1988) where many people lived in large apartment buildings constructed of brick and concrete slabs. [9]After a moderate earthquake of magnitude 6.9 weakened the buildings, a strong aftershock of magnitude 5.8 completed the demolition.

[10]In contrast to aftershocks, small earthquakes called foreshocks often precede a major earthquake by days or in some cases years. [11]Monitoring of foreshocks to predict forthcoming earthquakes has been attempted with limited success.

—Adapted from Lutgens, Frederick K. and Tarbuck, Edward J.,
Essentials of Geology, 11th ed., pp. 338–339.

_____ **1.** The thought pattern of paragraph 1 is
    a. cause and effect.
    b. generalization and example.
    c. definition and example.

...tern of paragraph 2 is
...effect.

...ion and example

...lought pattern of paragraph 3 is
...cause and effect.
   generalization and example.
c. contrast.

4. The thought pattern of paragraph 4 is
   a. cause and effect.
   b. contrast.
   c. definition and example

5. On what basis are aftershocks and foreshocks contrasted? _____

8 Summary of Key Concepts of Mo... Thought Patterns

LO1 LO2 LO3 LO4   Assess your comprehension of thought patterns. Complete the following two-column notes of terms and definitions with information from the chapter.

Term	Definition/Examples
Comparison	
Words and phrases of comparison	
Contrast	
Words and phrases of contrast	
Cause	
Effect	
Words and phrases of cause and effect	
Generalization and example	
Definition and example	
Words and phrases of example	

g questions and prompts.

what is the difference between comparison and contrast?

_____

_____

LO2 n words, what is the difference between a cause and an effect?

_____

_____

LO1 LO3 In your own words, what are the similarities and differences between these two
LO4 thought patterns: *generalization and example* and *definition and example*?

_____

_____

_____

_____

_____

_____

LO2 In the space below, create a concept map based on the information in the
paragraph.

According to research, meditation can have positive emotional and physical
effects. Regular meditation leads to increased control over one's emotions. Regular meditation also contributes to lower blood pressure and cholesterol levels.

LO1 LO2 Summarize the two most important ideas in this chapter that will help you
LO3 LO4 improve your reading comprehension.
LO5 LO6

_____

_____

Fact and Opinion

LO LEARNING OUTCOMES

After studying this chapter you should be able to:

- **LO1** Define *Fact* and *Opinion* and Identify Their Differences
- **LO2** Ask Questions to Identify Facts
- **LO3** Analyze Biased Words to Identify Opinions
- **LO4** Analyze Qualifiers to Identify Opinions
- **LO5** Analyze Supposed "Facts"
- **LO6** Read Critically: Evaluate Details as Fact or Opinion in Context
- **LO7** Develop Textbook Skills: Fact and Opinion in Textbooks
- **LO8** Apply Information Literacy Skills: Academic, Personal, and Career Applications of Fact and Opinion

Before Reading About Fact and Opinion

You are most likely already familiar with the commonly used words *fact* and *opinion*, and you probably already have an idea about what each one means. Take a moment to clarify your current understanding about fact and opinion by writing a definition for each one in the spaces below:

Fact: _____

_____

Opinion: _____

_____

_____

As you work through this chapter, compare what you already know about fact and opinion to new information that you learn using the following method.

On a blank page in your notebook draw a line down the middle of the page to form two columns. Label one side "Fact" and the other "Opinion." Below each heading, copy the definition you wrote for each one. As you work through the chapter, record new information you learn about facts and opinions in their corresponding columns.

LO1   Define *Fact* and *Opinion* and Identify Their Differences

Fact: The average American child will witness 12,000 violent acts on tele-
              vision each year, amounting to about 200,000 violent acts by age 18.
Opinion: American television programming is too violent.

Master readers must sort fact from opinion to properly understand and evaluate the information they are reading.

> A **fact** is a specific detail that is true based on objective proof. A
>   fact is discovered.
> An **opinion** is an interpretation, value judgment, or belief that
>   cannot be proved or disproved. An opinion is created.
> **Objective proof** can be physical evidence, an eyewitness account,
>   or the result of an accepted scientific method.

Most people's points of view and beliefs are based on a blend of fact and opinion. Striving to remain objective, many authors rely mainly on facts. The main purpose of these authors is to inform. For example, textbooks, news arti-cles, and medical research rely on facts. In contrast, editorials, advertisements, and fiction often mix fact and opinion. The main purpose of these types of writ-ing is to persuade or entertain.

Separating fact from opinion requires you to think critically because opin-ion is often presented as fact. The following clues will help you separate fact from opinion.

Fact	Opinion
Is objective	Is subjective
Is discovered	Is created
States reality	Interprets reality
Can be verified	Cannot be verified
Is presented with unbiased words	Is presented with biased words
Example of a fact	*Example of an opinion*
Spinach is a source of iron.	Spinach tastes awful.

A fact is a specific, objective, and verifiable detail; in contrast, an opinion is a biased, personal view created from feelings and beliefs.

> **EXAMPLE** Read the following statements, and mark each one **F** if it states a fact or **O** if it expresses an opinion.

_____ **1.** The most beautiful spot on earth is a serene lake nestled in the foothills of the Appalachian Mountains.

_____ **2.** Tippah Lake is located just outside of the small town of Ripley, Mississippi, in the foothills of the Appalachian Mountains.

EXPLANATION The first sentence expresses an opinion in the form of a personal interpretation about what is beautiful. The second sentence is a statement of fact that gives the location of the lake. <

Practice 1

Read the following statements and mark each one **F** if it states a fact or **O** if it expresses an opinion.

_____ **1.** Living in a large city is detrimental to one's psychological well-being.

_____ **2.** New York City offers an array of cultural experiences including Broadway theatre, historic sites such as Ellis Island and the Statue of Liberty, and many museums such as the Children's Museum of Manhattan.

LO2 Ask Questions to Identify Facts

To test whether a statement is a fact, ask these three questions:

- Can the statement be proved or demonstrated to be true?
- Can the statement be observed in practice or operation?
- Can the statement be verified by witnesses, manuscripts, or documents?

If the answer to any of these questions is no, the statement is not a fact. Instead, it is an opinion. Keep in mind, however, that many statements blend both fact and opinion.

> **EXAMPLE** Read the following statements and mark each one **F** if it states a fact or **O** if it expresses an opinion.

_____ 1. In the 1700s women sewed lead weights into the bottoms of their bathing gowns to prevent the gowns from floating up and exposing their legs.

_____ 2. Bikinis reveal too much skin and are indecent.

_____ 3. Paul Newman acted in more than 65 movies in a career that spanned more than 50 years.

_____ 4. Paul Newman's distinguished film career and admirable charity work made him an undeniable American hero.

EXPLANATION Compare your answers to the ones below.

1. **F:** This statement can be easily verified by doing research.

2. **O:** This is a statement of personal opinion. Words and phrases such as *too much* and *indecent* are judgments that vary from person to person.

3. **F:** This statement contains two easily verified facts.

4. **O:** Several words in this statement—*distinguished, admirable,* and *undeniable*—reveal that it is an opinion based on personal views. ◄

Practice 2

Read the following statements and mark each one **F** if it states a fact, **O** if it expresses an opinion, or **F/O** if it expresses both a fact and an opinion.

_____ 1. Ninety-five percent of the world's consumers live outside the United States.

_____ 2. During the creation of his novel *Carrie*, Stephen King threw the novel into the trash, and his wife dug it out and convinced him to finish it.

_____ 3. Low-carbohydrate diets such as Atkins and South Beach are ineffective and dangerous.

_____ 4. Balto was a dog who, in the winter of 1925, led a dogsled team through a blizzard to get medicine to Nome, Alaska, because of a fatal diphtheria epidemic; a statue stands in his honor in Central Park, New York, at 67th Street and Fifth Avenue, just inside the Park.

_____ 5. Cats can be irritating pets because they are independent and unaffectionate.

_____ **6.** Newspapers are the most reliable source for news.

_____ **7.** Danica Sue Patrick is an American auto racing driver, currently competing in the IndyCar Series, the ARCA Racing Series, and the NASCAR Nationwide Series.

_____ **8.** Danica Patrick is also a beautiful woman who has appeared on the cover of _Sports Illustrated_.

_____ **9.** Regular dental flossing reduces gum disease.

_____ **10.** People who live in the Northeast part of the United States are much more open-minded and liberal than people who live in the South.

LO3 Analyze Biased Words to Identify Opinions

Be on the lookout for biased words. **Biased words** express opinions, value judgments, and interpretations. They are often loaded with emotion. The box contains a small sample of these kinds of words.

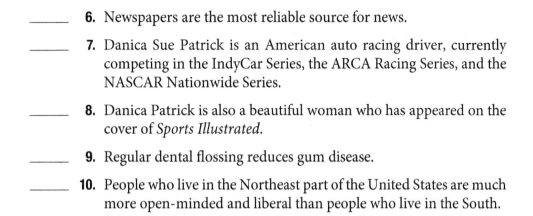

Biased Words					
amazing	best	favorite	great	miserable	stupid
awful	better	frightful	greatest	more	ugly
bad	disgusting	fun	handsome	most	unbelievable
beautiful	exciting	good	horrible	smart	very

Realize that a sentence can include both facts and opinions. The part of the sentence that includes a biased word may be an opinion about another part of the sentence that is a fact.

> **EXAMPLE** Read the following sentences. Underline the biased words.

1. John Coltrane was a jazz musician whose quartet produced hit albums that remain the most innovative and expressive jazz music of our time.

2. Even though marijuana use is widespread in America, it should not be legalized.

EXPLANATION In the first sentence, the first part "John Coltrane was a jazz musician whose quartet produced hit albums" is a fact that can be proved. The second part of the sentence, however, expresses an opinion about his music using the biased words *most innovative* and *expressive*. In the second sentence, the widespread use of marijuana is well documented, but the idea that "it should not be legalized" is an opinion. ◁

Practice 3

Read the following two sentences. Underline the biased words.

1. The works of Joan Didion, one of the most brilliant writers of this genera-tion, should be required reading in a liberal arts education.

2. Writing is a satisfying process that can lead to alarming self-discoveries, comforting insights, and much needed wisdom.

LO4 Analyze Qualifiers to Identify Opinions

Be on the lookout for words that qualify an idea. A qualifier may express an absolute, unwavering opinion using words like *always* or *never*. Other times a qualifier expresses an opinion in the form of a command as in *must*, or the desirability of an action with a word like *should*. Qualifiers may indicate differ-ent degrees of doubt with words such as *seems* or *might*. The box contains a few examples of these kinds of words.

Words That Qualify Ideas

all	could	likely	never	possibly, possible	sometimes
always	every	may	often	probably, probable	think
appear	has/have to	might	only	seem	usually
believe	it is believed	must	ought to	should	

Remember that a sentence can include both fact and opinion. Authors use qualifiers to express opinions about facts.

▷ **EXAMPLE** Read the following sentences. Underline the qualifiers.

1. Dissatisfaction with work often spills over into relationships; most people are not able to separate work problems from their relationship lives.

2. In his book *Messages: Building Interpersonal Communication Skills*, Joseph A. DeVito states, "Commitment may take many forms; it may be an engage-ment or a marriage; it may be a commitment to help the person or be with the person, or a commitment to reveal your deepest secrets." (1999, p. 264)

EXPLANATION

1. The qualifiers in this sentence are *often* and *most*.

2. The qualifiers in this sentence are *may* and *many*. ◀

Practice 4

Read the following sentences. Underline the qualifiers.

1. Oral hygiene is the only way to avoid possible gum disease; you must brush your teeth three times a day and floss at least once daily.

2. All citizens should save some portion of their earnings for their probable retirement.

LO5 Analyze Supposed "Facts"

Beware of **false facts,** or statements presented as facts that are actually untrue. At times, an author may mislead the reader with a false impression of the facts. Political and commercial advertisements often present facts out of context, exaggerate the facts, or give only some of the facts. For example, Governor People boasts that under his leadership, his state has attained the highest literacy rates ever achieved. Although his state's literacy rates did reach their highest historical levels, the actual rise was slight, and his state's literacy levels remained the lowest in the country. The governor misled people by leaving out important facts.

Sometimes an author deliberately presents false information. Journalist Jayson Blair concocted a host of false facts in many of the articles he wrote for the *New York Times.* For example, in his five articles about the capture and rescue of Private Jessica Lynch, Blair fabricated many facts. First, he wrote his stories as if he had conducted face-to-face interviews, yet he never traveled to meet the family and he conducted all of his interviews by telephone. Then, in a March 27, 2003, article, he described Lynch's father as being "choked up as he stood on his porch here overlooking the tobacco fields and cattle pastures." The statement was false: He never witnessed such a scene, and the Lynch home does not overlook tobacco fields or cattle pastures. Blair's use of false facts ruined his career and damaged the reputation of the prestigious *New York Times.*

Most often, however, false facts are mere errors. Read the following two examples of false facts:

1. Thomas Alva Edison invented the first light bulb.

2. The common cold is most commonly spread by coughing and sneezing.

Research quickly proves the first statement to be a false fact; light bulbs were being used 50 years before Edison patented his version of the light bulb. The second statement is a false fact because studies show that a cold is more likely to be spread by physical contact such as shaking hands or sharing a phone than by inhaling particles in the air. Often some prior knowledge of the topic is needed to identify false facts. The more you read, the more masterful you will become at evaluating facts as true or false.

False facts can be used to mislead, persuade, or entertain. For example, read the following claims about a nutritional supplement that allegedly prevents a wide range of illnesses including colds, flus, cancer, irritable bowel syndrome, *Candida albicans,* and heart disease.

BodyWise

[1]Every day your body is under attack and the results can be deadly. [2]The best thing you can do is to bolster your immune system so it can defend itself from infection and foreign invaders. [3]We believe BodyWise International's all natural AG-Immune formula is the most powerful product ever created to promote a healthy immune system . . . and a healthier future. [4]And while it's [sic] primary ingredient, Ai/E10^{TM}, has proven to be clinically effective for use with both immune and autoimmune disorders, you don't have to be immune system challenged to enjoy the amazing benefits of this exciting new supplement. [5]Think of it as a prudent preventative measure that promotes optimal health by increasing the activity of natural killer (NK) cells—your body's last line of defense against illness and disease. [6]AG-Immune has already changed the lives of thousands of people across North America. [7]Imagine what it could do for you: [8]"One day I happened to notice that, on the cover of The Ultimate Nutrient booklet, *candida* was listed as one of the areas Ai/E10^{TM} was clinically successful in treating. [9]I began taking two a day and literally—within 36 hours—the pain began to dissipate. [10]After only three weeks, my symptoms were completely gone! [11]I have been on BodyWise for almost eight years and at the risk of sounding over-dramatic, I have to say, the products have definitely changed my quality of life."

—Adapted from *United States of America, Plaintiff, v. Body Wise International, Inc.,* and *Jesse A. Stoff, M.D., Defendants,* United States District Court, Central District of California, Southern Division. Civil Action No.: SACV-05-43 (DOC) (Anx).

The Federal Trade Commission sued and won a settlement against the company for false advertisement. The company could not support its claims to prevent or improve disease symptoms with scientific evidence. Note the biased words the author used to describe the effectiveness of the supplement: *attack, deadly, best, bolster, most powerful, healthier, amazing benefits, exciting, prudent,* and *optimal,* to name a few.

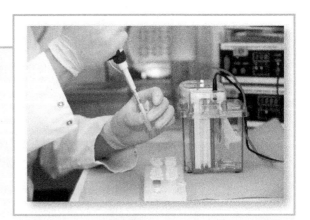

VISUAL *VOCABULARY*

The best synonym for "clinically" is _____.

   a. accidentally
   b. scientifically
   c. humanly

▶ Ai/E10™ has proven to be clinically effective for use with both immune and autoimmune disorders.

In addition to thinking carefully about false facts, beware of opinions worded to sound like facts. Remember that facts are specific details that can be researched and verified as true. However, opinions may be introduced with phrases like *in truth, the truth of the matter,* or *in fact.* Read the following two statements:

1. In truth, reproductive cloning is expensive and highly inefficient.

2. More than 90% of cloning attempts fail to produce viable offspring, and cloned animals tend to have much weaker immune function and higher rates of infection, tumor growth, and other disorders; in fact, reproductive cloning is expensive and highly inefficient.

—Adapted from "Cloning Fact Sheet," *Human Genome Program,*
U.S. Department of Energy.

The first statement is a general opinion that uses the biased words *expensive, highly,* and *inefficient.* The second statement is a blend of fact and opinion. It begins with the facts, but then uses the phrase *in fact* to introduce the opinion.

> **EXAMPLES**   Read the following statements and mark each one as follows:

F if it states a fact

O if it states an opinion

F/O if it combines fact and opinion

_____ **1.** Public funding for art education, at both national and local levels, has declined in recent years.

_____ **2.** Diet Pepsi tastes better than Diet Coke.

_____ **3.** Microwave popcorn is a nutritious, low-calorie, and tasty snack food.

_____ **4.** T'ai chi and yoga include relaxation and breathing techniques that improve mental and physical health.

_____ **5.** With humankind's ability to produce synthetic fibers that can clothe us with beauty and comfort, humans should refrain from murdering animals so their hides, coats, or furs can be used as clothing.

EXPLANATIONS

  1. This is a statement of fact that can be researched.

  2. This is a statement of opinion that includes the biased word *better*. Taste preferences are a matter of personal opinion.

  3. This is a blend of fact and opinion. Popcorn is a low-calorie snack food, and its nutritional value can be verified; however, the value word *tasty* states an opinion.

  4. This is a statement of fact that can be verified through research.

  5. This is a statement that blends fact and opinion. The biased words *beauty, should,* and *murdering* are used. ◀

> **EXAMPLE**   Look at the following cartoon. Then write one fact and one opinion about the cartoon.

Fact: _____

         _____

© 2004 Jeff Parker/Cagle Cartoons, Inc.

Opinion: _____

_____

EXPLANATION Compare your answers to the ones below.

Fact: Many Americans ignore the Surgeon General's warning against smoking. The percentage of Americans who smoke has declined since 1964.

Opinion: The Surgeon General's warning against smoking has had a significant effect on American smoking behaviors. People who smoke are foolish. ◄

Practice 5

A. Read the following statements and mark each one as follows:

F if it states a fact

O if it expresses an opinion

F/O if it combines fact and opinion

_____ **1.** I believe capital punishment is a crime against humanity.

_____ **2.** Executives of large corporations receive outrageously large salaries that unfairly reward them for successes created by lower paid rank-and-file workers.

_____ **3.** *E. coli*, influenza, tuberculosis, measles, mumps, and smallpox are just a few of the diseases that are preventable through vaccinations.

_____ **4.** More than 8 million Africans are infected with tuberculosis, with nearly 3 million dying each year; wealthier and more developed countries, such as the United States, should help fund widespread vaccination programs in Africa.

_____ **5.** Astrology offers information that is effective in making important life decisions.

B. Read the following short reviews of destinations, restaurants, movies, and plays. Mark each one as follows:

F if it states a fact

O if it expresses an opinion

F/O if it combines fact and opinion

_____ **6.** The 14th Street Bar and Grill in Boulder, Colorado, offers excellent food, average service, and a spectacular view of the Rocky Mountains.

_____ **7.** Drago's Seafood in Metairie, Louisiana, offers Creole cuisine ranging from $21 to $24, with lobster and seafood as the main entrees.

_____ **8.** Judson College, the nation's sixth-oldest women's college, offers a challenging and high-quality liberal arts education.

_____ **9.** One bat can eat as many as one thousand insect pests, such as mosquitoes, in an hour.

_____ **10.** *TMZ TV*, a television magazine show that delves into the private lives of celebrities, stands as an embarrassing example of the public's interest in gossip and the misfortune of other people.

L06

Read Critically: Evaluate Details as Fact or Opinion in Context

Because the printed word seems to give authority to an idea, many of us accept what we read as fact. Yet much of what is published is actually opinion. Master readers question what they read. Reading critically is noting the use of fact and opinion in the context of a paragraph or passage, the author, and the type of source in which the passage is printed.

Evaluate the Context of the Passage

> **EXAMPLE** Read the passage and identify each sentence as follows:

F if it states a fact

O if it expresses an opinion

F/O if it combines fact and opinion

Vermicomposting

[1]Composting is an excellent way to recycle organic materials like food scraps and yard clippings. [2]Vermicomposting uses red worms to decompose organic material and create fertilizer for gardens. [3]In addition, it provides an easy, clean, odor-free, and environmentally correct way to get rid of garbage. [4]The worms are able to eat over half their body weight in one day, and their waste material, known as castings, is full of nutrients and microbes that promote plant growth. [5]Everyone should use vermicomposting.

1. _____   2. _____   3. _____   4. _____   5. _____

EXPLANATION Compare your answers to the ones below.

1. **F/O:** Composting is a way to recycle organic materials like food scraps and yard clippings; however, the word *excellent* is a biased word.

2. **F:** This statement can be verified.

3. **F/O:** Vermicomposting is a way to get rid of garbage; however, the words *easy, clean,* and *environmentally correct* are biased words or phrases.

4. **F:** This statement can be checked and verified as true.

5. **O:** This statement expresses an opinion with the words *everyone* and *should.* ◀

Practice 6

Read the passage and identify each sentence as follows:

F if it states a fact

O if it expresses an opinion

F/O if it combines fact and opinion

What Makes a Home Energy Star?

[1]ENERGY STAR is the government-backed symbol for energy efficiency; homes that earn the ENERGY STAR are significantly more energy efficient than standard homes. [2]ENERGY STAR builders achieve this high efficiency for you by selecting from a variety of features such as the following:

Tight Construction and Ducts

[3]Advanced techniques for sealing holes and cracks in the home's "envelope" and in heating and cooling ducts help reduce drafts, moisture, dust, pollen, pests, and noise. [4]A tightly sealed home improves comfort and indoor air quality while lowering utility and maintenance costs.

Effective Insulation Systems

[5]Properly installed and inspected insulation in floors, walls, and attics ensures even temperatures throughout the house, while using less energy. [6]The result is lower utility costs and a quieter, more comfortable home.

Efficient Heating and Cooling Equipment

[7]An energy-efficient, properly installed heating and cooling system uses less energy to operate, which reduces your utility bills. [8]This system can also be quieter, reduce indoor humidity, and improve the overall comfort of your home.

High Performance Windows

[9]Energy-efficient windows employ advanced technologies, such as protective coatings and improved frame assemblies, to help keep heat in during the winter and out during the summer. [10]These windows also block damaging ultraviolet sunlight that can discolor carpets and furnishings.

—Adapted from U. S. Environmental Protection Agency. *Energy Star®
Qualified New Homes.* EPA 430-F-09-053.

1. _____   2. _____   3. _____   4. _____   5. _____

6. _____   7. _____   8. _____   9. _____   10. _____

VISUAL *VOCABULARY*

Energy construction materials, including insulation, replace a tornado destroyed home.
The best definition of **insulation** is material that _____ heat, electricity, or sound.

 a. isolates
 b. enhances
 c. blocks

Evaluate the Context of the Author

Even though opinions can't be proved true like facts can, many opinions are still sound and valuable. To judge the accuracy of the opinion, you must consider the source: the author of the opinion. Authors offer two types of valid opinions: informed opinions and expert opinions.

An author develops an **informed opinion** by gathering and analyzing evidence.
An author develops an **expert opinion** through much training and extensive knowledge in a given field.

> **EXAMPLE** Read the topic and study the list of authors who have written their opinions about the topic. Identify each person as **IO** if he or she is more likely to offer an informed opinion and **EO** if he or she is more likely to offer an expert opinion.

How to Lose Weight Safely and Effectively

_____ **1.** Michael F. Roizen, MD, and Mehmet C. Oz, MD, authors of *You: On a Diet.*

_____ **2.** An advice columnist such as Ann Landers or Dear Abby responding to a reader's question.

_____ **3.** Martha Stewart giving cooking tips on her nationally syndicated talk show.

_____ **4.** A student essay based on research.

EXPLANATION

1. Drs. Roizen and Oz are considered experts in the field of weight loss. One way to identify an expert opinion is to note if the person giving the opinion holds an advanced degree or title or has published articles or books about the topic being discussed. Both Roizen and Oz have the education and the achievement of being successful authors about this topic.

2. Advice columnists offer informed opinions on a wide range of topics. They often cite experts in their advice.

3. Martha Stewart has had extensive experience cooking and writing cookbooks and can provide an expert opinion about food preparation.

4. A student offers an informed opinion based on research. ◀

Evaluate the Context of the Source

Often people turn to factual sources to find the factual details needed to form informed opinions and expert opinions. A medical dictionary, an English handbook, and a world atlas are a few excellent examples of factual sources.

▶ **EXAMPLE** Read the following passage from a college psychology textbook. Answer the questions that follow.

Interpreting Dreams

Textbook
Skills

[1]You may have wondered whether dreams, especially those that frighten us or that recur, have hidden meanings. [2]Sigmund Freud believed that dreams function to satisfy unconscious sexual and aggressive desires. [3]Because such wishes are unacceptable to the dreamer, they have to be disguised and therefore appear in dreams in symbolic forms. [4]Freud claimed that objects such as sticks, umbrellas, tree trunks, and guns symbolize the male sex organ; objects such as chests, cupboards, and boxes represent the female sex organ. [5]Freud differentiated between the **manifest content** of a dream—the content of the dream as recalled by the dreamer—and

the **latent content**—or the underlying meaning of the dream—which he considered more significant.

[6]Beginning in the 1950s, psychologists began to move away from the Freudian interpretation of dreams. [7]For example, Hall (1953) proposed a **cognitive theory of dreaming**. [8]He suggested that dreaming is simply thinking while asleep. [9]Advocates of Hall's approach argued for a greater focus on the manifest content. [10]The actual dream itself is seen as an expression of a broad range of the dreamer's concerns rather than as an expression of sexual impulses (Webb, 1975).

[11]Well-known sleep researcher J. Allan Hobson (1988) rejects the notion that nature would equip humans with the capability of having dreams that would require a specialist to interpret. [12]Hobson and McCarley (1977) advanced the **activation-synthesis hypothesis of dreaming**. [13]This hypothesis suggests that dreams are simply the brain's attempt to make sense of the random firing of brain cells during REM-sleep. [14]Just as people try to make sense of input from the environment during their waking hours, they try to find meaning in the conglomeration of sensations and memories that are generated internally by this random firing of brain cells. [15]Hobson (1989) believes that dreams also have psychological significance, because the meaning a person imposes on the random mental activity reflects that person's experiences, remote memories, associations, drives, and fears.

—Wood, Samuel E., Wood, Ellen Green, and Boyd, Denise,
Mastering the World of Psychology, 3rd ed., p. 127.

_____ **1.** Sentence 1 states
    a. a fact.   c. a fact and an opinion.
    b. an opinion.

_____ **2.** Sentence 3 states
    a. a fact.   c. a fact and an opinion.
    b. an opinion.

_____ **3.** Sentence 6 states a
    a. a fact.   c. a fact and an opinion.
    b. an opinion.

_____ **4.** Overall, the theories of Freud, Hall, Hobson, and McCarley offer
    a. informed opinions.   c. factual details.
    b. expert opinions.

EXPLANATION Compare your answers to the following:

1. Sentence 1 states (b) an opinion. Many readers may have never "wondered" about dreams. This statement cannot be verified or proven.

2. Sentence 3 states the expert (b) opinion of Sigmund Freud—which is a partial explanation of his theory of dream interpretation.

3. Sentence 6 states (a) fact—an event in the history of dream interpretation.

4. Overall, the theories of Freud, Hall, Hobson, and McCarley offer (b) expert opinions. Scientific theories are plausible explanations for a fact or occurrence that can be observed. Thus, theories are not themselves facts, but reasonable explanations by experts supported by facts. As seen in this passage, conflicting theories about an occurrence can exist. ◄

Practice 7

Read the passage and then answer the questions that follow it.

Phobias

[1]All of us have experienced that gnawing feeling of fear in the pit of our stomach. [2]Perhaps we feared failing a test, losing a job, or disappointing a loved one, and each of these circumstances caused us to experience legitimate fear. [3]In contrast, a significant number of us experience fear for no known or logical reason. [4]According to the National Institute of Mental Health, millions of Americans, as many as one out of ten, suffer from phobias. [5]F. J. McGuigan, in his book *Encyclopedia of Stress,* defines a phobia as "an irrational, obsessive, and intense fear that is focused on a specific circumstance, idea, or thing." [6]Experts discuss phobias in terms of three subgroups: agoraphobia, social phobia, and specific phobia. [7]Agoraphobia is defined by *Merriam-Webster's Collegiate Dictionary* as the "abnormal fear of being helpless in an embarrassing or unescapable situation that is characterized especially by the avoidance of open or public places." [8]For example, McGuigan states that people who suffer agoraphobia tend to avoid crowds, tunnels, bridges, public transportation, and elevators. [9]In the textbook *Psychology and Life,* authors Richard Gerrig and Philip Zimbardo write that social phobia occurs as a person anticipates a public situation in which he or she will be observed by others. [10]People who suffer from social phobias fear public embarrassment. [11]"Finally, specific phobias occur in response to a specific object or situation." [12]For example, some people have an irrational fear of snakes, insects, or heights.

_____ **1.** Sentence 1 is
    a. a fact.   b. an opinion.

_____ **2.** In sentence 4, the National Institute of Mental Health is offered as
    a. a factual resource.   b. an informed opinion.

_____ **3.** In sentence 5, the *Encyclopedia of Stress* offers
    a. a factual resource.   b. an opinion.

_____ **4.** In sentence 7, *Merriam-Webster's Collegiate Dictionary* acts as
    a. an expert opinion.   b. a factual resource.

_____ **5.** In sentence 9, Gerrig and Zimbardo's definition is
    a. an informed opinion.   b. an expert opinion.

_____ **6.** Overall, this paragraph is
    a. a factual resource.   c. an expert opinion.
    b. an informed opinion.

VISUAL *VOCABULARY*

1. Identify the meaning of the word parts:

agora means _____

_____

phobia means _____

2. What type of phobia is agoraphobia? _____

_____

▲ Maya overcame agoraphobia and now enjoys city life.

L07 Develop Textbook Skills: Fact and Opinion in Textbooks

Textbook Skills

Most textbook authors are careful to present only ideas based on observation, research, and expert opinion.

In addition, textbook authors often use pictures, drawings, or graphics to make the relationship between the main idea and supporting details clear. Although most of these graphics are based on factual data and expert opinions, they still require careful analysis to discern fact from opinion as you interpret them.

⊙ **EXAMPLE**   Read the following passage and graphic illustration from a college environmental studies textbook. Identify the sentences in the passage and the statements about the graphic as follows:

F if it states a fact.

O if it states an opinion.

F/O if it combines fact and opinion.

¹Transit Options Help Cities

²Traffic jams on roadways cause air pollution, stress, and countless hours of lost personal time. ³They also cost the U.S. economy an estimated $74 billion each year in fuel and lost productivity.

⁴In general, however, the United States lags behind most nations in mass transit. ⁵Many countries, rich and poor alike, have extensive bus systems that ferry citizens within and between towns and cities cheaply and effectively. ⁶Curitiba, Brazil, a metropolis of 2.5 million people, has an outstanding bus system that is used each day by three-quarters of the population. ⁷Japan, China, and many European nations have developed modern high-speed "bullet" trains, whereas the United States has long starved its only national passenger rail network, Amtrak, of funding.

—Adapted from Withgott, Jay H. and Laposata, Matthew, *Essential Environment: The Science Behind the Stories,* pp. 406–407.

1. _____   2. _____   3. _____   4. _____   5. _____

6. _____   7. _____

_____   **8.** Automobiles require more energy consumption than all kinds of rail transit combined.

_____   **9.** The costs of driving in large cities need to be reduced.

_____   **10.** Buses are cheaper and more energy efficient and therefore better than automobiles.

EXPLANATION   Compare your answer to the ones that follow.

1. **O:** The word *Help* states a value judgment, which is based on expert opinion and facts.

2. **F:** This sentence states a commonly known, accepted, and provable fact.

3. **F:** This statement can be proved true.

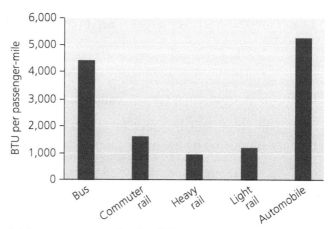

(a) Energy consumption for different modes of transit

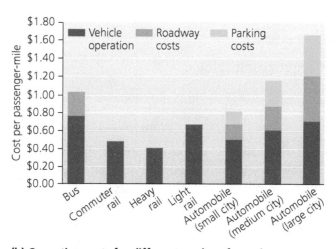

(b) Operating costs for different modes of transit

▲ Rail transit consumes far less energy per passenger mile **(a)** than bus or automobile transit. Rail transit involves fewer costs per passenger mile **(b)** than bus or automobile transit. Data from Litman, T., 2005. *Rail transit in America: A comprehensive evaluation of benefits.* Victoria, BC: Victoria Transport Policy Institute.

4. **F/O:** This statement can be proved true by comparing mass transit in the United States with mass transit in most nations, but it contains the qualifier *In general* and the biased phrase *lags behind*.

5. **F/O:** This statement is largely fact but also includes the value judgments *extensive, cheaply, and effectively.*

6. **F/O:** This statement is largely fact but also includes the value judgment *outstanding.*

7. **F/O:** This statement is largely fact but also includes the biased word *starved*.

8. **F:** This is a factual statement as illustrated by the first graph.

9. **O:** This is an opinion; it states a belief that something should be done.

10. **F/O:** This statement includes facts (*cheaper* and *more energy efficient*) that are supported by the graphs, but it also includes the value judgment *better*. ◀

Practice 8

A. Read the following passage from a history textbook. Mark selected sentences as follows:

F if it states a fact

O if it expresses an opinion

F/O if it combines fact and opinion

Women and World War II

Textbook
Skills

¹World War II had a dramatic impact on women. ²Easily the most visible change involved the sudden appearance of large numbers of women in uniform. ³The military organized women into auxiliary units with special uniforms, their own officers, and amazingly, equal pay. ⁴By 1945, more than 250,000 women had joined the Women's Army Corps (WAC), the Army Nurses Corps, the Women Accepted for Voluntary Emergency Service (WAVES), the Navy Nurses Corps, the Marines, and the Coast Guard. ⁵Most women who joined the armed services either filled traditional women's roles, such as nursing, or replaced men in non-combat jobs.

⁶Women also substituted for men on the home front. ⁷For the first time in history, married working women outnumbered single working women, as 6.3 million women entered the workforce during the war. ⁸The war challenged the conventional image of female behavior, as "Rosie the Riveter" became the popular symbol of women who abandoned traditional female occupations to work in defense industries.

⁹Women paid a price for their economic independence, though. ¹⁰Outside employment did not free wives from domestic duties. ¹¹The same women who put in full days in offices and factories went home to cook, clean, shop, and care for their children. ¹²They had not one job,

but two, and the only way they could fill both was to sacrifice relaxation, recreation, and sleep. **13**Outside employment also raised the problem of child care. **14**A few industries, such as Kaiser Steel, offered day-care facilities, but most women had to make their own informal arrangements.

—Adapted from Martin, James Kirby, Roberts, Randy J., Mintz, Steven, McMurry, Linda O., and Jones, James H., *America and Its Peoples, Volume 1: A Mosaic in the Making*, 3rd ed., pp. 875–876.

_____	**1.** Sentence 1	_____	**5.** Sentence 8
_____	**2.** Sentence 2	_____	**6.** Sentence 9
_____	**3.** Sentence 3	_____	**7.** Sentence 12
_____	**4.** Sentence 4		

B. Study the image of "Rosie the Riveter." Then identify each sentence based on the picture as follows:

F if it states a fact

O if it expresses an opinion

F/O if it combines fact and opinion

—"We Can Do It!" poster by J. Howard Miller. *Produced by Westinghouse for the War Production Co-Ordinating Committee, NARA Still Picture Branch (NWDNS-179-WP-1563)*, National Archives and Records Administration. © Courtesy of National Archives, photo war & conflict #798_we_can_do_it

_____ **8.** Some women gave up their traditional feminine dress to enter the workforce.

_____ **9.** "Rosie the Riveter" has the look of a strong, competent woman dressed in overalls and bandanna.

_____ **10.** "Rosie the Riveter" is the ideal patriotic woman.

Apply Information Literacy Skills

 ## Academic, Personal, and Career Applications of Fact and Opinion

The ability to separate fact from opinion is a key information literacy skill. For example, while the Internet has become a major resource for academic, personal, and career information, the nature of the Internet suggests that anyone can publish anything at any time. Knowing the difference between fact and opinion improves your ability to find, evaluate, and use information. In all areas of your life, you need to determine the facts. You need to recognize bias. You need to determine the accuracy of information. And you need to judge the trustworthiness of a source. Thus, you will use the skills that you have learned in this chapter in several ways:

- Recognize your own need to identify fact and opinion.
- Analyze a source to determine its reliability.
- Determine an author's use of fact and opinion to develop a main idea.

Academic Application

Assume you are taking a college course in psychology. You are currently studying the unit on aggression. The passage that follows is part of your required textbook reading.

- **Before Reading:** Skim the passage. Predict the author's stance on how or if bodily discomfort affects aggressive behaviors.
- **During Reading:** Underline the key facts. Enclose statements of opinion in (parenthesis).

■ **After Reading:** In the space following the passage, state the author's stance and proof of how bodily discomfort affects aggressive behaviors. Give reasons for your judgment.

Pain, Heat, and Aggression

Forms of bodily discomfort—such as heat, humidity, air pollution, crowds, and offensive odors—also lower the threshold for aggressive behavior. During the late 1960s and early 1970s, when tensions in the United States ran high over the war in Vietnam and the rise of the civil rights movement, national leaders worried about "the long, hot summer." The phrase was a code for the fear that the summer's heat would cause simmering tensions to explode. Their fears were justified. An analysis of disturbances in 79 cities between 1967 and 1971 found that riots were far more likely to occur on hot days than on cold ones.

Similarly, in major American cities from Houston, Texas, to Des Moines, Iowa, the hotter it is on a given day or a given average year, the greater the likelihood that violent crimes will occur. Smaller "crimes" increase, too: In the desert city of Phoenix, Arizona, drivers in non-air-conditioned cars are more likely to honk their horns in traffic jams than drivers in air-conditioned cars. Even on the baseball field, heat and hostility go together. In major league baseball games when the temperature rises above 90 degrees, significantly more batters are hit by pitched balls and (pitchers are more likely to intentionally retaliate against a batter when the pitcher's teammates have been hit by the opposing team earlier in the game.)

(As you know by now, one must be cautious about interpreting events that take place in natural settings outside the laboratory. The scientist in you might be tempted to ask whether increases in aggression are due to the temperature itself or merely to the fact that more people are apt to be outside (getting in one another's way) on hot days than on cold or rainy days. So how might we determine that it's the heat causing the aggression and not merely the greater opportunity for contact?) We can bring the phenomenon into the laboratory; (in fact, it is remarkably easy to do so.) In one such experiment, students took the same test under different conditions: Some worked in a room at normal room temperature, while others worked in a room where the temperature reached 90 degrees. The students in the hot room not only reported feeling more aggressive, but also expressed more hostility toward a stranger whom they were asked to describe and evaluate.

—Adapted from Aronson, Elliot, Wilson, Timothy D., and Akert, Robin M.,
Social Psychology, 8th ed., pp. 336–337.

Author's stance on heat and aggressive behaviors: _____

_____

_____

Personal Application

Assume you receive a call from an unknown person claiming to be from the Social Security Administration. This person begins to ask you to confirm your personal information. However, before you give out your sensitive, personal information, you analyze the situation and decide to hang up the phone. You then search the Internet for information on identity theft and find the following article.

- **Before Reading:** Skim the page. Evaluate the source. Then rate it on the following scale for trustworthiness.
- **During Reading:** Highlight details useful for detecting if you are a target of identity theft.
- **After Reading:** Make an informed opinion about the intent of the caller.

Evaluation of Source:	Untrustworthy			Trustworthy	
Office of the General Inspector, Social Security Administration	1	2	3	4	5

Scams Involving the Impersonation
of an SSA Employee

We sometimes receive reports where individuals have been contacted by someone pretending to be an SSA employee. The intent of this type of call may be to steal your identity and/or money from your bank accounts. The caller generally asks you for personal information such as your Social Security number, date of birth, your mother's maiden name, or your bank or financial account information.

The impersonator may state that "the SSA computers are down" or may refer to enrollment in the Medicare prescription drug program. The intent of this type of call may be to steal your identity and/or money from your bank accounts. You should not provide any of this information to these individuals.

It is possible that an SSA employee may contact you to follow up on a previous application for SSA/Medicare Part D benefits or to follow up on other business you initiated with SSA. If you are unsure as to the authenticity of someone who claims to be an SSA employee, please call SSA to verify the reason for the contact and the person's identity prior to providing any information to the caller.

If you wish to report a call from someone you suspect is impersonating an SSA employee, please provide us with the following details:

- Caller's alleged name
- Caller's telephone number
- Time and date the call was made
- Information requested by the caller
- Other identifying information or details about the content of the call

—Office of the Inspector General Social Security Administration.

Informed Opinion: _____

_____

Career Application

Assume you are a worker's compensation insurance claims administrator in the Human Resources department of your local general hospital. One of the ICU nurses has reported an incident to which you must respond.

- **Before Reading:** Use the reporter's questions *who, what, when, where, why,* and *how* to get an idea of the nature of the incident.
- **During Reading:** Highlight the relevant facts.
- **After Reading:** In the space following the passage, make a recommendation for action to respond to the incident.

Employee Incident Report

Name:	Isabella Davis	**Date of Accident:**	Continuous trauma
Age:	32	**Time:**	March 2013–July 2013
Position:	Critical Care Nurse	**Location:**	ICU

Case One: Worker injured her lower back while working in the ICU due to a shortage of handling partners or lifting machines. Worker has received medical care and has submitted a medical report indicating the trauma to her back has caused a temporary disability that will keep her from working for up to three months. In addition to salary compensation, her settlement should also include medical and rehabilitation expenses.

Recommendation for Action: _____

_____

_____

_____

REVIEW TEST 1

Score (number correct) _____ x 20 = _____ %

Visit MyReadingLab to take this test online and receive feedback and guidance on your answers.

Read the following article from a college health textbook. Answer the questions that follow.

Textbook
Skills

Do Restaurants and Food Marketers Encourage Overeating?

[1]When you go out to your local restaurant, do you think your dinner looks the same as one your grandmother might have ordered 50 years ago? [2]Would you be surprised to learn that today's serving portions are significantly larger than those of past decades? [3]Today's popular restaurant foods dwarf their earlier counterparts. [4]A 25 ounce prime-rib dinner served at one local steak chain, for example, contains nearly 3,000 calories and 150 grams of fat in the meat alone. [5]Add a baked potato with sour cream or butter, a salad loaded with creamy dressing, and fresh bread with real butter, and the meal may surpass the 5,000-calorie mark and ring in at close to 300 grams of fat. [6]In other words, it exceeds what most adults should eat in 2 days!

[7]And that is just the beginning. [8]Soft drinks, once commonly served in 12-ounce sizes, now come in "big gulps" and 1-liter bottles. [9]Cinnamon buns used to be the size of a dinner roll; now one chain sells them in giant, butter-laden, 700-calorie portions.

[10]What accounts for the increased portion sizes of today? [11]Restaurant owners might say that they are only giving customers what they want. [12]While there may be some merit to this claim, it's also true that bigger portions can justify higher prices, which help increase an owner's bottom line.

[13]A quick glance at the fattening of Americans provides growing evidence of a significant health problem. [14]According to Donna Skoda, a dietitian and chair of the Ohio State University Extension Service, "People are eating a ton of extra calories. [15]For the first time in history, more people are overweight in America than are underweight. [16]Ironically, although the U.S. fat intake has dropped in the past 20 years from an average of 0 to 33 percent of calories, the daily calorie intake has risen from 1,852 calories per day to over 2,000 per day. [17]In theory, this translates into a weight gain of 15 pounds a year." [18]Skoda and others say that the main reason Americans are gaining weight is that people no longer recognize a normal serving size. [19]The National Heart, Lung, and Blood Institute has developed a pair of "Portion Distortion" quizzes that show how today's portions compare with those of 20 years ago. [20]Test yourself online at http://hin.nhlbi.nih.gov/portion to see whether you can guess the differences between today's meals and those previously considered normal. [21]Just one example is the difference between an average cheeseburger 20 years ago and the typical cheeseburger of today. [22]According to the "Portion Distortion" quiz, today's cheeseburger has 590 calories—257 more calories than the cheeseburger of 20 years ago!

—Adapted from Donatelle, Rebecca, J.,
Access to Health, 11th ed., p. 292.

_____ **1.** Sentence 3 states
   a. a fact.   c. a fact and an opinion.
   b. an opinion.

_____ **2.** Sentence 11 states
   a. a fact.   c. a fact and an opinion.
   b. an opinion.

_____ **3.** Sentence 12 states
   a. a fact.   c. a fact and an opinion.
   b. an opinion.

_____ **4.** Sentence 15 states
   a. a fact.   c. a fact and an opinion.
   b. an opinion.

_____ **5.** In the article, Donna Skoda offers
   a. an informed opinion based on personal experience.
   b. an expert opinion based on education and professional experience.
   c. factual details only.

REVIEW TEST 2

Score (number correct) _____ x 10 = _____ %

Visit MyReadingLab to take this test online and receive feedback and guidance on your answers.

Fact and Opinion

Textbook Skills

Read the review and answer the questions that follow it.

From the Pen of the Mighty King

¹Stephen King, with his fantastical imagination, has built an impressive body of literary work worthy of recognition. ²The scope of his writing includes short stories, novels, screenplays for movies and television series, nonfiction, illustrated novels, a comic book, and a children's cookbook. ³However, he may be most widely known for those stories that explore the darkness of our fury and fears. ⁴In fact, an editor for Barnes & Noble stated on the bookseller's website, "Stephen King proves once again why he is the reigning master of dark fiction" in their review of his novel *Dreamcatcher*. ⁵His first novel, *Carrie*, the novel he allegedly threw in the trash, reveals the macabre side of his imagination. ⁶(Thank God his wife allegedly dug it out, flung it back and said, "finish it!") 7*Carrie* is a dark, dark tale fueled by the ferocity of an adolescent experience; the story encompasses outcasts, bullies, guilt, anger, sin, mayhem, death, justice, and fear. ⁸In *Carrie*, King revealed his ability to make nightmares seem real. ⁹In contrast, King also has the ability to probe into common human experiences with wit and tenderness, as in his short story "The Body," also made into a Hollywood movie, *Stand By Me*. ¹⁰In this story, King's pen renders a compelling portrait of a young boy's end of innocence, his conflict with mortality, and his induction into adulthood. ¹¹Stephen King's body of work has made him the 2003 recipient of *The National Book Foundation Medal for Distinguished Contribution to American Letters*.

_____ **1.** Sentence 1 is a statement of
    a. fact.   c. a combination of fact and opinion.
    b. opinion.

_____ **2.** Sentence 2 is a statement of
    a. fact.   c. a combination of fact and opinion.
    b. opinion.

_____ **3.** Sentence 3 is a statement of
     a. fact.   c. a combination of fact and opinion.
     b. opinion.

_____ **4.** Sentence 5 is a statement of
     a. fact.   c. a combination of fact and opinion.
     b. opinion.

_____ **5.** Sentence 6 is a statement of
     a. fact.   c. a combination of fact and opinion.
     b. opinion.

_____ **6.** Sentence 7 is a statement of
     a. fact.   c. a combination of fact and opinion.
     b. opinion.

_____ **7.** Sentence 9 is a statement of
     a. fact.   c. a combination of fact and opinion.
     b. opinion.

_____ **8.** Sentence 10 is a statement of
     a. fact.   c. a combination of fact and opinion.
     b. opinion.

_____ **9.** Sentence 11 is a statement of
     a. fact.   c. a combination of fact and opinion.
     b. opinion.

_____ **10.** The editor from Barnes & Noble in sentence 4 offers
     a. an informed opinion.   c. a fact.
     b. an expert opinion.

REVIEW TEST 3

Score (number correct) _____ x 10 = _____ %

Visit MyReadingLab to take this test online and receive feedback and guidance on your answers.

Fact and Opinion

Before you read this passage from a college sociology textbook, skim the passage and answer the Before Reading questions. Read the passage. Then answer the After Reading questions.

Vocabulary Preview

truism (1): a statement whose truth is well known
primacy (16): the state of being first in rank or importance
reaffirms (23): states again firmly and positively

The Politics of Immigrants: Power, Ethnicity, and Social Class

Textbook Skills

[1]That the United States is the land of immigrants is a **truism**. [2]Every schoolchild knows that since the English Pilgrims landed on Plymouth Rock, group after group has sought relief from hardship by reaching U.S. shores. [3]Some, such as the Irish immigrants in the late 1800s and early 1900s, left to escape brutal poverty and famine. [4]Others, such as the Jews of czarist Russia, fled religious persecution. [5]Some sought refuge from lands ravaged by war. [6]Others, called entrepreneurial immigrants, came primarily for better economic opportunities. [7]Still others were **sojourners** who planned to return home after a temporary stay. [8]Some, not usually called immigrants, came in chains, held in bondage by earlier immigrants.

[9]Today, the United States is in the midst of its second largest wave of immigration. [10]In the largest wave, immigrants accounted for 15 percent of the U.S. population. [11]Almost all of those immigrants in the late 1800s and early 1900s came from Europe. [12]In our current wave, immigrants make up 13 percent of the U.S. population, with a mix that is far more diverse. [13]Immigration from Europe has slowed to a trickle, with twice as many of our recent immigrants coming from Asia as from Europe (Statistical Abstract 2011:Tables 38, 42). [14]In the past 20 years, about 20 million immigrants have settled legally in the United States, and another 11 million are here illegally (Statistical Abstract 2011: Tables 43, 45).

[15]In the last century, U.S.-born Americans feared that immigrants would bring socialism or communism with them. [16]Today's fear is that the millions of immigrants from Spanish-speaking countries threaten the **primacy** of the English language. [17]Last century brought a fear that immigrants would take jobs away from U.S.-born citizens. [18] This fear has returned. [19]In addition, African Americans fear a loss of political power as immigrants from Mexico and Central and South America swell the Latino population.

[20]What path do immigrants take to political activity? [21]In general, immigrants first organize as a group on the basis of ethnicity rather than class. [22]They respond to common problems, such as discrimination and issues associated with adapting to a new way of life. [23]This first step in

political activity is their cultural identity. [24]As sociologists Alejandro Portes and Rubén Rumbaut (1990) note, "By mobilizing the collective vote and by electing their own to office, immigrant minorities have learned the rules of the democratic game and absorbed its values in the process."

[25]Immigrants, then, don't become "American" overnight. [26]Instead, they begin by fighting for their own interests as an ethnic group—as Irish, Italians, and so on. [27]However, according to Portes and Rumbaut, once a group gains representation somewhat proportionate to its numbers, a major change occurs. [28]At this point, social class becomes more significant than race–ethnicity. [29]Note that the significance of race–ethnicity in politics does not disappear, but that it recedes in importance.

[30]Irish immigrants to Boston illustrate this pattern. [31]Banding together on the basis of ethnicity, they built a power base that put the Irish in political control of Boston. [32]As the significance of ethnicity faded, social class became prominent. [33]Ultimately, they saw John F. Kennedy, one of their own, from the upper class, sworn in as president of the United States. [34]Even today, being "Irish" continues to be a significant factor in Boston politics.

—Henslin, James M., *Sociology: A Down-to-Earth Approach*, 11th ed., p. 423.

Before Reading

Vocabulary in Context

_____ **1.** What does the word **sojourners** mean in sentence 7?
a. people staying for a while   c. people looking for jobs
b. people touring the country   d. people seeking to escape

After Reading

Main Idea and Implied Central Idea

_____ **2.** The main idea of paragraph 1 (sentences 1–8) is stated in
a. sentence 1.   c. sentence 3.
b. sentence 2.   d. sentence 4.

_____ **3.** Which of the following sentences best states the implied central idea of the passage?
a. The United States is a land of immigrants and has been from the start.

b. Immigrants politically align with their ethnic group first and then shift to their social class.

c. The United States is in the midst of its second largest wave of immigration.

d. Many people fear that the Latinos making up the second greatest wave of immigration will change the United States.

Supporting Details

_____ **4.** According to the author, the attitude of U.S.-born citizens toward immigrants is

a. welcoming because of the hardships suffered by immigrants.

b. based on a common love for the country.

c. fearful but for different reasons.

d. hostile as both groups fight for political power.

Transitions

_____ **5.** The relationship of ideas between sentences 2 and 3 is one of

a. time order.   c. contrast.

b. cause and effect.   d. generalization and example.

_____ **6.** The relationship of ideas within sentence 27 is one of

a. time order.   c. contrast.

b. cause and effect.   d. addition.

Thought Patterns

_____ **7.** The primary thought pattern that organizes paragraph 2 (sentences 9–14) is

a. cause and effect.   c. contrast.

b. time order.   d. examples.

Fact and Opinion

_____ **8.** Sentence 3 is

a. a fact.   c. a mixture of fact and opinion.

b. an opinion.

_____ **9.** Sentence 10 is

a. a fact.   c. a mixture of fact and opinion.

b. an opinion.

_____ **10.** The statement "once a group gains representation somewhat proportionate to its numbers, a major change occurs" is

    a. a fact.   c. a mixture of fact and opinion.

    b. an opinion.

SUMMARY RESPONSE

Restate the author's central idea in your own words. In your summary, follow the thought pattern used by the author. Begin your summary response with the following: *The central idea of "The Politics of Immigrants: Power, Ethnicity, and Social Class" by Henslin is . . .*

WHAT DO YOU THINK?

What do you think about the changing population demographics in the United States? Assume you work for the local newspaper in your area, and write an opinion editorial that addresses this topic. In your article, respond to the following two excerpts from the passage.

- "Today's fear is that the millions of immigrants from Spanish-speaking countries threaten the primacy of the English language." (sentence 16)

- "However, according to Portes and Rumbaut, once a group gains representation somewhat proportionate to its numbers, a major change occurs. At this point, social class becomes more significant than race–ethnicity." (sentences 27–28)

REVIEW TEST 4

Score (number correct) _____ x 10 = _____ %

Visit MyReadingLab to take this test online and receive feedback and guidance on your answers.

Fact and Opinion

Textbook Skills

Before Reading: Survey the following passage adapted from a college nutrition textbook. Skim the passage, noting the words in bold print. Answer the Before Reading questions that follow the passage. Then read the passage. Next answer the After Reading questions. Use the discussion and writing topics as activities to do after reading.

Vocabulary Preview

saturated (1): of or relating to an organic compound, especially a fatty acid, containing the maximum number of hydrogen atoms and only single bonds between the carbon atoms

unsaturated (2): of or relating to an organic compound with a double or triple bond that links two atoms, usually of carbon

hydrogenation (4): the adding of hydrogen to an unsaturated fatty acid to make it more saturated and solid at room temperature

hydrogen (6): a colorless, tasteless, odorless, flammable gaseous substance that is the simplest and most abundant element

configuration (7): pattern, design

reformulated (13): changed, remade

cholesterol (17): a soft, waxy substance found among the lipids (fats) in the bloodstream and in the body's cells

What Is *Trans* Fat and Where Do You Find It?

[1]At one time, saturated fats from animal sources, like lard, and highly **saturated** tropical plant oils, like coconut and palm oils, were staples in home cooking and commercial food preparation. [2]These saturated fats work well in commercial food products because they provide a rich, flaky texture to baked goods and are more resistant to rancidity than the **unsaturated** fats found in oils. [3](The double bonds in unsaturated fats make them more susceptible to being damaged by oxygen, and thus, becoming rancid.) [4]Then, in the early twentieth century, a German chemist discovered the technique of **hydrogenation** of oils, which caused the unsaturated fatty acids in the oils to become more saturated. [5]*Trans fats* were born.

[6]The process of hydrogenation involves heating an oil and exposing it to **hydrogen** gas, which causes some of the double bonds in the unsaturated fatty acid to become saturated with hydrogen. [7]Typically, the hydrogens of a double bond are lined up in a *cis (cis* = same) **configuration**, that is, they are all on the same side of the carbon chain in the fatty acid. [8]During hydrogenation, some hydrogens cross to the opposite side of the carbon chain, resulting in a *trans (trans* = cross) configuration. [9]The newly configured fatty acid is now a *trans fatty acid.*

[10]*Trans* fats provide a richer texture, a longer shelf life, and better resistance to **rancidity** than unsaturated fats, so food manufacturers use them in many commercially made food products. [11]The first partially hydrogenated shortening, Crisco, was made from cottonseed oil, and became available in 1911.

[12]*Trans* fats came into even more widespread commercial use when saturated fat fell out of favor in the 1980s. [13]Research had confirmed that saturated fat played a role in increased risk of heart disease, so food manufacturers **reformulated** many of their products to contain less saturated fat. [14]The easiest solution was to replace the saturated fat with *trans* fats. [15]Everything from cookies, cakes, and crackers to fried chips and doughnuts used *trans* fats to maintain their texture and shelf life. [16]*Trans* fats were also frequently used for frying at fast-food restaurants.

[17]We now know that *trans* fats are actually worse for heart health than saturated fat because they not only raise the LDL **cholesterol** levels, but they also lower HDL cholesterol in the body. [18]*Trans* fat currently provides an estimated 2.5 percent of the daily calories in the diets of adults in the United States. [19]Of this amount, about 25 percent of them are coming from naturally occurring *trans* fats that are found in meat and dairy foods. [20]We don't yet know if the naturally occurring *trans* fats have the same heart-unhealthy effects as do those that are created through hydrogenation. [21]*Trans* fats use should be kept as low as possible in the diet.

[22]The major sources of *trans* fats are commercially prepared baked goods, margarines, fried potatoes, snacks, shortenings, and salad dressings. [23]Whole grains, fruits, and vegetables don't contain any *trans* fats, so consuming a plant-based diet with minimal commercially prepared foods will go a long way toward preventing *trans* fat (and saturated fat) from overpowering your diet.

—Adapted from Blake, Joan Salge, *Nutrition and You*, 1st ed., p. 147.

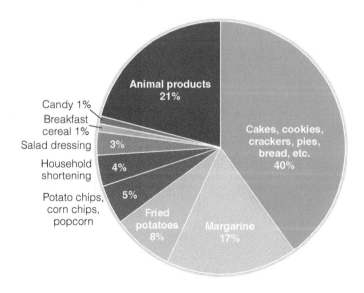

◀ **Major Food Sources of Trans Fat for U.S. Adults**
Commercially made baked goods and snack items are the major contributors of trans fat in the diet.

—Source FDA, Questions and Answers About Trans Fat Nutrition Labeling, 2003.

Before Reading

Vocabulary in Context

Use context clues to state in your own words the definition of the following terms. Indicate the context clue you used.

1. In sentences 2 and 10 what does the word **rancidity** mean? _____

_____

2. Identify the context clue used for the word **rancidity** in sentences 2 and 10.

_____

After Reading

Implied Central Idea

3. Using your own words, write a sentence that best states the implied main

idea of the passage. _____

_____

_____

Main Idea and Supporting Details

_____ **4.** In paragraph 4 (sentences 12–16), sentence 16 is a
   a. main idea.   c. minor supporting detail.
   b. major supporting detail.

Transitions

_____ **5.** The relationship of ideas between sentence 15 and sentence 16 is
   one of
   a. cause and effect.   c. time order.
   b. listing.   d. definition and example.

_____ **6.** The relationship of ideas within sentence 23 is one of
   a. time order.   c. cause and effect.
   b. contrast.   d. definition and example.

Thought Patterns

_____ **7.** The overall thought pattern for this passage is
   a. time order.   c. space order.
   b. definition and example.   d. comparison and contrast.

Fact and Opinion

_____ **8.** Sentence 4 is a statement of
      a. fact.   c. fact and opinion.
      b. opinion.

_____ **9.** Sentence 14 is a statement of
      a. fact.   c. fact and opinion.
      b. opinion.

_____ **10.** Read the caption for the graphic. The caption is a statement of
      a. fact.   c. fact and opinion.
      b. opinion.

SUMMARY RESPONSE

Restate the author's central idea in your own words. In your summary, follow the thought pattern used by the author. Begin your summary response with the following: _The central idea of "What Is Trans Fat and Where Do You Find It?" by Blake is_ . . .

WHAT DO YOU THINK?

Assume you taking a college-level health course. Your professor has assigned weekly written responses to what you are learning through your studies. This week, you have decided to respond to what you have learned about a healthful diet and trans fats. You have narrowed your written response to two topics. Choose one of these topics and write several paragraphs using information from the passage about trans fats:

- Evaluate your own diet and discuss ways in which your diet is healthful or needs to change to become healthful.
- Persuade people who consume a diet high in trans fats to change to a diet balanced with grains, fruits, vegetables, and protein.

After Reading About Fact and Opinion

Before you move on to the Mastery Tests on fact and opinion, take time to reflect on your learning and performance by answering the following questions. Write your answers in your notebook.

- How has my knowledge base or prior knowledge about fact and opinion changed?

- Based on my studies, how do I think I will perform on the Mastery Test(s)? Why do I think my scores will be above average, average, or below average? (Note: An additional fourth Mastery Test may be found in MyReadingLab.)

- Would I recommend this chapter to other students who want to learn about fact and opinion? Why or why not?

Test your understanding of what you have learned about fact and opinion by completing the Chapter 9 Review.

Name _____ Section_____

Date _____ **Score** (number correct) _____ x 10 = _____ %

Visit MyReadingLab to take this test online and receive feedback and guidance on your answers.

A. Read the following statements and mark each one as follows:

F if it states a fact

O if it expresses an opinion

F/O if it combines fact and opinion

_____ **1.** The barbell squat is the best exercise to sculpt beautiful, toned, firm legs.

_____ **2.** The barbell squat develops the quadriceps muscles (the front upper leg), the hamstring muscles (back of upper leg), and the gluteal muscles (the buttocks).

_____ **3.** In today's fast-paced, high-stress society, too many people eat to satisfy emotional needs.

_____ **4.** Because nutritional supplements prevent nutritional deficiencies, everyone should take supplements.

_____ **5.** Vitamin C is a water-soluble vitamin that may aid dieters by suppressing cortisol, a hormone that aids in fat storage and breaks down muscle tissue.

B. Read the following short reviews. Mark each one as follows:

F if it states a fact

O if it expresses an opinion

F/O if it combines fact and opinion

_____ **6.** "The Lottery" by Shirley Jackson

One story that has achieved international renown largely because of its shattering epiphany is "The Lottery" by Shirley Jackson (1919–1965), who often combines the chilling aspects of Poe with climactic meaningfulness. "The Lottery" exists on a number of levels. While it rewards the discerning reader with an epiphany that widens and deepens with each reading, it also offers a suspenseful and realistic surface tale of an annual prize-drawing ceremony in a typical, peaceful small town, with the nature of the "prize" carefully withheld until the horrifying climax.

—Janaro, Richard P. and Altshuler, Thelma C., *The Art of Being Human,* 10th ed., p. 97.

413

_____ **7.** *Slumdog Millionaire* (Britain, 2008)

The cast of this film featured many nonprofessionals from the actual slums of Mumbai, India. The film also featured a handful of experienced actors in the major roles. The two lovers are portrayed by Patel, who is British, but of Indian descent, and Pinto, who is Indian, but whose professional career was primarily in modeling. He had done a little acting prior to this role, but she had done virtually none. Yet their tender love scenes are believable—touching and innocent and sweet. Sometimes youth, good looks, and charm can be enough.

—Giannetti, Louis, *Understanding Movies*, 12th ed., p. 274.

_____ **8.** *Statistical Abstract of the United States, 2007*

The *Statistical Abstract of the United States,* published since 1878, is the authoritative and comprehensive summary of statistics on the social, political, and economic organization of the United States. Sources of data include the Census Bureau, Bureau of Labor Statistics, Bureau of Economic Analysis, and many other Federal agencies and private organizations.

—United States. *The 2007 Statistical Abstract: The National Data Book.* U.S. Census Bureau.

_____ **9.** The *Encyclopedia of Earth,* http://www.eoearth.org/

The *Encyclopedia of Earth* is an electronic reference about the Earth, its natural environments, and their interaction with society. The *Encyclopedia* is a free, fully searchable collection of articles. Articles are written by scholars, professionals, educators, and experts who collaborate and review each other's work.

_____ **10.** Gladwell, Malcolm, *What the Dog Saw*, Little, Brown, and Co., 2009

Gladwell's latest book, *What the Dog Saw*, a package of his favorite articles from the *New Yorker* since he joined as a staff writer in 1996, is divided into three sections: The first deals with what he calls obsessives and minor geniuses; the second with flawed ways of thinking; the third on how we make predictions about people: will they make a good employee, are they capable of great works of art, or are they the local serial killer? Brought together, the pieces form a dazzling record of Gladwell's art, according to Ian Sample of the *Guardian*.

Name _____ Section_____

Date _____ **Score** (number correct) _____ x 5 = _____ %

Visit MyReadingLab to take this test online and receive feedback and guidance on your answers.

A. Read the list of statements and mark each one as follows:

F if it states a fact; **O** if it expresses an opinion; **F/O** if it combines fact and opinion

_____ **1.** Capital punishment is immoral and cruel. It should be outlawed in a civilized society.

_____ **2.** Any criminal, no matter how hardened, can be and should be rehabilitated to reenter society.

_____ **3.** As of January 2007, 3,350 men and women were on death rows across the United States.

_____ **4.** Capital punishment is the only form of justice for heinous crimes against humanity.

_____ **5.** A majority of nations have ended capital punishment in law or practice.

B. Read the paragraph from a college humanities textbook. Identify the numbered sentences as follows:

F if it states a fact; **O** if it states an opinion; **F/O** if it combines fact and opinion

Wynton Marsalis

Textbook
Skills

[6]Since the early 1980s, trumpeter Wynton Marsalis (b. 1961) has distinguished himself as a performer and a composer, crossing over freely from jazz to symphonic music. [7]Classically trained at The Julliard School, he was just 20 when he assembled his own band. [8]His love of classical concert music—notably Bach, Mozart, and Beethoven—has earned him an enormous reputation in both fields. [9]He has won nine Grammy awards. [10]In 1983, he won in both the symphonic and jazz categories, the first artist ever to do so, and in 1997 he became the first jazz composer ever to win the Pulitzer Prize.

—Adapted from Janaro, Richard P. and Altshuler, Thelma C.,
The Art of Being Human, 10th ed., p. 179.

6. _____   **7.** _____   **8.** _____   **9.** _____   **10.** _____

C. Read the following passage from a college history textbook. Identify each numbered sentence as follows:

F if it states a fact; **O** if it expresses an opinion; **F/O** if it combines fact and opinion

Trailblazing

[11]In 1811 and 1812 fur trappers marked out the Oregon Trail, the longest and most famous pioneer route in American history. [12]This trail crossed about 2000 miles from Independence, Missouri, to the Columbia River country of Oregon. [13]During the 1840s, 12,000 pioneers traveled the Trail's entire length to Oregon.

[14]Travel on the Oregon Trail was a tremendous test of human endurance. [15]The journey by wagon train took six months. [16]Settlers encountered prairie fires, sudden blizzards, and impassable mountains. [17]Cholera and other diseases were common; food, water, and wood were scarce. [18]Only the stalwart dared brave the physical hardship of the westward trek.

—Martin, James Kirby, Roberts, Randy J., Mintz, Steven, McMurry,
Linda O., and Jones, James H., *America and Its Peoples,
Volume 1: A Mosaic in the Making,* 3rd ed., p. 425.

11. _____   12. _____   13. _____   14. _____   15. _____

16. _____   17. _____   18. _____

D. Study the picture and its caption. Mark each idea as follows:

F if it states a fact; **O** if it expresses an opinion; **F/O** if it combines fact and opinion

◀ Life along the westward trails was a tremendous test of human endurance.

_____ 19. Pioneers encountered arid desert, difficult mountain passes, dangerous rivers, and quicksand.

_____ 20. Still, despite the hardships of the experience, few emigrants ever regretted their decision to move west.

—Text and image adapted from Martin, James Kirby, Roberts, Randy J., Mintz,
Steven, McMurry, Linda O., and Jones, James H., *America and Its Peoples,
Volume 1: A Mosaic in the Making,* 3rd ed., p. 425.

Name _____ Section_____

Date _____ **Score** (number correct) _____ x 10 = _____ %

Visit MyReadingLab to take this test online and receive feedback and guidance on your answers.

A. The following passage and the figure in section B were published together in a health textbook. Read the passage, and identify the numbered sentences as follows:

F if it states a fact

O if it expresses an opinion

F/O if it combines fact and opinion

Content and Information Regulation

**Textbook
Skills**

[1]Direct content regulation emerged from government efforts to balance the free flow of information and ideas against the negative effects of media products. [2]Part of the news media's role, as H. L. Mencken said, "is to comfort the afflicted and afflict the comfortable." [3]Content regulation tries to reduce unjustified, unnecessary, and unreasonable harm to people from media content. [4]Such regulation can occur before or after distribution. [5]Some types of speech, such as political speech, are more protected than others, such as commercial speech.

—Folkerts, Jean and Lacy, Stephen, *The Media in Your Life: An Introduction to Mass Communication*, 2nd ed., p. 327.

1. _____   2. _____   3. _____   4. _____   5. _____

VISUAL *VOCABULARY*

The business conversation of this real estate agent is an example of _____ speech.

  a. political
  b. commercial

B. Study the graph. Read the statements that are based on the figure. Then identify each one as follows:

Textbook Skills

F if it states a fact

O if it expresses an opinion

F/O if it combines fact and opinion

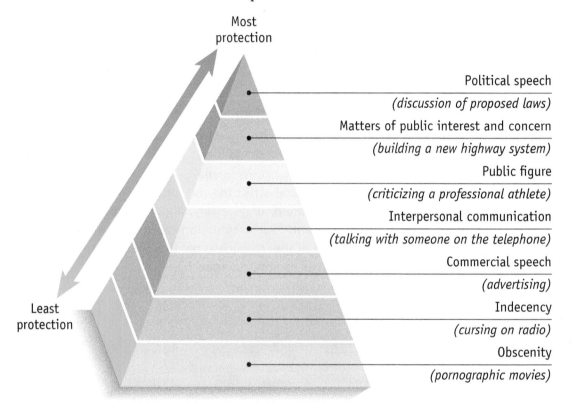

Most protection

Political speech
(discussion of proposed laws)

Matters of public interest and concern
(building a new highway system)

Public figure
(criticizing a professional athlete)

Interpersonal communication
(talking with someone on the telephone)

Commercial speech
(advertising)

Indecency
(cursing on radio)

Obscenity
(pornographic movies)

Least protection

▲ **Levels of Protected Communication**

—Folkerts, Jean and Lacy, Stephen, *The Media in Your Life: An Introduction to Mass Communication*, 2nd ed., p. 327. "Levels of Protected Communication" by Todd F. Simon. Reprinted by permission of author.

_____ **6.** Political speech includes discussions of proposed laws.

_____ **7.** This chart outlines the levels of protected speech.

_____ **8.** Talking with someone on a telephone has a degree of protection.

_____ **9.** Obscenity should not be protected communication.

_____ **10.** According to the graphic, political communication receives more protection than commercial communication; thus a politician's speech is a more important form of communication than is a commercial.

9 Summary of Key Concepts of Fact and Opinion

LO1 Assess your comprehension of fact and opinion. Complete the following two-column notes of terms and definitions with information from the chapter.

Term	Definition
A fact	
An opinion	
Objective proof	
An informed opinion	
An expert opinion	
A fact	
An opinion	
Biased words	
A qualifier	

Test Your Comprehension of Fact and Opinion

(LO1)   Respond to the following questions and prompts.

In your own words, what is the difference between a fact and an opinion?

_____

_____

(LO2) (LO3)   In your own words, what is the difference between an informed opinion and
(LO4)   an expert opinion? _____

_____

_____

_____

_____

(LO1) (LO2)   In your own words, describe how to distinguish between fact and opinion.
(LO3) (LO5)
_____

_____

_____

_____

_____

(LO6)   Identify the following two statements as fact or opinion. Then explain the
importance of knowing the difference between fact and opinion.

_____ Most fast food is high in calories and fat and low in nutrition.

_____ Fast food tastes great.

_____

_____

_____

_____

(LO1) (LO2)   Summarize the two most important ideas in this chapter that will help you
(LO3) (LO4)   improve your reading comprehension. _____
(LO5) (LO6)
(LO7) (LO8)   _____

_____

Tone and Purpose

10

LO LEARNING OUTCOMES

After studying this chapter, you should be able to:

LO1 Define Tone and Purpose

LO2 Recognize How Tone Is Established

LO3 Identify Subjective and Objective Tone Words

LO4 Determine the General Purpose in the Main Idea

LO5 Determine the Primary Purpose of a Passage

LO6 Recognize Irony Used for Special Effects

LO7 Develop Textbook Skills: Recognize an Author's Tone and Purpose

LO8 Apply Information Literacy Skills: Academic, Personal, and Career Applications of Tone and Purpose

Before Reading About Tone and Purpose

Study the chapter learning outcomes and underline words that relate to ideas you have already studied. Did you underline the following terms: subjective, objective, and main idea? What you already know about these topics will help you learn about tone and purpose. Use the blanks that follow to write a short one- or two-sentence summary about each topic:

Subjective words: _____

_____ .

Objective words: _____

_____ .

Main idea: _____

_____ .

Define *Tone* and *Purpose*

Read the following two paragraphs. As you read, think about the difference in the tone and purpose of each one:

> Youth substance abuse can lead to many other problems, including the development of delinquent behavior, anti-social attitudes, and health-related issues. These problems not only affect the child, but can also influence the child's family, community, and ultimately society.
>
> —Executive Office of the President of the United States, "Juveniles and Drugs." Executive Office of the President. Office of National Drug Control Policy.

> My name is Sheanne; I am 17 years old, and I am an alcoholic. I began drinking when I was 9 years old. My older cousins used to party pretty hard, and it seemed so cool, like they were having so much fun. They always got a kick out of giving me a beer on the sly, and I loved being part of the scene. By the time I was 11, I was guzzling hard booze. I fought with my family all the time, and school was a blur. Then last year, drunk as usual, I insisted on driving home from a late-night party. My twin sister, Shannon, rode with me. I don't remember what happened; I blacked out. Shannon died in that crash. I have been sober for 305 days. Every day is a struggle. Take my advice: Don't drink! If you do, don't drink and drive!
>
> —Sheanne's speech to a high school audience

The differences in the tone and purpose of these two paragraphs are clear. The first paragraph from a government agency was written to inform the public about juveniles and drug abuse, using unbiased words and an objective, formal tone. The second paragraph approaches the same subject, drug abuse, with a different purpose—to persuade youth to avoid alcohol abuse. Sheanne conveys a painful personal experience using biased words and a subjective, informal tone.

Every text is created by an author who has a specific attitude toward the chosen topic and a specific reason for writing and sharing that attitude. The author's attitude is conveyed by the tone. **Tone** is the emotion or mood of the author's written voice. Understanding tone is closely related to understanding the author's reason for writing about the topic. This reason for writing is known as the author's **purpose.** Tone and purpose work together to convey the author's meaning.

Tone and purpose are greatly influenced by the audience the author is trying to reach. The audience for the first paragraph is members of the general public who need factual information; the objective presentation of facts best serves such a wide-ranging audience. The audience for the second example is teenagers who need to be persuaded; the informal, personal approach is much more likely to reach this audience. Tone and purpose are established with word choice. Master readers read to understand the author's tone and purpose. To identify tone and purpose, you need to build on several skills you have already studied: vocabulary, fact and opinion, and main ideas.

> **Tone** is the author's attitude toward the topic.
> **Purpose** is the reason the author writes about a topic.

 ## Recognize How Tone Is Established

The author's attitude is expressed by the tone of voice he or she assumes in the passage. An author carefully chooses words that will make an impact on the reader. Sometimes an author wants to appeal to reason by using an objective tone, and just gives facts and factual explanations. At other times, an author wants to appeal to emotions by using a subjective tone to stir the reader to feel deeply.

Study the following list of words that describe the characteristics of tone.

Characteristics of Tone Words			
Objective Tone	**Shows no feelings for or against a topic**	**Subjective Tone**	**Shows favor for or against a topic**
unbiased	—remains impartial	biased	—makes it personal
neutral	—focuses on facts	emotional	—focuses on feelings
formal	—uses higher level words	informal	—uses conversational language
	—avoids personal pronouns *I* and *you*		—uses personal pronouns *I* and *you*
	—creates distance between writer and reader		—creates a connection between writer and reader
An objective tone is impartial, unbiased, neutral and most often formal.		A subjective tone is personal, biased, emotional, and often informal.	

For example, in an effort to share reliable information, textbooks strive for an objective tone, one that is matter-of-fact and neutral. The details given in an objective tone are likely to be facts. In contrast, sharing an author's personal world view through fiction and personal essays often calls for a subjective tone. A subjective tone uses words that describe feelings, judgments, or opinions. The details given in a subjective tone are likely to include experiences, senses, feelings, and thoughts.

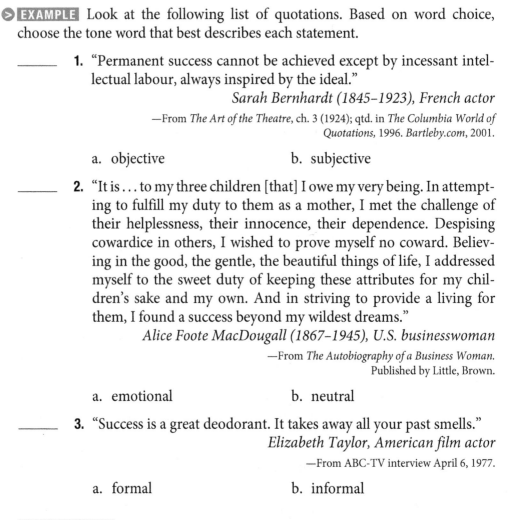

> **EXAMPLE** Look at the following list of quotations. Based on word choice, choose the tone word that best describes each statement.

_____ 1. "Permanent success cannot be achieved except by incessant intellectual labour, always inspired by the ideal."

Sarah Bernhardt (1845–1923), French actor

—From *The Art of the Theatre*, ch. 3 (1924); qtd. in *The Columbia World of Quotations*, 1996. *Bartleby.com*, 2001.

    a. objective   b. subjective

_____ 2. "It is . . . to my three children [that] I owe my very being. In attempting to fulfill my duty to them as a mother, I met the challenge of their helplessness, their innocence, their dependence. Despising cowardice in others, I wished to prove myself no coward. Believing in the good, the gentle, the beautiful things of life, I addressed myself to the sweet duty of keeping these attributes for my children's sake and my own. And in striving to provide a living for them, I found a success beyond my wildest dreams."

Alice Foote MacDougall (1867–1945), U.S. businesswoman

—From *The Autobiography of a Business Woman*. Published by Little, Brown.

    a. emotional   b. neutral

_____ 3. "Success is a great deodorant. It takes away all your past smells."

Elizabeth Taylor, American film actor

—From ABC-TV interview April 6, 1977.

    a. formal   b. informal

EXPLANATIONS

1. (b) subjective: Sarah Bernhardt establishes a subjective tone through the use of biased language with words such as *incessant, intellectual, labor, inspire,* or *ideal.*

2. (a) emotional: MacDougall expresses a passionate drive for success.

3. (b) informal: Taylor uses colloquial language (commonly spoken words) for a witty effect.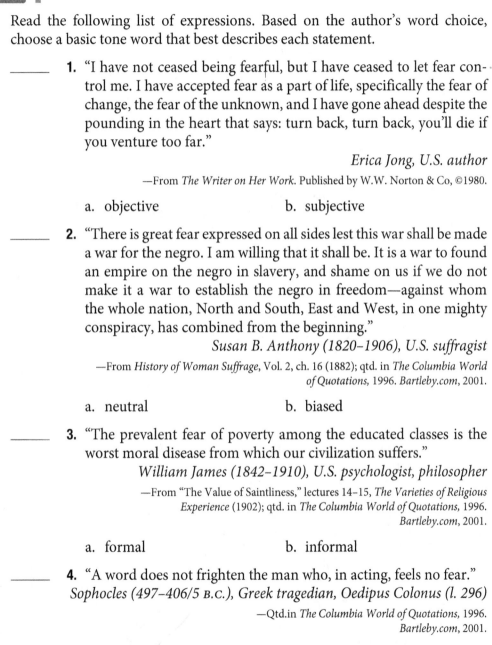

Practice 1

Read the following list of expressions. Based on the author's word choice, choose a basic tone word that best describes each statement.

_____ **1.** "I have not ceased being fearful, but I have ceased to let fear control me. I have accepted fear as a part of life, specifically the fear of change, the fear of the unknown, and I have gone ahead despite the pounding in the heart that says: turn back, turn back, you'll die if you venture too far."

Erica Jong, U.S. author

—From *The Writer on Her Work*. Published by W.W. Norton & Co, ©1980.

a. objective   b. subjective

_____ **2.** "There is great fear expressed on all sides lest this war shall be made a war for the negro. I am willing that it shall be. It is a war to found an empire on the negro in slavery, and shame on us if we do not make it a war to establish the negro in freedom—against whom the whole nation, North and South, East and West, in one mighty conspiracy, has combined from the beginning."

Susan B. Anthony (1820–1906), U.S. suffragist

—From *History of Woman Suffrage*, Vol. 2, ch. 16 (1882); qtd. in *The Columbia World of Quotations*, 1996. *Bartleby.com*, 2001.

a. neutral   b. biased

_____ **3.** "The prevalent fear of poverty among the educated classes is the worst moral disease from which our civilization suffers."

William James (1842–1910), U.S. psychologist, philosopher

—From "The Value of Saintliness," lectures 14–15, *The Varieties of Religious Experience* (1902); qtd. in *The Columbia World of Quotations*, 1996. *Bartleby.com*, 2001.

a. formal   b. informal

_____ **4.** "A word does not frighten the man who, in acting, feels no fear."

Sophocles (497–406/5 B.C.), Greek tragedian, Oedipus Colonus (l. 296)

—Qtd.in *The Columbia World of Quotations*, 1996. *Bartleby.com*, 2001.

a. emotional   b. neutral

_____ **5.** Around us fear, descending
Darkness of fear above
And in my heart how deep unending
Ache of love!

> *James Joyce (1882–1941), Irish writer,*
> *"On the Beach at Fontana" (l. 9–12)*
>
> —From *Oxford Book of Modern Verse*, Yeats, ed. (1936); qtd. in *The Columbia World of*
> *Quotations*, 1996. *Bartleby.com*, 2001.

a. objective   b. emotional

 ## Identify Subjective and Objective Tone Words

Recognizing tone and describing an author's attitude deepens your comprehension and helps you become a master reader. A small sample of words used to describe tone are listed here. Look up the meanings of any words you do not know; developing your vocabulary helps you better understand an author's word choice to establish tone.

Subjective			Objective
admiring	disbelieving	persuasive	accurate
angry	discouraged	pleading	factual
annoyed	disdainful	poetic	impartial
anxious	dramatic	reverent	matter-of-fact
approving	earnest	rude	straightforward
argumentative	elated	sad	truthful
arrogant	entertaining	sarcastic	
assured	fearful	self-pitying	
belligerent	friendly	serious	
biting	funny	sincere	
bitter	gloomy	supportive	
bored	happy	suspenseful	
bubbly	hostile	sympathetic	
calm	humorous	tender	
candid	idealistic	tense	
cold	informal	thoughtful	
comic	informative	threatening	
complaining	irritated	timid	
confident	joking	urgent	
cynical	jovial	warning	
demanding	joyful	wistful	
direct	lively	wry	
disappointed	loving		

> EXAMPLE Read the following quotations. Choose a word that best describes the tone of each statement.

cautionary	confident	critical	joyous	reverent

1. "Queenliness is an attitude that starts on the inside and works its way out. The way you hold your head up makes you a queen . . . I know who I am. I am confident. I know God. I can take care of myself. I share my life with others, and I love—I am worthy of the title Queen."

    Queen Latifah, actress, singer, rap artist

    —From *Ladies First: Revelations of a Strong Woman* by Queen Latifah and Karen Hunter. Published by Pocket Books, ©1999.

    Tone: _____

2. "Music puts me in touch with something beyond the intellect, something otherworldly, something sacred."

    Sting, musician

    —"Mystery and Religion of Music," Published by Berklee College of Music, ©1999.

    Tone: _____

3. "After a century of striving, after a year of debate, after a historic vote, health care reform is no longer an unmet promise. It is the law of the land. It is the law of the land."

    President Barack Obama

    —Remarks by the President on Health Insurance Reform at the Department of the Interior, 23 March 2010.

    Tone: _____

4. "Americans wanted us to get at the root of this problem, which is cost. Instead, Democrats are spending trillions more on a system that already costs too much and forcing seniors, small business owners and middle class families to pay for it. You can call that a lot of things. You might even call it historic. But you can't call it reform."

    Senator Mitch McConnell, Republican-Kentucky, Minority Leader

    —Remarks in press release regarding health care bill, 23 March 2010.

    Tone: _____

5. "As though a deep gulf were yawning below, As crossing thin ice, Take heed how ye go."

Confucius

—*The Sayings of Confucius.* Vol. XLIV, Part 1. *The Harvard Classics.*
New York: P.F. Collier & Son, 1909–14; *Bartleby.com,* 2001.

Tone: _____

VISUAL *VOCABULARY*

Use a tone word to describe the mood of President Obama and his team as they work to pass the health care reform bill in 2010.

_____

_____

EXPLANATION   Compare your answers to the following: (1) confident, (2) reverent, (3) joyous, (4) critical, (5) cautionary. ◀

Practice 2

Read the following items. Based on the author's word choice, choose a word from the box that best describes the tone of each statement.

emotional	humble	matter-of-fact	reflective	respectful

1.   **Harvard University, Cambridge, May 28, 1896**
                    President Booker T. Washington

MY DEAR SIR: Harvard University desires to confer on you at the approaching Commencement an honorary degree; but it is our custom to confer degrees only on gentlemen who are present. Our Commencement occurs this year on June 24, and your presence would be desirable from about noon till about five o'clock in the afternoon. Would it be possible for you to be in Cambridge on that day?

Believe me, with great regard,

Very truly yours,

CHARLES W. ELIOT.

—From Washington, Booker, *Up from Slavery: An Autobiography*,
ch. XVII, p. 4 (1901); *Bartleby.com*, 2000.

Tone: _____

2. "This was a recognition that had never in the slightest manner entered into my mind, and it was hard for me to realize that I was to be honoured by a degree from the oldest and most renowned university in America."

Booker T. Washington, President of Tuskegee College

—From *Up from Slavery: An Autobiography*,
ch. XVII, p. 5 (1901); *Bartleby.com*, 2000.

Tone: _____

3. "As I sat upon my veranda, with this letter in my hand, tears came into my eyes. My whole former life—my life as a slave on the plantation, my work in the coal-mine, the times when I was without food and clothing, when I made my bed under a sidewalk, my struggles for an education, the trying days I had had at Tuskegee, days when I did not know where to turn for a dollar to continue the work there, the ostracism and sometimes oppression of my race,—all this passed before me and nearly overcame me."

Booker T. Washington, President of Tuskegee College

—From *Up from Slavery: An Autobiography*,
ch. XVII, p. 5 (1901); *Bartleby.com*, 2000.

Tone: _____

4. "As this was the first time that a New England university had conferred an honorary degree upon a Negro, it was the occasion of much newspaper comment throughout the country."

Booker T. Washington, President of Tuskegee College

—From *Up from Slavery: An Autobiography*,
ch. XVII, p. 10 (1901); *Bartleby.com*, 2000.

Tone: _____

5. "If my life in the past has meant anything in the lifting up of my people and the bringing about of better relations between your race and mine, I assure you from this day it will mean doubly more."

Booker T. Washington, President of Tuskegee College

—From *Up from Slavery: An Autobiography,*
ch. XVII, p. 9 (1901); *Bartleby.com*, 2000.

Tone: _____

LO4 Determine the General Purpose in the Main Idea

In Chapter 3, you learned that a main idea is made up of a topic and the author's controlling point. You identified the controlling point by looking for thought patterns and biased (tone) words. The next two sections will build on what you have learned. First, you will study the relationship between the general purpose and the author's main idea. Then you will apply what you have learned to figure out an author's primary purpose.

Many reasons can motivate a writer. These can range from the need to take a stand on a hotly debated issue to the desire to entertain an audience with an amusing story. Basically, an author writes to share a main idea about a topic. An author's main idea, whether stated or implied, and the author's purpose are directly related. One of the following three general purposes will drive a main idea: to inform, to persuade, and to entertain.

- **To inform.** When a writer sets out to inform, he or she shares knowledge and information or offers instruction about a particular topic. A few tone words typically used to describe this purpose include *objective, matter-of-fact,* and *straightforward.* Authors use facts to explain or describe the main idea to readers. Most textbook passages are written to inform. The following topic sentences reflect the writer's desire to inform.

  1. A sensible weight management program combines a healthful diet and regular exercise.
  2. *Narrative of the Life of Frederick Douglass, an American Slave, Written by Himself* records Douglass's life as a slave in the United States.

In sentence 1, the topic is weight management, and the words that reveal the controlling point are *sensible, healthful,* and *regular.* The author uses a tone that is unbiased and objective, so the focus is on the information. In sentence 2, the topic is Frederick Douglass's autobiography, and the words that reveal the controlling point are *records, life,* and *slave.* Again, the author chooses words that are matter-of-fact and suggest that factual details will follow. Both topic sentences indicate that the author's purpose is to provide helpful information.

- **To persuade.** A writer who sets out to persuade tries to bring the reader into agreement with his or her view on the topic. A few of the tone words typically used to describe this purpose include *argumentative, persuasive, forceful, controversial, positive, supportive, negative,* and *critical.* Authors combine facts with emotional appeals to sway the reader to their point of view. Politicians and advertisers often write and speak to persuade. The following topic sentences reflect the writer's desire to persuade.

3. Resistance training is the best method of shaping the body.
4. *Narrative of the Life of Frederick Douglass, an American Slave, Written by Himself* should be required reading in American public high schools.

In sentence 3, the topic is resistance training. The word that reveals the author's controlling point is *best.* In sentence 4, the topic is Douglass's autobiography. The words that reveal the controlling point are *should be,* which are followed by a recommendation for action. The author is offering a debatable personal opinion about what should be required high school reading. In both of these sentences, the authors are out to convince others to agree with them.

- **To entertain.** A writer whose purpose is to entertain sets out to captivate or interest the audience. A few of the tone words typically used to describe this purpose include *amusing, entertaining, lively, humorous,* and *suspenseful.* To entertain, authors often use expressive language and creative thinking. Most readers are entertained by material that stirs an emotional reaction such as laughter, sympathy, or fear. Thus, authors engage readers creatively through vivid images, strong feelings, or sensory details (such as sights, sounds, tastes, textures, and smells). Both fiction and nonfiction writers seek to entertain. The following topic sentences reflect the writer's desire to entertain.

5. Leona had the fashion style of a cantaloupe.
6. Anton woke up to the cozy aromas of coffee, bacon, and freshly baked bread, just as he had every day of his twenty years, yet today promised to be very different. He just knew it.

You may have found identifying the topic and controlling point a little more challenging in these two sentences. Often, when writers entertain, they imply the main idea. And when they use an implied main idea, they rely much more heavily on tone words. Sentence 5 deals with the topic of Leona and her fashion style. In this sentence, the author focuses the topic with the phrase "style of a cantaloupe." The use of *cantaloupe* (a biased word when used in this context) offers a strong clue that the author's purpose is to entertain. The author seeks to amuse the reader with the contrast between style and cantaloupe. Surprising contrasts often amuse the reader. Authors also use other methods to entertain, including exaggerations, vivid details, and dramatic descriptions.

Sentence 6 deals with the topic of Anton's experience. In this case, the words that reveal the author's controlling point are *cozy, aromas, freshly baked,* which are pleasant sensory details, and *promised* and *different*. However, the main idea is not really about Anton's experience. The point seems to be about a change or hope for change in Anton's life.

These six sentences show that a topic can be approached in a variety of ways. The author chooses a topic and a purpose. The purpose shapes the focus of the main idea. The author carefully chooses tone words to express the main idea in light of the purpose. Each of these choices then controls the choices of supporting details and the thought pattern used to organize them.

> **EXAMPLES** Read each of the following paragraphs. Annotate them for main idea and tone. Then identify the author's purpose as follows:

I = to inform   P = to persuade   E = to entertain

_____ **1.** ¹Darla shivered, pulled her jacket's fuzzy collar up to the tops of her ears, and tucked her chin into its warmth; her arms and legs felt heavy and difficult to move as she started across the street. ²It was only November, and already she longed for the bright, long days of June and July. ³She dreaded the looming blackness of January and February. ⁴She did not mesh well with the rhythm of their abbreviated days and unending nights.

⁵Ah, she thought to herself, I am so incredibly tired. ⁶She felt the familiar cravings for something sweet and crunchy; she mentally pictured the box of Cocoa Puffs sitting on the pantry shelf, and she longed to be home. ⁷She didn't care that she was already beginning to show her dreaded winter weight, she was going to have a bowl, or maybe two, as soon as she could.

_____ **2.** ¹Some people suffer from symptoms of depression during the winter months, with symptoms subsiding during the spring and summer months. ²This may be a sign of Seasonal Affective Disorder (SAD). ³SAD is a mood disorder linked to two factors: episodes of depression and the seasonal variations of daylight.

⁴Some experts believe as seasons change, a shift in our "biological internal clocks" occurs, partly because of the changes in

sunlight patterns. [5]This may cause our biological clocks to be out of "step" with our daily schedules. [6]The most difficult months for some SAD sufferers seem to be January and February. [7]In addition, younger persons and women seem to be at higher risk.

—Adapted from "Symptoms of Depression" from Mental Health America. Copyright © 2010. Used by permission of Mental Health America.

_____ **3.** No one knows how many people suffer from SAD (seasonal affective disorder), but it is a very real and potentially debilitating condition. If you are afflicted with SAD, know that you are not alone, and realize that there are some remedies you can take. Spending time outdoors, exercise, social activity, and a nutritious diet (avoiding simple carbohydrates like cookies and candy) have been shown to help. Light therapy and cognitive behavioral therapy (CBT)—a type of talk therapy—can offer relief in more extreme cases. Be patient. You won't suddenly "snap out of" depression, but your mood will improve gradually. Most important, if you're feeling blue this winter, and if the feelings last for several weeks, talk to a health care provider. "It's true that SAD goes away on its own, but that could take 5 months or more. Five months of every year is a long time to be impaired and suffering," says Dr. Matthew Rudorfer, a mental health expert at the National Institutes of Health. "SAD is generally quite treatable, and the treatment options keep increasing and improving." So those of us who suffer from SAD can turn to those options with hope. And those of us who sympathize with SAD sufferers can pledge our support for funding more research into this condition.

—Adapted from News in Health http://newsinhealth.nih.gov/issue/Jan2013/Feature1

4. Study each of the photographs of people in public speaking situations. Label the purpose of each speaker with one of the following:

E = to entertain   **I** = to inform   **P** = to persuade

a. _____   b. _____   c. _____

EXPLANATIONS Passages 1 through 3 used the same topic: seasonal affective disorder (SAD). However, the purpose of each passage differed. Note how the difference in purpose affected the selection and presentation of supporting details.

1. The topic is Darla's experience with SAD. This topic is implied. In the first paragraph, the author uses vivid details, descriptions, and appeals to the senses *to entertain* the reader through an unfolding dramatic event.

2. In the second paragraph, the author's purpose is simply *to inform* the reader about the symptoms of seasonal affective disorder (SAD).

3. However, in the third paragraph, the author attempts to *persuade* the reader that there is hope for those suffering from SAD and to take steps to deal with it. The writer also tries to persuade those not suffering from SAD to support funding research for more treatment options. The persuasive tone is established and carried through by the words *remedies, therapy, relief,* and *improve.*

4. a. P, to persuade   b. I, to inform   c. E, to entertain ◔

Practice 3

Read the following topic sentences. Label each according to its purpose:

I = to inform   **P** = to persuade   **E** = to entertain

_____ 1. Understanding the aging process and those who seem to defy it is vital to our future.

_____ 2. According to Elisabeth Kübler-Ross, people go through five stages of grief.

_____ 3. To experience the hospitality and delights of a true summer resort away from the daily stresses, take a trip back in time to Mackinac Island in Michigan.

_____ 4. The sun spilled its brilliance from above so that every leaf, blade of grass, and ripple of water on the lake shimmered with no regard for my great grief.

LO5 Determine the Primary Purpose of a Passage

In addition to the three general purposes, authors often write to fulfill a more specific purpose. The following table offers several examples of specific purposes.

General and Specific Purposes

To Inform	To Entertain	To Persuade
to analyze	to amuse	to argue for
to clarify	to delight	to argue against
to discuss	to frighten	to criticize
to establish		to convince
to explain		to inspire (motivate a change)

Often a writer has two or more purposes in one piece of writing. Blending purposes adds interest and power to a piece of writing. Take, for example, the popular documentary show *MythBusters* on the Discovery Channel. The show attempts to inform and entertain, but its primary purpose is to argue. The show uses fact, research, and testing to debunk urban legends. When an author has more than one purpose, only one purpose is in control overall. This controlling purpose is called the **primary purpose.**

You have studied several reading skills that will help you grasp the author's primary purpose. For example, the author's primary purpose is often suggested by the main idea, the thought pattern, and the tone of the passage. Read the following topic sentence. Identify the author's primary purpose by considering the main idea, thought pattern, and tone.

_____ Spanking must be avoided as a form of discipline due to its long-term negative effects on the child.
   a. to discuss the disadvantages of spanking
   b. to argue against spanking as a means of discipline
   c. to make fun of those who use spanking as a means of discipline

This topic sentence clearly states a main idea "against spanking" using the tone words *must* and *negative*. The details will be organized using the thought pattern "long-term effects." Based on the topic sentence, the author's primary purpose is (b) to argue against spanking as a means of discipline. Even when the main idea is implied, tone and thought patterns point to the author's primary purpose.

You should also take into account titles, headings, and prior knowledge about the author. For example, it's easy to see that Jay Leno's primary purpose is to entertain us with his book *If Roast Beef Could Fly*. The title is funny, and we know Jay Leno is a comedian. A master reader studies the general context of the passage to find out the author's primary purpose.

Primary purpose is the author's main reason for writing the passage.

EXAMPLE Read the following paragraphs. Identify the primary purpose of each.

1.   **Coacoochee**

Coacoochee. A Seminole warrior, nicknamed "Wildcat" and "Shrieky Scream," led raids against Americans, including Captain Dummett and Sergeant Ormond on the Halifax River. Famous for escaping jail in St. Augustine [Florida], he was banished to Mexico where he died at 49 of smallpox. His mother said he was made of Florida sands.

—*Images of America: Ormond Beach,* published by
The Ormond Beach Historical Trust, 1999, p. 15

_____ The main purpose of this paragraph is
   a. to share historical information about Coacoochee, a Seminole Indian.
   b. to amuse the reader with entertaining details about Coacoochee.
   c. to convince readers that Coacoochee was a hero.

Textbook
Skills

2.   **Smartphones**

Perhaps the most potentially revolutionary application of computer miniaturization is found in the expanding capabilities of portable telephones. Indeed, what was recently merely a telephone has evolved into a small hand-held general purpose computer known as a smartphone on which telephony is only one of many applications. These "phones" are equipped with a rich array of sensors and interfaces including cameras, microphones, compasses, touch screens, accelerometers (to detect the phone's orientation and motion), and a number of wireless technologies to communicate with other smartphones and computers. The potential is enormous. Indeed, many argue that the smartphone will have a greater effect on society than the PC.

—Brookshear, J. Glenn, *Computer Science: An Overview,* p. 9.

_____ The main purpose of this passage is
   a. to offer entertaining details about people's use of smartphones.
   b. to persuade the reader to buy a smartphone.
   c. to explain what a smartphone is.

Textbook
Skills

3.   **Should Children Pledge Allegiance?**

[1]A government that is built upon respect for the dignity and the rights of every human being deserves the allegiance or loyalty of its citizens. [2]The United States is built upon respect for the dignity and the rights of every human being. [3]Therefore, the United States deserves the allegiance of its citizens. [4]In addition, an effort to develop in citizens an appreciation for such an allegiance is acceptable. [5]That effort, however, must not harm the dignity of the individual. [6]In addition, the effort must not cause the individual to act against his or her personal beliefs. [7]Sadly, requiring students to recite the pledge of allegiance in school does, in some cases, cause students to act against their personal beliefs. [8]And, in some cases, when students refuse to act against their beliefs in this way, they have been abused. [9]Therefore, requiring students to recite the pledge of allegiance is not acceptable.

—Adapted from Ruggerio, Vincent Ryan, *The Art of Thinking:*
A Guide to Critical and Creative Thought, 7th ed., p. 200.

_____ The main purpose of this paragraph is
   a. to argue against requiring students to recite the pledge of allegiance.
   b. to entertain the reader with a clever view about requiring students to recite the pledge of allegiance.
   c. to inform the reader about the pledge of allegiance.

EXPLANATION

1. The first paragraph is taken from a book produced by the historical society of the small coastal town of Ormond Beach, Florida. The purpose is (a), to share historical information about Coacoochee, a Seminole Indian.

2. The second paragraph comes from a college computer science textbook. The main purpose is (c), to explain what a smartphone is.

3. The third paragraph is taken from a college textbook on critical thinking. Its main purpose is (a), to argue against requiring students to recite the pledge of allegiance.

Practice 4

Read the passage from a college finance textbook. Answer the questions that follow it.

Textbook
Skills

Personal Financial Planning

[1]Where does it all go? [2]It seems like the last paycheck is gone before the next one comes in. [3]Money seems to burn a hole in your pocket, yet you don't believe that you are living extravagantly. [4]Last month you made a pledge to yourself to spend less than the month before. [5]Somehow, though, the weeks seem to go by, and you are again in the same position as you were last month. [6]Your money is gone. [7]Is there any way to plug the hole in your pocket?

[8]As with any campaign, the first step is to gather information. [9]How much income do you earn? [10]How much is left after withholding taxes? [11]What are your expenses? [12]For many people, the first obstacle is to correctly assess their true expenses. [13]Calculating your net income is easy; just look at your pay statement. [14]But expenses are sly little creatures. [15]Each one seems so harmless and worthwhile, but combined together they can be a pack of piranhas that quickly gobble up your modest income. [16]What can you do to gain control of your personal finances?

[17]The solution is simple, but not easy. [18]The solution is simple because others have blazed the path; however, your task is not easy, because it takes self-discipline and there may be no immediate reward. [19]The result is often like a diet: easy to get started, but hard to carry through.

[20]Your tools are the personal balance statement, the personal cash flow statement, and a budget. [21]These three personal financial statements show you where you are, predict where you will be after three months or a year, and help you control those pesky expenditures; the potential benefits are reduced spending, increased savings and investments, and peace of mind from knowing that you are in control.

—From Madura, Jeff. *Personal Finance*, 2nd ed., pp. 27–28.

_____ 1. The purpose of sentence 8 in the second paragraph is
  a. to inform the reader that financial planning is similar to any operating plan.
  b. to state a point against extravagant spending.
  c. to entertain the reader with a vivid detail about planning.

_____ 2. The main purpose of the second paragraph is
  a. to explain to the reader that everyone struggles with financial problems.
  b. to convince the reader that personal financial planning is necessary.
  c. to amuse the reader with a real-life story.

_____ **3.** The main purpose of the passage overall is
   a. to explain and illustrate the process of personal financial planning.
   b. to offer an amusing approach with real life details to the topic "personal financial planning."
   c. to argue against extravagant spending.

Recognize Irony Used for Special Effects

Irony is a tone often used in both conversation and written text. An author uses **irony** when he or she says one thing but means something else. Irony is the contrast between what is stated and what is implied, or between actual events and expectations.

Irony is often used to entertain and enlighten. For example, in the novel _Huckleberry Finn_ by Mark Twain, the boy Huckleberry Finn believes he has done something wrong when he helps his older friend Jim escape slavery. The ironic contrast lies between what Huckleberry Finn thinks is wrong and what really is wrong: slavery itself. Twain set up this ironic situation to reveal the shortcomings of society.

Irony is also used to persuade. In her essay "I Want a Wife," Judy Brady seems to be saying she wants a wife to take care of the children, do the household chores, and perform all the other countless duties expected of a wife in the mid-twentieth century. However, she doesn't really want a wife; she wants equality with men. As she describes the role of a wife as a submissive servant, she argues against the limitations that society has placed on women.

Due to the powerful effects of irony, authors use it in many types of writing. You may come across irony in fiction, essays, poetry, comedy routines, and cartoons. When authors use irony, they imply their main ideas and rely heavily on tone. Thus you need to understand two common types of irony so that you can see and enjoy their effects: verbal irony and situational irony.

> **Verbal irony** occurs when the author's words state one thing but imply the opposite.

- During a disagreement, your friend says, "I can't wait to hear your next great idea!"
- After eating large portions of a full-course meal, a diner says, "Good thing I wasn't hungry."
- After completing a challenging exam, a student says, "Well, that was easy."

> **Situational irony** occurs when the events of a situation differ from what is expected.

- A popular singer suffers from severe stage fright.
- The person voted "most likely to succeed" in high school becomes a homeless drifter.
- A wealthy person never takes a vacation or goes out to expensive restaurants.

> EXAMPLES Read the items, and identify the type of irony used in each.

_____ 1. Referring to Katharine Hepburn, in a theater review of *The Lake*, Dorothy Parker wrote, "She runs the gamut of emotions from A to B."

—In *The Columbia World of Quotations*,
1996; *Bartleby.com*, 2001.

a. verbal irony   c. no irony
b. situational irony

_____ 2. In O. Henry's "The Gift of the Magi," a wife sells her long hair for money to buy a chain for her husband's pocket watch, which he pawns to buy combs for her long hair.
a. verbal irony   c. no irony
b. situational irony

_____ 3. "C-O-P-D (Chronic Obstructive Pulmonary Disease) is the fourth leading cause of death in the United States. It is a serious lung disease that takes away the breath of 12 million Americans."

—*Kenneth P. Moritsugu, Acting Surgeon General,*
U.S. Department of Health and Human Services

—From Remarks at 52nd International Respiratory Congress.
11 Nov. 2006. Washington, D.C.

a. verbal irony   c. no irony
b. situational irony

EXPLANATIONS Compare your answers with these:

1. (a) verbal irony: Dorothy Parker is known for her ironic wit. In this case, Parker's biting wit arises out of the contrast between the word *gamut* and

the phrase "A to B." The word *gamut* means "scope" or "range," and sets up the expectation that Parker is going to imply that Ms. Hepburn displays an impressive breadth of emotion; however, she surprisingly limits Hepburn's range of emotion to the first two letters of the alphabet. What initially seems to be a compliment ends as a humorous insult.

2. (b) situational irony: This situation is ironic because the very special gifts the wife and husband gave each other are useless because of the sacrifices they made.

3. (c) no irony: The author directly states facts without implying any other meaning than the one stated.

Practice 5

Read the items below and identify the type of irony used in each.

_____ 1. "I love working sixteen-hour days for minimum wage."
   a. verbal irony   c. no irony
   b. situational irony

_____ 2. A recent college graduate takes a job as an intern in a company as a stepping-stone into a salaried position with full benefits. However, the intern's supervisor feels threatened by the efficiency and skill of the intern and denies her the full-time position.
   a. verbal irony   c. no irony
   b. situational irony

_____ 3. "Notice—By Order of the Author. Persons attempting to find a motive in this narrative will be prosecuted; persons attempting to find a moral in it will be banished; persons attempting to find a plot in it will be shot."

   —Mark Twain, *Huckleberry Finn* (1884).

   a. verbal irony   c. no irony
   b. situational irony

_____ 4. A student studies for weeks for final exams and earns the highest grade point average in her classes.
   a. verbal irony   c. no irony
   b. situational irony

_____ **5.** On his way home from an Alcoholics Anonymous meeting, a reformed alcoholic is killed in an automobile accident by a drunk driver who walks away from the accident with only minor injuries.
a. verbal irony
c. no irony
b. situational irony

LO7   Develop Textbook Skills: Recognize an Author's Tone and Purpose

Textbook
Skills

Read the following passage from the textbook *Access to Health*. Then answer the questions about the author's tone and purpose.

Societal Causes of Violence

[1]Although the underlying causes of violence and abuse are as varied as the individual crimes and people involved, several social, cultural, and individual factors seem to increase the likelihood of violent acts (see Figure 10.1). [2]Included among those factors most commonly listed are the following:

Poverty. [3]Low socioeconomic status and poor living conditions can create an environment of hopelessness, leaving one feeling trapped and seeing violence as the only way to obtain what is needed or wanted.

Unemployment. [4]It is a well-documented fact that when the economy goes sour, violent crime, suicide, assault, and other crimes increase.

Parental influence. [5]Violence is cyclical. [6]Children raised in environments in which shouting, slapping, hitting, and other forms of violence are commonplace are more apt to "act out" these behaviors as adults. [7]Horrifying reports in recent years have made this pattern impossible to ignore.

Cultural beliefs. [8]Cultures that objectify women and empower men to be tough and aggressive tend to have increased rates of violence in the home.

The media. [9]A daily dose of murder and mayhem can take a toll on even resistant minds.

Discrimination/oppression. [10]Whenever one group is oppressed by another, seeds of discontent are sown and hate crimes arise.

Religious differences. [11]Religious persecution has been a part of the human experience since the earliest times. [12]These battles between right and wrong, good and evil, and the attempt to impose beliefs on others have often led to violence.

Breakdown in the criminal justice system. [13]Overcrowded prisons, lenient sentences, early releases from prisons, and trial errors subtly encourage violence in a number of ways.

Stress. [14]People who suffer from inordinate amounts of stress or are in crisis are more apt to be highly reactive, striking out at others or acting irrationally.

—Text and graphic from Donatelle, Rebecca J. and Davis, Lorraine G., *Health: The Basics*, 7th ed., pp. 94–95 and Figure 4.1 (p. 95).

_____ **1.** The author's primary purpose for this section of the textbook is
    a. to inform.   c. to persuade.
    b. to entertain.

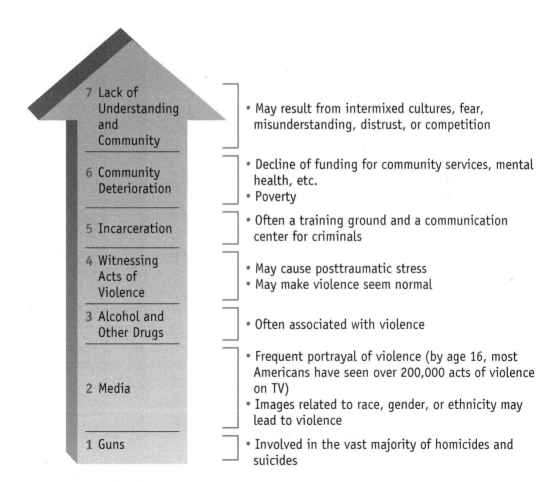

7 Lack of Understanding and Community
• May result from intermixed cultures, fear, misunderstanding, distrust, or competition

6 Community Deterioration
• Decline of funding for community services, mental health, etc.
• Poverty

5 Incarceration
• Often a training ground and a communication center for criminals

4 Witnessing Acts of Violence
• May cause posttraumatic stress
• May make violence seem normal

3 Alcohol and Other Drugs
• Often associated with violence

2 Media
• Frequent portrayal of violence (by age 16, most Americans have seen over 200,000 acts of violence on TV)
• Images related to race, gender, or ethnicity may lead to violence

1 Guns
• Involved in the vast majority of homicides and suicides

Figure 10.1 Correlates to Violence

_____ **2.** The overall tone of the text is
　　　　　a. biased.　　　　　　　　　　b. objective.

_____ **3.** The purpose of Figure 10.1, "Correlates to Violence," is
　　　　　a. to inform.　　　　　　　　　c. to persuade.
　　　　　b. to entertain.

_____ **4.** The tone of sentence 6 is
　　　　　a. ironic.　　　　　　　　　　c. sarcastic.
　　　　　b. angry.　　　　　　　　　　d. matter-of-fact.

_____ **5.** The tone of sentence 7 is
　　　　　a. irritated.　　　　　　　　　c. firm.
　　　　　b. matter-of-fact.　　　　　　d. sarcastic.

Apply Information Literacy Skills

 ## Academic, Personal, and Career Applications of Tone and Purpose

The ability to determine information's tone and purpose is an important information literacy skill. Considering the tone and purpose of information improves your ability to find, evaluate, and use relevant ideas. For example, think about the topic of health care. We view a politician's claim differently than we view a comedian's joke or a medical doctor's opinion. Tone and purpose affect meaning. As a student, consumer, citizen, and worker, you may come across materials such as textbook passages, advertisements, reports, or memos. Skimming for the purpose of the information helps you know where to focus your attention and how to react. Also, you may access or create particular types of documents for specific purposes such as brochures, journals, letters, recordings, or videos. Or you may think about how to use a part of a text, such as a quotation, in your own writings or speech. Therefore, you will use the skills that you have learned in this chapter in academic, personal, and career situations:

- Recognize your own need to identify tone and purpose.
- Analyze tone and purpose to determine the relevance of an idea.
- Determine the use of tone and purpose to develop a main idea.

Academic Application

Assume you are taking an American history college course, and your class is studying the unit about women's history. One of the course requirements is for each student to give a five-minute speech about a female public figure who influenced American history. You have chosen to speak about Eleanor Roosevelt. You would like use a quotation to either introduce or conclude your speech.

- **Before Reading:** Skim the quotes to identify the tone and purpose of each one.
- **During Reading:** Label the quotes to indicate your ranking of each quote's usability.
- **After Reading:** In the space following the passage, indicate which quote(s) you will use to help you make your point. Explain your choice.

Quote 1: "No one can make you feel inferior without your consent."

—"Eleanor Roosevelt." BrainyQuote.com.

Quote 2: "We all create the person we become by our choices as we go through life. In a real sense, by the time we are adults, we are the sum total of the choices we have made."

—"Eleanor Roosevelt." WisdomQuotes.com.

Quote 3: "Women must become more conscious of themselves as women and of their ability to function as a group. At the same time they must try to wipe from men's consciousness the need to consider them as a group or as women in their everyday activities, especially as workers in industry or the professions".

—"Eleanor Roosevelt." The Eleanor Roosevelt Papers Project. George Washington University.

_____

_____

_____

_____

Personal Application

Assume you are interested in buying a hybrid vehicle to replace your current car. You have found the following three sources of information about hybrid vehicles on the Internet.

- **Before Reading:** Skim the screen shot to get an overview of each source's title. Then, in the space provided, write down the search term that you think was used.
- **During Reading:** Highlight details that identify the purpose of the source.
- **After Reading:** In the space following the passage, describe the usefulness of each site as a source of information for purchasing a hybrid vehicle.

Search Term: _____.

HowStuffWorks "5 Reasons Not to **Buy a Hybrid**"
www.howstuffworks.com/5-reasons-to-not-buy-hybrid.htm ▾
Yeah, you read that title right: Five reasons to not **buy a hybrid car** -- so, are we crazy? Maybe a little bit. But don't all those Hollywood stars drive hybrids?

What You Should Know About Hybrids - Edmunds.com
www.edmunds.com › Car Reviews › 2013 New Car Buying Guides ▾
Edmunds 2013 **Car Buying** Guide offers things to consider when shopping for ... What You Should Know Before **Buying a Hybrid** | View Other **Buying** Guides ...

Hybrid **Buying** Guide - **Buying A Hybrid** | Hybrid Cars
www.hybridcars.com/hybrid-guide/ ▾
7 days ago – Data also revealed South Carolina, Tennessee, Kentucky and Mississippi are the fastest growing states for **hybrid car** registrations.

Hybrid Car Owners Not **Buying** Again - ABC News
abcnews.go.com › ABC News Blogs › Business › Consumer Report
Apr 10, 2012 – Image credit: Jim R. Bounds/Bloomberg via Getty Images) Once you "go **hybrid**," it seems you can turn back after all. Only 35 percent of **hybrid** ...

The Most Cost-Effective **Hybrid Cars** - Forbes
www.forbes.com/sites/.../2012/11/.../the-most-cost-effective-hybrid-cars/ ▾
Nov 20, 2012 – While most fuel-saving gas/electric-powered **hybrid cars** carry a substantial ... Still, the company determined that **buyers** of 11 out of 25 hybrids ...

Green **Cars**/Hybrids **Buying** Guide - **Cars**.com
www.cars.com/guides/best-gas-mileage/ ▾
Cars.com's Green **Car/Hybrid Buying** Guide includes photos, invoice prices, expert reviews and **car** ratings. View all Green **Cars**/Hybrids and see **Cars**.com's ...

The Downsides Of **Owning A Hybrid Vehicle** - Reasons Hybrid Cars ...
4wheeldrive.about.com › ... › Hybrid 4x4 Trucks/4WD SUVs ▾
These are the Cons - the worst things about **owning a Hybrid vehicle**. These are the top reasons that Hybrid cars aren't more popular.

5 Reasons to **Buy a Hybrid Car** - My Money (usnews.com)
www.usnews.com › Money › My Money ▾
Mar 24, 2011 – Yes, they're more expensive, but for some people, that cost is justified.

Hybrid-Car Competition Heats Up: Does the Toyota Prius Finally ...
business.time.com/.../hybrid-car-competition-heats-up-does-the-toyota-p... ▾
Feb 5, 2013 – In January, Ford sold five times as many **hybrid vehicles** as it did the year ... the majority of consumers (71%) indicated that the next car they **buy** ...

Tech **car buying** guide | **Car** Tech - CNET Reviews
reviews.cnet.com › Reviews › Car Tech ▾
Oct 30, 2012 – You are probably going to be focused on fuel economy if you are **buying** a daily driver, so seriously consider a hybrid. Today's **hybrid cars** get ...

Student Response:

_____

_____

_____

_____

_____

_____

_____

Career Application

Assume you are the office manager of a company. Your assistant manager, Evan Jones, is being considered for a promotion to manage a neighboring office of the same company. He has asked you to write a letter of recommendation. You have written the following two drafts.

- **Before Reading:** Skim both drafts to determine if the purpose is clear and the tone is appropriate.
- **During Reading:** Underline words that need to be revised to clarify purpose or to improve tone.
- **After Reading:** In the space following the passage, discuss which draft is more effective and why.

Draft 1:

To Whom It May Concern:

Evan Jones has worked for me for the last 4 years. His responsibilities have included accounting, planning and projecting future trends, developing and presenting new ideas. He has also worked as lead project coordinator for 7 out 10 of our department's largest projects during the last 2 years. Evan shows up on time, and never takes unwarranted or unplanned personal time. Evan also has a good rapport within our office. Evan has potential to be a great office manager. I recommend him for this position.

Sincerely,

Richard Perez

Draft 2:

To Whom It May Concern:

Evan Jones is a good worker. He always shows up on time, he rarely (if ever) leaves early, and gets along great with everyone. Evan always gets the job done! He would be a great addition to your team. Evan will make a great office manager, and I recommend you hire him.

Sincerely,

Richard Perez

_____

_____

_____

_____

REVIEW TEST 1

Score (number correct) _____ x 10 = _____ %

Visit MyReadingLab to take this test online and receive feedback and guidance on your answers.

Author's Purpose

A. Read the topic sentences. Label each one according to its purpose as follows:

I = to inform   **P** = to persuade   **E** = to entertain

_____ 1. A wedding should be viewed as one of the happiest of events, and we worked very hard to behave as if that were true for us, too—but more and more, the day felt like a collision of families in slow motion.

_____ 2. Americans consume more calories per person than does any other group of people in the world.

_____ 3. The Federal Drug Administration has a moral responsibility to the public that includes regulating alternative or herbal medicines.

_____ 4. "The process by which money that you currently hold accumulates interest over time is referred to as compounding."

—Madura, Jeff. *Personal Finance,* 2nd ed., p. 61.

_____ 5. A dollar received today is worth more than a dollar received tomorrow because it can be saved and invested; the time value of money is one of the strongest forces on earth—so save and invest.

—Adapted from Madura, Jeff. *Personal Finance,* 2nd ed., p. 59.

_____ 6. Adults with higher levels of education and income generally have more favorable health behaviors in terms of cigarette smoking, leisure-time physical activity, and body weight status; therefore, it is imperative that all people are afforded the opportunity for higher education.

_____ **7.** In 2009 a total of 2,437,163 deaths occurred in the United States; life expectancy at birth was 78.5 years, and the top five leading causes of deaths were heart disease, malignant neoplasms (cancer), chronic lower respiratory diseases, cerebrovascular diseases, and accidents.

—Centers for Disease Control and Prevention.

_____ **8.** One way to achieve the status of expert on a subject is through first-hand experience; thus I think it honest and helpful to offer myself as an expert of the highest order on the subject of smoking cessation, having quit over a dozen times.

B. Read the following items. Identify the primary purpose of each.

Editorial Cartoon Published in a Newspaper

© Clay Bennett Editorial Cartoon used with the permission of Clay Bennett, the Washington Post Writers Group and the Cartoonist Group.

_____ **9.** The primary purpose of this cartoon is
   a. to inform the reader about the quality of public education.
   b. to entertain the reader by mocking the public education system.
   c. to persuade the reader to oppose the emphasis on testing in public education.

Graphic from a Health Textbook

Textbook
Skills

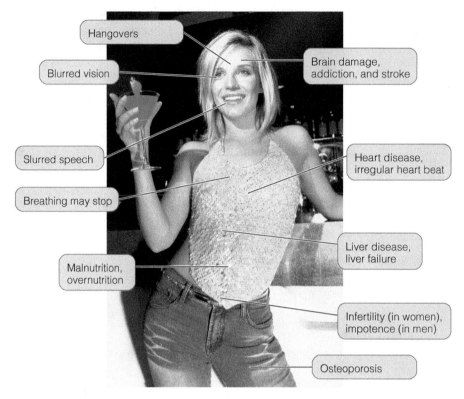

—Donatelle, Rebecca, J. and Davis, Lorraine G.,
Access to Health, 7th ed., p. 380.

_____ **10.** The primary purpose of this graphic is
   a. to persuade readers to abstain from alcohol consumption.
   b. to inform readers about the various negative effects of alcohol
      on the body.
   c. to interest readers with an interesting illustration.

REVIEW TEST 2

Score (number correct) _____ x 25 = _____ %

Visit MyReadingLab to take this test online and receive feedback and guidance on your answers.

Read the following passage from a college history textbook. Answer the questions that follow.

Native Americans

[1]Native Americans are the first true Americans, and their status under U.S. law is unique. [2]Under the U.S. Constitution, Indian tribes are considered distinct governments. [3]This situation has affected Native Americans' treatment by the Supreme Court in contrast to other groups of ethnic minorities. [4]And minority is a term that accurately describes American Indians. [5]It is estimated that there were as many as 10 million Indians in the New World at the time Europeans arrived in the 1400s. [6]The actual number of Indians is hotly contested. [7]Estimates vary from a high of 150–200 million to a low of 20–50 million throughout North and South America. [8]By 1900, the number of Indians in the continental United States had plummeted to less than 2 million. [9]Today, there are 2.8 million.

[10]Many commentators would agree that for years Congress and the courts manipulated Indian law to promote the westward expansion of the United States. [11]The Northwest Ordinance of 1787, passed by the Continental Congress, specified that "good faith should always be observed toward the Indians; their lands and property shall never be taken from them without their consent, and their property rights, and liberty, they shall never be invaded or disturbed, unless in just and lawful wars authorized by Congress." [12]These strictures were not followed. [13]Instead, over the years, "American Indian policy has been described as 'genocide-at-law' promoting both land acquisition and cultural extermination." [14]During the eighteenth and nineteenth centuries, the U.S. government isolated Indians on reservations as it confiscated their lands and denied them basic political rights. [15]Indian reservations were administered by the federal government. [16]And Native Americans often lived in squalid conditions.

[17]With passage of the Dawes Act in 1887, however, the government switched policies to promote assimilation over separation. [18]Each Indian family was given land within the reservation. [19]The rest was sold to whites, thus reducing Indian lands from about 140 million acres to about 47 million. [20]Moreover, to encourage Native Americans to assimilate, Indian children were sent to boarding schools off the reservation, and native languages and rituals were banned. [21]Native Americans didn't become U.S. citizens nor were they given the right to vote until 1924.

[22]At least in part because tribes were small and scattered (and the number of Indians declining), Native Americans formed no protest movement in reaction to these drastic policy changes. [23]It was not until the 1960s that Indians began to mobilize. [24]During this time, Indian activists, many trained by the American Indian Law Center at the University of New Mexico, began to file hundreds of test cases in the federal courts involving tribal fishing rights, tribal land claims, and the taxation of tribal profits.

[25]Native Americans have won some very important victories concerning hunting, fishing, and land rights. [26]Native American tribes all over America have sued to reclaim lands they say were stolen from them by the United States, often more than 200 years ago. [27]Today, these land rights allow Native Americans to play host to a number of casinos across the country.

—Adapted from Sabato, Larry J. and O'Connor, Karen, *American Government: Continuity and Change*, 2008 ed., pp. 226–227.

_____ 1. The overall purpose of the passage is to
  a. inform the reader with an overview of the history of Native Americans.
  b. amuse the reader with graphic details from the history of Native Americans.
  c. persuade the reader to support the Native American cause.

_____ 2. The overall tone of the passage is
  a. informal.   b. formal.

_____ 3. The overall tone of the passage is
  a. neutral.   b. biased.

_____ 4. Overall, the difficulties faced by the Native American reveals
  a. verbal irony.   c. no irony.
  b. situational irony.

REVIEW TEST 3

Score (number correct) _____ x 10 = _____ %

Visit MyReadingLab to take this test online and receive feedback and guidance on your answers.

Author's Purpose and Tone

Textbook Skills

Before Reading: Survey the following passage from a college film study textbook. Skim the passage, noting the words in **bold** print. Answer the Before Reading questions that follow the passage. Next, read the passage. Then answer the After Reading questions. Use the discussion and writing topics as activities to do after the reading.

Vocabulary Preview

bravura (3): daring; dash; brilliant technique
iconography (23): the different images of a person that make up one's view of him or her

persona (24): the outer personality that an individual presents to others
archetypal (27): like the model on which all others are based
exemplar (28): something worthy of imitation; a model
breadth (37): freedom from narrowness or restriction

Star Types

[1]At about the turn of the nineteenth century, George Bernard Shaw wrote a famous essay comparing the two foremost stage stars of the day—Eleonora Duse and Sarah Bernhardt. [2]Shaw's comparison is a useful springboard for a discussion of the different kinds of film stars. [3]Bernhardt, Shaw wrote, was a **bravura** personality, and she managed to tailor each different role to fit this personality. [4]This is what her fans both expected and desired. [5]Her personal charm was larger than life, yet undeniably captivating. [6]Her performances were filled with brilliant effects that had come to be associated with her personality over the years. [7]Duse, on the other hand, possessed a more quiet talent, less dazzling in its initial impact. [8]She was totally different with each role, and her own personality never seemed to intrude on the playwright's character. [9]Hers was an invisible art. [10]Her impersonations were so totally believable that the viewer was likely to forget it was an impersonation. [11]In effect, Shaw was pointing out the major distinctions between a personality star and an actor star.

[12]Personality stars commonly refuse all parts that go against their type, especially if they're leading men or leading ladies. [13]Performers like Tom Hanks almost never play cruel or psychopathic roles, for example, because such parts would conflict with their sympathetic image. [14]If a star is locked into his or her type, any significant departure can result in box-office disaster. [15]For example, when Pickford tried to abandon her little girl roles in the 1920s, her public stayed at home. [16]They wanted to see Little Mary or nothing. [17]She retired in disgust at the age of forty, just when most players are at the peak of their powers.

[18]On the other hand, many stars prefer to remain in the same mold, playing variations on the same character type. [19]John Wayne was the most popular star in film history. [20]From 1949 to 1976, he was absent from the top ten only three times. [21]"I play John Wayne in every part regardless of the character, and I've been doing okay, haven't I?" he once asked. [22]In the public mind, he was a man of action—and violence—rather than words. [23]His **iconography** is steeped in a distrust of sophistication and intellectuality. [24]His name is virtually synonymous with

masculinity—though his **persona** suggests more of the warrior than the lover, a man's man rather than a lady's man. [25]As he grew older, he also grew more human, developing his considerable talents as a comedian by mocking his own **macho** image. [26]Wayne was fully aware of the enormous influence a star can wield in transmitting values, and in many of his films, he embodied a right-wing ideology that made him a hero to conservative Americans, including Ronald Reagan, Newt Gingrich, Oliver North, and Pat Buchanan.

[27]Yet, as Garry Wills points out in his cultural study, *John Wayne's America: The Politics of Celebrity*, Wayne actually disliked horses, though in the popular imagination, he was the **archetypal** Westerner on a horse. [28]He also consciously evaded the military draft during World War II, yet his roles in such popular films as *The Sands of Iwo Jima* firmly established him as a military **exemplar**. [29]"From now on," Wills points out, "the man who evaded service in World War II would be the symbolic man who won World War II." [30]In short, a star's iconographical status can actually contradict historical truth. [31]In a 1995 poll, John Wayne (who had been dead for over sixteen years) was named America's all-time favorite movie star.

[32]The top box-office attractions tend to be personality stars. [33]They stay on top by being themselves, by not trying to impersonate anyone. [34]Gable insisted that all he did in front of the camera was to "act natural." [35]Similarly, Marilyn Monroe was always at her best when she played roles that exploited her indecisiveness, her vulnerability, and her pathetic eagerness to please.

[36]On the other hand, there have been many stars who refuse to be typecast and attempt the widest array of roles possible. [37]Such actor stars as Johnny Depp and Reese Witherspoon have sometimes undertaken unpleasant character roles rather than conventional leads to expand their range, for variety and **breadth** have traditionally been the yardsticks by which great acting is measured.

—Adapted from Giannetti, Louis, *Understanding Movies*, 12th ed., pp. 260, 264, 265.

Before Reading

Vocabulary in Context

1. In sentence 25, what does the word **macho** mean? _____

2. Identify the context clues used for the word **macho** in sentence 25.

_____

After Reading

Central Idea

_____ **3.** Which sentence best states the central idea of the passage?
- a. sentence 1
- b. sentence 11
- c. sentence 12
- d. sentence 32

Supporting Details

_____ **4.** One of the differences between personality stars and actor stars is
- a. their talent.
- b. their looks.
- c. the types of movies they star in.
- d. the kinds of roles they play.

Transitions

_____ **5.** The relationship of ideas within sentence 14 is
- a. cause and effect.
- b. time order.
- c. comparison.
- d. listing.

Thought Patterns

_____ **6.** The overall thought pattern for the passage is
- a. cause and effect.
- b. time order.
- c. contrast.
- d. definition and example.

Fact and Opinion

_____ **7.** Sentence 31 is a statement of
- a. fact.
- b. opinion.
- c. fact and opinion.

Tone and Purpose

_____ **8.** The tone of sentence 28 is
- a. argumentative.
- b. objective.
- c. ironic.

_____ **9.** The overall tone of the passage is
- a. witty.
- b. objective.
- c. sarcastic.

_____ **10.** The primary purpose of the passage is
- a. to persuade the reader that actor stars are more worthy of their admiration than personality stars.

b. to inform and explain about the different types of movie actors.

c. to entertain the reader with stories of Hollywood movie stars.

SUMMARY RESPONSE

Restate the author's central idea in your own words. In your summary, state the author's tone and purpose. Begin your summary response with the following: *The central idea of "Star Types" by Giannetti is . . .*

WHAT DO YOU THINK?

Choose one of the following topics and write an entry for a movie blog:

- Select two of your favorite movie stars and analyze whether each is a personality star or an actor star.

- Explain why you think people are attracted to movie stars. Why do we afford them celebrity status? What do they give moviegoers in return?

REVIEW TEST 4

Score (number correct) _____ x 10 = _____ %

Visit MyReadingLab to take this test online and receive feedback and guidance on your answers.

Author's Purpose and Tone

Textbook
Skills

Before Reading: Survey the following passage adapted from the college textbook *The West: Encounters & Transformations.* Skim the passage, noting the words in **bold** print. Answer the Before Reading questions that follow the passage. Then, read the passage. Next, answer the After Reading questions. Use the discussion and writing topics as activities to do after reading.

Vocabulary Preview

SS (2): abbreviation for the German word *Schutzstaffel,* which translates as Protective Squadron, a personal guard unit for Hitler, responsible for the mass murder of Jews and others deemed undesirable

Einsatzgruppen (3): strike or task force, SS units given the task of murdering Jews and Communist Party members in the areas of the Soviet Union occupied by Germany during World War II

indoctrinated (8): instructed, taught

Roma (12): gypsies

conglomerate (15): corporation, business

ghettos (20): in certain European cities, a section to which Jews were formally restricted

extermination (21): execution, death

culled (25): picked

The Death Camps: Murder by Assembly Line

[1]On January 20, 1942, senior German officials met in a villa in Wannsee, outside Berlin, to finalize plans for killing every Jew in Europe. [2]**SS** lieutenant colonel Adolf Eichmann (1906–1962) listed the number of Jews in every country; even the Jewish populations in neutral countries such as Sweden and Ireland showed up on the target list. [3]The Wannsee Conference marked the beginning of a more systematic approach to murdering European Jews, one that built on the experience gained by the **Einsatzgruppen** in the Soviet war.

[4]To accomplish mass murder, the Einsatzgruppen had become killing machines. [5]By trial and error, they discovered the most efficient ways of identifying and rounding up Jews, shooting them quickly, and burying the bodies. [6]But the Einsatzgruppen actions also revealed the limits of conventional methods of killing. [7]Shooting took time, used up valuable ammunition, and required large numbers of men.

[8]Moreover, even the best-trained and carefully **indoctrinated** soldiers eventually cracked under the strain of shooting unarmed women and children at close range. [9]A systematic approach was needed, one that would utilize advanced killing technology and provide a comfortable distance between the killers and the killed. [10]This perceived need resulted in a key Nazi innovation: the death camp.

[11]The death camp was a specialized form of a concentration camp. [12]From 1933 on, Hitler's government had sentenced communists, Jehovah's Witnesses, the **Roma**, and anyone else defined as an enemy of the **regime** to forced labor in concentration camps. [13]After the war began, the concentration camp system expanded dramatically. [14]Scattered throughout Nazi-controlled Europe, concentration camps became an essential part of the Nazi war economy. [15]Some firms, such as the huge chemical **conglomerate** I. G. Farben, established factories inside or right next to camps, which provided vital supplies of forced labor. [16]All across Europe during the war, concentration camp inmates died in huge numbers from the brutal physical labor, torture, and diseases brought on by malnutrition and inadequate housing and sanitary facilities. [17]But it was only in Poland that the Nazis constructed death camps, specialized concentration camps with only one purpose—murder, primarily the murder of Jews.

[18]The death camps marked the final stage in a vast assembly line of murder. [19]In early 1942 the trains conveying victims to the death camps began to rumble across Europe.

[20]Jewish **ghettos** across Nazi-occupied Europe emptied as their inhabitants moved in batches to their deaths. [21]Individuals selected for **extermination** followed orders to gather at the railway station for deportation to "work camps" farther east. [22]They were then packed into cattle cars, more than 100 people per car, all standing up for the entire journey. [23]Deprived of food and water, with hardly any air, and no sanitary facilities, often for several days, many Jews died en route. [24]The survivors stumbled off the trains into a nightmare world. [25]At some camps, SS guards **culled** stronger Jews from each transport to be worked to death as slave laborers. [26]Most, however, walked straight from the transport trains into a reception room, where they were told to undress, and then herded into a "shower room"—actually a gas chamber. [27]Carbon monoxide gas or a pesticide called Zyklon-B killed the victims. [28]After the poison had done its work, Jewish slaves emptied the chamber and burned the bodies in vast crematoria, modeled after industrial bake ovens. [29]The Nazis thus constructed a vast machine of death.

—Levack, Brian, Muir, Edward, Veldman, Meredith, and Maas, Michael, *The West: Encounters & Transformations,* Atlas Edition, Combined Edition, 2nd ed., pp. 870–871.

Before Reading

Vocabulary in Context

1. In sentence 12, what does the word **regime** mean? _____

_____

2. Identify the context clue used for the word **regime** in sentence 12. _____

_____

After Reading

Central Idea

_____ 3. Which sentence best states the central idea of the passage?
   a. sentence 1   c. sentence 4
   b. sentence 3   d. sentence 29

Supporting Details

_____ **4.** According to the passage, the death camps were constructed
   a. across Europe.   c. in Berlin.
   b. only in Poland.   d. in Jewish ghettos.

Transitions

_____ **5.** The relationship between sentence 5 and sentence 6 is
   a. time order.   c. listing.
   b. contrast.   d. definition and example.

Thought Patterns

_____ **6.** The thought pattern for paragraph 4 (sentences 11–17) is
   a. listing.   c. contrast.
   b. time order.   d. definition and example.

Fact and Opinion

_____ **7.** Sentence 8 is a statement of
   a. fact.   c. fact and opinion.
   b. opinion.

Tone and Purpose

_____ **8.** The tone of sentence 18 is
   a. matter-of-fact.   c. bitter.
   b. condemning.   d. understanding.

_____ **9.** The overall tone of the passage is
   a. horrified.   c. condemning.
   b. neutral.   d. sorrowful.

_____ **10.** The primary purpose of the passage is
   a. to persuade the reader about the brutality of the Nazi death camps.
   b. to shock the reader with graphic details about the Nazi death camps.
   c. to inform the reader about the Nazi commitment to exterminating Jews and others they deemed undesirable.

Restate the author's central idea in your own words. In your summary, state the author's tone and purpose. Begin your summary response with the following: *The central idea of "Death Camps: Murder by Assembly Line" by Levack, Muir, Veldman, and Maas is . . .*

Assume that a local chapter of the American Jewish League is sponsoring an essay contest in honor of those who suffered and died under the Nazi regime and to educate the next generation about the consequences of prejudice. There is a $250 cash prize for the winner of the contest. Consider the following points and write a 500-word essay:

- Identify the extreme effect of prejudice and hatred exhibited by the Nazi regime.
- Identify and discuss a current regime and its actions of terror that should be stopped.

After Reading About Tone and Purpose

Before you move on to the Mastery Tests on tone and purpose, take time to reflect on your learning and performance by answering the following questions. Write your answers in your notebook.

- How has my knowledge base or prior knowledge about tone and purpose changed?
- Based on my studies, how do I think I will perform on the Mastery Test(s)? Why do I think my scores will be above average, average, or below average? (Note: An additional fourth Mastery Test may be found in MyReadingLab.)
- Would I recommend this chapter to other students who want to learn about tone and purpose? Why or why not?

Test your understanding of what you have learned about tone and purpose by completing the Chapter 10 Review.

Name _____ Section_____

Date _____ **Score** (number correct) _____ x 20 = _____ %

Visit MyReadingLab to take this test online and receive feedback and guidance on your answers.

Read the poem and then answer the questions that follow it.

Fear Not the Fall

by Billie Jean Young

Fear not the fall.
Better to fall from the strength
of the sound of one's voice
speaking truth to the people
than to spend a lifetime
mired in discontent,
groveling in the sty of certainty
of acceptance,
of pseudo-love,
of muteness,
and easy-to-be-around-ness.

Better to fall screaming—
arms flailing,
legs askew
clawing in your intensity
for the right to be—
than silently,
like a weakened snowbird,
sentenced to the boredom of earth
too sick to sing.

—From Young, Billie Jean, "Fear Not the Fall" from *Fear Not the Fall: Poems and a Two-Act Drama*. Used by permission of NewSouth Books, Montgomery, AL, p. 112

_____ **1.** In the first stanza, the words *strength, sound, speaking,* and *truth* are best described by the tone word
a. confident.   c. afraid.
b. humble.   d. angry.

_____ **2.** In the second stanza, the words *screaming, flailing, askew, clawing,* and *intensity* are best described by the tone word
a. composed.   c. hostile.
b. defeated.   d. sad.

_____ **3.** The tone of the last three lines of the second stanza is
  a. hateful.   c. solemn.
  b. cold.   d. neutral.

_____ **4.** The phrase "fear not the fall" is ironic because
  a. the poem states "fear not" but implies the opposite.
  b. people often warn against falling or failing, but this poem advises "fear not."
  c. the poem suggests that failure is certain.

_____ **5.** The overall purpose of this poem is
  a. to persuade the reader to risk living honestly and avoid settling for security.
  b. to inform the reader about the effect of fear and the need to directly face fear.
  c. to entertain the reader with a personal experience about the fear of falling.

Name _____ Section_____

Date _____ **Score** (number correct) _____ x 20 = _____ %

Visit MyReadingLab to take this test online and receive feedback and guidance on your answers.

Read the following passage from a college literature textbook. Then answer the questions.

Textbook
Skills

Blues

¹Among the many song forms to have shaped the way poetry is written in English, no recent form has been more influential than the blues. ²Originally a type of folk music developed by black slaves in the South, blues songs have both a distinctive form and tone. ³They traditionally consist of three-line stanzas in which the first two identical lines are followed by a concluding, rhyming third line.

⁴To dream of muddy water—trouble is knocking at your door.
⁵To dream of muddy water—trouble is knocking at your door.
⁶Your man is sure to leave you and never return no more.

⁷Early blues lyrics almost always spoke of some sadness, pain, or deprivation—often the loss of a loved one. ⁸The melancholy tone of the lyrics, however, is not only world-weary but also world-wise. ⁹The blues expound the hard-won wisdom of bitter life experience. ¹⁰They frequently create their special mood through down-to-earth, even gritty, imagery drawn from everyday life. ¹¹Although blues reach back into the nineteenth century, they were not widely known outside African American communities before 1920 when the first commercial recordings appeared. ¹²Their influence on both music and song from that time was rapid and extensive. ¹³By 1930 James Weldon Johnson could declare, "It is from the blues that all that may be called American music derives its most distinctive characteristic." ¹⁴Blues have not only become an enduring category of popular music; they have helped shape virtually all the major styles of contemporary pop—jazz, rap, rock, gospel, country, and of course, rhythm-and-blues.

¹⁵The style and structure of blues have also influenced modern poets. ¹⁶Not only African American writers like Langston Hughes, Sterling A. Brown, Etheridge Knight, and Sonia Sanchez have written blues poems, but white poets as dissimilar as W. H. Auden, Elizabeth Bishop, Donald Justice, and Sandra McPherson have employed the form. ¹⁷The classic touchstones of the blues, however, remain the early singers like

Robert Johnson, Ma Rainey, Blind Lemon Jefferson, Charley Patton, and—perhaps preeminently—Bessie Smith, "the Empress of the Blues."

—Kennedy, X. J. and Gioia, Dana, *Literature: An Introduction to Fiction, Poetry, and Drama*, 3rd Compact edition, pp. 586–587.

_____ 1. Which term best describes the tone of sentence 1?
a. objective b. subjective

_____ 2. The tone of sentence 2 and sentence 3 is
a. objective. b. subjective.

_____ 3. The tone of the words *preeminently* and *Empress of the Blues* in sentence 17 is
a. mocking. c. objective.
b. understated. d. admiring.

_____ 4. Which word describes the overall tone of the passage?
a. humorous
b. informal
c. academic
d. argumentative

_____ 5. The overall purpose of this passage is
a. to inform the reader about the general importance, history, and characteristics of the blues.
b. to entertain the reader with lively details about the lives of blues singers and artists.
c. to persuade the reader that blues is the most important form of music and poetry in the English language.

Name _____ Section_____

Date _____ **Score** (number correct) _____ x 20 = _____ %

Visit MyReadingLab to take this test online and receive feedback and guidance on your answers.

Read the following passage from a college communications textbook. Then, answer the questions.

Advertisement's Purpose

Textbook
Skills

¹Although most advertisements promote a product or service, not all do. ²Advertisements fall into three categories: business ads, public service ads, and political ads.

³**Business ads** try to influence people's attitudes and behaviors toward the product and services a business sells, toward the business itself, or toward an idea that the business supports. ⁴Most of these ads try to persuade customers to buy something, but sometimes a business tries to improve its image through advertising. ⁵This often occurs when a company has been involved in a highly publicized incident that might negatively affect its image. ⁶Exxon had to rebuild its image after the *Valdez* accident in 1989, in which an Exxon tanker spilled millions of gallons of oil in Prince William Sound and damaged the Alaska Coast.

⁷**Public service ads** promote behaviors and attitudes that are beneficial to society and its members. ⁸These ads may be either national or local and usually are the product of donated labor and media time or space. ⁹The Advertising Council produces the best known public service ads. ¹⁰The council, which is supported by advertising agencies and the media, was formed during World War II to promote the war effort. ¹¹It now runs about twenty-five campaigns a year. ¹²These campaigns must be in the public interest, timely, noncommercial, nonpartisan, nonsectarian, and nonpolitical.

¹³**Political ads** aim to persuade voters to elect a candidate to political office or to influence the public on legislative issues. ¹⁴These advertisements run at the local, state, and national levels. ¹⁵They incorporate most forms of media but use newspapers, radio, television, and direct mail most heavily. ¹⁶During a presidential election year, more than $1 billion is spent on political ads.

—Folkerts, Jean and Lacy, Stephen, *The Media in Your Life: An Introduction to Mass Communication*, 2nd ed., pp. 428–429.

_____ **1.** The tone of the first paragraph (sentences 1–2) is
a. neutral.   c. bitter.
b. approving.   d. bored.

_____ **2.** The purpose of sentence 6 is
    a. to condemn Exxon for spilling millions of gallons of oil.
    b. to keep the reader entertained with a vivid detail.
    c. to illustrate the need for a business ad to improve a company's image.

_____ **3.** The tone of sentence 16 is
    a. shocked.   c. matter-of-fact.
    b. shameful.   d. abrupt.

_____ **4.** Which word best describes the overall tone of this passage?
    a. unbiased   b. biased

_____ **5.** The overall purpose of this passage is
    a. to inform the reader about different types of advertising.
    b. to persuade the reader that advertising serves beneficial purposes.
    c. to entertain the reader with interesting details about advertising.

VISUAL _VOCABULARY_

This advertisement is an

example of a _____

_____

—Library of Congress, Prints & Photography Division,
Yanker Poster Collection, POS6-U.S., no. 1384.

10 Summary of Key Concepts of Tone and Purpose

LO1 LO3 Assess your comprehension of tone and purpose. Complete the following two-column notes of terms and definitions with information from the chapter.

Term	Definition
Tone	
Objective tone words	
Subjective tone words	
The author's purpose	
The primary purpose	
The Purpose: To Inform	
The Purpose: To Entertain	
The Purpose: To Persuade	
Verbal irony	
Situational irony	

Test Your Comprehension of Tone and Purpose

Respond to the following questions and prompts.

(LO2) (LO4)
(LO5)
In your own words, what is the relationship between tone and purpose?

_____

_____

_____

_____

(LO2) In your own words, what is the difference between verbal and situational irony?

_____

_____

(LO6) (LO7) Use a checklist to help you determine the tone and purpose of passages. Select a passage to analyze; then complete the following checklist with information from the passage.

Title of Passage:

	Yes	No	Examples (words or phrases)/Explanations
Subjective Tone			
Objective Tone			
Irony			
Verbal Irony			
Situational Irony			
Primary Purpose			
To Inform			
To Persuade			
To Entertain			

(LO7) Summarize the two most important ideas in this chapter that will help you improve your reading comprehension. _____

_____

_____

Inferences

LO LEARNING OUTCOMES

After studying this chapter, you should be able to:

LO1 Describe Inferences as Educated Guesses

LO2 Define a Valid Inference

LO3 Apply the VALID Approach to Make Inferences and Avoid Invalid Conclusions

LO4 Make Inferences Based on Creative Expressions

LO5 Develop Textbook Skills: Inferences and Visual Aids in Textbooks

LO6 Apply Information Literacy Skills: Academic, Personal, and Career Applications of Inferences

Before Reading About Inferences

Predict what you need to learn based on the learning outcomes for this chapter by completing the following chart.

What I Already Know	What I Need to Learn
_____	_____.
_____	_____.
_____	_____.

Copy the following study outline in your notebook. Leave ample blank spaces between each topic. Use your own words to fill in the outline with information about each topic as you study about inferences.

Reading Skills Needed to Make VALID Inferences

   I. **V**erify facts.

   II. **A**ssess prior knowledge.

   III. **L**earn from text.
      a. Context clues
      b. Thought patterns
      c. Implied main ideas

   IV. **I**nvestigate bias.

   V. **D**etect contradictions.

Describe Inferences as Educated Guesses

Read the following paragraph.

> As Professor De Los Santos handed out the graded essays, Kassie's stomach rumbled with a familiar queasiness. She avoided looking around and focused with intensity on the opened textbook, not really seeing the pages that were before her. Aaron, who sat next to her, exclaimed with pleasure as he received his paper. "Unbelievable," he said as he turned to Kassie in surprise, "I thought I had blown this assignment." Kassie did not look up or respond to him, but continued staring at her book as she listened intently for her name. A girl with short, spiky hair across the room frowned after she received her paper and asked, "Dr. De Los Santos, may we rewrite this assignment?" The professor shook her head. Finally, Kassie heard her name, looked up, and took her essay. "Good job, Kassie," Dr. De Los Santos said as she handed her the paper, "Your work shows much improvement." Kassie smiled and carefully read each suggestion the teacher had written on her essay.

Which of the following statements might be true, based on the ideas in the passage?

_____ Kassie is extremely nervous about her essay.

_____ The girl with short, spiky hair is not satisfied with the grade she received.

_____ Aaron did not put much effort into his essay.

_____ Kassie's grade was "A" on her essay.

Did you choose the first two statements? Congratulations! You just made a set of educated guesses, or **inferences**. An author suggests or **implies** an idea, and the reader comes to a conclusion and makes an inference about what the author means.

In the paragraph about Kassie, the first two statements are firmly based on the information in the passage. However, the last two statements are not backed by the supporting details. The facts only suggest that Aaron thought he hadn't performed well on the assignment. He could have put a great deal of effort into the work; perhaps he underestimated his abilities. We just don't have enough information to make either assumption. Likewise, the passage does not suggest that Kassie made an "A," only that her work had improved.

Define a Valid Inference

People constantly draw conclusions about what they notice. We observe, gather information, and make inferences all the time.

> An **inference** or **conclusion** is an idea that is suggested by the facts or details in a passage.

For example, study the photo, and then answer the accompanying question.

VISUAL *VOCABULARY*

This businessman is wearing a face mask because

_____

_____

_____

If you wrote *of air pollution*, you made an inference based on the clues given by the visual details of the situation.

A **valid inference** is a rational judgment based on details and evidence. The ability to make a valid inference is a vital life skill. Making valid inferences aids us in our efforts to care for our families, succeed in our jobs, and even guard our health.

For example, doctors strive to make inferences about our health based on our symptoms. In the case of a heart attack, a doctor notes the observable symptoms such as pressure or pain in the center of the chest, shortness of breath, a cold sweat, nausea, or lightheadedness. To confirm the diagnosis, the doctor checks the patient's heart rate and blood pressure, takes a blood sample and performs a test called an electrocardiogram. If her educated guess (a guess based on evidence) is correct, she prescribes the best treatment she deems necessary.

> A **valid inference** is a logical conclusion based on evidence.

> ⊙ **EXAMPLE** Read the following passage. Write **V** beside the three valid inferences. (**Hint:** valid inferences are firmly supported by the details in the passage.)

Pollen and Allergies

¹For the past two weeks a heavy dusting of yellow pollen from the pine trees coated all the cars in the parking lot at Robert's job site. ²The thick layering of pine pollen masked the fact that the oak and juniper trees were also pollinating. ³In addition, every yard in Robert's neighborhood was covered with the purple flowering heads of Bermuda grass. ⁴Interestingly, Robert linked the obvious pine pollen to allergy flare-ups, until he read a scientific report that stated that the heaviness of pine pollen causes it to fall to the ground rather than be carried by the wind like most allergy-causing pollen. ⁵The same report stated that some of the most widely known plants that cause allergic reactions are Kentucky bluegrass, Johnson grass, Bermuda grass, redtop grass, orchard grass, and sweet vernal grass. ⁶Trees that produce allergenic pollen include oak, ash, elm, hickory, pecan, box elder, and mountain cedar. ⁷An allergic reaction includes frequent sneezing, clear and watery nasal discharge and congestion, itchy eyes, nose, and throat, and watery eyes. ⁸For over a week, Robert has been experiencing these symptoms.

_____ **1.** Robert is experiencing an allergic reaction to pollen.

_____ **2.** Pine pollen is a major source of allergic reactions.

_____ **3.** Robert's yard consists of Bermuda grass.

_____ **4.** Robert's allergy attack is caused by the pollen from oak trees, juniper trees, or Bermuda grass.

_____   **5.** Kentucky bluegrass does not grow where Robert lives.

_____   **6.** Robert suffers with allergy attacks from pollen every year.

EXPLANATION Statements 1, 3, and 4 are firmly based on the information in the passage. It is reasonable to infer that Robert is experiencing an allergic reaction to pollen based on his symptoms and the fact that Robert's yard consists of Bermuda grass since "every" yard in his neighborhood does. It is also reasonable to infer that either one or some combination of the pollens from the oak trees, juniper trees, and Bermuda grass is causing his allergic reaction, based on the list of plants known to cause allergic reactions.

Statements 2, 5, and 6 are not based on the information in the passage. It is unreasonable to assume that pine pollen is a major source of allergic reactions because of information in the scientific report explaining that this pollen drops to the ground and is not carried by the wind and thus not breathed in by humans. It is also wrong to infer that Kentucky bluegrass does not grow where Robert lives simply because it is not present in the yards in his neighborhood or at his place of business. Finally, it is incorrect to infer that Robert experiences an allergic reaction to pollen every year. The passage only focuses on the last few weeks of Robert's life, so we do not have enough information to know whether he has suffered from these symptoms before. ◉

Practice 1

Each of the following items contains a short passage and three inferences. In each item, only one inference is valid. In the space provided, write the letter of the inference that is clearly supported by each passage.

_____   **1.** Jermaine and his office coworkers all arrived at work at the same time Monday morning. As usual, Jermaine unlocked the only entrance to the building, and then everyone unlocked their offices to begin their work routine. Immediately, Jermaine and his coworkers discovered that their computers and printers were missing from their offices. Each one reported that they had locked their offices with their computers and printers securely inside before they left on Friday. As they looked around the office, nothing indicated a forced entry. Jermaine called the police to report the theft of the computers and printers.
a. Jermaine stole the computers.
b. The office computers and printers were stolen by someone who had access to the office keys.
c. Jermaine and his coworkers were not surprised to find the computers and printers were missing.

_____ **2.** Alex and Mindy sit opposite each other in a booth at a diner. Mindy's face is streaked with tears. Alex's face is turned away as if in deep thought. His mouth is drawn into a thin frown, and his arms are folded across his chest. They do not speak to one another. As the waitress fills their coffee cups, Alex's frown turns into a smile, and he orders a large breakfast. Mindy shakes her head to indicate that she does not want anything to eat. As fresh tears begin to flow, she quickly ducks her head.

    a. Alex and Mindy are having a fight.

    b. Mindy is more upset than is Alex.

    c. Alex is insensitive to Mindy's feelings.

_____ **3.** The patrol officer flashes his lights to pull over the sedan that has been weaving across the center line that divides the two-way traffic. After inspecting the driving license of Laurel, the young woman behind the wheel, he asks her to step out of the car, stand with her arms outstretched, and touch the tip of her nose with an index finger. She loses her balance as she tries to do so.

    a. Laurel is drunk.

    b. The police officer is harassing Laurel.

    c. The police officer suspects that Laurel has been driving while under the influence of alcohol.

LO3 Apply the VALID Approach to Make Inferences and Avoid Invalid Conclusions

Two of the most common pitfalls of making inferences are ignoring the facts and relying too much on personal opinions and bias. Often we are tempted to read too much into a passage because of our own prior experiences or beliefs. Of course, to make a valid inference, we must use clues based on logic and our experience. However, the most important resource must be the written text. As master readers, our main goal is to find out what the author is stating or implying. Master readers learn to use a VALID thinking process to avoid drawing false inferences or coming to invalid conclusions.

> An **invalid conclusion** is a false inference that is not based on the details or facts presented in the text or on reasonable thinking.

The VALID approach is made up of 5 steps:

Step 1. **V**erify and value the facts.

Step 2. **A**ssess prior knowledge.

Step 3. **L**earn from the text.

Step 4. **I**nvestigate for bias.

Step 5. **D**etect contradictions.

Step 1: Verify and Value the Facts

Develop a devotion to finding the facts. In Chapter 9, you learned to identify facts and to beware of false facts. You learned that authors may mix fact with opinion or use false information for their own purposes. Just as authors may make this kind of mistake, readers may, too. Readers may draw false inferences by mixing the author's facts with their own opinions or by misreading the facts. So it is important to find, verify, and stick to factual details. Once you have all the facts, only then can you begin to interpret the facts by making inferences.

> **EXAMPLE** Read the following short passage. Then write **V** next to the two valid inferences firmly supported by the facts.

Child Passenger Safety

[1]Motor vehicle injuries are the leading cause of death among children in the United States. [2]But many of these deaths can be prevented. [3]In the United States during 2009, 1,314 children ages 14 years and younger died as occupants in motor vehicle crashes, and approximately 179,000 were injured. [4]That's an average of almost 4 deaths and 490 injuries each day. [5]More than two-thirds of the fatally injured children were riding with a drinking driver. [6]Of the children ages 0 to 14 years who were killed or seriously injured in motor vehicle crashes, nearly half were unrestrained.

[7]Restraint use among young children often depends upon the driver's restraint use. [8]Almost 40% of children riding with unbelted drivers were themselves unrestrained. [9]Child restraint systems are often used incorrectly; one study found that 72% of nearly 3,500 observed child restraint systems were misused in a way that could be expected to increase a child's risk of injury during a crash. [10]All children younger than 13 years should

ride in the back seat. [11]Putting children in the back seat places them in the safest part of the vehicle in the event of a crash.

> —Adapted from United States, Department of Human and Health Services. "Child Passenger Safety: Fact Sheet." *National Center for Injury Prevention and Control, Centers for Disease Control and Prevention.*

_____ **1.** Most of the deaths and injuries related to motor vehicle crashes among children could be prevented.

_____ **2.** Placing children in age-appropriate restraint systems could reduce serious and fatal injuries by half.

_____ **3.** Parents are the chief cause of deaths and injuries related to motor vehicle crashes among children.

EXPLANATION The first two statements are correct inferences based on the facts. However, there is no hint or clue that parents are the chief cause of these injuries and deaths. Children often ride in vehicles with people other than their parents. The third statement goes beyond the facts without any reason to do so. ◀

VISUAL *VOCABULARY*

Fill in the blanks with words from the passage "Child Passenger Safety" that best complete the caption.

This child is _____

restrained, _____ the child's risk of injury during a crash.

Step 2: Assess Prior Knowledge

Once you are sure of the facts, the next step is to draw on your prior knowledge. What you have already learned and experienced can help you make accurate inferences.

> **EXAMPLE 1** Read the following passage from a college science textbook. Identify the facts. Check those facts against your own experience and understanding. Write **V** next to the four inferences firmly supported by the facts in the passage.

Textbook
Skills

The Flow of Energy and the Food Chain

[1]Energy stored by plants moves through the ecosystem in a series of steps of eating and being eaten, the **food chain**. [2]Food chains are descriptive diagrams—a series of arrows, each pointing from one species to another for which it is a source of food. [3]For example, grasshoppers eat grass, clay-colored sparrows eat the grasshoppers, and marsh hawks prey upon the sparrows. [4]We write this relationship as follows:

[5]grass $\longrightarrow$ grasshopper $\longrightarrow$ sparrow $\longrightarrow$ marsh hawk

[6]However, the food chain is not linear. [7]Resources are shared, especially at the beginning of the food chain. [8]The same plant is food for a variety of animals and insects, and the same animal is food for several predators. [9]Thus food chains link to form a **food web**, the complexity of which varies within and among ecosystems.

—Adapted from Smith, Thomas and Smith, Robert Leo,
Elements of Ecology, 4th ed., p. 329.

_____ **1.** An *ecosystem* is a community of organisms and its environment functioning as a unit.

_____ **2.** Grasshoppers eat only grass.

_____ **3.** Plant life is the basis of the food chain used as an example.

_____ **4.** The phrase *prey upon* in sentence 3 means "feed on."

_____ **5.** The survival of the marsh hawk could be dependent upon the availability of grasshoppers.

_____ **6.** Grass is always a basic element in a food chain or food web.

EXPLANATION Items 1, 3, 4, and 5 are sound inferences based on information in the passage. However, we have no evidence that grasshoppers eat only grass (item 2), nor that grass is always a basic element in a food chain or food web (item 6). In fact, sentence 9 states that ecosystems vary as does their complexity. For example, the food chain in a lake or ocean would not necessarily include grass. <

> **EXAMPLE 2** Study the editorial cartoon. In the space provided, write an inference that is firmly supported by the details.

© 2009 Steve Greenberg/Cagle Cartoons, Inc.

_____

_____

EXPLANATION Consider the following inference solidly based on the cartoon (and prior knowledge about fossil fuels and the environment): Global use of fossil fuels by industries is killing the planet. ◀

Step 3: Learn from the Text

When you value and verify facts, you are learning from the text. A valid inference is always based on what is stated or implied by the details in the text; in contrast, an invalid inference goes beyond the evidence. Thus, to make a valid inference, you must learn to rely on the information in the text. Many of the skills you have studied in previous chapters work together to enable you to learn from the text. For example, context clues unlock the meaning of an author's use of vocabulary. Becoming aware of thought patterns teaches you to look for the logical relationship between ideas. Learning about stated and implied main ideas trains you to examine supporting details. (In fact, you use inference skills to find the implied main idea.) In addition, tone and purpose reveal the author's bias and intent. (Again, you often use inference skills to grasp the author's tone and purpose.) As you apply these skills to your reading process, you are carefully listening to what the author has to say. You are learning from the text. Only after you have learned from the text can you make a valid inference. The following examples show you how you learn from the text.

> **EXAMPLE** Read the following short passage. Answer the questions that follow.

[1]In 1906, the Louvre installed a newly acquired collection of sculpture from Iberia (Spain and Portugal) that dated to the sixth and fifth centuries BCE, and these archaic figures became a powerful influence on his work over the next year. [2]Even more influential were his repeated visits to the **ethnographic** museum where African art brought back from France's colonies was displayed. [3]Picasso greatly admired the expressive power and unfamiliar formal qualities of African masks, and he bought several pieces and kept them in his studio. [4]Picasso's wide-ranging studies culminated in 1907 in *Les Demoiselles D'Avignon*, one of the most radical and complex paintings of the twentieth century.

—Adapted from Stokstad, Marilyn and Cothren, Michael. *Art: A Brief History*, 5th ed., pp. 517–518.

_____ **1.** The best synonym for the word **ethnographic** in sentence 2 is
  a. cultural.   c. historic.
  b. scientific.

_____ **2.** What is the primary relationship of ideas within sentence 1?
  a. addition   c. contrast
  b. cause and effect

_____ **3.** The author's tone is
  a. sarcastic.   c. admiring.
  b. pleading.

_____ **4.** The author's purpose is to
  a. inform.   c. persuade.
  b. entertain.

_____ **5.** Which of the following is a valid inference?
  a. Picasso was not an original artistic thinker.
  b. Picasso did not achieve much after 1907.
  c. Picasso was open to artistic ideas.

Practice 2

Read the following passages from college textbooks. Then answer the questions that follow.

Textbook
Skills

Alcohol, Cancer, and Heart Disease

[1]Heavy drinking is associated with an increased risk for several cancers—notably, cancer of the mouth, esophagus, pharynx, larynx, liver, and pancreas. [2]An analysis of multiple studies published in the mid-1990s found that having two alcoholic drinks per day (any type of alcohol) increased a woman's chances of developing breast cancer by nearly 25 percent. [3]The reasons for this are unclear. [4]However, researchers **speculate** that alcohol influences the metabolism of estrogen and that prolonged exposure to high levels of estrogen increases breast cancer risk, particularly for women on hormone replacement therapy (HRT). [5]The effect of one drink per day on increased risk is a matter of debate. [6]Most experts feel that one drink per day does not increase risk. [7]But before you decide to toss out all your alcohol, you should know that there is increasing evidence that a glass of red wine seems to provide protection against heart disease.

—Donatelle, Rebecca, J. and Davis, Lorraine G.,
Access to Health, 7th ed., p. 442.

_____ **1.** The best meaning of the word **speculate** in sentence 4 is
 a. know.   c. think.
 b. study.

_____ **2.** What is the relationship of ideas between sentence 3 and sentence 4?
 a. listing   c. contrast
 b. cause and effect

_____ **3.** What is the primary thought pattern of the paragraph?
 a. contrast   c. time order
 b. cause and effect

_____ **4.** Which of the following best describes the author's tone and purpose?
 a. to convince the reader to avoid consuming wine
 b. to inform the general public about the possible link between alcohol and increased risk of cancer
 c. to entertain the reader with interesting facts about the possible effects of alcohol

Google

Textbook
Skills

[1]Founded in 1998, Google Inc. has become one of the world's most recognized technology companies. [2]Its core service, the Google search engine, is used by millions of people to find documents on the World Wide Web. [3]In addition, Google provides electronic mail service (called Gmail), an Internet based video sharing service (called YouTube), and a host of other Internet services (including Google Maps, Google Calendar, Google Earth, Google Books, and Google Translate).

[4]However, in addition to being a prime example of the **entrepreneurial** spirit, Google also provides examples of how expanding technology is challenging society. [5]For example, Google's search engine has led to questions regarding the extent to which an international company should comply with the wishes of individual governments; YouTube has raised questions regarding the extent to which a company should be liable for information that others distribute through its services as well as the degree to which the company can claim ownership of that information; Google Books has generated concerns regarding the scope and limitations of intellectual property rights; and Google Maps has been accused of violating privacy rights.

—Adapted from Brookshear, J. Glenn, *Computer Science: An Overview*, 11th ed., p. 9.

_____ **1.** The best meaning of the word **entrepreneurial** in sentence 4 is
    a. patriotic.   c. artistic.
    b. business.

_____ **2.** What is the relationship of ideas between sentence 4 and sentence 5?
    a. definition and example
    b. generalization and example
    c. classification

_____ **3.** What is the primary thought pattern of the passage?
    a. classification
    b. cause and effect
    c. contrast

_____ **4.** Which of the following statements best describes the author's tone and purpose?
    a. to inform the reader about the nature of Google
    b. to persuade the reader to use Google services
    c. to entertain the reader with interesting facts about Google

Step 4: Investigate for Bias

One of the most important steps in making a valid inference is confronting your biases. Each of us possesses strong personal views that influence the way we process information. Often our personal views are based on prior experiences. For example, if we have had a negative prior experience with a used car salesperson, we may become suspicious and stereotype all used car salespeople as dishonest. Sometimes, our biases are based on the way in which we were raised. Some people register as Democrats or Republicans and vote for only Democratic or Republican candidates simply because their parents were dedicated supporters of one party. To make a valid inference, we must investigate our response to information for bias. Our bias can shape our reading of the author's meaning. To investigate for bias, note biased words and replace them with factual details as you form your conclusions.

> **EXAMPLE** Reword each of the following statements to eliminate the use of biased words.

1. Simon Cowell is best known for his roles as a brutally honest judge on the silly TV talent shows *The X Factor* and *American Idol*.

   _____

   _____

2. Surprisingly, Simon Cowell won the prestigious International Emmy award because he completely reshaped 21st century television and music around the world.

   _____

   _____

EXPLANATION Compare your answers to the following:

1. Simon Cowell is known for his roles as judge on the TV talent shows *The X Factor* and *American Idol*. The following biased words were deleted: *best*, *brutally honest*, and *silly*.
2. Simon Cowell won the International Emmy award because he has influenced 21st century television and music around the world. The following biased words were deleted: *Surprisingly*, *prestigious*, *completely reshaped*. <

Practice 3

Study the photo and caption that appears in a college sociology textbook. Reword the caption to eliminate any bias.

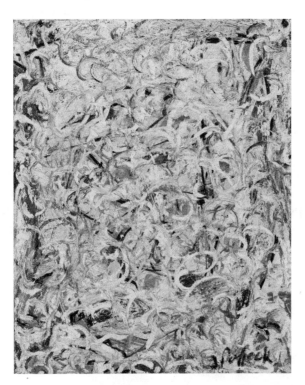

◀ **Jackson Pollock,** *Shimmering Substance.* **(1946)** Many of Pollock's postwar works— huge paintings that pulse with power—show an obsession with heat and light, surely no coincidence in the dawn of the nuclear age.

—Levack, Brian, Muir, Edward, Veldman, Meredith, and Maas, Michael, *The West: Encounters & Transformations,* Atlas Edition, Combined Edition, 2nd ed., p. 910.

Textbook
Skills

_____

_____

Step 5: Detect Contradictions

Have you ever misjudged a situation or had a wrong first impression? For example, have you ever assumed a person was conceited or rude only to find out later that he or she was acutely shy? Many times, there may be a better explanation for a set of facts than the first one that comes to mind. The master reader hunts for the most reasonable explanation. The best way to do this is to consider other explanations that could logically contradict your first impression.

> **EXAMPLE 1** Read the following list of symptoms. Then, in the blank, write as many explanations for the symptoms as you can.

- Fatigue
- Muscle and joint pain
- Erythema migrans (bull's-eye skin rash)
- Swollen lymph nodes
- Chills and fever
- Headache

EXPLANATION Some people may think the symptoms describe the flu, but it is actually a list of symptoms for the first stage of Lyme disease. The symptom that clearly identifies Lyme disease is the bull's-eye rash; however, not everyone who has the disease has this symptom, and others may have this symptom but not have Lyme disease. Thus Lyme disease can be misdiagnosed in its earliest stage. A reader who does not think about other possible views can easily jump to a wrong conclusion. Master readers consider all the facts and all the possible explanations for those facts. ◀

> **EXAMPLE 2** Study the graphic. In the space provided, write an inference that is firmly supported by the details.

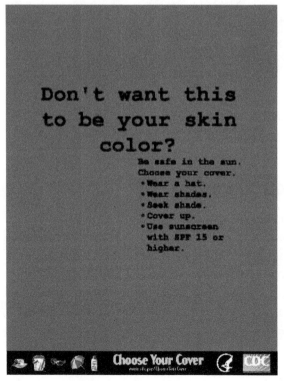

—"Don't Want This to Be Your Skin Color?" CDC
http://www.cdc.gov/cancer/skin/pdf/poster-red.pdf

_____

_____

EXPLANATION This poster implies that protection against the sun's harmful UV rays is necessary. Consider the following statement of an inference firmly based on the information in the poster: "You should protect yourself from severe sunburn and sun damage by covering up with one or more of the following: a hat, clothing, sunscreen, and sunglasses." ◁

Practice 4

Read the following passage. Investigate the list of inferences that follow for bias. Underline biased words. Mark each inference as follows: **V** for a valid inference firmly supported by the facts, **I** for an invalid inference.

Marching for the Vote:
The Woman Suffrage Parade of 1913

[1]On Monday, March 3, 1913, clad in a white cape astride a white horse, lawyer Inez Milholland led the great woman suffrage parade down Pennsylvania Avenue in the nation's capital. [2]Behind her stretched a long line with nine bands, four mounted brigades, three heralds, about twenty-four floats, and more than 5,000 marchers. [3]The procession began late, but all went well for the first few blocks. [4]Soon, however, the crowds, mostly men in town for the following day's inauguration of Woodrow Wilson, surged into the street making it almost impossible for the marchers to pass. [5]Occasionally only a single file could move forward. [6]Women were jeered, tripped, grabbed, shoved, and many heard "indecent epithets" and "barnyard conversation." [7]Instead of protecting the parade, the police "seemed to enjoy all the ribald jokes and laughter and participated in them." [8]One policeman explained that they should stay at home where they belonged. [9]The men in the procession heard shouts of "Henpecko" and "Where are your skirts?" [10]As one witness explained, "There was a sort of spirit of levity connected with the crowd. [11]They did not regard the affair very seriously."

—Adapted from Harvey, "Marching for the Vote: The Woman Suffrage Parade of 1913," *American Women*, 18 June 2003, Library of Congress.

_____ **1.** The word *suffrage* in sentence 1 means "right to vote."

_____ **2.** Nearly all of the 5,000 marchers were women.

_____   **3.** The police supported women's right to vote.

_____   **4.** Men opposed a woman's right to vote.

_____   **5.** Many men in the crowd opposed the women's right to vote.

 ## Make Inferences Based on Creative Expression

As you have learned, nonfiction writing, such as in textbooks and news articles, directly states the author's point. Everything is done to make sure that the meanings are clear and unambiguous (not open to different interpretations). However, in many other types of writing, both fiction and nonfiction, authors use creative expression to suggest layers of meaning. Creative expressions are also known as literary devices. The following chart shows a few common literary devices, their meanings, and an example of each.

Creative Expression: Literary Devices

Literary Device	Meanings	Example
Connotations of words	The emotional meaning of words	My home is for sale.
Metaphor	A direct comparison	Lies are sinkholes.
Personification	Giving human traits to things that are not human	The sun woke slowly.
Simile	An indirect comparison	Lies are like sticky webs.
Symbol	Something that stands for or suggests something else	A skull and crossbones is a symbol for poison and death.

By using these devices, a writer creates a vivid mental picture in the reader's mind. When a creative expression is used, a reader must infer the point the writer is making from the effects of the images. The following paragraph is the introduction to an essay about anger. Notice its use of literary devices. After you read, write a one-sentence statement of the author's main idea for this paragraph.

A Growing Anger

[1]At first, Julio sat quietly shaking his head; then his forehead crumpled into a wadded frown, and his mouth flattened into a pencil-thin

line. ²As the speaker continued, Julio's heartbeat sounded like drums beating in his ears, and his entire body flushed as a searing heat rushed up from his toes to the roots of his hair. ³His jaw tightened and his fists clenched and unclenched as he constantly shifted his weight in his chair. ⁴Finally, unable to contain himself any longer, he abruptly rose, jostling the table and tumbling the wine glasses. ⁵His body trembled, and his voice shook as he exclaimed, "You have no idea what you are talking about." ⁶Just as suddenly, he thudded back into his chair, fists still clenched, and stared without seeing at the white tablecloth bloodied with spilled wine.

_____

_____

This paragraph uses several creative expressions. *Forehead crumpled into a wadded frown* and *mouth flattened into a pencil-thin line* are metaphors. The author is showing the physical effects of anger by directly comparing Julio's frown to a crumpled wad and his mouth to a thin pencil line. The phrase *heartbeat sounded like drums* is a simile that indirectly compares the sound of Julio's heartbeat to a drum. The author chooses words that have rich connotations in the phrase *flushed as a searing heat rushed,* suggesting that Julio is becoming inflamed and passionate about what he is hearing. And finally, the author uses personification with the phrase *tablecloth bloodied with spilled wine.* The phrase suggests that the tablecloth is injured rather than merely soiled and that the wine bled instead of spilled. All of these details work to create a vivid mental image, and based on these details, the reader must come to the conclusion that Julio becomes increasingly angry. To understand plays, novels, short stories, and poems, a master reader must use inference skills.

> **EXAMPLE** Read the following poem written by Sara Teasdale. Answer the questions that follow.

Spring in War-Time

I feel the spring far off, far off,
The faint, far scent of bud and leaf
Oh, how can spring take heart to come
To a world in grief,
Deep grief?   5

The sun turns north, the days grow long,
Later the evening star grows bright—
How can the daylight linger on
For men to fight,
Still fight?   10

The grass is waking in the ground,
Soon it will rise and blow in waves—
How can it have the heart to sway
Over the graves,
New graves?   15

Under the boughs where lovers walked
The apple-blooms will shed their breath—
But what of all the lovers now
Parted by Death,
Grey Death?   20

—Sara Teasdale

1–3. Choose **three** inferences that are most firmly based on the words in the poem by writing a **V** next to each one.

_____   **a.** The speaker is describing a war that has been going on for a long time.

_____   **b.** The speaker is waiting for her lover to return from the war.

_____   **c.** The speaker of the poem is angry and resentful.

_____   **d.** The line "The grass is waking in the ground" means that the grass will soon begin growing.

_____   **e.** The speaker is ironically contrasting the life brought by spring with the death brought by war.

_____   **4.** Based on the details of the poem, you can infer that the speaker is
a. against the war.
b. proud of the men fighting.
c. eager for spring to come.

EXPLANATION

1–3. The valid references are a, d, and e.

4. Based on the details in the poem, you can infer that the speaker is against the war because she speaks of grief, graves, and death.

Practice 5

Read the poem written by Robert Frost. Then choose the inferences that are most logically based on the details in the poem.

Textbook
Skills

The Road Not Taken

by Robert Frost

Two roads diverged in a yellow wood,
And sorry I could not travel both
And be one traveler, long I stood
And looked down one as far as I could
To where it bent in the undergrowth;

Then took the other, as just as fair,
And having perhaps the better claim,
Because it was grassy and wanted wear;
Though as for that the passing there
Had worn them really about the same,

And both that morning equally lay
In leaves no step had trodden black.
Oh, I kept the first for another day!
Yet knowing how way leads on to way,
I doubted if I should ever come back.

I shall be telling this with a sigh
Somewhere ages and ages hence:
Two roads diverged in a wood, and I—
I took the one less traveled by,
And that has made all the difference.

—From *Mountain Interval* by Robert Frost. New York: Henry Holt, 1920.

_____ **1.** The best meaning of the word **diverged** in the first line is
       a. parted.   c. merged.
       b. ended.

_____ **2.** In the poem, the roads represent
       a. travelers.   c. choices.
       b. fears.

_____ **3.** The second verse describes the "other" road he took as
       a. less traveled than the first road.
       b. completely untraveled by others.
       c. worn with the constant travel of others.

_____   **4.** In the first two lines of the third verse, the speaker implies that
        a. others had traveled on both roads earlier that day.
        b. no other person had traveled on either road that day.
        c. he already regrets his decision to take the other road.

_____   **5.** What can you infer about the speaker of the poem?
        a. He is an individualist.
        b. He has many regrets.
        c. He conforms to the leadership of others.

LO5 Develop Textbook Skills: Inferences and Visual Aids in Textbooks

Textbook Skills

Textbook authors often use pictures, photos, and graphs to imply an idea. These visuals are used to reinforce the information in that section of the textbook.

> **EXAMPLE** Study this figure, taken from the textbook *Psychology and Life*. Then answer the question.

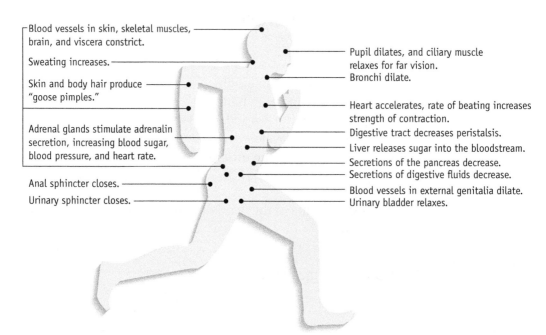

Blood vessels in skin, skeletal muscles, brain, and viscera constrict.

Sweating increases.

Skin and body hair produce "goose pimples."

Adrenal glands stimulate adrenalin secretion, increasing blood sugar, blood pressure, and heart rate.

Anal sphincter closes.
Urinary sphincter closes.

Pupil dilates, and ciliary muscle relaxes for far vision.
Bronchi dilate.

Heart accelerates, rate of beating increases strength of contraction.
Digestive tract decreases peristalsis.
Liver releases sugar into the bloodstream.
Secretions of the pancreas decrease.
Secretions of digestive fluids decrease.
Blood vessels in external genitalia dilate.
Urinary bladder relaxes.

▲ **The Body's Reaction to Stress**

—Gerrig, Richard J. and Zimbardo, Philip G., *Psychology and Life*, 19th ed. Figure 13.7, (p. 407).

_____ **1.** What do you think is the topic or title of the chapter?
 a. Jogging and Fitness   c. Emotion, Stress, and Health
 b. Cardiovascular Health

 2. Write a caption in a complete sentence that best states the main idea of the figure.

 _____

 _____

EXPLANATION

 1. This figure appeared in a chapter with the title "Emotion, Stress, and Health," choice (c).

 2. The figure shows at least 15 different ways in which stress affects the human body. Consider the following statement of the figure's main idea: Stress produces a wide range of physiological changes in the body. ◀

Practice 6

Study this figure, taken from the textbook _Life on Earth_ and read the list of statements about the figure. Write a **V** in the blanks next to the four inferences that are most firmly based on the figure.

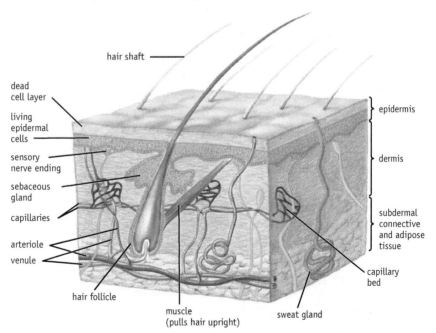

—Audesirk, Teresa, Audesirk, Gerald, and Byers, Bruce E., _Life on Earth,_
5th ed., Figure 19.9 (p. 363).

_____ **1.** This figure appears in the chapter titled "The Organization of the Animal Body."

_____ **2.** This figure appears in the chapter titled "Animal Behavior."

_____ **3.** The epidermis is one thin layer of living cells.

_____ **4.** The epidermis is the outer layer of skin.

_____ **5.** Mammalian skin is made up of three layers.

_____ **6.** Skin contains muscle tissue.

_____ **7.** Human skin differs from mammalian skin.

_____ **8.** Skin is not an organ.

Apply Information Literacy Skills

 ## Academic, Personal, and Career Applications of Inferences

Information literacy relies upon the ability to make inferences. For example, think about how to find information about a specific topic, such as online dating safety tips. First, you rely on what you need to know to direct your search. Do you need to know the traits of suspicious activity? What are ways to protect yourself from fraud? Next, you make an educated guess about the key words related to online dating that would help you find the information you need. Then, once you locate information, you infer the reliability of the source. You look for clues to determine if the source is biased or factual. As you read the information, you infer the importance and relevance of details based on your need to know. Ultimately, you decide the best way to apply or use what you have learned. Thus, you will use the skills that you have learned in this chapter in academic, personal, and career situations:

- Recognize your own need to make an inference.
- Determine if a conclusion is valid.
- Use inferences to create meaning.

Academic Application

Assume you are taking the college course Introduction to Hospitality. Your professor has assigned the following passage and exercise from your textbook.

- **Before Reading:** Skim the passage. Read the questions in the "Check Your Knowledge" section of the passage.

- **During Reading:** Underline the details in the passage that will help you complete the exercise.

- **After Reading:** In the space following the passage, answer the "Check Your Knowledge" questions.

Moments of Truth

Giving great service is a very difficult task; few businesses give enough priority to training associates in how to provide service. We suffer from an overreliance on technology so that service providers are often not motivated to give great service. For example, when checking a guest into the hotel, the front-desk associate may greet the guest but then look down at the computer for the remainder of the service encounter, even when asking for the guest's name. Or consider the reservations associate who says nothing when asked for a specific type of guest room because he is waiting for the computer to indicate availability.

"Moments of truth" is a term coined by Jan Carlson. When Carlson became president of Scandinavian Airline System (SAS), it was ranked at the bottom of the European airline market. He quickly realized that he had to spend a lot of time on the front line coaching SAS associates in how to handle guest encounters, or as he called them, "moments of truth." As a result of his efforts, SAS was soon ranked at the top of the European airlines for service. Service commitment is a total organizational approach that makes the quality of service, as perceived by the customer, the number one driving force for the operation of the business.

Every hospitality organization has thousands of moments of truth every day.

This leads to tremendous challenges in maintaining the expected levels of service. Let's look at just some of the moments of truth in a restaurant dining experience:

1. Guest calls the restaurant for a table reservation.
2. Guest tries to find the restaurant.
3. Guest parks.

4. Guest is welcomed.
5. Guest is informed that the table is not ready.
6. Guest either waits or goes to the lounge for a cocktail.
7. Guest tries to attract the bartender's attention for a cocktail because there are no seats available.
8. Guest is called over a loudspeaker or paged.
9. Guest is seated at the table.
10. Server takes order.
11. Server brings beverages or food.
12. Server clears food or beverages.
13. Server brings check.
14. Guest pays for meal.
15. Guest departs restaurant.

From your own experiences, you can imagine just how many moments of truth there are in a restaurant dining experience.

Check Your Knowledge

Why is service so important?
What is a moment of truth?

—Adapted from Walker, John R. *Introduction to Hospitality*, 6th ed., pp. 25–26.

_____

_____

_____

_____

Personal Application

Assume you have a newly divorced friend who is beginning to date again. She has asked for your advice about online dating. You don't know much about it, so you search for safety tips about online dating. You have found the following article.

- **Before Reading:** Skim the passage. Note the information about the source. Rate the reliability of the information by circling one of the following: Very Reliable, Somewhat Reliable, or Not Reliable. Be prepared to explain your reasons.

- **During Reading:** Underline the key details.

▪ **After Reading:** In the space following the passage, explain what types of dangers your friend should be aware of when dating online. State your reasons.

Source information: OnGuardOnline.gov is the federal government's website to help you be safe, secure, and responsible online.

Online Dating Scams

Millions of Americans use dating sites, social networking sites, and chat rooms to meet people. And many forge successful relationships. But scammers also use these sites to meet potential victims. They create fake profiles to build online relationships, and eventually convince people to send money in the name of love. Some even make wedding plans before disappearing with the money.

An online love interest who asks for money is almost certainly a scam artist.

- How to Recognize a Scam Artist
- What You Can Do About It

How to Recognize a Scam Artist

The relationship may not be what you think, especially if your sweetheart:

- Wants to leave the dating site immediately and use personal email or IM
- Claims love in a heartbeat
- Claims to be from the U.S., but is traveling or working overseas
- Plans to visit, but is prevented by a traumatic event or a business deal gone sour

Scammers also like to say they're out of the country for business or military service.

What You Can Do About It

You may lose your heart, but you don't have to lose your shirt, too. Don't wire money to cover:

- Travel
- Medical emergencies
- Hotel bills
- Hospital bills for a child or other relative

- Visas or other official documents
- Or losses from a temporary financial setback

Don't send money to tide someone over after a mugging or robbery, and don't do anyone a favor by making an online purchase or forwarding a package to another country. One request leads to another, and delays and disappointments will follow. In the end, the money will be gone along with the person you thought you knew.

—OnGuardOnline.gov

_____

_____

_____

_____

Career Application

Assume you have recently earned your B.A. in engineering and have applied for a job with a company that has many positions in different locations. There are two job opportunities to work with this company. One job is at the local office and starts at a lower position and salary. The other job is for Head Engineering Technician and would offer more pay, but would require you to move. As you think about which job to take, consider the following facts about your personal situation: Will this decision affect just you, or do you have a family? Do you own a home that would need to be sold in order for you to move? What are the pros and cons about living in the new location? What are the pros and cons about staying in your current location?

- **Before Reading:** Skim the following job outlook information you found while trying to make your decision. Evaluate the source.
- **During Reading:** Complete a comparison–contrast chart of the details for both jobs. Be sure to include the "facts about your personal situation."
- **After Reading:** In the space following the passage, indicate which job you will take. State you reasons.

Job Outlook

Employment of electrical and electronic engineering technicians is expected to grow 2 percent from 2010 to 2020, resulting in little or no change for this occupation.

Some of these technicians work in traditional manufacturing industries, many of which are growing slowly or declining. However, employment growth for electrical and electronic engineering technicians will likely occur in engineering services firms as companies seek to contract out these services as a way to lower costs. They also work closely with electrical and electronics and computer hardware engineers in the computer systems design services industry. Demand is expected to be high for technicians in this industry as computer and electronics systems become more integrated. For example, computer, cellular phone, and global positioning systems (GPS) technologies are being included in automobiles and various portable and household electronics systems.

—Bureau of Labor Statistics.

Local position   **Out of town, senior position**

My Decision: _____

REVIEW TEST 1

Score (number correct) _____ × 20 = _____%

Visit MyReadingLab to take this test online and receive feedback and guidance on your answers.

Making Inferences

Read the poem and then answer the questions that follow.

My Heart Leaps up When I Behold

by William Wordsworth (1807)

My heart leaps up when I behold
  A rainbow in the sky:
So was it when my life began;
So is it now I am a man;

So be it when I shall grow old,
   Or let me die!
The Child is father of the Man;
I could wish my days to be
Bound each to each by natural piety.

—Wordsworth, William, *The Complete Poetical Works.*
London: Macmillan and Co., 1888; Bartleby.com, 1999.
www.bartleby.com/145/.

_____ **1.** Based on the context of the poem, the best synonym for the word
piety is
a. youthfulness.   c. goodness.
b. courage.   d. law.

_____ **2.** What emotion does the title of the poem suggest?
a. fear   c. doubt
b. confidence   d. joy

_____ **3.** The rainbow represents
a. nature.   c. youthfulness.
b. mankind.   d. old age.

_____ **4.** In the line "The Child is the father of the Man," the poet suggests
a. mankind is as innocent as a child.
b. the person we are as an adult is connected to the person we are
as a child.
c. life passes by too quickly.

_____ **5.** Overall, the poet expresses
a. faith in the goodness of human beings.
b. a life-long love of nature.
c. a fear of death.

REVIEW TEST 2

Score (number correct) _____ × 20 = _____%

Visit MyReadingLab to take this test online and receive feedback and guidance on your answers.

Read the following passage from a college computer science textbook. Complete the activities that follow.

The Invention of the Desktop

[1]A major step toward popularizing computing was the development of desktop computers. [2]The origins of these machines can be traced to the computer hobbyists who built homemade computers from combinations of chips. [3]It was within this "underground" of hobby activity that Steve Jobs and Stephen Wozniak built a commercially viable home computer and, in 1976, established Apple Computer, Inc. (now Apple Inc.) to manufacture and market their products. [4]Other companies that marketed similar products were Commodore, Heathkit, and Radio Shack. [5]Although these products were popular among computer hobbyists, they were not widely accepted by the business community, which continued to look to the well-established IBM for the majority of its computing needs.

[6]In 1981, IBM introduced its first desktop computer, called the personal computer, or PC, whose underlying software was developed by a newly formed company known as Microsoft. [7]The PC was an instant success and legitimized the desktop computer as an established commodity in the minds of the business community. [8]Today, the term PC is widely used to refer to all those machines (from various manufacturers) whose design has evolved from IBM's initial desktop computer, most of which continue to be marketed with software from Microsoft. [9]At times, however, the term *PC* is used interchangeably with the generic terms *desktop* or *laptop*.

— Brookshear, J. Glenn, *Computer Science: An Overview,*
11th ed., pp. 7–8.

1–3. Write **V** for *valid* by the three inferences that are most firmly supported by the ideas in the passage.

_____ **a.** The term "underground" means that computer technology was originally popular with small numbers of people, not mainstream America.

_____ **b.** IBM had the trust of the business community.

_____ **c.** If IBM had not invented its personal computer, businesses would not have desktops.

_____ **d.** Apple computers are better than PCs because they were invented first.

_____ **e.** The success of Microsoft might be traced to the use of its software by IBM.

4–5. Complete the concept map with information from the passage.

Two Types of Desktop Computers	
• Began as homemade computers • Steve Jobs and Stephen Wozniak built a commercial home computer, started Apple Computer • Popular with _____	• IBM built personal computer (PC) • Used software from newly formed Microsoft • Popular with _____

REVIEW TEST 3

Score (number correct) _____ × 10 = _____%

Visit MyReadingLab to take this test online and receive feedback and guidance on your answers.

Making Inferences

Textbook
Skills

Before you read the following passage from a college health textbook, skim the passage. Answer the Before Reading questions that follow the passage. Then read the passage and answer the After Reading questions.

Vocabulary Preview

incentive (8): motivation, reason
cardiorespiratory (18): of or relating to the heart and respiratory system
calisthenics (20): exercises
elevate (21): raise
duration (23): length, period of time

Exercise Prescription

[1]Doctors often prescribe medications to treat certain diseases. [2]For every individual there is an appropriate dosage of medicine to cure an illness. [3]Similarly, for each individual, there is a correct dosage of exercise to best promote physical fitness. [4]An **exercise prescription** should be tailored to meet the needs of the individual. [5]It should include fitness goals, mode of exercise, a warm-up, a primary conditioning period, and a cool-down.

[6]Establishing short-term and long-term fitness goals is an important part of an exercise prescription. [7]Goals serve as motivation to start an exercise program. [8]Further, reaching your fitness goals improves self-esteem

and provides the **incentive** to make a lifetime commitment to regular exercise. [9]A logical and common type of fitness goal is a performance goal. [10]Increased flexibility is an example of a performance goal. [11]You should set both long-term and short-term performance goals, and you should be tested to determine when you have achieved them. [12]In addition to performance goals, consider setting exercise **adherence** goals. [13]That is, set a goal to exercise a specific number of days per week. [14]Exercise adherence goals are important because fitness will improve only if you exercise regularly. [15]The most important rule in setting goals is that you must create realistic ones. [16]Set fitness goals that you can reach so you will be encouraged to continue exercising.

[17]Every exercise prescription includes at least one mode, or type, of exercise. [18]For example, to improve **cardiorespiratory** fitness, you could select from a wide variety of exercise modes such as running, swimming, or cycling.

[19]A warm-up is a brief (5–15 minute) period of exercise that occurs before the workout. [20]It generally involves light **calisthenics** or stretching. [21]The purpose of a warm-up is to **elevate** muscle temperature and increase blood flow to those muscles that will be used in the workout. [22]A warm-up can also reduce the strain on the heart and may reduce the risk of muscle and tendon injuries.

[23]The primary conditioning period includes the mode of exercise and the frequency, intensity, and **duration** of the workout. [24]The frequency of exercise is the number of times per week that you exercise. [25]In general, the suggested number is three to five times per week. [26]The intensity of exercise is the amount of stress or overload placed on the body during the exercise. [27]The method of measuring intensity varies with the type of exercise. [28]For example, the heart rate is a standard means of tracking intensity during training to improve cardiorespiratory fitness. [29]In strength training, the number of repetitions that can be performed before muscle fatigue occurs is used. [30]In addition, flexibility is measured by the degree of tension or discomfort felt during the stretch.

[31]Another key **component** of the exercise prescription is the duration of exercise. [32]This is the amount of time spent in performing the primary workout. [33]Note that the duration of exercise does not include the warm-up or cool-down. [34]In general, research has shown that 20 to 30 minutes per exercise session is the least amount of time needed to improve physical fitness.

[35]The cool-down is a 5- to 15-minute period of low-intensity exercise that immediately follows the primary workout. [36]For instance, a period of

slow walking might be used as a cool-down after a running workout. [37]A cool-down accomplishes several goals. [38]First, the cool-down allows blood to be returned from the muscles back toward the heart. [39]During exercise, large amounts of blood are pumped to the working muscles. [40]Once exercise ends, blood tends to remain in large blood vessels located around the muscles that were worked. [41]This is known as pooling. [42]Failure to redistribute pooled blood after exercise could result in you feeling lightheaded or even fainting. [43]Finally, some experts argue that post-exercise soreness may be reduced as a result of a cool-down.

—Powers, Scott K. and Dodd, Stephen L., *Total Fitness and Wellness Student Textbook Component*, 3rd ed., pp. 65–69.

Before Reading

Vocabulary in Context

_____ **1.** The word **adherence** in sentence 12 means
  a. obedience.   c. time.
  b. esteem.

_____ **2.** The word **component** in sentence 31 means
  a. benefit.   c. factor.
  b. goal.

Concept Maps

Finish the concept map with information from the passage.

Components of the Exercise Prescription

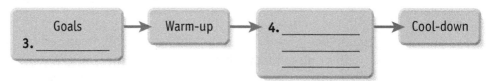

Goals
3. _____   →   Warm-up   →   4. _____   →   Cool-down
               _____
               _____

After Reading

Central Idea and Main Idea

_____ **5.** Which sentence best states the main idea of the passage?
  a. sentence 3   c. sentence 6
  b. sentence 5

Supporting Details

_____ **6.** Sentence 28 is a
   a. major supporting detail.
   b. minor supporting detail.

Transitions

_____ **7.** What thought pattern describes the relationship between sentences 35 and 36?
   a. cause and effect   c. definition and example
   b. time order

Thought Patterns

_____ **8.** The thought pattern used in the fifth paragraph (sentences 23–30) is
   a. cause and effect.   c. definition and example.
   b. time order.

Tone and Purpose

_____ **9.** The author's tone and purpose in the passage are
   a. to inform with objective details.
   b. to entertain with subjective details.
   c. to persuade with discouraging details.

Inferences

10. Write **V** for valid by the inference that is most firmly based on the information in the passage.

_____ A performance goal that is set too high can become a block to motivation.

_____ Sudden and intense exercise helps increase muscle mass more than a slower build up.

_____ In order to experience a complete workout, each exercise period should be at least two hours.

SUMMARY RESPONSE

Restate the author's central idea in your own words. In your summary, state the author's tone and purpose. Begin your summary response with the following: *The central idea of "Exercise Prescription" by Scott K. Powers and Stephen L. Dodd is . . .*

> ### WHAT DO YOU THINK?

Assume you are a personal trainer and create a personal exercise prescription for one or both of the following two potential clients:

- Shantel, age 45, no known medical problems or limitations, has a desk job, and is 30 pounds overweight

- Richard, age 17, no known medical problems or limitations, trying out for a position on his high school track team, is at a good weight, but is out of shape

---

> ### REVIEW TEST 4

Score (number correct) _____ × 10 = _____%

Visit MyReadingLab to take this test online and receive feedback and guidance on your answers.

Making Inferences

Textbook
Skills

Before Reading: Survey the following passage adapted from the college text-book *Essentials of Sociology*. Skim the passage, noting the words in **bold** print. Answer the Before Reading questions that follow the passage. Then read the passage. Next answer the After Reading questions. Use the discussion and writing topics as activities to do after reading.

Vocabulary Preview

fundamental (3): basic
intricate (7): complex
socializes (8): teaches
essence (11): core, real meaning
vanquish (12): conquer, defeat
protagonist (14): hero
encapsulated (15): summarize
predicament (17): dilemma, problem
voluptuous (18): fullness and beauty of form

Lara Croft, Tomb Raider: Changing Images of Women in the Mass Media

[1]The mass media reflect women's changing role in society. [2]Portrayals of women as passive, as subordinate, or as mere background

objects remain, but a new image has broken through. [3]Although this new image exaggerates changes, it also illustrates a **fundamental** change in gender relations. [4]Lara Croft is an outstanding example of this change.

[5]Like books and magazines, video games are made available to a mass audience. [6]And with digital advances, they have crossed the line from what is traditionally thought of as games to something that more closely resembles interactive movies. [7]Costing an average of $10 million to produce and another $10 million to market, video games now have **intricate** subplots and use celebrity voices for the characters (Nussenbaum 2004). [8]Sociologically, what is significant is that the content of video games **socializes** their users. [9]As they play, gamers are exposed not only to action but also to ideas and images. [10]The gender images of video games communicate powerful messages, just as they do in other forms of the mass media.

[11]Lara Croft, an adventure-seeking archeologist and star of *Tomb Raider* and its many sequels, is the **essence** of the new gender image. [12]Lara is smart, strong, and able to utterly **vanquish** foes. [13]With both guns blazing, she is the cowboy of the twenty-first century, the term *cowboy* being purposefully chosen, as Lara breaks stereotypical gender roles and dominates what previously was the domain of men.

[14]She was the first female **protagonist** in a field of muscle-rippling, gun-toting **macho-caricatures** (Taylor 1999). [15]Yet the old remains powerfully **encapsulated** in the new. [16]As the photos on [the next] page make evident, Lara is a fantasy girl for young men of the digital generation.

[17]No matter her foe, no matter her **predicament**, Lara oozes sex. [18]Her form-fitting outfits, which flatter her **voluptuous** physique, reflect the mental images of the men who fashioned this digital character.

[19]Lara has caught young men's fancy to such an extent that they have bombarded corporate headquarters with questions about her personal life. [20]Lara is the star of two movies and a comic book. [21]There is even a Lara Croft candy bar.

[22]A sociologist who reviewed this text said, "It seems that for women to be defined as equal, we have to become symbolic males—warriors with breasts." [23]Why is gender change mostly one-way—females adopting traditional male characteristics? [24]To see why men get to keep their gender roles, these two questions should help:

[25]Who is moving into the traditional territory of the other? [26]Do people prefer to imitate power or powerlessness? [27]Finally, consider just

how far stereotypes have actually been left behind. [28]The ultimate goal of the video game, after foes are vanquished, is to see Lara in a nightie.

—Henslin, James M., *Essentials of Sociology: A Down-to-Earth Approach*, 7th ed., p. 72.

▲ The mass media not only reflect gender stereotypes but also they play a role in changing them. Sometimes they do both simultaneously. The images of Lara Croft not only reflect women's changing role in society, but also, by exaggerating the change, they mold new stereotypes.

Before Reading

Vocabulary in Context

1–2. Study the following chart of word parts. Then read the passage for context clues to help you define the meaning of the word. Next, use your own words to define the terms. Finally, identify the context you used to determine the word's meaning.

Root	Meaning	Suffix	Meaning
macho	male	*-ure*	act, function
caricare	to load	*-s*	plural

1. In sentence 14, **macho-caricatures** are _____

   _____.

2. What is the context clue used to determine the meaning of **macho-caricatures**

   in sentence 14? _____

   _____

After Reading

Implied Central Idea

_____ **3.** Which sentence best states the main idea of the passage?
   a. The mass media reflect women's changing role in society.
   b. Lara Croft encapsulates the changing roles of women in society.
   c. Lara Croft is a stereotype of feminine sexuality.
   d. Lara Croft appeals mostly to men.

Supporting Details

_____ **4.** Sentence 7 is a
   a. major supporting detail.   b. minor supporting detail.

Transitions

_____ **5.** The relationship within sentence 5 is
   a. cause and effect.   c. comparison.
   b. listing.   d. definition and example.

Thought Patterns

_____ **6.** The main thought pattern for the second paragraph (sentences 5–10) is
   a. listing.   c. cause and effect.
   b. space order.   d. generalization and example.

Tone and Purpose

_____ **7.** The author's tone and purpose in the passage are
   a. to inform the reader with objective details.
   b. to entertain with subjective observations.
   c. to persuade with graphic details.

Inferences

8–10. Write **V** for valid by the three inferences that are most firmly based on the information in the passage and the images of Lara Croft.

_____ Lara Croft has developed a strong following among male consumers of entertainment.

_____ Lara Croft does not appeal to women consumers of entertainment.

_____ Lara Croft video games and movies contain violence and sexuality.

_____ Lara Croft breaks completely free of female stereotypes.

_____ Lara Croft is an aggressive action figure and main character in a series of video games, movies, and a comic book.

Restate the author's central idea in your own words. In your summary, state the author's tone and purpose. Begin your summary response with the following: *The central idea of "Lara Croft, Tomb Raider: Changing Images of Women in the Mass Media" by Henslin is...*

Assume you are a concerned parent and you have decided to write an article about the messages contained in movies and video games to your local newspaper. Consider using one of the following topics for your article:

- Discuss what one may learn about our culture by playing video games, or a particular video game.
- Write a review of a movie or video game based on the message it may send about violence or gender. Take a stand in support of or in opposition to the movie or video game.

After Reading About Inferences

Before you move on to the Mastery Tests on inferences, take time to reflect on your learning and performance by answering the following questions. Write your answers in your notebook.

- How has my knowledge base or prior knowledge about inferences changed?
- Based on my studies, how do I think I will perform on the Mastery Test(s)? Why do I think my scores will be above average, average, or below average? (Note: An additional fourth Mastery Test may be found in MyReadingLab.)
- Would I recommend this chapter to other students who want to learn more inferences? Why or why not?

Test your understanding of what you have learned about inferences by completing the Chapter 11 Review.

Name _____ Section _____

Date _____ **Score** (number correct) _____ × 20 = _____%

Visit MyReadingLab to take this test online and receive feedback and guidance on your answers.

Read the following passage, adapted from a college biology textbook. Then write **V** for valid by the five inferences most soundly based on the information.

Textbook
Skills

Matters of the Heart

[1]Cardiovascular disease, which impairs the heart and blood vessels, is the leading cause of death in the United States, killing nearly 1 million Americans annually. [2]And no wonder. [3]Your heart must contract vigorously more than 2.5 billion times during your lifetime without once stopping to rest, forcing blood through vessels whose total length would encircle the globe twice. [4]Because these vessels may become constricted, weakened, or clogged, the cardiovascular system is a prime candidate for malfunction.

Atherosclerosis Obstructs Blood Vessels

[5]*Atherosclerosis* causes the walls of the large arteries to thicken and lose their elasticity. [6]This change is caused by deposits called *plaques,* which are composed of cholesterol and other fatty substances as well as calcium and fibrin. [7]Plaques are deposited within the wall of the artery between the smooth muscle and the tissue that lines the artery. [8]A plaque may rupture through the lining into the interior of the vessel, stimulating platelets to adhere to the vessel wall and initiate blood clots. [9]These clots further obstruct the artery and may completely block it. [10]Or a clot may break loose and clog a narrower artery "downstream." [11]Arterial clots are responsible for the most serious consequences of atherosclerosis: heart attacks and strokes.

[12]A *heart attack* occurs when one of the coronary arteries is blocked. [13](Coronary arteries supply the heart muscle itself.) [14]Deprived of nutrients and oxygen, a heart muscle whose blood supply is curtailed by a blocked artery dies rapidly and painfully. [15]Heart attacks are the major cause of death from atherosclerosis.

[16]About 1.1 million Americans suffer heart attacks each year, and about half a million people die from them. [17]But atherosclerosis also causes plaques and clots to form in arteries throughout the body. [18]If a clot or plaque obstructs an artery that supplies the brain, it can cause a stroke, in which brain function is lost in the area deprived of blood and its vital oxygen and nutrients.

Treatment of Atherosclerosis

[19]The exact cause of atherosclerosis is unclear, but it is promoted by high blood pressure, cigarette smoking, genetic predisposition, obesity, diabetes, lack of exercise, and high blood levels of a certain type of cholesterol bound to a carrier molecule called low-density lipoprotein (LDL). [20]If LDL-bound cholesterol levels are too high, cholesterol may be deposited in arterial walls. [21]In contrast, cholesterol bound to high-density lipoprotein (HDL) is metabolized or excreted and hence is often called "good" cholesterol. [22]Treatment of atherosclerosis includes the use of drugs or changes in diet and lifestyle to lower blood pressure and blood cholesterol levels.

—Text and Figure E20-1 (p. 382) below from Audesirk, Teresa, Audesirk, Gerald, and Byers, Bruce E., *Life on Earth*, 5th ed.

_____ A synonym for coronary artery is blood vessel.

_____ Plaque is a sticky substance that hardens in the arteries.

_____ Cardiovascular diseases include heart attacks and strokes.

_____ Most heart attacks come on suddenly.

_____ Cholesterol promotes a healthy heart.

_____ The tendency to develop heart problems can be inherited.

_____ Lifestyle choices have a significant effect on the health of the heart.

_____ Most people are too busy to exercise.

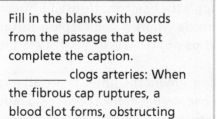

VISUAL *VOCABULARY*

Fill in the blanks with words from the passage that best complete the caption.

_____ clogs arteries: When the fibrous cap ruptures, a blood clot forms, obstructing the _____ .

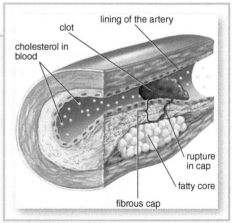

clot

lining of the artery

cholesterol in blood

rupture in cap

fatty core

fibrous cap

▶ **Figure E20-1**

Name _____ Section _____

Date _____ **Score** (number correct) _____ × 25 = _____%

Visit MyReadingLab to take this test online and receive feedback and guidance on your answers.

Read the poem, and then answer the questions that follow.

Mr. Flood's Party

by Edwin Arlington Robinson

Old Eben Flood, climbing along one night
Over the hill between the town below
And the forsaken upland *hermitage   a dwelling where one lives alone
That held as much as he should ever know
On earth again of home, paused *warily.   cautiously
The road was his with not a native near;
And Eben, having leisure, said aloud,
For no man else in Tilbury Town to hear:

"Well, Mr. Flood, we have the harvest moon
Again, and we may not have many more;
The bird is on the wing, the poet says,
And you and I have said it here before.
Drink to the bird." He raised up to the light
The jug that he had gone so far to fill,
And answered huskily: "Well, Mr. Flood,
Since you propose it, I believe I will."

Alone, as if enduring to the end
A valiant armor of scarred hopes outworn,
He stood there in the middle of the road
Like Roland's ghost winding a silent horn.
Below him, in the town among the trees,
Where friends of other days had honored him,
A phantom salutation of the dead
Rang thinly till old Eben's eyes were dim.

Then, as a mother lays her sleeping child
Down tenderly, fearing it may awake,
He set the jug down slowly at his feet
With trembling care, knowing that most things break;
And only when assured that on firm earth
It stood, as the uncertain lives of men
Assuredly did not, he paced away,

And with his hand extended paused again:
"Well, Mr. Flood, we have not met like this
In a long time; and many a change has come
To both of us, I fear, since last it was
We had a drop together. Welcome home!"
*Convivially returning with himself,   sociably
Again he raised the jug up to the light;
And with an acquiescent quaver said:
"Well, Mr. Flood, if you insist, I might.

"Only a very little, Mr. Flood—
For auld lang syne. No more, sir; that will do."
So, for the time, apparently it did,
And Eben evidently thought so too;
For soon amid the silver loneliness
Of night he lifted up his voice and sang,
Secure, with only two moons listening,
Until the whole harmonious landscape rang—

"For auld lang syne." The weary throat gave out,
The last word wavered; and the song being done,
He raised again the jug regretfully
And shook his head, and was again alone.
There was not much that was ahead of him,
And there was nothing in the town below—
Where strangers would have shut the many doors
That many friends had opened long ago.

—From E. A. Robinson, *Collected Poems.* New York, The Macmillan Company, 1921.

_____ **1.** The poem suggests that the narrator is
        a. young and distrustful.   c. middle-aged and frightened.
        b. old and lonely.

_____ **2.** In the second and fifth stanzas, Eben Flood is talking to
        a. a friend.   c. himself.
        b. God.

_____ **3.** In the second stanza, the narrator implies that Eben
        a. went to town to buy liquor. c. loves poetry and birds.
        b. lives in town.

_____ **4.** Overall, the poet suggests that Eben Flood is
        a. well known and well respected by the townspeople.
        b. lonely because he has outlived those who knew him.
        c. fearful of death.

Name _____ Section _____

Date _____ **Score** (number correct) _____ × 20 = _____%

Visit MyReadingLab to take this test online and receive feedback and guidance on your answers.

Read the following passage taken from the novel *A Wasted Day* by Richard Hardin Davis. Using inference skills, mark each of the statements that follow:

T for true

F for false

UK for unknown based on the information given

From *A Wasted Day*

[1]When its turn came, the private secretary, somewhat apologetically, laid the letter in front of the Wisest Man in Wall Street.

[2]"From Mrs. Austin, probation officer, Court of General Sessions," he explained. [3]"Wants a letter about Spear. [4]He's been convicted of theft. [5]Comes up for sentence Tuesday."

[6]"Spear?" repeated Arnold Thorndike.

[7]"Young fellow, stenographer, used to do your letters last summer going in and out on the train."

[8]The great man nodded. [9]"I remember. [10]What about him?"

[11]The habitual gloom of the private secretary was lightened by a grin.

[12]"Went on the loose; had with him about five hundred dollars belonging to the firm; he's with Isaacs & Sons now, shoe people on Sixth Avenue. [13]Met a woman, and woke up without the money. [14]The next morning he offered to make good, but Isaacs called in a policeman. [15]When they looked into it, they found the boy had been drunk. [16]They tried to withdraw the charge, but he'd been committed. [17]Now, the probation officer is trying to get the judge to suspend sentence. [18]A letter from you, sir, would—"

[19]It was evident the mind of the great man was elsewhere. [20]Young men who, drunk or sober, spent the firm's money on women who disappeared before sunrise did not appeal to him. [21]Another letter submitted that morning had come from his art agent in Europe. [22]In Florence he had discovered the Correggio he had been sent to find. [23]It was undoubtedly genuine, and he asked to be instructed by cable. [24]The price was forty thousand dollars. [25]With one eye closed, and the other keenly regarding the inkstand, Mr. Thorndike decided to pay the price; and with the facility of long practice dismissed the Correggio, and snapped his mind back to the present.

[26]"Spear had a letter from us when he left, didn't he?" he asked. [27]"What he has developed into, SINCE he left us—" he shrugged his shoulders. [28]The secretary withdrew the letter, and slipped another in its place.

[29]"Homer Firth, the landscape man," he chanted, "wants permission to use blue flint on the new road, with turf gutters, and to plant silver firs each side. [30]Says it will run to about five thousand dollars a mile."

[31]"No!" protested the great man firmly, "blue flint makes a country place look like a cemetery. [32]Mine looks too much like a cemetery now. [33]Landscape gardeners!" he exclaimed impatiently. [34]"Their only idea is to insult nature. [35]The place was better the day I bought it, when it was running wild; you could pick flowers all the way to the gates." [36]Pleased that it should have recurred to him, the great man smiled. [37]"Why, Spear," he exclaimed, "always took in a bunch of them for his mother. [38]Don't you remember, we used to see him before breakfast wandering around the grounds picking flowers?" [39]Mr. Thorndike nodded briskly. [40]"I like his taking flowers to his mother."

[41]"He SAID it was to his mother," suggested the secretary gloomily.

[42]"Well, he picked the flowers, anyway," laughed Mr. Thorndike. [43]"He didn't pick our pockets. [44]And he had the run of the house in those days. [45]As far as we know," he dictated, "he was satisfactory. [46]Don't say more than that."

[47]The secretary scribbled a mark with his pencil. [48]"And the landscape man?"

[49]"Tell him," commanded Thorndike, "I want a wood road, suitable to a farm; and to let the trees grow where God planted them."

[50]As his car slid downtown on Tuesday morning the mind of Arnold Thorndike was occupied with such details of daily routine as the purchase of a railroad, the Japanese loan, the new wing to his art gallery, and an attack that morning, in his own newspaper, upon his pet trust. [51]But his busy mind was not too occupied to return the salutes of the traffic policemen who cleared the way for him. [52]Or, by some genius of memory, to recall the fact that it was on this morning young Spear was to be sentenced for theft. [53]It was a charming morning. [54]The spring was at full tide, and the air was sweet and clean. [55]Mr. Thorndike considered whimsically that to send a man to jail with the memory of such a morning clinging to him was adding a year to his sentence. [56]He regretted he had not given the probation officer a stronger letter. [57]He remembered the young man now, and favorably. [58]A shy, silent youth, deft in work, and at other times conscious and embarrassed. [59]But that, on the part of a stenographer, in the presence of the Wisest Man in Wall Street, was not unnatural. [60]On occasions, Mr. Thorndike had put even royalty—frayed, impecunious royalty, on the lookout for a loan—at its ease.

—From E. A. Robinson, *Collected Poems*. New York, The Macmillan Company, 1921.

_____ 1. Arnold Thorndike is a successful Wall Street businessman.

_____ 2. Spear developed a drinking problem after leaving Thorndike's employ.

_____ 3. Spear is actually innocent of any wrongdoing.

_____ 4. Arnold Thorndike is very concerned with money and status.

_____ 5. The secretary takes delight in the misfortune of Spear.

11 Summary of Key Concepts About Inferences

(LO1) (LO2)
(LO3)
Assess your comprehension of inferences. Complete the following two-column notes of terms and definitions with information from the chapter.

Term	Definition
Inference	_____ _____
Valid inference	_____
Invalid conclusion	_____ _____
The 5-step VALID Thinking Process	Step 1: _____ Step 2: _____ Step 3: _____ Step 4: _____ Step 5: _____

Test Your Comprehension of Inferences

Respond to the following questions and prompts. Answers may vary.

(LO2) (LO3)
In your own words, what is the difference between a valid and an invalid inference? _____

_____

_____

_____

Complete the following three-column notes about creative expression. Use your own examples.

Creative Expression: Literary Devices

Literary Device	Meaning	Example
Connotations of words	_____	_____
	_____	_____
	_____	_____
	_____	_____
Metaphor	_____	_____
	_____	_____
Personification	_____	_____
	_____	_____
	_____	_____
Simile	_____	_____
Symbol	_____	_____
	_____	_____

LO1 LO2 LO3 LO4 LO5 LO6 Describe how you will use what you have learned about inferences in your reading process to comprehend textbook material. _____

_____

_____

_____

_____

LO1 LO2 LO3 LO4 LO5 LO6 Summarize the two most important ideas in this chapter that will help you improve your reading comprehension. _____

_____

_____

The Basics of Argument

LO LEARNING OUTCOMES

After studying this chapter, you should be able to:

- **LO1** Define the Terms *Argument, Claim,* and *Evidence*
- **LO2** Identify the Author's Claim and Supports
- **LO3** Determine Whether the Supports Are Relevant
- **LO4** Determine Whether the Supports Are Adequate
- **LO5** Analyze the Argument for Bias
- **LO6** Develop Textbook Skills: The Logic of Argument in Textbooks
- **LO7** Apply Information Literacy Skills: Academic, Personal, and Career Applications of the Basics of Argument

 ## Before Reading About the Basics of Argument

Many of the same skills you learned to make valid inferences will help you master the basics of argument. Take a moment to review the five steps in the VALID approach to making sound inferences. Fill in the following blanks with each of the steps.

Step 1. _____

Step 2. _____

Step 3. _____

Step 4. _____

Step 5. _____

Use your prior knowledge about valid inferences, other reading skills, and the learning outcomes to create at least three questions that you can answer as you study:

1. _____
_____?

2. _____
_____?

3. _____
_____?

Compare the questions you created based on your prior knowledge and the chapter learning outcomes with the following questions. Then write the ones that seem the most helpful in your notebook, leaving enough space between questions to record your answers as you read and study the chapter.

How will verifying and valuing the facts help me decide if supports in an argument are relevant? How will learning from the text help me decide if supports in an argument are adequate? How does an argument use bias? What is the relationship between main ideas and the author's claim? How does opinion affect an argument? What is the connection between tone, purpose, and the basics of argument?

LO1 Define the Terms *Argument*, *Claim*, and *Evidence*

Have you noticed how many of us enjoy debating ideas and winning arguments? Many television shows such as the talk show *The View* and political programs such as *The Rachel Maddow Show* or *The O'Reilly Factor* thrive on conflict and debate. Likewise, talk radio devotes hours of air time to debating cultural and political issues on shows like *Rush Limbaugh* and *The Bill Press Show*. In everyday life, a couple may argue about spending priorities. Colleagues may argue how best to resolve a workplace dispute. One politician may argue in favor of corporate tax cuts while another politician argues against any kind of tax cut. Certain topics stir debate and argument. For many, sports contests can cause heated debate, and topics such as religion and evolution often evoke powerful discussions.

Some people are so committed to their ideas that they become emotional, even angry. However, effective **argument** is reasoned: it is a process during which a claim is made and logical details are offered to support that claim.

> An **argument** is made up of two types of statements:
> **1.** The author's claim—the main point of the argument
> **2.** The supports—the evidence or reasons that support the author's claim

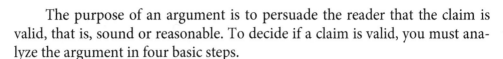

The purpose of an argument is to persuade the reader that the claim is valid, that is, sound or reasonable. To decide if a claim is valid, you must analyze the argument in four basic steps.

1. Identify the author's claim and supports.

2. Determine whether the supports are relevant.

3. Determine whether the supports are adequate.

4. Analyze the argument for bias.

 ## Step 1: Identify the Author's Claim and Supports

Read the following claim:

> Competitive sports provide several benefits to participants and should be financed by public funds.

The claim certainly states the speaker's point clearly, but it probably wouldn't inspire most of us to support or become involved in competitive sports. Instead, our first response to the claim is likely to be, "What are the benefits to participants of competitive sports?" We need reasons before we can decide whether or not we think the claim is valid.

Read the following statements:

1. Competitive sports teach participants physical, social, emotional, and psychological skills.

2. Competitive sports set standards against which participants can measure growth and ability.

3. Competitive sports allow participants to experience the connection between effort and success.

These three sentences offer the supports for the author's claim. We are now able to understand the basis of the argument, and we now have details about which we can agree or disagree.

Writers frequently make claims that they want us to accept as valid. To assess whether the claim is valid, a master reader first identifies the claim and the supports.

> **EXAMPLES**

A. Read each of the following groups of ideas. Mark each statement **C** if it is an author's claim or **S** if it provides support for the claim.

1. _____   a. Staph is a particularly dangerous type of bacteria.

   _____   b. Staph may cause skin infections that look like pimples or boils, which may be red, swollen, painful, or have pus or other drainage.

   _____   c. Some strains of staph have developed antibiotic resistance, making a staph infection sometimes difficult to treat.

2. _____   a. Aerobic training such as walking, biking, and swimming strengthens the heart and lungs.

   _____   b. A comprehensive fitness program must combine aerobic and anaerobic training.

   _____   c. Anaerobic training, using free weights, weight machines, and resistance bands, builds muscles and bones.

3. _____   a. All Siamese cats are domesticated cats.

   _____   b. All domesticated cats are excellent pets.

   _____   c. Therefore, all Siamese cats are excellent pets.

B. Political cartoons offer arguments through the use of humor. The cartoonist has a claim to make and uses the situation, actions, and words in the cartoon as supporting details. Study the cartoon reprinted here. Then write a claim based on the supports in the cartoon.

© 2010 Mike Keefe/Cagle Cartoons, Inc.

_____

_____

_____

_____

EXPLANATIONS

A. Compare your answers to these.

   1. In this example the opinion is phrased *particularly dangerous* and then supported with the evidence. Thus (a) is the claim and (b) and (c) are the supports.

   2. The use of the word *must* identifies (b) as the claim; the other sentences provide support.

   3. The word *therefore* signals the conclusion or claim.

B. Several claims may be suggested by the details in the cartoon. One possible claim is "Gang life leads to death or prison." ◄

Practice 1

A. Read the following groups of ideas. Mark each statement **C** if it is an author's claim or **S** if it provides support for the claim.

   1. _____   a. As many as 9 million Americans have their identities stolen each year.

      _____   b. Identity theft is a serious crime that affects millions of people each year.

   2. _____   a. Exposure to media violence causes increases in aggression and violence.

      _____   b. By the time a typical child finishes elementary school, he or she will have seen around 8,000 murders and more than 100,000 other acts of violence on TV.

   3. _____   a. The use of cell phones while driving contributes to 25% of all traffic crashes.

      _____   b. A federal law should be passed to ban talking on a cell phone while driving.

4. _____ a. Concealed handguns are not an effective form of self-defense.

_____ b. A recent study found that someone carrying a gun for self-defense was 4.5 times more likely to be shot during an assault than a victim without a gun.

B. Study the following editorial cartoon. Write a claim based on the details of the cartoon.

CAGLECARTOONS.COM

© 2010 Jeff Parker/Cagle Cartoons, Inc.

Step 2: Determine Whether the Supports Are Relevant

In Step 1, you learned to identify the author's claim and supports. The next step is to determine whether the supports are relevant to the claim. Remember, a claim, like any main idea, is made up of a topic and a controlling point. Irrelevant supports change the topic or ignore the controlling point. Relevant supports will answer the reporter's questions (*Who? What? When? Where? Why?* and *How?*). Use these questions to determine whether the supports for a claim are relevant.

For example, read the following argument a student makes about her grades. Identify the support that is irrelevant to her claim.

> [1]I deserve a higher grade than the one I received. [2]Even though I have missed some classes, I made sure to get all the lecture notes from class-mates. [3]I turned in all my assignments on time, and my test scores average at the A-level. [4]It's not my fault I missed so many classes. [5]My mother became seriously ill, and she is the one who watches my children for me so I can come to school. [6]I also had car problems.

By turning this student's claim into a question, she and her teacher can test her ability to offer valid reasons: "How have I shown I have mastery of the course material?" Sentences 2 and 3 offer relevant examples of her mastery of the course material. However, sentences 4, 5, and 6 state irrelevant supports that shift the focus away from her grade. The argument is about her grade based on an appeal to pity or emotions.

When evaluating an argument, it is important to test each piece of supporting evidence to determine whether it is relevant.

> **EXAMPLES**

A. Read the following lists of claims and supports. Mark each support **R** if it is relevant to the claim or **N** if it is not relevant to the claim.

1. Claim: All police should be equipped with Taser guns.
   Supports:

   _____ a. Taser guns were developed by two brothers who wanted their mother to own a weapon for self-defense with which she could feel comfortable.

   _____ b. The Taser gun is a *nonlethal* stun gun that disables suspects for five seconds by shooting them with 50,000 volts of electricity.

   _____ c. Human rights activists warn that Taser guns can be abused as instruments of torture, especially since they leave no significant or enduring mark on the skin.

   _____ d. Police officers in Miami, Florida, and Seattle, Washington, have had no incidents or sharply lower incidents of fatal police shootings since they began using Taser guns.

   _____ e. The electrical shock caused by Taser guns has no long-term negative effect.

B. Argument is also used in advertisements. It is important for you to be able to understand the points and supports of ads. Many times advertisers appeal to emotions, make false claims, or give supports that are not relevant because their main aim is to persuade you to buy their product. Study the following mock advertisement for Cabre, a fictitious brand of red wine. Mark each of the statements **R** if it is relevant to the claim or **N** if it is not relevant to the claim.

◀ Cabre! To a happy and long life. Recent research suggests that one glass of red wine daily may do more than reduce the risk of high levels of cholesterol. The grape skin and seeds appear to hold a natural cancer-fighting chemical.*

*Research conducted on animals only.

2. Claim: Moderate consumption of red wine may have some health benefits. Supports:

_____ a. A beautiful woman drinks red wine.

_____ b. Red wine may reduce the risk of high levels of cholesterol.

_____ c. The grape skin and seeds appear to hold a natural cancer-fighting chemical.

_____ d. The woman is happy.

_____ e. Research was conducted on animals only.

EXPLANATIONS

A. 1. Items *b*, *d*, and *e* are relevant to the claim. Items *a* and *c* are not relevant. The reason the Taser guns were created is not important to their use by police officers; and a warning about the possibility of Taser guns being used as instruments of torture is not the issue.

B. **2.** Items *a*, *d*, and *e* are not relevant to the claim that moderate consumption of red wine may have some health benefits. Advertisers often use beautiful models who appear to be pleased with the product, but neither beauty nor personal preference of the model is relevant to health issues. Items *b* and *c* are relevant to the claim. However, interestingly, the smallest line of print in this mock advertisement discloses that the research only involved animals. Thus the "research" is not relevant to the claim. In fact, the disclaimer could lead a reasonable reader to discard all of the supports as not relevant. ◉

Practice 2

A. Read the following lists of claims and supports. Mark each support **R** if it is relevant to the claim or **N** if it is not relevant to the claim.

1. Claim: The need for organ and tissue donors is critical.
Supports:

_____ a. According to the Organ Procurement and Transplantation Network (OPTN), as of June 4, 2013, over 118,000 people were on a waiting list for an organ transplant.

_____ b. According to the OPTN, only 6,891 transplants took place between January and March of 2013.

_____ c. Each day 18 people on the waiting list die.

_____ d. The organs needed for transplant include heart, kidneys, pancreas, lungs, liver, and intestines; the tissues needed are cornea, skin, bone marrow, heart valves, and connective tissue.

_____ e. To become an organ donor, fill out and carry a donor card, indicate your intent to donate on your driver's license, and tell your family about your decision.

—Adapted from "Organ Donation," *FirstGov*.
http://www.organdonor.gov

2. Claim: Binge drinking is dangerous and irresponsible.
Supports:

_____ a. Binge drinking is commonly defined as drinking large quantities of alcohol in a short period of time: 5 drinks in a row for men; 4 drinks in a row for women.

_____ b. Many young people do not think it is important to have alcohol at a party.

_____ c. Eating a large meal before drinking slows down the effect of the alcohol.

_____ d. The intent and purpose of binge drinking is to become intoxicated and to lose control.

_____ e. Binge drinking is linked to vandalism, confrontations with police, injuries, alcohol poisoning, and death.

3. Claim: If expressions of religion are allowed in national government institutions, then prayer should be allowed in public schools.
   Supports:

   _____ a. Banning prayer in public schools leads to moral decline.

   _____ b. Congress prays at the opening of each session.

   _____ c. Federal officials, including the president of the United States, take their oaths of office upon a Bible.

   _____ d. Moses and the Ten Commandments are prominently displayed in the Supreme Court building.

   _____ e. A majority of Americans favor prayer in schools.

4. Claim: Volunteers perform many selfless acts.
   Supports:

   _____ a. Volunteers promote worthwhile causes and improve the lives of others.

   _____ b. Volunteers boost their own sense of self-worth and well-being.

   _____ c. Volunteers conserve funds for charities, nonprofits, and other community organizations by contributing their time.

   _____ d. They share their skills and expertise.

   _____ e. Volunteers improve their reputations and promote their careers.

B. Study the public service poster sponsored by the White House Office of National Drug Control Policy on the following page. Read the claim, and then mark each support **R** if it is relevant to the claim or **N** if it is not relevant to the claim.

Claim: Steer Clear of Pot.

Supports:

_____ a. Stoners laugh a lot, eat junk food, and don't bug anyone.

_____ b. It's dangerous to drive stoned.

_____ c. An estimated 38,000 high school seniors in the United States reported in 2001 that they had crashed while driving under the influence of marijuana.

_____ d. Everyone smokes pot.

_____ e. Research shows that smoking weed affects a driver's perception, coordination, and reaction time.

—United States Executive Office of the President. "Steer Clear of Pot." The White House Office of National Drug Control Policy. Free Resources. <http://abovetheinfluence .com/facts/drugsmarijuana>

Now that you have practiced identifying relevant supports in a list format, you are ready to isolate relevant supports in reading passages. In a passage, the thesis statement states the author's claim. Each of the supporting details must be evaluated as relevant or irrelevant supports for the thesis statement.

> **EXAMPLE**   Read the following passage.

Shell Eggs from Farm to Table

[1]Eggs are among the most nutritious foods on earth and can be part of a healthy diet; however, they are perishable just like raw meat, poultry, and fish. [2]Unbroken, clean, fresh shell eggs may contain *Salmonella enteritidis* (SE) bacteria that can cause foodborne illness. [3]While the number of eggs affected is quite small, several cases of foodborne illness have surfaced in the last few years. [4]To be safe, eggs must be properly handled and cooked.

[5]Bacteria can be present on the exterior of a shell egg because the egg exits the hen's body through the same passageway as feces are excreted; thus, eggs are washed and sanitized at the processing plant. [6]Bacteria can be present inside an uncracked, whole egg. [7]This interior contamination may be due to bacteria within the hen's ovary or oviduct before the shell forms around the yolk and white. [8]*Salmonella enteritidis* doesn't make the hen sick. [9]It is also possible for eggs to become infected by *Salmonella enteritidis* fecal contamination through the pores of the shells after they have been laid.

[10]Researchers say that, if present, the *Salmonella enteritidis* is usually in the yolk or yellow; however, experts cannot rule out the bacteria's presence in egg whites. [11]As a result, everyone is advised against ingesting raw or undercooked egg yolks and whites or products containing raw or undercooked eggs.

—Adapted from "Egg Products Preparation," Food Safety and Inspection Service, U.S. Department of Agriculture, 7 March 2007.

1. Underline the thesis statement (the sentence that states the author's claim).

_____ **2.** Which sentence is *not* relevant to the author's point?
     a. sentence 2   c. sentence 3
     b. sentence 6   d. sentence 8

EXPLANATION

1. Sentence 4 is the central idea and states the author's claim.

2. The sentence that is *not* relevant to the author's point is *(d)*, sentence 8. The author's claim focuses on the health risks associated with eggs, not with the health of the hens laying the eggs. ◀

Practice 3

Read the following passages and respond to the two questions following each of them.

The Street Outreach Program

1Today, in communities across the country, some young people are living on the streets, running from or being asked to leave homes characterized by abuse, neglect, or parental drug or alcohol abuse. **2**Once on the streets, such youth are at risk of being sexually exploited or abused by adults for pleasure or profit.

3To prevent the sexual abuse or exploitation of these young people by providing them with services that help them leave the streets, Congress established the Education and Prevention Services to Reduce Sexual Abuse of Runaway, Homeless, and Street Youth Program, through the Violence Against Women Act of the Violent Crime Control and Law Enforcement Act of 1994. **4**That program created Grants for the Prevention of Sexual Abuse and Exploitation (also known as the Street Outreach Program). **5**Naturally, not all at-risk youth can be reached through this program.

6The Street Outreach Program offers many services including the following: street-based education and outreach, access to emergency shelter, survival aid, individual assessments, treatment and counseling, prevention and education activities, information and referrals, crisis intervention, and follow-up support.

7The Education and Prevention Services to Reduce Sexual Abuse of Runaway, Homeless, and Street Youth Program should be supported with increased funding.

—Excerpted from "Family and Youth Services Bureau Street Outreach Program," Administration for Children and Families.

1. Underline the thesis statement (the sentence that states the author's claim).

_____ 2. Which sentence is *not* relevant to the author's point?
   a. sentence 3   c. sentence 5
   b. sentence 4   d. sentence 6

Preventing Identity Theft Is Your Responsibility!

[1]As with any crime, you can't guarantee that you will never be a victim, but you can take responsibility to minimize your risk. [2]To protect yourself against identity theft, you should take the following steps.

[3]First, don't give out personal information on the phone, through the mail, or over the Internet unless you've initiated the contact or are sure you know whom you're dealing with. [4]Identity thieves may pose as representatives of banks, Internet service providers (ISPs) and even government agencies to get you to reveal your SSN, mother's maiden name, account numbers, and other identifying information.

[5]Second, secure personal information in your home, especially if you have roommates, employ outside help, or are having service work done in your home. [6]Don't carry your SSN card; leave it in a secure place.

[7]Third, guard your mail and trash from theft. [8]Deposit outgoing mail in post office collection boxes or at your local post office rather than in an unsecured mailbox. [9]Promptly remove mail from your mailbox. [10]If you're planning to be away from home and can't pick up your mail, call the U.S. Postal Service to request a vacation hold. [11]You can have the amount of junk mail delivered to your home reduced by contacting Mail Preference Service, PO Box 643, Carmel, NY 10512.

[12]Finally, to thwart an identity thief who may pick through your trash or recycling bins to capture your personal information, tear or shred your charge receipts, copies of credit applications, insurance forms, physician statements, checks and bank statements, expired charge cards that you're discarding, and credit offers you get in the mail.

—Adapted from "Protecting Against Identity Theft,"
Federal Trade Commission, 2003.

3. Underline the thesis statement (the sentence that states the author's claim).

_____ 4. Which sentence is *not* relevant to the author's point?
   a. sentence 8   c. sentence 10
   b. sentence 9   d. sentence 11

Step 3: Determine Whether the Supports Are Adequate

In Step 1 you learned to identify the author's claim and supports. In Step 2 you learned to make sure the supports are relevant. In Step 3 you must determine whether the supports are adequate. A valid argument is based not only on a claim and relevant support but also on the amount and quality of the support given. That is, supports must give enough evidence for the author's claim to be convincing. Just as you used the reporter's questions to determine whether supports are relevant, you can use them to test whether supports are adequate. Supporting details fully explain the author's controlling point about a topic. Remember, those questions are *Who? What? When? Where? Why?* and *How?*

For example, you may argue, "A low-carbohydrate diet is a more healthful diet. I feel much better since I stopped eating so much bread and pasta." However, the reporter's question "Why?" reveals that the support is inadequate. The answer to "Why is a low-carbohydrate diet a more healthful diet?" should include expert opinions and facts, not just personal opinion. Often in the quest to support a claim, people oversimplify their reasons. Thus, they do not offer enough information to prove the claim. Instead of logical details, they may offer false causes, false comparisons, forced choices, or leave out facts that hurt the claim. You will learn more about inadequate argument in Chapter 13.

In Chapter 11, you studied how to avoid invalid conclusions and make valid inferences (see pages 474–485). The same thinking steps you use to make valid inferences help you identify valid claims: consider the facts, don't infer anything that is not there, and make sure nothing contradicts your conclusion.

> **EXAMPLE** Read the list of supports.

- Increasing levels of greenhouse gases like carbon dioxide (CO_2) in the atmosphere since pre-industrial times are well documented and understood.

- The atmospheric buildup of CO_2 and other greenhouse gases is largely the result of human activities such as the burning of fossil fuels.

- An "unequivocal" warming trend of about 1.0 to 1.7°F occurred from 1906–2005. Warming occurred in both the Northern and Southern Hemispheres, and over the oceans.

- The major greenhouse gases emitted by human activities remain in the atmosphere for periods ranging from decades to centuries. It is therefore virtually certain that atmospheric concentrations of greenhouse gases will continue to rise over the next few decades.

- Increasing greenhouse gas concentrations tend to warm the planet.

—U.S. Environmental Protection Agency. "Climate Change: Science: State of Knowledge."

Write **V** for valid by the claim that is adequately supported by the evidence.

_____ a. The earth's surface temperature is going to rise at least 1 degree Fahrenheit in the next century.

_____ b. Human activities have changed the global climate and may lead to wide-ranging negative effects on humans, animals, and ecosystems.

_____ c. Coastal regions will be covered with water because of global warming and melting polar regions.

_____ d. Big oil companies such as Saudi Aramco, ExxonMobil, and BP are responsible for global warming.

EXPLANATION   Choices (a) and (c) jump to conclusions about the future effects of global warming, and choice (d) uses the evidence to jump to conclusions about the role of big oil companies in the cause of global warming. More evidence is needed to support any one of those claims. The only logical conclusion based on the evidence is (b). ◄

Practice 4

A. Read the list of supports taken from an article about using corn as an alternative energy. Then write **V** next to the claim that is adequately supported by the evidence.

▫ Dwindling foreign oil, rising prices at the gas pump, and hype from politically well-connected U.S. agribusiness have combined to create a frenzied rush to convert food grains into ethanol fuel.

▫ Using corn or any other biomass for ethanol requires huge regions of fertile land, plus massive amounts of water and sunlight to maximize crop production.

▫ If the entire national corn crop were used to make ethanol, it would replace a mere 7% of U.S. oil consumption—far from making the U.S. independent of foreign oil.

▫ The environmental impacts of corn ethanol production include severe soil erosion of valuable food cropland; the heavy use of nitrogen fertilizers and pesticides that pollute rivers; and the required use of fossil fuels, releasing large quantities of carbon dioxide into the atmosphere, adding to global warming.

▫ More than 40 percent of the energy contained in one gallon of corn ethanol is expended to produce it, and that expended energy to make ethanol comes mostly from highly valuable oil and natural gas.

▫ Growing crops for fuel squanders land, water, and energy vital for human food production.

—Pimentel, David. "Corn Can't Save Us: Debunking the Biofuel Myth."
Reproduced by the permission of David Pimentel.

_____ a. Ethanol made from corn and other biomasses is an acceptable alternative energy form.

_____ b. The United States is too dependent on foreign oil.

_____ c. Fuels made from biomasses can reduce the United States's dependency on foreign oil.

_____ d. The use of corn and other biofuels to solve our energy problem is an ethically, economically, and environmentally unworkable sham.

B. Study the following graph. Then write **V** by the claim that is adequately supported by the evidence in the graph.

Recidivism of U.S. Prisoners

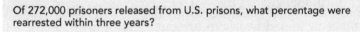

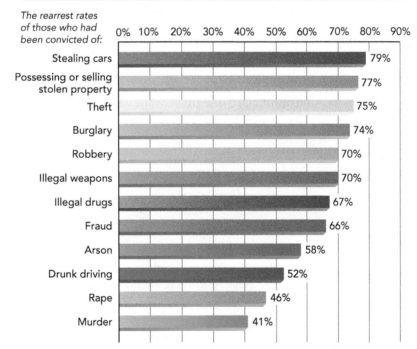

Note: The individuals were not necessarily rearrested for the same crime for which they had originally been imprisoned.

Source: By the author. Based on _Sourcebook of Criminal Justice Statistics_ 2003:Table 6.50.

—Henslin, James M., _Sociology: A Down-to-Earth Approach,_ 11th ed., p. 10.

_____ **a.** Convicted criminals should receive longer prison sentences.

_____ **b.** Criminals who commit property crimes like stealing cars and burglary are more likely to get caught.

_____ **c.** There is too much crime in the United States.

_____ **d.** Prisons do not rehabilitate criminals and change their behavior.

LO5 Step 4: Analyze the Argument for Bias

In Step 1, you learned to identify the author's claim and supports. In Step 2, you learned to make sure the supports are relevant to the claim. In Step 3, you learned to avoid false inferences and identify valid claims based on adequate supports. Again, the skills you use to make sound inferences help you determine whether an argument is valid. In Step 4, you must also check for the author's bias for or against the topic. Authors may use emotionally slanted language or biased words to present either a favorable or a negative view of the topic under debate. In addition, authors may include only the details that favor the stances they have taken. A valid argument relies on objective, factual details. As you evaluate the argument for the author's bias, ask the following questions:

- Does the author provide mostly positive or negative supports?
- Does the author provide mostly factual details or rely on biased language?
- Does the writer include or omit opposing views?

> **EXAMPLE** Read the paragraph. Then answer the questions.

The Immorality of Using Animals in Medical Research

¹Animals should not be used in medical research. ²The lives of hundreds of thousands of mice, rabbits, birds, dogs, cats, horses, and pigs, among others, have been sacrificed in the quest to save human lives. ³Hundreds of thousands more have suffered the pain and distress of being infected with diseases, blinded with chemicals, electrically shocked, or injected with drugs, all for the sake of improving the longevity and quality of human life. ⁴The basic premise that humans are superior life forms falls short when one considers that animals are used in these horrific experiments because they possess enough physiological similarities

to humans to make the research findings worthwhile for humans. [5]For example, much of what is known about the human immune system came from studies with mice, and understandings about the human cardio-vascular system came from studies with dogs. [6]Even if humans believe themselves more worthy because they are self-aware creatures capable of reasoning, able to establish complex social orders, and gifted with written language, humans prove themselves to be mere animals when they inflict pain upon defenseless fellow creatures for personal gain, in an instinctive grapple for "survival of the fittest." [7]Non-human animals are sentient beings, capable of intense suffering. [8]This fact alone makes the cost they pay too high—and human morals too low.

_____ **1.** Overall, the passage relies on
     a. factual details.   b. emotionally slanted language.

_____ **2.** Which of the following sentences includes an opposing view?
     a. sentence 5   c. sentence 7
     b. sentence 6   d. sentence 8

_____ **3.** In this passage, the author expressed a biased attitude
     a. in favor of using animals in medical research.
     b. in favor of finding alternatives to using animals in medical research.
     c. against the belief that humans are a superior life form.
     d. against the belief that animals are capable of suffering.

EXPLANATION

1. Although the author uses emotionally slanted words occasionally, overall, the passage relies on (a) factual details that can be verified through research. Some of the biased words are _should not, sacrificed, horrific, mere, defenseless,_ and _grapple._

2. (b) Sentence 6 refers to the opposing view that humans are superior to other animals and thus their lives are more worthy of saving. The sentence even lists a few of the reasons the opposition holds this belief.

3. In this passage, the author expresses a bias (c) against the belief that humans are a superior life form by emphasizing the human willingness to inflict pain and suffering on other creatures.

Practice 5

Read the paragraph. Then answer the questions.

School Uniforms Benefit Students

[1]School uniforms should be mandatory in all public schools. [2]Uniforms promote school spirit and school values by establishing a group identity and making students feel as if they are part of a team. [3]School uniforms promote modesty and eliminate the distraction of sexually provocative clothing. [4]They contribute to the sense that school is a place of order and work, as well as foster a respect for authority. [5]In such an environment, students are likely to approach learning more seriously. [6]School uniforms also minimize cliques based on socioeconomic differences; they increase attendance and reduce dropout rates. [7]In addition, school uniforms increase student safety in several ways. [8]Gang- and drug-related activity decline; students are less likely to bring weapons to school undetected; and teachers and administrators are more able to distinguish their students from outsiders. [9]For those who cannot afford uniforms or oppose uniforms on the basis of legitimate religious or philosophical beliefs, an "opt-out" policy should be in place so that students with the support of their families can apply for exemptions.

_____ **1.** Overall, the passage offers supports that are
      a. mainly positive.   b. mainly negative.

_____ **2.** Which of the following sentences refers to an opposing view?
      a. sentence 6   c. sentence 8
      b. sentence 7   d. sentence 9

_____ **3.** In this passage, the author expressed a biased attitude
      a. in favor of individual competition.
      b. in favor of freedom of expression.
      c. against the "opt-out" policy.
      d. against cliques based on socioeconomic differences.

LO6 Develop Textbook Skills: The Logic of Argument in Textbooks

Textbook Skills

Most of the subjects you will study in college rely on research by experts, and these experts may have differing views on the same topic. Often textbooks spell out these arguments. Sometimes textbook authors will present several experts' views. But occasionally, only one view will be given. In this case, be aware that there may be other sides to the story.

Textbook arguments are usually well developed with supports that are relevant and adequate. These supports may be studies, surveys, expert opinions, experiments, theories, examples, or reasons. Textbooks may also offer graphs, charts, and photos as supports. A master reader tests passages in textbooks for the logic of the arguments they present. The exercise that follows is designed to give you practice evaluating the logic of arguments in textbooks.

Practice 6

Read the following passage from a college environmental studies textbook and study the graphic that accompanies it. Mark each statement in the passage **C** if it is an author's claim or **S** if it provides support for a claim. (**_Hint:_** Three sentences contain both a claim and evidence that supports the claim. Mark those sentences **C/S**.) Then write a sentence that states a logical conclusion that can be drawn from the graphic about fuel usage.

Responding to Climate Change

[1]Today, most of the world's people recognize that our fossil fuel consumption is altering the planet that our children will inherit. [2]From this point onward, our society will be focusing on the difficult question of how

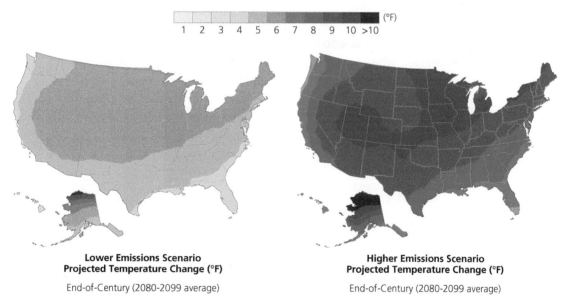

Lower Emissions Scenario
Projected Temperature Change (°F)

End-of-Century (2080-2099 average)

Higher Emissions Scenario
Projected Temperature Change (°F)

End-of-Century (2080-2099 average)

FIGURE 14.17 ▲ Average temperatures across the United States are predicted to rise by 4–6 °F by the end of this century under a low-emissions scenario, and 7–11 °F under a high-emissions scenario. Data from Karl, T.R., et al., eds., 2009. _Global climate change impacts in the United States._ U.S. Global Change Research Program and Cambridge University Press.

best to respond to the challenges of climate change. [3]The good news is that everyone—not just leaders in government and business, but everyday people, and especially today's youth—can play a part in this all-important search for solutions.

[4]We can respond to climate change in two fundamental ways. [5]One is to pursue actions that reduce greenhouse gas emissions, so as to lessen the severity of climate change. [6]This strategy is called *mitigation* because the aim is to mitigate, or alleviate, the problem. [7]Examples include improving energy efficiency, switching to clean and renewable energy sources, preventing deforestation, recovering landfill gas, and encouraging farm practices that protect soil quality.

[8]Alternatively, we can pursue strategies to cushion ourselves from the impacts of climate change. [9]This strategy is called *adaptation* because the goal is to adapt to change.

[10]Erecting a seawall like the Maldives' Great Wall of Mal is one example of adaptation. [11]Other examples include restricting coastal development; adjusting farming practices to cope with drought; and modifying water management practices to deal with reduced river flows, glacial outburst floods, or salt contamination of groundwater.

[12]We need to pursue adaptation because even if we could halt all our emissions right now, the greenhouse gas pollution already in the atmosphere would continue driving global warming until the planet's systems reach a new equilibrium, with temperature rising an estimated 0.6°C (1.0°F) more by the end of the century. [13]Because we will face this change no matter what we do, it will be wise to develop ways to minimize its impacts. [14]We also need to pursue mitigation, because if we do nothing to diminish climate change, it will eventually overwhelm any efforts we might make to adapt. [15]The sooner we begin reducing our emissions, the lower the level at which they will peak, and the less we will alter climate.

—Withgott, Jay H. and Laposata, Matthew, *Essential Environment: The Science Behind the Stories*, 4th ed., pp. 315–317.

_____   **1.** sentence 1

_____   **2.** sentence 2

_____   **3.** sentence 3

_____   **4.** sentence 4

_____   **5.** sentence 5

_____   **6.** sentence 6

_____ **7.** sentence 7

_____ **8.** sentence 8

_____ **9.** sentence 9

_____ **10.** sentence 10

_____ **11.** sentence 12

_____ **12.** sentence 13

_____ **13.** sentence 14

_____ **14.** sentence 15

15. _____

_____

Apply Information Literacy Skills

 ## Academic, Personal, and Career Applications of the Basics of Argument

Learning the basics of argument is an important information literacy skill. In every area of your life, you make and hear claims that may or may not be based on solid evidence. In your academic life, you sharpen your thinking skills as you examine the logic of, and seek evidence for, the specific claims in content courses. For example, historians may offer opposing views on the purpose of the United States' role in Afghanistan. Different news journals will report stories with varying viewpoints and supporting details. In your personal life, you need to determine which claims are valid as you weigh important decisions—from deciding who to vote for to everyday issues such as finding child care, choosing products to purchase, or selecting investments to make. In your career life, you will seek information to test claims raised by supervisors, coworkers, or customers. Thus, you will use the skills that you have learned in this chapter in academic, personal, and career situations.

- Recognize your own need to make or evaluate a claim.
- Determine if a claim is supported by sound evidence.
- Support or reject a claim based on the validity of the evidence.

Academic Application

Assume you are taking a college course in environmental studies. The following article from the Environmental Protection Agency is part of your weekly reading assignment. Your professor has given you the following question to answer based on your reading: "Why is bottled water a billion-dollar industry even though people have access to free, clean water?"

- **Before Reading:** Skim the passage. Circle the major claims about bottled water.

- **During Reading:** Underline the major supports you will use to answer the question posed by your professor.

- **After Reading:** In the space following the passage, answer the question based on your annotations.

Bottle Water Basics

Bottled water is the fastest growing drink choice in the United States. And Americans spend billions of dollars each year to buy it (Beverage Marketing Corporation, 2004). Some people drink bottled water as an alternative to other beverages. Others drink it because they prefer its taste or think it is safer than their tap water.

Drinking water (both bottled and tap) can reasonably be expected to contain at least small amounts of some contaminants. The presence of contaminants does not necessarily indicate that the water poses a health risk. For example, minerals such as magnesium and calcium give water a distinctive flavor, and are essential to the body. At high levels, however, these and other contaminants, such as pesticides or microbes from human wastes, can cause adverse effects or illness.

Bottled water is much more expensive, per gallon, than tap water. Because of this, consider whether you are buying it as a healthy alternative to bottled beverages, for its taste, or for other reasons.

Many people prefer bottled water because of its taste. The taste of all water has to do with the way it is treated and the quality of its source, including its natural mineral content. Most bottled water comes from a ground water source, where water quality varies less from day to day, or is treated and immediately bottled. Bottled water from a dedicated source or plant may have a more consistent taste than tap water, which mostly comes from surface sources and must travel through pipes to reach homes.

Ground water is typically less vulnerable to contamination than water from surface sources. However, ground water can still contain naturally high amounts of certain contaminants. These may include radioactive elements, arsenic, and nitrates, or may be vulnerable to contamination from human activities, such as industrial waste, faulty septic systems, and underground gas or chemical tanks.

One of the key taste differences between tap water and bottled water is due to how the water is disinfected. Tap water may be disinfected with chlorine, chloramine, ozone, or ultraviolet light to kill disease-causing germs. Water systems use the disinfectants chlorine and chloramine because they are effective and inexpensive, and they continue to disinfect as water travels through pipes to homes and businesses. Bottled water that is disinfected is typically disinfected using ozone or other technologies such as ultraviolet light or chlorine dioxide. Ozone is preferred by bottlers, though it is more expensive than chlorine, because it does not leave a taste and because bottlers do not need to worry about maintaining disinfectant in water sealed in a container. Untreated water, whether from a bottle or from a tap, will have the characteristic taste of its source.

—Adapted from *Bottle Water Basics*. Environmental
Protection Agency.

Why is bottled water a billion-dollar industry even though people have access

to free, clean water? _____

_____

Personal Application

Assume a member of your household has decided to purchase a firearm and plans to keep it in your home. This decision has raised your awareness about the gun control debate. You have been researching the issue to determine your own stand. You have come across the following advertisement sponsored by a anti-gun control group called Freedom Fighters.

- **Before Reading:** Skim the advertisement. Write at least one question you need answered to determine your response to the claim and supports of this argument.

- **During Reading:** Underline the facts that support the claim. Circle the opinions given in support of the claim.

■ **After Reading:** In the space following the advertisement, record the main claim of the advertisement and answer the questions about the argument.

Before reading questions: _____

_____

_____

_____

MORE GUNS, LESS CRIME!

" A free people ought. . . to be armed. . . " George Washington (Speech of January 7, 1790 in the Boston Independent Chronicle, January 14, 1790)

- The United States has the most highly armed civilian population.
- United States ranks 24th in the world in terms of its murder rate.
- States that allow law-abiding citizens to carry concealed handguns have a 60% decrease in multiple-victim public shootings and a 78% decrease in victims per attack.
- The Constitution of the United States guarantees citizens the right to own guns!

After reading evaluation of advertisement:

Claim: _____

_____

Are the supports for the argument mostly fact or opinion? Explain. _____

_____

_____

_____

Are the supports for the argument adequate? Explain. _____

_____

_____

Career Application

Assume you are a supervisor of a local credit union. One of your employees who has a disability has made a claim that he does not have access to reasonable accommodation. To evaluate the claim, you have researched the Americans with Disabilities Act (ADA) on The U.S. Equal Employment Opportunity Commission's website as a resource.

- **Before Reading:** Skim the Americans with Disabilities Act, as amended. Then skim the incident report.
- **During Reading:** Underline key details in the ADA that you can use to evaluate the incident report. Put question marks by the details in the report that raise questions. Double underline details in the report that refute the employee's claim or supports that argue that reasonable accommodation would cause undue hardship on the business.
- **After Reading:** In the space following the passage, record your conclusion about the incident report.

The Americans with Disabilities Act, as amended

The ADA prohibits discrimination on the basis of disability in all employment practices. It is necessary to understand several important ADA definitions to know who is protected by the law and what constitutes illegal discrimination:

Individual with a Disability

An individual with a disability under the ADA is a person who has a physical or mental impairment that substantially limits one or more major life activities, has a record of such impairment, or is regarded as having a disability. An entity subject to the ADA regards someone as having a disability when it takes an action prohibited by the ADA based on an actual or perceived impairment, except if the impairment is both transitory (lasting or expected to last six months or less) and minor. Major life activities are basic activities that most people in the general population can perform with little or no difficulty such as walking, breathing, seeing, hearing, speaking, learning, thinking, and eating. Major life activities also include the operation of a major bodily function, such as functions of the immune system normal cell growth, brain, neurological, and endocrine functions.

"Qualified"

An individual with a disability is "qualified" if he or she satisfies skill, experience, education, and other job-related requirements of the position held or desired, and who, with or without reasonable accommodation, can perform the essential functions of that position.

Reasonable Accommodation

Reasonable accommodation may include, but is not limited to, making existing facilities used by employees readily accessible to and usable by persons with disabilities; job restructuring; modification of work schedules; providing additional unpaid leave; reassignment to a vacant position; acquiring or modifying equipment or devices; adjusting or modifying examinations, training materials, or policies; and providing qualified readers or interpreters. Reasonable accommodation may be necessary to apply for a job, to perform job functions, or to enjoy the benefits and privileges of employment that are enjoyed by people without disabilities. An employer is not required to lower production standards to make an accommodation. An employer generally is not obligated to provide personal use items such as eyeglasses or hearing aids. A person who only meets the "regarded as" definition of disability is not entitled to receive a reasonable accommodation.

Undue Hardship

An employer is required to make a reasonable accommodation to a qualified individual with a disability unless doing so would impose an undue hardship on the operation of the employer's business. Undue hardship means an action that requires significant difficulty or expense when considered in relation to factors such as a business' size, financial resources, and the nature and structure of its operation.

—Adapted from The U.S. Equal Employment Opportunity Commission. "Federal Laws Prohibiting Job Discrimination Questions And Answers."

Incident Report Form

Background Information

Employee Name: _____   **Date of Incident:** _____

Supervisor: _____   **Location:** _____

Type of Discrimination or Harassment: ___Age ___x___Disability ___Gender

___Marital Status ___National Origin ___Physical Attribute ___Race ___Sexual

Claim: The employee claims that only one of the two entrances/exits to the credit union is accessible by wheelchair. The door that has the wheelchair ramp is located at the front entrance of the store, which is not connected to the parking lot in the back where the employees are required to park. This makes it difficult for the employee to enter the building from the parking where he is required to park. Although there is an adequate sidewalk that connects the rear parking lot to the front entrance with the ramp, the employee claims that this is not reasonable to use during times of severe weather. The employee suggests building another ramp at the rear entrance of the credit union. However, an initial survey of the space for building an additional ramp at the rear entrance indicates the building will require larger renovations. This will be a significant expense that the company will not recoup.

Response/Recommendation to Harassment Incident Report: _____

_____

_____

_____

_____

REVIEW TEST 1

Score (number correct) _____ × 10 = _____ %

Visit MyReadingLab to take this test online and receive feedback and guidance on your answers.

Argument

A. Study the following mock advertisement. Then study the claim and supports based on it. Mark each support **R** if it is relevant to the claim or **N** if it is not relevant to the claim. Then answer the questions.

JUST SAY, "NO THANKS!"

- In 1999, 61% of adults in the United States were overweight or obese.

- Approximately 300,000 deaths each year in the United States may be attributable to obesity.

- Overweight and obesity are associated with heart disease, certain types of cancer, type 2 diabetes, stroke, arthritis, breathing problems, and psychological disorders, such as depression.

- Choose a diet that is low in saturated fat and cholesterol and moderate in total fat.

- Exercise three times a week for 30 minutes.

—Data from "Fact Sheet: What You Can Do," Overweight and Obesity.
United States Office of the Surgeon General, 11 Jan. 07.

Claim: The health risks associated with obesity can be reduced by diet choices.
Supports:

_____ **1.** In 1999, 61% of adults in the United States were overweight or obese.

_____ **2.** A meal consisting of a cheeseburger, French fries, and soda is high in saturated fat, total fat, and cholesterol.

_____ **3.** Overweight and obesity are associated with heart disease, certain types of cancer, type 2 diabetes, stroke, arthritis, breathing problems, and psychological disorders, such as depression.

_____ **4.** Exercise helps reduce obesity.

_____ **5.** Overall, the relevant supports are
    a. statements of factual details.
    b. statements using biased language.

B. Read the following group of ideas from a government website. Mark each statement **C** if it is an author's claim or **S** if it provides support for the claim.

_____   **6.** One small chocolate chip cookie (50 calories) is equivalent to walking briskly for 10 minutes.

_____   **7.** The difference between a large gourmet chocolate chip cookie and a small chocolate chip cookie could be about 40 minutes of raking leaves (200 calories).

_____   **8.** One hour of walking at a moderate pace (20 min/mile) uses about the same amount of energy that is in one jelly-filled doughnut (300 calories).

_____   **9.** A fast-food meal containing a double-patty cheeseburger, extra-large fries, and a 24 oz. soft drink is equal to running $2^1/_2$ hours at a 10 min/mile pace (1,500 calories).

_____   **10.** Food intake should be balanced with activity.

"Overweight and Obesity: What You Can Do," United States Office of the Surgeon General, 11 Jan. 07.

REVIEW TEST 2

Score (number correct) _____ × 20 = _____ %

Visit MyReadingLab to take this test online and receive feedback and guidance on your answers.

Argument

Read the following passage and then answer the questions.

Study Examines Spanking Among Minnesota Parents

[1]Parents can effectively replace physical punishment with different methods of discipline. [2]When parents use nurturing and teaching methods instead of spanking, their children become less aggressive and violent. [3]Those are the findings of an 8-year study led by the University of Minnesota's Extension Service in Goodhue County. [4]Researchers followed 1,000 parents of children younger than 13 to learn about their attitudes toward spanking.

[5]"If you hit your children, it will be very difficult to teach them not to hit others because they have experienced it from the most important person in their lives," said retired sociologist Ron Pitzer, who led the study.

[6]During the study, a public awareness and educational campaign called "Kids: Handle with Care" sent the message to Goodhue County residents that it is never okay to spank a child. [7]The message was circulated through newspaper articles, radio programs, restaurant table tent cards, grocery bags and carts, church programs, parade floats, and a county fair exhibit.

[8]The following results were reported among Goodhue County parents at the conclusion of the study:

- [9]The use of physical punishment dropped from 36 percent to 12 percent.
- [10]Parents who spanked their children reported a sizeable increase in their children's aggressiveness.
- [11]Parents who reduced physical punishment reported their children were less aggressive.
- [12]Parents who attended classes were better at setting limits and enforcing consequences, and they were more calm and nurturing. [13]Their children were more obedient, communicated more openly, had a better attitude, and were calmer.
- [14]Fathers matched or exceeded mothers in alternative, more positive discipline methods.

[15]The findings indicate that the county-wide educational effort was successful in helping make the decision to eliminate spanking, resulting in happier parents and happier children.

—Adapted from "Study Examines Spanking Among Minnesota Parents," Children's Bureau Express, U.S. Department of Human and Health Services, Apr. 2002.

_____ **1.** Which sentence states the author's claim?
   a. sentence 1   c. sentence 4
   b. sentence 3   d. sentence 5

Mark each of the following sentences (**2–5**) **C** if it is a claim or **S** if it provides support for the claim.

_____ **2.** sentence 5

_____ **3.** sentence 6

_____ **4.** sentence 7

_____ **5.** In this passage, the author expresses a biased attitude
   a. in favor of spanking children as a form of punishment.
   b. against the use of physical punishment as a form of discipline.

VISUAL *VOCABULARY*

An antonym for the word
nurturing is _____.

   a. disengaged
   b. involved
   c. needed

▶ A father who is **nurturing** has
a positive impact on his child's
development.

REVIEW TEST 3

Score (number correct) _____ × 10 = _____ %

Visit MyReadingLab to take this test online and receive feedback and guidance on your answers.

Argument

Before Reading Skim the following passage from a college psychology textbook. Answer the Before Reading questions that follow the passage. Then read
the passage. Next answer the After Reading questions. Use the discussion and
writing topics as activities to do after reading.

Vocabulary Preview

polygraph (1): a device that records, or graphs, many ("poly") measures of
   physical arousal
false positives (16): mistaken identifications of persons as having a particular
   characteristic
implicate (17): to imply a connection with wrongdoing

Do Lie Detectors Really Detect Lies?

   [1]The **polygraph** or "lie detector" test is based on the assumption
that people will display physical signs of arousal when lying; so most polygraph machines make a record of the suspect's heart rate, breathing rate,
perspiration, and blood pressure. [2]Occasionally, voice-print analysis is also

employed. [3]Thus, the device really acts as an emotional arousal detector rather than a direct indicator of truth or lies. [4]But does it work?

[5]Without a doubt, wrongdoers sometimes confess when confronted with polygraph evidence against them. [6]Yet, critics have pointed out several problems with the polygraphic procedure that could easily land innocent people in prison and let the guilty walk free (Aftergood, 2000). [7]For example, polygraph subjects know when they are suspects, so some will give heightened responses to the critical questions even when they are innocent. [8]On the other hand, some people can give **deceptive** responses because they have learned to control or distort their emotional responses. [9]To do so, they may employ simple physical movements, drugs, or biofeedback training—a procedure in which people are given moment-to-moment information on certain biological responses, such as perspiration or heart rate (Saxe et al., 1985). [10]Either way, a polygraph examiner risks incorrectly identifying innocent people as guilty and failing to spot the liars.

[11]Important statistical issues call the polygraph procedure into further question. [12]Even if the examination were 95 percent accurate, a 5 percent error rate could lead to the misidentification of many innocent people as being guilty. [13]To illustrate, imagine that your company arranges for all 500 of your employees to take a polygraph test to find out who has been stealing office supplies. [14]Imagine also that only about 4 percent (20 out of 500 people) are really stealing, which is not an unreasonable estimate. [15]If the lie detector test is 95 percent accurate, it will correctly spot 19 of these 20 thieves. [16]But the test will also give 5 percent **false positives**, falsely fingering 5 percent of the innocent people. [17]Of the 480 innocent employees, the polygraph will inaccurately **implicate** 24 as liars. [18]That is, you could end up with more people falsely accused of lying than people correctly accused of lying. [19]This was borne out in a field study of suspected criminals who were later either convicted or declared innocent. [20]The polygraph results were no better than a random coin flip (Brett et al., 1986).

[21]An equally serious concern with polygraphy is that there are no generally accepted standards either for administering a polygraph examination or for interpreting its results. [22]Different examiners could conceivably come to different conclusions based on the same polygraph record. [23]For these reasons, the U.S. Congress has outlawed most uses of polygraph tests in job screening and in most areas of the government, except for high-security-risk positions. [24]National Academies of Science (2003) has gone even further in a report saying that the polygraph is too crude to be useful for screening people to identify possible terrorists or other national security risks.

^{25}As far as criminal investigations are concerned, we find a patchwork of laws on the admissibility of polygraph evidence among the states. ^{26}Few have gone so far as imposing complete bans and 20 more allow such evidence only on agreement of both sides—although, in a few states, polygraph results are still routinely admissible in court (Gruben & Madsen, 2005).

—Adapted from Zimbardo, Philip G., Johnson, Robert L., and Hamilton, Vivian McCann, *Psychology: Core Concepts,* 7th ed., pp. 405–406.

Before Reading

Vocabulary in Context

_____ **1.** Based on the context of the passage, what is the best meaning of the word **deceptive** (sentence 8)?
a. useful   c. false
b. emotional   d. understandable

Tone and Purpose

_____ **2.** The overall tone of the passage is
a. objective.   b. biased.

_____ **3.** The primary purpose of the passage is to
a. inform.   c. persuade.
b. entertain.

After Reading

Central Idea and Main Idea

_____ **4.** Which sentence best states the implied central idea of the passage?
a. The polygraph assumes that people display physical signs of arousal when lying.
b. People who lie may still pass a polygraph test.
c. Better guidelines are needed for polygraph use.
d. The polygraph should not be considered or used as a lie detector.

Supporting Details

_____ **5.** In the third paragraph (sentences 11–20), sentence 11 states a
a. main idea.   c. minor supporting detail.
b. major supporting detail.

Transitions

_____ **6.** The relationship of ideas within sentence 7 is
a. time order.   c. comparison.
b. listing.   d. cause and effect.

Thought Patterns

_____ **7.** The overall thought pattern of the passage is
a. time order.   c. comparison.
b. listing.   d. cause and effect.

Fact and Opinion

_____ **8.** Sentence 23 is a statement of
a. fact.   c. fact and opinion.
b. opinion.

Inferences

_____ **9.** Based on the information in the passage, the reader can infer that
a. there is no relation between emotional arousal and lying.
b. many companies use polygraphs to help stop office theft.
c. a lie detector less than 100% accurate will falsely accuse some people of lying.
d. there is a need for better-trained polygraph examiners.

Argument

_____ **10.** Which sentence is not relevant to the authors' claim?
a. sentence 2   c. sentence 12
b. sentence 6   d. sentence 21

SUMMARY RESPONSE

Restate the author's claim in your own words. In your summary, state the author's tone and purpose. Begin your summary response with the following: *The central idea of "Do Lie Detectors Really Detect Lies?" by Zimbardo, Johnson, and McCann is . . .*

WHAT DO YOU THINK?

Assume you live in a state where polygraph results are allowed, but the legislature is considering outlawing them. Write a letter to a state legislator stating your position on whether to continue allowing them or to ban them. Consider the following in points in your argument:

- Is the argument to outlaw polygraph results valid?
- Does the fact that a "lie detector" test can sometimes make a guilty person confess to his or her crime justify its use?

REVIEW TEST 4

Score (number correct) _____ × 10 = _____ %

Visit MyReadingLab to take this test online and receive feedback and guidance on your answers.

Argument

Textbook Skills

Skim the following passage adapted from a college textbook about world civilizations. Answer the Before Reading questions that follow the passage. Then read the passage. Next, answer the After Reading questions.

Vocabulary Preview

migratory (4): moving, traveling
ecological (6): natural, environmental
imperialism (6): government or authority of an empire
immunities (7): protections

The Great Exchange

[1]The arrival of the Spaniards and the Portuguese in the Americas began one of the most extensive and profound changes in the history of humankind. [2]The New World, which had existed in isolation since the end of the last ice age, was now brought into continual contact with the Old World. [3]The peoples and cultures of Europe and Africa came to the Americas through voluntary or forced immigration. [4]Between 1500 and 1850, perhaps 10 to 15 million Africans and 5 million Europeans crossed the Atlantic and settled in the Americas as part of the great **migratory** movement. [5]Contact also initiated a broader biological and ecological exchange that changed the face of both the Old World and the New World—the way people lived, what they ate, and how they died, indeed how many people there were in different regions—as the animals, plants, and diseases of the two hemispheres were transferred.

[6]It was historian Alfred Crosby who first called this process the *Columbian exchange*, and he has pointed out its profound effects as the

first stage of the "**ecological imperialism**" that accompanied the expansion of the West. [7]Long separated from the populations of the Old World and lacking **immunities** to diseases such as measles and smallpox, populations throughout the Americas suffered disastrous losses after initial contact. [8]Throughout North America, contact with Europeans and Africans resulted in epidemics that devastated the **indigenous** populations.

[9]Disease may have also moved in the other direction. [10]Some authorities believe that syphilis had an American origin and was brought to Europe only after 1492. [11]In general, however, forms of life in the Old World—diseases, plants, and animals—were more complex than those in the Americas and thus displaced the New World varieties in open competition. [12]The diseases of Eurasia and Africa had a greater impact on America than American diseases had on the Old World.

[13]With animals also, the major exchange was from the Old World to the New World. [14]Native Americans had domesticated dogs, guinea pigs, some fowl, and llamas, but in general domesticated animals were far less important in the Americas than in the Old World. [15]In the first years of settlement in the Caribbean, the Spanish introduced horses, cattle, sheep, chickens, and domestic goats and pigs, all of which were considered essential for civilized life as the Iberians understood it. [16]Some of these animals thrived in the New World. [17]For example, a hundred head of cattle abandoned by the Spanish in the Rio de la Plata area in 1587 had become 100,000 head 20 years later.

[18]In the exchange of foods, the contribution of America probably outweighed that of Europe, however. [19]New World plants such as tomatoes, squash, sweet potatoes, types of beans, and peppers, became essential foods in Europe. [20]Tobacco and cacao, or chocolate, both American in origin, became widely distributed throughout the world.

[21]Even more important were the basic crops such as potato, maize, and manioc, all of which yielded more calories per acre than all the Old World grains, except rice. [22]The high yield of calories per acre of maize and potatoes had supported the high population densities of the American civilizations. [23]After the Columbian voyages, these foods began to produce similar effects in the rest of the world. [24]After 1750, the world population experienced a dramatic rise. [25]The reasons were many, but the contribution of the American foodstuff was a central one.

—Adapted from Stearns, Peter N., Adas, Michael B., Schwartz, Stuart B., and Gilbert, Marc Jason, *World Civilizations: The Global Experience Combined Volume, Atlas Edition*, 5th ed., p. 526.

Before Reading

Vocabulary in Context

Use context clues to state in your own words the definition of the following term. Indicate the context clue you used.

1. In sentence 8, what does the word **indigenous** mean?

_____

2. Identify the context clue used for the word **indigenous** in sentence 8.

_____

Tone and Purpose

_____ **3.** What is the overall tone and purpose of the passage?
  a. to inform the reader about the impact of the Columbian exchange
  b. to persuade the reader that the Columbian exchange benefited America more than Europe
  c. to engage the reader with little known facts about early American history

After Reading

Central Idea

4. Use your own words to state the central idea of the passage: _____

_____

_____

Main Idea and Supporting Details

_____ **5.** Sentence 17 states a
  a. main idea.   c. minor supporting detail.
  b. major supporting detail.

Transitions

_____ **6.** The relationship between sentences 8 and 9 is
  a. cause and effect.   c. time order.
  b. addition.   d. contrast.

Thought Patterns

_____ **7.** The overall thought pattern of the passage is
   a. cause and effect.   c. time order.
   b. listing.   d. contrast.

Fact and Opinion

_____ **8.** Sentence 1 is a statement of
   a. fact.   c. fact and opinion.
   b. opinion.

Inferences

_____ **9.** Based on the context of the information in the second paragraph (sentences 6–8), the term "ecological imperialism" in sentence 6 implies that
   a. natural resources exchanged between America and Europe dramatically changed the natural environments of both regions.
   b. Europe damaged the natural resources of America.
   c. the immigration of Europeans brought diseases and caused epidemics that weakened the resistance of native peoples to European control.

Argument

_____ **10.** The following list of statements contains one claim and several supports from the third paragraph (sentences 9–12). Identify the support that is **not** relevant to the claim.
   a. Disease may have also moved in the other direction (from America to the Old World).
   b. Some authorities believe that syphilis had an American origin and was brought to Europe only after 1492.
   c. The diseases of Eurasia and Africa had a greater impact on America than American diseases had on the Old World.

SUMMARY RESPONSE

Restate the author's claim in your own words. In your summary, state the author's tone and purpose. Begin your summary response with the following: _The central idea of "The Great Exchange" by Stearns, Adas, Schwartz, and Gilbert is . . ._

WHAT DO YOU THINK?

Assume you are taking a college course in world civilizations. Your professor has assigned the following essay: Take a stand in support of or in opposition to the following claim by the Office of the United States Trade Representative: "American families benefit from trade and open markets every day. Trade delivers a greater choice of goods—everything from food and furniture to computers and cars—at lower prices." Offer examples to support your stance.

Consider the following points in your argument:

- Is the claim valid?
- How do American families benefit from free trade and open markets?
- What is the alternative to free trade and open markets?

After Reading About the Basics of Argument

Before you move on to the Mastery Tests on the basics of argument, take time to reflect on your learning and performance by answering the following questions. Write your answers in your notebook.

- How has my knowledge base or prior knowledge about the basics of argument changed?
- Based on my studies, how do I think I will perform on the Mastery Test(s)? Why do I think my scores will be above average, average, or below average? (Note: An additional fourth Mastery Test may be found in MyReadingLab.)
- Would I recommend this chapter to other students who want to learn more about the basics of argument? Why or why not?

Test your understanding of what you have learned about the basics of argument by completing the Chapter 12 Review.

Name _____ Section _____

Date _____ **Score** (number correct) _____ × 20 = _____%

Visit MyReadingLab to take this test online and receive feedback and guidance on your answers.

Read the following passage and examine the graphic in this excerpt from a college sociology textbook. Then answer the questions.

Who Smokes, and Why?

Textbook Skills

[1]Nicotine use—with its creeping side effects of emphysema and cancer—kills about 400,000 Americans each year (Centers for Disease Control and Prevention 2011). [2]This is the equivalent of five fully loaded, 200-passenger jets with full crews crashing each and every day—leaving no survivors. [3]Who in their right mind would take the risk that their plane will not be among those that crash? [4]Yet this is the risk that smokers take.

[5]Nicotine is, by far, the most lethal of all recreational drugs. [6]Smoking causes cancer of the bladder, cervix, esophagus, kidneys, larynx, lungs, and other body organs. [7]Smokers are more likely to have heart attacks and strokes, and even to come down with cataracts and pneumonia (Surgeon General 2005; Centers for Disease Control and Prevention 2010c). [8]The list of health problems related to smoking goes on and on.

[9]Then there is secondhand smoke, which is estimated to kill 45,000 nonsmokers a year (Surgeon General 2006; Centers for Disease Control and Prevention 2010d). [10]This is the equivalent of another fully loaded jet going down every two days. [11]An antismoking campaign that stresses tobacco's health hazards has been so successful that smoking is banned on public transportation and in most offices, restaurants, and, in some states, even bars.

[12]Millions of Americans wouldn't think of flying if they knew that even one jet were going to crash—yet they continue to smoke. [13]Why? [14]The two major reasons are addiction and advertising. [15]Nicotine may be as addictive as heroin (Tolchin 1988).

[16]The second reason is advertising. [17]Cigarette ads were banned from television and radio in 1970, but cigarettes continue to be advertised in newspapers and magazines and on billboards. [18]Cigarette companies spend huge amounts to encourage Americans to smoke—about $12 billion a year. [19]This comes to $43 for every man, woman, and child in the entire country (Centers for Disease Control 2010c).

—Henslin, James M., *Sociology: A Down-to-Earth Approach*, 11th ed., p. 557.

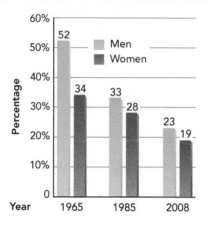

Figure 19.11 Who Is Still Smoking?

The Percentage of Americans Age 18 and over Who Smoke Cigarettes

Source: By the author. Based on *Statistical Abstract of the United States* 2011:Table 200, and earlier years.

_____ **1.** Which of the following sentences is a claim that is adequately supported by the details?

   a. sentence 1   c. sentence 5

   b. sentence 2   d. sentence 12

_____ **2.** Which of the following is a logical conclusion based on the details in the passage?

   a. There will always be people who smoke.

   b. Nicotine is the most dangerous substance people take in.

   c. People are more afraid of dying in a plane crash than of cancer caused by nicotine.

   d. People are swayed by both anti- and pro-smoking arguments.

3–5. Based on the information in the graphic, place an **X** by the three statements that assert logical conclusions.

_____ Smoking has decreased in general by about half.

_____ Women find quitting smoking harder than men.

_____ The anti-smoking campaign has had even more success with men than with women.

_____ The rate of smoking will continue to decrease.

_____ Most men used to smoke.

Name _____ Section _____

Date _____ **Score** (number correct) _____ × 20 = _____%

Visit MyReadingLab to take this test online and receive feedback and guidance on your answers.

Read the following passage from a college history textbook and then answer the questions.

Is There a Right to Privacy?

Textbook
Skills

[1]Nowhere does the Bill of Rights say that Americans have a right to privacy. [2]Clearly, however, the First Congress had the concept of privacy in mind when it created the first 10 amendments. [3]For example, freedom of religion implies the right to exercise private beliefs, and protections against "unreasonable searches and seizures" make persons secure in their homes. [4]In addition, private property cannot be seized without "due process of law." [5]In 1928, Justice Brandeis hailed privacy as "the right to be left alone—the most comprehensive of the rights and the most valued by civilized men."

[6]The idea that the Constitution guarantees a right to privacy was first expressed in a 1965 case involving the conviction of a doctor and family planning specialist for disseminating birth control devices in violation of a little-used Connecticut law. [7]The state reluctantly brought them to court. [8]They were convicted. [9]After wrestling with the privacy issue in *Griswold* v. *Connecticut*, seven Supreme Court justices finally decided that various portions of the Bill of Rights cast "penumbras" (or shadows), unstated liberties implied by the stated rights. [10]These protected a right to privacy, including a right to family planning between husband and wife. [11]Supporters of privacy rights argued that this ruling was a reasonable interpretation of the Fourth Amendment. [12]There were many critics of the ruling. [13]They claimed that the Supreme Court was inventing protections not specified by the Constitution.

[14]The most important application of the privacy rights, however, came not in the area of birth control but in the area of abortion. [15]The Supreme Court unleashed a constitutional firestorm in 1973 that has not yet abated.

—Edwards, George C. III, Wattenberg, Martin P., and Lineberry, Robert L., *Government in America: People, Politics, and Policy*, 5th ed., Brief Version p. 103.

_____ **1.** The claim of the entire passage is stated in
    a. sentence 1.   c. sentence 3.
    b. sentence 2.   d. sentence 15.

_____ **2.** The claim of the second paragraph is stated in
    a. sentence 6.   c. sentence 9.
    b. sentence 11.   d. sentence 13.

_____ **3.** In the first paragraph, sentence 4 states
    a. a detail that is relevant.
    b. a detail that is not relevant.

_____ **4.** In the second paragraph, sentence 7 states
    a. a detail that is relevant.
    b. a detail that is not relevant.

_____ **5.** In the second paragraph, sentence 12 states
    a. a detail that is relevant.
    b. a detail that is not relevant.

VISUAL *VOCABULARY*

Which is the best synonym for
disseminated? _____

a. blown
b. gathered
c. spread

▶ Upon maturation, the dandelion turns into the well-known puffball containing seeds that are **disseminated** by the wind.

Name _____ Section _____

Date _____ **Score** (number correct) _____ × 20 = _____%

Visit MyReadingLab to take this test online and receive feedback and guidance on your answers.

Read the following passage adapted from a college humanities textbook. Then answer the questions.

Transcending Self-Interest: Altruism

Textbook Skills

[1]It is hard to deny that self-interest is sometimes necessary. [2]Can there be a place for altruism, or a greater concern for the welfare of others than for oneself? [3]Some say no, arguing that even if reason in the Socratic sense requires us to place others before ourselves, what appears to be an altruistic or selfless act really springs from secretly selfish motives.

[4]To be sure, many examples of altruistic deeds require no questioning of motives, as when a firefighter loses his life in a daring rescue attempt, or in a case involving a random shooting at an elementary school when a teacher shields the body of a child and receives a fatal bullet. [5]In such instances, the cynics are quiet, later observing that the number of people willing to die for others is trivially small. [6]The deaths of three hundred firefighters in the disaster of September 11, 2001, may have changed the attitude of many such cynics. [7]Nor can we ever know how many of the thousands who perished did so because they stayed to help others.

[8]In the everyday world, altruism does exist: donating an organ to save a stranger's life, or diving into the sea to try to save someone in distress. [9]During the insurgencies in the Sudan, when millions of innocent women, men, and children were slaughtered in acts of "ethnic cleansing," Doctors Without Borders, humanitarian medical personnel, worked tirelessly to save as many lives as they could, even though they faced being shot for their efforts or becoming infected with disease themselves.

[10]In the corporate world of today, where workers may become aware of defective auto parts, unsanitary food preparation, or the advertising of products they know carry a health risk, cases of altruistic whistle-blowing exist. [11]There are no easy moral victories here. [12]If nothing else, we learn from them that doing the right thing takes not only courage but the willingness to stand quite alone.

—Janaro, Richard P. and Altshuler, Thelma C., *The Art of Being Human*, 10th ed., p. 368.

_____ **1.** Sentence 4 is a statement that is
   a. a claim.
   b. a support for a claim.
   c. both a claim and support for it.

_____ **2.** Sentence 6 is a statement that is
   a. a claim.
   b. a support for a claim.
   c. both a claim and support for it.

_____ **3.** Sentence 8 is a statement that is
   a. a claim.
   b. a support for a claim.
   c. both a claim and support for it.

_____ **4.** Sentence 9 is a statement that is
   a. a claim.
   b. a support for a claim.
   c. both a claim and support for it.

_____ **5.** Sentence 10 is a statement that is
   a. a claim.
   b. a support for a claim.
   c. both a claim and support for it.

12 Summary of Key Concepts about the Basics of Argument

 Assess your comprehension of the basics of argument. Complete the question-answer study notes with information from the chapter.

What is an effective argument?	_____ _____
What two types of statements make up an argument?	(a) _____ (b) _____ _____
What is an invalid conclusion?	_____ _____
What are the four steps to analyze an argument?	(1) _____ (2) _____ (3) _____ (4) _____
What is a claim made without providing adequate support for the claim?	_____

Test Your Comprehension of the Basics of Argument

Respond to the following questions and prompts.

In your own words, explain the relationship between making an inference and

analyzing an argument. _____

_____

_____

_____

_____

 Create a valid argument. Assume you are going to create and distribute a brochure about distracted driving. You have found the following photograph to use in your brochure. Using details from the photo, write a claim and two supports that clearly support the claim.

Claim: _____

Support 1: _____

Support 2: _____

Describe how you will use what you have learned about the basics of argument in your reading process to comprehend written material in various sources such as textbooks or websites. _____

_____

_____

Summarize the two most important ideas in this chapter that will help you

improve your reading comprehension. _____

_____

_____

Advanced Argument: Persuasive Techniques

LEARNING OUTCOMES

After studying this chapter you should be able to:

LO1 Define Biased Arguments: Fallacy and Propaganda

LO2 Detect Fallacies Based on Irrelevant Arguments: *Personal Attack, Straw Man,* and *Begging the Question*

LO3 Detect Propaganda Techniques Based on Irrelevant Arguments: *Name-Calling, Testimonials, Bandwagon,* and *Plain Folks*

LO4 Detect Fallacies Based on Inadequate Arguments: *Either-Or, False Comparison,* and *False Cause*

LO5 Detect Propaganda Techniques Based on Inadequate Arguments: *Card Stacking, Transfer,* and *Glittering Generalities*

LO6 Develop Textbook Skills: Examine Biased Arguments in Textbooks

LO7 Apply Information Literacy Skills: Academic, Personal, and Career Applications of Advanced Argument: Persuasive Techniques

Before Reading About Advanced Argument

In this chapter, you will build on the concepts you studied in Chapter 12 about the basics of argument. Take a moment to review the four steps in analyzing an argument. Fill in the following blanks with each of the steps.

Step 1. _____

Step 2. _____

Step 3. _____

Step 4. _____

To help you master the material in the chapter, create a three-column chart in your notebook. In the left column copy the headings as in the example that follows. Leave enough room between each heading to fill in definitions and examples as you work through the chapter.

General definition: A fallacy is

Fallacy	Definition	Example
Personal attack		
Straw man		

General definition: Propaganda is

Propaganda technique	Definition	Example
Name-calling		
Testimonials		

LO1   Define Biased Arguments: Fallacy and Propaganda

Much of the information that we come in contact with on a daily basis is designed to influence our thoughts and behaviors. Advertisements, editorials, and political campaigns offer one-sided, biased information to sway public opinion.

This biased information is based on two types of reasoning: the use of **fallacies** in logical thought and the use of **propaganda**. A master reader identifies and understands the use of these persuasion techniques in biased arguments.

What Is a Fallacy in Logical Thought?

You have already studied logical thought in Chapter 12. Logical thought or argument is a process that includes an author's claim, relevant support, and a valid conclusion. A **fallacy** is an error in the process of logical thought. A fallacy leads to an invalid conclusion. You have also studied two general types of fallacies: irrelevant details and inadequate details. By its nature, a fallacy is not persuasive because it weakens an argument. However, fallacies are often used to convince readers to accept an author's claim. In fact, the word *fallacy* comes from a Latin word that means "to deceive" or "trick." You will learn more about irrelevant and inadequate arguments in the next sections of this chapter.

Fallacies are not to be confused with false facts. A fact, true or false, is stated without bias, and facts can be proven true or false by objective evidence. In contrast, a fallacy is an invalid inference or biased opinion about a fact or set of facts. Sometimes the word *fallacy* is used to refer to a false belief or the reasons for a false belief.

A **fallacy** is an error in logical thought.

> **EXAMPLE** Read the following sets of ideas. Mark each statement as follows:

UB for unbiased statements
B for biased arguments

_____ **1.** Henry Ford invented the automobile.

_____ **2.** Jamal had been wearing his lucky shirt during every game in which he scored a winning point, and when he didn't wear his lucky shirt, he did not score. Now he wears his lucky shirt every game without fail.

_____ **3.** Joanne lies all the time because she is incapable of telling the truth.

_____ **4.** Based on eyewitness accounts and the statement of Marji Thompson, the police report stated that Thompson had thought the car was in drive when it was actually in reverse. When she stepped on the gas, she backed into the car parked behind her, damaging her back bumper and the front bumper and hood of the other car.

_____ **5.** Four-time winner of NASCAR's Nextel Cup Championship, Jeff Gordon set new standards in the sport during the 2007 season with 6 victories, 21 top-five finishes, a record-breaking 30 top-ten finishes, and a 7.3 average finishing position with one DNF (Did Not Finish). Even though he came in second place behind Jimmie Johnson for the title during the season's Chase, Gordon has more career wins than almost all other drivers; only Richard Petty with seven wins has more victories.

EXPLANATION

1. This statement is unbiased (UB), but it is not true. The automobile was not invented by Henry Ford. The automobile evolved from inventors' efforts worldwide; the modern automobile is the result of over 100,000 patents. Ford did invent an improved assembly line.

2. This is a biased argument (B) based on a fallacy in logical thought. By not considering other reasons for his success, Jamal has identified a false cause and made an invalid inference. You will learn more about the fallacy of false cause later in this chapter.

3. This is a biased argument (B) based on a fallacy in logical thought. The statement about Joanne uses circular thinking; the statement restates the claim as its own proof. The phrase "lies all the time" is the claim, which is restated by the phrase "incapable of telling the truth." No factual evidence is given.

4. This is an unbiased statement (UB). Every detail can be verified through the police report and eyewitness accounts of the incident.

5. This is an unbiased statement (UB). This statement is factual and can be proven with eyewitness accounts and newspaper reports. ◀

Practice 1

Read the following sets of ideas. Mark each statement as follows:

> **UB** for unbiased statements
> **B** for biased arguments

_____ 1. The flea is the smallest insect.

_____ 2. Watching violent programs causes youth to become violent criminals.

_____ 3. Convicted felons should not have the right to vote because they have broken the law.

_____ 4. Cars that run on hydrogen are not dependent upon imported oil.

What Is Propaganda?

Propaganda is a means by which an idea is widely spread. The word *propaganda* comes from a Latin term that means to "propagate" or "spread." **Propaganda** is a biased argument that advances or damages a cause. Propaganda is often used in politics and advertising.

Read the following two descriptions of a mock sandwich called The Two-Fisted Bacon Burger. The first description is an advertisement for the sandwich. The second is the nutritional information for a meal that would include the sandwich and a small order of fries.

Advertisement: You're gonna love The Two-Fisted Bacon Burger! Two juicy 1/2 lb. patties fully loaded with crisp smokehouse bacon, mayo, ketchup, and thick-sliced cheddar cheese inside a fresh, soft bun. Nothing compares! Two handfuls of lip-smacking, mouth-watering pleasure. Get the combo! The Two-Fisted Bacon Burger with small fries is umm, umm, *delicious*!

Nutritional Facts:

	Calories	Calories from fat	Total fat (g)	Saturated fat (g)	Trans fat (g)	Cholesterol (mg)	Sodium (mg)	Carbs (g)	Fiber (g)	Sugar (g)	Protein (g)
The Two-Fisted Bacon Burger	1601	944	78.48	31.06	0	389	1398	18.8	.6	2	118.82
Small French Fries	271	130	14.5	3.4	3.7	0	165	31.9	3.4	0	4

The advertisement uses tone words that appeal to the senses of hunger—smell, taste, and vision—such as *two-fisted, juicy, crisp, smokehouse, thick-sliced, fresh, soft, lip-smacking, mouth-watering,* and *umm, umm, delicious.* These words are meant to tempt the customer into purchasing the sandwich. (For more about tone, see Chapter 10, "Tone and Purpose.") In contrast, the nutritional facts reveal objective data. These facts might keep someone who is concerned about a healthful diet from buying and eating this meal.

This advertisement is an example of **propaganda**. Propaganda uses fallacies to spread biased information.

> **Propaganda** is an act of persuasion that systematically spreads biased information that is designed to support or oppose a person, product, cause, or organization.

Propaganda uses a variety of techniques that are based on **emotional appeal**. If you are not aware of these techniques, you may be misled by the way information is presented and come to invalid conclusions. Understanding propaganda techniques will enable you to separate factual information from emotional appeals so that you can come to valid conclusions.

> **Emotional appeal** is the arousal of emotion to give meaning or power to an idea.

> **EXAMPLE** Read the following sets of ideas. Mark each statement as follows:

> **UB** for unbiased statements
> **B** for biased arguments

_____   1. Studies show that green tea contains antioxidants and polyphenols, as well as a wide variety of vitamins and minerals.

_____   2. A vote for Senator Manness is a vote for the worker on the job, the teacher in the classroom, the nurse in the hospital, the ordinary person trying to make ends meet.

_____   3. Certain foods, such as chocolate, nuts, and soft drinks, cause acne.

_____   4. Mueller's dried pasta is America's favorite pasta.

_____   5. Zora Neale Hurston, author of *Their Eyes Were Watching God*, records the unique customs and speech of the rural black town of Eatonville, Florida, where she was born and raised.

EXPLANATION

1. This is an unbiased statement (UB). It is factual and can be proven with objective evidence and expert opinions.

2. This is a biased argument (B) using the emotional appeal of propaganda. The statement uses the "plain folks" appeal. Senator Manness is identified as an everyday person with the same values as everyday people. You will learn more about this propaganda technique later in this chapter.

3. This is an unbiased statement (UB); however, it is a false fact. Current research does not support this claim.

4. This is a biased argument (B) using the emotional appeal of the propaganda techniques of "transfer" and "bandwagon." You will learn more about these propaganda techniques later in this chapter.

5. This is an unbiased statement (UB). This statement offers factual information that can be verified by reading the novel and researching African American customs and speech. ◀

Practice 2

Read the following sets of ideas. Mark each statement as follows:

> **UB** for unbiased statements
> **B** for biased arguments

_____ **1.** Look like Sandra Bullock, Heidi Klum, or Jennifer Lopez—use Love Your Hair for silky, shimmering hair.

_____ **2.** Be a true patriot; buy Liberty Bonds to support our troops.

_____ **3.** People with apple-shaped figures are at greater risk for heart disease, stroke, diabetes, and some types of cancer.

_____ **4.** Research exists both for and against milk consumption; while many experts agree that milk contains important vitamins and minerals for healthy bones, such as vitamin D and calcium, other experts say milk contributes to heart disease and obesity.

Detect Fallacies Based on Irrelevant Arguments: *Personal Attack, Straw Man,* and *Begging the Question*

Writing based in logical thought offers an author's claim and relevant supporting details, and it arrives at a valid conclusion. Fallacies and propaganda offer irrelevant arguments based on irrelevant details. Irrelevant details draw attention away from logical thought by ignoring the issue or changing the subject.

Personal Attack

Personal attack is the use of abusive remarks in place of evidence for a point or argument. Also known as an *ad hominem* attack, a personal attack attempts to discredit the point by discrediting the person making the point.

For example, Maurice Long, a recovering alcoholic, decides to run for mayor. His opponent focuses attention on Maurice's history of alcohol abuse and ignores his ideas about how to make the community stronger with statements like "Don't vote for a Long record of poor decisions," or "Don't give the keys to the city to the town drunk." However, Maurice's past struggle with alcoholism has nothing to do with his current ability to work as a public servant, making this argument a personal attack.

⊘ **EXAMPLE** Read this discussion between a husband and wife, and then underline two uses of the logical fallacy of *personal attack*.

Budget Woes

[1]"Glenn, I am more than concerned about the amount of money you are spending," Jean says in a concerned but polite voice.

[2]"Oh, really?" Glenn replies with surprise.

[3]"How can you be surprised? [4]We worked out this budget together, so you must know that you are spending more than we can afford," Jean retorts with exasperation.

[5]"I seem surprised because I have worked hard to stay within the budget, but the cost of gas at the pump has skyrocketed and is much more expensive than what we figured, and . . . " Glenn says defensively.

[6]Jean interrupts, "Stop! [7]The price of gas is not the issue; you are eating out every day at lunch while the pantry is full of groceries you purchased, with my credit card, by the way, so you could save money by taking your lunch. [8]You are playing golf twice a week, while you promised to cut back to playing only once a week."

[9]"Well, I only agreed to that budget because you are such a control freak and have to have everything your way," Glenn shouts, then continues in a controlled, measured voice. [10]"The budget is unreasonable; we make enough money to live comfortably. [11]I wish you wouldn't worry so much."

[12]"What! [13]Well, maybe I wouldn't get so 'freaked out' if you weren't such a manipulator." [14]Jean's voice trembles with emotion as she continues. [15]"You shouldn't have agreed to the budget if you didn't think it was realistic. [16]It's not fair to agree with me knowing you are going to do as you please; we have to be honest with each other."

[17]"Okay, okay, so let's sit down together later tonight and create a budget that we can both live with," Glenn says as he embraces his wife.

EXPLANATION   Although much of this conversation is emotional, most of it is based on facts. However, sentences 9 and 13 sink into an exchange of personal attacks. Glenn accuses his wife of being a *control freak*, and she responds by calling him a *manipulator*. ◑

Straw Man

A **straw man** is a weak argument substituted for a stronger one to make the argument easier to challenge. A straw man fallacy distorts, misrepresents, or falsifies an opponent's position. The name of the fallacy comes from the idea that it is easier to knock down a straw man than a real man who will fight back. The purpose of this kind of attack is to shift attention away from a strong argument to a weaker one that can be more easily overcome. Study the following example.

Governor Goodfeeling is campaigning against a movement by the populace to limit the size of public school classes to 15 students per teacher. His opponents run political advertisements that state the following:

"Governor Goodfeeling would rather invest in special interest tax breaks than our children's future. Governor Goodfeeling uses taxpayer money to fund her campaign against class-size reductions."

This passage doesn't mention Governor Goodfeeling's reason for opposing the limit on class size: the state does not have the additional $2.3 billion needed to implement such a major reform without a drastic tax increase. Her opponents used straw man fallacies to put forth views that do not address the governor's line of reasoning and are easier to attack than her valid stand against smaller class sizes.

⊙ **EXAMPLE** Read the following paragraph and then underline the logical fallacy of *straw man*.

> [1]For the past five years, Senator Richy and his political party have consistently blocked action on the Patient's Bill of Rights while Americans have suffered mercilessly from HMO abuse and neglect. [2]For every day that Congress delays, medical treatment for tens of thousands of Americans is effectively denied or delayed by insurance companies. [3]Those, like Senator Richy, who stand against the Patients' Bill of Rights stand against the spirit of the original Bill of Rights and other fundamental freedoms, such as the freedom of speech, religion, and the freedom from unreasonable searches and seizures.

EXPLANATION The third sentence sets up a straw man, a misleading notion that those who oppose the Patients' Bill of Rights oppose basic constitutional rights. This approach effectively draws attention away from the actual reasons Senator Richy opposed this bill and denies the public an honest discussion of the facts involved in the issue. ⊙

Begging the Question

Begging the question restates the point of an argument as the support and conclusion. Also known as *circular reasoning*, begging the question assumes that an unproven or unsupported point is true. For example, the argument "Exercise is tiring because it is strenuous" begs the question. The point "Exercise is tiring" is assumed to be true because it is restated in the term *strenuous* without specific supports that give logical reasons or explanations. Compare the same idea stated without begging the question: "I find exercise such as weight-lifting tiring because I have little endurance and strength."

> **EXAMPLE** Read the following paragraph. Underline the irrelevant argument of *begging the question*.

It's the Law for a Reason

¹Current laws that mandate the use of bicycle helmets must not be repealed. ²Properly fitted helmets protect the brain against debilitating injuries. ³According to the Centers for Disease Control and Prevention, more than 500,000 people in the United States are treated in emergency rooms, and more than 700 people die as a result of bicycle-related injuries annually. ⁴In addition, if bicycle helmet laws are repealed, then these laws would cease to exist.

EXPLANATION Sentence 4 is a statement of begging the question. To say *these laws would cease to exist* is a restatement of the word *repeal*, which means "cancel." As a master reader, you want to know the reasons that explain how helmet laws have reduced the risks or incidents of injuries. ◁

Practice 3

Identify the fallacy in each of the following items. Write **A** if it begs the question, **B** if it constitutes a personal attack, or **C** if it is a straw man.

_____ **1.** Health care is a universal right because everyone deserves adequate health care.

_____ **2.** Sarah Clinton is a fatal cancer to the Republican party.

_____ **3.** Opponents of health reform are afraid of the facts themselves. Their attempt to drown out opposing views is simply un-American.

_____ **4.** "Nothing is not an option. You didn't send me to Washington to do nothing," President Obama, in defense of his $800 billion economic stimulus package in 2009.

LO3 Detect Propaganda Techniques Based on Irrelevant Arguments: *Name-Calling, Testimonials, Bandwagon,* and *Plain Folks*

Name-Calling

Name-calling uses negative labels for a product, idea, or cause. The labels are made up of emotionally loaded words and suggest false or irrelevant details that cannot be verified. Name-calling is an expression of personal opinion. For example, a bill for censorship of obscene speech on television and radio may be labeled "anti-American" to generate opposition to the bill. The "anti-American" label suggests that any restriction placed on the right of public speech is *against basic American values,* for which the Revolutionary War was fought.

> **EXAMPLE** Read the following paragraph. Underline the irrelevant details that use *name-calling.*

[1]State Attorney John Q. Private's appointment to the U.S. Court of Appeals for the Sixth Circuit should not be confirmed. [2]Private is an ideological zealot with a long history of undermining legal and constitutional protections for ordinary Americans. [3]He has diligently opposed reproductive rights, environmental protections, and the separation of church and state. [4]In addition, he has consistently showed favoritism for big tobacco and the gun lobby. [5]It is clear that Private is a right-wing conservative, a partisan who values corporate interests more than the interests of the people.

EXPLANATION The paragraph offers little factual evidence to support the assertion that John Q. Private should not be confirmed to the U.S. Court of Appeals. Phrases such as *undermining legal and constitutional protections* and *diligently opposed reproductive rights, environmental protections, and the separation of church and state* are emotionally laden accusations that remain unsupported with evidence. The author couples these biased generalizations with name-calling. Sentences 2 and 5 label John Q. Private an *ideological zealot,* a *right-wing conservative,* and a *partisan.* <

Testimonials

Testimonials use irrelevant personal opinions to support a product, idea, or cause. Most often the testimonial is provided by a celebrity whose only qualification as a spokesperson is fame. For example, a famous actor promotes a certain brand of potato chips as his favorite, or a radio talk show host endorses a certain type of mattress.

> **EXAMPLE** Read the following paragraph. Underline the irrelevant details that use a *testimonial.*

The Brilliance of a Smile

[1]SmileBrite offers the fastest and best whitening results of all the leading paint-on and strip whiteners. [2]SmileBrite's secret is in its method

of application and its secret combination of ingredients, which include peroxide. [3]Film star Julia Famous loves SmileBrite: "SmileBrite is safe and effective; I trust my smile to SmileBrite." [4]This special formula is gentle and will not damage the tooth's enamel, yet delivers tremendous results in just a few applications.

EXPLANATION Sentences 1, 2, and 4 offer details about SmileBrite that can be verified. However, sentence 3 uses the testimonial of a famous actress. Being a famous actress doesn't make the spokesperson an expert on the safety or effectiveness of a product. A dentist, dental hygienist, or scientific researcher could offer a relevant expert opinion.

Practice 4

Identify the propaganda technique used in each of the following items. Write **A** if the sentence is an example of name-calling or **B** if it is a testimonial.

_____ **1.** Senator Fleming is a big-government socialist who works against the American way.

_____ **2.** "I'm winning at losing weight. Winning at losing on Weight Watchers. Weight Watchers—because it works!"—Jennifer Hudson

_____ **3.** "When my husband lost his job, we lost our health insurance. Then, my five-year-old was diagnosed with a brain tumor. When my husband finally got a new job several months later, the company's health insurance denied payment to treat our daughter, saying she had a pre-existing condition. We need health reform!"—Jennifer Cortez

_____ **4.** The city commissioners are a bunch of bums.

Bandwagon

The **bandwagon** appeal uses or suggests the irrelevant detail that "everyone is doing it." This message plays on the natural desire of most individuals to conform to group norms for acceptance. The term *bandwagon* comes from the 19th-century use of a horse-drawn wagon that carried a musical band to lead circus parades and political rallies. To *jump on the bandwagon* meant to follow the crowd, usually out of excitement and emotion stirred up by the event rather than out of thoughtful reason or deep conviction.

> **EXAMPLE** Read the following paragraph. Underline the irrelevant details that use the *bandwagon* appeal.

A Matter of Honor

¹Tyrell hated to write. ²He often struggled with finding a topic, and once he found a topic, he then struggled with finding the words to express his ideas. ³He knew he was in danger of failing his composition course, and the stress made it even harder for him to think of an idea for his major research project. ⁴While he was searching the Internet for ideas, he came across a Web site that sold research essays. ⁵As he paid for an essay, downloaded, and printed it out, he thought to himself, "No big deal, everybody cheats at least once in their college career."

EXPLANATION In sentence 5, Tyrell uses the bandwagon fallacy to justify his cheating. Finding permission in "everybody cheats" is not valid reasoning. The emotional appeal is the relief that you are one of "everybody," not an individual who has decided to engage in dishonest and unethical behavior. <

Plain Folks

The **plain folks** appeal uses irrelevant details to build trust based on commonly shared values. Many people distrust the wealthy and powerful, such as politicians and the heads of large corporations. Many assume that the wealthy and powerful cannot relate to the everyday concerns of plain people. Therefore, the person or organization in power puts forth an image to which everyday people can more easily relate. For example, a candidate may dress in simple clothes, pose for pictures doing everyday chores like shopping for groceries, or talk about his or her own humble beginnings to make a connection with "plain folks." These details strongly suggest that "you can trust me because I am just like you." The appeal is to the simple, everyday experience, and often the emphasis is on a practical or no-nonsense approach to life.

> **EXAMPLE** Read the following paragraph. Underline the irrelevant details that appeal to *plain folks*.

For the Good of the Children

¹Helen McCormick, a well-known multimillionaire, is running for the school board. ²Every day she dresses in sensible shoes and a conservative business suit and goes door to door in neighborhoods populated with young families with school-age children. ³As she visits with them, she

reminds them of her success and attributes it to hard work and a good education, even though she inherited her fortune and has never held a job. [4]Her newspaper ads run the slogan "I am committed to public education. [5]My own children attend public school; help me help our children." [6]On the day of the election, Helen stands on the corner of the busiest intersection holding a sign that reads, "Helen cares about our children."

EXPLANATION Candidate Helen is described as wearing clothes that many "plain folks" also wear: *sensible shoes and a conservative business suit.* In sentence 3, the candidate asserts ideals valued by many people: *hard work and a good education.* She emphasizes her common bond with voters by stating *My own children attend public school; help me help our children.* Helen sets a friendly tone with the use of her first name. In addition, Helen's willingness to go door to door and stand on the street corner indicates she is humble and working hard for every vote. All of these details suggest that this multimillionaire, Helen, is just one of the "plain folks." ◄

Practice 5

Label each of the following items according to the propaganda techniques they employ:

| A. plain folks | C. testimonial |
| B. bandwagon | D. name-calling |

_____ **1.** An owner of a local car dealership stars in a commercial for his business dressed in jeans and a flannel shirt with his sleeves rolled up.

_____ **2.** Nine out of ten customers express deep satisfaction with Relora, the natural way to ease tension and lose weight.

_____ **3.** Don't be a butt head; stop smoking today!

_____ **4.** "Proactive keeps your skin acne free. Proactive means clear skin," says Jessica Simpson.

LO4 Detect Fallacies Based on Inadequate Arguments: *Either-Or, False Comparison,* and *False Cause*

In addition to offering relevant supporting details, logical thought relies on adequate supporting details. A valid conclusion must be based on sufficient support. Fallacies and propaganda offer inadequate arguments that lack details.

Inadequate arguments oversimplify the issue and do not give a person enough information to draw a proper conclusion.

Either-Or

Either-or assumes that only two sides of an issue exist. Also known as the *black-and-white fallacy*, either-or offers a false dilemma because more than two options are usually available. For example, the statement "If you don't vote for social security reform, you don't care about the elderly" uses the either-or fallacy. The statement assumes only one reason for not voting for social security reform—not caring about the elderly. Yet it may be that a person doesn't approve of the particular reform being considered, prefers another solution or perhaps believes the current social security program is strong and serves the elderly as well as could be expected. Either-or leaves no room for the middle ground or other options.

> **EXAMPLE** Read the following paragraph taken from President Bush's Address to the Joint Session of Congress and the American people on September 20, 2001. Then, underline the logical fallacy of *either-or*.

> [1]Our response involves far more than instant retaliation and isolated strikes. [2]Americans should not expect one battle, but a lengthy campaign, unlike any other we have ever seen. [3]It may include dramatic strikes, visible on TV, and covert operations, secret even in success. [4]We will starve terrorists of funding, turn them one against another, drive them from place to place, until there is no refuge or no rest. [5]And we will pursue nations that provide aid or safe haven to terrorism. [6]Every nation, in every region, now has a decision to make. [7]Either you are with us, or you are with the terrorists. [8]From this day forward, any nation that continues to harbor or support terrorism will be regarded by the United States as a hostile regime.
>
> —George W. Bush, *The White House*, 20 Sept. 2001.

EXPLANATION President Bush's address is in direct response to the September 11, 2001, terrorist attacks on the United States. No one would dispute that the shocking, horrific loss that resulted from that attack demanded a strong response. However, Bush's use of the either-or fallacy in sentence 7 is undeniable. A reader may choose to assume that Bush is speaking only of terrorists and those who actively support their acts of terror. However, his use of this either-or statement allows his critics to infer that he equates those who may disagree with America's response to the situation with terrorists. In addition, his statement leaves no room for a country to take a neutral stance. This issue is difficult and emotional, which places an even greater responsibility on writers, speakers, listeners, and readers to analyze such statements and ideas for logical soundness. ◀

False Comparison

False comparison assumes that two things are similar when they are not. This fallacy is also known as a *false analogy*. An analogy is a point-by-point comparison that is used to explain an unfamiliar concept by comparing it to a more familiar one.

For example, some people have compared the human heart to a plumbing system. The heart is thought of as a pump that sends blood throughout the body to vital organs, and the arteries and veins are compared to pipes that carry this nutrient-enriched fluid to its destination and take away waste material. However, the analogy breaks down when one considers all the differences between a mechanical plumbing system and the human anatomy. First, the heart is not totally responsible for transporting the blood throughout the body. For instance, arteries dilate and contract and move in a wavelike manner to regulate and move blood through the body. Also, the relationship between the pressure, volume, and rate of the heartbeat is very different from the workings of a mechanical pump. A false comparison occurs when the differences outweigh the similarities.

▶ **EXAMPLE** Read the following paragraph. Underline the logical fallacy of *false comparison*.

> [1]Here at Great Foods we are in business to win. [2]We want to win customers and profits. [3]We do what it takes to make our products the best and to satisfy our customers. [4]We only hire the most talented and competitive workers, and we give them rigorous training in sales and service. [5]Just like a football team, we at Great Foods are a committed team, playing hard to beat the competition and build a loyal following.

EXPLANATION This paragraph draws a false comparison between a business and a football team. While a business may compete against other businesses for customers, the analogy breaks down upon closer examination. For example, in football, one team always wins and the other clearly loses; in contrast, two similar businesses can thrive in close proximity to each other. Furthermore, for a business to make a profit, the customer may lose a bargain. In football, each player is assigned a distinct role; oftentimes in a business, an employee may fulfill a variety of roles. In football, the rules of the game are fixed and known to all who play. However, in business, the rules may vary based on who is in charge and the type of business, and customers may not always understand the rules ("the fine print") until after a purchase is made. This false comparison relies on superficial similarities and oversimplifies the complexities of running a successful business. ◀

False Cause

False cause, also known as **Post Hoc,** assumes that because events occurred around the same time, they have a cause-and-effect relationship. For example, a black cat crossing your path, walking under a ladder, and breaking a mirror are said to cause bad luck. What are the other possible causes? The Post Hoc fallacy is the false assumption that because event B *follows* event A, event B *was caused by* event A. A master reader does not assume a cause without thinking about other possible causes.

▶ **EXAMPLE** Read the following paragraph. Underline the logical fallacy of *false cause.*

> ¹Leanne, a single mother of two children, decided to continue her education and become a registered nurse. ²The long hours of study required a drastic change in her lifestyle. ³Before enrolling in college, her lifestyle had been moderately active, and, as a conscientious mother, she had prepared well-balanced, healthy meals. ⁴However, once she began her college career, her lifestyle became much more sedentary due to the long hours of attending class and studying at home. ⁵In addition, she found that she was eating on the go (although she usually ordered healthful meals such as salad and grilled chicken sandwiches). ⁶Over the course of her four-year college career, she gained forty pounds. ⁷Leanne thought she probably had a thyroid problem, since her mother had had one. ⁸When she went to the doctor, she discovered she did not. ⁹Her weight gain was caused by her lack of exercise and poor diet. ¹⁰Leanne started exercising regularly and eating better. ¹¹Within six months, she had lost the extra weight.

EXPLANATION Leanne jumped to a false conclusion about the cause of her weight gain. She had attributed her weight gain to a medical condition, when the real cause was changes in her lifestyle. ◀

Practice 6

Identify the fallacy in each of the following items. Write **A** if the sentence states a false cause, **B** if it makes a false comparison, or **C** if it employs the either-or fallacy.

_____ **1.** Gossip is just like murder; it destroys a life.

_____ **2.** Every time I made spaghetti for dinner, my husband and I fought, so I don't fix spaghetti anymore.

_____ **3.** I failed the test because the teacher doesn't like me.

_____ **4.** A father said to his son, "I will only pay for your education if you decide to become a doctor."

_____ **5.** Either you give me a raise, or I am going to quit immediately.

_____ **6.** Which logical fallacy does the World War II poster reprinted here use?

—© Courtesy of National Archives, photo NWDNS-188-p. 42.

Detect Propaganda Techniques Based on Inadequate Arguments: *Card Stacking, Transfer,* and *Glittering Generalities*

Card Stacking

Card stacking omits factual details in order to misrepresent a product, idea, or cause. Card stacking intentionally gives only part of the truth. For example, a commercial for a snack food labels the snack "low in fat," which suggests that it is healthier and lower in calories than a product that is not low in fat. However, the commercial does not mention that the snack is loaded with sugar and calories.

> **EXAMPLE** Read the following list of details about the product Carblaster. Place a check beside the detail(s) that would be omitted by *card stacking*.

_____ **1.** Carblaster guarantees weight loss by blocking as much as 45 grams of carbohydrates from entering the body.

_____ **2.** Carblaster contains the miracle ingredient *phaselous vulgaris,* an extract from the northern white kidney bean.

_____ **3.** The extract hinders an enzyme in the body that breaks down carbohydrates into glucose.

_____ **4.** Side effects can include severe gastrointestinal distress, heartburn, excessive gas, and diarrhea.

EXPLANATION The detail that would be left out by a writer or speaker using the method of card-stacking is the last detail in the list: *Side effects can include severe gastrointestinal distress, heartburn, excessive gas, and diarrhea.* Consumers might choose to avoid the risk of such side effects and not buy the product. ◁

Transfer

Transfer creates an association between a product, idea, or cause with a symbol or image that has positive or negative values. This technique carries the strong feelings we may have for one thing over to another thing.

Symbols stir strong emotions, opinions, or loyalties. For example, a cross represents the Christian faith; a flag represents a nation; and a beautiful woman or a handsome man represents acceptance, success, or sex appeal. Politicians and advertisers use symbols like these to win our support. For example, a political candidate may end a speech with a prayer or the phrase "God bless America," to suggest that God approves of the speech. Another example of transfer is the television spokesperson who wears a white lab coat and quotes studies about the health product she is advertising.

Transfers can also be negative. For example, a skull and crossbones together serve as a symbol for death. Therefore, placing a skull and crossbones on a bottle transfers the dangers of death to the contents of the bottle.

> **EXAMPLE** Read the following paragraph. Underline the irrelevant details that use *transfer*.

Senator Edith Public

[1]Senator Edith Public is running for reelection to represent California in the Senate and is the guest of honor at a lavish Hollywood-sponsored fundraising party, which is being covered by CNN. [2]She is introduced by Ron Massey, a highly popular film actor. [3]And as she speaks, she is surrounded by some of the best known, most successful producers, directors, and actors in Hollywood. [4]Senator Public says, "Thank you, Ron, for the warm and enthusiastic support. [5]I know that all of you in this room are concerned about education, the environment, and national health care. [6]As you know, the polls indicate that millions of hardworking Americans across this country are also concerned about these very issues. [7]I promise to work hard to encourage funding for research for alternative sources of energy, to increase national funding for public education, and to pass a Patients' Bill of Rights.

EXPLANATION Senator Edith Public is hoping that the public's affection and respect for these individuals will transfer to her and motivate the fans to vote for her. Interestingly, in her speech, the senator uses the plain folks appeal in the phrase *hardworking Americans* and the bandwagon appeal in her allusion to the polls that show these issues to be popular with the public. <

Glittering Generalities

Glittering generalities offer general positive statements that cannot be verified. A glittering generality is the opposite of name-calling. Often words of virtue and high ideals are used, and the details are inadequate to support the claim. For example, words like *truth, freedom, peace,* and *honor* suggest shining ideals and appeal to feelings of love, courage, and goodness.

> **EXAMPLE** Read the following paragraph. Underline the irrelevant details that use *glittering generalities*.

People for Democracy

[1]People for Democracy is a nonprofit organization dedicated to actively preserving the rights of democracy, which are under dire attack by the conservative fanatics who are currently in control of the government. [2]People for Democracy dedicate our time, energies, and talents to fight tirelessly and courageously for the rights and freedoms that make the United States a vibrant and diverse democracy. [3]We are pro-life, fighting for a woman's right to choose. [4]We advocate civil rights, fighting, like Lincoln, for the equal rights of all. [5]We defend constitutional liberties, ensuring separation of church and state. [6]We will not rest as long as radical demagogues threaten our way of life. [7]Our fight is the fight for freedom and justice.

EXPLANATION Most of the glittering generalities used to describe this fictitious organization call to mind American virtues; even the name of the organization is chosen to communicate democratic ideals. The paragraph offers no substantive details but relies on glittering generalities, which include the following: sentence 1 uses *preserving the rights of democracy;* sentence 2 uses *fight tirelessly and courageously, rights and freedoms,* and *vibrant and diverse democracy;* sentence 4 uses *equal rights of all;* sentence 6 uses *our way of life;* and sentence 7 states *Our fight is the fight for freedom and justice.* Sentence 1 and 6 also use name-calling with the labels *conservative fanatics* and *radical demagogues,* and sentence 4 uses the technique of transfer by mentioning President Lincoln, a revered martyr for all these values. ◁

Practice 7

Label each of the following items according to the propaganda techniques they employ:

    A. transfer   C. card stacking
    B. glittering generality

_____ **1.** A vote for Joan Willis is a vote for honesty, dedication, and fairness.

_____ **2.** Nike has long offered high-priced celebrity athletic shoes, including Michael Jordan's Air Jordans, LeBron James's Nike LeBrons, and Air Yeezy designed by Kanye West.

_____ **3.** Dewdrop deodorant will increase your confidence and poise with its light and refreshing scent.

_____ **4.** An individual dressed in a white medical coat holds a box of pain reliever and says, "Need immediate relief? Take Pain-away. Guaranteed to relieve headache pain in minutes."

_____ **5.** Use Curl Right to turn frizzy hair into luscious, long-lasting curls. Curl Right's alcohol-free and vitamin-enriched formula restores your hair's natural moisture and vitality. Curl Right gives that hard-to-handle hair lasting volume and styling control.

LO6 Develop Textbook Skills: Examine Biased Arguments in Textbooks

Textbook Skills

Textbooks strive to present information in a factual, objective manner with relevant and adequate support, in keeping with their purpose to inform. However, textbook authors may choose to present biased arguments for your examination. As a master reader, you are expected to evaluate the nature of the biased argument as well as the author's purpose for including the biased argument.

◐ EXAMPLE The following passage appears in a college humanities textbook. As you read the passage, underline biased information. After you read, answer the questions.

Beethoven's Ninth

[1]Beethoven's Ninth, and final, symphony was composed around 1818, when he was totally deaf. [2]It is easily four times the length of a late Mozart symphony, and twice that of even the *Eroica*. [3]Not the journey of a young man's soul coping with the sobering realities of life, the Ninth Symphony is rather the final statement of a gigantic mentality that has struggled for years with both physical and creative suffering—of a person who has labored to find and capture it all, as Michelangelo, two centuries earlier, had sought perfection in marble, and as Einstein, a century later, would seek the ultimate equation for unifying the interactions among all the forces in the universe.

[4]During the first three movements of the Ninth, Beethoven gives us one haunting melody after another, complex rhythms, intricate harmonies, and bold dissonance. [5]He seems to be striving to find a musical equivalent to every feeling that can be experienced. [6]By the fourth movement he appears to have concluded that the orchestra alone was not enough to express the sounds he must have heard in the far recesses of his silent world. [7]He needed human voices.

[8]Other composers before him had written large choral works: Bach's *Passion According to Saint Matthew*, Haydn's *Creation*, and

Mozart's *Requiem*, to name three supreme examples. [9]But Beethoven pushes the human voice farther than many have believed possible.

[10]There remains considerable controversy about the final movement of the Ninth. [11]Some critics say it takes us as close to the gates of heaven as we can get in this earthly lifetime. [12]Some have called it a musical embarrassment, totally unsingable. [13]One soprano, after attempting it, vehemently declared that Beethoven had no respect whatever for the female voice. [14]Others have suggested that in his deafness Beethoven heard extraordinary sounds that were not contained within the boundaries of music and for which there were no known instruments, not even the human voice. [15]Perhaps such sentiments over-romanticize the work. [16]But perhaps not. [17]No one will ever know what Beethoven was hearing.

[18]The musical setting for Friedrich von Schiller's "Ode to Joy," the main theme of the fourth movement, has attained the stature of an international hymn. [19]By far, the majority opinion about this music is that it transcends its own "unsingability" and any breach of musical taste it may commit. [20]Asking whether one "likes it" seems beside the point. [21]One can only feel humbled by its majesty. [22]Listening to Beethoven's Ninth Symphony is discovering what human creativity really means.

[23]The premiere performance of the work in Vienna, at that time the capital of European music, was attended by every Viennese musical luminary. [24]By now fully convinced of the composer's genius, they were eager to discover what new sounds the great man could possibly bring forth from an inner world that was barred forever from the real sounds of humanity and nature. [25]Beethoven was the co-conductor.

[26]Witnesses to the event have left behind stories of the performance, especially of how the maestro conducted with sustained vigor, hearing his own orchestra no doubt; for when the "other" orchestra had finished the work and the enthusiastic applause began, Beethoven had not yet put down his baton. [27]When at last he realized what was happening, he started to walk from the stage, perhaps feeling his music had not communicated. [28]The other conductor caught up with him and turned him around in time to see the huge audience on its feet, shouting, crying "Bravissimo!" [29]Beethoven simply bowed his head. [30]No one will ever know what it was he had heard, just as he could not have known what they had heard.

[31]Nonetheless, that moment lives on in the history of the humanities as a rare meeting of souls in that strange space where the spirit of art lives.

—Janaro, Richard P. and Altshuler, Thelma C., *The Art of Being Human*, 10th ed., pp. 168–169.

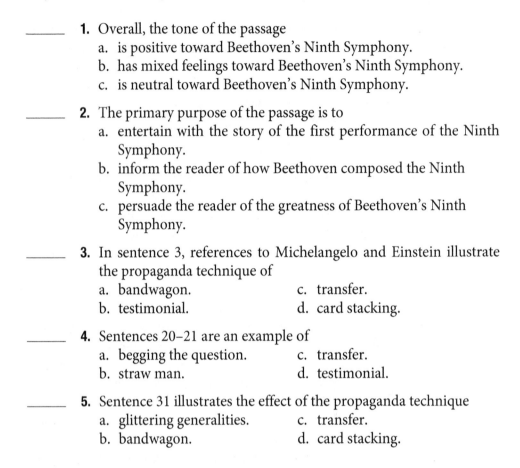

_____ **1.** Overall, the tone of the passage
    a. is positive toward Beethoven's Ninth Symphony.
    b. has mixed feelings toward Beethoven's Ninth Symphony.
    c. is neutral toward Beethoven's Ninth Symphony.

_____ **2.** The primary purpose of the passage is to
    a. entertain with the story of the first performance of the Ninth Symphony.
    b. inform the reader of how Beethoven composed the Ninth Symphony.
    c. persuade the reader of the greatness of Beethoven's Ninth Symphony.

_____ **3.** In sentence 3, references to Michelangelo and Einstein illustrate the propaganda technique of
    a. bandwagon.   c. transfer.
    b. testimonial.   d. card stacking.

_____ **4.** Sentences 20–21 are an example of
    a. begging the question.   c. transfer.
    b. straw man.   d. testimonial.

_____ **5.** Sentence 31 illustrates the effect of the propaganda technique
    a. glittering generalities.   c. transfer.
    b. bandwagon.   d. card stacking.

EXPLANATION The biased information includes the following words: _final statement, gigantic mentality, struggled, suffering, labored, sought perfection, seek, ultimate, haunting, complex, intricate, bold, striving, every feeling, not enough, far recesses, silent world, pushes, farther, believed possible, controversy, gates of heaven, embarrassment, unsingable, vehemently, no respect, extraordinary, not contained, over-romanticize, attained, stature, hymn, transcends, breach, musical taste, humbled, majesty, discovering, creativity, every, musical luminary, fully convinced, genius, eager, new, great, maestro, vigor, enthusiastic applause, huge, shouting, crying "Bravissimo!," simply, lives on, rare, strange, spirit of art._

1. This list of biased words indicates the overall positive tone (a) of the passage.

2. The primary purpose of the passage is to (c) persuade the reader of the greatness of Beethoven's Ninth Symphony.

3. The references to Michelangelo and Einstein are an example of (c) transfer, as they create an association with two very positive figures.

4. Sentences 20–21 ("Asking whether one 'likes it' seems beside the point. One can only feel humbled by its majesty") is an example of the straw man technique (b) because the author is addressing the weaker argument of "liking" the symphony so he can say that it is not the point.

5. Sentence 31 illustrates (a) glittering generalities, such as "history of the humanities," "meeting of souls" and "spirit of art." ◀

Practice 8

The following passage appears in a college sociology textbook. As you read the passage, underline biased words. Then answer the questions.

The McDonaldization of Society

Textbook
Skills

[1]The significance of the McDonald's restaurants that dot the United States—and, increasingly, the world—goes far beyond quick hamburgers, milk shakes, and salads. [2]As sociologist George Ritzer (1993, 1998, 2001) says, our everyday lives are being "McDonaldized." [3]Let's see what he means by this.

[4]The McDonaldization of society does not refer just to the robotlike assembly of food. [5]This term refers to the standardization of everyday life, a process that is transforming our lives. [6]Want to do some shopping? [7]Shopping malls offer one-stop shopping in controlled environments. [8]Planning a trip? [9]Travel agencies offer "package" tours. [10]They will transport middle-class Americans to ten European capitals in fourteen days. [11]All visitors experience the same hotels, restaurants, and other scheduled sites—and no one need fear meeting a "real" native. [12]Want to keep up with events? [13]USA Today spews out McNews—short, bland, non-analytical pieces that can be digested between gulps of the McShake or the McBurger.

[14]Efficiency brings dependability. [15]You can expect your burger and fries to taste the same whether you buy them in Minneapolis or Moscow. [16]Although efficiency also lowers prices, it does come at a cost. [17]Predictability washes away spontaneity, changing the quality of our lives. [18]It produces flat, bland versions of what used to be unique experiences. [19]In my own travels, for example, had I taken packaged tours I never would have had the eye-opening experiences that have added so much to my appreciation of human diversity. [20](Bus trips with chickens in Mexico, hitchhiking in Europe and Africa, sleeping on a granite table in a nunnery in Italy and in a cornfield in Algeria are not part of tour agendas.)

[21]For good or bad, our lives are being McDonaldized, and the predictability of packaged settings seems to be our social destiny. [22]When education is rationalized, no longer will our children have to put up with real professors, who insist on discussing ideas endlessly, who never come to decisive answers, and who come saddled with idiosyncrasies. [23]At some point, such an approach to education is going to be a bit of quaint history.

[24]Our programmed education will eliminate the need for discussion of social issues—we will have packaged solutions to social problems, definitive answers that satisfy our need for closure. [25]Computerized courses will teach the same answers to everyone—the approved, "politically correct" ways to think about social issues. [26]Mass testing will ensure that students regurgitate the programmed responses.

[27]Our coming prepackaged society will be efficient, of course. [28]But it also means that we will be trapped in the "iron cage" of bureaucracy—just as Weber warned would happen.

—Henslin, James M., *Sociology: A Down-to-Earth Approach,* 11th ed., p. 173.

_____ **1.** Overall, the tone of the passage
  a. is positive toward standardization in our lives.
  b. is negative toward standardization in our lives.
  c. remains neutral toward standardization in our lives.

_____ **2.** The author's purpose is to
  a. persuade the reader that standardization has bad effects.
  b. inform the reader of the causes and effects of standardization.
  c. entertain the reader with a new outlook on society.

_____ **3.** Sentence 4 is an example of the propaganda technique
  a. bandwagon.
  b. testimonial.
  c. name calling.
  d. plain folks.

_____ **4.** Sentence 13 is an example of
  a. bandwagon.
  b. glittering generalities.
  c. testimonial.
  d. transfer.

LO7 Academic, Personal, and Career Applications of Advanced Argument: Persuasive Techniques

Understanding the techniques of persuasion is an important literacy information skill. Information is often used to sway you to believe or do something. Examining persuasive techniques empowers your thinking. You are better able to form valid conclusions in your academic life, as well as make valid decisions in your personal and career lives. As a college student, you evaluate the use of persuasive techniques in areas such as history, art, and literature. In your personal life, you sift through the everyday uses of persuasive techniques. Family, friends, advertisers, or politicians may use these techniques to influence your thoughts and actions. In your career life, you may confront persuasive techniques in the workplace. Job applicants, proposals, marketing strategies, or sales reports may tap into the power of persuasive techniques to achieve goals. Thus you will use the skills that you have learned in this chapter in many ways:

- Identify persuasive techniques.
- Evaluate a claim and its supports to determine the use of persuasive techniques or sound logic.
- Support or reject a claim based on persuasive techniques.

Academic Application

Assume you are taking a college course in American history. Part of your grade is based on reading the following debate concerning women's suffrage and answering one of the questions for discussion.

- **Before Reading:** Skim this chapter to review the various persuasive techniques. Predict how the information you have learned may help you analyze the strategies used in each argument. Read the "For Discussion" questions and decide which one you will respond to.
- **During Reading:** Underline specific details of each argument that directly support one side of the debate. Circle words or phrases that clearly use persuasive techniques.
- **After Reading:** In the space following the debate, answer the "For Discussion" question you have chosen to write about.

Different Voices: The Debate Over Women's Suffrage

The debate over a woman's right to vote did not divide along gender lines. Many men supported women's suffrage, and many women, including Britain's Queen Victoria, regarded it as a violation of the natural order. The excerpts below present arguments in the women's suffrage debate. The best-selling British novelist Mary Ward—or, as she always presented herself, Mrs. Humphry Ward (1857–1920)—wrote the first document, a letter to the editor of an influential magazine, in 1889. Many well-known and influential women signed the letter. The second excerpt comes from a French suffragist pamphlet published in 1913.

An Anti-Suffrage Argument: Mrs. Humphry Ward

We, the undersigned, wish to appeal to the common sense and the educated thought of the men and women of England against the proposed extension of the Parliamentary suffrage to women. While desiring the fullest possible development of the powers, energies and education of women, we believe that their work for the State, and their responsibilities towards it, must always differ essentially from those of men, and that therefore their share in the working of the State machinery should be different from that assigned to men. . . . To men belong the struggle of debate and legislation in Parliament; the working of the army and navy; all the heavy, laborious, fundamental industries of the State, such as those of mines, metals, and railways; the lead and supervision of English commerce, the service of that merchant fleet on which our food supply depends.

At the same time we are heartily in sympathy with all the recent efforts which have been made to *give* women a more important part in those affairs of the community where their interests and those of men are equally concerned; where it is possible for them not only to decide but to help in carrying out, and where, therefore, judgment is weighted by a true responsibility, and can be guided by experience and the practical information which comes from it. As voters for or members of School Boards, Boards of Guardians, and other important public bodies, women *have* now opportunities for public usefulness which must promote the growth of character, and at the same time strengthen among them the social sense and habit. But we believe that the emancipation process has now reached the limits fixed by the physical constitution of women, and by the fundamental difference which must always exist between their main occupations and those of men. The care of the sick and the insane, the treatment of the poor; the education of children: in all these matters, and others besides, they have made good their claim to a larger and more extended powers. We rejoice in it. But when it comes to questions of foreign or colonial policy, or of grave constitutional change, then we maintain that the necessary and normal experience of women does not and can never provide them with such materials for sound judgment as are open to men.

In conclusion: nothing can be further from our minds than to seek to depreciate the position or the importance of women. It is because we are keenly alive to the enormous value of their special contribution to the community, that we oppose what seems to us likely to endanger that contribution. We are convinced that the pursuit of a mere outward equality with men is for women not only vain but demoralizing. It leads to a total misconception of women's true dignity and special mission. It tends to personal struggle and rivalry, where the only effort of both the great divisions of the human family should be to contribute the characteristic labour and the best gifts of each to the common stock.

A Pro-Suffrage Argument: The French Union for Women's Suffrage

We are going to try to prove that the vote for women is a just, possible and desirable reform. . . .

A woman has responsibility in the family; she ought to be consulted about the laws establishing her rights and duties with respect to her husband, her children, her parents.

Women work—and in ever greater numbers; a statistic of 1896 established that . . . the number of women workers was 35 percent of the total number of workers, both male and female.

If she is in business, she, like any businessman, has interests to protect. . . .

If a woman is a worker or a domestic, she ought to participate as a man does in voting on unionization laws, laws covering workers' retirement, social security, the limitation and regulation of work hours, weekly days off, labor contracts, etc.

Finally, her special characteristics of order, economy, patience and resourcefulness will be as useful to society as the characteristics of man and will favor the establishment of laws too often overlooked until now.

The woman's vote will assure the establishment of important social laws. All women will want:

To fight against alcoholism, from which they suffer much more than men;

To establish laws of health and welfare;

To obtain the regulation of female and child labor;

To defend young women against prostitution;

Finally, to prevent wars and to submit conflicts among nations to courts of arbitration.

Sources: (1) Mrs. Humphry Ward, "An Appeal against Female Suffrage," *Nineteenth Century* 147 (June 1889): 781–785. (2) A report presented to Besancon Municipal Council by the Franc-Comtois Group of the Union Française pour Le Suffrage des Femmes. Besancon, March 1913, 6–9.

For Discussion

1. In her "Anti-Suffrage Argument," Mary Humphry Ward states that women do not have the life experiences to make political decisions. For example, she says, " . . . the necessary and normal experience of women does not and can never provide them with such materials for sound judgment as are open to men." Do you agree or disagree with this view? Explain why or why not. Feel free to use details from either article to support your point.

2. In the "Pro-Suffrage Argument," The French Union for Women's Suffrage asserts that women are uniquely equipped to contribute to the political process. The argument states, " . . . her special characteristics of order, economy, patience and resourcefulness will be as useful to society as the characteristics of man and will favor the establishment of laws too often overlooked until now." Do you agree or disagree with this view? Explain why or why not. Feel free to use details from either article to support your point.

_____

_____

_____

_____

_____

_____

Personal Application

Assume you live in Manhattan, where the city is attempting to enforce a limitation on the size of a soft drink you may buy. Do you agree with banning giant soft drinks, or do you think that the choice should be left to the individual? Read the following article, and then respond with your view about the issue.

- **Before Reading:** Skim the article and analyze the photograph. Write a caption for the photograph with emotional words that convey the intended impact of the image.
- **During Reading:** Underline key details that will help you respond to the issue.
- **After Reading:** Respond to the article with your comments. State your argument for or against the big-soda ban.

Caption for photograph: _____

Top NY Court Will Review Bloomberg's Big-Soda Ban

ALBANY, N.Y. (AP)—The state's highest court agreed Thursday to hear New York City's appeal of a ruling that blocked Mayor Michael Bloomberg's effort to stop many eateries from selling super-sized, sugary drinks.

The Court of Appeals granted a request by city officials to challenge a mid-level court decision that struck down the measure in August.

Arguments and a decision by the top court are expected next year.

The lower court said the city Board of Health exceeded its authority by putting a 16-ounce size limit on high-calorie soft drinks. The cap would have applied to restaurants, stadiums and many other places.

Bloomberg said he was confident the top court would uphold the board's rule, which he said will help save lives.

"Obesity is the only major public health issue we face that is getting worse, and sugary drinks are a major driver of the crisis," Bloomberg said. "The related epidemics of obesity and diabetes are killing at least 5,000 New Yorkers a year and striking hardest in black and Latino communities and low-income neighborhoods."

The American Beverage Association said it's confident the lower court decisions will be upheld.

"The courts have agreed the Board of Health did not have the authority to pass this regulation," spokesman Christopher Gindlesperger said. "We look forward to a final resolution of this issue."

—Virtanen, Michael. "Top NY Court Will Review Bloomberg's Big-Soda Ban." Associated Press. 17 Oct. 2013. Reproduced by the permission of the YGS group.

Pro or Anti Big-Soda Ban? _____

_____

_____

_____

_____

Career Application

Assume you own a hotel on one of Florida's popular beaches. Your state is debating whether to legalize casino gambling. You are interested in this issue as it will affect not only your business, but also the growth of your community.

- **Before Reading:** Skim this chapter to review the various persuasive techniques. Skim the article and predict the purpose of the article.
- **During Reading:** Underline the details that support the argument against casino gambling.
- **After Reading:** In the space following the article, respond to the question.

Say No to Casinos!

After years of high unemployment and a shaky economy, the State of Florida is looking for ways to raise revenues and generate new jobs. Legalized casino gambling, such as in Las Vegas, Nevada, or Atlantic City, New Jersey, is once again being offered as a viable solution.

Those in favor of casinos claim that gambling establishments will bring in hundreds of millions of dollars for the state, tens of thousands of new jobs, tax relief for property owners, and more money for services like public education.

However, casino gambling is a predatory industry. Research documents that over half of their profits come from problem gamblers. Experts estimate that 1.2% of U.S. adults are pathological gamblers and another 1.5% are problem gamblers. Furthermore, the likelihood of becoming a pathological or problem gambler doubles for someone living within 50 miles of a casino.

Statistics show that casinos bring increased crime (such as prostitution), drug addiction, and higher rates of bankruptcy, divorce, mental problems, and suicides. These problems are costly. Community Research Partners (CRP) outline several negative impacts of casinos in a 2010 report, "The Social Impact of Casinos." Pathological and problem gamblers cost society around $5 billion each year. However, another $40 billion occurs in lifetime costs due to reduced productivity, social services, and credit losses. While state revenues may increase due to casinos, this money is typically used to cover the social cost of gambling. Thus, the revenue generated from casinos will not offset the cost of providing additional services such as counseling for compulsive gamblers or additional police to deal with increased crime.

The CRP also point out the effects of casinos on the local economy. Local businesses are often hurt as gamblers stay and spend all their money at the casino. On the one hand, casinos may, at first, increase construction, hospitality, and tourism dollars spent in the area. On the other hand, the number of restaurants, bars, and shops near the casinos decline. For example, Atlantic City had 242 local restaurants and bars in 1977 (the year before the first casino opened). By 1996, the number was down to 142. In addition, most jobs at casinos are low paying, unskilled jobs that do not offer opportunities for advancement.

Despite these many negatives, those in favor of casinos say that people should have the right to participate in the amusement of their choice. They say it is not the place of government to dictate such personal choices.

I would challenge supporters of casinos to seriously consider the serious consequences of gambling. And before any vote takes place, state officials should educate the public about the risks associated with gambling. In addition, the state should offer a clear plan to use state dollars to address the social issues associated with gambling.

In the end, an educated public will conclude that legalizing casino gambling is not be the solution to improve Florida's economy. The cost is too great—in both dollars and community well-being.

After Reading: Do you think legalized casino gambling will benefit or harm the community? Take one side of the issue. Give and explain supports for your side of the argument.

Response: _____

_____

_____

_____

REVIEW TEST 1

Score (number correct) _____ x 20 = _____ %

Visit MyReadingLab to take this test online and receive feedback and guidance on your answers.

Biased Arguments

Read the following sets of ideas. Write **UB** if the statement is unbiased, or **B** if the idea is a biased argument.

_____ 1. Facebook is the largest social media network, with more than 900 million users worldwide.

_____ 2. Facebook is a great way for people to share information about themselves.

_____ 3. Many Facebook users become obsessed and spend too much time on the social network.

_____ 4. Users must be careful about who they "friend" and allow to see their personal information.

_____ 5. The number one reason people quit Facebook is a concern for privacy.

Score (number correct) _____ x 5 = _____ %

Visit MyReadingLab to take this test online and receive feedback and guidance on your answers.

Biased Arguments: Fallacies in Logical Thought and Propaganda

A. Write the letter of the fallacy next to its definition.

a. begging the question   d. false cause

b. personal attack   e. false comparison

c. straw man   f. either-or

_____ 1. In this fallacy, the original argument is replaced with a weaker version that is easier to challenge than the original argument.

_____ 2. This fallacy assumes two things are similar when they are not.

_____ 3. This fallacy assumes that because events occurred around or near the same time, they have a cause-and-effect relationship.

_____ 4. This fallacy assumes that only two sides of an issue exist.

_____ 5. This fallacy restates the point of an argument as the support and conclusion.

_____ 6. This fallacy uses abusive remarks in place of evidence for a point or argument.

B. Write the letter of the propaganda technique next to its definition.

a. plain folks   e. name-calling

b. bandwagon   f. glittering generality

c. testimonial   g. card stacking

d. transfer

_____ 7. This technique uses irrelevant personal opinions to support a product, idea, or cause.

_____ 8. This technique uses or suggests the irrelevant detail that "everyone is doing it."

_____ 9. This technique omits factual details in order to misrepresent a product, idea, or cause.

_____ **10.** This technique uses irrelevant details to build trust based on commonly shared values.

_____ **11.** This technique creates an association between a product, idea, or cause with a symbol or image that has positive or negative values.

_____ **12.** This technique uses negative labels for a product, idea, or cause.

_____ **13.** This technique offers general positive statements that cannot be verified.

C. Write the letter of the fallacy used in each of the following items.

_____ **14.** If you don't like the rules of the house, get out and live on your own.
   a. begging the question   c. personal attack
   b. either-or   d. straw man

_____ **15.** The teacher doesn't care if you pass or fail—he still gets paid.
   a. false cause   c. begging the question
   b. either-or   d. personal attack

_____ **16.** Studying for final exams is like running in a marathon.
   a. false comparison   c. begging the question
   b. straw man   d. false cause

_____ **17.** Every time you get into serious trouble, Sam and Maurice are nearby. You are not allowed to see either one of them again.
   a. straw man   c. false cause
   b. either-or   d. personal attack

D. Write the letter of the propaganda technique used in each of the following items.

_____ **18.** A vote for Social Security Reform is a vote for peace of mind.
   a. bandwagon   c. plain folks
   b. glittering generalities   d. transfer

_____ **19.** A decorated war hero and proven military leader, General Smithenhouser says, "I fought shoulder to shoulder with Senator Treat in the trenches of Viet Nam and in the mountains of Afghanistan. I tell you, you will find no greater man for president of the United States. I pledge my full support to his candidacy."
   a. bandwagon   c. plain folks
   b. glittering generalities   d. transfer

_____ **20.** If you long for fluffy, light biscuits just like the ones fresh from your grandmother's oven, then buy Country Biscuits.
   a. bandwagon
   b. glittering generalities
   c. plain folks
   d. transfer

REVIEW TEST 3

Score (number correct) _____ x 10 = _____ %

Visit MyReadingLab to take this test online and receive feedback and guidance on your answers.

Advanced Argument

Textbook
Skills

Before Reading: Survey the following passage adapted from a college psychology textbook. Skim the passage, noting the words in **bold** print, and answer the Before Reading questions. Then answer the After Reading questions and respond to the writing prompt.

Vocabulary Preview

ambiguity (6): unclearness; vagueness
pathological (14): caused by disease
perpetrator (16): someone who commits a crime or other offense
deter (17): keep from doing
flammable (24): able to catch fire
volatile (28): unstable; explosive
trajectory (38): path of something that moves

Is Terrorism "a Senseless Act of Violence, Perpetrated by Crazy Fanatics"?

[1]The terrorist attacks of September 11, 2001, and suicide bombings in Israel, Iraq, London, Madrid, and elsewhere around the world raise questions for which there are no easy answers. [2]Terrorism is really about psychology. [3]It typically involves a relatively small group of people working as a network who take dramatic, violent actions against a larger group with the intention of spreading fear of death among them and inducing anxiety and uncertainty about their government's ability to protect them. [4]Terrorists do not want to conquer other nations' land, as in traditional

wars, but to conquer the minds of their enemies by making them feel victimized and fearful of random attacks.

[5]The reasons for terrorist violence are many and complex. [6]However, media sources of such claims try to simplify complexity and reduce **ambiguity** to simple frameworks. [7]They often exaggerate fears for viewers and listeners. [8]"If it bleeds, it leads," is a classic statement about what it takes to be the lead TV news item. [9]When they or the general public do not understand something, there is a readiness to label it "senseless." [10]That only means it does not make sense to them or that there is no solid evidence for the motivations behind it.

[11]Obviously this is an extreme generalization and simplification of a complex social-political-cultural issue. [12]Unfortunately, the easiest and most simplistic response is to **demonize** those who perpetrate evil deeds—but that blinds us to the power of the situation to create aggression in ordinary people, as we have seen in the Milgram and Stanford Prison research. [13]More important, it prevents us from dealing with the situations that nurture violence. [14]Labeling others as "evil" or **"pathological"** usually prevents any attempt to understand the reasons for their actions, instead making them into objects of scorn or disdain. [15]Again, it is a related mistake to think of violence and terrorism as "senseless." [16]On the contrary, destructive deeds always make sense from the **perpetrator**'s frame of reference. [17]As Shakespeare's Hamlet said, there is "method" in madness: We must understand the method in the minds of potential terrorists if we are to **deter** them.

[18]A summary of recent perspectives on what moves people to kill themselves and innocent bystanders is available in a thorough report by *New York Times* correspondent Sarah Kershaw (2010). [19]Research has shown that aggressive behavior can be **induced** by situations that create prejudice, conformity, frustration, threat, or wounded pride (Aronson, 2004; Baumeister et al., 1996). [20]There is no evidence that terrorists, even suicide bombers, are pathological. [21]Rather, they are filled with anger and desire for revenge against what they perceive as injustice. [22]They are often well educated, in stable relationships, and now likely to be from both sexes. [23]In many cases, they become part of a systematic training program to learn the skills necessary to effectively destroy one's perceived enemy and accept being a martyr for a cause they believe is just (Merari, 2006).

[24]The **flammable** combination of poverty, powerlessness, and hopelessness is the tinder that the September 11 attacks were intended to ignite,

says Jonathan Lash (2001), president of the World Resources Institute in Washington, D.C. [25]Much of the world lives in poverty and hunger and sees no way out. [26]Ethnic hatred and wars aggravate their plight. [27]Moreover, the number of people living in these miserable conditions is increasing, as most of the world's population explosion is occurring in poorer countries. [28]And, to make matters more **volatile**, says Lash, a large proportion of these desperate people depend directly on resources that are rapidly being depleted: fisheries, forests, soils, and water resources. [29]As a result, every day, thousands flee their traditional homelands and stream into the largest and poorest cities. [30]Most are young—a result of the high birth rates in the Third World. [31]Mr. Lash warns that urban slums, filled with restless, jobless young men, are "tinderboxes of anger and despair; easy recruiting grounds" (p. 1789). [32]We have seen this in recent violent riots in the slums outside Paris by young immigrants without jobs and educational opportunities.

[33]Understanding terrorism requires the combined insights of many perspectives—and not just those from psychology. [34]Issues of money, power, resources, and ancient grudges must be considered as well. [35]When we expand our view of terrorism, we can see that long-standing hostilities arise from religious, ethnic, and racial prejudices and from poverty, powerlessness, and hopelessness. [36]To arrive at this understanding, however, we must view terrorism from historical, economic, and political perspectives—again, not to excuse violent acts but to understand their origins. [37]We cannot understand, for example, the tensions between Christianity and Islam without knowing about the 200-year war that the Western world calls the Crusades (1095 to 1291) or the fall of the six-centuries-old Ottoman Empire (1300 to 1922) at the end of World War I. [38]Although such events may seem remote, they changed the **trajectory** of history, and their religious significance continues to fuel conflict in the Middle East today.

—Adapted from Zimbardo, Philip G., Johnson, Robert L., and Hamilton, Vivian McCann, *Psychology: Core Concepts*, 7th ed., pp. 508–510.

Before Reading

Vocabulary

_____   **1.** What is the best meaning of the word **induced** in sentence 19?
   a. prevented   c. punished
   b. eased   d. caused

Tone and Purpose

_____ **2.** The authors' tone and purpose is to
   a. entertain readers by recounting shocking acts of terrorism.
   b. inform readers how we can fight terrorism.
   c. persuade readers to understand the causes of terrorism.

After Reading

Central Idea

_____ **3.** Which sentence best states the authors' central idea?
   a. sentence 1   c. sentence 5
   b. sentence 2   d. sentence 18

Supporting Details

_____ **4.** According to the passage, the purpose of terrorist acts is to
   a. overthrow governments.   c. erase poverty.
   b. acquire land.   d. spread fear.

Thought Patterns

_____ **5.** The thought pattern of paragraph 4 (sentences 18–23) is
   a. time order.   c. comparison.
   b. cause and effect.   d. classification.

Fact and Opinion

_____ **6.** Sentence 33 is a statement of
   a. fact.   c. fact and opinion.
   b. opinion.

Inferences

_____ **7.** Based on the details in the passage, which of the following is a valid inference?
   a. Reducing poverty worldwide is one way to prevent terrorism.
   b. Terrorism is a very recent phenomenon in history.
   c. We will never be able to prevent terrorism because we can't erase events from the past.
   d. The emotion of envy plays a major role in causing terrorism.

Argument

_____ **8.** Sentence 9 discusses the propaganda technique of
   a. name calling.   c. bandwagon.
   b. testimonial.   d. plain folks.

_____ **9.** Sentence 12 discusses the fallacy of
   a. straw man.   c. false comparison.
   b. begging the question. d. personal attack.

_____ **10.** Sentence 17 uses the technique of
   a. testimonial.   c. card stacking.
   b. transfer.   d. glittering generalities.

SUMMARY RESPONSE

Restate the authors' central idea in your own words. Include key major details in your summary. Begin your summary response with the following: *The central idea of "Is Terrorism a Senseless Act of Violence, Perpetrated by Crazy Fanatics?" by Zimbardo, Johnson, and McCann is . . .*

WHAT DO YOU THINK?

Assume you are taking a college course in political science, and your professor has assigned an essay on terrorism. Write an essay in which you state your views about the most effective way to deal with terrorists. Include the following in your essay:

- Identify causes of terrorism.
- Determine whether the authors' claim that understanding the causes of terrorism is necessary to deal with it effectively is relevant.
- Support your stance with details from the passage.

REVIEW TEST 4

Score (number correct) _____ x 10 = _____ %

Visit MyReadingLab to take this test online and receive feedback and guidance on your answers.

Advanced Argument

Textbook
Skills

Before Reading: Survey the following passage adapted from a college sociology textbook. Skim the passage, noting the words in **bold** print. Answer the Before Reading questions that follow the passage. Then read the passage. Next, answer the After Reading questions. Use the discussion and writing topics as activities to do after reading.

Vocabulary Preview

rampant (3): uncontrolled
nomadic (5): wandering
ethnocentric (7): belief in the superiority of one's own ethnic group
immunity (15): resistance
accommodated (21): adjusted to
intervene (29): interfere
pacification (31): soothing, subduing

Native Americans

¹"I don't go so far as to think that the only good Indians are dead Indians, but I believe nine out of ten are—and I shouldn't inquire too closely in the case of the tenth. ²The most vicious cowboy has more moral principle than the average Indian."

—Teddy Roosevelt, 1886 President of the United States, 1901–1909

³This quote from Teddy Roosevelt provides insight into the **rampant** racism of earlier generations. ⁴Yet, even today, thanks to countless grade B Westerns, some Americans view the original inhabitants of what became the United States as wild, uncivilized savages, a single group of people subdivided into separate tribes. ⁵The European immigrants to the colonies, however, encountered diverse groups of people with a variety of cultures—from **nomadic** hunters and gatherers to people who lived in wooden houses in settled agricultural communities. ⁶Altogether, they spoke over 700 languages. ⁷Each group had its own norms and values—and the usual **ethnocentric** pride in its own culture. ⁸Consider what

happened in 1744, when the colonists of Virginia offered college scholarships for "savage" lads. [9]The Iroquois replied:

[10]"Several of our young people were formerly brought up at the colleges of Northern Provinces. [11]They were instructed in all your sciences. [12]But when they came back to us, they were bad runners, ignorant of every means of living in the woods, unable to bear either cold or hunger, knew neither how to build a cabin, take a deer, or kill an enemy . . . [13]They were totally good for nothing."

[14]They added, "If the English gentlemen would send a dozen or two of their children to Onondaga, the great Council would take care of their education, bring them up in really what was the best manner and make men of them." (Nash 1974; in McLemore 1994)

[15]Native Americans, who numbered about 10 million, had no **immunity** to the diseases the Europeans brought with them. [16]With deaths due to disease—and warfare, a much lesser cause—their number was reduced to about one-twentieth its original size. [17]A hundred years ago, the Native American population reached a low point of a half million. [18]Native Americans, who now number about 2 million, speak 150 different languages. [19]Like Latinos and Asian Americans, they do not think of themselves as a single people who fit neatly within a single label.

[20]At first, relations between the European settlers and the Native Americans were by and large peaceful. [21]The Native Americans **accommodated** the strangers, as there was plenty of land for both the newcomers and themselves. [22]As Native Americans were pushed aside and wave after wave of settlers continued to arrive, however, Pontiac, an Ottawa chief, saw the future—and didn't like it. [23]He convinced several tribes to unite in an effort to push the Europeans into the sea. [24]He almost succeeded, but failed when the English were reinforced by fresh troops.

[25]A pattern of deception developed. [26]The U.S. government would make treaties to buy some of a tribe's land, with the promise to honor forever the tribe's right to what it had not sold. [27]European immigrants, who continued to pour into the United States, would disregard these boundaries. [28]The tribes would resist, with death tolls on both sides. [29]The U.S. government would then **intervene**—not to enforce the treaty but to force the tribe off its lands. [30]In its relentless drive westward, the U.S. government embarked on a policy of **genocide**. [31]It assigned the U.S. cavalry the task of "**pacification**," which translated into

slaughtering Native Americans who "stood in the way" of this territorial expansion.

—Henslin, James M., *Essentials of Sociology: A Down-to-Earth Approach,* 7th ed., pp. 247–248.

Before Reading

Vocabulary in Context

Use context clues to state in your own words the definition of the following term. Indicate the context clue you used.

1. In sentence 30, what does the word **genocide** mean? _____

_____

2. Identify the context clue used for the word **genocide** in sentence 30.

_____

Tone and Purpose

_____ **3.** What is the overall tone and purpose of the passage?
  a. to inform the reader about the historical relationship between Native Americans, European settlers, and the U.S. government
  b. to persuade the reader that Native Americans have endured a pattern of racism that continues today
  c. to entertain the reader with surprising details about Native American history

After Reading

Central Idea

4. Use your own words to state the central idea of the passage: _____

_____

_____

Main Idea and Supporting Details

_____ **5.** Sentence 15 states a
  a. main idea.   c. minor supporting detail.
  b. major supporting detail.

Transitions

_____ **6.** The relationship between sentences 4 and 5 is
- a. cause and effect.
- b. addition.
- c. time order.
- d. contrast.

Thought Patterns

_____ **7.** The overall thought pattern of the passage is
- a. cause and effect.
- b. listing.
- c. time order.
- d. contrast.

Fact and Opinion

_____ **8.** Sentences 1 and 2 are statements of
- a. fact.
- b. opinion.
- c. fact and opinion.

Inferences

_____ **9.** Based on the information in sentence 31, the U.S. government's use of "pacification" implies that
- a. the U.S. government tried to coexist peacefully with Native Americans.
- b. the U.S. government used a glittering generality as a propaganda technique to describe its violent actions against Native Americans.
- c. the Native Americans initiated violence and caused the actions taken against them by the U.S. government.

Argument

_____ **10.** Sentences 1 and 2 are examples of the logical fallacy
- a. begging the question.
- b. straw man.
- c. false comparison.
- d. personal attack.

SUMMARY RESPONSE

Restate the author's central idea in your own words. Include key major details in your summary. Begin your summary response with the following: *The central idea of "Native Americans" by Henslin is . . .*

WHAT DO YOU THINK?

Assume your community is going to celebrate the various ethnic groups that live in your area during the traditional Fourth of July celebration. You have been asked to represent your ethnic group by giving a short speech that explains your heritage. Write a draft of your speech that is at least three paragraphs long. In your speech, include the following details:

- Define your ethnic group.
- Describe the core values of your culture.
- Explain how a key tradition reflects those values.

After Reading About Advanced Argument

Before you move on to the Mastery Tests on advanced argument, take time to reflect on your learning and performance by answering the following questions. Write your answers in your notebook.

- How has my knowledge base or prior knowledge about advanced argument—persuasive techniques changed?
- Based on my studies, how do I think I will perform on the Mastery Test(s)? Why do I think my scores will be above average, average, or below average? (Note: An additional fourth Mastery Test may be found in MyReadingLab.)
- Would I recommend this chapter to other students who want to learn more about advanced argument—persuasive techniques? Why or why not?

Test your understanding of what you have learned about advanced argument—persuasive techniques by completing the Chapter 13 Review.

Name _____ Section_____

Date _____ **Score** (number correct) _____ x 10 = _____ %

Visit MyReadingLab to take this test online and receive feedback and guidance on your answers.

Write the letter of the fallacy used in each statement.

_____ **1.** If you cannot perform the duties listed on your job description, you'll have to find another job.
a. begging the question   c. personal attack
b. either-or   d. straw man

_____ **2.** The government doesn't care about you. You are just a student who doesn't pay taxes.
a. false cause   c. begging the question
b. either-or   d. personal attack

_____ **3.** Falling in love is like jumping off the high diving board.
a. false comparison   c. begging the question
b. straw man   d. false cause

_____ **4.** Whenever you eat ice cream, you get irritable. We're not having dessert anymore.
a. straw man   c. false cause
b. either-or   d. personal attack

_____ **5.** Most politicians are like alcoholics—drunk on power, in denial, and unwilling to stop their addiction to lying.
a. false comparison   c. straw man
b. begging the question   d. false cause

_____ **6.** *Parent to teenager:* "You can't be trusted because you have proven you are untrustworthy."
a. straw man   c. begging the question
b. personal attack   d. either-or

_____ **7.** My grandmother says that to cure a wart you should cut a potato in half, rub the wart with the cut potato, and then bury the potato at night during a full moon. The wart will go away within a week.
a. false cause   c. either-or
b. straw man   d. personal attack

_____ **8.** *Speaker 1:* I propose a solution that will address the concerns of both developers and environmentalists. In every new neighborhood, developers will set aside green areas that can be used as parks or environmental havens. Funds to offset the cost of these green areas could be raised by a nominal county tax and donations from the Green-Friendly Organization.

Speaker 2: My opponent's solution to everything is to raise taxes.

a. begging the question   c. false comparison

b. personal attack   d. straw man

_____ **9.** My Lexus is my favorite car of all those that I have ever owned because I like it so much.

a. straw man   c. begging the question

b. personal attack   d. either-or

_____ **10.** City commissioner Jerome Little is a political bully who is determined to protect the wealthy at the expense of the middle class.

a. personal attack   c. false cause

b. straw man   d. either-or

Name _____ Section_____

Date _____ **Score** (number correct) _____ x 20 = _____ %

Visit MyReadingLab to take this test online and receive feedback and guidance on your answers.

A. Identify the propaganda technique used in each statement. Some techniques are used more than once.

a. plain folks
c. testimonial
b. bandwagon
d. name-calling

_____ **1.** The founder of our company is just like you; she understands the pressures of everyday life, so she made sure that we offer affordable goods in the most efficient way possible to save you money and time.

_____ **2.** Don't delay! Buy a lot in this gated community before they are all gone. Lots are moving quickly! Don't miss out on this opportunity to live in one of the most sought-after neighborhoods.

_____ **3.** Of course Gerald Homey would vote for an increase in minimum wage; he is the puppet of labor unions.

B. Read each fictitious advertisement. Then identify the detail from the list that was omitted from the ad for the purpose of card stacking.

_____ **4.** For Sale: This two-year-old female Yorkie terrier has been neutered, house-trained, and has had all the required vaccinations. She is bright, energetic, and loving. She weighs three pounds and has silver coloring.
a. The family is moving to a condominium where no pets are allowed.
b. The terrier is a thoroughbred with registered papers.
c. The terrier has a feisty personality with a history of biting.

_____ **5.** Ageless Solutions is a miracle supplement that turns back the aging process. With a secret blend of natural ingredients, including vitamin D, the recommended daily dosage helps the body rebuild bone, protecting you from osteoporosis and other bone diseases.
a. Ageless Solutions contains a complete daily dose of several necessary vitamins, including vitamin A, vitamin C, riboflavin, niacin, and folic acid.

b. Certain batches of Ageless Solutions have been recalled due to labeling errors that led to excessive dosages of vitamin D. Taking excessive amounts of this vitamin can cause weakness, fatigue, headaches, nausea, vomiting, diarrhea, mental status changes, and even coma in severe cases.

c. Ageless Solutions has been clinically tested with proven results.

Name _____ Section_____

Date _____ **Score** (number correct) _____ x 10 = _____ %

Visit MyReadingLab to take this test online and receive feedback and guidance on your answers.

Propaganda Techniques

A. Identify the propaganda technique used in each statement. A technique may be selected more than once or not at all.

a. plain folks	d. transfer
b. bandwagon	e. name-calling
c. testimonial	f. glittering generality

_____ 1. Sandra's Fruitcake is just like the one your mother made every Christmas. For the same fresh-baked, homemade taste, buy Sandra's Fruitcake.

_____ 2. A candidate says, "If you like what George Washington, Abraham Lincoln, and Martin Luther King, Jr. stood for, then you will cast your vote for me."

_____ 3. I would never recommend Professor Higgins; he is anti-American and subversive.

_____ 4. Please, Mother, I have to have a pair of low-riding jeans and a midriff shirt; it's what everybody is wearing.

_____ 5. Actress Heather McCoy says, "True Blond leaves my hair silky, shiny, and much more manageable."

_____ 6. The owner of a national fast-food chain, dressed in a cotton short-sleeved shirt, sits at a table in one of his restaurants, surrounded by working-class people who are happily eating hamburgers and French fries. He says, "My wife and I started this business 30 years ago, and we are still here for you. Drop on in. We'll be glad to see you."

_____ 7. Famous race car driver Rick Ellington states, "I only use ValvoClean on the race track and on the road."

_____ 8. Supplies Limited. Only a few special edition Bag Babies are left. No more shipments expected before Christmas. Hurry before they are all gone.

_____ 9.

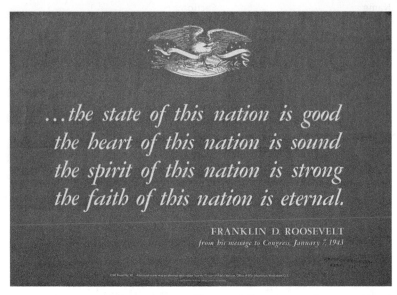

...*the state of this nation is good*
the heart of this nation is sound
the spirit of this nation is strong
the faith of this nation is eternal.

FRANKLIN D. ROOSEVELT
from his message to Congress, January 7, 1943

—From World War II Poster Collection, Office of War Information (OWI)
The New Hampshire State Library.

B. Read this fictitious advertisement. Then identify the detail that was omitted for the purpose of card stacking.

_____ 10. Fun Water will turn your backyard into a water park for your children and their friends. Simply hook your water hose to Fun Water and watch the fun begin. Fun Water throws a sheet of water down a brightly colored slide that gently slopes into a shallow pool. Your children will slip and slide their way to fun all summer long.
   a. Fun Water is a highly popular, fast-selling product.
   b. Fun Water doesn't waste water because it recycles and reuses water.
   c. Several children have experienced minor injuries using Fun Water.

13 Summary of Key Concepts about Advanced Argument: Persuasive Techniques

 Assess your comprehension of advanced arguments and persuasive techniques. Complete the two-column notes with information from the chapter.

Fallacy	
Irrelevant details	
Inadequate details	
Propaganda	
Emotional appeal	
Personal attack	
Straw man	
Begging the question	
Name-calling	
Testimonials	
Bandwagon	

Plain folks	
Either-or	
False comparison	
False cause	
Card stacking	
Transfer	
Glittering generalities	

Test Your Comprehension of Advanced Argument: Persuasive Techniques

Respond to the following questions and prompts.

(LO1) (LO2) (LO3) (LO4) (LO5) In your own words, explain the relationship among the following terms: *fallacy, irrelevant details, emotional appeal, inadequate details*, and *propaganda*.

_____

_____

_____

_____

(LO1) (LO2) (LO3) (LO4) (LO5) (LO6) (LO7) Summarize the two most important ideas in this chapter that will help you improve your reading comprehension. _____

_____

_____

Additional Readings

The Connection Between Reading and Writing

The link between reading and writing is vital and natural. Written language allows an exchange of ideas between a writer and a reader. Thus, writing and reading are two equal parts of the communication process. In fact, reading is a form of listening or receiving information. And writing is like speaking—the sending of information. So a master reader makes every effort to understand and respond to the ideas of the writer. Likewise, a master writer makes every effort to make ideas clear so the reader can understand and respond to those ideas. Most writers find that reading improves their writing. Reading builds prior knowledge and fuels ideas for writing.

Because of this close relationship between reading and writing, both share similar thinking steps in their processes. In Chapter 1, you learned that the reading process has three phases: Before Reading, During Reading, and After Reading. The writing process also has three phases that occur before, during, and after writing: Prewriting, Drafting, and Proofing. By coordinating these two sets of process, you can improve both your reading and your writing. For example, the following statements sum up one way to connect reading and writing:

Reading is a prewriting activity. Drafting is an after reading activity.

Once you think of reading as a prewriting activity, you become a responsive or active reader during the reading process. In fact, you can begin using your writing skills as you read by annotating the text.

Annotating a Text

The word *annotate* suggests that you "take notes" in your book. Writing notes in the margin of a page of your own book as you read keeps you focused and improves your comprehension. You can quickly note questions where they occur, move on in your reading, and later return to clarify answers. In addition, after reading, your annotations help you review and respond to the material. The following suggestions offer one way to annotate a text:

How to Annotate a Text

- Circle important terms.
- Underline definitions and meanings.
- Note key ideas with a star or a check.
- Place question marks above words that are unknown or confusing.
- Number the steps in a process or items in a list.
- Write summaries at the end of long sections.
- Write recall questions in the margin near their answers.
- Write key words and meanings in the margin.

> **EXAMPLE** The passage from a college communications textbook on page 624 is marked up as an example of an annotated text. Read the passage. Study the annotations. Then work with a peer or in a small group and create a summary of the text based on the annotations. See below to review how to write a summary.

Writing a Summary

Writing a summary is an effective step in the reading and studying process.

A **summary** is a brief, clear restatement of a longer passage.

A summary includes only the passage's most important points. Often a summary is made up of the main idea and major supporting details. The length of a summary should reflect your study needs and the kind of passage you are trying to understand. For example, a paragraph might be summarized in a sentence or two, an article might be summarized in a paragraph, and a textbook chapter might be summarized in a page or two.

You can discover how well you understand a passage by writing a summary of it as an after reading activity. Use the annotations you make during reading to create your summary.

For example, read the following summary of "Recognize Culture Shock" from a college communications textbook. Underline the words and phrases that were annotated in the longer section on page 624:

> [1]Culture shock is the "psychological reaction you experience when you're in a culture very different from your own." [2]When you are in culture shock, you can't communicate effectively and don't know even simple customs. [3]For example, you don't know how to ask for a favor, how to order a meal, or how to dress. [4]Anthropologist Kalervo Oberg coined the term "culture shock" and identifies its four stages. [5]Stage one, "the honeymoon," is filled with excitement and adventure. [6]Stage two, "the crisis," brings confusion and frustration due to unfamiliar customs and surroundings. [7]Stage three, "the recovery," is the process of learning how to function. [8]And stage four, "the adjustment," brings independence and enjoyment. [9]As the process indicates, culture shock can be overcome.

This summary includes the author's main idea and the major supporting details. However, this summary also brings in a few minor supporting details. For example, sentence 3 gives examples of customs that a person would not know. Including these details makes the summary longer than may be necessary. The version on page 625 includes only the main idea and the major supporting details.

Recognize Culture Shock (Culture shock) refers to the psychological reaction you experience when you're in a culture very different from your own (Furnham & Bochner, 1986). Culture shock is normal; most people experience it when entering a new and different culture. Nevertheless, it can be unpleasant and frustrating. Part of this results from feelings of alienation, conspicuousness, and difference from everyone else. When you lack knowledge of the rules and customs of the new society, you cannot communicate effectively. You're apt to blunder frequently and seriously. In your culture shock you may not know basic things:

1. ■ how to ask someone for a favor or pay someone a compliment
2. ■ how to extend or accept an invitation for dinner
3. ■ how early or how late to arrive for an appointment
4. ■ how long you should stay when visiting someone
5. ■ how to distinguish seriousness from playfulness and politeness from indifference
6. ■ how to dress for an informal, formal, or business function
7. ■ how to order a meal in a restaurant or how to summon a waiter

7 basic communication tasks & simple customs you may not know

Anthropologist Kalervo Oberg (1960), who first used the term culture shock, notes that it occurs in stages. These stages are useful for examining many encounters with the new and the different. Going away to college, moving in together, or joining the military, for example, can also result in culture shock. In explaining culture shock, we use the example of moving away from home into your own apartment to illustrate its four stages.

Who first used the term "culture shock"?

1. Stage One: The Honeymoon At first you experience fascination, even enchantment, with the new culture and its people. You finally have your own apartment. You're your own boss. Finally, on your own! When in groups of people who are culturally different, this stage is characterized by cordiality and friendship in these early and superficial relationships. Many tourists remain at this stage because their stay in foreign countries is so brief.

How many stages are there?

2. Stage Two: The Crisis Here, the differences between your own culture and the new one create problems. No longer do you find dinner ready for you unless you do it yourself. Your clothes are not washed or ironed unless you do them yourself. Feelings of frustration and inadequacy come to the fore. This is the stage at which you experience the actual shock of the new culture. One study of foreign students coming from over 100 different countries studying in 11 different countries found that 25 percent of the students experienced depression (Klineberg & Hull, 1979).

What are the labels for each stage?

3. Stage Three: The Recovery During this period you gain the skills necessary to function effectively. You learn how to shop, cook, and plan a meal. You find a local laundry and figure you'll learn how to iron later. You learn the language and ways of the new culture. Your feelings of inadequacy subside.

4. Stage Four: The Adjustment At this final stage, you adjust to and come to enjoy the new culture and the new experiences. You may still experience periodic difficulties and strains, but on a whole, the experience is pleasant. Actually, you're now a pretty decent cook. You're even coming to enjoy it. You're making a good salary so why learn to iron?

Culture shock can be overcome!

—DeVito, Joseph A. *The Interpersonal Communication Book,* 10th ed., p. 59. Printed and Electronically reproduced by permission of Pearson Education, Inc., Upper Saddle River, New Jersey.

[1]Culture shock is the "psychological reaction you experience when you're in a culture very different from your own." [2]When you are in culture shock, you can't communicate effectively and don't know even simple customs. [3]Anthropologist Kalervo Oberg coined the term "culture shock" and identifies its four stages: stage one is "the honeymoon"; stage two is "the crisis"; stage three is "the recovery"; and stage four is "the adjustment." [4]Culture shock can be overcome.

Remember, the length of the summary depends on your study needs as well as the length of the passage you are summarizing.

A Reading-Writing Plan of Action

Can you see how annotating a text lays the ground upon which you can build a written response? The steps you take during reading feed into the process of writing a response after reading.

Remember, reading and writing is a conversation between the writer and the reader. One writes; the other reads. But the conversation often doesn't end there. A reader's response to a piece of writing keeps the dialogue going. When you write a summary, your response is to restate the author's ideas. It's like saying to the author, "If I understood you correctly, you said . . . " When you offer your own views about the author's ideas, you are answering the author's implied question, "What do you think?" In your reading and writing classes, your teacher often steps into the conversation. He or she stands in for the author and becomes the reader of your written response. In this case, your teacher evaluates both your reading and writing abilities. Your teacher checks your response for accuracy in comprehension of the author's message and development of your ability to write. The following chart illustrates this exchange of ideas.

The Conversation Among Writers and Readers

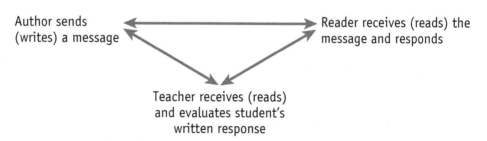

Author sends (writes) a message

Reader receives (reads) the message and responds

Teacher receives (reads) and evaluates student's written response

In each skill chapter of this textbook, the question "What Do You Think?" is posed after Review Tests 3 and 4. This question also appears after each reading selection in this section. The "What Do You Think?" writing assignments after each reading selection prompt you to respond to what you have read. This activity creates a writing situation and gives you a purpose for your written response. Just like a vocabulary word makes more sense in context than in a list, a writing assignment in context is more meaningful than an isolated topic or set of disconnected questions. The goal of "What Do You Think?" is to strengthen your connection between reading and writing. Because reading and writing are two distinct processes, it is helpful to have a guide that shows how to efficiently coordinate them. The following chart lays out a reading-writing plan of action. Note that the chart breaks the reading-writing process into a series of 6 steps. Keep in mind that any step can be repeated as needed. Also, you can move back and forth between steps as needed.

Study the 6-Step Reading-Writing Action Plan. Then work with a peer or small group of classmates and discuss the relationship between reading and writing, and how you will put this plan to use.

A 6-Step Reading-Writing Action Plan

Read		Write
1. Survey and Question	**BEFORE**	**4. Prewrite**
Call on Prior Knowledge Identify Topic Identify Key or New Words Identify Thought Patterns Note Visual Aids Skim Introductions and Conclusions		Build Prior Knowledge* Gather Information* Read and Annotate* Brainstorm Ideas Choose Your Topic Generate Your Details Create a Concept Map Outline Ideas
2. Read	**DURING**	**5. Draft**
Monitor Comprehension Fix Confusion Annotate Text		Write Introduction, Body, and Conclusion
3. Review and Recite	**AFTER**	**6. Revise and Proofread**

Recall Key Words and Ideas
Create Concept Maps
Create Outlines
Write a Summary
Write a Response
		Revise to Organize
		Revise for Exact Wording
		Correct Errors
		    Fragments and Run-ons
		    Spelling
		    Punctuation

---

*Prewriting steps accomplished during reading

1 Sex, Lies and Conversation: Why Is It So Hard for Men and Women to Talk to Each Other?

by Deborah Tannen

Deborah Tannen is University Professor of Linguistics in the Department of Linguistics at Georgetown University in Washington, D.C. Tannen, the author of nineteen published books and nearly a hundred articles and the recipient of five honorary doctorates, is an expert on the nature of human language. She lectures worldwide and is also a frequent guest on television and radio news and information shows. Tannen is perhaps best known to the general public, however, as the author of *You Just Don't Understand: Women and Men in Conversation.* This groundbreaking book about gender-based communication was on the *New York Times* best-seller list for nearly four years, including eight months as the number one best-selling book. It was also a best-seller in Brazil, Canada, England, Germany, Holland, and Hong Kong. *You Just Don't Understand* offers helpful insights about gender differences in communication style. This article, adapted from *You Just Don't Understand: Women and Men in Conversation,* appeared in *The Washington Post.*

Vocabulary Preview

anecdotes (paragraph 1): illustrations, stories
concurred (paragraph 1): agreed
crystallizes (paragraph 2): becomes well defined
havoc (paragraph 2): chaos, disorder
tangible (paragraph 4): concrete, real, touchable
inequities (paragraph 4): injustices
socialization (paragraph 8): training to gain skills necessary to function successfully in society
attuned (paragraph 12): adjusted, in tune with
analogous (paragraph 13): similar, comparable
alienated (paragraph 14): separated
requisite (paragraph 19): necessary, essential
paradox (paragraph 22): contradiction
ethnic (paragraph 26): cultural

1   I was addressing a small gathering in a suburban Virginia living room—a women's group that had invited men to join them. Throughout the evening, one man had been particularly talkative, frequently offering ideas and **anecdotes,** while his wife sat silently beside him on the couch. Toward the end of the evening, I commented that women frequently complain that their husbands don't talk to them. This man quickly **concurred.** He gestured toward his wife and said, "She's the talker in our family." The room burst into laughter; the man looked puzzled and hurt. "It's true," he explained. "When I come home from work I have nothing to say. If she didn't keep the conversation going, we'd spend the whole evening in silence."

2   This episode **crystallizes** the irony that although American men tend to talk more than women in public situations, they often talk less at home. And this pattern is wreaking **havoc** with marriage.

3   The pattern was observed by political scientist Andrew Hacker in the late '70s. Sociologist Catherine Kohler Riessman reports in her new book "Divorce Talk" that most of the women she interviewed—but only a few of the men—gave lack of communication as the reason for their divorces. Given the current divorce rate of nearly 50 percent, that amounts to millions of cases in the United States every year—a virtual epidemic of failed conversation.

4   In my own research, complaints from women about their husbands most often focused not on **tangible inequities** such as having given up the chance for a career to accompany a husband to his, or doing far more than their share of daily life-support work like cleaning, cooking, social arrangements and errands. Instead, they focused on communication: "He doesn't listen to me," "He doesn't talk to me." I found, as Hacker observed years before, that most wives want their husbands to be, first and foremost, conversational partners, but few husbands share this expectation of their wives.

5   In short, the image that best represents the current crisis is the stereotypical cartoon scene of a man sitting at the breakfast table with a newspaper held up in front of his face, while a woman glares at the back of it, wanting to talk.

Linguistic Battle of the Sexes

6   How can women and men have such different impressions of communication in marriage? Why the widespread imbalance in their interests and expectations?

7   In the April issue of *American Psychologist,* Stanford University's Eleanor Maccoby reports the results of her own and others' research showing that children's development is most influenced by the social structure of peer interactions. Boys and girls tend to play with children of their own gender, and their sex-separate groups have different organizational structures and interactive norms.

8   I believe these systematic differences in childhood **socialization** make talk between women and men like cross-cultural communication, heir to all the attraction and pitfalls of that enticing but difficult enterprise. My research on men's and women's conversations uncovered patterns similar to those described for children's groups.

9   For women, as for girls, intimacy is the fabric of relationships, and talk is the thread

from which it is woven. Little girls create and maintain friendships by exchanging secrets; similarly, women regard conversation as the cornerstone of friendship. So a woman expects her husband to be a new and improved version of a best friend. What is important is not the individual subjects that are discussed but the sense of closeness, of a life shared, that emerges when people tell their thoughts, feelings, and impressions.

10   Bonds between boys can be as intense as girls', but they are based less on talking, more on doing things together. Since they don't assume talk is the cement that binds a relationship, men don't know what kind of talk women want, and they don't miss it when it isn't there.

11   Boys' groups are larger, more inclusive, and more **hierarchical,** so boys must struggle to avoid the subordinate position in the group. This may play a role in women's complaints that men don't listen to them. Some men really don't like to listen, because being the listener makes them feel one-down, like a child listening to adults or an employee to a boss.

12   But often when women tell men, "You aren't listening," and the men protest, "I am," the men are right. The impression of not listening results from misalignments in the mechanics of conversation. The misalignment begins as soon as a man and a woman take physical positions. This became clear when I studied videotapes made by psychologist Bruce Dorval of children and adults talking to their same-sex best friends. I found that at every age, the girls and women faced each other directly, their eyes anchored on each other's faces. At every age, the boys and men sat at angles to each other and looked elsewhere in the room, periodically glancing at each other. They were obviously **attuned** to each other, often mirroring each other's movements. But the tendency of men to face away can give women the impression they aren't listening even when they are. A young woman in college was frustrated: Whenever she told her boyfriend she wanted to talk to him, he would lie down on the floor, close his eyes, and put his arm over his face. This signaled to her, "He's taking a nap." But he insisted he was listening extra hard. Normally, he looks around the room, so he is easily distracted. Lying down and covering his eyes helped him concentrate on what she was saying.

13   **Analogous** to the physical alignment that women and men take in conversation is their topical alignment. The girls in my study tended to talk at length about one topic, but the boys tended to jump from topic to topic. The second-grade girls exchanged stories about people they knew. The second-grade boys teased, told jokes, noticed things in the room and talked about finding games to play. The sixth-grade girls talked about problems with a mutual friend. The sixth-grade boys talked about 55 different topics, none of which extended over more than a few turns.

Listening to Body Language

14   Switching topics is another habit that gives women the impression men aren't listening, especially if they switch to a topic about themselves. But the evidence of the 10th-grade boys in my study indicates otherwise. The 10th-grade boys sprawled across their chairs with bodies parallel and eyes straight ahead, rarely looking at

each other. They looked as if they were riding in a car, staring out the windshield. But they were talking about their feelings. One boy was upset because a girl had told him he had a drinking problem, and the other was feeling **alienated** from all his friends.

15 Now, when a girl told a friend about a problem, the friend responded by asking probing questions and expressing agreement and understanding. But the boys dismissed each other's problems. Todd assured Richard that his drinking was "no big problem" because "sometimes you're funny when you're off your butt." And when Todd said he felt left out, Richard responded, "Why should you? You know more people than me."

16 Women perceive such responses as belittling and unsupportive. But the boys seemed satisfied with them. Whereas women reassure each other by implying, "You shouldn't feel bad because I've had similar experiences," men do so by implying, "You shouldn't feel bad because your problems aren't so bad."

17 There are even simpler reasons for women's impression that men don't listen. Linguist Lynette Hirschman found that women make more listener-noise, such as "mhm," "uhuh," and "yeah," to show "I'm with you." Men, she found, more often give silent attention. Women who expect a stream of listener noise interpret silent attention as no attention at all.

18 Women's conversational habits are as frustrating to men as men's are to women. Men who expect silent attention interpret a stream of listener noise as overreaction or impatience. Also, when women talk to each other in a close, comfortable setting, they often overlap, finish each other's sentences and anticipate what the other is about to say. This practice, which I call "participatory listenership," is often perceived by men as interruption, intrusion and lack of attention.

19 A parallel difference caused a man to complain about his wife, "She just wants to talk about her own point of view. If I show her another view, she gets mad at me." When most women talk to each other, they assume a conversationalist's job is to express agreement and support. But many men see their conversational duty as pointing out the other side of an argument. This is heard as disloyalty by women, and refusal to offer the **requisite** support. It is not that women don't want to see other points of view, but that they prefer them phrased as suggestions and inquiries rather than as direct challenges.

20 In his book "Fighting for Life," Walter Ong points out that men use "agonistic" or warlike, oppositional formats to do almost anything; thus discussion becomes debate, and conversation a competitive sport. In contrast, women see conversation as a ritual means of establishing rapport. If Jane tells a problem and June says she has a similar one, they walk away feeling closer to each other. But this attempt at establishing rapport can backfire when used with men. Men take too literally women's ritual "troubles talk," just as women mistake men's ritual challenges for real attack.

The Sounds of Silence

21 These differences begin to clarify why women and men have such different

expectations about communication in marriage. For women, talk creates intimacy. Marriage is an orgy of closeness: you can tell your feelings and thoughts, and still be loved. Their greatest fear is being pushed away. But men live in a hierarchical world, where talk maintains independence and status. They are on guard to protect themselves from being put down and pushed around.

22   This explains the **paradox** of the talkative man who said of his silent wife, "She's the talker." In the public setting of a guest lecture, he felt challenged to show his intelligence and display his understanding of the lecture. But at home, where he has nothing to prove and no one to defend against, he is free to remain silent. For his wife, being home means she is free from the worry that something she says might offend someone, or spark disagreement, or appear to be showing off; at home she is free to talk.

23   The communication problems that endanger marriage can't be fixed by mechanical engineering. They require a new conceptual framework about the role of talk in human relationships. Many of the psychological explanations that have become second nature may not be helpful, because they tend to blame either women (for not being assertive enough) or men (for not being in touch with their feelings). A sociolinguistic approach by which male-female conversation is seen as cross-cultural communication allows us to understand the problem and forge solutions without blaming either party.

24   Once the problem is understood, improvement comes naturally, as it did to the young woman and her boyfriend who seemed to go to sleep when she wanted to talk. Previously, she had accused him of not listening, and he had refused to change his behavior, since that would be admitting fault. But then she learned about and explained to him the differences in women's and men's habitual ways of aligning themselves in conversation. The next time she told him she wanted to talk, he began, as usual, by lying down and covering his eyes. When the familiar negative reaction bubbled up, she reassured herself that he really was listening. But then he sat up and looked at her. Thrilled, she asked why. He said, "You like me to look at you when we talk, so I'll try to do it." Once he saw their differences as cross-cultural rather than right and wrong, he independently altered his behavior.

25   Women who feel abandoned and deprived when their husbands won't listen to or report daily news may be happy to discover their husbands trying to adapt once they understand the place of small talk in women's relationships. But if their husbands don't adapt, the women may still be comforted that for men, this is not a failure of intimacy. Accepting the difference, the wives may look to their friends or family for that kind of talk. And husbands who can't provide it shouldn't feel their wives have made unreasonable demands. Some couples will still decide to divorce, but at least their decisions will be based on realistic expectations.

26   In these times of resurgent **ethnic** conflicts, the world desperately needs cross-cultural understanding. Like charity, successful cross-cultural communication should begin at home.

—Reproduced by permission of Deborah Tannen.

VISUAL *VOCABULARY*

_____ Which phrase best expresses the meaning
of *rapport* in the caption?

   a. a bond

   b. an idea

   c. a commitment

▶ Women see conversation as a way
to establish rapport.

Choose the best meaning of each word in **bold** type. Use context clues to make
your choice.

Vocabulary
in Context   _____
1. The word **Linguistic** in the heading "Linguistic Battle of the Sexes"
(above paragraph 6) relates to

   a. gender.   c. relationship.

   b. language.   d. education.

Vocabulary
in Context   _____
2. "Boys' groups are larger, more inclusive, and more **hierarchical**, so
boys must struggle to avoid the subordinate position in the group."
(paragraph 11)

   a. ranked   c. logical

   b. brutal   d. submissive

Central Idea   _____
and Main Ideas
3. Which sentence is the best statement of the central idea of the
passage?

   a. "Given the current divorce rate of nearly 50 percent, that
amounts to millions of cases in the United States every year—a
virtual epidemic of failed conversation." (paragraph 3)

   b. "My research on men's and women's conversations uncovered patterns similar to those described for children's groups."
(paragraph 8)

   c. "A sociolinguistic approach by which male-female conversation
is seen as cross-cultural communication allows us to understand the problem and forge solutions without blaming either
party." (paragraph 23)

   d. "Like charity, successful cross-cultural communication should
begin at home." (paragraph 26)

Central Idea and Main Ideas _____

4. Which sentence is the best statement of the implied main idea of paragraphs 14 through 20?
  a. Men and women have different views of communication in marriage.
  b. Men switch topics more often than women do during a conversation.
  c. Women and men differ in their use of body language during the communication process.
  d. Women are more effective listeners than men.

Supporting Details _____

5. According to Catherine Kohler Riessman, which of the following reasons did most women give for their divorces?
  a. giving up the chance for a career to follow a husband
  b. doing far more than their share of daily life-support work like cleaning
  c. sexual infidelity
  d. lack of communication

Supporting Details _____

6. Men reassure each other by
  a. making direct eye contact when they communicate.
  b. making listener-noise such as "mhm," "uhuh," and "yeah" to show "I'm with you."
  c. implying "you shouldn't feel bad because your problems aren't so bad."
  d. practicing "participatory listenership."

Transitions _____

7. "Little girls create and maintain friendships by exchanging secrets; similarly, women regard conversation as the cornerstone of friendship. So a woman expects her husband to be a new and improved version of a best friend." (paragraph 9)

The relationship of ideas between these two sentences is
  a. time order.   c. comparison and contrast.
  b. cause and effect.

Transitions _____

8. "The misalignment begins as soon as a man and a woman take physical positions." (paragraph 12)

The relationship of ideas within this sentence is
  a. time order.   c. comparison and contrast.
  b. cause and effect.

Thought Patterns _____

9. The overall thought pattern used in this passage is
  a. a discussion of the differences in the ways men and women communicate.

b. an argument against the various ways men use communication.

c. a narrative that illustrates the different problems men and women face as they attempt to communicate.

d. a step-by-step description of how to effectively communicate with the opposite sex.

Thought Patterns _____ **10.** The main thought pattern used in paragraph 24 is

a. comparison.   c. time order.

b. definition and example.

Fact and Opinion _____ **11.** Overall, the ideas in this passage are mainly based on

a. the opinions and experiences of ordinary men and women.

b. fictitious or hypothetical details.

c. the research and observation of the author and other experts in the field of linguistics and communication.

Fact and Opinion _____ **12.** "Like charity, successful cross-cultural communication should begin at home." (paragraph 26)

This sentence is a statement of

a. fact.   c. fact and opinion.

b. opinion.

Tone and Purpose _____ **13.** Which word best expresses the overall tone of the passage?

a. biased   c. balanced

b. condescending   d. emotional

Tone and Purpose _____ **14.** The overall tone of paragraph 1 is

a. dismayed.   c. scornful.

b. humorous.   d. neutral.

Tone and Purpose _____ **15.** The tone of paragraph 26 is

a. mocking.   c. hopeful.

b. objective.   d. persuasive.

Tone and Purpose _____ **16.** The author's main purpose is

a. to persuade men and women to change their communication styles.

b. to entertain readers with amusing incidents of miscommunication between men and women.

c. to inform the reader about the differences in communication styles between men and women so that they can better understand one another.

Inferences _____   **17.** Based on the information in the article, generally men
- a. do not listen as well as women.
- b. are more competitive than women.
- c. prefer intimacy over independence, unlike women.

Inferences _____   **18.** The author implies that generally women
- a. are more comfortable and better at giving advice than are men.
- b. are more interested in establishing networks of support than are men.
- c. are more skilled at effective communication than are men.

Inferences _____   **19.** The details in paragraphs 21–26 imply that
- a. men are just as emotional as women.
- b. the hurt and tension between men and women are often based on misunderstanding the communication purpose of the other.
- c. women need to communicate more than men.

Argument _____   **20.** Men live in a hierarchical world, where talk maintains independence and status.

Which statement does *not* support this claim?
- a. Men are on guard to protect themselves from being put down and pushed around.
- b. Men use "agnostic" or warlike, oppositional formats to do almost anything.
- c. He said, "You like me to look at you when we talk, so I'll try to do it."

Mapping

Complete the chart with information from the passage.

Communication Approach of Men	Communication Approach of Women
Establish bonds based on _____	Establish bonds based on talking
Jump from topic to topic	Talk at length about one topic
Expect silent attention	Practice "participatory listenership"
"Agnostic" or warlike, oppositional formats	Ritual means of establishing rapport
Discussion becomes debate	Talk creates _____

WHAT DO YOU THINK?

Do you think men and women differ in the way they communicate? Explain why or why not with examples you have observed. Given that men and women do differ in their approach to communication, how do these differences affect communication at work or school? Assume a friend of yours is having difficulty communicating with a boss or friend of the opposite sex. Write a letter to your friend in which you give advice based on what you learned from this article to help him or her communicate more effectively. Begin your letter with a summary of the author's main idea and major supporting details.

MASTER READER SCORECARD

"Sex, Lies and Conversation"

Skill	Number Correct	Points			Total
Vocabulary					
Vocabulary in Context (2 items)	_____	×	4	=	_____
Comprehension					
Central Idea and Main Ideas (2 items)	_____	×	4	=	_____
Supporting Details (2 items)	_____	×	4	=	_____
Transitions (2 items)	_____	×	4	=	_____
Thought Patterns (2 items)	_____	×	4	=	_____
Fact and Opinion (2 items)	_____	×	4	=	_____
Tone and Purpose (4 items)	_____	×	4	=	_____
Inferences (3 items)	_____	×	4	=	_____
Argument (1 item)	_____	×	4	=	_____
Mapping (2 items)	_____	×	10	=	_____
		Comprehension Score			_____

Prude or Prudent? The Debate Over Access to Plan B

Kathleen Parker

An American journalist, Kathleen Parker started her column in 1987 as a staff writer for *The Orlando Sentinel*. Her column was nationally syndicated in 1995, and she joined The Washington Post Writers Group in 2006. In addition, she has contributed articles to *The Weekly Standard, Town & Country, Cosmopolitan,* and *Fortune Small Business*. She also serves on the Board of Contributors for *USA Today* and writes for that newspaper's op-ed page. In 2008, Random House published her book *Save the Males: Why Men Matter, Why Women Should Care*. In the following piece, Parker weighs in on making the controversial birth control method known as Plan B legally available to young females without the consent of their parents. Do you think the Plan B morning-after pill should be available to 15-year-old girls?

Vocabulary Preview

proffered (paragraph 2): offered, submitted, proposed
discretion (paragraph 4): freedom to decide
advocates (paragraph 14): supporters, backers, activists
underpinnings (paragraph 14): foundations, supports
prudishness (paragraph 16): narrow minded, reserved, easily shocked by sex
paranoid (paragraph 16): fearful, distrustful
delusion (paragraph 16): false belief, fantasies, mistaken ideas
marginalizing (paragraph 18): disregarding, demoting, sidelining

1   They lost me at the word "women."

2   As so often happens in contemporary debate, arguments being **proffered** in support of allowing teenagers as young as 15 (and possibly younger) to buy the "morning-after pill" without adult supervision are false on their premise.

3   Here's an experiment to demonstrate.

4   Question 1: Do you think that women should have access to Plan B, also known as the morning-after pill, to be used at their own **discretion**? *Yes!*

5   Question 2: Do you think that girls as young as 11 or 12 should be able to buy the morning-after pill without any adult supervision? Didn't think so.

6   Question 3: If you answered yes to Question 2, are you a parent? Didn't think so.

7   Perhaps a few parents answered yes to Question 3, but not many, I suspect. Yet, repeatedly in the past several days, we've heard the argument that any interference with the over-the-counter sale of Plan B to any female of *any age* is blocking a woman's right to self-determination. Fifteen-year-olds, where the Obama administration wants to set the limit, are girls, not women. And female parts do not a woman make any more than a correspondingly developed male makes the proud possessor a man.

8   The debate arose after a federal judge last month ordered the government to remove all obstacles to over-the-counter sales of Plan B. Administration policy is that children as young as 15 can buy the drug without a prescription or parental knowledge. They would have to show identification proving they are 15, which, as critics of such restrictions have pointed out, is problematic for many teenagers.

9   Apparently the Obama administration agrees that young girls shouldn't use so serious a drug, even though proclaimed medically "safe," without adult supervision. The Justice Department has given notice that it will appeal the judge's decision, a move that could potentially backfire and, in fact, remove all age barriers.

10   The dominant question is legitimate: Even if we would prefer that girls not be sexually active so early in life, wouldn't we rather they block a pregnancy before it happens than wait and face the worse prospect of abortion?

11   The pros are obvious: Plan B, if taken within three days of unprotected sex, greatly reduces the chance of pregnancy. If a child waits too long to take the pill, however, a fertilized egg could reach the uterine wall and become implanted, after which the drug is useless.

12   You see how the word "child" keeps getting in the way.

13   There's no point debating whether such young girls should be sexually active. Obviously, given the potential consequences, both physical and psychological, the answer is no. Just as obvious, our culture says quite the opposite: As long as there's an exit, whether abortion or Plan B, what's the incentive to await mere maturity?

14   **Advocates** for lifting age limits on Plan B, including Planned Parenthood President Cecile Richards, insist that the pill is universally safe and, therefore, all age barriers should be dropped. From a strictly utilitarian viewpoint, this may be well-advised. But is science the only determining factor when it comes to the well-being of our children? Even President Obama, who once boasted that his policies would be based on science and not emotion, has parental **qualms** about children buying serious drugs to treat a situation that has deeply psychological **underpinnings**.

15   What about the right of parents to protect their children? A 15-year-old can't get Tylenol at school without parental permission, but we have no hesitation about children taking a far more serious drug without oversight?

16   These are fair questions that deserve more than passing scrutiny—or indictments of **prudishness**. A *Slate* headline about the controversy goes: "The Politics of Prude." More to the point: The slippery

slope to parental **autonomy** is no **paranoid delusion**. Whatever parents may do to try to delay the ruin of childhood innocence, the culture says otherwise: Have sex, take a pill, don't tell mom.

17   Where, finally, do we draw the increasingly blurred line for childhood?

18   Americans may disagree about what is sexually appropriate for their children. And everyone surely wishes to prevent children from having babies. But public policy should be aimed at involving, rather than **marginalizing**, parents.

19   To say that this controversy is strictly political is no argument against debate. Politics is the debate about the role of government in our lives. And the debate about Plan B is fundamentally about whether government or parents have ultimate authority over their children's well-being.

—"Prude or prudent? The debate over access to Plan B" by Kathleen Parker from *The Washington Post*, May 3, 2013. Used by permission of *The Washington Post* and protected by the Copyright Laws of the United States.

Choose the best meaning of each word in **bold**. Use context clues to make your choice.

Vocabulary in Context   _____   **1.** "Even President Obama, who once boasted that his policies would be based on science and not emotion, has parental **qualms** about children buying serious drugs to treat a situation that has deeply psychological underpinnings." (paragraph 14)
    a. confidence   c. misgivings
    b. powers   d. understandings

Vocabulary in Context   _____   **2.** "The slippery slope to parental **autonomy** is no paranoid delusion." (paragraph 16)
    a. control   c. weakness
    b. trust   d. independence

Central Idea   _____   **3.** Which of the following sentences best states the central idea of the passage?
    a. "As so often happens in contemporary debate, arguments being proffered in support of allowing teenagers as young as 15 (and possibly younger) to buy the 'morning-after pill' without adult supervision are false on their premise." (paragraph 2)
    b. "The pros are obvious: Plan B, if taken within three days of unprotected sex, greatly reduces the chances of pregnancy." (paragraph 11)
    c. "The slippery slope to parental autonomy is no paranoid delusion." (paragraph 16)

d. "And the debate about Plan B is fundamentally about whether government or parents have ultimate authority over their children's well-being." (paragraph 19)

Main Idea _____ **4.** Which of the following sentences states the main idea of paragraph 8?
a. "The debate arose after a federal judge last month ordered the government to remove all obstacles to over-the-counter sales of Plan B."
b. "Administration policy is that children as young as 15 can buy the drug without a prescription or parental knowledge."
c. "They would have to show identification proving they are 15, which, as critics of such restrictions have pointed out, is problematic for many teenagers."

Supporting Details _____ **5.** According to the author, who plans to appeal the judge's decision to remove all obstacles to the sales of over-the-counter Plan B?
a. President Obama   c. Planned Parenthood
b. the Justice Department   d. School officials

Supporting Details _____ **6.** According to the author, lifting age limits on Plan B is a slippery slope away from
a. parental authority.   c. prudishness.
b. children's rights.   d. women's rights.

Transitions _____ **7.** "The pros are obvious: Plan B, if taken within three days of unprotected sex, greatly reduces the chance of pregnancy." (paragraph 11)

The relationship of ideas **within** this sentence is
a. classification.   c. comparison and contrast.
b. generalization and example. d. space order.

Transitions _____ **8.** "Here's an experiment to demonstrate. Question 1: Do you think that women should have access to Plan B, also known as the morning-after pill, to be used at their own discretion?" (paragraphs 3 and 4)

The relationship of ideas **between** these sentences is
a. cause and effect.   c. comparison and contrast.
b. time order.   d. generalization and example.

Thought Patterns _____ **9.** The thought pattern of paragraph 13 is
a. time order.   c. generalization and example.
b. listing.   d. classification.

Thought
Patterns _____ **10.** The overall thought pattern of the passage is

      a. description.   c. argument.

      b. cause and effect.   d. definition and example.

Fact and
Opinion _____ **11.** "The debate arose after a federal judge last month ordered the government to remove all obstacles to over-the-counter sales of Plan B." (paragraph 8)

      This sentence is a statement of

      a. fact.   c. fact and opinion.

      b. opinion.

Fact and
Opinion _____ **12.** "You see how the word 'child' keeps getting in the way." (paragraph 12)

      This sentence is a statement of

      a. fact.   c. fact and opinion.

      b. opinion.

Fact and
Opinion _____ **13.** Throughout the passage, the author relies mostly on

      a. fact.   c. fact and opinion.

      b. opinion.

Tone and
Purpose _____ **14.** The overall tone of the passage is

      a. neutral.   c. humorous.

      b. sarcastic.   d. persuasive.

Tone and
Purpose _____ **15.** The overall purpose of the author is

      a. to inform girls about their right to buy Plan B.

      b. to entertain the reader with the details of the controversial sales of Plan B to young girls.

      c. to clarify to the reader the fundamental issue in the debate about the sales of Plan B.

Inferences _____ **16.** Based on the details in paragraphs 14, we can infer that Planned Parenthood President Cecile Richards is focused on

      a. the scientific evidence of the physical safety of Plan B.

      b. the emotional effects of teenage girls engaged in unprotected sex.

      c. the rights of parents to be involved in their child's health care.

      d. the rights of adult women to control decisions about their bodies.

Inferences _____ **17.** Based on the details in the passage, we can infer that
a. the author agrees that there should be no barriers to the sales of Plan B to young girls.
b. the author opposes the removal of barriers to the sales of Plan B to young girls.
c. the author is neutral about the issue of unrestricted sales of Plan B to young girls.
d. the author is calling for more debate about the issue of unrestricted sales of Plan B to young girls.

Inferences _____ **18.** Based on the details in the passage, we can infer that
a. most teenage girls are having unprotected sex.
b. Plan B always prevents an unwanted pregnancy.
c. parents cannot be trusted to help their daughter cope with an unwanted pregnancy.
d. the law concerning Plan B restricts parents' right to information about their daughters' use of the after-morning pill.

Argument _____ **19.** The following list contains a claim and list of supports for that claim. Which item states the claim?
a. "Whatever parents may do to try to delay the ruin of childhood innocence, the culture says otherwise: Have sex, take a pill, don't tell mom." (paragraph 16)
b. "Americans may disagree about what is sexually appropriate for their children." (paragraph 18)
c. "And everyone surely wishes to prevent children from having babies." (paragraph 18)
d. "But public policy should be aimed at involving, rather than marginalizing, parents." (paragraph 18)

Argument _____ **20.** "Wouldn't we rather they block a pregnancy before it happens than to wait and face the worse prospect of an abortion?" (paragraph 10)

This question is an example of the persuasive technique
a. false cause.   c. either-or.
b. personal attack.   d. plain folks.

Concept Mapping

Complete the following Pro and Con chart with information from the passage.

The Debate Over Youth Access to Plan B

Pro (for)	Con (against)
_____	If a child waits too long to take the pill, pregnancy may occur.
_____	Plan B is a serious drug used _____
	_____
	_____
Plan B empowers girls to control _____	Plan B _____ by restricting
_____	their right to know about their child's health decision.

WHAT DO YOU THINK?

Assume you are the parent of a teenage daughter. You have decided to take a stand on this issue by writing to your elected representatives in the House and Senate. Write a letter that states your support of or opposition to the sales of over-the-counter Plan B. Explain your reasons.

MASTER READER SCORECARD

"Prude or Prudent? The Debate Over Access to Plan B"

Skill	Number Correct		Points		Total
Vocabulary					
Vocabulary in Context (2 items)	_____	×	4	=	_____
Comprehension					
Central Idea and Main Idea (2 items)	_____	×	4	=	_____
Supporting Details (2 items)	_____	×	4	=	_____
Transitions (2 items)	_____	×	4	=	_____
Thought Patterns (2 items)	_____	×	4	=	_____
Fact and Opinion (3 items)	_____	×	4	=	_____
Tone and Purpose (2 items)	_____	×	4	=	_____
Inferences (3 items)	_____	×	4	=	_____
Argument (2 items)	_____	×	4	=	_____
Mapping (5 items)	_____	×	4	=	_____
			Comprehension Score		_____

3 Binge Drinking, a Campus Killer

by Sabrina Rubin Erdely

Sabrina Rubin Erdely, an investigative journalist, graduated from the University of Pennsylvania in 1994. Currently a senior staff writer at *Philadelphia* magazine and a contributing writer for *Cosmopolitan*, Erdely's work has earned her a number of awards, including nomination for the National Magazine Award in public interest writing. In the article reprinted here, Erdely explores the nationwide chronic problem of binge drinking on college and university campuses.

Vocabulary Preview

indulgences (paragraph 1): pleasures, excesses
surmise (paragraph 11): conclude, speculate
gratification (paragraph 11): satisfaction, pleasure
concoctions (paragraph 15): mixture, blend, brew
defibrillation (paragraph 18): an electrical shock applied to restore the heart's
  rhythm
equivalent (paragraph 19): equal, corresponding
illicit (paragraph 38): illegal, illegitimate, banned

1   Pregame tailgating parties, post-exam celebrations and Friday happy hours—not to mention fraternity and sorority mixers—have long been a cornerstone of the collegiate experience. But on campuses across America, these **indulgences** have a more alarming side. For some of today's college students, binge drinking has become the norm.

2   This past February I headed to the University of Wisconsin-Madison, rated the No. 2 party school in the nation by the college guide *Princeton Review,* to see the party scene for myself. On Thursday night the weekend was already getting started. At a **raucous** off-campus gathering, 20-year-old Tracey Middler struggled to down her beer as fist-pumping onlookers yelled, "Chug! Chug! Chug!"

3   In the kitchen, sophomore Jeremy Budda drained his tenth beer. "I get real wasted on weekends," he explained. Nearby, a 19-year-old estimated, "I'll end up having 17, 18 beers."

4   Swept up in the revelry, these partiers aren't thinking about the alcohol-related tragedies that have been in the news. All they're thinking about now is the next party. The keg is just about empty.

5   As the 19-year-old announces loudly, these college students have just one objective: "to get drunk!"

6   The challenge to drink to the very limits of one's endurance has become a celebrated staple of college life. In one of the most extensive reports on college drinking thus far, a 1997 Harvard School of Public Health study found that 43 percent of college students admitted binge drinking in the preceding two weeks. (Defined as four drinks in a sitting for a woman and five for a man, a drinking binge is when one drinks enough to risk health and well-being.)

7   "That's about five million students," says Henry Wechsler, who co-authored the study. "And it's certainly a cause for concern. Most of these students don't realize they're engaging in risky behavior." University of Kansas Chancellor Robert Hemenway adds, "Every year we see students harmed because of their involvement with alcohol."

8   Indeed, when binge drinking came to the forefront last year with a rash of alcohol-related college deaths, the nation was stunned by the loss. There was Scott Krueger, the 18-year-old fraternity pledge at the Massachusetts Institute of Technology, who died of alcohol poisoning after downing the equivalent of 15 shots in an hour. There was Leslie Baltz, a University of Virginia senior, who died after she drank too much and fell down a flight of stairs. Lorraine Hanna, a freshman at Indiana University of Pennsylvania, was left alone to sleep off her night of New Year's Eve partying. Later that day her twin sister found her dead—with a blood-alcohol content (BAC) of 0.429 percent. (Driving with a BAC of 0.1 percent and above is illegal in all states.)

9   Experts estimate that excessive drinking is involved in thousands of student deaths a year. And the Harvard researchers found that there has been a dramatic change in why students drink: 39 percent drank "to get drunk" in 1993, but 52 percent had the same objective in 1997.

10   "What has changed is the across-the-board *acceptability* of intoxication," says Felix Savino, a psychologist at UW-Madison. "Many college students today see not just drinking but being *drunk* as their primary way of socializing."

11   The reasons for the shift are complex and not fully understood. But researchers **surmise** that it may have something to do with today's instant-**gratification** life-style—and young people tend to take it to the extreme.

12   In total, it is estimated that America's 12 million undergraduates drink the equivalent of six million gallons of beer a week. When that's combined with teenagers' need to drink secretly, it's no wonder many have a dangerous relationship with alcohol.

13   The biggest predictor of bingeing is fraternity or sorority membership. Sixty-five percent of members qualified as binge drinkers, according to the Harvard study.

14   August 25, 1997, was meant to be a night the new Sigma Alpha Epsilon pledges at Louisiana State University in Baton Rouge would never forget, and by 8 P.M. it was certainly shaping up that way. The revelry had begun earlier with a keg party. Then they went to a bar near campus, where pledges consumed massive quantities of alcohol.

15   Among the pledges were Donald Hunt, Jr., a 21-year-old freshman and Army veteran, and his roommate, Benjamin Wynne, a 20-year-old sophomore. Friends since high school, the two gamely drank the

alcoholic **concoctions** offered to them and everyone else.

16   Before long, many in the group began vomiting into trash cans. (Donald Hunt would later allege in a lawsuit that these "vomiting stations" were set up for that very purpose, something the defendants adamantly deny.) About 9:30, **incapacitated** pledges were taken back to sleep it off at the frat house.

17   The 911 call came around midnight. Paramedics were stunned at what they found: more than a dozen young men sprawled on the floor, on chairs, on couches, reeking of alcohol. The paramedics burst into action, shaking the pledges and shouting, "Hey! Can you hear me?" Four couldn't be roused, and of those, one had no vital signs: Benjamin Wynne was in cardiac arrest.

18   Checking to see that nothing was blocking Wynne's airway, the paramedics began CPR. Within minutes they'd inserted an oxygen tube into his lungs, hooked up an I.V., attached a cardiac monitor and begun shocking him with **defibrillation** paddles, trying to restart his heart.

19   Still not responding, Wynne was rushed by ambulance to Baton Rouge General Hospital. Lab work revealed that his blood-alcohol content was an astonishing 0.588 percent, nearly six times the legal driving limit for adults—the **equivalent** of taking about 21 shots in an hour.

20   Meanwhile, three other fraternity pledges were undergoing similar revival efforts. One was Donald Hunt. He would suffer severe alcohol poisoning and nearly die.

21   After working furiously on Wynne, the hospital team admitted defeat. He was pronounced dead of acute alcohol poisoning.

22   One simple fact people tend to lose sight of is that alcohol is a poison—often pleasurable, but a toxin nonetheless. And for a person with little experience processing this toxin, it can come as something of a physical shock.

23   In general, a bottle of beer has about the same alcohol content as a glass of wine or shot of liquor. And the body can remove only the equivalent of less than one drink hourly from the bloodstream.

24   Many students are not just experimenting once or twice. In the Harvard study, half of binge drinkers were "frequent binge drinkers," meaning they had binged three or more times in the previous two weeks.

25   It also is assumed by some that bingeing is a "guy thing," an activity that, like cigar smoking and watching televised sports, belongs in the realm of male bonding. Statistics, however, show that the number of heavy-drinking young women is significant. Henry Wechsler's Harvard study found that a hefty 48 percent of college men were binge drinkers, and women were right behind them at 39 percent.

26   Howard Somers had always been afraid of heights. Perhaps his fear was some sort of an omen. On an August day in 1997 he helped his 18-year-old daughter, Mindy, move into her dorm at Virginia Tech. As they unloaded her things in the eighth-floor room, Somers noted with unease the position of the window. It opened inward like an oven door, its lip about level with her bed. He mentioned it, but Mindy dismissed his concern with a smile.

27 "I have gone through more guilt than you can imagine," Somers says now quietly. "Things I wish I had said or done. But I never thought this would happen. Who would?"

28 Mindy Somers knew the dangers of alcohol and tried to stay aware of her limits. She'd planned not to overdo it that Friday night, since her mother was coming in that weekend to celebrate Mindy's 19th birthday on Sunday. But it was Halloween, the campus was alive with activity, and Mindy decided to stop in at several off-campus parties.

29 When she returned to her room at 3 A.M., she was wiped out enough to fall into bed fully clothed. Mindy's bed was pushed lengthwise against the long, low window. Her roommate and two other girls, who were on the floor, all slept too soundly to notice that sometime after 4 A.M. Mindy's bed was empty.

30 When the paperboy found her facedown on the grass at 6:45 A.M., he at first thought it was a Halloween prank. Police and EMTs swarmed to the scene in minutes. Somers was pronounced dead of massive chest and abdominal injuries. She had a blood-alcohol content of 0.21 percent, equal to her having drunk about five beers in one hour.

31 Police surmised that Mindy had tried to get out of bed during the night but, disoriented, had slipped out the window, falling 75 feet to her death. "It was a strange, tragic accident," Virginia Tech Police Chief Michael Jones says.

32 A terrible irony was that the week prior to Mindy's death had been Virginia Tech's annual Alcohol Awareness Week.

33 While binge drinking isn't always lethal, it does have other, wide-ranging effects.

Academics is one realm where it takes a heavy toll.

34 During my trip to Wisconsin most students told me they didn't plan on attending classes the following day. "Nah, I almost never go to class on Friday. It's no big deal," answered Greg, a sophomore. According to a survey of university administrators, 38 percent of academic problems are alcohol-related, as are 29 percent of dropouts.

35 Perhaps because alcohol increases aggression and impairs judgment, it is also related to 25 percent of violent crimes and roughly 60 percent of vandalism on campus. According to one survey, 79 percent of students who had experienced unwanted sexual intercourse in the previous year said that they were under the influence of alcohol or other drugs at the time. "Some people believe that alcohol can provide an excuse for inappropriate behavior, including sexual aggression," says Jeanette Norris, a University of Washington researcher. Later on, those people can claim, "It wasn't me—it was the booze."

36 Faced with the many potential dangers, college campuses are scrambling for ways to reduce binge drinking. Many offer seminars on alcohol during freshman orientation. Over 50 schools provide alcohol-free living environments. At the University of Michigan's main campus in Ann Arbor, for instance, nearly 30 percent of undergrads living in university housing now choose to live in alcohol-free rooms. Nationwide several fraternities have announced that by the year 2000 their chapter houses will be alcohol-free.

37 After the University of Rhode Island topped the *Princeton Review* party list two

years in a row, administrators banned alcohol at all student events on campus; this year URI didn't even crack the top ten. Some campuses respond even more severely, unleashing campus raids and encouraging police busts.

38   Researchers debate, however, if such "zero-tolerance" policies are helpful or if they might actually result in more secret, off-campus drinking. Other academics wonder if dropping the drinking age to 18 would take away the **illicit** thrill of alcohol and lower the number of kids drinking wildly. Others feel this would just create more drinking-related fatalities.

39   Whatever it takes, changing student behavior won't be easy. "What you've got here are people who think they are having fun," Harvard's Henry Wechsler explains. "You can't change their behavior by preaching at them or by telling them they'll get hurt."

40   Around 2 A.M. at UW-Madison a hundred kids congregate at a downtown intersection in a nightly ritual. One girl is trying to pull her roommate up off the ground. "I'm not that drunk," the one on the ground insists. "I just can't stand up."

41   Two fights break out. A police car cruises by and the crowd thins, some heading to after-hours parties. Then maybe at 3 or 4 A.M. they'll go home to get some sleep, so they will be rested for when they start to drink again. Tomorrow night.

—Sabrina Rubin Erdely, "Binge Drinking, A Campus Killer." From *Reader's Digest*, November 1998. Reproduced by the permission of the author.

Choose the best meaning of each word in **bold** type. Use context clues to make your choice.

Vocabulary in Context   _____   **1.** "At a **raucous** off-campus gathering, 20-year-old Tracey Middler struggled to down her beer as fist-pumping onlookers yelled, 'Chug! Chug! Chug!'" (paragraph 2)

a. fun   c. illegal
b. dangerous   d. wild

Vocabulary in Context   _____   **2.** "About 9:30, **incapacitated** pledges were taken back to sleep it off at the frat house." (paragraph 16)

a. mindless   c. dangerous
b. disabled   d. young

Central Idea and Main Ideas   _____   **3.** Which sentence is the best statement of the implied central idea of the article?

a. Binge drinking is a normal and widespread trend in American college life.
b. Parents, educators, and researchers are unable to stop the dangerous trend of college binge drinking.
c. College students indulge in binge drinking to have fun and assert adultlike independence.

d. The national problem of binge drinking among college students is an alarming and escalating threat to their physical and academic well-being that has college campuses scrambling for solutions.

Central Idea _____
and Main Ideas

4. Which sentence states the main idea of paragraph 6?
   a. "The challenge to drink to the very limits of one's endurance has become a celebrated staple of college life."
   b. "In one of the most extensive reports on college drinking thus far, a 1997 Harvard School of Public Health study found that 43 percent of college students admitted to drinking in the preceding two weeks."
   c. "Defined as four drinks in a sitting for a woman and five for a man, a drinking binge is when one drinks enough to risk health and well-being."

Supporting _____
Details

5. Which university—"rated as the No. 2 party school in the nation"—did the author visit to research her article?
   a. Harvard
   b. Princeton
   c. University of Wisconsin-Madison
   d. University of Pennsylvania

Supporting _____
Details

6. For a man, binge drinking is defined by downing how many drinks in one sitting?
   a. 4   c. 8
   b. 5   d. 12

Transitions _____

7. "On Thursday night the weekend was already getting started. At a raucous off-campus gathering, 20-year-old Tracey Middler struggled to down her beer as fist-pumping onlookers yelled, 'Chug! Chug! Chug!'" (paragraph 2)

   What is the relationship of ideas between these two sentences?
   a. time order   c. example
   b. contrast

Transitions _____

8. "In general, a bottle of beer has about the same alcohol content as a glass of wine or shot of liquor." (paragraph 23)

   Which term best describes the relationship of ideas within this sentence?
   a. time order   c. comparison
   b. example

Thought Patterns _____ **9.** The overall thought pattern used by the author to organize her article is
   a. examples of binge drinking and its consequences.
   b. an argument to eliminate alcohol from college and university campuses.
   c. a discussion of the causes of binge drinking.
   d. a narrative about binge drinking.

Thought Patterns _____ **10.** The thought pattern in paragraph 11 is
   a. example.   c. time order.
   b. cause and effect.

Fact and Opinion _____ **11.** Overall, the ideas in this passage
   a. are based on research and statistics.
   b. are based on research and the personal observations of the author.
   c. objectively present the views of college students.
   d. angrily describe the causes and effects of binge drinking.

Fact and Opinion _____ **12.** "Many college students today see not just drinking but being *drunk* as their primary way of socializing." (paragraph 10)

   This sentence is a statement of
   a   fact.   c. fact and opinion.
   b. opinion.

Tone and Purpose _____ **13.** The overall tone of the passage is
   a. sympathetic.   c. objective.
   b. humorous.   d. outraged.

Tone and Purpose _____ **14.** The tone of paragraph 8 is
   a. harsh.   c. matter-of-fact.
   b. regretful.   d. disgusted.

Tone and Purpose _____ **15.** The tone of paragraph 27 is
   a. angry.   c. humble.
   b. puzzled.   d. remorseful.

Tone and Purpose _____ **16.** The author's main purpose is
   a. to persuade parents, educators, and students to take action against binge drinking.
   b. to shock readers with alarming details about binge drinking.
   c. to inform readers about the depth and scope of the alarming national trend of binge drinking among college students.

Inferences _____ **17.** From paragraphs 8 and 9, we can conclude that
   a. deaths from binge drinking are inevitable.
   b. universities and colleges are responsible for the thousands of student deaths that occur each year.
   c. thousands of lives could be saved each year if binge drinking could be controlled.
   d. college students understand the risks associated with binge drinking.

Inferences _____ **18.** Based on the details about Mindy Somers (paragraphs 28–32), we can conclude that
   a. Mindy engaged in binge drinking frequently.
   b. Virginia Tech's annual Alcohol Awareness Week did not effectively educate Mindy about the dangers of binge drinking.
   c. Mindy's father should have known about the risks related to her drinking habits.
   d. binge drinking is always lethal.

Inferences _____ **19.** The details in paragraphs 2, 3, and 34 imply that
   a. the weekend binge drinking cycle probably begins on Thursday.
   b. most college students do not "get wasted" during the week.
   c. most college students are more interested in partying than in studying.
   d. males are more likely to binge and miss classes than are females.

Argument _____ **20.** The following list of ideas from paragraphs 9–11 contains a claim and supports for that claim. In the space, write the letter of the claim for the argument.
   a. "The Harvard researchers found that there has been a dramatic change in why students drink: 39 percent drank 'to get drunk' in 1993, but 52 percent had the same objective in 1997."
   b. "What has changed is the across-the-board *acceptability* of intoxication," says Felix Savino, a psychologist at UW-Madison.
   c. "Researchers surmise that it may have something to do with today's instant-gratification life-style—and young people tend to take it to the extreme."
   d. "Many college students today see not just drinking but being *drunk* as their primary way of socializing."

Mapping

Complete the concept map below. Fill in the blanks with the central idea and the missing supporting details from "Binge Drinking, a Campus Killer."

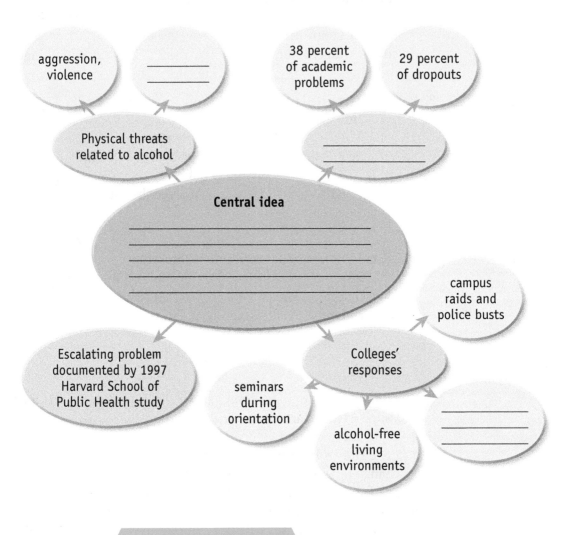

Do you think binge drinking is a problem at your college or university? What do you think is the best solution to binge drinking on college campuses? Assume you are a member of your Student Government Association (SGA). SGA has decided to raise awareness about this issue, so you have been asked to write an article for publication in the college and local newspapers. In your editorial, advise college students about the dangers of binge drinking and suggest ways to avoid the dangers based on what you have learned from reading this article. Begin your editorial with a summary of the author's main ideas and major supporting details. Also identify and discuss some obvious and underlying reasons for student binge drinking.

MASTER READER SCORECARD

"Binge Drinking, a Campus Killer"

Skill	Number Correct	Points			Total
Vocabulary					
Vocabulary in Context (2 items)	_____	×	4	=	_____
Comprehension					
Central Idea and Main Ideas (2 items)	_____	×	4	=	_____
Supporting Details (2 items)	_____	×	4	=	_____
Transitions (2 items)	_____	×	4	=	_____
Thought Patterns (2 items)	_____	×	4	=	_____
Fact and Opinion (2 items)	_____	×	4	=	_____
Tone and Purpose (4 items)	_____	×	4	=	_____
Inferences (3 items)	_____	×	4	=	_____
Argument (1 item)	_____	×	4	=	_____
Mapping (4 items)	_____	×	5	=	_____
		Comprehension Score			_____

Is Substance Abuse a Social Problem?

by John D. Carl

Textbook
Skills

John D. Carl holds a Ph.D. in Sociology from the University of Oklahoma. His work history includes not only colleges but hospitals, schools, churches, and prisons. This passage is taken from his textbook *Think: Social Problems*. Carl's passion for sociology is evident as he expresses his goal for writing: "the goal of this book is rather simple: To teach students to view social problems critically and to use sociological thinking to help them do that." How would you evaluate the use of drugs in America?

Vocabulary Preview

plethora (paragraph 1): large or excessive amount or number
inebriation (paragraph 1): intoxicated, drunk
gratification (paragraph 9): satisfaction, fulfillment
socialization (paragraph 10): training or developing skills needed to function
   successfully in society

Basics of Drug Use in America

1   As you can imagine, drug use and abuse creates a **plethora** of social problems for society. These problems are not only because of the extra costs associated with trying to help people "kick the habit" but also due to the lost productivity, destroyed relationships, and personal injury that such abuse can cause. Of all the drugs available in the United States, tobacco and alcohol are the two most commonly used. Recent surveys have shown that 20.6 percent of Americans over 18 are current smokers. In addition, 23 percent of adults drink alcohol at a dangerous level, and even among youth, 91 percent of drinkers 12 to 14 years old admit to binge drinking. College students in particular fall into the binge-drinking scene, as many students view **inebriation** as a rite of passage. This attitude has created a serious issue for schools, as alcohol-related hospitalizations and deaths are regular occurrences on many college campuses. In fact, numerous colleges are now making it illegal for anyone to consume alcohol on campus, regardless of their age.

Characteristics of Drug Users

Age

If you think teenagers and college students make up the majority of "users," you're mistaken. It's true that almost 20 percent of 18- to 25-year olds frequently use illegal drugs, compared to 5.8 percent of those 26 and older. However, a 2007 survey on drug use showed that 42 percent of Americans over 26 have used marijuana, while only about 16 percent of young adults have tried this drug. Researchers attribute this pattern to the aging baby boomer population who grew up in a culture of drug use.

3   Even if the researchers are correct in saying that anti-drug ads have been counterproductive, teen drug use has been steadily decreasing since the turn of the millennium. In 1999, it was estimated that more than half of high school seniors used illicit drugs, mostly marijuana. Even pre-teen drug use was high, as one fourth of eighth graders admitted to having been drunk at least once, and 44 percent reported that they smoked cigarettes. Compare those numbers to the current ones that estimate 44 percent of all high school seniors admit to alcohol use, and 18 percent admit to marijuana use.

Race

4   Although drug abuse occurs among all races in the United States, it is more prevalent in some races than others. Asians currently show the lowest rate of drug use among persons 12 and older (3.6 percent); Native Americans and Alaska Natives have the highest percentage of drug use in the United States (13.7 percent).

Socioeconomic Status

5   How does drug use effect socioeconomic status? Certainly, there are many studies that show the connection between illegal drug use and dropping out of school, lower educational attainment, unemployment, and low rates of advancement in one's career. However, in terms of earnings, research suggests that lower incomes

for drug users takes time to **manifest** itself. In other words, the effect of drug use has little impact on the individual when he or she is younger, but increases over time. This is in part due to the fact that early in their work lives, drug users tend to take jobs with little potential for growth. Over time, that choice keeps them from advancing, unlike their non-user peers.

Prescription Drug Use

6   As government and private organizations work to thwart current forms of drug use, Americans are finding new ways to get high. The most current trend in drug abuse is the misuse of prescription drugs. According to the Centers for Disease Control and Prevention, more than 1.8 billion prescription drugs were ordered or provided in 2006, the most frequently prescribed drugs being analgesics, or painkillers. Although these drugs are created and prescribed with the intention of healing or providing relief, they are sometimes abused rather than used appropriately.

7   The three types of prescription drugs that are most commonly abused are opiates (medically prescribed to treat pain), central nervous system depressants (prescribed to treat anxiety and sleep disorders), and stimulants (prescribed to treat disorders such as narcolepsy and attention deficit disorder). Although the use of these types of drugs can help an individual, abuse of these drugs can be extremely harmful to a user's body.

8   Amphetamines, such as Adderall or Ritalin, are some of the most widely abused prescription drugs, especially among teens.

Ritalin, a drug prescribed to individuals with attention deficit disorder, has been used without a prescription by as many as 1 in 10 teenagers. As you may already know, some of the most frequent abuse of amphetamines occurs on college campuses. Whereas some students might drink a can of Red Bull to stay alert for a long night of studying, others might turn to amphetamines. One student even admitted to me that he took Adderall to stay awake when he needed to pull all-nighters.

Why Do We Use Drugs?

9   Our bodies have natural defenses against infection and disease; when we're in pain, our brains produce chemicals that dull the ache and make us feel happy. So, why do we need drugs? Some suggest that this is the wrong question. People have always used drugs and will likely continue to use them. Most of society's legal efforts to control drug use fail; the issue becomes how to control use while avoiding the harmful aspects of drug abuse. The causes of drug abuse are difficult to determine and often involve claims that abusers cannot delay **gratification** and have low self-control. However, many people do not agree that addiction is a sign of moral or psychological weakness. Treating addiction as a medical condition—as opposed to a moral failure—arose in the 20th century and resulted in a number of treatment programs and models. In general, these models hold two common beliefs: (1) Individuals have biological predispositions to addiction, and (2) these predispositions can be overcome through treatment.

Socialization

Sociological theory and medical 10 research are aware that determining why people use drugs is a complex issue. Researcher Denise Kandel suggests that there is an interaction between how a person is socialized and with whom they interact. Recall that we are socialized by a variety of individuals. Parents provide long-term values, and their use of drugs has the potential to influence their children. However, one's peers provide even more powerful **socialization**. Teens who get involved in drugs and/or alcohol generally have peers who are users. The selection of one's peer group provides the foundation for the likelihood of use by adolescents. This happens in part because they bond to users and learn to share their values and behaviors. Of course, we choose our friends not merely based on who we live near, but also by who interests us. In this way, people who get into drug-using groups in a sense choose their path, although, at the same time, they are being steered toward this path by their group. This is a dynamic process that usually starts with minor alcohol use, such as beer or wine, moves to cigarettes and hard alcohol, then to marijuana, and possibly to harder drugs. To put it simply, people can drift into drugs through a process of being socialized into their use.

Another part of drug socialization 11 stems from the fact that the United States is increasingly becoming a medicalized society. Medicalization is the process by which we expand the use of medical terms and solutions to non-medical problems. Medical personnel often claim that certain social components are diseases in need of treatment. Such an attitude expands the power of the medical community, but also increases the public's desire for medical solutions. This leads us to seek a pill to solve our problems. In 2006 alone, more than 1.8 billion prescription drugs were ordered or provided. Does that necessarily make things better? It's clear that what it does do is help socialize us into a mind-set whereby drug use is common.

12   At what point do we change from a culture of drug users to a culture of drug abusers? When so many people seem motivated to abuse substances and modify their behavior with drugs, it's easy to see how this problem can spread to the greater society. A student of mine who had an alcoholic husband put it this way: "Living with an addict is like living with an elephant in your house. It stinks up the place, makes lots of messes, and it's too big to simply act like it's not there because doing that will destroy your family, your children, and your sense of reality." The social problems of substance abuse are not just individual issues.

Go Global: The Mexican Drug War

13   The real Mexican-American War ended in 1848, but lately a new, covert war has begun. Like any other war, this conflict has resulted in casualties: 6,300 bodies in 2008 alone. This time, however, the Mexican and U.S. governments are working together, battling the rampant drug trafficking that goes on at the border.

14   It's not just drugs that officials are worried about. According to the Federal Bureau of Alcohol, Tobacco, Firearms and Explosives, roughly 90 percent of guns seized in raids of Mexican dealers are traced back to the United States. Drug traffickers cross the border on three-day shopping visas, purchase large quantities of assault weapons and ammunition from local merchants, then return home. It's estimated that nearly 2,000 firearms cross the border into Mexico daily.

15   Americans aren't just providing drug cartels with guns; they're also providing them with money. The majority of drugs cultivated in Mexico are sold to Americans, and Mexican drug dealers generate profits of $15 billion to $25 billion a year solely from the United States.

16   Mexico's drug war isn't only an issue south of the border. The U.S. Justice Department has stated that Mexican drug trafficking organizations represent the greatest organized crime threat to the United States. President Obama has been working with Mexican President Felipe Calderon to build a more aggressive offense against drug lords. "We are absolutely committed to working in partnership with Mexico to make sure that we are dealing with this **scourge** on both sides of the border," Obama said after meeting with Calderon. "You can't fight this war with just one hand. You can't have Mexico making an effort and the United States not making an effort."

17   So far, the President has sent Congress a war-spending request for $350 million to increase security along the United States-Mexico border. More efforts from the U.S. government are expected to be initiated as violence from the Mexican drug war continues to spread.

—Adapted from Carl, John D. *Think Social Problems*, pp. 144–147. Copyright © 2011 by Pearson Education, Inc. Printed and Electronically reproduced by permission of Pearson Education, Inc., Upper Saddle River, New Jersey.

Choose the best meaning of each word in **bold**. Use context clues to make your choice.

Vocabulary in Context _____ 1. "However, in terms of earnings, research suggests that lower incomes for drug users takes time to **manifest** itself." (paragraph 5)
a. list   c. clear
b. reveal   d. hide

Vocabulary in Context _____ 2. "'We are absolutely committed to working in partnership with Mexico to make sure that we are dealing with this **scourge** on both sides of the border,' Obama said . . ." (paragraph 16)
a. whip   c. misery
b. law   d. issue

Central Idea _____ 3. Which of the following sentences from paragraph 1 states the central idea of the passage?
a. "As you can imagine, drug use and abuse creates a plethora of social problems for society."
b. "These problems are not only because of the extra costs associated with trying to help people 'kick the habit' but also due to the lost productivity, destroyed relationships, and personal injury that such abuse can cause."
c. "Of all the drugs available in the United States, tobacco and alcohol are the two most commonly used."
d. "Recent surveys have shown that 20.6 percent of Americans over 18 are current smokers."

Central Idea _____ 4. Which of the following sentences states the central idea of paragraphs 6 through 8?
a. "As government and private organizations work to thwart current forms of drug use, Americans are finding new ways to get high." (paragraph 6)
b. "The most current trend in drug abuse is the misuse of prescription drugs." (paragraph 6)
c. "The three types of prescription drugs that are most commonly abused are opiates (medically prescribed to treat pain), central nervous system depressants (prescribed to treat anxiety and sleep disorders), and stimulants (prescribed to treat disorders such as narcolepsy and attention deficit disorder)." (paragraph 7)
d. "Amphetamines, such as Adderall or Ritalin, are some of the most widely abused prescription drugs, especially among teens." (paragraph 8)

Supporting Details _____ **5.** According to the passage, which of the following has the greatest influence on an individual's drug use?

    a. parents   c. peers

    b. doctors   d. one's self

Supporting Details _____ **6.** According to the passage, how much money has President Obama requested from Congress to increase security along the United States-Mexican border?

    a. $15 billion   c. $1.8 billion

    b. $25 billion   d. $350 million

Transitions _____ **7.** "Although the use of these types of drugs can help an individual, abuse of these drugs can be extremely harmful to a user's body." (paragraph 7)

The relationship of ideas within this sentence is

    a. addition.   c. comparison and contrast.

    b. cause and effect.   d. generalization and example.

Transitions _____ **8.** "Recent surveys have shown that 20.6 percent of Americans over 18 are current smokers. In addition, 23 percent of adults drink alcohol at a dangerous level, and even among youth, 91 percent of drinkers 12 to 14 years old admit to binge drinking." (paragraph 1)

The relationship of ideas between these sentences is

    a. cause and effect.   c. comparison and contrast.

    b. addition.   d. generalization and example.

Thought Patterns _____ **9.** The overall thought pattern for paragraphs 2 through 5 is

    a. cause and effect.   c. comparison and contrast.

    b. classification.   d. definition and example.

Thought Patterns _____ **10.** The thought pattern for paragraph 4 is

    a. cause and effect.   c. comparison and contrast.

    b. classification.   d. generalization and example.

Thought Patterns _____ **11.** The thought pattern for paragraph 5 is

    a. cause and effect.   c. comparison and contrast.

    b. classification.   d. generalization and example.

Fact and Opinion _____ **12.** "Recent surveys have shown that 20.6 percent of Americans over 18 are current smokers." (paragraph 1)

This sentence is a statement of

    a. fact.   c. fact and opinion.

    b. opinion.

Fact and Opinion   _____ **13.** "Living with an addict is like living with an elephant in your house." (paragraph 12)

This sentence is a statement of
a. fact.   c. fact and opinion.
b. opinion.

Fact and Opinion   _____ **14.** "This leads us to seek a pill to solve our problems." (paragraph 11)

This sentence is a statement of
a. fact.   c. fact and opinion.
b. opinion.

Fact and Opinion   _____ **15.** "This time, however, the Mexican and U.S. governments are working together, battling the rampant drug trafficking that goes on at the border." (paragraph 13)

This sentence is a statement of
a. fact.
b. opinion.
c. fact and opinion.

Tone   _____ **16.** The overall tone of the passage is
a. informal.   b. formal.

Tone   _____ **17.** The overall tone of the author is
a. light-hearted.   c. dismayed.
b. belittling.   d. balanced.

Purpose   _____ **18.** The author's purpose is to
a. inform the student about the sociological perspective of drug use in America.
b. entertain the student with interesting facts about drug use in America.
c. persuade the student to take a stand against drug abuse in America.

Inferences   _____ **19.** Based on the details in paragraphs 7 and 8, we can infer that Adderall and Ritalin are
a. opiates.
b. depressants.
c. stimulants.
d. analgesics.

Argument _____ **20.** Identify the persuasive technique used in the following statements:

"Living with an addict is like living with an elephant in your house. It stinks up the place, makes lots of messes, and it's too big to simply act like it's not there because doing that will destroy your family, your children, and your sense of reality."(paragraph 12)

a. false analogy
b. personal attack
c. begging the question
d. transfer

Outlining

Complete the following formal outline with information from the passage.

Central Idea: _____

_____

   I. Basics of Drug Use in America

  II. _____

     A. Age

     B. _____

     C. _____

  III. Prescription Drug Use

  IV. Why Do We Use Drugs?

   V. Socialization

  VI. _____

WHAT DO YOU THINK?

Did you learn any new information from this passage? If so, what did you learn? If you already knew all of the information in the passage, which parts of the passage are the most important and why? Do you think the United States is largely responsible for the drug trafficking across the Mexico–U.S. border? Why or why not? Assume you are taking a college course in sociology, and your professor has handed out study topics for a unit review worth 25% of your final grade. When you and your study group divided the topics up among yourselves to answer and share with the group, you drew the following two topics: (1) Write a short essay that discusses and illustrates how a person is socialized into using drugs; (2) Give several reasons to support or oppose President Obama's request for money to increase security along the United States–Mexico border.

"Is Substance Abuse a Social Problem?"

Skill	Number Correct	Points		Total
Vocabulary				
Vocabulary in Context (2 items)	_____	× 4	=	_____
Comprehension				
Central Idea (2 items)	_____	× 4	=	_____
Supporting Details (2 items)	_____	× 4	=	_____
Transitions (2 items)	_____	× 4	=	_____
Thought Patterns (3 items)	_____	× 4	=	_____
Fact and Opinion (4 items)	_____	× 4	=	_____
Tone and Purpose (3 items)	_____	× 4	=	_____
Inferences (1 item)	_____	× 4	=	_____
Argument (1 item)	_____	× 4	=	_____
Outlining (5 items)	_____	× 4	=	_____
		Comprehension Score		_____

An Account of Alfred C. Cooley's Plight in the Face of Hurricane Katrina

Sandra Offiah-Hawkins

> Sandra Offiah-Hawkins is a Senior Professor at Daytona State College in Daytona Beach, Florida, where she has taught English and reading for more than twenty-one years. She is a Kellogg Scholar and has attended, spoken, chaired/co-chaired at state, national, and international conferences (including the University of Santiago de Compostella, in Spain, The University of Ireland in Dublin, and the International Conference on Research and Access in Developmental Education in Puerto Rico). She has also performed as the lead actress in *I Leave You Love,* based on the life and legacy of eighty-year-old Dr. Mary McLeod Bethune, and as Mama in *A Raisin in the Sun*. The following real-life account is one of many non-fiction articles she has written.

Vocabulary Preview

caravan (paragraph 1): group of travelers, procession, motorcade
paternal (paragraph 8): related through father
holocaust (paragraph 12): destruction of human life, complete destruction

1   I am **aghast** by the sudden series of events. There is no time to figure out the next day, for there is no time to visualize where we are going to all sleep this night—new, used, and old cars line up along Interstate 10 and Highway 1 as we all travel 10 miles an hour and wait in five-mile long lines in hopes of getting gas before the stations run out. There are thirty-five of us traveling in a **caravan**: a Dodge Caravan, a Ford Taurus, a 2000 Grand Prix, and a Toyota CRV just to name a few. All the relatives we can contact in New Orleans on this day August 27, 2005, are with us; we have been asked to leave our homes immediately, for the strong winds, the deluging rain, the terrible wrath of Hurricane Katrina is headed straight to New Orleans—our home.

2   All of us leave our worldly possessions that day, bringing with us essentials for two days: I never think for a minute this is the end of what I have called home in the Ninth Ward for more than 50 years; all of us feel this is going to be a "James Brown turnaround." I never think the wife

and children I have been blessed with over the past 30 years would never again know life as they had known it in New Orleans.

3   Throughout my life, I have known suffering: I suffer from Sickle Cell Anemia; my parents were told that I would not live past age 16, but here I am! Within the last eight years, I have had two hip replacements as well as operations on my shoulder and on my left eye. I have been placed in a situation of sometimes raising my four daughters as a single parent, and for many years, I have cared for my aging parents. Now this—the unanticipated fury of Katrina.

4   Once the storm hits, the power, as expected, is off for days in New Orleans, so it is Tuesday evening or Wednesday before we find out the Levee has broken. Since we left home on Saturday, we have been traveling—first to Alexandria, Louisiana, where we sleep wherever there is a space on the floor at Dora Ann's house, my sister's former daughter-in-law's home. The next day, we plan our next move: my parents, sisters, and one brother stay there, but the remaining sixteen of us head East on I-10 towards Memphis, Tennessee, to the home of Stanley Trotter, my ex-wife's cousin, where there were now 20 people sharing a house.

5   As the sixteen of us from New Orleans sit and watch television, we see the water begin to cover the roof of the familiar Circle Food Store, on North Clayborne Avenue and St. Bernard Avenue near the home we just abandoned; we realize now, we will not be returning home.

6   It is extremely difficult for anyone watching the news, but it has to be most difficult for those of us witnessing everything we have worked for being destroyed right before our eyes; we have no idea what we should do or where we should go from here; we begin to mourn for friends and neighbors gone from our lives forever. We continue watching as the Super Dome and Convention Center prove to be inadequate for the more than three thousand people seeking shelter and assistance; we listen to the reports of water leaks and criminals raping people in the Dome; we watch the people standing along the bridge in the smoldering heat with no sanitation, no food, no water; we see dead people floating in the water; we see another person dead in a wheelchair—not even covered. "Why is help so slow to arrive?" we cry out at the television.

7   My heart is truly heavy, and I can barely watch or believe what I am witnessing on television. During this time, I think of my brother and his adult son, Robert Jr., both of whom remained in New Orleans when we left: I pray to God they survive—not knowing until days later that they have located a car and driven to Alexandria to be with my parents and other siblings; I pray to God they survive—not knowing that they have returned to help the people and the cleanup efforts in the areas hit hardest by Katrina and the tornadoes that followed.

8   My mind drifts in time back to my uncles' and aunts' homes in Picayune, Mississippi, less than an hour's drive from New Orleans, and I think about all of my relatives living there: my cousins, my grandmothers, and **paternal** grandfather—I contemplate memories of Pilgrim

Bound Baptist Church and other churches as the neighborhood readies for the 5th Sunday Singing. Every fifth Sunday, all the churches in the area gather as members from the various congregations hope for an opportunity to be placed on the program to sing two selections each. Reverend Woods, the announcer, is always filled with the Holy Spirit as he listens to the lyrics of songs and hymns both old and new: "What a Friend We Have in Jesus," "Amazing Grace," "Do Lord Remember Me," and "Jesus Paid It All." My father, brothers, and I would often travel to participate in the program as an all-male guest quartet from New Orleans, LA.

9 Oh, I will never forget those days—they remain an inspiring part of my life because I had an opportunity to meet many people; some I had forgotten until now: Mrs. Jewel had a candy store next door to where my grandmother, aunt, and uncle lived; only a few blocks away, Bossie Boys, a place where teenagers would meet and dance on the weekends, was located just a few feet from my Uncle Bishop's barber shop.

10 In the wake of Katrina, we move to Atoka, Tennessee, and it does not take long for people to hear about the sixteen people who fled New Orleans. I shall never forget—Mrs. Snead of St. Mark Baptist Church and Pastor McGee alert church members, the fire department, and other social agencies about our plight; church members help us get food and clothing and raise money so that we can begin reestablishing ourselves; through the Red Cross, we are able to obtain proper documentation for identification. No, I shall never forget—all the blessings that flowed from throughout the community to my family during these darkest hours.

11 Finally people are allowed to return briefly to New Orleans to check out their property and help others during the aftermath of Katrina—I am anxious. My son-in-law Javelle and I rent a van to go back and **salvage** what we can. On the way, a police cruiser clocks my speed on the highway at 89 mph in a 70 mph zone; I tell the officer who I am, where I am going and why I am going there; he makes me prove that I have lived in New Orleans all of my life; then, he voids my ticket with a warning to slow down. How ironic—I have to prove that I am a "real" life-long New Orleans "native."

12 Getting off of Highway 610 at Franklin Avenue, we can see the marks of high water levels, and so much trash—garbage and debris strewn everywhere—we see the damage, the loss, and oh so much more—we see a **holocaust**: we see wind damage; we see cars flipped on their sides; we see homes with nothing more than a frame of what once was; we see X's marked on still-standing homes, with a number 1, 2, 3, or more to indicate the dead inside.

13 When you have a near death experience, it is said, your life flashes before you. That is exactly my experience during Katrina. Burdens are heavy, I cannot sleep, and I worry about my family; days pass, and I know the end of my life is near: I now realize that it is the end of my life as I have known it—as I walk in what was once my parent's home on Clouet Street. I see just how high the water had come, and there, I raise my hands to lift several pictures off the wall.

—Reproduced by permission of Sandra Offiah-Hawkins.

Choose the best meaning of each word in **bold**. Use context clues to make your choice.

Vocabulary in Context _____ 1. "I am **aghast** by the sudden series of events." (paragraph 1)
- a. excited
- b. puzzled
- c. horrified
- d. unaffected

Vocabulary in Context _____ 2. "My son-in-law Javelle and I rent a van to go back and **salvage** what we can." (paragraph 11)
- a. sell
- b. destroy
- c. recover
- d. fix

Implied Central Idea _____ 3. Which sentence best states the author's implied central idea?
- a. Hurricane Katrina destroyed Alfred C. Cooley's home in New Orleans.
- b. Hurricane Katrina dramatically and unexpectedly changed the lives of Alfred C. Cooley, his family, and other victims of the storm.
- c. Alfred C. Cooley and his family suffered more than most who lived through Hurricane Katrina.
- d. The people of New Orleans did not receive adequate help during Hurricane Katrina.

Supporting Details _____ 4. When the family evacuated New Orleans they took
- a. essentials for two days.
- b. nothing.
- c. everything they owned.
- d. supplies for a month.

Supporting Details _____ 5. How many years had Alfred C. Cooley lived in New Orleans before Hurricane Katrina?
- a. 16
- b. around 35
- c. more than 50
- d. less than 1

Supporting Details _____ 6. Who returns with Cooley to check out his family's property in New Orleans?
- a. Dora Ann, his sister's former daughter-in-law
- b. Stanley Trotter, his ex-wife's cousin
- c. Mrs. Snead of St. Mark Baptist Church
- d. Javelle, his son-in-law

Transitions _____ 7. "Throughout my life, I have known suffering: I suffer from Sickle Cell Anemia." (paragraph 3)

The primary relationship of ideas **within** this sentence is
- a. time order.
- b. cause and effect.
- c. comparison and contrast.
- d. generalization and example.

Transitions _____ **8.** "My parents were told that I would not live past age 16, but here I am!" (paragraph 3)

The primary relationship of ideas **within** this sentence is
a. cause and effect.
b. time order.
c. comparison and contrast.
d. generalization and example.

Transitions _____ **9.** "No, I shall never forget—all the blessings that flowed from throughout the community to my family during these darkest hours. Finally people were allowed to return briefly to New Orleans . . ." (paragraphs 10–11)

The relationship of ideas **between** these sentences is
a. cause and effect.
b. time order.
c. comparison and contrast.
d. generalization and example.

Thought Patterns _____ **10.** The main thought pattern used in paragraph 1 is
a. space order.
b. cause and effect.
c. definition and example.
d. comparison and contrast.

Thought Patterns _____ **11.** The overall thought pattern of passage is
a. time order.
b. cause and effect.
c. comparison and contrast.
d. definition and example.

Fact and Opinion _____ **12.** "I am aghast by the sudden turn of events." (paragraph 1)

This sentence is a statement of
a. fact.
b. opinion.
c. fact and opinion.

Fact and Opinion _____ **13.** "There are thirty-five of us traveling in a caravan: a Dodge Caravan, a Ford Taurus, a 2000 Grand Prix, and a Toyota CRV just to name a few." (paragraph 1)

This sentence is a statement of
a. fact.
b. opinion.
c. fact and opinion.

Fact and Opinion _____ **14.** "In the wake of Katrina, we move to Atoka, Tennessee, and it does not take long for people to hear about the sixteen people who fled New Orleans." (paragraph 10)
a. fact.
b. opinion.
c. fact and opinion.

Tone and Purpose _____ **15.** "The overall tone of paragraphs 8 and 9 is
a. objective.
b. sarcastic
c. homesick.
d. positive.

Tone and
Purpose

_____ **16.** The main tone of the entire passage is
   a. neutral.   c. argumentative.
   b. appreciative.   d. distressed.

Tone and
Purpose

_____ **17.** The overall purpose of the author is
   a. to entertain the reader with a personal story about living through Hurricane Katrina.
   b. to inform the reader about the suffering caused by Hurricane Katrina.
   c. to persuade the reader to give aid to the survivors of Hurricane Katrina.

Inferences

_____ **18.** Based on the details in paragraph 10, we can infer that Cooley
   a. was reluctant to ask for help.
   b. resented having to rely on others for help.
   c. felt grateful to the people who helped them.
   d. begged others for help.

Inferences

_____ **19.** Based on the details in the passage, we can infer that the Cooley family
   a. did not suffer significant losses from Hurricane Katrina.
   b. suffered the loss of the lives of family members.
   c. will be able to rebuild their lives in New Orleans.
   d. was wise to evacuate New Orleans in the face of Katrina.

Argument

_____ **20.** Which logical fallacy is used in the following sentence?

"...all of us believe this is going to be a 'James Brown turnaround.'" (paragraph 2)
   a. either-or   c. false comparison
   b. personal attack   d. false cause

Outlining

Complete the following outline with information from the passage.

An Account of Alfred C. Cooley's Plight

   I. Evacuating _____

      A. Traveling in a _____

      B. Leaving worldly possessions behind

   II. _____

      A. _____

      B. Operations: two hip replacements, shoulder, left eye

III. Since we left home

IV. Watching the news

V. Remembering Picayune

VI. In the wake of Katrina

    A. Getting help in _____

    B. Returning briefly to New Orleans

WHAT DO YOU THINK?

Have you or someone you know survived a natural disaster such as a hurricane, tornado, flood, or wildfire? How did you prepare for or respond to the event? What type of natural disaster is more likely to occur in your area? What advice would you give, or what steps would you take to prepare for a natural disaster? Write a letter to the editor of your local paper to warn about the dangers of a natural disaster that could strike your area. Include steps your readers could take to prepare.

MASTER READER SCORECARD

"An Account of Alfred C. Cooley's Plight"

Skill	Number Correct	Points		Total
Vocabulary				
Vocabulary in Context (2 items)	_____	× 4	=	_____
Comprehension				
Implied Central Idea (1 item)	_____	× 4	=	_____
Supporting Details (3 items)	_____	× 4	=	_____
Transitions (3 items)	_____	× 4	=	_____
Thought Patterns (2 items)	_____	× 4	=	_____
Fact and Opinion (3 items)	_____	× 4	=	_____
Tone and Purpose (3 items)	_____	× 4	=	_____
Inferences (2 items)	_____	× 4	=	_____
Argument (1 item)	_____	× 4	=	_____
Outlining (5 items)	_____	× 4	=	_____
		Comprehension Score		_____

6 Night Diving

Bucky McMahon

> Travel and adventure writer Bucky McMahon also writes about unusual
> events that happen to him closer to home. In "Night Diving" he tells us of his
> experiences going night diving in a Florida sink hole close to his home. In
> this interesting essay, the writer explores how being submerged in darkness
> can be filled with as much beauty and exploration as highly visual diving
> environments. This essay teaches the reader that sometimes a simple night
> dive can be just as awe inspiring as grand works of art.

Vocabulary Preview

circumspectly (paragraph 1): watchful and discreet; cautious

query (paragraph 4): a question

foraging (paragraph 5): to look for food

gobies (paragraph 5): small fish whose fins form a suction disc

hypnagogic (paragraph 6): drowsiness

auditory (paragraph 6): the sense of hearing

interlocutors (paragraph 6): a person who engages in dialogue or questioning;
in comedy, the announcer or straight man who sets up the comedian for joke
answers

ectoplasmic (paragraph 6): in spiritualism, the shadowy ghost form in a seance
that rises above the person communicating with the dead

narcosis (paragraph 6): stupor; drowsiness; drug-induced slowness

fritz (paragraph 7): Slang; for an electronic device to become inoperable

Sistine Chapel (paragraph 7): a small church in the Vatican in Rome, the ceiling of
which is decorated with Michelangelo's fresco showing God, angels, and Adam

foreshortened (paragraph 7): a painter's technique of perspective used to make
close objects larger

1   There are two kinds of people at northern Florida's Emerald Sink after dark: those
who get naked and jump out of trees, and
those who put on rubber suits and go night
scuba diving. There's not a lot of mingling
amongst us. Mostly the two groups stalk **circumspectly** around each other's campfire at
the sinkhole's rim, like two species of shore
birds that can't eat each other's eggs and
don't want to mate. Country music twangs

from truck radios, goosed girls shriek in the dark, and sometimes a bandy-legged skinny-dipper will approach a group of divers suiting up on their tarp to peck at a particularly tasty-looking piece of scuba equipment and ask, "How much you pay for that?"

2   If it's a cave diver's complicated rig of **redundant** everything, the answer is "plenty." But most of us are just open-water divers packing the basic budget night-diving gear: a dependable, handheld D-battery powered primary light; a smaller, clamp-on C-battery-powered backup light; and a glow-in-the-dark (chemilumines-cent) light-stick, which will be attached to a sunken log at the sinkhole's center, mark-ing a direct route to the surface.

3   Emerald Sink is shaped roughly like a flask. A thirty-foot-wide tube drops straight down sixty feet to the debris cone (where the sunken part of the sinkhole lies), and then opens up to a wider cavern angling down to 180 feet. My dive buddy and I like to putter around just below the summit of this black cone, drifting in and out of the cavern zone, probing our flash-lights into cave entrances, and congratu-lating ourselves for not going into them. If Dracula were a kind of giant blind catfish, any one of these caves could be his castle.

4   There's a surprising amount of graffiti down here, mostly lovers' initials and fra-ternal insignia, though at a depth of eighty feet someone has gone to considerable trou-ble to carve this **query** in big block letters on the algae-darkened limestone: "WHAT ARE YOU LOOKING AT, _____?"

5   Good question. If we were night div-ing in the ocean, on a reef or around a

wreck, we might see shy nocturnal creatures openly **foraging**. Out of their hidey-holes octopuses would unravel, moray eels unreel and lobsters and other crustaceans creep forth in complete confidence. On the reef, divers' lights would blend a whole new pal-ette of colors. Coral that appears dark blue by daylight becomes brilliant red by night, and the little purple **gobies** that flitted about it earlier would seem orange and sleep soundly on their side. Often in the ocean at night, you can swim through cosmic con-stellations of bioluminescent microorgan-isms—the famed phosphorescence that makes divers glow like velvet Elvises.

6   But Emerald Sink is just your basic freshwater swimming hole close to home, and, alas, there's not much to look at. Yet even when there's nothing to see—especially when there's nothing to see—night scuba diving offers a meditatively fruitful sensory-deprivation experience. As the mind soaks in the **solution** of darkness, it becomes sus-ceptible to **hypnagogic auditory** hallucina-tions. Beyond the bubble and squeak of the regulator, you hear things: deeply internal-ized **interlocutors** waft up from the uncon-scious, clearing their throat and shaking their shipwrecked cocktails from the other world. A few times during the seance atmo-sphere of a deep night dive at Emerald, I've heard the insistent ringing of a spiritualist's **ectoplasmic** telephone. And, I swear, one time I heard, down around 180 feet, where the **narcosis** kicks in, the distant flushing of the Devil's toilet.

7   On a night dive, once you've achieved neutral buoyancy, you can simply lie back on a black cushion, sighting up the tele-scopic tube of the sink at the dime-sized

disc of the night sky. It glows faint and gray, like a Fifties TV set about to go on the **fritz**. On a good night you'll see a rippling moon looking back at you through the veins of thin black branches, and if you wait long enough, you're sure to see naked souls falling out of the trees, a veritable redneck **Sistine Chapel** of **foreshortened** bare limbs kicking up faraway clouds of turbulence as the angels toss them out of Heaven.

—"Night Diving" from *Night Diver* by Bucky McMahon. Reproduced by the permission of Bucky McMahon.

Choose the best meaning of each word in **bold**. Use context clues to make your choice.

Vocabulary in Context _____ **1.** "If it's a cave diver's complicated rig of **redundant** everything, the answer is 'plenty.'" (paragraph 2)
   a. expensive   c. needing skill to use
   b. duplicated for safety   d. complex

Vocabulary in Context _____ **2.** "As the mind soaks in the **solution** of darkness, it becomes susceptible to hypnagogic auditory hallucinations." (paragraph 6)
   a. answer   c. puzzle
   b. sink-like   d. liquid for chemical experiments

Central Idea _____ **3.** Which of the following sentences best states the central idea of the passage?
   a. "Emerald Sink is shaped roughly like a flask." (paragraph 3)
   b. "If Dracula were a kind of giant blind catfish, any one of these caves could be his castle." (paragraph 3)
   c. "Yet even when there's nothing to see—especially when there's nothing to see—night scuba diving offers a meditatively fruitful sensory-deprivation experience." (paragraph 6)
   d. "And, I swear, one time I heard, down around 180 feet, where the narcosis kicks in, the distant flushing of the Devil's toilet." (paragraph 6)

Central Idea _____ **4.** Which of the following sentences states the central idea of paragraphs 5 and 6?
   a. "If we were night diving in the ocean, on a reef or around a wreck, we might see shy nocturnal creatures openly foraging." (paragraph 5)
   b. "Often in the ocean at night, you can swim through cosmic constellations of bioluminescent microorganisms—the famed phosphorescence that makes divers glow like velvet Elvises." (paragraph 5)

c. "But Emerald Sink is just your basic freshwater swimming hole close to home, and, alas, there's not much to look at." (paragraph 6)

d. "A few times during the seance atmosphere of a deep night dive at Emerald, I've heard the insistent ringing of a spiritualist's ectoplasmic telephone." (paragraph 6)

Supporting Details _____ **5.** According to the author, what kinds of people make up the two kinds of swimmers at the sinkhole?
a. high school and college students
b. rap fans and rock fans
c. small town and big city dwellers
d. divers and rural partiers

Supporting Details _____ **6.** According to the author, which of the following is *not* a part of the basic budget night-diving gear?
a. a diving suit   c. a backup light
b. a primary light   d. a light-stick

Transitions _____ **7.** "There are two kinds of people at northern Florida's Emerald Sink after dark: those who get naked and jump out of trees, and those who put on rubber suits and go night scuba diving." (paragraph 1)

The relationship of ideas **within** this sentence is
a. classification.   c. comparison and contrast.
b. cause and effect.   d. space order.

Transitions _____ **8.** "A few times during the seance atmosphere of a deep night dive at Emerald, I've heard the insistent ringing of a spiritualist's ectoplasmic telephone. And, I swear, one time I heard, down around 180 feet, where the narcosis kicks in, the distant flushing of the Devil's toilet." (paragraph 6)

The relationship of ideas **between** these sentences is
a. cause and effect.   c. comparison and contrast.
b. time order.   d. generalization and example.

Thought Patterns _____ **9.** The thought pattern of paragraph 1 is
a. time order.   c. classification.
b. cause and effect.   d. listing.

Thought Patterns _____ **10.** The overall thought pattern of the passage is
a. description.   c. argument.
b. cause and effect.   d. definition and example.

Fact and
Opinion

_____ **11.** "Emerald Sink is shaped roughly like a flask." (paragraph 3)

This sentence is a statement of
a. fact.   c. fact and opinion.
b. opinion.

Fact and
Opinion

_____ **12.** "Yet even when there's nothing to see—especially when there's nothing to see—night scuba diving offers a meditatively fruitful sensory-deprivation experience." (paragraph 6)

This sentence is a statement of
a. fact.   c. fact and opinion.
b. opinion.

Tone and
Purpose

_____ **13.** "Mostly the two groups stalk circumspectly around each other's campfire at the sinkhole's rim, like two species of shore birds that can't eat each other's eggs and don't want to mate." (paragraph 1)

The tone of this sentence is
a. objective.   c. humorous.
b. bitter.   d. argumentative.

Tone and
Purpose

_____ **14.** The overall tone of the passage is
a. neutral and objective.   c. argumentative.
b. appreciative and reflective.   d. sarcastic and critical.

Tone and
Purpose

_____ **15.** The overall purpose of the author is
a. to persuade skinny-dippers to become divers.
b. to argue that diving is dangerous.
c. to reflect on ideas generated by experiences in Nature.
d. to criticize partying teenagers who are bored by the sinkhole.

Inferences

_____ **16.** Based on the details in paragraphs 5 and 6, we can infer that
a. ocean diving is more interesting than sinkhole diving.
b. ocean diving is less dangerous than sinkhole diving.
c. the author is afraid of the hallucinations caused by sinkhole diving.
d. the author enjoys unusual states of mind.

Inferences

_____ **17.** Based on the details in the passage, we can infer that
a. the author does not respect the people jumping into the sinkhole.
b. the enjoyment of Nature can create religious experiences.
c. the people swimming can't afford expensive diving equipment.
d. cave diving is so risky that it is unpleasant.

Inferences _____ **18.** Based on the details in the passage, we can infer that
   a. uneducated people wouldn't appreciate Michelangelo's Sistine Chapel.
   b. cave diving isn't all that interesting.
   c. the author is afraid to go further down into the cave.
   d. both groups of sinkhole users enjoy the water in different ways.

Argument _____ **19.** The following sentences from paragraph 6 contain a claim and list of supports for that claim. Which sentence states the claim?
   a. "As the mind soaks in the solution of darkness, it becomes susceptible to hypnagogic auditory hallucinations."
   b. "Beyond the bubble and squeak of the regulator, you hear things: deeply internalized interlocutors waft up from the unconscious, clearing their throat and shaking their shipwrecked cocktails from the other world."
   c. "A few times during the seance atmosphere of a deep night dive at Emerald, I've heard the insistent ringing of a spiritualist's ectoplasmic telephone."
   d. "And, I swear, one time I heard, down around 180 feet, where the narcosis kicks in, the distant flushing of the Devil's toilet."

Argument _____ **20.** The graffiti carved eighty feet underwater in the sinkhole in big block letters on the algae-darkened limestone in paragraph 4 is an example of the fallacy of
   a. false cause.   c. straw man.
   b. personal attack.   d. glittering generality.

Outlining

Complete the following outline with information from the passage.

Night Diving

   I. Two kinds of people at northern Florida's Emerald Sink after dark

   A. _____

   B. Night divers

II. Diving gear

    A. D-battery powered primary light

    B. Clamp-on C-battery-powered backup light

    C. Glow-in-the-dark light-stick

III. _____

    A. Shaped like _____

    B. A thirty-foot tube drops straight down sixty feet to the debris cone

    C. Divers putter just below the summit of the black cone, drifting in and out of the cavern zone

    D. Surprising amount of graffiti

    E. Basic freshwater swimming hole

IV. Night scuba, a sensory-deprivation experience

    A. Hypnagogic auditory hallucinations

    B. _____ buoyancy

    C. The telescopic tube of the sink

    D. The dime-size disc of the night sky

    E. Glows faint and gray

    F. A rippling moon

    G. Veins of thin black branches

    H. _____ falling out of trees

    I. Redneck Sistine Chapel

WHAT DO YOU THINK?

Assume you are taking a college writing course, and your professor has asked you to write reflectively about the reasons you enjoy one of your favorite pastimes. Describe your favorite activity, hobby, or interest. As you describe the activity, explain why you enjoy the experience.

"Night Diving"

Skill	Number Correct		Points		Total
Vocabulary					
Vocabulary in Context (2 items)	_____	×	4	=	_____
Comprehension					
Central Ideas (2 items)	_____	×	4	=	_____
Supporting Details (2 items)	_____	×	4	=	_____
Transitions (2 items)	_____	×	4	=	_____
Thought Patterns (2 items)	_____	×	4	=	_____
Fact and Opinion (2 items)	_____	×	4	=	_____
Tone and Purpose (3 items)	_____	×	4	=	_____
Inferences (3 items)	_____	×	4	=	_____
Argument (2 items)	_____	×	4	=	_____
Outlining (5 items)	_____	×	4	=	_____
			Comprehension Score		_____

7 Fannie Lou Hamer

by Maya Angelou

> Poet, writer, performer, teacher, and director, Maya Angelou was raised in Stamps, Arkansas, then moved to San Francisco. In addition to her bestselling autobiographies, beginning with *I Know Why the Caged Bird Sings*, she has also written a cookbook, *Hallelujah! The Welcome Table*, and five poetry collections, including *I Shall Not Be Moved* and *Shaker, Why Don't You Sing?* The following passage appears in *Letter to My Daughter*, Angelou's first original collection in 15 years. In this collection of essays, she shares lessons based on the distilled knowledge of a lifetime well-lived. If you could choose a public figure to honor, whom would you choose? What lessons could be learned from this person's life?

Vocabulary Preview

imperative (paragraph 2): of vital importance, urgent
sequestered (paragraph 3): placed in isolation
laud (paragraph 5): praise
avert (paragraph 5): turn away
embolden (paragraph 11): encourage

1   "All of this on account we want to register, to become first-class citizens, and if the Freedom Democratic Party is not seated now, I question America, is this America, the land of the free and the home of the brave, where we have to sleep with our telephones off the hooks because our lives be threatened daily because we want to live as decent human beings, in America? Thank you."

—FANNIE LOU HAMER

2   It is important that we know that those words come from the lips of an African American woman. It is **imperative** that we know those words come from the heart of an American.

3   I believe that there lives a burning desire in the most **sequestered** private heart of every American, a desire to belong to a great country. I believe that every citizen wants to stand on the world stage and represent a noble country where the mighty do not always crush the weak and the dream of a democracy is not the sole possession of the strong.

4   We must hear the questions raised by Fannie Lou Hamer forty years ago. Every American everywhere asks herself, himself, these questions Hamer asked:

5 What do I think of my country? What is there, which elevates my shoulders and stirs my blood when I hear the words, the United States of America: Do I praise my country enough? Do I **laud** my fellow citizens enough? What is there about my country that makes me hang my head and **avert** my eyes when I hear the words the United States of America, and what am I doing about it? Am I relating my disappointment to my leaders and to my fellow citizens, or am I like someone not involved, sitting high and looking low? As Americans, we should not be afraid to respond.

6 We have asked questions down a pyramid of years and given answers, which our children memorize, and which have become an integral part of the spoken American history. Patrick Henry remarked, "I know not what course others may take, but as for me, give me liberty or give me death."

7 George Moses Horton, the nineteenth century poet, born a slave, said, "Alas, and was I born for this, to wear this brutish chain? I must slash the handcuffs from my wrists and live a man again."

8 "The thought of only being a creature of the present and the past was troubling. I longed for a future too, with hope in it. The desire to be free, awakened my determination to act, to think, and to speak."

—FREDERICK DOUGLASS

9 The love of democracy motivated Harriet Tubman to seek and find not only her own freedom, but to make **innumerable** trips to the slave South to gain the liberty of many slaves and instill the idea into the hearts of thousands that freedom is possible.

10 Fannie Lou Hamer and the Mississippi Democratic Freedom Party were standing on the shoulders of history when they acted to unseat evil from its presumed safe perch on the backs of the American people. It is fitting to honor the memory of Fannie Lou Hamer and surviving members of the Mississippi Democratic Freedom Party. For their gifts to us, we say thank you.

11 The human heart is so delicate and sensitive that it always needs some **tangible** encouragement to prevent it from faltering in its labor. The human heart is so robust, so tough, that once encouraged it beats its rhythm with a loud unswerving insistency. One thing that encourages the heart is music. Throughout the ages we have created songs to grow on and to live by. We Americans have created music to **embolden** the hearts and inspire the spirit of people all over the world.

12 Fannie Lou Hamer knew that she was one woman and only one woman. However, she knew she was an American, and as an American she had a light to shine on the darkness of racism. It was a little light, but she aimed it directly at the gloom of ignorance.

13 Fannie Lou Hamer's favorite was a simple song that we all know. We Americans have sung it since childhood . . .

14 "This little light of mine, I'm going to let it shine, Let it shine,

15 Let it shine,

16 Let it shine.

—Angelou, Maya. "Fannie Lou Hamer" from *Letter to My Daughter*, pp. 83–85. Copyright © 2008 by Maya Angelou. Used by permission of Random House, Inc.

Choose the best meaning of each word in **bold**. Use context clues to make your choice.

Vocabulary _____ **1.** "The love of democracy motivated Harriet Tubman to seek and
in Context   find not only her own freedom, but to make **innumerable** trips to
                      the slave South to gain the liberty of many slaves and instill the idea
                      into the hearts of thousands that freedom is possible." (paragraph 9)
                      a. few   c. immense
                      b. specific   d. countless

Vocabulary _____ **2.** "The human heart is so delicate and sensitive that it always needs
in Context   some **tangible** encouragement to prevent it from faltering in its
                      labor." (paragraph 11)
                      a. obvious   c. subtle
                      b. important   d. indescribable

Central Idea _____ **3.** Which of the following sentences states the central idea of the
                      passage?
                      a. "It is important to know that those words come from the lips of
                         an African American woman." (paragraph 2)
                      b. "We must hear the questions raised by Fannie Lou Hamer forty
                         years ago." (paragraph 4)
                      c. "It is fitting to honor the memory of Fannie Lou Hamer and
                         surviving members of the Mississippi Democratic Freedom
                         Party." (paragraph 10)
                      d. "However, she knew she was an American, and as an American
                         she had a light to shine on the darkness of racism." (paragraph 12)

Main Idea _____ **4.** Which of the following sentences states the main idea of paragraph 11?
                      a. "The human heart is so delicate and sensitive that it always
                         needs some tangible encouragement to prevent it from faltering
                         in its labor."
                      b. "The human heart is so robust, so tough, that once encouraged
                         it beats its rhythm with a loud unswerving insistency."
                      c. "One thing that encourages the heart is music."
                      d. "Throughout the ages we have created songs to grow on and to
                         live by."

Supporting _____ **5.** According to the passage, who said "I must slash the handcuffs
Details   from my wrists . . ."?
                      a. Patrick Henry   c. Fannie Lou Hamer
                      b. George Moses Horton   d. Frederick Douglass

Supporting   _____   **6.** According to the passage, Harriet Tubman was motivated by
Details
             a. fear of slavery.
             b. the shoulders of history.
             c. love of democracy.
             d. the work of Fannie Lou Hamer.

Transitions   _____   **7.** "It was a little light, but she aimed it directly at the gloom of ignorance." (paragraph 12)

The relationship of ideas within this sentence is
             a. cause and effect.
             b. listing.
             c. comparison and contrast.
             d. generalization and example.

Transitions   _____   **8.** "Fannie Lou Hamer knew that she was one woman and only one woman. However, she knew she was an American, and as an American she had a light to shine on the darkness of racism." (paragraph 12)

The relationship of ideas between these sentences is
             a. cause and effect.   c. comparison and contrast.
             b. listing.   d. generalization and example.

Thought   _____   **9.** "The human heart is so delicate and sensitive that it always needs
Patterns   some tangible encouragement to prevent it from faltering in its labor. The human heart is so robust, so tough, that once encouraged it beats its rhythm with a loud unswerving insistency." (paragraph 11)

The thought pattern established by these two sentences is
             a. cause and effect.   c. comparison and contrast.
             b. listing.   d. definition and example.

Thought   _____   **10.** The overall thought pattern for paragraph 5 is
Patterns
             a. cause and effect.   c. comparison and contrast.
             b. listing.   d. definition and example.

Fact and   _____   **11.** "It is imperative that we know those words come from the heart of
Opinion   an American." (paragraph 2)

This sentence is a statement of
             a. fact.   c. fact and opinion.
             b. opinion.

Fact and Opinion _____ **12.** "I believe that there lives a burning desire in the most sequestered private heart of every American, a desire to belong to a great country." (paragraph 3)

This sentence is a statement of
a. fact.   c. fact and opinion.
b. opinion.

Fact and Opinion _____ **13.** "We must hear the questions raised by Fannie Lou Hamer forty years ago." (paragraph 4)

This sentence is a statement of
a. fact.   c. fact and opinion.
b. opinion.

Tone _____ **14.** The overall tone of the author is
a. complaining.   c. bitter.
b. balanced.   d. inspirational.

Tone _____ **15.** The tone of the words of Fannie Lou Hamer in the first paragraph is
a. challenging.   c. frightened.
b. accepting.   d. respectful.

Purpose _____ **16.** The purpose of the author is
a. to inform the reader about the racism faced by African Americans such as Fannie Lou Hamer.
b. to entertain the reader with the words and deeds of highly regarded civil rights leaders.
c. to persuade the reader to appreciate and be inspired by Fannie Lou Hamer and the history she represents.

Inferences _____ **17.** Based on the details in the passage, we can infer that Fannie Lou Hamer was working to
a. gain freedom for slaves.
b. be officially represented in the political process.
c. be seated in a restaurant.
d. produce music to further the civil rights movement.

Inferences _____ **18.** Based on the details in the passage, we can infer that
a. there will always be injustice and oppression.
b. determined individuals can significantly impact society for the good.
c. freedom always comes through violence and loss of life.
d. citizens should love their country unconditionally.

Argument _____ **19.** Identify the persuasive technique used in the following sentence:

"I believe that every citizen wants to stand on the world stage and represent a noble country where the mighty do not always crush the weak and the dream of a democracy is not the sole possession of the strong." (paragraph 3)
a. false cause
b. personal attack
c. glittering generality
d. black and white fallacy

Argument _____ **20.** Read the claim and supports taken from the passage. Then identify the detail that does not support the claim.

" . . . give me liberty or give me death." (paragraph 6)
a. false cause   c. glittering generality
b. personal attack   d. black and white fallacy

Summarizing

Complete the following summary of the passage:

(1) _____ and surviving members of the Mississippi Democratic Freedom Party should be honored because they stood on the historical shoulders of **(2)** _____, **(3)** _____, **(4)** _____, and **(5)** _____ to shine a light on the gloom of ignorance and the darkness of racism.

WHAT DO YOU THINK?

Do you think it is important to pay tribute to people who have impacted our lives? Why or why not? Whom would you choose to honor for his or her impact on society? Assume you are taking a college course in sociology. Your professor sponsors a course webpage on which he posts samples of student essays about social issues. The current topic is as follows: After reading Maya Angelou's essay "Fannie Lou Hamer," write your own tribute (400–750 words) to a person who has had a significant impact on society. In your essay, identify the social problem and describe how this person made a difference.

MASTER READER SCORECARD

"Fannie Lou Hamer"

Skill	Number Correct	Points			Total
Vocabulary					
Vocabulary in Context (2 items)	_____	×	4	=	_____
Comprehension					
Central Idea and Main Idea (2 items)	_____	×	4	=	_____
Supporting Details (2 items)	_____	×	4	=	_____
Transitions (2 items)	_____	×	4	=	_____
Thought Patterns (2 items)	_____	×	4	=	_____
Fact and Opinion (3 items)	_____	×	4	=	_____
Tone and Purpose (3 items)	_____	×	4	=	_____
Inferences (2 items)	_____	×	4	=	_____
Argument (2 items)	_____	×	4	=	_____
Outlining (5 items)	_____	×	4	=	_____
		Comprehension Score			_____

Human Development

Richard J. Gerrig with Philip G. Zimbardo

> Suppose you were asked to make a list of all the ways in which you believe you have changed this past year. What sorts of things would you put on your list? Developmental psychology studies the changes in physical and mental functioning that occur across the entire lifespan. Each stage of life brings significant change. The following passage is a section of the chapter "Human Development Across the Life Span" from the college textbook *Psychology & Life*.

Vocabulary Preview

puberty (paragraph 2): the process through which sexual maturity is attained

menarche (paragraph 2): the onset of menstruation

maturation (paragraph 3): the continuing influence of heredity throughout development; the age-related physical and behavioral changes characteristic of a species

cognitive development (paragraph 6): the development of processes of knowing, including imagining, perceiving, reasoning, and problem solving

scheme (paragraph 8): Piaget's term for a cognitive structure that develops as infants and young children learn to interpret the world and adapt to their environment

assimilation (paragraph 8): according to Piaget, the process whereby new cognitive elements are fitted in with old elements or modified to fit more easily; this process works in tandem with accommodation

accommodation (paragraph 8): according to Piaget, the process of restructuring or modifying cognitive structures so that new information can fit into them more easily; this process works in tandem with assimilation

object permanence (paragraph 10): the recognition that objects exist independently of an individual's action or awareness; an important cognitive acquisition of infancy

egocentrism (paragraph 11): in cognitive development, the inability of a young child at the preoperational stage to take the perspective of another person

centration (paragraph 11): preoperational children's tendency to focus their attention on only one aspect of a situation and disregard other relevant aspects

reversibility (paragraph 13): capability of reestablishing the original condition after a change by the reverse of the change

Physical Development in Adolescence

1   The first concrete indicator of the end of childhood is the pubescent growth spurt. At around age 10 for girls and age 12 for boys, growth hormones flow into the bloodstream. For several years, the adolescent may grow 3 to 6 inches a year and gain weight rapidly as well. The adolescent's body does not reach adult proportions all at once. Hands and feet grow to full adult size first. The arms and legs come next, with the torso developing most slowly. Thus an individual's overall shape changes several times over the teenage years.

2   Another important process that occurs during adolescence is **puberty**, which brings about sexual maturity. (The Latin word *pubertas* means "covered with hair" and signifies the growth of hair on the arms and legs, under the arms, and in the genital area.) Puberty for males brings about the production of live sperm; for girls it leads to **menarche**, the onset of menstruation. In the United States, the average time for menarche is between the ages of 12 and 13, although the normal range extends from 11 to 15. For boys, the production of live sperm first occurs, on average, between the ages of 12 and 14, but again there is considerable variation in this timing. These physical changes often bring about an awareness of sexual feelings.

3   Some other important physical changes happen inside adolescents' brains. Researchers once thought that most brain growth was over within the first few years of life. However, recent studies using brain imaging techniques have demonstrated continuing development within the adolescent brain. Researchers have documented particularly important changes in the limbic system—which regulates emotional processes—and the frontal lobes—the areas responsible for planning and control of emotions. However, **maturation** of the limbic system precedes maturation of the frontal lobes. The relative timing of changes within those regions may explain one of most salient aspects of social development in adolescence: Adolescents tend to engage in risky behavior. Let's explore this insight.

4   We'll return to social aspects of risky behavior when we review social development. For now, our focus is on physical development. Researchers speculate that maturation of the limbic system readies adolescents to go out into the world.

5   Evolutionarily speaking, adolescence is the period in which independence skills are acquired to increase success upon separation from the protection of the family. In that evolutionary context, it makes sense that regions of the frontal cortex that inhibit and control the emotional drive toward independence would mature somewhat later in life. To survive apart from their families, adolescents would have to take some initial risks. The difficulty is that in contemporary times people no longer typically leave their families during adolescence. Thus, the evolutionary impulse toward novelty seeking and risk taking no longer has an adaptive function. Fortunately, as people develop from adolescence into adulthood, the frontal lobes achieve maturity. New connections form between the frontal lobes and limbic system. Those new connections enable individuals to exercise more

cognitive control over their emotional impulses.

Cognitive Development in Adolescence

6   How does an individual's understanding of physical and social reality change across the life span? **Cognitive development** is the study of the processes and products of the mind as they emerge and change over time. We begin our discussion of cognitive development with the pioneering work of the late Swiss psychologist Jean Piaget.

Piaget's Insights into Mental Development

7   For nearly 50 years, Jean Piaget developed theories about the ways that children think, reason, and solve problems. Piaget used simple demonstrations and sensitive interviews with his own children and with other children to generate complex theories about early mental development. His interest was not in the amount of information children possessed but in the ways their thinking and inner representations of physical reality changed at different stages in their development.

8   **Building Blocks of Developmental Change** Piaget gave the name *schemes* to the mental structures that enable individuals to interpret the world. **Schemes** are the building blocks of developmental change. Piaget characterized the infant's initial schemes as *sensorimotor intelligence*—mental structures or programs that guide sensorimotor sequences, such as sucking, looking, grasping, and pushing. With practice, elementary schemes are combined, integrated, and differentiated into ever-more-complex,

diverse action patterns, as when a child pushes away undesired objects to seize a desired one behind him or her. According to Piaget, two basic processes work in tandem to achieve cognitive growth—assimilation and accommodation. **Assimilation** modifies new environmental information to fit into what is already known; the child accesses existing schemes to structure incoming sensory data. **Accommodation** restructures or modifies the child's existing schemes so that new information is accounted for more completely. The balanced application of assimilation and accommodation permits children's behavior and knowledge to become less dependent on concrete external reality, relying more on abstract thought.

Stages in Cognitive Development 9 Piaget believed that children's cognitive development could be divided into a series of four ordered, discontinuous stages. All children are assumed to progress through these stages in the same sequence, although one child may take longer to pass through a given stage than does another.

Sensorimotor Stage The sensorimo- 10 tor stage extends roughly from birth to age 2. In the early months, much of an infant's behavior is based on a limited array of inborn schemes, like sucking, looking, grasping, and pushing. The most important cognitive acquisition of the infancy period is the ability to form mental representations of absent objects—those with which the child is not in direct sensorimotor contact. **Object permanence** refers to children's understanding that objects exist and behave independently of their actions or awareness.

11   **Preoperational Stage** The preoperational stage extends roughly from 2 to 7 years of age. The big cognitive advance in this developmental stage is an improved ability to represent mentally objects that are not physically present. Piaget believed that young children's preoperational thought is marked by **egocentrism**, the child's inability to take the perspective of another person. They also experience **centration**—they tend to focus (center) their attention on only one aspect of a situation and disregard other relevant aspects.

12   **Concrete Operations Stage** The concrete operations stage goes roughly from 7 to 11 years of age. At this stage, the child has become capable of mental operations, actions performed in the mind that give rise to logical thinking. Concrete operations allow children to replace physical action with mental action. For example, if a child sees that Adam is taller than Zara and, later, that Zara is taller than Tanya, the child can reason that Adam is the tallest of the three—without physically manipulating the three individuals.

13   Another hallmark of the concrete operations period is called **conservation**: They know that the physical properties of objects do not change when nothing is added or taken away, even though the objects' appearances change. One of the newly acquired operations children can bring to bear on conservation tasks is reversibility. **Reversibility** is the child's understanding that both physical actions and mental operations can be reversed.

14   **Formal Operations Stage** The formal operations stage covers a span roughly from age 11 on. In this final stage of cognitive growth, thinking becomes abstract. Adolescents can see how their particular reality is only one of several imaginable realities. They begin to ponder deep questions of truth, justice, and existence. They seek answers to problems in a systematic fashion: Adolescents also begin to be able to use the types of advanced **deductive** logic. Unlike their younger siblings, adolescents have the ability to reason from abstract premises ("If A, then E" and "not E") to their logical conclusions ("not A").

Social Development and Erikson's Psychosocial Stages

15   **Social development** includes the ways in which individuals' social interactions and expectations change across the life span. To begin our discussion on social development, we will describe Erik Erikson's life span theory. Erik Erikson (1902–1994) was trained by Sigmund Freud's daughter, Anna Freud. He proposed that every individual must successfully navigate a series of psychosocial stages. Erikson identified eight stages in the life cycle. At each stage, a particular crisis comes into focus, as shown in the following table. Although each conflict never completely disappears, it needs to be sufficiently resolved at a given stage if an individual is to cope successfully with the conflicts of later stages.

Social Development in Adolescence

16   Because the individual has reached a certain level of physical and mental maturity, new social and personal challenges

present themselves. We will first consider the general experience of adolescence and then turn to the individual's changing social world.

17 **The Experience of Adolescence** The traditional view of adolescence predicts a uniquely tumultuous period of life, characterized by extreme mood swings and unpredictable, difficult behavior: "storm and stress." This view can be traced back to romantic writers of the late 18th and early 19th centuries, such as Goethe. The storm-and-stress conception of adolescence was strongly propounded by G. Stanley Hall, the first psychologist of the modern era to write at length about adolescent development. Following Hall, the major proponents of this view have been psychoanalytic theorists working within the Freudian tradition. Some of them have argued that not only is extreme turmoil a normal part of adolescence but that failure to exhibit such turmoil is a sign of arrested development. Anna Freud wrote that "to be normal during the adolescent period is by itself abnormal."

18 Two early pioneers in cultural anthropology, Margaret Mead (1928) and Ruth Benedict (1938), argued that the storm-and-stress theory is not applicable to many non-Western cultures. They described cultures in which children gradually take on more and more adult responsibilities without any sudden stressful transition or period of indecision and turmoil. Contemporary research has confirmed that the experience of adolescence differs across cultures. Those cross-cultural differences argue against strictly biological theories of adolescent experience. Instead, researchers focus on the transitions children are expected to make in different cultures.

Most researchers reject "storm and 19 stress" as a biologically programmed aspect of development. Nonetheless, people typically do experience more extreme emotions and more conflict as they pass from childhood into adolescence. When we discussed physical development we noted that brain areas that control emotional responses show growth during adolescence. That brain maturation may explain why adolescents experience both extreme positive and extreme negative emotions. You can understand the conflicts adolescents have with their parents if you recall Erikson's claim that the essential task of adolescence is to discover one's true identity. For cultures like the majority culture in the United States, one consequence is that children attempt to achieve independence from their parents. Parents and their adolescent children must weather a transition in their relationship from one in which a parent has unquestioned authority to one in which the adolescent is granted reasonable independence to make important decisions. Consider the results of a study that followed 1,330 adolescents from age 11 to age 14 (McGue et al., 2005). As 14-year-olds, these adolescents reported greater conflict with their parents than they had at age 11. At age 14, the adolescents' parents were less involved in their lives; the adolescents had less positive regard for their parents and they believed that their parents had less positive regard for them. These data illustrate some of the relationship costs that arise when children strive for independence.

20   Still, adolescents' conflicts with their parents often do not lead to harmful outcomes. Most adolescents at most times are able to use their parents as ready sources of practical and emotional support. For that reason, many adolescents have conflicts with their parents that leave their basic relationship unharmed. When conflict occurs in the context of otherwise positive relationships, there may be few negative consequences. However, in the context of negative relationships, adolescent conflict can lead to other problems such as social withdrawal and delinquency. Thus, family contexts may explain why some adolescents experience unusual levels of "storm and stress."

21   Now that we've considered the general adolescent experience, let's turn to the increasing importance of peers in adolescents' social experience.

22   **Peer Relationships** Much of the study of social development in adolescence focuses on the changing roles of family (or adult caretakers) and friends. We have already seen that attachments to adults form soon after birth. Children also begin to have friends at very young ages. Adolescence, however, marks the first period in which peers appear to compete with parents to shape a person's attitudes and behaviors. Adolescents participate in peer relations at the three levels of friendships, cliques, and crowds. Over the course of these years, adolescents come to count increasingly on their one-on-one friendships to provide them with

help and support. Cliques are groups that most often consist of 6 to 12 individuals. Membership in these groups may change over time, but they tend to be drawn along lines of, for example, age and race. Finally, crowds are the larger groups such as "jocks" or "nerds" that exist more loosely among individuals of this age. Through interaction with peers at these three levels, adolescents gradually define the social component of their developing identities, determining the kinds of people they choose to be and the kinds of relationships they choose to pursue.

23   The peer relationships that adolescents form are quite important to social development. They give individuals opportunities to learn how to function in what can often be demanding social circumstances. In that sense, peer relationships play a positive role in preparing adolescents for their futures. At the same time, parents often worry—with reasonable cause—about negative aspects of peer influence. We noted earlier that adolescents are likely to engage in risky behavior. That tendency increases when adolescents are under the influence of their peers.

24   To study developmental changes in peer influence, researchers recruited three groups of participants: Adolescents (age 13 to 16), young adults (ages 18 to 22), and adults (ages 24 and older). Participants in each age range played a video game called "Chicken." In this game, players act as drivers. They must decide how soon to stop their car when a light changes from green to yellow. Their goal is to achieve as much distance as they can

before the light turns red and a wall pops up. If they don't stop in time, they'll crash into the wall. About half of the participants played the game alone. The other half played in groups of three—each participant played in turn while the other two watched. Adolescents were far more likely to engage in risky driving (within the context of the video game) when in the presence of their peers.

25　　This study confirms a general tendency for adolescents to demonstrate peer influence as a shift toward riskier behaviors. However, some adolescents are more susceptible to peer influence than others—and that susceptibility has consequences. In a longitudinal study, students who were more susceptible to their close friends' influence at the study's outset were more likely to have problems with drugs and alcohol 1 year later. We note, once again, that adolescence need not be a time of storm and stress. However, research of this type indicates the patterns of behavior that indicate some adolescents are at risk.

—Gerrig, Richard J., Zimbardo, Philip G., Svartdal, Frode, Brennen, Tim, Donaldson, Roger, and Archer, Trevor. *Psychology and Life*, © 2012 by Pearson Education, Inc. Printed and Electronically reproduced by permission of Pearson Education, Inc., Upper Saddle River, New Jersey.

Choose the best meaning of each word in **bold**. Use context clues to make your choice.

Vocabulary in Context _____ **1.** "Another hallmark of the concrete operations period is called **conservation**: They know that the physical properties of objects do not change when nothing is added or taken away, even though the objects' appearances change." (paragraph 13)
a. concentration　　c. destruction
b. preservation　　d. moderation

Vocabulary in Context _____ **2.** "They seek answers to problems in a systematic fashion: Adolescents also begin to be able to use the types of advanced **deductive** logic." (paragraph 14)
a. reasonable　　c. realistic
b. provable　　d. unverifiable

Main Idea _____ **3.** Which of the following sentences best states the central idea of Piaget's insights into mental development? (paragraphs 7–9)
a. "For nearly 50 years, Jean Piaget developed theories about the ways that children think, reason, and solve problems." (paragraph 7)
b. "His interest was not in the amount of information children possessed but in the ways their thinking and inner representations

of physical reality changed at different stages in their development." (paragraph 7)

c. "The balanced application of assimilation and accommodation permits children's behavior and knowledge to become less dependent on concrete external reality, relying more on abstract thought." (paragraph 8)

d. "Piaget believed that children's cognitive development could be divided into a series of four ordered, discontinuous stages." (paragraph 9)

Main Idea _____ 4. Which of the following sentences states the main idea of paragraph 15?

a. "Erikson identified eight stages in the life cycle."

b. "At each stage, a particular crisis comes into focus, as shown in the following table."

c. "Although each conflict never completely disappears, it needs to be sufficiently resolved at a given stage if an individual is to cope successfully with the conflicts of later stages."

Supporting Details _____ 5. According to the author, why do adolescent children have conflict with their parents during this stage of their development?

a. discovering their identity   c. rebellion against authority

b. hormones   d. mood swings

Supporting Details _____ 6. According to the author, social development in adolescence is influenced by which one of the following options?

a. parents   c. culture

b. school   d. peers

Transitions _____ 7. "Instead, researchers focus on the transitions children are expected to make in different cultures. Most researchers reject 'storm and stress' as a biologically programmed aspect of development." (paragraphs 18 and 19)

The relationship of ideas **between** these sentences is

a. cause and effect.   c. comparison and contrast.

b. time order.   d. generalization and example.

Transitions _____ 8. "Now that we've considered the general adolescent experience, let's turn to the increasing importance of peers in adolescents' social experience." (paragraph 21)

The relationship of ideas **within** this sentence is

a. classification. c. comparison.

b. generalization and example d. space order.

Thought Patterns _____ **9.** The thought pattern of paragraph 24 is

a. time order. c. generalization and example.

b. listing d. description.

Thought Patterns _____ **10.** The overall thought pattern of the passage is

a. description. c. process.

b. cause and effect. d. definition and example.

Fact and Opinion _____ **11.** "Maturation of the limbic system precedes maturation of the frontal lobes." (paragraph 3)

This sentence is a statement of

a. fact. c. fact and opinion.

b. opinion.

Fact and Opinion _____ **12.** "All children are assumed to progress through these stages in the same sequence, although one child may take longer to pass through a given stage than does another." (paragraph 9)

This sentence is a statement of

a. fact. c. fact and opinion.

b. opinion.

Fact and Opinion _____ **13.** Throughout the passage, the author relies mostly on

a. fact. c. fact and opinion.

b. opinion.

Tone and Purpose _____ **14.** The overall tone of the passage is

a. informative. c. humorous.

b. sarcastic. d. persuasive.

Tone and Purpose _____ **15.** The overall purpose of the author is

a. to inform the reader of the mental development of adolescent children.

b. to entertain the reader with the reckless social development of adolescents.

c. to explain the physical, cognitive, and social development of adolescent children.

Inferences _____ **16.** Based on the details in paragraph 14, we can infer that the formal operations stage of development means that a child from age 11 on has the ability to:

    a. form mental representations of absent object.

    b. replace physical action with mental action.

    c. assimilate and accommodate new information.

    d. think abstractly and solve problems.

Inferences _____ **17.** Based on the details in the passage, we can infer Erikson believed

    a. that biology dictates adolescent behavior.

    b. in the storm-and-stress conception of adolescence.

    c. the experience of adolescence differs across cultures.

    d. failure to exhibit turmoil during adolescent development is a sign of arrested development.

Inferences _____ **18.** Based on the details in the passage, we can infer that Margaret Mead and Ruth Benedict believed:

    a. harmful adolescent behavior is lessened when children gradually take on adult responsibility.

    b. adolescent children will always act out against parental authority.

    c. to be normal during the adolescent period is by itself abnormal.

    d. cross-cultural differences argue against strictly biological theories of adolescent experience.

Argument _____ **19.** The following list contains a claim and list of supports for that claim. Which item states the claim?

    a. "At age 14, the adolescents' parents were less involved in their lives; the adolescents had less positive regard for their parents and they believed that their parents had less positive regard for them." (paragraph 19)

    b. "Still, adolescents' conflicts with their parents often do not lead to harmful outcomes." (paragraph 20)

    c. "Most adolescents at most times are able to use their parents as ready sources of practical and emotional support." (paragraph 20)

    d. "When conflict occurs in the context of otherwise positive relationships, there may be few negative consequences." (paragraph 20)

Argument _____ **20.** The following list contains a claim and list of supports for that claim. Which item states the claim?

   a. "For several years, the adolescent may grow 3 to 6 inches a year and gain weight rapidly as well." (paragraph 1)
   b. "The adolescent's body does not reach adult proportions all at once." (paragraph 1)
   c. "Hands and feet grow to full adult size first." (paragraph 1)
   d. "Thus an individual's overall shape changes several times over the teenage years." (paragraph 1)

Outlining

Complete the outline with information from the passage.

Human Development (Adolescent)

   I. Physical Development in Adolescence

   II. _____

      A. Piaget's Insights into Mental Development

         1. Sensorimotor stage

         2. Preoperational stage

         3. _____

         4. Formal operations stage

   III. _____

   IV. Social Development in Adolescence

      A. _____

         1. "Storm and stress" as a biologically programmed aspect of development

         2. Transitions children are expected to make in different cultures

      B. _____

WHAT DO YOU THINK?

Assume you are a parent of a 9-year-old child and are a member of his or her school's PTA. As an involved parent, you want to relay and discuss the important information you have just read about the physical, cognitive, and social development of adolescent children at your next PTA meeting. Write a brief essay to hand out to the other parents at the meeting using the information from the passage. Consider the following points to address in your essay:

- State the greatest influences during adolescence.
- Describe challenges an adolescent may face socially.
- Explain why parents and adolescents experience conflict at this stage in life.

MASTER READER SCORECARD

"Human Development"

Skill	Number Correct	Points		Total
Vocabulary				
Vocabulary in Context (2 items)	_____	× 4	=	_____
Comprehension				
Main Idea (2 items)	_____	× 4	=	_____
Supporting Details (2 items)	_____	× 4	=	_____
Transitions (2 items)	_____	× 4	=	_____
Thought Patterns (2 items)	_____	× 4	=	_____
Fact and Opinion (3 items)	_____	× 4	=	_____
Tone and Purpose (2 items)	_____	× 4	=	_____
Inferences (3 items)	_____	× 4	=	_____
Argument (2 items)	_____	× 4	=	_____
Mapping (5 items)	_____	× 4	=	_____
		Comprehension Score		_____

9 The Price of Greatness

by *Winston S. Churchill*

Winston S. Churchill (1874–1965) was the acclaimed Prime Minister of the United Kingdom. At the outbreak of the Second World War, he was appointed First Lord of the Admiralty—a post he had held earlier from 1911 to 1915. In May, 1940, he became Prime Minister and Minister of Defence and remained in office until 1945. Known for his magnificent oratory, Churchill also won the Nobel Prize for Literature in 1953, and Queen Elizabeth II conferred upon him the dignity of Knighthood. In 1963, President Kennedy conferred on him the honorary citizenship of the United States. The following passage is an excerpt from the speech he gave in 1943 when he received an honorary degree at Harvard. Do you think the United States has a responsibility to the world?

Vocabulary Preview

remorselessly (paragraph 2): showing no pity or compassion; continuing without lessening in strength or intensity

indisputable (paragraph 4): beyond doubt, undeniable

prodigious (paragraph 5): extraordinary, impressive

Parliamentarians (paragraph 5): members of a parliament, a type of governing body

anarchy (paragraph 6): disorder, chaos, rebellion

conceptions (paragraph 8): broad understandings, ideas, theories

vigilant (paragraph 10): watchful, on guard

munitions (paragraph 11): weapons, arms

plenary (paragraph 12): comprehensive, complete, fully represented

Bismarck (paragraph 16): Prime Minister of Prussia from 1862–1890, he oversaw the unification of Germany and designed the German Empire in 1871

amenity (paragraph 18): pleasantness, courtesy, advantage

1   Twice in my lifetime the long arm of destiny has reached across the oceans and involved the entire life and manhood of the United States in a deadly struggle.

2   There was no use in saying "We don't want it; we won't have it; our forebears left Europe to avoid these quarrels; we have founded a new world which has no contact

697

with the old." There was no use in that. The long arm reaches out **remorselessly**, and every one's existence, environment, and outlook undergo a swift and irresistible change. What is the explanation, Mr. President, of these strange facts, and what are the deep laws to which they respond? I will offer you one explanation—there are others, but one will suffice.

3   The price of greatness is responsibility. If the people of the United States had continued in a **mediocre** station, struggling with the wilderness, absorbed in their own affairs, and a factor of no consequence in the movement of the world, they might have remained forgotten and undisturbed beyond their protecting oceans: but one cannot rise to be in many ways the leading community in the civilized world without being involved in its problems, without being convulsed by its agonies and inspired by its causes.

4   If this has been proved in the past, as it has been, it will become **indisputable** in the future. The people of the United States cannot escape world responsibility. Although we live in a period so tumultuous that little can be predicted, we may be quite sure that this process will be intensified with every forward step the United States makes in wealth and in power. Not only are the responsibilities of this great Republic growing, but the world over which they range is itself contracting in relation to our powers of locomotion at a positively alarming rate.

5   We have learned to fly. What **prodigious** changes are involved in that new accomplishment! Man has parted company with his trusty friend the horse and has sailed into the azure with the eagles, eagles being represented by the infernal (loud laughter)—I mean internal—combustion engine. Where, then, are those broad oceans, those vast staring deserts? They are shrinking beneath our very eyes. Even elderly **Parliamentarians** like myself are forced to acquire a high degree of mobility.

6   But to the youth of America, as to the youth of all the Britains, I say "You cannot stop." There is no halting-place at this point. We have now reached a stage in the journey where there can be no pause. We must go on. It must be world **anarchy** or world order.

7   Throughout all this ordeal and struggle which is characteristic of our age, you will find in the British Commonwealth and Empire good **comrades** to whom you are united by other ties besides those of State policy and public need. To a large extent, they are the ties of blood and history. Naturally I, a child of both worlds, am conscious of these.

8   Law, language, literature—these are considerable factors. Common **conceptions** of what is right and decent, a marked regard for fair play, especially to the weak and poor, a stern sentiment of impartial justice, and above all the love of personal freedom, or as Kipling put it:

9   "Leave to live by no man's leave, underneath the law"—these are common conceptions on both sides of the ocean among the English-speaking peoples. We hold to these conceptions as strongly as you do.

10   We do not war primarily with races as such. Tyranny is our foe, whatever trappings or disguise it wears, whatever

language it speaks, be it external or internal, we must forever be on our guard, ever mobilized, ever **vigilant**, always ready to spring at its throat. In all this, we march together. Not only do we march and strive shoulder to shoulder at this moment under the fire of the enemy on the fields of war or in the air, but also in those realms of thought which are consecrated to the rights and the dignity of man.

11 At the present time we have in continual vigorous action the British and United States Combined Chiefs of Staff Committee, which works immediately under the President and myself as representative of the British War Cabinet. This committee, with its elaborate organization of Staff officers of every grade, disposes of all our resources and, in practice, uses British and American troops, ships, aircraft, and **munitions** just as if they were the resources of a single State or nation.

12 I would not say there are never divergences of view among these high professional authorities. It would be unnatural if there were not. That is why it is necessary to have a **plenary** meeting of principals every two or three months. All these men now know each other. They trust each other. They like each other, and most of them have been at work together for a long time. When they meet they thrash things out with great candor and plain, blunt speech, but after a few days the President and I find ourselves furnished with sincere and united advice.

13 This is a wonderful system. There was nothing like it in the last war. There never has been anything like it between two allies. It is reproduced in an even more tightly-knit form at General Eisenhower's headquarters in the Mediterranean, where everything is completely intermingled and soldiers are ordered into battle by the Supreme Commander or his deputy, General Alexander, without the slightest regard to whether they are British, American, or Canadian, but simply in accordance with the fighting need.

14 Now in my opinion it would be a most foolish and **improvident** act on the part of our two Governments, or either of them, to break up this smooth-running and immensely powerful machinery the moment the war is over. For our own safety, as well as for the security of the rest of the world, we are bound to keep it working and in running order after the war—probably for a good many years, not only until we have set up some world arrangement to keep the peace, but until we know that it is an arrangement which will really give us that protection we must have from danger and aggression, a protection we have already had to seek across two vast world wars.

15 I am not qualified, of course, to judge whether or not this would become a party question in the United States, and I would not presume to discuss that point. I am sure, however, that it will not be a party question in Great Britain. We must not let go of the securities we have found necessary to preserve our lives and liberties until we are quite sure we have something else to put in their place, which will give us an equally solid guarantee.

16 The great **Bismarck**—for there were once great men in Germany—is said to have observed towards the close of his life that the most potent factor in human

society at the end of the nineteenth century was the fact that the British and American peoples spoke the same language.

17   That was a pregnant saying. Certainly it has enabled us to wage war together with an intimacy and harmony never before achieved among allies.

18   This gift of a common tongue is a priceless inheritance, and it may well someday become the foundation of a common citizenship. I like to think of British and Americans moving about freely over each other's wide estates with hardly a sense of being foreigners to one another. But I do not see why we should not try to spread our common language even more widely throughout the globe and, without seeking selfish advantage over any, possess ourselves of this invaluable **amenity** and birthright.

—"The Price of Greatness" from Curtis Brown, Ltd. (UK) by Winston S Churchill. Reproduced by the permission of Curtis Brown, Ltd. (UK).

Choose the best meaning of each word in **bold**. Use context clues to make your choice.

Vocabulary in Context _____ 1. "The price of greatness is responsibility. If the people of the United States had continued in a **mediocre** station, struggling with the wilderness, absorbed in their own affairs, and a factor of no consequence in the movement of the world . . . " (paragraph 3)
    a. unusual
    b. commonplace
    c. special
    d. extreme

Vocabulary in Context _____ 2. "Throughout all this ordeal and struggle which is characteristic of our age, you will find in the British Commonwealth and Empire good **comrades** to whom you are united by other ties besides those of State policy and public need." (paragraph 7)
    a. enemies
    b. soldiers
    c. friends
    d. ideas.

Central Idea _____ 3. Which of the following sentences states the central idea of the passage?
    a. "Twice in my lifetime the long arm of destiny has reached across the oceans and involved the entire life and manhood of the United States in a deadly struggle." (paragraph 1)
    b. "The price of greatness is responsibility." (paragraph 3)
    c. "It must be world anarchy or world order." (paragraph 6)
    d. "This gift of a common tongue is a priceless inheritance, and it may well someday become the foundation of a common citizenship." (paragraph 18)

Supporting
Details   _____   **4.** According to the passage prodigious changes in the world have occurred because of
  a. world wars.
  b. law.
  c. high mobility.
  d. the establishment of the United States.

Supporting
Details   _____   **5.** According to Bismarck, what was the most potent fact in human society at the end of the nineteenth century?
  a. free movement
  b. the great men of Germany
  c. the common values of Britain and the U.S.
  d. the common tongue of Britain and the U.S.

Transitions   _____   **6.** "We hold to these conceptions as strongly as you do." (paragraph 9)

The relationship of ideas within this sentence is
  a. cause and effect.   c. comparison and contrast.
  b. time order.   d. generalization and example.

Transitions   _____   **7.** "There is no halting-place at this point. We have now reached a stage in the journey where there can be no pause." (paragraph 6)

The relationship of ideas between these sentences is
  a. cause and effect.   c. comparison and contrast.
  b. time order.   d. generalization and example.

Thought
Patterns   _____   **8.** The thought pattern for paragraph 3 is
  a. cause and effect.   c. comparison and contrast.
  b. time order.   d. definition and example.

Thought
Patterns   _____   **9.** The thought pattern for paragraph 4 is
  a. cause and effect.   c. comparison and contrast.
  b. time order.   d. definition and example.

Fact and
Opinion   _____   **10.** "Certainly it has enabled us to wage war together with an intimacy and harmony never before achieved among allies." (paragraph 17)

This sentence is a statement of
  a. fact.   c. fact and opinion.
  b. opinion.

Fact and
Opinion   _____   **11.** "At the present time we have in continual vigorous action the British and United States Combined Chiefs of Staff Committee, which

works immediately under the President and myself as representative of the British War Cabinet." (paragraph 11)

This sentence is a statement of
a. fact.   c. fact and opinion.
b. opinion.

Fact and _____   **12.** "Now in my opinion it would be a most foolish and improvident
Opinion   act on the part of our two Governments, or either of them, to break
                       up this smooth-running and immensely powerful machinery the
                       moment the war is over." (paragraph 14)

This sentence is a statement of
a. fact.   c. fact and opinion.
b. opinion.

Tone   _____   **13.** The overall tone of the author is
a. neutral.   c. arrogant.
b. critical.   d. approving.

Tone   _____   **14.** The tone of the author in paragraph 15 is
a. humiliated.   c. confident.
b. arrogant.   d. timid.

Purpose _____   **15.** The primary purpose of the author is
a. to inform the audience of the accomplishments of Great Britain
    and the United States during the war.
b. to celebrate the shared values, accomplishments, and responsi-
    bilities of Great Britain and the United States during and after
    the war.
c. to persuade the audience to support the war efforts of Great
    Britain and the United States.

Inferences _____ **16.** Based on the details in paragraph 14, we can infer that **improvident**
means
a. wise.   c. important.
b. fateful.   d. careless.

Inferences _____ **17.** Based on the details in the passage, we can conclude that Churchill
believes that the United States is responsible for
a. World War II.
b. the security of the rest of the world after the war.
c. our powers of locomotion.
d. the gift of a common language.

Argument   _____   **18.** Identify the persuasive technique used in the following sentence:

"Man has parted company with his trusty friend the horse and has sailed into the azure with the eagles." (paragraph 5)

a. plain folks   c. glittering generality
b. either-or   d. false cause

Argument   _____   **19.** Identify the persuasive technique used in the following sentence:

"It must be world anarchy or world order." (paragraph 6)

a. false comparison   c. plain folks
b. either-or   d. transfer

Argument   _____   **20.** Identify the persuasive technique used in the following sentence:

"Not only do we march and strive shoulder to shoulder at this moment under the fire of the enemy on the fields of war or in the air, but also in those realms of thought which are consecrated to the rights and the dignity of man." (paragraph 10)

a. glittering generality   c. false cause
b. either-or   d. false comparison

Summarizing

Complete the following summary with information from the passage.

According to Winston Churchill in his speech given when he received an honorary degree at Harvard, the people of the United States cannot escape world _____. The responsibilities of the United States grow as its wealth and power increase, and the changes brought by _____ shrink the range of the world. The shared _____ and the common _____ of Great Britain and the United States built a smooth-running and immensely powerful machinery of war that should continue until _____ _____.

> **WHAT DO YOU THINK?**

Do you agree with Churchill's claim that a "gift of a common tongue" [the English language] is a priceless inheritance, and it may well someday become the foundation of a common citizenship? Why or why not? Why would a common language help secure world peace and prosperity? Do you think the United States should create a law that makes English its official language? Or do you think the United States should encourage its citizens to learn more than one language? If so, which language should be learned? Assume that your local Board of Education is considering adding learning a foreign language as a requirement for graduation from high school. Write a letter to the board in favor of or in opposition to this proposal. If you support the proposal, identify the language you believe should be taught and why. If you oppose the proposal, explain why students should learn only English.

MASTER READER SCORECARD

From "The Price of Greatness"

Skill	Number Correct	Points		Total
Vocabulary				
Vocabulary in Context (2 items)	_____	× 4	=	_____
Comprehension				
Central Idea (1 item)	_____	× 4	=	_____
Supporting Details (2 items)	_____	× 4	=	_____
Transitions (2 items)	_____	× 4	=	_____
Thought Patterns (2 items)	_____	× 4	=	_____
Fact and Opinion (3 items)	_____	× 4	=	_____
Tone and Purpose (3 items)	_____	× 4	=	_____
Inferences (2 items)	_____	× 4	=	_____
Argument (3 items)	_____	× 4	=	_____
Summarizing (5 items)	_____	× 4	=	_____
		Comprehension Score		_____

10

Real People in the "Age of the Common Man"

by Jacqueline Jones, Peter H. Wood, Thomas Borstelmann, Elaine Tyler May, and Vicki L. Ruiz

> In the preface of the *Created Equal* textbook from which this passage comes, the authors state, "*Created Equal* tells the dramatic, evolving story of America in all its complexity—a story of a diverse people 'created equal' yet struggling to achieve equality." The following excerpt addresses the American ideal of equality and the concept of the "common man." What do you think the term "common man" meant during the 1800s? How would you define the "common man" in America today?

Vocabulary Preview

hierarchy (paragraph 1): formally ranked group, chain of command
suffrage (paragraph 1): right to vote, act of voting
egalitarian (paragraph 1): democratic, equal, free
denigrate (paragraph 3): belittle, scorn, degrade
assimilate (paragraph 8): integrate, blend in, conform
interlopers (paragraph 9): intruders, trespassers
deference (paragraph 17): respect, submission
subversive (paragraph 19): rebellious, defiant
atole (paragraph 25): hot sweet drink made from corn dough
vanguard (paragraph 30): front line, forerunner
advocate (paragraph 35): supporter, activist

1   In the early 1830s, a wealthy Frenchman named Alexis de Tocqueville visited the United States and wrote about the contradictions he saw. In his book *Democracy in America* (published in 1835), Tocqueville noted that the United States lacked the rigid **hierarchy** of class privilege that characterized European nations. With universal white manhood **suffrage**, white men could vote and run for office regardless of their class or religion. However, Tocqueville also noted some sore spots in American democratic values and practices. He commented on the plight of groups deprived of the right to vote; their lack of freedom stood out starkly in the otherwise **egalitarian** society of the United States. He sympathized with the southeastern Indians uprooted from their

homelands. He raised the possibility that conflicts between blacks and whites might eventually lead to bloodshed. He even contrasted the situation of young unmarried white women, who seemed so free-spirited, with that of wives, who appeared cautious and dull. He concluded, "In America a woman loses her independence forever in the bonds of matrimony." In other words, Tocqueville saw America for what it was: a blend of freedom and slavery, of independence and dependence.

Wards, Workers, and Warriors: Native Americans

2   Population growth in the United States—and on the borderlands between the United States and Mexican territory—put pressure on Indian societies. Yet different cultural groups responded in different ways to this pressure. Some, like the Cherokee, conformed to European American ways and became sedentary farmers. Others were forced to work for whites. Still others either waged war on white settlements and military forces or retreated farther and farther from European American settlements in the hope of avoiding clashes with the intruders.

3   Nevertheless, prominent whites continued to **denigrate** the humanity of all Indians. In the 1820s Henry Clay claimed that Indians were "essentially inferior to the Anglo-Saxon race . . . and their disappearance from the human family will be no great loss to the world." In 1828 the House of Representatives Committee on Indian Affairs surveyed the Indians of the South and concluded that "an Indian cannot work" and that all Indians were lazy

and notable for their "thirst for spirituous liquours." According to the committee, when European American settlers depleted reserves of wildlife, Indians as a group would cease to exist.

Members of the Cherokee Nation 4 bitterly denounced these assertions. "The Cherokees do not live upon the chase [for game]," they pointed out. Neither did the Creek, Choctaw, Chickasaw, and Seminole—the other members of the Five Civilized Tribes, so called for their varying degrees of conformity to white people's ways.

Charting a middle course between 5 the Indian and European American worlds was Sequoyah, the son of a white Virginia trader-soldier and a Cherokee woman. A veteran of Andrew Jackson's campaign against the Creek in 1813–1814, Sequoyah moved to Arkansas in 1818, part of an early Cherokee migration west. In 1821 he finished a Cherokee syllabary (a written language consisting of syllables and letters, in contrast to pictures, or pictographs). The product of a dozen years' work, the syllabary consisted of 86 characters. In 1828 the Cherokee Phoenix, a newspaper based on the new writing system, began publication in New Echota, Georgia.

Sequoyah's written language enabled 6 the increasingly dispersed Cherokee to remain in touch with each other on their own terms. At the same time, numerous Indian cultural groups lost their struggle to retain even modest control over their destinies. In some areas of the continent, smallpox continued to ravage native populations. In other regions, Indians became wards of, or dependent on, whites, living with and working for white families. Other groups, living close to whites, adopted their trading practices. In Spanish California, the Muquelmne Miwok in the San Joaquin delta made a living by stealing and then selling the horses of Mexican settlers.

7   In other parts of California, Spanish missionaries conquered Indian groups, converted them to Christianity, and then forced them to work in the missions. In missions up and down the California coast, Indians worked as weavers, tanners, shoemakers, bricklayers, carpenters, blacksmiths, and other artisans. Some herded cattle and raised horses. Indian women cooked for the mission, cleaned, and spun wool. They wove cloth and sewed garments.

8   Nevertheless, even Indians living in or near missions resisted the cultural change imposed by the intruders. Catholic missionaries complained that Indian women such as those of the Chumash refused to learn Spanish. The refusal among some Indians to **assimilate** completely signaled persistent, deep-seated conflicts between native groups and incoming settlers. In 1824 a revolt among hundreds of newly converted Indians at the mission La Purisima Concepción north of Santa Barbara revealed a rising militancy among native peoples.

9   After the War of 1812, the U.S. government had rewarded some military veterans with land grants in the Old Northwest. Federal agents tried to clear the way for these new settlers by ousting Indians from the area. Overwhelmed by the number of whites, some Indian groups such as the Peoria and Kaskaskia gave up their lands to the **interlopers**. Others took a stand against the white intrusion. In 1826 and

1827 the Winnebago attacked white families and boat pilots living near Prairie du Chien, Wisconsin. Two years later, the Sauk chief Black Hawk (known to Indians as Maka-tai-me-she-kia-kiak) assembled a coalition of Fox, Winnebago, Kickapoo, and Potawatomi. Emboldened by the prospect of aid from British Canada, they clashed with federal troops and raided farmers' homesteads and miners' camps.

10   In August 1832 a force of 1,300 U.S. soldiers and volunteers struck back, killing 300 Indian men, women, and children encamped on the Bad Axe River in western Wisconsin. The massacre, the decisive point of what came to be called the Black Hawk War, marked the end of armed Indian resistance north of the Ohio River and east of the Mississippi.

Slaves and Free People of Color

11   In the 1820s the small proportion of free blacks within the southern population declined further. Southern whites perceived free blacks as an unwelcome and dangerous presence, especially given the possibility that they would conspire with slaves to spark a rebellion. For these reasons some states began to outlaw private manumissions (the practice of individual owners freeing their slaves) and to force free blacks to leave the state altogether.

12   One free black who inspired such fears was Denmark Vesey. Born on the Danish-controlled island of Saint Thomas in 1767, Vesey was a literate carpenter as well as a religious leader. In 1799 he won $1,500 in a Charleston, South Carolina, lottery and used some of the money to buy his freedom. In the summer of 1822, a Charleston

court claimed to have unearthed evidence of a "diabolical plot" hatched by Vesey together with plantation slaves from the surrounding area.

13   Yet the historical record strongly suggests that no plot ever existed. Black "witnesses" who feared for their own lives provided inconsistent and contradictory testimony to a panel of judges. Authorities never located any material evidence of a plan, such as stockpiles of weapons. Under fire from other Charleston elites for rushing to judgment, the judges redoubled their efforts to **embellish** vague rumors of black discontent into a tale of a well-orchestrated uprising and to implicate growing numbers of black people. As a result of the testimony of several slaves, 35 black men were hanged and another 18 exiled outside the United States. Of those executed, Vesey and 23 other men said nothing to support even the vaguest charges of the court.

14   In the North, some blacks were granted the right to vote after emancipation in the late eighteenth century; however, many of those voting rights were lost in the early nineteenth century. New Jersey (in 1807), Connecticut (1818), New York (1821), and Pennsylvania (1838) all revoked the legislation that had let black men cast ballots. Free northern blacks continued to suffer under a number of legal restrictions. Most were not citizens and therefore perceived themselves as oppressed like the slaves in the South.

15   A new group of black leaders in the urban North began to link their fate to that of their enslaved brothers and sisters in the South. In Boston, North Carolina-born David Walker published his fiery *Walker's Appeal* to the Coloured Citizens of the World in 1829. Walker called for all blacks to integrate fully into American society, shunning racial segregation whether initiated by whites or by blacks themselves. Reminding his listeners of the horrors of the slave trade, he declared that black people were ready to die for freedom: "I give it as a fact, let twelve black men get well armed for battle, and they will kill and put to flight fifty whites."

Northern black leaders disagreed 16 among themselves on the issues of integration and black separatism—for example, whether blacks should create their own schools or press for inclusion in the public educational system. A few leaders favored leaving the country altogether, believing that black people would never find peace and freedom in the United States. Founded by whites in New Jersey in 1817, the American Colonization Society (ACS) paid for black Americans to settle Monrovia (later named Liberia) on the west coast of Africa. The ACS drew support from a variety of groups: whites in the upper South who wanted to free their slaves but believed that black and white people could not live in the same country, and some slaves and free people of color convinced that colonization would give them a fresh start. A small number of American-born blacks settled in Liberia. However, most black activists rejected colonization. They had been born on American soil, and their forebears had been buried there. Maria Stewart, an African American religious leader in Boston, declared, "But before I go [to Africa] the bayonet shall pierce me through."

Northern whites sought to con- 17 trol black people and their movements.

Outspoken black men and women such as Walker and Stewart alarmed northern whites who feared that if blacks could claim decent jobs, white people would lose their own jobs. African Americans who worked outdoors as wagon drivers, peddlers, and street sweepers were taunted and in some cases attacked by whites who demanded **deference** from blacks in public. In October 1824 a white mob invaded a black neighborhood in Providence, Rhode Island. They terrorized its residents, destroyed buildings, and left the place "almost entirely in ruins." The catalyst for the riot had come the previous day, when a group of blacks had refused to yield the inside of the sidewalk—a cleaner place to walk—to white passersby.

18   The South's silence was broken in 1831 when white Southerners took steps to reinforce the institution of slavery, using both violent and legal means. That year Nat Turner, an enslaved preacher and mystic, led a slave revolt in Southampton, Virginia. In the 1820s the young Turner had looked skyward and had seen visions of "white spirits and black spirits engaged in battle . . . and blood flowed in streams." Turner believed that he had received divine instructions to lead other slaves to freedom, to "arise and prepare myself, and slay my enemies with their own weapons." In August he and a group of followers that eventually numbered 80 moved through the countryside, killing whites wherever they could find them. Ultimately, nearly 60 whites died at the hands of Turner's rebels. Turner himself managed to evade capture for more than two months. After he was captured, he was tried, convicted, and sentenced to death. A white man named Thomas Gray interviewed Turner in his jail cell and recorded his "confessions" before he was hanged.

Published in 1832 by Gray, *The Con-* 19 *fessions of Nat Turner* reached a large, horrified audience in the white South. According to Gray, Turner said that he had exhibited "uncommon intelligence" when he was a child. As a young man, he had received inspiration from the Bible, especially the passage "Seek ye the kingdom of Heaven and all things shall be added unto you." Perhaps most disturbing of all, Turner reported that, since 1830, he had been a slave of "Mr. Joseph Travis, who was to me a kind master, and placed the greatest confidence in me; in fact, I had no cause to complain of his treatment to me." Turner's "confessions" suggested the **subversive** potential of slaves who were literate and Christian and those who were treated kindly by their masters and mistresses.

After the Turner revolt, a wave of 20 white hysteria swept the South. In Virginia near where the killings had occurred, whites assaulted blacks with unbridled fury. The Virginia legislature seized the occasion to defeat various antislavery proposals. Thereafter, all the slave states moved to strengthen the institution of slavery. For all practical purposes, public debate over slavery ceased throughout the American South.

Legal and Economic Dependence: The Status of Women

In the political and economic realms, 21 the egalitarian impulse rarely affected the status of women in a legal or practical sense. Regardless of where they lived, enslaved women and Indian women had almost no rights under either U.S. or Spanish law. Still, legal systems in the United States and the Spanish borderlands differed in their treatment of women. In the United States, most of the constraints that white married women had experienced in the colonial period still applied in the 1820s. A husband controlled the property that his wife brought to the marriage, and he had legal authority over their children. Indeed, the wife was considered her husband's possession. She had no right to make a contract, keep money she earned, vote, run for office, or serve on a jury. In contrast, in the Spanish Southwest, married women could own land and conduct business on their own. At the same time, however, husbands, fathers, and local priests continued to exert much influence over the lives of these women.

22   European American women's economic subordination served as a rationale for their political inferiority. The "common man" concept rested on the assumption that only men could ensure American economic growth and well-being. According to this view, men had the largest stake in society because only they owned property. That stake made them responsible citizens.

23   Yet women contributed to the economy in myriad ways. Although few women earned cash wages in the 1820s, almost all adult women worked. In the colonial period, society had highly valued women's labor in the fields, the garden, and the kitchen. However, in the early nineteenth century, work was becoming increasingly identified as labor that earned cash wages. This attitude proved particularly common in the Northeast, where increasing numbers of workers labored under the supervision of a boss. As this belief took root, men began valuing women's contributions to the household economy less and less. If women did not earn money, many men asked, did they really work at all?

24   In these years, well-off women in the northeastern and mid-Atlantic states began to think of themselves as consumers and not producers of goods. They relied more and more on store-bought cloth and household supplies. Some could also afford to hire servants to perform housework for them. Privileged women gradually stopped thinking of their responsibilities as making goods or processing and preparing food. Rather, their main tasks were to manage servants and create a comfortable home for their husbands and children. They saw their labor as necessary to the well-being of their families, even if their compensation came in the form of emotional satisfaction rather than cash.

25   In contrast, women in other parts of the country continued to engage in the same forms of household industry that had characterized the colonial period. In Spanish settlements, women played a central role in household production. They made all of their family's clothes by carding, spinning, and weaving the wool from sheep. They tanned cowhides and ground blue corn to make tortillas, or **atole**. They produced their own candles and soap, and they plastered the walls of the home.

26   Like women's work in general, the labor of wives and mothers in Spanish-speaking regions had great cultural significance. In the Mexican territory of California, women engaged in backbreaking efforts so that members of their families could wear

snow-white linen clothing. One community member recalled that "certainly to do so was one of the chief anxieties" of well-to-do households: "There was sometimes a great deal of linen to be washed for it was the pride of every Spanish family to own much linen, and the mothers and daughters almost always wore white." Women used homemade soap to scrub the clothes on the rocks of a nearby spring. Then they spread out the wet garments to dry on the tops of bushes that grew on the mountainside.

27   In the Spanish mission of San Gabriel, California, the widow Eulalia Perez cooked, sewed, ministered to the ill, and instructed children in reading and writing. As housekeeper, Perez kept the keys to the mission storehouse. She also distributed supplies to the Indians and the vaqueros (cowboys) who lived in the mission. She supervised Indian servants as well as soap makers, wine pressers, and olive oil producers.

28   At Mission San Diego, Apolonaria Lorenzana worked as a healer and cared for the church sacristy and priestly vestments. From the time she arrived in Monterey at age 7 (in 1800) until her death in the late nineteenth century, Lorenzana devoted her life to such labors. Although the priests tried to restrict her to administering the mission hospital, she took pride in her nursing abilities, "even though Father Sanchez had told me not to do it myself, but to have it done, and only to be present so that the servant girls would do it well."

29   Indian women also engaged in a variety of essential tasks. Sioux and Mandan women, though of a social rank inferior to men, performed a great deal of manual labor in their own villages. They dressed buffalo skins that the men later sold to traders. They collected water and wood, cooked, dried meat and fruit, and cultivated maize (corn), pumpkins, and squash with hoes made from the shoulder blades of elk. These women worked collectively within a network of households rather than individually within nuclear families.

30   Many women, regardless of ethnicity, were paid for their work with food and shelter but not money. Nevertheless, some women did work for cash wages during this era. New England women and children, for example, were the **vanguard** of factory wage-earners in the early manufacturing system. In Massachusetts in 1820, women and children constituted almost a third of all manufacturing workers. In the largest textile factories, they made up fully 80 percent of the workforce.

31   The business of textile manufacturing took the tasks of spinning thread and weaving cloth out of the home, where such tasks often were performed by unpaid, unmarried daughters, and relocated those tasks in factories, where the same workers received wages. The famous "Lowell mill girls" are an apt example. Young, unmarried white women from New Hampshire, Vermont, and Massachusetts, these workers moved to the new company town of Lowell, Massachusetts, to take jobs as textile machine operatives. In New England, thousands of young men had migrated west, tipping the sex ratio in favor of women and creating a reserve of female laborers. But to attract young women to factory work, mill owners had to reassure them (and their parents) that they would be safe and well cared for

away from home. To that end, they established boarding houses where employees could live together under the supervision of a matron—an older woman who served as their mother-away-from-home.

32 Company towns set rules shaping employees' living conditions as well as their working conditions. In the early 1830s, a posted list of "Rules and Regulations" covered many aspects of the lives of the young women living at the Poignaud and Plant boardinghouse at Lancaster, Massachusetts. The list told the women how to enter the building (quietly, and then hang up "their bonnet, shawl, coat, etc. etc. in the entry") and where to sit at the dinner table (the two workers with greatest seniority were to take their places at the head of the table). Despite these rules, many young women valued the friendships they made with their coworkers and the money they made in the mills. Some of these women sent their wages back home so that their fathers could pay off the mortgage or their brothers could attend school.

33 But not all women wage-earners labored in large mills. In New York City, single women, wives, and widows toiled as needle workers in their homes. Impoverished, sewing in tiny attics by the dim light of candles, these women were at the mercy of jobbers—merchants who parceled out cuffs, collars, and shirt fronts that the women finished. Other urban women worked as street vendors, selling produce, or as cooks, nurse-maids, or laundresses.

34 The new **delineation** between men's and women's work and workplaces intensified the drive for women's education begun after the Revolution. If well-to-do women were to assume domestic responsibilities while their husbands worked outside the home, then women must receive their own unique form of schooling, or so the reasoning went. Most ordinary women received little in the way of formal education. Yet elite young women had expanded educational opportunities, beginning in the early nineteenth century. Emma Willard founded a female academy in Troy, New York, in 1821, and Catharine Beecher established the Hartford Female Seminary two years later in Connecticut. For the most part, these schools catered to the daughters of wealthy families, young women who would never have to work in a factory to survive. Hailed as a means to prepare young women to serve as wives and mothers, the schools taught geography, foreign languages, mathematics, science, and philosophy, as well as the "female" pursuits of embroidery and music.

35 Out of this curriculum designed especially for women emerged women's rights activists, women who keenly felt both the potential of their own intelligence and the degrading nature of their social situation. Elizabeth Cady, an 1832 graduate of the Troy Female Seminary, later went on to marry Henry B. Stanton and bear seven children, but by the 1840s she strode onto the national stage as a tireless **advocate** of women's political and economic rights.

VISUAL *VOCABULARY*

_____ is hard won in many places across the world.

   a. suffrage
   b. assimilation
   c. subversion

Choose the best meaning of each word in **bold**. Use context clues to make your choice.

Vocabulary in Context _____ **1.** "Under fire from other Charleston elites for rushing to judgment, the judges redoubled their efforts to **embellish** vague rumors of black discontent into a tale of a well-orchestrated uprising and to implicate growing numbers of black people." (paragraph 13)
   a. decorate   c. adorn
   b. exaggerate   d. simplify

Vocabulary in Context _____ **2.** "The new **delineation** between men's and women's work and workplaces intensified the drive for women's education begun after the Revolution." (paragraph 34)
   a. description   c. discrimination
   b. unity   d. phase

Central Idea _____ **3.** Which of the following sentences from the first paragraph states the central idea of the passage?
   a. "In the early 1830s, a wealthy Frenchman named Alexis de Tocqueville visited the United States and wrote about the contradictions he saw."
   b. "With universal white manhood suffrage, white men could vote and run for office regardless of their class or religion."
   c. "However, Tocqueville also noted some sore spots in American democratic values and practices."
   d. "In other words, Tocqueville saw America for what it was: a blend of freedom and slavery, of independence and dependence."

Central Idea _____   **4.** Which of the following sentences states the central idea of paragraphs 2 through 10?

a. "Population growth in the United States—and on the borderlands between the United States and Mexican territory—put pressure on Indian societies." (paragraph 2)

b. "Charting a middle course between the Indian and European American worlds was Sequoyah, the son of a white Virginia trader-soldier and a Cherokee woman." (paragraph 5)

c. "Overwhelmed by the number of whites, some Indian groups such as the Peoria and Kaskaskia gave up their lands to the interlopers." (paragraph 9)

d. "The massacre, the decisive point of what came to be called the Black Hawk War, marked the end of armed Indian resistance north of the Ohio River and east of the Mississippi." (paragraph 10)

Implied _____
Central Idea   **5.** Which of the following sentences states the implied central idea of paragraphs 11 through 20?

a. Southern states enacted laws to support slavery and force free blacks to leave the region.

b. Northern states granted blacks the right to vote in the late eighteenth century only to revoke voting rights for blacks in the nineteenth century.

c. Black leaders disagreed about the issues of integration and black separation.

d. The United States enacted laws in the eighteenth and nineteenth century that enslaved blacks and limited the rights of free blacks.

Central Idea _____   **6.** Which of the following sentences states the central idea of paragraphs 21 through 35?

a. "In the political and economic realms, the egalitarian impulse rarely affected the status of women in a legal or practical sense." (paragraph 21)

b. "Yet women contributed to the economy in myriad ways." (paragraph 23)

c. "In these years, well-off women in the northeastern and mid-Atlantic states began to think of themselves as consumers and not producers of goods." (paragraph 24)

d. "The new delineation between men's and women's work and workplaces intensified the drive for women's education begun after the Revolution." (paragraph 34)

Supporting
Details   _____   **7.** According to the passage, Nat Turner led a slave revolt because he
    a. was beaten as a slave.
    b. was a literate Christian.
    c. believed he had divine instructions to act.
    d. had been sentenced to death.

Transitions   _____   **8.** "Most were not citizens and therefore perceived themselves as oppressed like the slaves in the South." (paragraph 14)

The relationship of ideas within this sentence is
    a. classification.   c. comparison and contrast.
    b. cause and effect.   d. time order.

Transitions   _____   **9.** "With universal white manhood suffrage, white men could vote and run for office regardless of their class or religion. However, Tocqueville also noted some sore spots in American democratic values and practices." (paragraph 1)

The relationship of ideas between these sentences is
    a. cause and effect.   c. comparison and contrast.
    b. classification.   d. generalization and example.

Thought
Patterns   _____   **10.** The overall thought pattern for the passage is
    a. cause and effect.   c. comparison and contrast.
    b. classification.   d. generalization and example

Thought
Patterns   _____   **11.** The thought pattern for paragraph 11 is
    a. cause and effect.   c. comparison and contrast.
    b. classification.   d. definition and example.

Fact and
Opinion   _____   **12.** "In the early 1830s, a wealthy Frenchman named Alexis de Tocqueville visited the United States and wrote about the contradictions he saw." (paragraph 1)

This sentence is a statement of
    a. fact.   c. fact and opinion.
    b. opinion.

Fact and
Opinion   _____   **13.** "Charting a middle course between the Indian and European American worlds was Sequoyah, the son of a white Virginia trader-soldier and a Cherokee woman." (paragraph 5)

This sentence is a statement of
    a. fact.   c. fact and opinion.
    b. opinion.

Fact and
Opinion

_____ **14.** "In Massachusetts in 1820, women and children constituted almost a third of all manufacturing workers." (paragraph 30)

This sentence is a statement of

a. fact.   c. fact and opinion.

b. opinion.

Tone

_____ **15.** The overall tone of the passage is

a. angry.   c. sympathetic.

b. neutral.   d. cold.

Purpose

_____ **16.** The primary purpose of the passage is

a. to inform.   c. to persuade.

b. to entertain.

Inferences

_____ **17.** Based on the details in the passage, we can infer that

a. discrimination against minorities occurred mostly in the South during the Age of the Common Man.

b. the Age of the Common Man favored white males.

c. women had more rights than other minority groups during the Age of the Common Man.

d. all the various groups of people attained freedom during the Age of the Common Man.

Argument

_____ **18.** Read the claim and supports taken from the passage. Then identify the detail that does not support the claim.

Claim: "In America a woman loses her independence forever in the bonds of matrimony." (paragraph 1)

a. "A husband controlled the property that his wife brought to the marriage, and he had legal authority over their children." (paragraph 21)

b. "Indeed, the wife was considered her husband's possession." (paragraph 21)

c. "She had no right to make a contract, keep money she earned, vote, run for office, or serve on a jury." (paragraph 21)

d. "Elizabeth Cady, an 1832 graduate of the Troy Female Seminary, later went on to marry Henry B. Stanton and bear seven children, but by the 1840s she strode on the national stage as a tireless advocate of women's political and economic rights." (paragraph 35)

Argument _____ **19.** Identify the persuasive technique used in the following sentence:

"In 1828 the House of Representatives Committee on Indian Affairs surveyed the Indians of the South and concluded that 'an Indian cannot work' and that all Indians were lazy and notable for their 'thirst for spirituous liquours.'" (paragraph 3)
a. false analogy   c. begging the question
b. personal attack   d. transfer

Argument _____ **20.** Identify the persuasive technique used in the following sentence:

"European American women's economic subordination served as a rationale for their political inferiority." (paragraph 22)
a. false analogy   c. begging the question
b. personal attack   d. transfer

Mapping

Complete the following concept map with information from the passage.

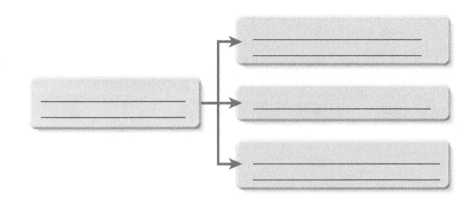

WHAT DO YOU THINK?

Now that you have read the passage, how would you define the Common Man in America during the first half of the 1800s? Do you think the idea of a Common Man still exists in America today? If so, how would you define the term today? Assume you are taking a college history course and you have been assigned an essay that connects what you are learning about history to current life. Choose one of the groups of people discussed in the passage and compare the status of that group during the Age of the Common Man to their current status today.

"Real People in the 'Age of the Common Man'"

Skill	Number Correct	Points		Total
Vocabulary				
Vocabulary in Context (2 items)	_____	× 4	=	_____
Comprehension				
Central Idea and Implied				
Central Idea (4 items)	_____	× 4	=	_____
Supporting Details (1 item)	_____	× 4	=	_____
Transitions (2 items)	_____	× 4	=	_____
Thought Patterns (2 items)	_____	× 4	=	_____
Fact and Opinion (3 items)	_____	× 4	=	_____
Tone and Purpose (2 items)	_____	× 4	=	_____
Inferences (1 item)	_____	× 4	=	_____
Argument (3 items)	_____	× 4	=	_____
Mapping (4 items)	_____	× 5	=	_____
		Comprehension Score		_____

3

Combined-Skills Tests

Part Three contains 5 tests. The purpose of these tests is twofold: to track your growth as a reader and to prepare you for the formal tests you will face as you take college courses. Each test presents a reading passage and questions that cover some or all of the following skills: vocabulary in context, central ideas, supporting details, thought patterns, fact and opinion, tone and purpose, inferences, and argument. These tests—and 5 additional combined-skills tests—can be found in MyReadingLab. By taking the tests in MyReadingLab, you will not only get additional practice and preparation, you will also receive feedback to right and wrong answers. This feedback will help reinforce why an answer is correct, and it will help you understand why an answer is incorrect.

Read the following passage. Then answer the questions.

Cults

[1]The term *cult* literally refers to any group of people with a particular religious or philosophical set of beliefs and identity. [2]In the strictest sense of the word, the Roman Catholic Church and Protestantism are cults within the larger religion of Christianity. [3]But most people associate the term *cult* with a negative connotation: a group of people whose religious or philosophical beliefs and behavior are so different from that of mainstream organizations that they are viewed with suspicion and seen as existing on the fringes of socially acceptable behavior. [4]Although many cults exist without much notice from more mainstream groups, at times members of cults have horrified the public with their actions.

[5]One of the most well-remembered and often cited examples of a cult gone horribly wrong was that of the People's Temple in Jonestown, Guyana, headed by Jim Jones. [6]Originally a Christian offshoot, the People's Temple became a cult under Jones's dictatorial leadership. [7]In 1978, when Jones felt threatened by reporters coming to Guyana, he instructed the entire cult of over 900 people to commit suicide by either drinking cyanide-laced drinks or shooting each other. [8]A total of 914 people died, including 274 children (Chidester, 2003).

[9]While the mainstream Mormon Church, or Church of Jesus Christ of Latter Day Saints, banned polygamy in the early 1900s, Warren Jeffs, the leader and "prophet" of the 10,000-member Fundamentalist Church of Jesus Christ of Latter Day Saints, was arrested in 2006 for arranging "marriages" of his adult male followers to underage girls and is currently serving a minimum 10-year sentence in the Utah State Prison (Winslow, 2007).

[10]Why would any person get so caught up in cult beliefs that polygamy, suicide, and in some cases, murder becomes a desired behavior? [11]What kind of person joins a cult in the first place? [12]Although there is no particular personality profile associated with cult membership, cult members do appear to have been in some psychological distress at the time of recruitment by the cult. [13]People who are under a lot of stress, dissatisfied with their lives, unassertive, **gullible**, dependent, feel a desire to belong to a group, and who are unrealistically **idealistic** ("we can solve all the world's problems if everyone will just love each other") are the

most likely targets of cult recruitment (Langone, 1996). [14]Young people rebelling against parental authority or trying to become independent of families are prime targets.

[15]Cult leaders also have certain techniques of persuasion that are common to most cult organizations. [16]The first step is usually something called "love-bombing" by current cult members, who shower the recruits with affection and attention and claim to understand just how the potential cult members feel. [17]Then efforts are made to isolate the recruits from family and friends who might talk them out of joining. [18]This is accomplished in part by keeping the recruits so busy with rigid rituals, ways of dress, meditations, and other activities that they do not allow the recruits time to think about what is happening. [19]All of these activities also serve to wear down the resistance of the recruits. [20]Cults also teach their members how to stop questioning thoughts or criticisms, which are typically seen as sins or extremely undesirable behavior. [21]Access to people and information outside the cult is either kept to a well-guarded minimum or totally shut off (Singer & Lalich, 1995; Zimbardo & Hartley, 1985).

[22]Commitments to the cult are small at first, such as attending a music concert or some other cult function. [23]Eventually, a major step is requested by the cult, such as quitting one's job, turning over money or property to the cult, or similar commitments. [24]Leaving a cult is quite difficult, as members of the cult in good standing will often track down a "deserter." [25]Parents, friends, and other family members have been known to hire special "deprogrammers" to help their loved one recover from cult membership, willingly or unwillingly. [26]Sometimes people actually have to "kidnap" their loved one out of the cult environment. [27]Nevertheless, as difficult as it is to leave, 90 percent or more of cult members do eventually get out (Barker, 1983; Galanter, 1983).

[28]Cults have existed all through recorded history and will probably continue to exist in the future. [29]In 1995, there were between 3,000 and 5,000 cults in the United States alone (Singer & Lalich, 1995). [30]Most cults do not pose a physical threat to their members or others, but the examples of the followers of Jim Jones, David Koresh, and Osama bin Laden clearly demonstrate that cults, like any group of people, can become deadly.

—Ciccarelli, Saundra K. and White, Noland J., *Psychology: An Exploration*, pp. 374–375.

Vocabulary _____ **1.** The best meaning of the word **gullible** as used in sentence 13 is
a. overly friendly.
b. strong-willed.
c. willing to believe anything.
d. highly imaginative.

Vocabulary _____ **2.** The best meaning of the word **idealistic** as used in sentence 14 is
   a. thinking deep thoughts.   c. feeling things deeply.
   b. thinking how things should be. d. feeling hurt.

Implied _____ **3.** Which sentence best states the authors' implied central idea?
Central Idea
   a. Cults are groups of people who hold a particular set of religious or philosophical beliefs.
   b. Cults are out of the mainstream and use extreme techniques to get and keep members.
   c. Cults should be outlawed because some have committed horrific acts.
   d. People join cults for various reasons, but they have trouble leaving.

Main Idea, _____ **4.** Sentence 9 states a
Supporting
Details
   a. main idea.   c. minor supporting detail.
   b. major supporting detail.

Thought _____ **5.** What is the thought pattern of paragraphs 1–3 (sentences 1–9)?
Patterns
   a. classification   c. comparison and contrast
   b. cause and effect   d. definition and example

Transitions _____ **6.** What is the relationship of ideas within sentence 4?
   a. cause and effect   c. contrast
   b. classification   d. time order

Purpose _____ **7.** The overall purpose of the passage is
   a. to entertain the reader with horrific stories of cults.
   b. to inform the reader about cults and their practices.
   c. to persuade the reader not to join a cult.

Tone _____ **8.** The tone of the authors toward cults is somewhat
   a. cynical.   c. respectful.
   b. supportive.   d. disapproving.

Fact and _____ **9.** Overall, the passage uses
Opinion
   a. fact.   c. fact and opinion.
   b. opinion.

Argument _____ **10.** Sentence 16 states
   a. a claim.   b. support for a claim.

Read the following excerpt from President Barack Obama's second inaugural speech on January 20, 2013. Then answer the questions.

Second Inaugural Speech
President Barack Obama

[1]Each time we gather to inaugurate a president, we bear witness to the enduring strength of our Constitution. [2]We affirm the promise of our democracy. [3]We recall that what binds this nation together is not the colors of our skin or the tenets of our faith or the origins of our names. [4]What makes us exceptional—what makes us American—is our allegiance to an idea, **articulated** in a declaration made more than two centuries ago:

[5]"We hold these truths to be self-evident, that all men are created equal, that they are endowed by their Creator with certain unalienable rights, that among these are Life, Liberty, and the pursuit of Happiness."

[6]Today we continue a never-ending journey, to bridge the meaning of those words with the realities of our time. [7]For history tells us that while these truths may be self-evident, they have never been self-executing; that while freedom is a gift from God, it must be secured by His people here on Earth.

[8]The patriots of 1776 did not fight to replace the tyranny of a king with the privileges of a few or the rule of a mob. [9]They gave to us a Republic, a government of, and by, and for the people, entrusting each generation to keep safe our founding creed.

[10]For more than two hundred years, we have.

[11]Through blood drawn by lash and blood drawn by sword, we learned that no union founded on the principles of liberty and equality could survive half-slave and half-free. [12]We made ourselves anew, and vowed to move forward together.

[13]Together, we determined that a modern economy requires railroads and highways to speed travel and commerce; schools and colleges to train our workers.

[14]Together, we discovered that a free market only thrives when there are rules to ensure competition and fair play.

[15]Together, we resolved that a great nation must care for the vulnerable, and protect its people from life's worst hazards and misfortune.

[16]Through it all, we have never **relinquished** our skepticism of central authority, nor have we succumbed to the fiction that all society's ills can

be cured through government alone. [17]Our celebration of initiative and enterprise; our insistence on hard work and personal responsibility, are constants in our character.

[18]But we have always understood that when times change, so must we; that fidelity to our founding principles requires new responses to new challenges; that preserving our individual freedoms ultimately requires collective action. [19]For the American people can no more meet the demands of today's world by acting alone than American soldiers could have met the forces of fascism or communism with muskets and militias. [20]No single person can train all the math and science teachers we'll need to equip our children for the future, or build the roads and networks and research labs that will bring new jobs and businesses to our shores. [21]Now, more than ever, we must do these things together, as one nation, and one people.

[22]This generation of Americans has been tested by crises that steeled our resolve and proved our resilience. [23]A decade of war is now ending. [24]An economic recovery has begun. [25]America's possibilities are limitless, for we possess all the qualities that this world without boundaries demands: youth and drive; diversity and openness; an endless capacity for risk and a gift for reinvention. [26]My fellow Americans, we are made for this moment, and we will seize it—so long as we seize it together.

Source: Read more: http://www.wjla.com/articles/2013/01/obama-inauguration-speech-transcript-84299.html#ixzz2Lu3jQW3n

Vocabulary _____ **1.** The best meaning of the word **articulated** as used in sentence 4 is
    a. expressed.   c. read.
    b. emphasized.   d. inserted.

Vocabulary _____ **2.** The best meaning of the word **relinquished** as used in sentence 16 is
    a. strengthened.   c. apologized for.
    b. flaunted.   d. given up.

Central Idea _____ **3.** Which sentence best states the author's central idea?
    a. sentence 1   c. sentence 5
    b. sentence 2   d. sentence 21

Supporting _____ **4.** Sentence 13 states a
Details
    a. main idea.   c. minor supporting detail.
    b. major supporting detail.

Thought _____ **5.** What is the thought pattern of paragraphs 5–9 (sentences 10–15)?
Patterns
    a. listing   c. comparison
    b. cause and effect   d. contrast

Purpose   _____   **6.** The overall purpose of the passage is to
- a. entertain with stories from American history.
- b. inform about American history.
- c. to persuade the audience to work together as in the past.

Tone   _____   **7.** The overall tone of the passage is
- a. cynical.
- b. inspiring.
- c. objective.
- d. cautious.

Fact and Opinion   _____   **8.** Sentence 22 is a statement of
- a. fact.
- b. opinion.
- c. fact and opinion.

Argument   _____   **9.** Sentence 10 is
- a. a claim.
- b. support for a claim.

Argument   _____   **10.** In sentence 25, the president uses the propaganda technique of
- a. bandwagon.
- b. plain folks.
- c. testimonial.
- d. glittering generalities.

TEST 3

Read the following passage, and then, answer the questions.

What Risks Are Involved in Tattooing?

[1]Despite the obvious popularity of body art, several complications can result from tattooing.

[2]Tattooing can cause infections. [3]Unsterile tattooing equipment and needles can transmit infectious diseases, such as hepatitis; thus the American Association of Blood Banks requires a one-year wait between getting a tattoo and donating blood. [4]Even if the needles are sterilized or never have been used, the equipment that holds the needles may not be sterilized reliably due to its design. [5]In addition, a tattoo must be cared for properly during the first week or so after the **pigments** are injected.

[6]Tattooing involves removal problems. [7]Despite advances in laser technology, removing a tattoo is a painstaking process, usually involving several treatments and considerable expense. [8]Complete removal without scarring may be impossible.

[9]Although allergic reactions to tattoo pigments are rare, when they happen they may be particularly troublesome because the pigments can

be hard to remove. **¹⁰**Occasionally, people may develop an allergic reaction to tattoos they have had for years.

¹¹Tattoos may also result in granulomas and keloids. **¹²**Granulomas are nodules that may form around material that the body perceives as foreign, such as particles of tattoo pigment. **¹³**If you are prone to developing keloids—scars that grow beyond normal boundaries—you are at risk of keloid formation from a tattoo. **¹⁴**Keloids may form any time you injure or traumatize your skin. **¹⁵**According to experts, tattooing or micropigmentation is a form of trauma, and keloids occur more frequently as a consequence of tattoo removal.

> —Adapted from "Tattoos and Permanent Makeup." U.S. Food and Drug Administration Center for Food Safety and Applied Nutrition Office of Cosmetics and Colors Fact Sheet. 29 November 2000; Updated 14 July 2006.

Vocabulary _____ **1.** The best meaning of the word **pigments** as used in sentence 5 is
  a. infections.   c. dyes.
  b. protections.   d. skin.

Central Idea _____ **2.** The sentence that best states the central idea of the passage is
  a. sentence 1.   c. sentence 5.
  b. sentence 2.   d. sentence 12.

Transitions _____ **3.** The relationship between sentences 11 and 12 is one of
  a. definition.   c. time order.
  b. cause and effect.   d. addition.

Transitions _____ **4.** The relationship of the ideas within sentence 3 is
  a. definition.   c. time order.
  b. cause and effect.   d. comparison and contrast.

Thought Patterns _____ **5.** What is the overall thought pattern of the passage?
  a. comparison and contrast   c. time order
  b. cause and effect   d. definition

Supporting Details _____ **6.** Sentence 6 is a
  a. main idea.
  b. major supporting detail.
  c. minor supporting detail.

Purpose _____ **7.** The author's main purpose in the passage is
  a. to inform.
  b. to entertain.
  c. to persuade.

Tone _____ **8.** The tone of the passage is
a. graphic.   c. objective.
b. judgmental.   d. pessimistic.

9–10. Complete the outline below with information from the passage.

Central idea: _____

   I. Tattooing can cause infections.

  II. Tattooing involves removal problems.

 III. _____

 IV. Tattooing may result in granulomas and keloids.

TEST 4

Read the passage from a history textbook, and then answer the questions.

The Stewardship of Natural Resources History:
Mapping Puget Sound and Western Washington

Textbook
Skills

[1]Nestled between two dramatic mountain ranges, the Olympics and the Cascades, the lush and mild Puget Sound region provided abundant natural resources for fishing, timbering, and farming for Native Americans for thousands of years before the arrival of British Captain George Vancouver and Lieutenant Peter Puget in 1792. [2]Seattle grew in the twentieth century as a trading port, particularly with east Asian markets, and as the original aircraft manufacturing site of Boeing Corporation. [3]With the permanently snow-capped volcanic peaks of the Cascade range visible on clear days, Seattle continued to attract new residents and tourists alike. [4]The population of the former frontier state of Washington nearly doubled from 1970 to 2003, topping 6 million.

[5]Seattle was also the departure point for most Americans traveling north to Alaska. [6]Passenger ferries crisscrossed Puget Sound, providing an alternative method of commuting to work in Seattle for residents of other area communities. [7]In the 1980s the city became associated with the extraordinary business success of computer software giant Microsoft and coffee retailer Starbucks. [8]Recreation Equipment Incorporated (REI)

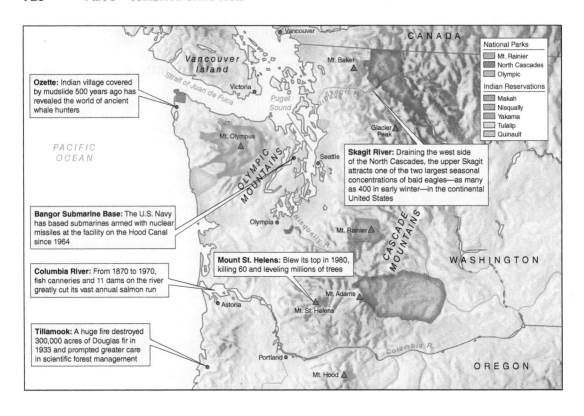

National Parks
- Mt. Rainier
- North Cascades
- Olympic

Indian Reservations
- Makah
- Nisqually
- Yakama
- Tulalip
- Quinault

Ozette: Indian village covered by mudslide 500 years ago has revealed the world of ancient whale hunters

Bangor Submarine Base: The U.S. Navy has based submarines armed with nuclear missiles at the facility on the Hood Canal since 1964

Columbia River: From 1870 to 1970, fish canneries and 11 dams on the river greatly cut its vast annual salmon run

Tillamook: A huge fire destroyed 300,000 acres of Douglas fir in 1933 and prompted greater care in scientific forest management

Skagit River: Draining the west side of the North Cascades, the upper Skagit attracts one of the two largest seasonal concentrations of bald eagles—as many as 400 in early winter—in the continental United States

Mount St. Helens: Blew its top in 1980, killing 60 and leveling millions of trees

---

began in Seattle as a consumer **cooperative** for buying products for outdoor activities such as rock-climbing and backpacking. [9]By 2000 REI had built stores across the United States.

—Jones, Jacqueline, Wood, Peter H., Borstelmann, Thomas, May, Elaine Tyler, and Ruiz, Vicki L., *Created Equal: A Social and Political History of the United States,* 2nd ed., p. 1019.

Vocabulary _____ **1.** The best meaning of the word **stewardship** in the title is
   a. duty.   c. management.
   b. need.   d. benefit.

Vocabulary _____ **2.** The best meaning of the word **cooperative** as used in sentence 8 is
   a. helper.   c. company.
   b. companion.   d. product.

Implied _____ **3.** Based on the title and the details, which sentence best states the
Main Idea   implied main idea of the passage?
   a. The Puget Sound region is a beautiful area that needs no stewardship.

    b. Stewardship is needed because commerce and development are harming the Puget Sound region.

    c. Under the stewardship of Native Americans, the Puget Sound region provided abundant natural resources for fishing, timbering, and farming.

    d. The natural environment of the Seattle area has greatly influenced the economic development of the area.

Thought Patterns _____ **4.** The main thought pattern of the passage is

    a. time order.   c. classification.

    b. cause and effect.   d. listing.

Tone _____ **5.** The tone of the passage is

    a. admiring.   c. critical.

    b. neutral.   d. persuasive.

Answer the following questions based on information in the map.

Supporting Details _____ **6.** Based on the map, where does the vast salmon run occur?

    a. Skagit River   c. Tillamook

    b. Puget Sound   d. Columbia River

Supporting Details _____ **7.** Based on the map, how many Indian reservations are in the region?

    a. two   c. five

    b. three   d. six

Purpose _____ **8.** The purpose of the map is

    a. to inform the reader about various historical resources, facts, and traits of the region.

    b. to persuade the reader that, historically, human activity has harmed the natural resources of the region.

    c. to entertain the reader with little known historical facts about the region.

Inference _____ **9.** Based on the information in the map, we can infer that

    a. the salmon run is more vast than it once was.

    b. Mount St. Helens is an active volcano.

    c. the fire at Tillamook was started by human activity.

    d. the Bangor Submarine Base has a nuclear power plant.

Argument _____ **10.** *Claim*: The Puget Sound region is rich in natural resources.

Which of the following statements is not relevant to the claim?

    a. An Indian village covered by mudslide 500 years ago has revealed the world of ancient whale hunters.

b. The U.S. Navy has based submarines with nuclear missiles at the facility on the Hood Canal since 1964.

c. The upper Skagit attracts one of the two largest seasonal concentrations of bald eagles—as many as 400 in early winter—in the continental United States.

d. Native Americans live on reservations that are smaller in size than the three national parks in the region.

TEST 5

Read the following passage. Then answer the questions.

Dating in Cyberspace

[1]There seems little doubt that the dating industry has changed dramatically as a result of new and increasing computer technology. [2]Some observers say that a quiet revolution has overtaken the world of romance as the increasingly popular electronic bulletin boards have transformed into what some call "online pickup joints." [3]One thing for sure, there is now relatively broad public contact with the online dating world. [4]Some 31 percent of American adults say they know someone who has used a dating Web site and 15 percent of American adults—about 30 million people—say they know someone who has been in a long-term relationship or married someone she or he met online (Madden & Lenhart, 2006). [5]Mate selection, by way of the computer and the Internet, has become pretty routine for a wide range of dating and dating-related behaviors among a variety of today's singles.

[6]For example, many single professionals are looking for a mate in cyberspace. [7]Modern life for the unmarried professional today is increasingly complicated and full, making finding a partner difficult, if not impossible, for those who are interested. [8]Today's professionals are marrying later; they travel thousands of miles each year for business reasons; they relocate frequently as they climb the corporate ladder; they run in and out of health and other exercise clubs on a tight schedule on their way to the office; they rarely date colleagues on the job; and many of them are fed up with singles' bars, blind dates, and family and friend fix-ups (rarely does what they want in a partner coincide with what family and friends think they need). [9]In addition, at both ends of the dating age spectrum, an increasing number of teenagers and people 50 years of age and older are growing segments of online daters.

¹⁰In this regard, some relationship experts predict that "niche dating sites" are the wave of the future for online dating. ¹¹They say that as more new dating sites come online, the best chance for success is to focus on a particular niche. ¹²In fact, there are already hundreds of such niche dating sites currently online. ¹³These sites run the **gamut** from sites specifically for Seventh Day Adventists, Big, Beautiful Women, Christians, Singles who are Deaf, Military Singles and their Admirers, and Singles over 40 to Single Parents, Single and Widowed Seniors, and one for every possible racial/ethnic and religious group. ¹⁴Ironically, it is the same technology that some people feel isolates us and is too invasive that is also responsible for bringing people together.

¹⁵Online dating has advantages as well as pitfalls. ¹⁶Some of the advantages of online dating are its accessibility, **autonomy**, and increasingly low cost. ¹⁷Subscribers can sit in the privacy of their homes and access tens of thousands of eligible mates, sifting through them as often as they like by specific "niche" characteristics such as age, race/ethnicity, religion, or body type. ¹⁸They can also remain anonymous as long as they like, thus allowing people to portray the persona they choose until they are ready to get involved. ¹⁹This can lead to more open expression because people do not have to worry about seeing or running into each other if the online relationship does not work. ²⁰It also saves the time and expense that might be spent on a bad blind or fix-up date, and it cuts out the need for barhopping. ²¹A pitfall is the potential for dishonesty and even harassment or violence if, for example, the online relationship does not work out (Madden & Lenhart, 2006; Nichcolas and Milewski, 1999). ²²When it does work, it can lead a couple to the altar. ²³Online Dating Magazine estimates that there are more than 280,000 marriages a year as a direct result of people meeting on an online dating service (Online Dating Magazine – January 2011).

—Schwartz, Mary Ann and Scott, Barbara Marliene, *Marriages and Families: Diversity and Change*, 2010, Census Update, p. 136.

Vocabulary _____ **1.** A synonym of the word **gamut** in sentence 13 is
a. range.   c. category.
b. network.   d. program.

Vocabulary _____ **2.** The best meaning of the word **autonomy** as used in sentence 16 is
a. ease of use.   c. success rate.
b. quickness.   d. independent control.

Main Idea/ _____ **3.** Sentence 3 states a
Details
a. main idea.   c. minor supporting detail.
b. major supporting detail.

Central Idea _____ **4.** Which sentence best states the authors' central idea?
    a. sentence 1   c. sentence 6
    b. sentence 5   d. sentence 23

Supporting _____ **5.** About how many adults know someone who has used a dating
Details   website?
    a. 15 percent   c. 31 percent
    b. 30 percent   d. 50 percent

Transitions _____ **6.** What is the relationship of ideas between sentences 12 and 13?
    a. cause and effect   c. comparison and contrast
    b. classification   d. generalization and example

Transitions _____ **7.** What is the relationship of ideas within sentence 18?
    a. cause and effect   c. definition
    b. classification   d. comparison and contrast

Purpose _____ **8.** The author's main purpose is
    a. to entertain the reader with stories of online dating.
    b. to inform the reader about online dating.
    c. to persuade the reader to use online dating.

Tone _____ **9.** The tone of the passage is
    a. cynical.   c. objective.
    b. amused.   d. disapproving.

Fact and _____ **10.** Sentence 23 is a statement of
Opinion   a. fact.   c. fact and opinion.
    b. opinion.

Text Credits

Aaron, Jane E., *The Little, Brown Compact Handbook*, 4th ed., © 2001. Printed and Electronically reproduced by permission of Pearson Education, Inc., Upper Saddle River, New Jersey.

Agee, Warren K., Ault, Philip H., and Emery, Edwin, *Introduction to Mass Communication*, 12th ed. Boston: Allyn and Bacon © 1997. Printed and Electronically reproduced by permission of Pearson Education, Inc., Upper Saddle River, New Jersey.

Anderson, Lydia E. and Bolt, Sandra B., *Professionalism: Skills for Workplace Success*, 2nd ed. Copyright © 2011. Printed and Electronically reproduced by permission of Pearson Education, Inc., Upper Saddle River, New Jersey.

Aronson, Elliot, Wilson, Timothy D., and Akert, Robin M., *Social Psychology*, 8th ed., © 2013 by Pearson Education, Inc. Printed and Electronically reproduced by Permission of Pearson Education, Inc., Upper Saddle River, New Jersey.

Audesirk, Teresa, Audesirk, Gerald, and Byers, Bruce E., *Life on Earth*, 5th ed., © 2009. Printed and Electronically reproduced by permission of Pearson Education, Inc., Upper Saddle River, New Jersey.

Audesirk, Gerald, Audesirk, Teresa, and Byers, Bruce E., *Biology: Life on Earth*, 8th ed., © 2008. Printed and Electronically reproduced by permission of Pearson Education, Inc., Upper Saddle River, New Jersey.

Audesirk, Gerald, Audesirk, Teresa, and Byers, Bruce E., *Biology: Life on Earth*, 9th ed., © 2011. Printed and Electronically reproduced by permission of Pearson Education, Inc., Upper Saddle River, New Jersey.

Barker, Larry Lee and Gaut, Deborah A., *Communication*, 8th ed., © 2001. Published by Pearson Education, Inc., Upper Saddle River, New Jersey.

Benokraitis, Nijole V., *Marriages and Families: Changes, Choices, and Constraints*, 4th ed. Copyright © 2002 by Pearson Education, Inc. Printed and Electronically reproduced by permission of Pearson Education, Inc., Upper Saddle River, New Jersey.

Bergman, Edward and Renwick, William, *Introduction to Geography: People, Places, and Environment*, 4th ed., © 2008. Printed and Electronically reproduced by permission of Pearson Education, Inc., Upper Saddle River, New Jersey.

Bergman, Edward and Renwick, William, *Introduction to Geography: People, Places, and Environment*. © 2011. Printed and Electronically reproduced by permission of Pearson Education, Inc., Upper Saddle River, New Jersey.

Bittinger, Marvin L. and Beecher, Judith A., *Introductory and Intermediate Algebra: A Combined Approach*, 2nd ed. Copyright © 2003 by Pearson Education, Inc. Printed and Electronically reproduced by permission of Pearson Education, Inc., Upper Saddle River, New Jersey.

Blake, Joan Salge, *Nutrition and You*, 1st ed. Copyright © 2008. Printed and Electronically reproduced by permission of Pearson Education, Inc., Upper Saddle River, New Jersey.

Blake, Joan Salge, *Nutrition and You*, 2nd ed. Copyright © 2012. Printed and Electronically reproduced by permission of Pearson Education, Inc., Upper Saddle River, New Jersey.

Brookshear, J. Glenn, *Computer Science: An Overview,* 11th ed. Published by Prentice Hall, © 2011.

Brownell, Judi, *Listening: Attitudes, Principles, and Skills*, 2nd ed. Copyright © 2002. Printed and Electronically reproduced by permission of Pearson Education, Inc., Upper Saddle River, New Jersey.

Carl, John D., *Think Social Problems*. Copyright © 2011 by Pearson Education, Inc. Printed and Electronically reproduced by permission of Pearson Education, Inc., Upper Saddle River, New Jersey.

Carl, John D., *Think Sociology*, 11th ed. Copyright © 2011 by Pearson Education, Inc. Printed and Electronically reproduced by permission of Pearson Education, Inc., Upper Saddle River, New Jersey.

Carlson, Neil R. and Buskist, William, *Psychology: The Science of Behavior*, 5th ed., Boston: Allyn and Bacon. Copyright © 1999. Printed and Electronically reproduced by permission of Pearson Education, Inc. Upper Saddle River, New Jersey.

Carson, Clayborne, Lapsansky-Werner, Emma J., and Nash, Gary B., "The Jazz Age" from *The Struggle for Freedom: A History of African-Americans, Volume II*. White Plains: Longman, 2007. Printed and Electronically reproduced by permission of Pearson Education, Inc., Upper Saddle River, New Jersey.

Ciccarelli, Saundra K. and White, Noland J., *Psychology: An Exploration*, © 2010 by Pearson Education, Inc. Printed and Electronically reproduced by permission of Pearson Education, Inc., Upper Saddle River, New Jersey.

Cook, Roy A., Yale, Laura J., and Marqua, Joseph J., *Tourism: The Business of Travel*, 4th ed., © 2010. Printed and Electronically reproduced by permission of Pearson Education, Inc., Upper Saddle River, New Jersey.

Craig, Albert M., Graham, William A., Kagan, Donald, Ozment, Steven, and Turner, Frank M., *The Heritage of World Civilizations, Brief*, 5th ed. Copyright © 2012. Printed and Electronically reproduced by permission of Pearson Education, Inc., Upper Saddle River, New Jersey.

DeVito, Joseph A., *Essentials of Human Communication*, 4th ed., © 2002. Printed and Electronically reproduced by permission of Pearson Education, Inc., Upper Saddle River, New Jersey.

DeVito, Joseph A., *The Interpersonal Communication Book*, 10th ed., © 2004. Printed and Electronically reproduced by permission of Pearson Education, Inc., Upper Saddle River, New Jersey.

DeVito, Joseph A., *The Interpersonal Communication Book*, 11th ed., © 2007. Printed and Electronically reproduced by permission of Pearson Education, Inc., Upper Saddle River, New Jersey.

DeVito, Joseph A., *Messages: Building Interpersonal Communication Skills*, 6th ed. Boston: Allyn and Bacon, © 2005. Printed and Electronically reproduced by permission of Pearson Education, Inc., Upper Saddle River, New Jersey.

Divine, Robert A., Frederickson, George M., Williams, R. Hal, and Breen, T. H., *The American Story*, 1st ed., Copyright © 2002 by Pearson Education. Printed and Electronically reproduced by permission of Pearson Education, Inc., Upper Saddle River, New Jersey.

Donatelle, Rebecca, J. and Davis, Lorraine G., *Access to Health*, 7th ed. Copyright © 2002. Printed and Electronically reproduced by permission of Pearson Education, Inc., Upper Saddle River, New Jersey.

Donatelle, Rebecca, J., *Access to Health*, 11th ed. Copyright © 2010. Printed and Electronically reproduced by permission of Pearson Education, Inc., Upper Saddle River, New Jersey.

Donatelle, Rebecca, J., *Access to Health*, 12th ed. Copyright © 2012. Printed and Electronically reproduced by permission of Pearson Education, Inc., Upper Saddle River, New Jersey.

Donatelle, Rebecca, J., *Access to Health*, 13th ed. Copyright © 2014. Printed and Electronically reproduced by permission of Pearson Education, Inc., Upper Saddle River, New Jersey.

Donatelle, Rebecca J., *Health: The Basics*, 5th ed. Copyright © 2003 by Pearson Education, Inc. Printed and Electronically reproduced by permission of Pearson Education, Inc. Upper Saddle River, New Jersey.

Donatelle, Rebecca J. and Davis, Lorraine G., *Health: The Basics*, 7th ed., © 2007. Printed and Electronically reproduced by permission of Pearson Education, Inc., Upper Saddle River, New Jersey.

Edgar, Robert R., Hackett, Neil J., Jewsbury, George F., Molony, Barbara S., and Gordon, Matthew, *Civilizations Past & Present*, Combined Volume, 12th ed. Copyright © 2008 by Pearson Education, Inc. Printed and Electronically reproduced by permission of Pearson Education, Inc., Upper Saddle River, New Jersey.

Edwards, George C. III, Wattenberg, Martin P., and Lineberry, Robert L., *Government in America: People, Politics, and Policy*, 5th ed., Brief Version. Copyright © 2000 by Pearson Education, Inc. Printed and Electronically reproduced by permission of Pearson Education, Inc., Upper Saddle River, New Jersey.

Ember, Carol R., Ember, Melvin R., and Peregrine, Peter, *Human Evolution and Culture: Highlights of Anthropology*, 7th ed. Copyright © 2012. Printed and Electronically reproduced by permission of Pearson Education, Inc., Upper Saddle River, New Jersey.

Faigley, Lester, *The Penguin Handbook*. © 2003. Published by Pearson Education, Inc., Upper Saddle River, New Jersey.

Fernandez-Armesto, Felipe, *The World: A History, Combined Volume*, 2nd ed. Copyright © 2010 by Pearson Education, Inc. Printed and Electronically reproduced by permission of Pearson Education, Inc., Upper Saddle River, New Jersey.

Folger, Joseph P., Poole, Marshall Scott, and Stutman, Randall K., *Working Through Conflict*, 4th ed. Published by Pearson Education, Inc., Upper Saddle River, New Jersey.

Folkerts, Jean and Lacy, Stephen, *The Media in Your Life: An Introduction to Mass Communication*, 2nd ed. Boston: Allyn and Bacon, 2001. Printed and Electronically reproduced by permission of Pearson Education, Inc., Upper Saddle River, New Jersey.

Fowler, H. Ramsey and Aaron, Jane E., *The Little, Brown Handbook*, 9th ed., Copyright © 2004 by Pearson Education, Inc. Printed and Electronically reproduced by permission of Pearson Education, Inc., Upper Saddle River, New Jersey.

Gerrig, Richard J. and Zimbardo, Philip G., *Psychology and Life*, 16th ed., © 2002. Printed and Electronically reproduced by permission of Pearson Education, Inc., Upper Saddle River, New Jersey.

Gerrig, Richard J. and Zimbardo, Philip G., *Psychology and Life*, 19th ed. © 2010. Printed and Electronically reproduced by permission of Pearson Education, Inc., Upper Saddle River, New Jersey.

Gerrig, Richard J., Zimbardo, Philip G., Svartdal, Frode, Brennen, Tim, Donaldson, Robert, and Archer, Trevor, *Psychology and Life*, © 2012 by Pearson Education, Inc. Printed and Electronically reproduced by permission of Pearson Education, Inc., Upper Saddle River, New Jersey.

Giannetti, Louis, *Understanding Movies*, 12th ed., © 2011. Printed and Electronically reproduced by permission of Pearson Education, Inc., Upper Saddle River, New Jersey.

Girdano, Daniel A., Dusek, Dorothy E., and Everly, Jr., George S., "Physical Effects of Modern Life" from *Controlling Stress and Tension*, 6th ed., Boston: Allyn and Bacon. Copyright © 2000. Printed and Electronically reproduced by permission of Pearson Education, Inc., Upper Saddle River, New Jersey.

Griffin, Ricky W. and Ebert, Ronald J., *Business*, 8th ed., © 2006. Printed and Electronically reproduced by permission of Pearson Education, Inc., Upper Saddle River, New Jersey.

Hackett, Neil J., *Civilizations Past & Present*, 12th ed., © 2008. Printed and Electronically reproduced by permission of Pearson Education, Inc., Upper Saddle River, New Jersey.

Hames, Joanne B. and Ekern, Yvonne, *Introduction to Law*, 4th ed., © 2010. Printed and Electronically reproduced by permission of Pearson Education, Inc., Upper Saddle River, New Jersey.

Henslin, James M., *Essentials of Sociology: A Down-to-Earth Approach*, 7th ed., © 2007 by Pearson Education, Inc. Reproduced by permission of Pearson Education, Inc., Upper Saddle River, New Jersey.

Henslin, James M., *Sociology: A Down-to-Earth Approach*, 10th ed., © 2008. Printed and Electronically reproduced by permission of Pearson Education, Inc., Upper Saddle River, New Jersey.

Henslin, James M., *Sociology: A Down-to-Earth Approach*, 11th ed., © 2012. Printed and Electronically reproduced by permission of Pearson Education, Inc., Upper Saddle River, New Jersey.

Jaffee, Michael L., *Understanding Parenting*, 2nd ed. Copyright © 1997. Reprinted by permission of Pearson Education, Inc., Upper Saddle River, New Jersey.

Janaro, Richard P. and Altshuler, Thelma C., *The Art of Being Human*, 10th ed., © 2012. Printed and Electronically reproduced by permission of Pearson Education, Inc., Upper Saddle River, New Jersey.

Jones, Jacqueline, Wood, Peter H., Borstelmann, Thomas, May, Elaine Tyler, and Ruiz, Vicki L., *Created Equal: A Social and Political History of the United States*, 2nd ed. Copyright © 2006 by Pearson Education, Inc. Printed and Electronically reproduced by permission of Pearson Education, Inc., Upper Saddle River, New Jersey.

Karren, Keith J., Hafen, Brent Q., Smith, Lee, and Frandsen, Kathryn, *Mind/Body Health: The Effects of Attitudes, Emotions, and Relationships*, 2nd ed., © 2002. Printed and Electronically reproduced by permission of Pearson Education, Inc., Upper Saddle River, New Jersey.

Kennedy, X. J. and Gioia, Dana, *Literature: An Introduction to Fiction, Poetry, and Drama*, 8th ed. Copyright © 2002 by Pearson Education, Inc. Reprinted by permission of Pearson Education, Inc.

Kennedy, X. J. and Gioia, Dana, *Literature: An Introduction to Fiction, Poetry, Drama*, 3rd Compact edition. Copyright © 2003 by Pearson Education, Inc. Printed and Electronically reproduced by permission of Pearson Education, Inc., Upper Saddle River, New Jersey.

Kishlansky, Mark, Geary, Patrick, and O'Brien, Patricia, "God Kings" from *Civilization in the West*, 4th ed., © 2001. Printed and Electronically reproduced by permission of Pearson Education, Inc., Upper Saddle River, New Jersey.

Kosslyn, Stephen M. and Rosenberg, Robin S., *Fundamentals of Psychology: The Brain, the Person, The World*. Boston: Allyn and Bacon, 2002. Printed and Electronically reproduced by permission of Pearson Education, Inc., Upper Saddle River, New Jersey.

Leathers, Dale and Eaves, Michael H., *Successful Nonverbal Communication: Principles and Applications*, 4th ed., © 2008. Printed and Electronically reproduced by permission of Pearson Education, Inc., Upper Saddle River, New Jersey.

Lefton, Lester A. and Brannon, Linda, *Psychology*, 8th ed. Boston: Allyn and Bacon, © 2003. Printed and Electronically reproduced by permission of Pearson Education, Inc., Upper Saddle River, New Jersey.

Levack, Brian, Muir, Edward, Veldman, Meredith, and Maas, Michael, *The West: Encounters & Transformations*, Atlas Edition, Combined Edition, 2nd ed. Copyright © 2008 by Pearson Education, Inc. Printed and Electronically reproduced by permission of Pearson Education, Inc., Upper Saddle River, New Jersey.

Levens, Michael R., *Marketing: Defined, Explained, Applied*, 2nd ed., © 2012. Printed and Electronically reproduced by permission of Pearson Education, Inc., Upper Saddle River, New Jersey.

Levinthal, Charles F., *Drugs, Behaviors, and Modern Society*, 3rd ed., Boston: Allyn and Bacon, Copyright © 2002. Printed and Electronically reproduced by permission of Pearson Education, Inc., Upper Saddle River, New Jersey.

Lutgens, Frederick K. and Tarbuck, Edward J., *Essentials of Geology*, 11th ed. Copyright © 2012 by Pearson Education, Inc. Printed and Electronically reproduced by permission of Pearson Education, Inc., Upper Saddle River, New Jersey.

Lutgens, Frederick K., Tarbuck, Edward J., and Tasa, Dennis, *Foundations of Earth Science*, 5th ed., © 2008 by Pearson Education, Inc. Printed and Electronically reproduced by permission of Pearson Education, Inc., Upper Saddle River, New Jersey.

Madura, Jeff. *Personal Finance*, 2nd ed., © 2004. Printed and Electronically reproduced by permission of Pearson Education, Inc., Upper Saddle River, New Jersey.

Madura, Jeff. *Personal Finance*, 3rd ed., © 2007. Printed and Electronically reproduced by permission of Pearson Education, Inc., Upper Saddle River, New Jersey.

Maier, Richard A. *Comparative Animal Behavior: An Evolutionary and Ecological Approach*. Published by Pearson Education.

Marieb, Elaine N., *Essentials of Human Anatomy and Physiology*, 9th ed., © 2009. Printed and Electronically reproduced by permission of Pearson Education, Inc., Upper Saddle River, New Jersey.

Marieb, Elaine N., *Essentials of Human Anatomy and Physiology*, 10th ed., © 2012. Printed and Electronically reproduced by permission of Pearson Education, Inc., Upper Saddle River, New Jersey.

Martin, James Kirby, Roberts, Randy J., Mintz, Steven, McMurry, Linda O., and Jones, James H., *America and Its Peoples, Volume 1: A Mosaic in the Making*, 3rd ed. Copyright © 1997 Printed and Electronically reproduced by permission of Pearson Education, Inc., Upper Saddle River, New Jersey.

Mayer, Richard E., *Journal of Educational Psychology*, American Psychological Association, © 2003. Reproduced with the permission of American Psychological Association.

Miller, Barbara, *Cultural Anthropology*, 4th ed., © 2007 by Pearson Education, Inc. Printed and Electronically reproduced by permission of Pearson Education, Inc., Upper Saddle River, New Jersey.

O'Connor, Karen, *American Government: Roots and Reform* 2012 Election Edition, © 2012. Printed and Electronically reproduced by permission of Pearson Education, Inc., Upper Saddle River, New Jersey.

Powell, Sara Davis, *Your Introduction to Education*, 2nd ed. Copyright © 2012. Printed and Electronically reproduced by permission of Pearson Education, Inc., Upper Saddle River, New Jersey.

Powers, Scott K. and Dodd, Stephen L., *From Total Fitness and Wellness Student Textbook Component*, 3rd ed., © 2003 by Pearson Education, Inc. Printed and Electronically reproduced by permission of Pearson Education, Inc., Upper Saddle River, New Jersey.

Pruitt, B. E. and Stein, Jane J., *Healthstyles: Decisions for Living Well*, 2nd ed., ©1999. Printed and Electronically reproduced by permission of Pearson Education, Inc., Upper Saddle River, New Jersey.

Riddell, Tom, Shackelford, Jean A., Stamos, Stephen C., and Schneider, Geoffrey, *Economics: A Tool for Critically Understanding Society*, 9th ed., © 2011. Printed and Electronically reproduced by permission of Pearson Education, Inc., Upper Saddle River, New Jersey.

Ruggerio, Vincent Ryan, *The Art of Thinking: A Guide to Critical and Creative Thought*, 7th ed. Copyright © 2004 by Pearson Education, Inc. Printed and Electronically reproduced by permission of Pearson Education, Inc., Upper Saddle River, New Jersey.

Sabato, Larry J. and O'Connor, Karen, *American Government: Continuity and Change*, © 2008 by Pearson Education, Inc. Printed and Electronically reproduced by permission of Pearson Education, Inc., Upper Saddle River, New Jersey.

Schmalleger, Frank J., *Criminal Justice*, 9th ed., © 2012. Printed and Electronically reproduced by permission of Pearson Education, Inc., Upper Saddle River, New Jersey.

Schmalleger, Frank J., *Criminal Justice: A Brief Introduction*, 9th ed. Copyright © 2012 by Pearson Education, Inc. Printed and Electronically reproduced by permission of Pearson Education, Inc., Upper Saddle River, New Jersey.

Schmalleger, Frank J., *Criminal Justice Today: An Introductory Text for the 21st Century*, 10th ed., © 2009. Printed and Electronically reproduced by permission of Pearson Education, Inc., Upper Saddle River, New Jersey.

Schwartz, Mary Ann and Scott, Barbara Marliene, *Marriages and Families: Diversity and Change*, 2010 Census Update, © 2012 by Pearson Education, Inc. Printed and Electronically reproduced by permission of Pearson Education, Inc., Upper Saddle River, New Jersey.

Shiraev, Eric B. and Levy, David A. *Cross-Cultural Psychology: Critical Thinking and Contemporary Applications*, 3rd ed., © 2007. Printed and Electronically reproduced by permission of Pearson Education, Inc., Upper Saddle River, New Jersey.

Smith, Thomas and Smith, Robert Leo, *Elements of Ecology*, 4th ed., © 2000. Printed and Electronically reproduced by permission of Pearson Education, Inc., Upper Saddle River, New Jersey.

Smith, Thomas and Smith, Robert Leo, *Elements of Ecology*, 6th ed., © 2006. Printed and Electronically reproduced by permission of Pearson Education, Inc., Upper Saddle River, New Jersey.

Solomon, Michael, Poatsy, Mary Anne, and Martin, Kendall. *Better Business*, 2nd ed., © 2012. Printed and Electronically reproduced by permission of Pearson Education, Inc., Upper Saddle River, New Jersey.

Sporre, Dennis J., *The Creative Impulse: An Introduction to the Arts*, 8th ed., © 2009. Printed and Electronically reproduced by permission of Pearson Education, Inc., Upper Saddle River, New Jersey.

Stearns, Peter N., Adas, Michael B., Schwartz, Stuart B., and Gilbert, Marc Jason, *World Civilizations: The Global Experience, Combined Volume, Atlas Edition*, 5th ed., © 2008. Printed and Electronically reproduced by permission of Pearson Education, Inc., Upper Saddle River, New Jersey.

Stokstad, Marilyn and Cothren, Michael. *Art: A Brief History*, 5th ed. © 2012. Published by Pearson Education, Inc., Upper Saddle River, New Jersey.

Walker, John R. *Introduction to Hospitality*, 6th ed. © 2012. Published by Pearson Education, Inc., Upper Saddle River, New Jersey.

Walker, John R. and Walker, Josielyn T., *Tourism: Concepts and Practices*, 1st ed., Copyright © 2011 by Pearson Education, Inc. Printed and Electronically reproduced by permission of Pearson Education, Inc., Upper Saddle River, New Jersey.

Wilen, William, Ishler, Margaret, Hutchinson, Janice, and Kindsvatter, Richard, *Dynamics of Effective Teaching*, 4th ed., © 1999. Published by Pearson Education, Inc., Upper Saddle River, New Jersey.

Withgott, Jay H. and Brennan, Scott R., *Essential Environment*, 2nd ed., © 2012. Printed and Electronically reproduced by permission of Pearson Education, Inc., Upper Saddle River, New Jersey.

Withgott, Jay H. and Brennan, Scott R., *Essential Environment: The Science Behind the Stories*, 3rd ed. Copyright © 2009 by Pearson Education, Inc. Printed and Electronically reproduced by permission of Pearson Education, Inc., Upper Saddle River, New Jersey.

Withgott, Jay H. and Laposata, Matthew, *Essential Environment: The Science Behind the Stories*, 4th ed. Copyright © 2012 by Pearson Education, Inc. Printed and Electronically reproduced by permission of Pearson Education, Inc., Upper Saddle River, New Jersey.

Wood, Samuel E., Wood, Ellen Green, and Boyd, Denise, *Mastering the World of Psychology*, 3rd ed. Copyright © 2008 by Pearson Education, Inc. Printed and Electronically reproduced by permission of Pearson Education, Inc., Upper Saddle River, New Jersey.

Woolfolk, Anita E., *Educational Psychology*, 8th ed., © 2001. Printed and Electronically reproduced by permission of Pearson Education, Inc., Upper Saddle River, New Jersey.

Woolfolk, Anita E., *Educational Psychology*, 10th ed., © 2007. Printed and Electronically reproduced by permission of Pearson Education, Inc., Upper Saddle River, New Jersey.

Zimbardo, Philip G., Johnson, Robert L., and Hamilton, Vivian McCann, *Psychology: Core Concepts*, 7th ed. Copyright © 2012. Printed and Electronically reproduced by permission of Pearson Education, Inc., Upper Saddle River, New Jersey.

Photo Credits

p. 21, Ken Seet/Fancy/Corbis; pp. v, 23, Savageultralight/Shutterstock; p. 31, Lisa F. Young/Shutterstock; p. 44, Steve Hix/Somos Images/Corbis; p. 50, Steffen Schmidt/Keystone/Corbis; p. 70, Coka/Fotolia; p. 94, Hervé Lewandowski/RMN-Grand Palais/Art Resource; p. 103, Simon Potter/Getty Images; p. 109, David Scharf/Science Source; p. 140, John A. Anderson/Shutterstock; pp. vi, 144, Buddy Mays/Corbis; p. 158, Kevin Lamarque/Reuters; p. 168, CB2/ZOB/WENN.com/Newscom; p. 202, Orlando Florin Rosu/Fotolia; p. 220, Wasan Srisawat/Shutterstock; p. 234, Andrew Goetz/Corbis; p. 241, Auremar/Shutterstock; pp. viii, 257, Ron Watts/Corbis; p. 268, Ludovic Maisant/Corbis; p. 270, Greg Smith/Corbis; p. 286, Matt Herring/Corbis; p. 290, MedicalRF.com/Corbis; p. 296, Dlillc/Corbis; pp. ix, 307, Philip Gendreau/Corbis; p. 319, Martin B. Withers/Corbis; p. 346 left, Ned Frisk Photography/Corbis; p. 346 right, Hugh Sitton/Corbis; p. 358, Will Hart/PhotoEdit, Inc.; p. 381, BSIP/Universal Images Group/Getty Images; pp. x, 387, Tyrone Turner/National Geographic Society/Corbis; p. 391, PBNJ Productions/Blend Images/Corbis; p. 395, National Archives and Records Administration; p. 416, E.O. Hoppe/Corbis; p. 417, Jose Luis Pelaez Inc/Blend Images/Corbis; p. 428, The White House; p. 433 left, Bikeriderlondon/Shutterstock; p. 433 middle, Image Source/Corbis; p. 433 right, Brooks Kraft/Corbis; p. 450, Image Source/Corbis; p. 466, Library of Congress Prints and Photographs Division [yan1996001397]; pp. xi, 471, Christine Schneider/Corbis; p. 476, Etsa/Corbis; p. 483, Jackson Pollock/Superstock; © 2013 The Pollock-Krasner Foundation/Artists Rights Society (ARS), New York; p. 506 left, Apic/Moviepix/Getty Images; p. 506 right, Paramount/Everett Collection; p. 524, Tom & Dee Ann McCarthy/Corbis; p. 527, The White House Office of National Drug Control Policy. Free Resources. http://www.freevibe.com/Drug_Facts/free-resources.asp; p. 542, Stephanie Frey/Shutterstock; p. 546, Brand X Pictures/Stockbyte/Getty Images; p. 549, Keith Brofsky/Stockbyte/Getty Images; p. 562, Matthias Ernert/Dpa/Corbis; p. 566, Don Mason/Blend Images/Getty Images; p. 584, © Courtesy of National Archives, photo NWDNS; p. 597, Burlingham/Shutterstock; p. 618, Office of War Information (OWI)/The New Hampshire State Library; p. 632, Medioimages/Photodisc/Getty Images; p. 713, David Turnley/Turnley/Corbis; p. 727, Pearson Education, Inc.

Index